GERONTOLOGY

A BEHAVIORAL SCIENCE
APPROACH

GERONTOLOGY

A BEHAVIORAL SCIENCE APPROACH

SECOND EDITION

Richard C. Crandall

Lake Superior State University

McGRAW-HILL, INC.

New York   St. Louis   San Francisco   Auckland   Bogotá
Caracas   Hamburg   Lisbon   London   Madrid   Mexico   Milan   Montreal
New Delhi   Paris   San Juan   São Paulo   Singapore   Sydney   Tokyo   Toronto

This book was set in Times Roman by Arcata Graphics/Kingsport.
The editors were Phillip A. Butcher and Katherine Blake;
the production supervisor was Richard A. Ausburn.
The cover was designed by Fern Logan.
Project supervision was done by The Total Book.
The photo editor was Elyse Rieder.
Arcata Graphics/Halliday was printer and binder.

Cover photo: Michael Keller, FPG International Corp.

GERONTOLOGY

A Behavioral Science Approach

1 2 3 4 5 6 7 8 9 0 HAL HAL 9 0 9 8 7 6 5 4 3 2 1

ISBN 0-07-013446-4

Library of Congress Cataloging-in-Publication Data

Crandall, Richard C.
  Gerontology: a behavioral science approach / Richard C. Crandall.
  —2nd ed.
    p.   cm.
  Includes bibliographical references and index.
  ISBN 0–07–013446–4
  1. Gerontology.   I. Title.
HQ1061.C67   1991
305.26—dc20   90–43310

To my mother,
who showed me both life and
death with dignity.

CONTENTS

PREFACE

This book was written during a very exciting time in gerontology. Since the publication of the first edition, knowledge about older persons has undergone numerous revisions—in part because some of the early gerontological knowledge was flawed and in part because the social changes occurring in society during this time period changed older persons. In addition to the change in many beliefs about older persons many new concepts have been brought into gerontology.

Admittedly, the first edition of this text was much easier to write than this one. Quite frankly, for the first edition the questions and answers were simpler. As those in gerontology are now aware, the days of simple questions and answers are long gone. Although this made the task of summarizing and synthesizing the research more difficult, I see this as a positive development, since it demonstrates the growth and maturity of gerontology.

For those who used the first edition, you will find that this book has been almost entirely rewritten. There are very few sections that have remained the same. There were very few sections that could remain the same given the changes that have taken place over the last few years. The organization of the book has changed somewhat. I have still made each chapter an independent unit, so that later chapters are not dependent on earlier chapters. In this way instructors can assign chapters according to their needs, rather than my organization.

This book is longer than the first edition, which was necessitated by the increase in knowledge and because I chose to cover many topics in greater depth than is normally found in introductory textbooks. The result is a book that is current, complete, and thorough in its coverage of gerontology. The book has two features that will help students in their research projects. First, students will find a large reference section at the end of each chapter. From these references students will be able to find original research as well as articles that summarize the research in a selected area. Second, I have pointed out where further research is needed.

As with the first book, there is a lesson to be learned from this book. The lesson is that most of us have the ability, at the individual level, to control the aging process and hence the type of life we lead in old age. Our life styles when we are younger will have an impact on factors such as our health, economic status, and life satisfaction when we are older.

I wish to thank Kathy Blake of McGraw-Hill for being there when problems arose, which she quickly and skillfully eliminated. A special thanks goes to Annette Bodzin of The Total Book, who edited the book and helped me say what I had intended to say but hadn't said.

I want to thank the following for reviewing drafts of the manuscript: Thomas E. DiMatteo, Ithaca College; Kenneth J. Doka, College of New Rochelle; Howard C. Eisner, University of Houston; Charles Hawkins, Central Washington University; James J. Kelly, California State University; Daniel J. Klenow, North Dakota State University; Daniel R. Krause, Roosevelt University; John Middleton, State University of New York; Andrew T. Nilsson, Eastern Connecticut State University; and Karen A. Roberto, University of Northern Colorado.

There are several others whom I want to acknowledge. First, my parents, who, even though my life didn't always turn out as they had hoped or expected, never stopped trusting, believing, supporting, encouraging, or loving me. Second, Sue, who has "covered for me" through three books. This will be the last one . . . probably. Third, to Amanda who was a little girl when I wrote the first edition and eagerly helped me alphabetize 3 × 5 cards for the glossary and references (not always accurately), and who now is a young woman and showing me how to use some of the more sophisticated aspects of computer programs. Fourth, to Jordan who wasn't born when the first edition was published and who at times has made me realize that I may have studied the wrong end of the age continuum.

Also, thanks to Shirley for bringing happiness to our family.

Richard C. Crandall

GERONTOLOGY

A BEHAVIORAL SCIENCE
APPROACH

PART **ONE**

INTRODUCTION TO GERONTOLOGY

Dean Abramson/Stock, Boston

CHAPTER 1

GERONTOLOGY: AN INTRODUCTION

Marianne Gontarz/The Picture Cube

INTRODUCTION

I was 24 years old and had just started teaching at a small college when I was provided with the opportunity to participate in a series of weekend seminars in gerontology at a major university. At the time I was more attracted to the university than to the seminars. I had just finished my undergraduate and graduate education without ever hearing about gerontology, and didn't see why I should use the material from the seminars in the courses I was teaching. Also, at the time I was young and thought myself invincible! Aging and the aged were not major concerns in my life.

Since that time students have often asked, "Why did you become a gerontologist?" Although I had given the question some thought, I didn't have an honest answer. Admittedly, there were times when an answer, rather than a blank stare, was appropriate, and I created an entertaining and acceptable answer for such occasions, but it wasn't a real answer.

In writing this introduction I had the opportunity to think about, for the first time in years, why I became a gerontologist. I have an answer and it is no more complex than I like it.

A major reason for writing this book was to share with you not only the facts, but some of the feelings that I have about gerontology. As someone trained to write technical, factual, scientific prose, writing about the facts was easy; writing about the feelings was more difficult. The feelings that I have about gerontology are difficult to describe. I can use terms such as "exciting" or "energizing," but these terms don't do justice to my feelings.

Instead of attempting to describe my feelings, it might be easier to describe their source. There are two sources, the first being the study of gerontology. When I began to study gerontology there were far more questions than answers, and many of the answers were not very good. Now, on a monthly basis, it is exciting to see lingering, nagging questions answered. It is like being part of a mystery and not just watching but helping the mystery unfold. Admittedly, in the last 20 years for every answer there have been several new questions, but that is part of the excitement. The second source is people. Probably most of what I feel about gerontology has come from the people I have had the opportunity to meet, both other gerontologists and older persons.

Even if you do not feel the excitement that I have, hopefully you will see the relevance of the course at an individual, family, and societal level.

At an individual level you will find that the course is very relevant. You will find that *you* have the ability to determine, to a significant extent, the quantity and quality of your life in old age. Your lifestyle, in areas such as exercise and nutrition, will have a significant impact on whether your old age is spent in a nursing home or running marathons. Your lifestyle, in terms of savings, will determine if you spend your "golden years" in a cheap, dingy apartment building in a dilapidated, crime-ridden section of a city, or in a sunbelt condominium surrounded by tennis courts, swimming pools, and golf courses. It is *never* too early or too late to start to ask yourself about the type of old age you want to have, and the lifestyle you will need to achieve it.

4

At the family level you will also find the course relevant. Although there is a tremendous amount of literature on the family with dependent children living at home, which reviews and offers suggestions to parents in areas ranging from how to avoid intergenerational conflicts to financing your child's college education, less literature exists on the family in old age. This is unfortunate since old age confronts us throughout our lives, first as grandchildren dealing with grandparents, then as adult children interacting with aged parents, and finally as we are ourselves "old." There are many relevant issues that need to be confronted at the family level. For example, many of you are aware that about the time a couple's childcaring responsibilities end they have to assume parent-caring responsibilities. There are many issues that caregivers face, such as whether to place a relative in a nursing home or maintain them at home, or whether to authorize a medical procedure that will prolong life (or dying—depending on your perspective).

At the societal level the course is also relevant. For example, the age at which most of you will be eligible to collect Social Security retirement benefits is 2 years later than the age at which I will be eligible. Additionally, recent changes in Social Security legislation were designed to discourage early retirement. Some writers have suggested that future changes will transform Social Security into a welfare program, with only poverty-level older persons being eligible for retirement benefits. Other issues at the societal level are, for example, preliminary attempts to enact legislation that would make adult children responsible for the cost of their parents' medical care. Existing family responsibility laws require parents to provide for their dependent children, and it has been suggested that adult children should be required to provide for their aged parents. Depending on your perspective, the changes noted above can be "good" or "bad." The point is that there are many changes taking place at the societal level that are relevant for all age groups.

All of the issues noted above will be discussed in further detail later in the book. This chapter has three purposes, presented in separate sections. The first section is to acquaint you with some terminology that will be used throughout the book. The second section examines the concept of life periods. Essentially, what is it about "old age" that is unique from other age categories? The last section will discuss the development of gerontology.

TERMINOLOGY

The study of aging and the aged has created the need for a special vocabulary. If gerontologists are to communicate effectively it is important that terms be clearly defined so that they can be used consistently.

The first term is **gerontology.** This word comes from the Greek *geras,* meaning "old age," and *logos,* a study or description of something. Thus, gerontology is the study of old age. It is a very broad term and encompasses the study of aging and older persons from a variety of perspectives including the psychological, socioeconomical, physiological, historical, and clinical (Achenbaum & Levin, 1989; Kastenbaum, 1987; U.S. Department of Health and Human Services, nd).

Another term frequently encountered in the literature is "social gerontology."

Social gerontology is a subfield of gerontology. It was first used by E. J. Steiglitz in 1943, and was then expanded by Clark Tibbitts (Kleemeir et al., 1967; Koller, 1967; Philibert, 1965; Tibbitts, 1960a, 1963). The social gerontologist is concerned with the reciprocal relationship between the individual and society. That is, how do individuals shape society through their behavior, and how does society influence individuals. Although social gerontologists are not interested in the physical aspects of aging per se, they are interested in the individual's reactions to physical changes, as determined by the societal values placed on certain physical conditions (Palmore, 1989).

Like social gerontology, the term **geriatrics** refers to a subfield of gerontology. Frequently geriatrics has been used to refer to the medical or nursing aspects of gerontology; it also refers to the application of gerontological knowledge in areas such as medicine, nursing, social work, or counseling (Butler, 1987b).

Educational gerontology is another subfield of gerontology and deals with two areas. The first is education for older persons. Interest here is not only in creating and offering education programs and courses, but also in ways of facilitating learning for older persons. The second area is gerontology courses and programs designed primarily for younger persons. Examples could be courses designed to reduce stereotypes about older persons in grade schools, and specialized gerontology courses at the college or university level in medicine, nursing, sociology, or psychology.

Ageism is another term that should be examined. Most are aware that sexism and racism are prejudice and discrimination based on sex and race; ageism is prejudice and discrimination based on age (Butler, 1969, 1987a). Technically, any age group can be subjected to ageism. In this course it refers to discrimination on the basis of "old" age. Ageism is often expressed through the use of derogatory terms, such as "old fogy," "coot," "fossil," "geezer," or "grump" (see Nuessel, 1982). Some consequences of ageism are job discrimination or inadequate health care.

Another term that we want to examine is **gerontophobia.** This comes from the Greek words *geras* for "old" and *phobos* for "fear." It is used to designate the fear of growing old or the fear or hatred of older persons (Bunzel, 1972; Comfort, 1967; Fischer, 1978).

Most, if not all of the terms listed above have a definition that most gerontologists would agree with. When these terms are used there is little doubt that individuals are talking about the same concepts. There are others where a variety of definitions exist, and there is no clear consensus over which definition is "right." Retired or poverty, for example, can have a variety of definitions, as we will see in this book.

Three terms with no consistent definition have already been used in this text and need to be defined. These are aging, aged, and older person.

Aging refers to the process of growing older. Technically, all human beings can be considered aging from the moment of conception. In fact, it can even be argued that aging starts before conception since both human sperm and egg cells show developmental changes prior to fusion (Hayflick, 1984). Generally, however, individuals are considered to be in a growth period for the first 25 to 30 years of their lives. At about age 25–30 a period of decline or aging will start to occur; it is at this time that most of the physical changes we experience make us less capable of coping with life. As we will see later in the book, some parts of the body start the aging process much earlier than others. Because the effects of the aging process are often not immediately noticeable, individuals are not socially defined as aging until the aging process produces noticeable effects, such as thinning or greying hair, facial wrinkles, or the need for bifocals (see Kastenbaum, 1984).

The terms **aged** or **older person** are more difficult to define. A 10 year old is likely to use these terms for someone past the age of 25. A 65 year old in good health may use the terms for those 75+ years of age. Some define anyone 10 to 15 years older than themselves as aged, older, or old. The problem in defining who is aged or older stems from the fact that researchers use different criteria to classify individuals. For some it is simple chronological age, although the specific age may vary. For others the classification may depend on certain social characteristics such as retirement. Other researchers may base the definition on physical functioning, in areas such as the filtration rate of the kidneys or the stroke volume of the heart. Others may base the definition on a combination of social, physical, or psychological characteristics.

For this book, I have decided to base the definition of "old age" on chronological age, and the specific age that will determine when someone is "old" or is an "older person" will be 65+ years of age. This is the "traditional" definition, and was more or less institutionalized by the Social Security Act of 1935 which made those 65 years of age eligible to collect full retirement benefits (Deming & Cutler, 1983; Uhlenberg, 1987). As a point of interest, in 1935 life expectancy for white males was 59.9 years and for white females it was 63.9 years; for black males and females the figures were 51.3 and 55.2 (U.S. Bureau of the Census, 1975).

We also need to confront what we are going to call those 65+ years of age. A variety of terms come to mind, such as senior citizens, elderly, mature adults, and elders. Initially this may seem like a simple issue, and not worth much time or attention. However, it has received a considerable amount of attention since the terminology assigned to a group can have a significant influence on how others see and react to it as well as on how members of the group see themselves.

Historically, the issue with blacks and women is significant, as terms used to characterize them helped to perpetuate racism and sexism. For example, certain descriptions of blacks (i.e., colored, Negro) and women (i.e., girls, gals) are covert ways of perpetuating racism and sexism. This holds true for those 65+ years of age. Terms such as geezer, fogy, or codger all evoke a negative image (see Covey, 1988; Kalab, 1985; Nuessel, 1984).

Some studies have asked those 65+ years of age what they prefer to be called. One study found that the three most preferred terms were senior citizen, mature American, and retired person (Harris & Associates, 1975). A similar study found that there were differences in preference according to variables such as sex (Barbato & Feezel, 1987). Another study examined the terms used in textbooks and found that, although there were differences by the type of book, no one term emerged as the most used or preferred (Kalab, 1985).

Researchers who have examined this controversy have suggested different terms: elders (Barbato & Feezel, 1987), older adults (Nuessel, 1987), and older persons

(Williams, 1986). This book will use older persons. I believe that this is a neutral way to accurately describe the segment of the population 65+ years of age, and also preserve its heterogeneity. Occasionally I will use "the aged" in place of older persons.

LIFE PERIODS

Those who study human beings search for patterns and regularities. One concept that has been developed to assist them is that of life periods. Students will also find that the terms life course, life span development, life path, life stages, life cycle, and developmental stages have been used by different researchers, with some using the terms interchangeably with life periods, while others distinguish among the terms. The basic concept is that throughout life there are periods that are separate and distinct from other periods in areas such as rights, roles, responsibilities, obligations, privileges, and physical and mental characteristics and capabilities. Throughout their lives, individuals move into and out of life periods as a result of factors such as chronological age, societal expectations, or physical, social, or psychological changes.

There are many ways to conceptualize life periods. One writer has established three major periods, with each period further subdivided. The first period is infancy, which would include the neonate (birth to 2 weeks), infant (to 1 year), toddler (1 to 3), and preschool child (3 to 5). The second period is the juvenile period, which subdivides into childhood (5 to 10), early adolescence (10 to 15), and late adolescence (15 to 20). The last period, making up almost three-fourths of the life cycle, is adulthood. This period has the most subdivisions since it is the longest; it is generally divided into early adulthood (20 to 25), middle adulthood (25 to 40), late adulthood (40 to 60), preretirement (60 to 65), retirement (65 to 70), and old age (70 plus) (Bromley, 1974).

Although there can be exceptions, gerontologists generally study the life periods that follow age 65. Gerontologists are interested in describing the physical, social, and psychological characteristics of these life periods. They are also interested in how changes in society produce new life periods or change existing life periods.

Members of almost all academic disciplines have been concerned with the concept of life periods. For example, psychologists have had an interest in life periods since at least the time of Freud and his psychosexual stages of development. Physiologists from Hippocrates and Galen to the present have noted that with advancing age the body undergoes a series of changes. For decades sociologists have observed that increasing age brings about changes in roles, rights, expectations, opportunities, behaviors, and responsibilities. Anthropologists have studied how the concept of life periods is present in all societies, but differs from society to society.

Components of the Life Period

The scientific concept of life periods involves three terms that should be explained: age grading, birth cohorts, and rites of passage.

Age Grading   Chronological age is an important variable in all societies because all societies make assumptions about the level of functioning of different age groups. Because of these assumptions, an age group may be denied or permitted to engage in certain forms of activities or behaviors. For example, in the United States those under 16 years of age are denied access to such rights as driving automobiles, drinking alcohol, and voting in local, state, or national elections. Older persons are also denied or given access to certain rights. For example, on reaching the age of 65 years most individuals have the right to collect Social Security or Medicare benefits. On the other side, older persons may be denied the opportunity to work because of ageism or mandatory retirement, or may be required to take a special driver's license exam.

Age grading divides life into different life periods. It is important to realize that although age grading is done primarily by chronological age, there is considerable variability based on factors such as social class, subculture, or sex. For example, individuals from the lower social classes generally progress through the life periods "faster," or at earlier chronological ages. They leave school, marry, have children, retire, and die at earlier ages than those in the upper social classes, who delay entry into the work force because of an extended period of education, which, in turn, delays marriage and parenthood. Those in the upper social classes also retire later and have a longer life expectancy. Also, different subcultures within the society may have different expectations for the same chronological age. For example, one subculture may expect 18-year-old females to be in school, while another may expect 18-year-old females to be married. Sex is another variable with considerable variability in age grading. Some believe that in contemporary American society women enter middle age and old age at an earlier chronological age than males (Neugarten & Hagestad, 1986).

At one time it was widely believed that life periods created a "timing of life events" (see Neugarten, 1979) which created expectations or patterns of behavior for individuals in certain life periods. This created a "road map" of when certain events, such as graduation from high school, marriage, the birth of a first child, retirement, or death should occur.

However, age grading is not static but dynamic and reacts to changes within a society which can alter or eliminate the timing of certain life events or even create new life periods. For example, in contemporary society many occupations have become increasingly complex, requiring an extended period of education. This may have created a new life period of youth, where individuals who are physically and mentally capable of marrying and entering the work force, delay marriage, parenthood, and workforce entry for several years because of the necessity for advanced education.

Another "new" life period has been created around retirement. In the past very few individuals lived long enough or had the financial resources to retire. Most individuals worked until they died or became too sick or debilitated to continue working. Thus, retirement was a time of poverty, illness, and disability for many. Currently, health and medical advances, coupled with Social Security and private pension plans, allow many individuals to have healthy, financially independent retirements. This category of young retirees is sometimes referred to as the "young-old." In fact, some gerontologists have divided "old age" into the young-old (55 to 74) and the old-old (75+) (Neugarten, 1974; Neugarten & Hagestad, 1976). The young-old are retired, healthy, and financially independent. This group tends to be active and recreationally oriented. The old-old have started to decline physically and need assistance in everyday living. Also, their financial resources are often strained or inadequate. Given the increase in the percentage of the population 85+ years of age, another life period of the oldest-old has been suggested (see Dannefer, 1988).

One last example of a new life period deals with the increasing amount of time married couples spend together after their children have left home. In the past, a shorter life expectancy, higher birthrate, and childbearing over a longer period of time, generally meant that one spouse in the marriage would be widowed before the last child had left home. Currently, a greater life expectancy, lower birthrate, and shortened period of childbearing means that prior to widowhood couples spend more time together after all of the children have left home in what is called the "empty nest."

In addition to new life periods, there can also be a changing rhythm in life periods (see Neugarten & Datan, 1973). For example, women in contemporary American society generally leave school later, marry earlier, have their last child earlier, and are widowed later than women in the past. Men leave school later, marry earlier, and retire earlier. Depending on the rate of social change in a society, different generations can have different life periods or they can have the same life periods occur at different chronological ages.

Research in the 1960s indicated that there was considerable consensus around certain areas of life periods such as the best age to get married or to retire (see Neugarten & Datan, 1973; Neugarten, Moore, & Lowe, 1968). That is, there were certain life-period events, such as marriage, that could occur "on-time" or "off-time." Off-time events were the most salient and obvious in statements such as, "I married late in life," "We had our family early," or "He was a young man when he died."

Now, however, some observers believe that the United States is becoming an "age-irrelevant" society (see Hall, 1980; Neugarten, 1979). We can see this as young couples delay parenthood or retired older persons go back to school. These researchers believe that it is becoming more common and acceptable for individuals to be off-time in certain life events. In a small, homogeneous society it would be more difficult to be off-time. However, in a large, heterogeneous society, such as the United States, it is much easier to be off-time.

One empirical study found a "loosening" of norms around the timing of certain life events, but reported that there was still considerable adherence to the timetables. This study noted that impressionistic observations of certain widely publicized factors, such as second and third marriages or careers, create the false belief that the United States is becoming an age-irrelevant society (Zepelin et al., 1986–1987). Another study found that although different age cohorts exhibited consensus over life events such as marriage and birth of the first child, they preferred different timings of the events (Fallo-Mitchell & Ryff, 1982).

Birth Cohorts A birth cohort is a group of individuals born in the same period of time. Terms such as "generation" and "age set" have also been used. In selecting a birth cohort researchers study individuals born in a certain year or group of years (e.g., 1910, 1910–1912).

In designating a birth cohort researchers are attempting to analyze cohort effect. They are trying to ascertain if being born in a certain time period and being exposed to certain events at a certain age, makes a cohort unique in areas such as attitudes, beliefs, or expectations. In other words, a cohort's age during a certain historical period is believed to make that cohort unlike others that either did not experience the event or that experienced it at a different age. Researchers believe that the age at which a particular event is experienced has a direct bearing on the development that takes place during a life period. For example, the depression had an impact on individuals who experienced it. However, the impact was different for those who experienced it at age 1, age 21, or age 71. For the very young it meant less food, clothing, and toys. For those about to enter the job market, it often meant frustration and feelings of inadequacy stemming from the inability to find a job. For older persons, it often meant feelings of hopelessness as they saw decades of saving vanish and increasing dependency on their adult children. Riley (1971) claimed that the differences in experiences can lead to "cohort-centrism," in which different birth cohorts view the same phenomena in distinctive ways.

Researchers now recognize that the historical period into which an individual is born, coupled with socialization and personal experiences, have an impact on future behavior. Thus variables such as the depression, World War II, the Vietnam War, the Civil Rights Movement, as well as other events, influence each birth cohort in distinctive ways. Obviously the heterogeneity of a birth cohort makes it impossible to have a perfect correlation between cohort and behavior, values, or attitudes. Nevertheless, the relationship in some instances is very strong.

The differences between birth cohorts have frequently been expressed as "generation gap." Just as parents of today who were growing up in the 1960s, 1970s, and 1980s often felt a generation gap between themselves and their parents, so they may now feel a similar gap between themselves and their children. The education, socialization, and personal experiences of their children make each generation unique in terms of concepts of reality, values, and behavior.

So far we have seen that age grading creates different life periods. Different rights, roles, responsibilities, obligations, and privileges are assigned to individuals on the basis of the life period they are in. We have also examined birth cohorts. A birth cohort simply refers to those individuals born in a certain time period. It is believed that the age at which certain historical events are experienced is important. Thus, because different birth cohorts experience the same historical event at different ages, each will be affected by an event in a different way.

In the next section we will examine how the change from one life period to another takes place.

Rites of Passage   Each life period has a different set of rights, roles, responsibilities, obligations, privileges, and physical and mental characteristics and capabilities. A variety of factors, such as chronological age, can create the expectation that a shift from one life period to another should take place. This shift from one life period to another generally takes place through the rites of passage.

Because the rites of passage bring with them new sets of expectations, in certain areas individuals learn to think of themselves and others as being "early," "late," or "on time" in regard to such milestones as having children, marrying, obtaining a job, completing an education, retiring, or dying (Neugarten & Datan, 1973; Neugarten & Hagestad, 1976). Even though, as mentioned previously, there may be a loosening of norms around the time of certain life events, being off-time in certain areas may be detrimental to individuals. For example, Neugarten and Hagestad (1976) pointed out that women who were widowed early and men who retired early often had greater difficulty in their social relationships than did individuals for whom these events occurred "on time."

The concept of rites of passage comes from anthropology (see Bettelheim, 1954; Eliade, 1958; VanGennep, 1960). In preliterate societies, the rites of passage consist of an elaborate ceremony in which individuals are symbolically transformed in status, roles, rights, opportunities, and responsibilities. In many preliterate societies there are only two life periods: childhood and adulthood. With the onset of menstruation, females usually undergo the rites of passage that transform them from the status of child to the status of adult. With males the rites of passage generally take place when the elders in the society deem them mature enough physically, socially, and psychologically to function as adults.

It should be pointed out that not only do biological changes, such as menstruation, bring about rites of passage, but the ascription of cultural meaning to the biological change is important. The onset of menstruation in a preliterate society generally signifies that a female is ready for marriage. The onset of menstruation in contemporary American society obviously does not have the same meaning.

In contemporary American society the rites of passage are generally not as formalized or public as in preliterate societies. The heterogeneity of American society and the numerous life periods contribute to this situation. However, formalized rites of passage do still occur in contemporary American society and can be seen in graduations, debutante balls, marriage ceremonies, and retirement dinners. Some of the less formalized rites of passage may be the acquisition of a house, parenthood, or a promotion. Physical changes, such as heart problems or arthritis may also signal a change in life periods.

Limitations of the Life Period Approach   Although the concept of life periods is a useful heuristic device, it has several limitations that must be taken into consideration.

First, it should be apparent that the life-period approach is culture-, time-, and generation-bound; that is, there is not one life-period approach that will fit all people in all societies for all times. The life-period approach is different from society to society. Moreover, within the same society different age cohorts may be exposed to a different number of life periods or the same life periods at different chronological ages.

Second, not only is the life-period approach limited by time, culture, and generation but also by such variables as social class, race, sex, and education.

Third, although the life-period approach is useful, it can mask the heterogeneity of older persons. Older individuals are not a homogeneous group in any factor but chronological age. For this reason there is considerable deviation from "normal" life periods. Additionally, the life period "old age" encompasses an enormous age range which allows for a tremendous variation in factors such as health or economic resources. The separation of the life period old age into several subcategories, such as young-old and old-old, is beneficial in recognizing the diversity of older persons.

Fourth, researchers have created numerous life-period approaches. Because researchers have studied different types of older persons, from different theoretical or academic frameworks, they have conceptualized each life period very differently. Some researchers have created their frameworks on the basis of chronological age; others have created frameworks based on social, psychological, or physiological criteria. For these reasons, there are a variety of life-period approaches that are often contradictory.

Fifth, often there is not an abrupt break between the life periods. Rather, there may be a considerable overlap of periods. In fact, individuals may have certain roles in one life period, which continue unchanged into the next life period. This overlap can make the categorization of individuals difficult for researchers and confusing for students.

THE DEVELOPMENT OF GERONTOLOGY

This section examines the growth and development of gerontology. First we will examine the growth of gerontology in several traditional disciplines and professions. Second, the growth and development of gerontology as a distinctive area of study will be examined. This sub-section will include information on gerontology as a discipline, and on the increase in gerontology organizations, courses, and programs. Third, occupations in gerontology will be previewed.

Academic Disciplines and Professions

The growth and development of gerontology in anthropology, biology, education, medicine, nursing, psychology, and sociology will be examined in this section.

Anthropology   Anthropologists have been fairly consistent in producing literature on aging and the aged, although not from an interest in the experience of being old in a preliterate society but because the older persons were often used as informants on the history and beliefs of their cultures (see Keith, 1985). Thus, there are numerous references to older persons scattered throughout anthropological literature. However, there was a lack of interest in older persons per se until 1965 when the American Anthropological Association held a meeting on aging and older persons (Arth, 1972). More recently the Association for Anthropology and Gerontology was founded to help "formalize" some of the "informal" work being done in the area (Fry, 1981*b*).

The "classic" work on older persons in preliterate societies was Leo Simmons' 1945 book *The Role of the Aged in Primitive Society* (see Hallowell, 1946; Simmons, 1946, 1960) based on information gathered from the Human Relations Area Files

(HRAF). After its publication, little was produced until the 1960s when several excellent works appeared (Fry, 1980).

Aging in Western Societies: A Survey of Social Gerontology (Burgess, 1960) reviewed what it was like to be an older person in several western societies and was the third book in a series. The first on the psychological aspects of aging was by Birren (1959*b*) and the second on the social aspects by Tibbitts (1960*b*). This series of books was updated in 1976, 1985, and 1990.

Margaret Clark and Barbara Anderson's excellent book *Culture and Aging* was published in 1967 and filled important gaps in the literature that signaled the start of a renewed interest in the anthropology of aging. Clark (1967) noted that the lack of anthropological material on aging stemmed from two factors. First, the area in anthropology that would most likely study older persons was that of culture and personality. This area was dominated primarily by Americans and until recently in America aging and the aged were not popular topics. The second reason why anthropologists ignored the second half of the life cycle was because the discipline of culture and personality was dominated by a psychoanalytic theoretical framework largely Freudian in nature, and as we will point out in the section on psychology, Freud did not consider the second half of the life cycle important.

Old People in Three Industrial Societies appeared in 1968 (Shanas et al., 1968). Sponsored by the International Gerontological Association, this was a cross-sectional study of the aged and their living condition in three societies: Denmark, Great Britain, and the United States.

The next major book was Cowgill and Holmes *Aging and Modernization,* published in 1972. The authors compiled a selection of papers to examine the impact of modernization on the status and treatment of older persons. Since the publication of this work, numerous other books and articles have been published. Fry (1981*a*) has compiled a bibliography of more than 500 references (see Fry, 1980, 1985; Keith, 1985).

Although some may believe that anthropological interest in aging and the aged is increasing at a time when preliterate societies are rapidly disappearing, it must be remembered that anthropologists can study any culture; it is the way anthropologists collect their information, primarily by living among and observing those they are studying, that makes anthropology unique. One example would be studies done on older persons who live in inner-city hotels in the United States (see Bohannan, 1981; Sokolovsky & Cohen, 1981).

Biology Research on the biological aspects of aging, especially longevity, has consistently generated a significant amount of literature (see Beauvoir, 1973). Biologists have extensively studied the aging process in both animals and human beings. Four early books on the biological aspects of aging were Minot's *The Problems of Age, Growth, and Death* (1908), Elie Metchnikoff's *The Prolongation of Life* (1908), Child's *Senescence and Rejuvenescence* (1915), and Pearl's *Biology of Death* (1922). It was Metchnikoff who created the term gerontology in 1903 to refer to the ''biologic study of senescence'' or ''the scientific study of old age'' (Achenbaum & Levin, 1989; Freeman, 1979).

More recently there have been three handbooks on the biological aspects of aging, the first published in 1977 (Finch & Hayflick) and the second in 1985 (Finch & Schneider) and the third in 1990 (Schneider & Rowe).

Education   One reason why the study of older persons was generally neglected by academicians in this country was because of the emphasis placed on education. To date, few other societies have placed such a high value on the education of its young. In the past, many people believed that through the universal education of the young, social problems would be eliminated, class conflicts would vanish, and the American dream would become a reality. Because they believed that a quasiperfect society would emerge through education, it became imperative to study the best ways to educate children and adolescents. Education was supposed to take young people and mold them into adults who would function smoothly in a future world. Thus, the study of child development was elevated to a new level of importance. Writers such as John Dewey, F. W. Parker, Edward Thorndike, and G. S. Hall wrote prolifically on the education of children. Older persons were considered unimportant since they were too rigid to change and since the future belonged to the young (see Curti, 1968; Jacobs, 1970).

Educators now generally view education as a lifelong process as can be seen in the changing age composition of those attending college; in 1972 about 8 percent of those attending college were 35+ years of age, by 1988 the figure was 17 percent (U.S. Bureau of the Census, 1990). This is due, in part, to the rapidly changing nature of contemporary society. Technological changes generally create obsolescence in those who do not continually participate in formal or informal education programs. In the past the knowledge and skills required for most occupations tended to remain fairly stable over a worker's life; currently occupational knowledge and skills are changing rapidly, and those who do not keep up are soon obsolete.

Education for older persons will be discussed more thoroughly in Chapter 10, "Religion and Education."

Medicine   Medicine has a long history but until recently it had little interest in older persons. Some claim that the "father of gerontology" was a medical scientist named Vladimir Korenchevsky (ca., 1880–1959) who recognized that individuals did not die from old age but rather from a "pathological interference" in the physiological process (Jacobs, 1970).

In 1909 Dr. Ignatz Nascher (ca., 1863–1944) created the term "geriatrics," in 1912 he founded the Society of Geriatry in New York City, and in 1914 published *Geriatrics: The Diseases of Old Age and Their Treatments.* While many during this time period saw the pathological conditions frequently associated with old age as "normal" and "untreatable," Dr. Nascher distinguished between senile conditions and senile pathology. In 1926 he noted that he was the only full-time specialist in geriatrics (Achenbaum, 1978; Butler, 1987b; Fischer, 1978; Haber, 1986).

In the early 1930s the chairman of the National Research Council's Division of Medical Sciences requested Dr. E. V. Cowdry, a Ph.D. in anatomy, to examine the problem of arteriosclerosis. In response to this request Dr. Cowdry edited and published

Arteriosclerosis in 1933, which noted that it was not a normal consequence of the aging process. Cowdry was also responsible for a second important book, *The Problems of Ageing*, which was published in 1939 (see Freeman, 1984). Cowdry is also considered by some to be the "father of gerontology" (see Bramwell, 1985).

The American Geriatrics Society (AGS) was founded in 1942 by a group of physicians who were interested in the health needs of older persons and publishes the *American Geriatrics Society Journal*. A second society is the National Geriatrics Society.

Edward J. Stieglitz's classic book *Geriatric Medicine* was published in 1943 and helped to generate further interest in gerontology (Butler, 1987*b*) presenting older persons in a most positive way (Haber, 1986).

Although interest continued to grow, in 1970 one-half of the medical schools in the United States made no mention of geriatrics in their catalogs. In 1978 a report by a committee of the Institute of Medicine concluded that gerontology and geriatrics were not adequately covered in the education of medical students (see Dans & Kerr, 1979; Institute of Medicine, 1978). By 1983 almost 90 percent of medical schools had instruction in geriatrics (Peterson, 1986), although frequently the courses were electives (Kroger et al., 1986; U.S. Congress, Office of Technology Assessment, 1987). In fact, a survey of educators and practitioners of medicine found little support for mandatory geriatric courses for students (Coccaro & Meyerson, 1984). The elective nature of geriatric courses is perhaps unfortunate since the older segment utilizes the medical profession more than other age groups. It is estimated that 40 percent of internists' patients are 65+ years of age and that they take up 60 percent of internists' time (see Peterson & Hansel, 1985; U.S. Congress, Office of Technology Assessment, 1987). The elective nature of courses is also unfortunate since studies have indicated that physicians have many misconceptions about older persons (see Ahmed et al., 1987; Goodwin, 1989; Michielutte & Diseker, 1984–1985; Murden & Meier, 1986; West & Levy, 1984). There have been a variety of proposals to incorporate geriatrics into medical school programs (see Duthie & Gambert, 1983; Goodenough, 1986; Papsidero et al., 1985; Ruchlin & Ullman, 1985; Sachs et al., 1984; Schimer et al., 1983; Simson & Wilson, 1984).

The growth of geriatric medicine has been hindered by the fact that traditionally it has been, and still remains, a low-status and low-paying specialty (see Steel, 1984). Also, physicians, like others in contemporary American society, often have negative attitudes toward older persons (Weiler et al., 1989). To an extent some of the negative attitudes can be eliminated by exposing medical students to older persons, especially in what might be called "quality time," and by involving them in programs that are designed to maintain the health of healthy older persons. It is also important for medical students to have role models in geriatric medicine (Weiler et al., 1989). An additional factor inhibiting growth is that there are few geriatric textbooks written for students; most have been written for the practitioner (Kroger et al., 1986).

There is also debate over the position of geriatrics in medicine. Some believe that it is a distinct body of knowledge and skills and should be an independent specialty, like pediatrics. Others believe that it belongs to specialties such as internal medicine or family practice medicine. Currently physicians cannot become board-certified in geriatrics, as they do in many other specialties. Because of this those who have the knowledge do not receive recognition; those without the knowledge can claim they possess it. In 1985 the American Board of Medical Specialties authorized the American Board of Family Practice and the American Board of Internal Medicine to offer "certificates" in geriatrics. The exam was first offered in 1988, and 4000 physicians took the exam (Besdine, 1989).

There is growth in geriatric medicine. There are currently ten postgraduate geriatric programs, with more being developed; 20 years ago the number was zero (Besdine, 1989). Also, in 1989 the *New England Journal of Medicine* started a section called "Current Concepts," which is devoted to addressing important topics in the "clinical practice of geriatric medicine."

Nursing Burnside (1988) noted that until recently there has been relatively little interest in gerontological nursing. Her review of articles in the *American Journal of Nursing* from 1900 to 1940 found only twenty-three articles, editorials, and book reviews related to older persons (see McConnell, 1988). This isn't surprising given the beliefs about older persons held by nursing at the time. One example was provided recently in an interview with a woman who became a nurse in the late 1930s or early 1940s. She noted that at that time older persons were simply considered to be patients who had "lived a long time," and that it had not been conceptualized that a specialized body of nursing knowledge was needed to address their needs (Career parallels, 1989).

The first nursing textbook, *Geriatric Nursing,* was published in 1950 by Newton and Anderson. In 1952 the term "gerontology" first appeared in the *Cumulative Index to Nursing Literature.*

Changes started to take place in the early 1960s. In 1961 the American Nurses' Association (ANA) recommended the formation of a group on geriatric nursing; in 1962 a group called Geriatric Nursing Practice was created. In 1966 the ANA established the Division of Geriatrics Nursing Practice (changed to Gerontological Nursing Practice in 1976). Also in 1966 Duke University offered the first gerontological nursing program.

By the late 1960s only 12 percent of nursing schools offered gerontology courses; another 72 percent incorporated an average of 12 hours of information on older persons in their courses. A study in the early 1970s found that out of 1072 nursing schools only twenty-seven had geriatrics as a specialty (Edel, 1986).

In 1973 the ANA offered the first nursing gerontological certificates: Gerontological Nurse Practitioner and Gerontological Nurse. By 1986 about 600 nurses had received the first, about 3500 the second. Originally the gerontological nurse practitioner (now called geriatric nurse practitioner) involved a training process that resulted in a certificate; it now cumulates in a master's degree.

In 1975 the first nursing gerontology journal was published, *Journal of Gerontological Nursing,* followed by *Geriatric Nursing* in 1979.

The second nursing gerontological textbook was published in 1976 by Burnside (see Burnside, 1988). There are now several textbooks in geriatric nursing.

Nurses spend an average of 32 percent of their time with patients 65+ years of age (Edel, 1986). Given the growth of the older population, this is likely to increase.

It is estimated that in the future there will be a severe shortage of nurses who have specialized knowledge in geriatrics. One of the reasons is that there is a lack of qualified faculty. Edel (1986) reported that 4.4 percent of nursing faculty have had courses in gerontology. Another study reported that there was a need for 2450 gerontological nursing faculty members. To date, surveys have only identified 420 (U.S. Congress, Office of Technology Assessment, 1987).

Psychology   Kaplan (1946) has noted that interest in the psychological aspects of aging goes back thousands of years. However, it is only recently that psychologists have studied gerontology from a scientific framework (see Birren, 1959a). The famous statistician Lambert Adolphe Jacques Quaetlet (ca., 1796–1874), who is sometimes called the "first" gerontologist (Birren & Woodruff, 1983), is often credited with initiating the first psychological studies on older persons in his book, *On Man and the Development of His Faculties*. In this book he described the development of individuals over a 60-year span. Francis Galton (ca., 1822–1911) was another early researcher who was interested in gerontology. In the 1880s he collected physical data from the individuals who visited the London International Health Exhibition. From these data on individuals between the ages of 5 to 80, he demonstrated the differences in physical characteristics by age in areas such as handgrip strength and hearing (Birren & Clayton, 1975; Chebotarev & Duplenko, 1972). Ivan Pavlov (ca., 1849–1936), who found that the conditioning of older animals differed from younger animals, is another frequently cited early researcher in the field of aging (Birren, 1961; Jacobs, 1970).

The man who influenced not only the study of the aged but also all of psychology was Sigmund Freud. Freud's beliefs were youth-oriented; thus he did not study or generate much interest in the study of the later part of the life cycle. He believed that the personality was formed by the time a child was 5 years of age (Back & Gergen, 1968; Hall & Lindzey, 1957). The personality in later life was only a reflection or modification of the earlier personality; hence Freud felt that it was the early life periods that should be studied. Even in dealing with older patients Freud was not as concerned with contemporary events as he was with childhood development. In his voluminous writings he had very little to say about old age, although he occasionally referred to old age and its relationship to the death instinct (see Riegel, 1959). There were also allusions in his writings to his own bitterness about growing old (see Shur, 1972).

One of Freud's major developments was his theory of psychoanalysis. Freud did not consider psychoanalysis an appropriate technique for older individuals. By "older" Freud meant 45 years of age or older (Pfeiffer, 1974). He believed that by the time the analyst broke through the rigid defense barriers, the psychoanalytic technique would be so protracted that new problems would have occurred as a natural consequence of old age. He also believed that the remaining life expectancy would not justify utilizing psychoanalytic techniques with older persons. This belief was widely held by psychoanalysists until 1919 when Karl Abraham noted that he had dealt successfully with older patients through the use of psychoanalysis (Abraham, 1960).

G. S. Hall (ca., 1844–1924), primarily known for his work on adolescence, published a book in 1922 called *Senescence*. Hall, who wrote the "first modern scientific treatment of adolescence" produced "the first major work in gerontology by an American social scientist" (Cole, 1984). The book is interesting in that it is devoid of academic references. The chapter called "Literature by and on the Aged" consists of autobiographies of aged individuals and biographies of aged individuals with special skills, strengths, or other unique traits. Hall drew his conclusions from his own survey since he found that there were no other scientific works available for consultation. In the conclusion to the book, Hall claims that the differences manifested by individuals in old age are as great, if not greater, than those exhibited in childhood and adolescence.

In the early 1930s, Walter R. Miles and his associates in the Stanford Later Maturity Project analyzed the psychological aspects of aging. The results of this project were published in 1939 by Edmund V. Cowdry in a book called *Problems of Aging*. This work was called the first systematic attempt to study aging (Tibbitts, 1960a).

In 1946 the American Psychological Association (APA) added a new division to its structure called "Maturity and Old Age." In 1955 this division held a conference on the psychological aspects of aging. Out of this conference came a book on aging called *Psychological Aspects of Aging*, edited by J. E. Anderson. This division is now called Division 20 (Adult Development and Aging), which has been very active in expanding the knowledge of the psychological aspects of aging.

In 1959 J. E. Birren edited and published the *Handbook of Aging and the Individual: Psychological and Biological Aspects*. This book has become a "classic" reference book in gerontology because of the sound scholarship in most of the articles.

In 1973 the APA's task force on aging published *The Psychology of Adult Development and Aging* edited by Carl Eisdorfer and M. Powell Lawton. This work summarized many of the developments in the area of aging. In 1977 the *Handbook of the Psychology of Aging* was published, with the second edition appearing in 1985, and the third in 1990 (Birren & Schaie, 1977, 1985, 1990). The purpose of these editions was to provide a review of the current state of knowledge in certain areas as well as a reference list for readers.

In 1986, after 5 years of planning, the APA developed a new journal, *Journal of Psychology and Aging*, which publishes ". . . original articles on adult development and aging" (Lawton & Kausler, 1986).

Sociology   Sociology was founded as an academic discipline in the 1830s by Auguste Comte. Its purpose was to discover social laws—the laws that governed human behavior. There was a belief among many early sociologists that it was their destiny to become the rulers of society. The idea seemed logical to them since they were the ones who studied society and knew the most about its functioning.

Charles Darwin had a significant influence on the development of early sociology. It was widely believed that just as animals progressed through a series of physical evolutions, so societies progressed through social evolutions. On the basis of this belief, sociologists began to create models that outlined the stages of societal development and to judge the evolution of societies. These sociologists who were concerned with the evolution of societies were called "social Darwinists." The goal of the social Darwinists was to direct society so that evolution would continue and nothing would happen to stop, redirect, or cause evolution to regress. This attitude worked against the aged in society. The more radical social Darwinists believed that individuals who could not survive via their own means should be allowed to perish. They maintained that if a society created welfare programs, then the misfits, throwbacks, and retarded would inbreed with the rest of the society and thus alter the course of evolution (see Hinkle & Hinkle, 1954; Hofstadter, 1967).

By the turn of the century, sociology was undergoing a number of significant changes. A new movement of social reform with an emphasis on culture and personality entered sociology. Writers such as W. I. Thomas, C. H. Cooley, and G. H. Mead added greatly to sociological knowledge about human behavior and how it was influenced by social forces. This was also a time when sociologists were trying to cast off earlier philosophical ties and make their discipline a science. Thus, new research techniques were constantly employed. New concepts began to create a framework that would make the study of aging easier. For example, sociological concepts such as social change, role, status, and position are frequently used in the gerontology literature today.

During the 1930s, sociology became problem-oriented. The depression arrived and thousands of older people were destitute because their savings had been wiped out and jobs were difficult to obtain. The problems of aging and the aged at last received a cursory glance by sociologists.

One of the first "good" sociology books on aging was *Social Adjustment in Old Age* edited by Otto Pollak and published in 1948. The book was the result of the work of a subcommittee of the Social Sciences Research Council, which was formed in 1923 to further research in the social sciences. In 1943 a subcommittee of this organization began to study old age. Part of its purpose was to lay a foundation and provide a framework for further research in the social aspects of aging. Pollak's book moved gerontology away from a problem-oriented approach to aging to the academic study of aging. This prompted E. W. Burgess, in the foreword to the book, to note that Pollak was writing in an area in which few studies existed.

In 1960 the *Handbook of Social Gerontology* was published by Clark Tibbitts. This book has been called a "landmark" in gerontology, and the foreword noted the ". . . newness and unorganized state of knowledge about psychosocial aging, the breadth of the subject matter to be covered, and the difficulties of introducing a new field of study and inquiry into the established academic structure. . . ." (Donahue, 1960). As noted earlier, this book was the second in a series (Birren, 1959*b*; Burgess, 1960).

Another important work in sociology was *Older People and Their Social World*, completed in 1965. This book resulted from a series of conferences held by the Midwest Sociological Society. Edited by Rose and Peterson, the book became a frequently cited source in gerontology with several "classic" articles.

Yet another major book in the development of gerontology was Cumming and Henry's book *Growing Old*, which was based on the Kansas City Studies of Adult Life that will be discussed in Chapter 4 in the sections on research projects and gerontological theory (Cumming & Henry, 1961). In the foreword to the book Talcott

Parsons noted that this was the most serious attempt to date to establish a theoretical framework for the social and psychological aspects of the aging process.

At the end of the 1960s, Matilda White Riley and Anne Foner published *Aging and Society: An Inventory of Research Findings* (1968), which condensed a great deal of empirical data of interest to sociologists. Riley, Riley, and Johnson edited a second volume called *Aging and the Professions* (1969), which presented an interpretation of the inventory findings for various professions that work with the aged. Riley, Johnson, and Foner produced the third, and last, volume in 1972, *A Sociology of Age Stratification,* which set forth their model of age stratification.

In 1976 the *Handbook of Aging and the Social Sciences* was published with the second edition appearing in 1985 (Binstock & Shanas, 1976, 1985), and the third in 1990 (Binstock & George, 1990).

The American Sociological Association has a section called the "Sociology of Aging." In addition, *Sociological Abstracts* has a section under the heading "Social Problems and Social Welfare" called "Social Gerontology."

The Growth and Development of Gerontology

We have examined the growth and development of gerontology in several traditional academic disciplines and professions. We now want to examine gerontology as a separate and distinctive area of study. First we will ask the question, "Is gerontology a discipline?" Second we will look at the growth and development of gerontological organizations. Third, the development of gerontology courses and programs, and the issues of accreditation and licensure, will be examined. Fourth, and last, occupations in gerontology will be examined.

Gerontology: What Is It?   There is currently a great deal of discussion about whether gerontology is a profession, a field, a discipline, a protodiscipline, or a subfield of other disciplines (Levine, 1981). This issue was first raised by Clark Tibbitts (1960a) when he suggested that "social gerontology" had the characteristics of a separate discipline. Now the issue is not around social gerontology, but gerontology. In the past it was assumed that gerontology would be studied by those in traditional disciplines and professions. That is, there would be sociologists, psychologists, and physicians who would have an interest in gerontology, but who would still identify with their traditional discipline or profession. Thus, if asked, "What are you?" they would answer sociologist, psychologist, or physician, not "gerontologist!"

This issue has been discussed and debated for three decades. There are those who claim that gerontology is not a discipline (Adelman, 1986; Johnson, 1980; Levine, 1981; Loeb, 1979; Peterson & Bolton, 1980) and those who have suggested that it is a discipline (Bramwell, 1985; Seltzer, 1985). There are compelling arguments for each side. In large part the issue is decided by the criteria that are used to determine the characteristics of a discipline, and the subjective determination of whether gerontology has satisfied the criteria. This issue is complex, subjective, and political. At this time, there does not appear to be a clear consensus for either position.

Gerontological Organizations Although there is debate about "what gerontology is" there is less debate about its growth (Weg, 1989). This growth can be seen in the increase in both the number and size of gerontological organizations.

In the last section it was noted that the professional organizations of many disciplines and professions have specialized groups that study aging and the aged. Division 20 of the APA would be one example. In addition to the organizations that are associated with certain disciplines and professions, there are also some organizations that can probably best be classified as multidisciplinary. This section will briefly examine the history of gerontological organizations, and three current multidisciplinary gerontological organizations.

The Society of Geriatry, founded in 1912 in New York City by Dr. Ignatz Nascher, was one of the first organizations formed to study aging and the aged. Although this society did not generate much interest or publish much literature in gerontology, it was nevertheless a beginning.

In 1938 three events occurred that increased academic interest in aging and the aged. First, the U.S.S.R. held a national conference on senescence; second, in France one of the first surveys of older people was conducted; and third, in Germany the first specialized journal in gerontology was published. A year later, in 1939, a group of English scientists formed an international association called the Club for Research on Aging. The club held conferences between 1939 and 1945.

The remainder of this section will examine three current gerontology organizations. There are *many* more that could have been examined (see Kerschner, 1987), but this list is not intended to be complete or comprehensive, but to give readers a perspective of three organizations.

The Gerontological Society was founded in the United States in 1945 with eighty members (Fischer, 1978); it grew out of the Club for Research on Aging (Achenbaum, 1978; Adler, 1958). The organization changed its name to the Gerontological Society of America (GSA) in 1981 to distinguish itself from local and state organizations. This was consistent with other national organizations such as the American Medical Association (AMA), the American Sociological Association (ASA), the American Psychological Association (APA), or the American Anthropological Association (AAA) (Brody, 1980).

The GSA is a multidisciplinary organization that is separated into four sections: biological sciences, clinical medicine, behavioral and social sciences, and social research, planning, and practice. The GSA has been instrumental in creating an interest in aging and the aged, and in coordinating and collecting relevant information. In 1957 with a grant from the National Institute of Mental Health, the society created a committee to provide a framework for future research, prepare college faculty for instruction in gerontology, train people to do research on aging, and give people the skills for working with the aged. The work of this committee was published in the three classic works previously discussed: *Handbook of Aging and the Individual: Psychological and Biological Aspects* edited by James E. Birren (1959*b*), *Handbook of Social Gerontology: Social Aspects of Aging* edited by Clark Tibbitts (1960*b*), and *Aging in Western Society: A Survey of Social Gerontology* edited by Ernest W. Burgess (1960) (Donahue, 1967). This series has since been updated three times, in the mid-1970s, the mid-1980s, and 1990 (Binstock & Shanas, 1976, 1985; Binstock & George, 1990; Birren & Schaie, 1977, 1985, 1990; Finch & Hayflick, 1977; Finch and Schneider, 1985; Schneider & Rowe, 1990).

The GSA currently publishes three regular publications for its members: *The Gerontologist,* the *Journals of Gerontology* (formerly the *Journal of Gerontology,* and now under one cover there are the following sections: Biological Sciences, Medical Sciences, Psychological Sciences,and Social Sciences), and *Gerontology News.*

The GSA has over 7000 members. In the past the GSA was one of the few organizations devoted to the study of gerontology and as such it had a distinctive purpose. Now, however, there are literally hundreds, if not thousands, of aged-related organizations. Part of its new purpose is to examine aging and the aged from an interdisciplinary perspective (Silverstone, 1988).

The GSA is only one organization dealing with older persons. A second multidisciplinary national organization dealing with older persons is the American Society on Aging, which was founded in 1954. This organization was formerly known as the Western Gerontological Society, but recently changed its name to reflect the fact that it had become a national organization. The society also has over 7000 members and publishes a quarterly journal called *Generations,* with each issue being devoted to one topic, and a bimonthly newspaper called *The Aging Connection* which reports current developments in gerontology and allows for debate and discussion of gerontological issues.

The last organization that will be discussed in this section is the Association for Gerontology in Higher Education (AGHE). Created in 1974, AGHE's purpose is primarily educational, and is directed at assisting in developing and establishing standards, and improving the quality of gerontology programs (Douglass, 1987).

Rather than individual members, only "accredited institutions of higher education" can belong to AGHE. It is an organization of colleges and universities which offer programs, degrees, and training, or which conducts research in gerontology. Currently, over 300 institutions are members.

AGHE has several publications, including the quarterly newsletter the *AGHE Exchange* and the *National Directory of Educational Programs in Gerontology.*

Gerontology Courses and Programs   The first gerontology course in the United States was offered in the late 1940s at the University of Chicago (Neugarten, 1988). In 1957 there were fifty-seven colleges and universities in the United States that offered gerontology courses. The majority of the courses were electives in academic or professional degrees. By 1967 the number had increased to 159. A study done in the mid-1980s found that 1155 campuses offered gerontology courses on a regular basis (Peterson, 1986; Standards Committee, 1989). In all probability the number has increased since this study was completed.

In addition to courses, there were also 709 gerontology programs, the first two being created in 1967 at North Texas State University and the University of South Florida (Bader et al., 1988). The AGHE defined a gerontology program "as one offering a degree, certificate, concentration, specialization, emphasis, or minor in gerontology, or one that is identified as a research and/or clinical training center in

gerontology/geriatrics'' (Standards Committee, 1989). There were 408 schools awarding some type of credential such as a certificate or degree. The survey reported that
the following number of degrees were being offered: associates 48, bachelors 187,
masters 151, and doctorates 22 (Peterson, 1987c).

Although gerontology programs have generally been developed independently of
one another, Peterson's study (1984) of master's degrees in gerontology reported
that most of the programs were similar in content, length, and requirements.

Several studies have been done on those who have obtained gerontology degrees,
the majority from master's degree programs (Friedsam & Martin, 1980; Hartford,
1980; Mangum & Rich, 1980; Peterson, 1984, 1985a, 1985b, 1987a, 1987b; Roberto
& Benschoff, 1987–1988). When graduate programs in gerontology were first created
there was concern that their graduates would be unemployable since the degree was
too specialized and at the time there were not any job designations or titles for
gerontologists. The studies have been consistent in reporting that graduates have
high employment rates, continue to work in gerontology full or part-time, and that
most were in management or administrative rather than service positions (Peterson,
1987a). Between 70 to 80 percent of those with master's degrees said that they held
their current job because of their gerontology degree (Peterson, 1985a; Roberto &
Benshoff, 1987–1988). Similar results have been found for graduates with bachelor's
degrees in gerontology (Fruit, 1985; Roberto & Benshoff, 1987–1988).

The high employment of gerontology graduates has been criticized as being somewhat misleading since many of those in these programs held jobs while taking courses
or had work experience that facilitated obtaining jobs after graduation (Krause, 1987).
When students were asked to comment on their master's programs, most were satisfied
with the length and content. The most common suggestion was that management or
administrative courses be offered, which given the positions most were in is not
surprising (see Peterson, 1985a, 1985b; Roberto & Benshoff, 1987–1988).

There are currently two major issues surrounding gerontology programs (see Seltzer,
1985). The first is whether gerontology programs in higher education should be accredited. Generally colleges and universities are accredited by a national or regional
organization and then within each college/university specific academic disciplines or
programs (i.e., education, engineering, social work, nursing, business, etc.) also receive accreditation from professional organizations. Colleges and universities that
have "accredited" programs are generally considered to have "better" programs
than those that are not accredited. Frequently, better employment opportunities exist
for graduates of accredited programs. For a program to be accredited the college/
university must meet certain standards in terms of financial support, curriculum content,
library resources, and faculty and staff. The purpose of accreditation is to assure a
higher quality program for students.

Euster (1989) has pointed out that in the past many have emphasized the quantity
of gerontology programs, not the quality. Now, with numerous gerontology programs
well established it is time to start examining quality. One way of determining quality
would be through accreditation.

In 1978 the Education Committee of the Western Gerontological Society (now
the American Society on Aging) published its suggestions on accreditation (Western

Gerontological Society, 1978). In 1980 GSA and AGHE published a report called *Foundation for Gerontological Education* (Johnson et al., 1980) which was the culmination of a project called "Foundation for Establishing Educational Program Standards in Gerontology." This project considered such questions as "Should programs in gerontology have a common core, and if yes, what should the core consist of?"

AGHE has also been active in attempting to establish standards for gerontology programs. One of the purposes of AGHE is to monitor gerontology programs and research in higher education with the ultimate goal of improving the quality, perhaps through the establishment of national standards and certification criteria (see Peterson, 1987c).

The second issue deals with licensure in gerontology. There are certain areas where individuals must pass some type of qualifying exam to be able to call themselves professionals. Generally, professional organizations administer these examinations and award licenses. These exams are generally taken after one has completed a program in higher education. For example, engineers can take an exam to be licensed as a "professional engineer." Teachers in the elementary and secondary schools need a teaching certificate in addition to a higher education degree. Accountants can take an exam to be called a certified public accountant (CPA), and nurses must pass an exam to be called a registered nurse. Additionally, licenses can be obtained in numerous other areas such as clinical psychology or social work.

The issue of licensure is again controversial. Those in favor note that currently "anyone" can call him- or herself a "gerontologist." This leads to individuals claiming knowledge and skills that they do not have (see Seltzer, 1985). It is unlikely that these individuals would be effective teaching gerontology courses or working with older persons. Bolton (1988) noted that a survey of gerontologists at the college and university level found that only 44 percent had any "formal" gerontological instruction. Of the 56 percent who did not have formal instruction, some noted that they qualified as gerontologists through self-study, work experience, personal interest, or observing family members. Bolton noted that there are few academic disciplines, if any, that would allow these nonformal methods to suffice as professional qualifications.

Those opposed to licensure claim that many eminent gerontologists have never had a gerontology course. Rather, they completed their academic degrees with specializations in areas other than gerontology (or before gerontology courses were offered at their institutions) and it was only after graduation that they became interested in gerontology. Through self-study and research they acquired their gerontological knowledge and skills (see Adelman, 1988; Atchley, 1988). Others have noted that gerontology is still evolving and that to impose rigid standards and guidelines at this state of development would be inappropriate (Beattie, 1978). These standards and guidelines may also impede the development of new innovative programs or programs with unique or specialized missions. It has also been noted that it is not rules and guidelines that create good programs but faculty and staff (Bolton, 1988).

In some cases it may not be a license that is required but the completion of a certain training or education program. Recently a series of articles described a program that developed standards, and then provided training to Area Agency on Aging personnel in Pennsylvania (Burroughs et al., 1986; Lago et al., 1986; Sharp et al., 1986;

Silverman et al., 1986). The basic concept is that certain areas of gerontology are defined by specific knowledge that should be required of personnel before employment.

A problem in the creation of accreditation and/or licensure in gerontology deals with which organization will create the standards, do the evaluations, and award accreditation or licenses. Additionally, other groups outside gerontology, such as social workers, may also oppose a gerontological organization creating standards that may affect their members.

This is currently a very political and sensitive issue in gerontology, and it is not likely to vanish. The consequences of either (or both) licensure or accreditation could be significant. For example, the federal government could decide that only licensed gerontologists, or those who graduated from an accredited gerontology program, could administer certain services to older persons. Or, organizations offering health insurance may state that they will only reimburse ''professional gerontologists'' for certain services (see Wilson et al., 1986). This could impact on other disciplines and professions that currently service these areas.

Occupations in Gerontology   We have examined the development of gerontology in some specific disciplines and professions such as anthropology, biology, nursing, and psychology. We have also explored the issue of gerontology as a separate discipline, and examined organizations, courses, and programs. This section will examine occupations in gerontology. Much of the material in this section is based on an article in *Occupational Outlook Quarterly* (Kahl, 1988) and David A. Peterson's book *Career Paths in the Field of Aging* (1987*b*). The specific areas that we will examine are teaching, research, social services, health services, program planning, and administration. There is considerable overlap among the areas. For example, a social worker may instruct gerontology courses, conduct research, and also work in a service area such as counseling with older persons. The social worker could be classified under the fields of teaching, research, and social services. Thus, while in a textbook the areas are neat and concise, in real life there is often considerable overlap.

Teaching   Studies of the two largest gerontological organizations indicated that about 12 to 14 percent of their members are employed primarily as teachers (Peterson, 1987*b*). Assuming that these teachers are instructing in gerontology programs, they are probably teaching some of the following frequently required courses in gerontology programs: introduction to social gerontology, psychology of aging, biology or physiology of aging, and sociology of aging. Other courses often required are dying and death, counseling older persons, health and diseases of aging, and public policy for the aged (Association for Gerontology in Higher Education, 1987). Rather than specific courses, gerontologists can also instruct segments of courses. For example, in a social problems' course the gerontologist would handle the segment on older persons, or in a substance abuse course would discuss the development and treatment of substance abuse in older persons. In addition, gerontologists also have the opportunity to create and instruct in short-term training programs, such as training respite workers to work with Alzheimer's families (Middleton, 1987).

Of institutions of higher education surveyed, about 50 percent offered at least one gerontology course. Larger public institutions had more courses than smaller private institutions. The number of faculty currently involved in gerontology instruction appears to be around 2600, with the largest departments being health, psychology and human development. Many of those employed in teaching have Ph.D.s or other doctorates (i.e., M.D., D.D.S., Ed.D., etc.). Most instructors teach an average of about two gerontology courses per year (Association for Gerontology in Higher Education, 1987).

Research   In the larger gerontological organizations from 4 to 19 percent of their members defined themselves primarily as researchers (Peterson, 1987*b*). There is a growing recognition that much of our information on older persons is inadequate and that if federal, state, and local programs are going to be effective, more knowledge is needed. Careers in this area generally require doctorates.

Social Services   There are a variety of careers in this area and the requirements can range from paraprofessional training to extensive graduate work. Essentially, those in social service careers provide services to older persons. The type of services will depend on the purpose and the amount of funding of the social service agency. Individuals working for social service agencies might find themselves primarily in an educational role, educating older persons on their eligibility for federal, state, or local programs such as Supplemental Security Income, meal-on-wheels, day care, food stamps, or respite programs. In addition to education, the individual could also assist eligible older persons to enroll in these programs. Other social service workers might manage nutrition programs, transportation services, day-care programs, or housing programs for older persons.

Social workers, or other qualified individuals, can provide counseling to older persons. They can also create and run programs in areas such as Alzheimer's, caregiver support groups, or grief counseling.

Health Services   Although traditionally the term ''health'' is associated with physicians or nurses, the field is much broader and encompasses many occupations. The social worker noted above could be classified in this area, as could psychologists, occupational or physical therapists, nutritionists, as well as many other health specialties. Other health areas could be in nursing homes as directors, recreation leaders, or perhaps as some type of ombudsperson who would attempt to resolve complaints of nursing home residents.

Program Planning   In the last decade we have seen the development of many new and creative programs to assist older persons. In addition, many traditional programs have changed, responding to the needs of older persons. Program planners work in a variety of agencies and try to determine ways to make existing programs better or to create new programs for older persons. For most this is a broad-based role that means that the individual has to work with older persons to understand some of their needs, and then be able to conceptualize a program to meet these needs and to secure funding to actually implement the program.

Administration   All of these programs for older persons discussed above require administrators. For each agency, someone has to allocate money, hire personnel, and essentially coordinate the programs within the agency. Often this means that the administrator assumes a variety of roles from chief executive officer, to accountant, to public relations director. This individual is also concerned with obtaining funding for the next fiscal year, and sources of funding often change from one year to the next. As funding in one area is no longer available, changing some programs and services may be necessary. Individuals in this position are concerned with demonstrating the need and the effectiveness of the programs they offer. Other administrative roles would be as nursing home administrator.

As was noted in an earlier section, many gerontologists find themselves in administrative roles. Individuals in the study on the two largest professional gerontological organizations reported that 23 percent of one and 43 percent of the other reported that they worked primarily in administrative roles (Peterson, 1987*b*).

Comment on Careers in Gerontology   The opportunities in gerontology are enormous, especially for those with entrepreneurial skills (see Coyle, 1985). Because many careers in gerontology are not well defined, gerontologists have the opportunity to create new areas, roles, and careers. For example, it may take an energetic student to convince an organization that it needs an "industrial gerontologist." The industrial gerontologist could provide services to an organization's employees in areas such as pre- and postretirement counseling, elder-care workshops, or information on local, state, or federal programs for older persons. Additionally, the individual could implement programs such as adult day care, an elder-care referral service (IBM Introduces, 1988), or retirement options (i.e., rehearsal retirement or phased retirement) that could benefit not only the organization but employees. The individual could also expand into areas such as grief counseling, which again would benefit employees and the organization. Depending on the individual's skills and the organization, the individual could also make suggestions in such areas as marketing or special services to older persons (see Jessup & Coberly, 1989).

SUMMARY

Knowledge of aging and the aged is almost certain to be relevant in your life since you will deal with it at a personal, family, and societal level.

In the first section of this chapter some basic terminology was defined. The term gerontology refers to the study of old age. Three subfields of gerontology were described. The first was social gerontology which refers to the social aspects of aging. The second subfield was geriatrics. Essentially in geriatrics, knowledge is applied, such as the diagnosis or treatment of a physical or mental disorder. The third subfield was educational gerontology which deals with educational programs for, or programs about, aging and the aged.

Ageism and gerontophobia were also discussed. Ageism refers to prejudice and discrimination based on age. Ageism can manifest itself in an area such as job discrimination. Gerontophobia is the fear of growing old, or the fear or hatred of older persons.

Two terms that were difficult to define were aging and aged. The term aging refers to the process of growing older. It is debatable as to when aging starts, but many would agree that we spend the first 25 to 30 years of our lives maturing and developing and the remaining years aging. The term aged is also difficult to define. Some prefer to base the definition on chronological age, while others use physical, social, or psychological characteristics. Others use a combination of several characteristics. For this book individuals are considered aged when they are 65+ years of age.

There is also debate over what to call those 65+ years of age. In this book they will generally be called "older persons," although at times they will be referred to as aged.

The second section of this chapter discussed the concept of life periods. Throughout life individuals enter into new life periods that are different from previous life periods in terms of rights, roles, responsibilities, obligations, privileges, and physical and mental characteristics. A variety of factors move individuals into and out of life periods, such as completing one's education or aging. It is important to recognize that different researchers conceptualize life periods in different ways. It is also important to recognize that the concept of life periods is dynamic, not static. That is, it is continually changing with existing life periods being modified and new life periods being added.

There are generally three components in life periods: age grading, birth cohorts, and rites of passage. Age grading simply notes that each society makes assumptions about the level of functioning of each age group. Based on these assumptions an age group may be permitted or denied to engage in certain activities. For example, certain age groups in the United States cannot drive motor vehicles, vote in local, state, or national elections, or be elected to certain political offices. In the past it was assumed that age grading created a "timing of life events." That is, age grading created standards of when certain things were expected to occur: graduation from high school or college, marriage, birth of children, retirement, and death. Age grading is currently controversial, with some researchers believing that we are becoming an age-irrelevant society. By this they mean that the age at which certain events are supposed to occur are no longer relevant. Others believe that although there are exceptions, age grading is still in effect.

The second concept that was considered under life periods was birth cohorts, or those born in the same year or group of years. The basic concept is that those born about the same time form a generation that shares values, beliefs, and experiences, which makes them different from other cohorts. The term "generation gap" has been used to express the differences between generations.

The last concept under life periods was rites of passage. This deals with the shift from one life period to another. Often the rites of passage are formal, such as graduation from college or retirement dinners. These mark the transition from student to worker or worker to nonworker. Many rites of passage are not formal ceremonies, but they are no less important. Becoming parents or having a major medical problem could signal the transition from one life period to another.

The third and last section in this chapter dealt with the development of gerontology. This area was subdivided into two parts: academic disciplines and professions, and the growth and development of gerontology.

In the first part the growth and development of gerontology in several disciplines and professions was examined: anthropology, biology, education, medicine, nursing, psychology, and sociology. The first major work in gerontology emerged in anthropology in the 1940s. Since that time anthropology has had more of an interest in the subject. Biology has had a persistent interest in gerontology, especially in the area of longevity. Education is a "newcomer" to gerontology. Traditionally it was concerned with the education of children, adolescents, and young adults. Recently, however, education has been conceptualized as a lifelong process, and education has become interested in developing programs for older persons. Medicine and nursing were both slow to develop an interest in geriatrics, perhaps because traditionally there have been so few older persons. This is changing in both professions with more courses and programs being developed. Psychology and sociology have also been slow to develop an interest in aging and the aged. Some excellent works did appear in both disciplines, but until recently there was not much of an interest by either. Both now have specialized groups that study older persons and the quality and quantity of research is growing.

The second part of this section examined the growth and development of gerontology. Four areas were examined. The first explored the question of where gerontology falls in terms of the traditional disciplines and professions. Some believe that gerontology is a separate and distinct discipline, while others do not. This is currently a controversial issue. The second area dealt with the growth and development of gerontological organizations. Gerontology organizations originated in the early part of this century and have continued to expand in both numbers and membership. Three organizations were examined: Gerontological Society of America, American Society on Aging, and the Association for Gerontology in Higher Education. The third area dealt with the growth of courses and programs in gerontology. The first course in gerontology was offered in the late 1940s; the first gerontology program in the late 1960s. Both courses and gerontology programs have proliferated which has brought up two concerns: accreditation and licensure. The basic concept behind accreditation is whether gerontology programs should be accredited by a national organization. The other issue is whether "gerontologists" should be licensed.

The last part of the chapter dealt with occupations in gerontology. Originally it was noted that there was hesitation to create degrees in gerontology since there were no job descriptions that called specifically for "gerontologists." However, it has been found that graduates of gerontology programs have found employment opportunities in areas such as teaching, research, social services, health services, program planning, and administration.

REFERENCES

Abraham, K. (1960). The applicability of psycho-analytic treatment to patients at an advanced age (1919). In E. Jones (Ed.), *Selected papers of Karl Abraham* (pp. 312–317). New York: Basic Books.

Achenbaum, W. A. (1978). *Old age in the new land.* Baltimore: Johns Hopkins University Press.

Achenbaum, W. A., & Levin, J. S. (1989). What does gerontology mean? *The Gerontologist,* **29**(3): 393–400.

Adelman, R. C. (1986). The dilemma of research training in gerontology. *Educational Gerontology,* **12**(6): 579–584.

Adelman, R. C. (1988). On the establishing of credentials in gerontology. *The Gerontologist,* **28**(2): 169.

Adler, M. (1958). History of the Gerontological Society. *Journal of Gerontology,* **13**(2): 94–100.

Ahmed, S. M., Kraft, I. A., & Porter, D. M. (1987). Attitudes of different professional groups toward geriatric patients. *Gerontology and Geriatrics Education,* **6**(4): 77–86.

Anderson, J. E. (1956). *Psychological aspects of aging.* Washington, DC: American Psychological Association.

Arth, M. (1972). Aging: A cross-cultural perspective. In R. Kastenbaum & S. Sherwood (Eds.), *Research planning and action for the elderly* (pp. 352–364). New York: Behavioral Publications, Inc.

Association for Gerontology in Higher Education and the Andrus Gerontology Center (1987). *Gerontology instruction in American institutions of higher education: A national survey.* Washington, DC: Association for Gerontology in Higher Education.

Atchley, R. C. (1988). Credentialing and licensing of gerontologists. *The Gerontologist,* **28**(2): 170–171.

Back, K. W., & Gergen, K. J. (1968). The self through the latter span of life. In C. Gordon & K. J. Gergen (Eds.), *The self in social interaction* (pp. 241–250). New York: Wiley.

Bader, J. E., Scott, F. G., & Kime, R. E. (1988). The first 20 years of The University of Oregon Center for Gerontology. *Educational Gerontology,* **14**(6): 471–480.

Barbato, C. A., & Feezel, J. D. (1987). The language of aging in different age groups. *The Gerontologist,* **27**(4): 527–531.

Beattie, W. M. (1978). Major concerns and future directions in gerontology higher education. In M. M. Seltzer, H. Sterns, & T. Hickey (Eds.), *Gerontology in higher education: Perspectives and issues.* Belmont, CA: Wadsworth.

Beauvoir, S. (1973). *The coming of age.* New York: Warner.

Besdine, R. W. (1989). The maturing of geriatrics. *The New England Journal of Medicine,* **320**(3): 181–182.

Bettelheim, D. (1954). *Symbolic wounds.* New York: Collier Books.

Binstock, R. H., & George, L. K. (Eds.) (1990). *Handbook of aging and the social sciences* (third edition). New York: Academic Press.

Binstock, R. H., & Shanas, E. (Eds.) (1976). *Handbook of aging and the social sciences.* New York: Van Nostrand Reinhold.

Binstock, R. H., & Shanas, E. (Eds.) (1985). *Handbook of aging and the social sciences* (second edition). New York: Van Nostrand Reinhold.

Birren, J. E. (1959a). Principles of research on aging. In J. E. Birren (Ed.), *Handbook of aging and the individual: Psychological and biological aspects* (pp. 3–42). Chicago: University of Chicago Press.

Birren, J. E. (Ed.) (1959b). *Handbook of aging and the individual: Psychological and biological aspects.* Chicago: University of Chicago Press.

Birren, J. E. (1961). A brief history of the psychology of aging. *The Gerontologist,* **1**(June): 69–77.

Birren, J. E., & Clayton, V. (1975). History of gerontology. In D. S. Woodruff & J. E. Birren (Eds.), *Aging: Scientific perspectives and social issues* (pp. 15–30). New York: Van Nostrand.

Birren, J. E., & Schaie, K. W. (Eds.) (1977). *Handbook of the psychology of aging.* New York: Van Nostrand Reinhold.

Birren, J. E., & Schaie, K. W. (Eds.) (1985). *Handbook of the psychology of aging* (second edition). New York: Van Nostrand Reinhold.

Birren, J. E., & Schaie, K. W. (Eds.) (1990). *Handbook of the psychology of aging* (third edition). New York: Academic Press.

Birren, J. E., & Woodruff, D. S. (1983). Aging: past and future. In D. S. Woodruff & J. E. Birren (Eds.), *Aging: Scientific perspectives and social issues* (second edition) (pp. 1–16). Monterey, CA: Brooks/Cole.

Bohannan, P. (1981). Food of old people in center-city hotels. In C. L. Fry (Ed.), *Dimensions: Aging, culture, and health* (pp. 185–200). Brooklyn: Bergin.

Bolton, C. (1988). Program standards and faculty development in gerontology instruction: A role for professional organizations. *Educational Gerontology*, **14**(6): 497–507.

Bramwell, R. D. (1985). Gerontology as a discipline. *Educational Gerontology*, **11**(4/6): 201–210.

Brody, E. M. (1971). Aging. In J. Turner (Ed.), *Encyclopedia of social work* (pp. 51–74). New York: National Association of Social Workers.

Brody, E. M. (1980). A message from the immediate past-president. *The Gerontologist*, **20**(6): 616.

Bromley, D. B. (1974). *The psychology of human ageing* (second edition). Baltimore: Penguin.

Bullough, B. (1987). Nursing. In G. L. Maddox (Ed.), *The encyclopedia of aging* (pp. 487–489). New York: Springer.

Bunzel, J. H. (1972). Note on the history of a concept—gerontophobia. *The Gerontologist*, **12**(2, Part I): 116, 203.

Burgess, E. W. (Ed.) (1960). *Aging in western societies: A survey of social gerontology*. Chicago: University of Chicago Press.

Burnside, I. M. (Ed.) (1976). *Nursing and the aged*. New York: McGraw-Hill.

Burnside, I. M. (Ed.) (1988). *Nursing and the aged* (third edition). New York: McGraw-Hill.

Burroughs, P., Young, J. E., Silverman, M., Ricci, E., Shore, B. K., & Lago, D. (1986). The development and evaluation of training standards for the aging network and academia: II. Summary of project products and the process of their validation. *Gerontology and Geriatrics Education*, **7**(2): 47–54.

Butler, R. N. (1969). Ageism: Another form of bigotry. *The Gerontologist*, **9**(4, Part I): 243–246.

Butler, R. N. (1987*a*). Ageism. In G. L. Maddox (Ed.), *The encyclopedia of aging* (pp. 22–23). New York: Springer.

Butler, R. N. (1987*b*). Geriatrics. In G. L. Maddox (Ed.), *The encyclopedia of aging* (p. 284). New York: Springer.

Career parallels history of gerontology (1989). *American Nurse*, **21**(4), 6.

Chebotarev, D. F., & Duplenko, Y. K. (1972). On the history of the home gerontology movement. In D. F. Chebotarev (Ed.), *The main problems of Soviet gerontology* (pp. 3–40). Kiev: USSR Academy of Social Sciences.

Clark, M. (1967). The anthropology of aging. *The Gerontologist*, **7**(1): 53–65.

Clark, M., & Anderson, B. G. (1967). *Culture and aging: An anthropological study of older Americans*. Springfield: Thomas.

Coccaro, E. F., & Meyerson, A. T. (1984). Attitudes of students, educators and practitioners of medicine towards gerontologic/geriatric training. *Gerontology and Geriatrics Education*, **4**(4): 29–37.

Cole, T. R. (1984). The prophecy of *Senescence:* G. Stanley Hall and the reconstruction of old age in America. *The Gerontologist*, **24**(4): 360–366.

Comfort, A. (1967). On gerontophobia. *Medical Opinion & Review*, **3**(9): 455–457.

Covey, H. C. (1988). Historical terminology used to represent older people. *The Gerontologist,* **28**(3): 291–297.

Cowgill, D. O., & Holmes, L. D. (Eds.) (1972). *Aging and modernization.* New York: Appleton-Century-Crofts.

Coyle, J. M. (1985). Entrepreneurial gerontology: creative marketing of gerontological skills. *Educational Gerontology,* **11**(2/3): 161–167.

Cumming, E., & Henry, W. F. (1961). *Growing old: The process of disengagement.* New York: Basic Books.

Curti, M. (1968). *The social ideas of American educators.* Totowa, NJ: Littlefield, Adams.

Dannefer, D. (1988). Differential gerontology and the stratified life course: Conceptual and methodological issues. In G. L. Maddox & M. P. Lawton (Eds.), *Annual review of gerontology and geriatrics, Volume Eight* (pp. 3–36). New York: Springer.

Dans, P. E., & Kerr, M. R. (1979). Gerontology and geriatrics in medical education. *New England Journal of Medicine,* **300**(5): 228–232.

Deming, M. B., & Cutler, N. E. (1983). Demography of the aged. In D. S. Woodruff & J. E. Birren (Eds.), *Aging: Scientific perspectives and social issues* (pp. 18–51). Monterey, CA: Brooks/Cole.

Donahue, W. (1960). Foreword. In C. Tibbitts (Ed.), *Social gerontology* (pp. v–vii). Chicago: University of Chicago Press.

Donahue, W. (1967). Development and current status of university instruction in social gerontology. In R. E. Kushner & M. E. Bunch (Eds.), *Graduate education in aging within the social sciences* (pp. 76–101). Ann Arbor: Division of Gerontology, University of Michigan.

Douglass, E. B. (1987). Association for Gerontology in Higher Education. In G. L. Maddox (Ed.), *The encyclopedia of aging* (pp. 40–41). New York: Springer.

Duthie, E. H., & Gambert, S. R. (1983). Geriatrics consultation: Implications for teaching and clinical care. *Gerontology and Geriatrics Education,* **4**(2): 59–66.

Edel, M. K. (1986). Recognize gerontological content. *Journal of Gerontological Nursing,* **12**(10): 28–32.

Eisdorfer, C., & Lawton, M. P. (Eds.) (1973). *The psychology of adult development and aging.* Washington, DC: American Psychological Association.

Eliade, M. (1958). *Rites and symbols of initiation: The mysteries of birth and rebirth.* New York: Harper and Row.

Estes, C. L. (1986). The challenge to gerontological education in an era of austerity. *Educational Gerontology,* **12**(6): 495–505.

Euster, G. L. (1989). Assessment of gerontology certificate program quality: A follow-up study of graduates. *Gerontology and Geriatrics Education,* **9**(4): 59–72.

Fallo-Mitchell, L., & Ryff, C. D. (1982). Preferred timing of female life events: Cohort differences. *Research on Aging,* **4**(2): 249–267.

Finch, C. E., & Hayflick, L. (Eds.) (1977). *Handbook of the biology of aging.* New York: Van Nostrand Reinhold.

Finch, C. E., & Schneider, E. L. (Eds.) (1985). *Handbook of the biology of aging* (second edition). New York: Van Nostrand Reinhold.

Fischer, D. H. (1978). *Growing old in America.* Oxford: Oxford University Press.

Freeman, J. T. (1979). *Aging: Its history and literature.* New York: Human Sciences Press.

Freeman, J. T. (1984). Edmund Vincent Cowdry, creative gerontologist: Memoir and autobiographical notes. *The Gerontologist,* **24**(6): 641–644.

Friedsam, H. J., & Martin, C. A. (1980). An applied program in social gerontology: A report on ten year's experience. *The Gerontologist,* **20**(5): 514–518.

Fruit, D. (1985). Are graduates of bachelor's degree programs in gerontology employed? A report of a national survey. *Educational Gerontology,* **11**(4/6: 237–245.

Fry, C. L. (Ed.) (1980). *Aging in culture and society: Comparative viewpoints and strategies.* Brooklyn: Bergin.

Fry, C. L. (Ed.) (1981a). *Dimensions: Aging, culture, and health.* Brooklyn: Bergin.

Fry, C. L. (1981b). Introduction: Anthropology and dimension of aging. In C. L. Fry (Ed.), *Dimensions: Aging, culture, and health* (pp. 1–11). Brooklyn: Bergin.

Fry, C. L. (1985). Culture, behavior, and aging in the comparative perspective. In J. E. Birren & K. W. Schaie (Eds.), *Handbook of the psychology of aging* (second edition) (pp. 216–244). New York: Van Nostrand Reinhold.

Goodenough, G. K. (1986). The relative value of geriatric training components in family practice preparation. *Gerontology and Geriatrics Education,* **7**(2): 1–7.

Goodwin, J. S. (1989). Knowledge about aging among physicians. *Journal of Aging and Health,* **1**(2): 234–243.

Haber, C. (1986). Geriatrics: A specialty in search of specialists. In D. VanTassel & P. N. Stearns (Eds.), *Old age in a bureaucratic society* (pp. 66–84). New York: Greenwood Press.

Hagestad, G. O., & Neugarten, B. L. (1985). Age and the life course. In R. H. Binstock & E. Shanas (Eds.), *Handbook of aging and the social sciences* (second edition) (pp. 35–61). New York: Van Nostrand Reinhold.

Hall, C. S., & Lindzey, G. (1957). *Theories of personality.* New York: Wiley.

Hall, E. (1980). Acting one's age: New rules for old: Bernice Neugarten interviewed. *Psychology Today,* **14**(4): 66–80.

Hallowell, A. (1946). Review of Leo Simmons' *The role of the aged in primitive society. Annals of the American Academy,* **244**: 229.

Harris, L., & Associates (1975). *The myth and reality of aging in America.* Washington, DC: National Council on the Aging.

Hartford, M. E. (1980). Study of the vocational interests of the first two masters degree classes of the Leonard Davis School 1975–1976. *The Gerontologist,* **20**(5): 526–533.

Hayflick, L. (1984). When does aging begin? *Research on Aging,* **6**(1): 99–103.

Hinkle, R. C., & Hinkle, G. J. (1954). *The development of modern sociology.* New York: Random House.

Hofstadter, R. (1967). *Social Darwinism in American thought.* Boston: Beacon Press.

IBM introduces elder care referral service for employees (1988). *Aging,* **358**: 26.

Institute of Medicine (1978). *Aging and medical education.* Washington, DC: National Academy of Sciences.

Jacobs, H. L. (1970). Education for aging. In A. M. Hoffman (Ed.), *The daily needs and interests of older people* (pp. 382–398). Springfield: Thomas.

Jessup, D. D., & Coberly, S. (1989). Gerontologists in business. *Generations,* **13**(3): 40–43.

Johnson, H. R. (1980). Introduction. In C. Tibbitts, H. Friedsam, P. Kerschner, G. Maddox, & H. McClusky (Eds.), *Academic gerontology: Dilemmas of the 1980s.* Ann Arbor: University of Michigan Institute of Gerontology.

Johnson, H. R., Britton, J. H., Lang, C. A., Seltzer, M. M., Stanford, E. P., Yancik, R., Maklan, C. W., & Middlesworth, A. B. (1980). Foundations for gerontological education. *The Gerontologist,* **20**(3 Part 2): 1–61.

Kahl, A. (1988). Careers in the field of aging. *Occupational Outlook Quarterly,* **32**(3): 3–21.

Kalab, K. A. (1985). Textbook references to the older population. *Educational Gerontology,* **11**(4/6): 225–235.

Kaplan, O. J. (1946). The psychology of maturity. In P. L. Harriman (Ed.), *The encyclopedia of psychology* (pp. 370–378). New York: Philosophical Library.

Kastenbaum, R. (1984). When aging begins: A lifespan developmental approach. *Research on Aging,* **6**(1): 105–117.

Kastenbaum, R. (1987). Gerontology. In G. L. Maddox (Ed.), *The encyclopedia of aging* (pp. 288–290). New York: Springer.

Keith, J. (1985). Age in anthropological research. In R. H. Binstock & E. Shanas (Eds.), *Handbook of aging and the social sciences* (second edition) (pp. 231–262). New York: Van Nostrand Reinhold.

Kerschner, P. A. (1987). Membership organizations. In G. L. Maddox (Ed.), *The encyclopedia of aging* (pp. 424–427). New York: Springer.

Kleemeir, R. W., Havighurst, R. J., & Tibbitts, C. (1967). Social gerontology. In R. E. Kushner & M. E. Bunch (Eds.), *Graduate education in aging within the social sciences* (pp. 37–52). Ann Arbor: University of Michigan Press.

Koller, M. R. (1968). *Social gerontology.* New York: Random House.

Krause, D. (1987). Careers in gerontology: Occupational fact or academic fancy. *The Gerontologist,* **27**(1): 30–33.

Kroger, M. H., Papsidero, J. A., Isaacs, F., & Gesten, F. C. (1986). The content of textbooks in geriatric medicine: Some directions for improvement. *Gerontology and Geriatrics Education,* **7**(1): 37–53.

Kuhn, M. E. (1987). Gray Panthers. In G. L. Maddox (Ed.), *The encyclopedia of aging* (p. 297). New York: Springer.

Lago, D., Silverman, M., Eisele, F., Ricci, E., & Britton, J. H. (1986). The development and evaluation of training standards for the aging network and academia: III. Conclusions and implications. *Gerontology and Geriatrics Education,* **7**(2): 55–65.

Lawton, M. P., & Kausler, D. H. (1986). Editorial. *Journal of Psychology and Aging,* **1**(1): 3.

Levine, M. (1981). Editorial: Does gerontology exist? *The Gerontologist,* **21**(1): 2–3.

Loeb, M. B. (1979). Gerontology is not a profession—the oldest or the youngest. In H. L. Sterns, E. F. Ansello, B. M. Sprouse, & R. Layfield-Faux (Eds.), *Gerontology in higher education: Developing institutional and community strength.* Belmont, CA: Wadsworth.

McConnell, E. S. (1988). Outlook for gerontological nursing as a specialty. In M. A. Matteson & E. S. McConnell (Eds.), *Gerontological nursing: Concepts and practice* (pp. 123–136). Philadelphia: Saunders.

Mangum, W. P., & Rich, T. A. (1980). Ten years of career training in gerontology: The University of South Florida experience. *The Gerontologist,* **20**(5): 519–525.

Michielutte, R., & Diseker, R. A. (1984–1985). Health care provider's perceptions of the elderly and levels of interest in geriatrics as a specialty. *Gerontology and Geriatrics Education,* **5**(2): 65–85.

Middleton, L. (1987). Training respite workers for Alzheimer's families. *Aging,* **356**: 24–26.

Moody, H. R. (1976). Philosophical presuppositions of education for old age. *Educational Gerontology,* **1**(1): 1–16.

Murden, R. A., & Meier, D. E. (1986). Medical student outlook on practice in nursing homes. *Gerontology and Geriatrics Education,* **7**(2): 29–37.

Neugarten, B. L. (1974). Age groups in American society and the rise of the young-old. *Annals of the American Academy of Political and Social Science,* **415**(September): 187–198.

Neugarten, B. L. (1979). Time, age, and the life cycle. *American Journal of Psychiatry,* **136**(7): 887–894.

Neugarten, B. L. (1988). The aging society and my academic life. In M. W. Riley (Ed.), *Sociological lives* (pp. 91–106). Newbury Park, CA: Sage.

Neugarten, B. L., & Datan, N. (1973). Sociological perspectives on the life cycle. In P. B. Baltes & K. W. Schaie (Eds.), *Life-span developmental psychology: Personality and socialization* (pp. 53–69). New York: Academic Press.

Neugarten, B. L., & Hagestad, G. (1986). Age and the life course. In R. H. Binstock & E. Shanas (Eds.), *Handbook of aging and the social sciences* (pp. 35–55). New York: Van Nostrand Reinhold.

Neugarten, B. L., Moore, J. W., & Lowe, J. C. (1968). Age norms, age constraints, and adult socialization. In B. L. Neugarten (Ed.), *Middle age and aging: A reader in social psychology* (pp. 22–28). Chicago: University of Chicago Press.

Newton, K., & Anderson, H. C. (Eds.) (1950). *Geriatric nursing.* St. Louis: Mosby.

Nuessel, F. H. (1982). The language of ageism. *The Gerontologist,* **22**(3): 273–276.

Nuessel, F. H. (1984). Old age needs a new name. *Aging,* **346:** 4–6.

Nuessel, F. H. (1987). On the Barbato and Feezel article. *The Gerontologist,* **27**(6): 809.

Palmore, E. B. (1989). Social gerontology: An essential part of the "backbone." *Gerontology and Geriatrics Education,* **9**(4): 27–45.

Papsidero, J. A., Isaacs, F., & Reinhardt, M. (1985). Comprehensive assessment of the elderly patient: A clinical course of study for medical students. *Gerontology and Geriatrics Education,* **5**(4): 1–15.

Peterson, D. A. (1984). Are master's degrees in gerontology comparable? *The Gerontologist,* **24**(6): 646–651.

Peterson, D. A. (1985*a*). Employment experience of gerontology master's degree graduates. *The Gerontologist,* **24**(5): 514–519.

Peterson, D. A. (1985*b*). Graduates' perceptions of gerontology master's degree curricula. *Gerontology and Geriatrics Education,* **5**(3): 19–28.

Peterson, D. A. (1986). Extent of gerontology instruction in American institutions of higher education. *Educational Gerontology,* **12**(6): 519–529.

Peterson, D. A. (1987*a*). Job placement and career advancement of gerontology master's degree graduates. *The Gerontologist,* **27**(1): 34–38.

Peterson, D. A. (1987*b*). Career paths in the field of aging. Lexington, MA: Lexington Books.

Peterson, D. A. (1987*c*). Gerontology credentials: Extent and consistency. *Gerontology and Geriatrics Education,* **7**(3/4): 5–15.

Peterson, D. A. & Bolton, C. R. (1980). *Gerontology instruction in higher education.* New York: Springer.

Peterson, M. C., & Hansel, N. K. (1985). Perceived adequacy of geriatric training in a family practice residency program. *Gerontology and Geriatrics Education,* **6**(1): 9–15.

Pfeiffer, E. (1974). Use of drugs which influence behavior in the elderly. In R. H. Davis (Ed.), *Drugs and the elderly* (pp. 33–51). Los Angeles: Ethel Percy Andrus Gerontology Center.

Philibert, M. (1965). The emergence of social gerontology. *Journal of Social Issues,* **21**(4): 4–12.

Pollak, O. (1948). *Social adjustment in old age.* New York: Social Science Research Council.

Riegel, K. F. (1959). Personality theory in aging. In J. E. Birren (Ed.), *Handbook of aging and the individual* (pp. 797–830). Chicago: University of Chicago Press.

Riley, M. W. (1971). Social gerontology and the age stratification of society. *The Gerontologist,* **11**(1, Part 1): 79–87.

Riley, M. W. (1987). On the significance of age in sociology. *American Sociological Review,* **52**(1): 1–14.

Riley, M. W., & Foner, A. (1986). *Aging and society, Volume one: An inventory of research findings*. New York: Russell Sage Foundation.

Riley, M. W., Johnson, M., & Foner, A. (1972). *Aging and society, Volume Three: A sociology of age stratification*. New York: Russell Sage Foundation.

Riley, M. W., Riley, J. W., & Johnson, M. E. (1969). *Aging and society, Volume Two: Aging and the professions*. New York: Russell Sage Foundation.

Roberto, K. A., & Benshoff, J. J. (1987–1988). A comparison of graduates with bachelor's and master's degrees in gerontology. *Gerontology and Geriatrics Education*, **8**(1/2): 53–63.

Rose, A. M., & Peterson, W. A. (Eds.) (1965). *Older people and their social world*. Philadelphia: F. A. Davis.

Ruchlin, H. S., & Ullman, A. (1985). Preparing medical students to effectively care for the elderly. *Gerontology and Geriatrics Education*, **5**(4): 69–76.

Sachs, L. A., McPherson, C., & Donnerberg, R. (1984). Influencing medical students' attitudes toward older adults: A curriculum proposal. *Gerontology and Geriatrics Education*, **4**(4): 91–96.

Schimer, M. R., Sterns, H. L., & Gerson, L. W. (1983). Promoting faculty support and participation in geriatric teaching programs. *Gerontology and Geriatrics Education*, **4**(2): 51–57.

Schneider, E. L., & Rowe, J. W. (Eds.) (1990). *Handbook of the biology of aging* (third edition). New York: Academic Press.

Seltzer, M. M. (1985). Issues of accreditation of academic gerontology programs and credentialing of workers in the field of aging. *Gerontology and Geriatrics Education*, **5**(3): 7–18.

Shanas, E., Townsend, P., Wedderburn, D., Friis, H., Milhoj P., & Stehouwer, J. (1968). *Old people in three industrial societies*. New York: Atherton.

Sharp, S. J., Britton, J. H., Lago, D., Ricci, E., Silverman, M., Shore, B. K., & Young, J. E. (1986). The development and evaluation of training standards for the aging network and academia: I. Background and rationale. *Gerontology and Geriatrics Education*, **7**(2): 39–45.

Shur, M. (1972). *Freud: Living and dying*. New York: International Universities Press.

Silverman, M., Shore, B. K., & Jewell, I. K. (1986). The development and evaluation of training standards for the aging network and academia: IV. One year follow-up evaluation of the implementation of the training standards. *Gerontology and Geriatrics Education*, **7**(2): 67–89.

Silverstone, B. (1988). Editorial: Aging in tomorrow's world. *The Gerontologist*, **28**(5): 577–578.

Simmons, L. W. (1946). Attitudes toward aging and the aged: Primitive societies. *Journal of Gerontology*, **1**(1): 72–93.

Simmons, L. W. (1960). Aging in preindustrial society. In C. Tibbitts. (Ed.), *Handbook of social gerontology* (pp. 62–91). Chicago: University of Chicago Press.

Simson, S., & Wilson, L. B. (1984). Education in prevention, health promotion and aging in medical and nursing schools. *Gerontology and Geriatrics Education*, **5**(1): 43–52.

Smith, L. (1988). The world according to AARP. *Fortune*, **117**(5): 96–98.

Sokolovsky, J., & Cohen, C. (1981). Being old in the inner city: Support systems of the SRO aged. In C. L. Fry (Ed.), *Dimensions: Aging, culture, and health* (pp. 163–184). Brooklyn: Bergin.

Standards Committee of the Association for Gerontology in Higher Education (1989). *AGHE standards and guidelines for gerontology programs*. Washington, DC: Association for Gerontology in Higher Education.

Steel, K. (1984). Geriatric medicine is coming of age. *The Gerontologist,* **24**(4): 367–372.

Tibbitts, C. (1960*a*). Origin, scope, and field of social gerontology. In C. Tibbitts (Ed.), *Handbook of social gerontology* (pp. 3–26). Chicago: University of Chicago Press.

Tibbitts, C. (Ed.) (1960*b*), *Handbook of social gerontology: Social aspects of aging.* Chicago: University of Chicago Press.

Tibbitts, C. (1963). Introduction: Social gerontology: origin, scope, and trends. *International Social Science Journal,* **15**(6): 339–354.

Uhlenberg, P. (1987). A demographic perspective on aging. In P. Silverman (Ed.), *The elderly as modern pioneers* (pp. 183–204). Bloomington: Indiana University Press.

U.S. Bureau of the Census (1975). *Historical statistics of the United States, colonial times to 1970.* Washington, DC: U.S. Government Printing Office.

U.S. Bureau of the Census (1990). *Statistical Abstract of the United States: 1990.* Washington, DC: U.S. Government Printing Office.

U.S. Congress, Office of Technology Assessment (1987). *Life-sustaining technologies and the elderly.* Washington, DC: U.S. Government Printing Office.

U.S. Department of Health and Human Services (nd). Age words: A glossary on health and aging. Washington, DC: U.S. Government Printing Office.

VanGennep, A. (1960). *The rites of passage.* Chicago: University of Chicago Press.

Weg, R. B. (1989). The backbone of academic gerontology: Introduction. *Gerontology and Geriatrics Education,* **9**(4): 1–7.

Weiler, P. G., Orgren, R. A., & Olafson, L. (1989). Medical education and interest in geriatrics. *Educational Gerontology,* **15**(5): 441–451.

West, H. L., & Levy, W. J. (1984). Knowledge of aging in the medical profession. *Gerontology and Geriatrics Education,* **4**(4): 97–105.

Western Gerontological Society, Education Committee (1978). Draft standards and guidelines. *Generations,* **3**: 43–51.

Wilensky, H. L., & Lebeaux, C. N. (1965). *Industrial society and social welfare.* New York: Free Press.

Williams, T. F. (1986). Geriatrics: The fruition of the clinician reconsidered. *The Gerontologist,* **26**(4): 345–349.

Wilson, C. C., Netting, F. E., & Thibault, J. M. (1986). Jack of all trades: Master of none? *Gerontology and Geriatrics Education,* **6**(4): 27–39.

Zepelin, H., Sills, R. A., & Heath, M. W. (1986–1987). Is age becoming irrelevant? An exploratory study of perceived age norms. *International Journal of Aging and Human Development,* **24**(4): 241–256.

CHAPTER **2**

DEMOGRAPHY

Judy Gelles/Stock, Boston

INTRODUCTION

In the first chapter we defined gerontology and explored its development and history. We also examined occupations in gerontology. It is now time to begin an examination of some of the characteristics of older persons. This chapter will examine demography, which is the study of the composition and distribution of a population or subpopulation of a society. Demographers are generally involved in three areas of study.

First, they are interested in determining the characteristics of a society's population, such as median age, percentage of minority members, distribution of individuals between rural and urban areas, ratio of males to females, or percentage that is 65+ years of age.

A second area of interest is in the examination of how the society's population characteristics influence the society. For example, demographers would be concerned with how an increase in older persons influences attitudes and social policies toward older persons.

The third area that demographers give attention to is how certain changes in the society, such as increasing technology, affect or change the population's characteristics. For example, demographers would study the impact industrialization had on the desirability of children, or the average age at retirement.

The remainder of this chapter is separated into two sections. The first section examines the size and growth of the older population and the factors that have contributed to the growth of the older population: birth rate, immigration, and mortality and life expectancy. Future demographic projections will also be provided. The second section will present a demographic profile of the older population. Specifically we will examine sex ratio, marital status, race and ethnicity, labor force participation, economic status, education, geographic distribution, social support ratio, and living arrangements.

SIZE AND GROWTH OF THE OLDER POPULATION

As we will see shortly, there are many areas concerning older individuals that demographers can examine. Of all the areas perhaps the most dramatic concerns the growth of the population segment that is 65+ years of age. Some figures are presented in Table 2-1 for different years.

As Table 2-1 indicates, there has been a significant increase in both the number and percentage of this population. In 1870 there were slightly over one million older persons and they composed 3 percent of the population; by 1988 there were over thirty million older persons and they composed 12.3 percent of the population. In absolute numbers, the size of the older population is currently larger than the total population of the United States in 1850.

While this percentage of older persons is the highest in the history of the United States, there are several European countries that have a larger percentage: Sweden (16.9), Norway (15.5), United Kingdom (15.1), Denmark (14.9), West Germany (14.5), Austria (14.1), Belgium (13.4), Greece (13.1), Italy (13.0), Luxembourg (12.7), France (12.4), Hungary (12.5). Some developing countries have a compara-

TABLE 2-1
NUMBER AND PERCENT OF THE
POPULATION 65+ YEARS OF AGE
(Numbers in Thousands)

Year	Number	Percentage
1870	1153	3.0
1880	1723	3.5
1890	2417	3.9
1900	3084	4.0
1910	3950	4.3
1920	4933	4.7
1930	6634	5.4
1940	9019	6.8
1950	12,270	8.1
1960	16,560	9.2
1970	19,980	9.8
1980	25,549	11.3
1988	30,367	12.3

Source: U.S. Bureau of the Census, 1975, 1990.

tively low percentage of older persons: Guatemala (2.9), Bangladesh (3.1), Philippines (3.4), Indonesia (3.5), Mexico (4.3) (Soldo & Agree, 1988).

Another way to examine the growth of the aged segment of the population is to examine the changing population composition of the society. This is done in Table 2-2 which shows the percent of the population in different age categories for 1900, 1970, and 1988.

As can be seen, the decline is primarily in the younger age categories. In fact, in 1900 the segment of the population from 0 to 19 years of age composed 44.3 percent of society; by 1970 it had declined to 37.8 percent; in 1988 it composed 28.9 percent. When we examine the segment of the population that is 65+ years of age we can see that it went from 4 percent of the total population in 1900, to 9.8 percent in 1970, to 12.3 percent in 1988.

The increase in the aged population can be seen in another figure, median age, which is simply the age at which half the population is older and half younger. Table 2-3 presents the figures on median age from 1820 to the present.

The increase in the median age indicates that the entire population is "aging." This is also true of the segment 65+ years of age. There are two ways to demonstrate the aging of the aged population. The first is shown in Table 2-4 which presents the number and percentage of the total population in the age groups 65–74, 75–84, and 85+ from 1900 to 1990.

In examining the increases we can see that from 1900 to 1990 the segment 65–74 increased from 2.9 percent to 7.2 percent of the total population. The percentages for the segment 75–84 were 1.0 and 4.1 and for the segment 85+ were 0.2 and 1.3.

TABLE 2-2
PERCENT OF POPULATION BY AGE CATEGORY

	Year		
	1900	1970	1988
Under 5	12.06	8.4	7.5
5–9	11.68	9.8	7.3
10–14	10.63	10.2	6.7
15–19	9.94	9.4	7.4
20–24	9.65	8.1	7.9
25–29	8.59	6.6	8.9
30–34	7.31	5.6	8.9
35–39	6.53	5.5	7.8
40–44	5.59	5.9	6.6
45–49	4.55	6.0	5.3
50–54	3.87	5.5	4.5
55–59	2.91	4.9	4.4
60–64	2.36	4.2	4.4
65+	4.05	9.8	12.3

Source: U.S. Bureau of the Census, 1975, 1990.

The second way to demonstrate the aging of the aged population is by examining only the population 65+ years of age, and then looking at the percentage each age category represents of the total aged population. This is done in Table 2-5.

Table 2-5 indicates that between 1960 and 1988 the percentage of "young" older persons (65–69) declined from 37.7 percent of the total population of older persons to 32.9 percent; the percentage of "old" older persons (85+) increased from 5.4 percent to 9.7 percent of the total aged population. The age group 85+ is currently

TABLE 2-3
MEDIAN AGE OF THE
POPULATION

Year	Median age
1820	16.7
1850	18.9
1870	20.2
1900	22.9
1920	25.3
1950	30.2
1960	29.4
1970	27.9
1980	30.0
1987	32.3

Source: U.S. Bureau of the Census, 1975, 1990.

TABLE 2-4
POPULATION 65+ YEARS OF AGE
(Numbers in Thousands)

Year	65–74		75–84		85+		65+ years total	
	Number	Percent	Number	Percent	Number	Percent	Number	Percent
1900	2189	2.9	772	1.0	123	0.2	3084	4.0
1920	3464	3.3	1259	1.2	210	0.2	4933	4.7
1940	6375	4.8	2278	1.7	365	0.3	9018	6.8
1950	8415	5.6	3278	2.2	577	0.4	12,270	8.1
1960	10,997	6.1	4633	2.6	929	0.5	16,559	9.2
1970	12,447	6.1	6124	3.0	1409	0.7	19,980	9.8
1980	15,578	6.9	7727	3.4	2240	1.0	25,545	11.3
1990*	18,035	7.2	10,349	4.1	3313	1.3	31,697	12.7

* Projected.
Source: U.S. Senate Special Committee on Aging, 1987–1988.

one of the fastest growing age groups in the country (U.S. Senate, 1987–1988). The major reasons for the increase in the aged segment of the population are birth rate, immigration, and mortality and life expectancy. These will be examined below.

Birth Rate

The birth rate (the number of children born for every 1000 individuals in the society) is influenced by factors such as the availability and reliability of birth control methods, legalized abortion, and the desirability of children. The number of children born in a particular time period will forever alter the composition of a population. A large number of children born in a relatively short period of time (such as the post-World War II "baby boom" ca., 1946–1964) will initially alter the composition of the population by lowering the median age. Over the next two decades the number of

TABLE 2-5
PERCENTAGE OF TOTAL AGED
POPULATION BY AGE CATEGORY

	1960	1988
65–69	37.7	33.9
70–74	28.7	26.0
75–79	18.6	19.4
80–84	9.6	11.9
85+	5.4	9.7
Total	100.0	100.0

Source: U.S. Bureau of the Census, 1975, 1990.

schools, teachers, and jobs would have to increase to accommodate the influx of young people into society. If the birthrate then dropped or returned to previous levels, the median age would start to climb as this segment of the society grew older. Again, changes in the society would be necessary, such as the closing of some schools, and the reduction in the number of teachers. As this segment grew older there would be other changes needed, such as new ways to finance Social Security and medical care for older persons.

In large part, the growth of the population 65+ years of age has been caused by two factors. First, a high pre-1920 birth rate and second, a decline in the birthrate in recent years.

Prior to 1920 the birthrate was higher than today. For example, in 1900 for every 1000 individuals there were 32.3 births. These individuals now compose the population that is 65+ years of age. Thus, a high pre-1920 birthrate contributed to the increase in the size and percentage of older persons in contemporary American society.

The second way the birthrate has influenced the growth of the percentage of persons 65+ years of age is by declining in recent years; in fact, it is widely believed that the decline in the birthrate is more important in increasing the percentage of older persons than the decline in the mortality rate (Soldo & Agree, 1988). The birthrate in 1988 was 15.9, or about half what it was in 1900 (see Table 2-6).

Immigration

Pre-1920 immigration also had an impact on the growth of the older segment of the population. Between 1900 and 1910 the average yearly immigration rate (the number

TABLE 2-6
BIRTH RATE FROM
1800 TO 1987
(Per 1000 Population)

Year	Rate
1800	55.0
1840	51.8
1880	39.8
1900	32.3
1920	29.5
1930	21.3
1940	19.4
1950	24.1
1960	23.7
1970	18.4
1980	15.9
1988	15.9

Source: U.S. Bureau of the Census, 1975, 1990.

of immigrants per 1000 residents) was 10.4. Until 1950, immigrants totaled about one-fourth of those reaching old age (Uhlenberg, 1987). Restrictions on immigration after World War I significantly reduced the impact of immigrants on the composition of the aged population.

In 1988 the immigration rate was 2.6 and the percentage of immigrants in each age category was more consistent with the existing composition of the population of the United States. For example, in 1988 about 28 percent of immigrants were under 16 years of age (in comparison with 29 percent of the population being 0 to 19 years of age). About 13 percent of immigrants were 65+ years of age. Again, this compares closely with the 12.3 percent of the existing population. With the current immigration rate being much lower than the rate at the turn of the century and the percentage of immigrants in each age category similar to societal percentages, current immigration has little influence on the age composition of the population. In fact, currently only about 10 percent of those turning 65 years of age were foreign born (Uhlenberg, 1987).

Mortality (Death) Rate and Life Expectancy

The last factors that have significantly influenced the growth of the segment of the population 65+ years of age are the mortality rate and life expectancy. Because of factors such as public health and medical improvements, the mortality rate has declined significantly for most age categories. The total mortality rate (the number of deaths per 100,000) was 1105 in 1960. By 1988 it had dropped to 944.0. Changes can be seen in almost every age category, with some of the most dramatic changes for those 65+ years of age. The decline in the death rate for younger individuals will initially decrease median age, but ultimately mean that more individuals will live to old age, thus increasing median age. A decline in the mortality rate for older persons means an increase in life expectancy, which will probably increase median age and the percentage of older persons (U.S. Bureau of the Census, 1980, 1990).

We can see the impact of the decline in the mortality rate on life expectancy. Life expectancy is the estimated average number of years an individual at a certain age can expect to live (U.S. Bureau of the Census, 1990). Although generally computed from birth, it can be computed for any age (see Fries, 1987). In 1900, a person could expect to live to about 48 years of age. The average life expectancy in 1988 was 74.9. Additionally, in 1900 four out of every 10 infants reached 65 years of age; currently it is 8 out of 10 (Soldo & Agree, 1988).

Another factor is having a significant influence here, namely medical advances. In the past the major medical advances benefited primarily the young who were freed from many fatal or chronically incapacitating "childhood" diseases. Recent medical advances are beginning to change this. For example, the risk of dying from two of the major causes of death, heart disease and stroke, have been declining in recent years. Additionally, the age at onset and survival time for those with cancer has been increasing. For example, from 1968 to 1982 the mean age for those dying from cancer increased by almost 2 years (Soldo & Agree, 1988).

Not only have there been medical advances but more people have access to health care through health insurance. Also, increasing knowledge of the consequences of lifestyle has resulted in selecting "healthier" lifestyles for many individuals (see Rosenwaike & Dolinsky, 1987).

Societies that go from high birth- and death rates to low birth- and death rates are sometimes said to have undergone demographic transition. The theory of demographic transition has three stages. The first stage is characterized by a high potential for growth. In this stage there is a high birthrate and a high death rate. Preindustrial societies are often examples of the first stage. Although the high birthrate provides the potential for growth, the high death rate offsets it and creates a society with little or no growth. The second stage occurs when the society is beginning to "modernize." New knowledge reduces the death rate, but the birthrate remains high. This creates a society with high growth. The high birthrate also creates a "young" population. The third and last stage characterizes a mature "modern" society. Both the birth- and death rates have been reduced. This is generally a low- or no-growth society, with an aging population.

Future Projections

The future is often difficult to predict. This is also true for demographers. To accurately calculate future population statistics demographers must predict factors that will impact on immigration, birth, and mortality rates (see Carter, 1988a). The complexity of accurately predicting these factors is easy for most to see. The impact of the immigration rate, which has the least influence of the three on the population's demographic composition, is the easiest to predict since it is established by law and rarely changes. However, predicting the birth- and mortality rates is more difficult. For example, since 1945 we have had two generations with different birthrates; one was the "baby boom" generation (ca. 1946–1964) and the other the "baby bust" generation.

There are several factors that impact on the birthrate. One is the economy. Generally, the better the economy the higher the birthrate; the worse the economy the lower the birthrate. We saw low birthrates in the depression, as well as some recent recessions. We saw high birthrates after World War II when there was economic growth. However, not only is it difficult to predict economic trends, but more recently the strength of the economy as a predictor of birthrate has been challenged. Another factor that influences the birthrate deals with the cost of raising children. At one time children were probably an economic asset; now they are an economic liability. Some societies offset the high cost of childrearing by providing parents with a monthly allowance per child and offering free health care and free educational costs through college. Other societies can offset the high cost of childrearing by offering certain tax advantages. These are social policy decisions and are determined largely by societal attitudes. If social attitudes change then we may see other changes that would decrease childrearing costs and increase the birthrate.

The future mortality rate is also difficult to predict. Because we have seen so many medical advances in the last few decades there is the tendency to believe that in the future the changes in this area will significantly reduce mortality in old age, thus increasing life expectancy and the number and percentage of older persons. However, there are numerous factors, which are difficult to predict that could interfere with our demographic projections and expectations; we will briefly consider two. The first deals with euthanasia. Many states have enacted "right-to-die" legislation, which essentially allows dying individuals to elect to forgo certain "life-sustaining technologies," which could include food and water. This is sometimes referred to as "passive" euthanasia. There is also a movement toward a more "active" form of euthanasia which would allow physicians to "induce" death in dying individuals. We do not know how widely these forms of euthanasia will be used. However, depending on the number of older persons who elected these as options, the percentage and number of older persons in the population could be affected.

A second potential impact is the HIV/AIDS epidemic (human immunodeficiency virus/acquired immunodeficiency syndrome). As of July 1989, about 1 percent of the reported cases of AIDS were individuals 65+ years of age (Schmidt & Kenen, 1989), and in 1988 it ranked as the fifteenth leading cause of death in the United States (Centers for Disease Control, 1989). Currently, the majority of those identified with AIDS are between 25 and 44 years of age (Schmidt & Kenen, 1989). If AIDS becomes a major cause of death in this age group, the initial impact would be to increase the percentage of older persons, because the death rate of younger age cohorts is increased, but ultimately there would be fewer individuals reaching old age, thus decreasing the percentage of older persons.

The major point of the above is that it is difficult to accurately make demographic projections. Because of this, demographers often calculate different sets of statistics, each based on different assumptions about future birth, immigration, and mortality rates. These are commonly referred to as low-, middle-, or high-series projections. In Table 2-7 you will find the middle-series projections for the total percentage of older persons and the median age, with the low-, and high-series projections given in parentheses.

To a large extent the projected figures are a reflection of prior birthrates. During the depression the birthrate was fairly low. As these individuals reach old age (ca. 1995–2005) the percentage of older persons is not projected to increase very much. However, as the baby boomers reach old age (ca. 2010–2030) we will see a rapid increase in the percentage of older persons. Initially the large influx of "young-

TABLE 2-7
PROJECTIONS OF THE PERCENTAGE OF
THOSE 65+ YEARS OF AGE FROM 2000 TO
2050

Year	Percentage	Median age
2000	13.0 (12.3–13.8)	36.3 (35.3–37.3)
2010	13.8 (12.4–15.3)	38.5 (36.0–40.7)
2020	17.3 (14.8–19.7)	39.3 (35.7–42.9)
2030	21.2 (17.3–25.4)	40.8 (36.0–45.5)
2040	21.7 (16.7–27.5)	41.6 (35.4–47.6)
2050	21.8 (15.8–29.2)	41.6 (35.2–48.5)

Source: U.S. Senate, 1987–1988; Soldo & Agree, 1988.

old'' will increase the percentage of older persons and lower the average age of the older population. As the "baby bust" generation reaches old age, the percentage will level off, but the average age of the older population will probably increase (i.e., the baby bust generation will be the young-old, while the baby boom generation will now be entering the old-old category).

Almost all demographic changes have consequences for a society. As was mentioned earlier, a "young" population needs more educational resources; an "old" population more health resources. Often these demographic changes take place so rapidly that it is difficult for society to prepare for or adjust to the changes. For example, in the 1960s there was a teacher shortage because of the baby boom; by the 1980s the baby bust generation created an excess of teachers. Some of the consequences of the increasing number and percentage of older persons will be discussed in subsequent chapters.

PROFILE OF THE OLDER POPULATION

We have seen that there has been an increase in the number and percentage of older persons. In this section we want to examine some of the demographic characteristics of the older population. Specifically, we will examine sex ratio, marital status, race and ethnicity, labor force participation, economic status, education, geographic distribution, social support ratio, and living arrangements.

Sex Ratio

The sex ratio is the number of males per 100 females in a population or subgroup of a population. A sex ratio of 95 means that for every 100 females there are 95 males. A sex ratio of 104 means that for every 100 females there are 104 males. In the United States, as in almost all "modern" countries, the sex ratio declines with increasing age. Some of the reasons for this decline are discussed in Chapter 6, "Physical Health," and Chapter 17, "Dying and Death." Table 2-8 presents the sex-ratio figures for several age categories.

The sex ratio declines with increasing age. This is because males have a higher death rate at all age categories, which contributes to a shorter life expectancy. The impact of a cumulative higher death rate is especially apparent in the 65+ age categories. The sex ratio indicates an unequal distribution between the sexes with increasing age.

The aged sex ratio has not always been below 100. In fact, it was not until about 1930 that it dropped below 100 for those 65+ years of age (Uhlenberg, 1987). Three factors produced a higher sex ratio for those 65+ years of age in the past. The first was the high female mortality rate associated with childbirth. Many women died as a result of childbearing complications, hence reducing the number of women reaching old age. Advances in medicine have significantly reduced maternal mortality. Second, in the past, life expectancy rates of men and women were similar, in part because of high maternal mortality rates. This started to change early in this century,

TABLE 2-8
RATIO OF MALES TO FEMALES
(Represents Number of Males per
100 Females)

Age	Ratio
All Ages	95.0
Under 14 years	104.9
14–24 years	102.4
25–44 years	98.9
45–64 years	92.0
65+ years	68.6
65–69	83
70–74	74
75–79	64
80–84	53
85+	40

Source: U.S. Senate, 1987–1988 and the U.S. Bureau of the Census, 1990.

TABLE 2-9
MARITAL STATUS OF THOSE 65+ YEARS
OF AGE
(Percent Distribution)

Status	Males	Females
Single	4.6	5.3
Married	77.7	41.5
Spouse present	75.1	39.9
Spouse absent	2.5	1.6
Widowed	13.9	48.7
Divorced	3.9	4.5

Source: U.S. Bureau of the Census, 1990.

and life expectancy for women is now several years greater than for men. Third, formerly there were more male than female immigrants. In 1900 about 70 percent of immigrants were male (Deming & Cutler, 1983). The figures are currently almost equal, and thus immigration has little impact on the aged sex ratio.

Since 1920 there have been significant gains in life expectancy for both males and females. However, recently, the rate for females has slowed, causing speculation that the gap in life expectancy may decrease. This would ultimately raise the sex ratio.

Marital Status

Above we examined the sex ratio for those 65+ years of age and noted the decline with increasing age. In this section we will examine marital status. Table 2-9 presents the figures.

Table 2-9 shows that while most older males are married most older females are not married. There is also a striking difference in the widowed category, with significantly more women being widowed. This is because in most marriages the male is older than the female and the male has a shorter life expectancy.

These figures mean that the probability of remarriage for older women is very low. In fact, eight times more older males remarry than older females (U.S. Senate, 1987–1988). These figures also have a bearing on living arrangements, with three-fourths of older males living with a spouse while the figure for older women is about 40 percent. By age 75, 68 percent of males are living with a spouse; for females the figure is 23 percent (U.S. Senate, 1987–1988).

Race and Ethnicity

Another way to examine the population characteristics of the society is to examine the race and ethnicity of those 65+ years of age. For the total white population, 13.2 percent are 65+ years of age, slightly above the figure for society in general. For nonwhites the figure is 8 percent; that is, 8 percent of the total nonwhite population is 65+ years of age. For the total black population 8.3 percent is 65+ years of age; for Hispanics it is 5.1 percent. For Asian and Pacific Islanders the figure is 6.1 percent; for Native Americans it is 5.2 percent (U.S. Bureau of the Census, 1990).

The percentages of older persons is lower for minority and ethnic groups for two reasons. First, most nonwhite segments of a society have a lower life expectancy. For example, the life expectancy figures for white males and females are 72.1 and 78.9. The figures for blacks are 65.1 and 73.8 (U.S. Bureau of the Census, 1990).

The second reason is that the percentage of older persons is lower for certain racial and ethnic groups than the nation as a whole since the figures include birthrate. As was mentioned earlier, a high birthrate tends to lower the percentage of the population 65+ years of age. The birthrates (per 1000 population) for whites and blacks are 14.5 and 21.6 (U.S. Bureau of the Census, 1990).

It is projected that the percentage of minority aged will increase. This will be primarily because of increases in life expectancy. For example, since 1900 black females have gained 40 years in life expectancy. For black males the figure is 33 years. For white females and white males the figures are 30 and 25 years (National Center for Health Statistics, 1988).

Labor Force Participation

The percentage of older employed males is 16.1; for females the figure is 7.7 percent. We can see the tremendous drop in labor force participation by examining comparable figures for the age category 50–54: 88.9 percent for males and 62 percent for females (U.S. Bureau of the Census, 1990). Thus, a high percentage of both males and females in their early 50s are in the labor force; for older persons the majority of both males and females are no longer in the labor force. We will examine this in more detail later in the book. Older persons leave the work force for both voluntary reasons, such as an adequate retirement income, and nonvoluntary reasons, such as poor health.

Projections in this area are difficult to make. Changes in Social Security are designed to discourage early retirement. However, early retirement appears to be a growing trend because many companies encourage workers to retire early, which private pension plans make possible.

Economic Status

There have been tremendous changes in this area in recent years. In 1959 35.2 percent of those 65+ years of age lived in poverty; in 1988 the figure was 12.0 percent. Older females are much more likely to find themselves in poverty than older males (U.S. Bureau of the Census, 1990).

Age is a factor in economic status. Basically, the young-old generally have higher Social Security and pension benefits and fewer are below the poverty line than the old-old. For example, 10.3 percent of those 65 to 74 years old live in poverty compared to 17.6 percent of those 85+ years of age (U.S. Senate, 1987–1988).

Race is also a factor. In 1987 the percentage of aged whites below the poverty level was 10.1. For blacks and Hispanics the percentages were 33.9 and 27.4 (U.S. Bureau of the Census, 1990).

We should see poverty continue to decline among older persons. Women have traditionally composed a disproportionate percentage of those in poverty. In the past three decades a greater percentage of women have been entering the work force. This will mean that in the future older women will have higher Social Security and private pension benefits than previous generations.

Education

The average number of years of school completed for older persons is below that of most younger individuals. Those 65+ years of age have completed an average of 12.1 years of education. The figure for those age 25–29 is 12.8 years. The difference is most noticeable in the percentages who have completed 4 or more years of college; for the aged the percentage is 10.6, for those age 25–29 it is 22.7 (U.S. Bureau of the Census, 1990).

Again there are differences by sex and race. For example, about 13 percent of older males and 8 percent of older females have completed 4 or more years of college. For blacks and Hispanics the percentages are 5.3 and 3.7 (U.S. Bureau of the Census, 1990).

Although for many older persons the levels of education are no longer a factor in salary, promotion, or other job related areas, the relatively low educational achievement still influences most individuals. This is because the lack of education often meant working at low-paying jobs which did not have private pension plans and making minimum contributions to Social Security. Additionally, lack of education may decrease the likelihood of knowledge of social services or of successfully completing or negotiating one's way through the bureaucracy that provides these services.

We will probably see the number of years of education increase for both young adults and the aged, with young adults continuing to have slightly more years of education than the aged.

Geographic Distribution

Another area that can be examined is the geographic distribution of older persons. As we will see, they are not evenly distributed throughout the states. As many would expect, Florida is the state with the highest percentage of older persons: 17.8 percent. It is followed by Pennsylvania and Iowa each with 14.9 percent, and Rhode Island with 14.7 percent. Alaska is the state with the lowest percentage of older persons, 3.8 percent, followed by Utah with 8.4 percent, Wyoming with 9.4 percent, Colorado with 9.5 percent, and Texas with 9.9 percent (U.S. Bureau of the Census, 1990).

The factors that contribute to the unique percentage of older persons in each state can vary. Florida, for example, has a large percentage of older persons because of a large in-migration of older persons. Alaska's small percentage of older persons can be accounted for in part by a large in-migration of younger individuals (see Montgomery et al., 1988). In Massachusetts between 1980 and 1986 the percentage of older persons increased from 12.8 to 13.7 percent due mostly to economic conditions that created an out-migration of younger persons (see Soldo & Agree, 1988).

As is apparent, the percentage of older persons in a state is affected by migratory patterns. The migration of older persons is a relatively new area of study in gerontology (Rogers & Watkins, 1987). In the 1950s it was assumed that older persons were basically geographically immobile (see Martin et al., 1987), and it was not until 1980 that the first collected work in this area appeared (Longino & Jackson, 1980).

There can be two types of migration: permanent and seasonal. Seasonal migrants are also often called "snowbirds." Many studies do not differentiate between the two. While the U.S. Bureau of the Census has recently started to examine permanent migrants, it has only conducted preliminary studies on seasonal migrants.

Developmental gerontologists have postulated a three-stage theory of migration. In the first stage primarily white, retired, young-old married couples in good health who have above average financial resources move from north to south, primarily for leisure pursuits. The second stage occurs when health or financial problems make independent living difficult. This is often after widowhood and the move is from south to north, generally back to their original communities near adult children. This is sometimes called "countermigration." The third stage occurs when independent living becomes impossible and the move is from the home to an institution (Carter, 1988b; Litwak & Longino, 1987).

Preliminary evidence tends to support the theory, although it needs further testing. This theory contradicts the traditional belief that the northern communities have benefited from the migration since individuals migrated south at a time when they were beginning to place demands on social services.

If this theory is correct, there are significant consequences for certain communities. For example, according to the theory older persons who have the most money and who place the fewest demands on community services leave northern communities and migrate south where they live until their health starts to deteriorate when they migrate back to their original communities. Thus, the southern communities have the "healthy and wealthy" migrants while the northern communities lose these individuals until they come back in need of health care and other local services (see Bryant & El-Altar, 1984).

There is growing interest in the snowbirds or seasonal migrants (Sullivan & Stevens, 1982). Snowbirds tend to be married, white, have above average financial resources and good health. They generally migrate to escape winter weather, or to be around friends. Older migrants from the west tend to migrate to Arizona. Older migrants from the east tend to migrate to Florida (Hogan, 1987; Martin et al., 1987; Rogers, 1989).

There have not been many studies on the economic consequences of snowbirds on the communities they migrate to. Snowbirds are consumers within the community, often add to the tax base, and do not compete with full-time residents for jobs.

However, many communities have expressed concern about the increasing number of snowbirds. These communities have noted that they place large demands on area facilities during peak times of the year. Road congestion and long lines at stores are two examples. Although preliminary studies indicate that snowbirds have a significant economic impact on the areas they migrate to (Happel et al., 1988), some area residents complain that permanent residents are forced to pay to expand roads, sewers, and water systems that are only needed 4 to 5 months out of the year. Additionally, the economic impact is not diverse, but specific to only certain areas and the jobs that are created are seasonal and generally poorly paid.

Studies are starting to emerge on the social consequences of seasonal migration. One study on Canadian snowbirds in Florida found that about 20 percent were lonely, with young-old, unmarried females in below average health, and with few area friends, as the most likely to report loneliness (Mullins et al., 1989).

It has been suggested that continued migration of older persons to sunbelt states will reduce these states' desirability. Essentially, older migrants will confront what they have gone south to escape: overcrowding, congestion, pollution, crime. Some have suggested that we will see more "aging in place," especially as more communities develop resources for older persons. Others have suggested that certain foreign countries may attract a significant number of older persons; generally countries where living expenses are lower than the United States.

Social Support Ratio

The social support ratio, also called the dependency ratio, compares a "working segment" of society with a "nonworking segment." It is a "crude" ratio and one that has many faults (see Gibson, 1989). However, because it is widely quoted it should be presented and discussed. The ratio we are interested in deals with the number of individuals 65+ years of age per 100 individuals 18 to 64 years of age (a youth dependency ratio can also be computed, which deals with the number of individuals 0 to 17 years of age per 100 individuals 18 to 64 years of age; a total dependency ratio can also be calculated which would be the number of individuals 0 to 17 and 65+ years of age per 100 individuals 18 to 64 years of age). The basic concept is that those age 18–64 are likely to be in the work force and those 65+ are likely to be out of the work force. Thus the ratio is used to indicate the working versus the nonworking or dependent segments of society.

A low dependency ratio would indicate that the working segment of society supports a small number of individuals 65+ years of age. A large ratio indicates that a large number of older individuals are dependent on those age 18–64.

In 1900 the dependency ratio was 7.4, meaning that for every 100 individuals 18 to 64 years old, there were 7.4 older persons (U.S. Senate, 1987–1988). The dependency ratio has been increasing in recent years. For example, in 1960 it was 17, in 1980 and 1988 the figures were 18.6 and 20 (U.S. Bureau of the Census, 1990; U.S. Senate, 1987–1988).

It is difficult to determine the impact the increase is going to have. Those who see the increase negatively believe it means that those age 18–64 will have to pay proportionally more of their incomes to support those 65+. That is, rather than 100 workers having to pay for 17 older persons they now have to pay for 20. This belief is correct to a certain extent for programs such as Social Security where the funds from current workers are used to pay the benefits to current retired workers. That is, the funds workers pay into the program are not used for "their" benefits but the benefits of those currently collecting benefits. When these workers retire, the funds of current workers will be used to pay their benefits. This type of system only works as long as the amount being collected from current workers exceeds the amount being paid to retired workers. The financial problems that have developed with Social Security were temporarily "solved" by raising the taxation rate and increasing the taxable salary base. An increase in the ratio would also have negative implications in a society where production was low.

Others believe that the increase in the social support ratio is not going to be detrimental to the society. They note that technology has made us a very productive society and that it is beneficial to get individuals out of the work force. Additionally, many of those 65+ years of age are not dependent on those age 18–64. Rather, they have placed money into pension plans and draw income from these plans. Additionally, they note that programs, such as Social Security, will not become burdensome to those age 18–64 because changes will be made in the program to prevent this from happening. We can currently see some of these changes, such as an increase in the age of eligibility or increasing the taxation of benefits. Other changes may be establishing an income level above which benefits would be reduced or eliminated.

In the future, the dependency ratio will shift from a high-young dependency ratio to a more even split between young-old. Table 2-10 shows the projected changes.

Living Arrangements

About 95 percent of older persons live in households. The other 5 percent are mostly in nursing homes, with a small percentage in other institutional facilities such as mental hospitals, prisons, or facilities for those who are developmentally disabled.

If we consider only those who live in households, we find that most older males

TABLE 2-10
ACTUAL AND PROJECTED DEPENDENCY RATIO

	Elderly	Young	Total
1900	7.4	76.3	83.7
1980	18.6	45.8	64.4
1990	20.6	41.9	62.5
2010	21.9	36.2	58.1
2020	28.7	36.9	65.6
2030	37.0	37.8	74.8
2050	38.0	36.6	74.6

Source: U.S. Senate, 1987–1988.

live with a spouse (75.1 percent) or other person (8.8 percent) while almost half of older women live alone (41.1 percent). In comparison, only 39.9 percent of older women live with a spouse and 19.6 percent live with someone else (U.S. Bureau of the Census, 1990). The reasons most older women live alone or with someone other than a spouse are first, because in most marriages males die before females and second, because surviving women have a longer life expectancy, are more likely to need assistance in daily living, and thus live with someone who can provide support.

As mentioned earlier, about 5 percent are in institutions, with most of those in nursing homes. Considering those in nursing homes who are 65+ years of age, we find that a relatively small percent are 65 to 74 years of age (16.1). The percentage increases with increasing age, and for the age category 75–84 the percentage is 38.7. For the age group 85+ the percentage is 45.2. We also find that females outnumber males. About 25 percent of nursing home residents 65+ years of age are male, and 75 percent female. Nursing homes are also predominately white. This is because whites have a longer life expectancy, and blacks and other racial and ethnic groups often receive more informal home care.

In the future we will probably see an increase in the percentage of older persons in nursing homes. An increase in life expectancy also means a greater likelihood of developing debilitating chronic conditions that will make independent living difficult or impossible.

SUMMARY

This chapter dealt with a demographic profile of older persons. Demography is the study of the composition and distribution of a population. In this chapter we were interested in the older population. This section was divided into two parts, the first which examined the growth of the older population, the second which examined certain demographic characteristics of older persons.

There has been a significant increase in the percentage of older persons. For example, in 1900 they composed 4 percent of the total population, by 1988 it was 12.2 percent. The increase has been brought about by four factors. The first two were caused by pre-1920s factors, the first being a high birthrate. The second was a high immigration rate, mostly of young immigrants. Both of these groups are now aged. The third is a decline in the current birthrate, which tends to increase the percentage of older persons. The last is a decreasing mortality rate, which means more individuals reach old age and live longer once they reach it.

Although difficult to project, the percentage of older persons will probably continue to increase, especially when the ''baby boom'' generation reaches old age.

The second part of the demographic section was a profile of the older population. Several characteristics were considered.

The sex ratio is the number of males per 100 females. The sex ratio goes down with increasing age, primarily because males have a shorter life expectancy than females. This has a bearing on marital status, and means that about three-fourths of older males are married and about 50 percent of older females are widowed.

Earlier we saw that about 12.3 percent of the total population is 65+ years of age. We can also examine the percentages by race or ethnic group. If we examine only whites, about 13 percent of the total white population is 65+ years of age. For blacks the figure is about 8 percent. Generally the percentage of older persons is lower for nonwhites than whites because they have a lower life expectancy and a higher birthrate.

In terms of labor force participation, about 16 percent of males and 7 percent of females 65+ years of age are employed. After age 65, labor force participation goes down.

Economic status was also examined. The percentage of older persons living in poverty has been significantly reduced from the recent past. Currently about 12.0 percent of older persons live in poverty. Poverty can vary by sex, race, and ethnic group. For example, aged women, blacks, and Hispanics are much more likely to live in poverty than white males.

Education was also examined. The average number of years of formal education for older persons is less than for young adults, although the difference has been reduced in recent years. There are still a significant number of older persons who lack the educational skills to successfully obtain needed or earned goods or services.

Older persons are not distributed equally throughout the United States. As expected, some sunbelt states, such as Florida, have a higher percentage of older persons than other states. The age composition of a state can be determined by many factors. For example, in Florida the large percentage of older persons is because of an in-migration of the old; in other states it may be because of an out-migration of the young. A three-stage theory of migration was examined.

The social support ratio was also examined. This is a crude ratio that compares the "working" segment of society with the "aged" segment. The basic concept is to examine how many are in the work force supporting the aged, and presumably nonworking segment of society. A high social support ratio means that there are several people working for every aged person; a low ratio is the reverse. The ratio has been declining in recent years. The implications were discussed.

The last variable examined was living arrangement. Basically it was noted that most older persons live in households; only about 5 percent are in nursing homes, mental institutions, prisons, or other facilities.

REFERENCES

Bouvier, L., Atlee, E., & McVeigh, F. (1975). The elderly in America. *Population Bulletin,* **30**(3).

Bryant, E. S., & El-Altar, M. (1984). Migration and redistribution of the elderly: A challenge to community services. *The Gerontologist,* **24**(6): 634–640.

Carter, J. (1988a). Policy implications of the impact of continuing mortality declines on support systems for the elderly in the United States. *Journal of Applied Gerontology,* **7**(4): 427–447.

Carter, J. (1988b). Elderly local mobility: An examination of determinants derived from the literature. *Research on Aging,* **10**(3): 399–419.

Centers for Disease Control (1989). First 100,000 cases of acquired immunodeficiency syndrome—United States. *Morbidity and Mortality Weekly Report,* **38**(32): 561–563.

Deming, M. B., & Cutler, N. E. (1983). Demography of the aged. In D. S. Woodruff & J.

E. Birren (Eds.), *Aging: Scientific perspectives and social issues* (pp. 18–51). Monterey, CA: Brooks/Cole.

Fries, J. (1987). Life expectancy. In G. L. Maddox (Ed.), *The encyclopedia of aging* (pp. 393–395). New York: Springer.

Gibson, D. E. (1989). Advancing the dependency ratio concept and avoiding the Malthusian trap. *Research on Aging*, **11**(2): 146–157.

Happel, S. K., Hogan, T. D., & Pflanz, E. (1988). The economic impact of elderly winter residents in the Phoenix area. *Research on Aging*, **10**(1): 119–133.

Hogan, T. D. (1987). Determinants of the seasonal migration of the elderly to sunbelt states. *Research on Aging*, **9**(1): 115–133.

Litwak, E., & Longino, C. F. (1987). Migration patterns among the elderly: A developmental perspective. *The Gerontologist*, **27**(3): 266–272.

Longino, C. F., & Jackson, D. J. (Eds.) (1980). Migration and the aged. *Research on Aging*, **2**(2): 131–280.

Martin, H. W., Hoppe, S. K., Larson, C. L., & Leon, R. L. (1987). Texas snowbirds: Seasonal migrants to the Rio Grande Valley. *Research on Aging*, **9**(1): 134–147.

Montgomery, R. J. V., Seccombe, K., Borgatta, E. F., & Kamo, Y. (1988). A profile of Alaska's seniors. *Research on Aging*, **10**(2): 275–296.

Mullins, L. C., Tucker, R., Longino, C. F., & Marshall, V. (1989). An examination of loneliness among elderly Canadian seasonal residents in Florida. *Journal of Gerontology: Social Sciences*, **44**(2): S80–S86.

National Center for Health Statistics (1988). *Health, United States, 1987*. Washington, DC: U.S. Government Printing Office.

Rogers, A. (1989). The elderly mobility transition. *Research on Aging*, **11**(1): 3–32.

Rogers, A., & Watkins, J. (1987). General versus elderly interstate migration and population redistribution in the United States. *Research on Aging*, **9**(4): 483–529.

Rosenwaike, I., & Dolinsky, A. (1987). The changing demographic determinants of the growth of the extreme aged. *The Gerontologist*, **27**(3): 275–280.

Schmidt, R. M., & Kenen, R. H. (1989). AIDS in an aging society: Ethical and psychosocial considerations. *Generations*, **13**(4): 36–39.

Soldo, B. J., & Agree, E. M. (1988). America's elderly. *Population Bulletin*, **43**(3): 1–51.

Sullivan, D. A., & Stevens, S. A. (1982). Snowbirds: Seasonal migrants to the sunbelt. *Research on Aging*, **4**(2): 159–177.

Uhlenberg, P. (1987). A demographic perspective on aging. In P. Silverman (Ed.), *The elderly as modern pioneers* (pp. 183–204). Bloomington: Indiana University Press.

U.S. Bureau of the Census (1975). *Historical statistics of the United States, colonial times to 1970*. Washington, DC: U.S. Government Printing Office.

U.S. Bureau of the Census (1980). *Statistical abstracts of the United States: 1980*. Washington, DC: U.S. Government Printing Office.

U.S. Bureau of the Census (1990). *Statistical abstracts of the United States: 1989*. Washington, DC: U.S. Government Printing Office.

U.S. Senate Special Committee on Aging (1987–1988). *Aging America: Trends and projections*. Washington, DC: U.S. Government Printing Office.

CHAPTER 3

OLDER PERSONS IN THE PAST AND IN PRELITERATE SOCIETIES

National Museums of Canada, Ottawa (71–1796)

INTRODUCTION

I still remember my early years in gerontology. There were two nonmedical gerontology journals (*The Gerontologist* and *The Journal of Gerontology*), I could read most of the new gerontology books that I was interested in, and at the gerontology conferences I attended most of the faces were familiar. It was in many ways comfortable, both professionally and personally. Professionally, I felt as though I could keep up with the research; personally there was a family atmosphere.

There has been a tremendous change in gerontology in a short period of time. The number of gerontology journals is probably now close to 100, with specialized journals now being published in areas such as religion, abuse, women, social policy, nutrition, social work, and housing. There are literally scores of new gerontology books being published monthly, and national gerontology conferences now often have several thousand participants.

I see these changes as positive changes for gerontology, and for society. Although gerontology is currently experiencing rapid growth, this has not always been true. In fact, until recently the study of older persons, with the possible exception of the area of longevity, has been largely ignored by researchers.

This chapter is separated into two sections. The first section provides a review of some of the reasons there was so little interest in older persons in the past; the second section will examine what it was like to be old in preliterate societies and in early American society.

EARLY INTEREST IN OLDER PERSONS

There were several factors that contributed to the lack of interest in older persons in the past. This section will examine some of these factors and will also discuss how these factors, as they changed, eventually contributed to an increased interest in older persons. Specifically we will examine the following: life expectancy, visibility of older persons, the life-period approach, urbanization, and the stigma of old age.

Life Expectancy

One of the major reasons there was so little research or writing on older persons in the past is because of life expectancy. As you recall from Chapter 2, "Demography," life expectancy is the estimated average number of years an individual at a certain age can expect to live (U.S. Bureau of the Census, 1990). Until recently life expectancy was relatively short. Thus, there was little reason to think about older persons. Table 3-1 presents life expectancy figures from prehistory to the present.

As can be seen, until the twentieth century the average life expectancy at birth was not very great. The life expectancy for Neanderthal men and women who lived 150,000 to 100,000 years ago was under 20 years of age. To date archaeological excavations have not found any Neanderthal skeletal remains where the individual was above the age of 50 (Cowgill, 1970; Fischer, 1978). Average life expectancy 8000 to 35,000 years ago in the Paleolithic Period was also under 20 years of age. Only about 1 percent of the skeletal remains from prehistoric periods are above the

TABLE 3-1
LIFE EXPECTANCY AT BIRTH
FROM PREHISTORY TO THE PRESENT

Time period	Life expectancy, years
Prehistoric men/women	18
Ancient Greece	20–30
Ancient Rome	22–30
Native Americans, Kentucky 500 B.C. to A.D. 500	<20
Middle Ages (England)	33
Nobility/Europe 1480–1579	30
1620 Massachusetts Bay Colony	35
Europe 1700	25–30
1800s England/Wales	41
1900 U.S.	47.3
1988 U.S.	74.9

Sources: Cowgill, 1970; Lerner, 1970; U.S. Bureau of the Census, 1975, 1990.

age of 50, and none have been found over the age of 65. Life expectancy in 1000 B.C. was still under 20 years of age (Cutler & Harootyan, 1975; Lerner, 1970). An examination of the skeletal remains of more than 1100 Native Americans who lived in what is now the state of Kentucky between 500 B.C. and A.D. 500 found that only three-tenths of a percent lived to be 50 years of age and that none reached 65 years of age. Even with the "rise of civilization" life expectancy did not initially increase very fast. Depending on the source, life expectancy was 20 to 30 years in ancient Greece and 15 to 30 years in ancient Rome (Cowgill, 1970; Lerner, 1970). In western society, life expectancy probably dropped after the fall of Rome until after the Middle Ages. This drop was brought about by an increase in urbanization, which increased sanitation problems that facilitated the spread of contagious diseases. Life expectancy was 33 years in England during the Middle Ages, 35 years in the Massachusetts Bay Colony (ca., 1628), and about 48 years in the United States in 1900 (Lerner, 1970). Currently it is about 75 years of age (U.S. Bureau of the Census, 1990).

The way life expectancy is calculated makes the above figures a little deceiving and in need of further explanation (also see the section on life expectancy in Chapter 17, "Dying and Death"). Life expectancy can be conceptualized as an "average" age of death. As a result, a society that has a high infant, child, and adolescent mortality rate has a low life expectancy because fewer individuals reach and die in old age. A low average life expectancy does not mean that the potential for a long life is not present, only that conditions within the society make it rare. Even for those who escaped the fatal childhood diseases, life was often difficult and short. Medical conditions, easily corrected with modern technology, often produce lingering illnesses which gradually weaken individuals and cause early death. The lack of modern technology means that most work is done with brute force, which often produces debilitating chronic conditions. The lack of a regular or adequate diet takes a toll. The point is that while the potential for a greater life expectancy is present, the conditions within the society prevent the potential from being realized for most individuals.

In the United States a variety of factors have recently increased life-expectancy figures. Essentially, the United States has experienced a demographic transition which has produced an aging of contemporary society (Meyers, 1987). In this transition, society has moved from a high birth rate and a high mortality rate—primarily from contagious diseases that affected infants, children, and adolescents—to a society that has a low birth rate and a low mortality rate.

Thus, in the past older persons received relatively little attention from writers, poets, philosophers, and scientists because there were so few of them.

Visibility of Older Persons

The above figures on life expectancy denote that until recently older persons composed a relatively small percentage of the population of most, if not all, societies. The percentage of older persons in the United States has significantly increased, as can be seen in Table 3-2 which presents information on the percentage of the population 65+ years of age and the median age for selected years.

As the percentage of older persons increased so did their visibility. As a result, older persons have gone from having a very low visibility to representing a significant proportion of the population.

Life-Period Approach

Even though people are living longer, and the percentage of the total population is growing larger, significant interest in older persons is a relatively recent phenomenon.

TABLE 3-2
PERCENT OF THE POPULATION 65+
YEARS OF AGE AND MEDIAN AGE
FOR SELECTED YEARS

Year	% 65+	Median age
1790	2.0	16.0
1820	. . .	16.7
1850	. . .	18.9
1900	4.0	22.9
1950	8.1	30.2
1970	9.8	27.9
1980	11.3	30.0
1988	12.3	32.3

Sources: U.S. Bureau of the Census, 1975, 1990; Fischer, 1978.

Another factor that will help us understand the reason for this recent interest is the concept of life periods. As was mentioned in Chapter 1, throughout life some periods are separate and distinct from others in areas such as rights, roles, responsibilities, obligations, privileges, and physical and mental characteristics. For example, we might think of retirement, widowhood, or physical decline as characteristics that often exist during the life period of old age.

As Philippe Aries (1965) pointed out in *Centuries of Childhood,* at one time the life-period approach did not distinguish between children and adults. Children were simply considered small adults. Thus, although children were clearly different from adults in many ways (e.g., physical size) early writers did not conceptualize a distinctive life period for children.

Although some writers would disagree (Achenbaum, 1978; Fischer, 1978), to some extent the same may have been true for older persons: there was not a separate life period of old age. Although there were clearly differences between "young" and "old" adults, with older individuals often being accorded special rights and privileges, many of the characteristics that we currently associate with the "aged" life period were not present. For example, sickness and death were more evenly distributed throughout life. This also meant that widowhood was not primarily a characteristic of the aged. Additionally, the lack of private or government pension plans meant that retirement was rare. Also, many of the special rights and privileges of older persons were not universally accorded, but reserved for only certain older persons, generally those who had obtained power and wealth.

Two additional factors can account for the failure to conceptualize a separate life period for older persons. First, many perceived aging as a natural, normal process which was of little interest to scientists or writers (see Brody, 1971; Carp, 1972). Second, because older persons were rare it was sometimes believed that a spiritual being (e.g., God) had caused their longevity. Because of this belief it may have been assumed that this was not an appropriate area for study.

However, as societies started to become more complex and develop more specialized roles, specific life periods evolved for several age groups, including older persons.

Urbanization

A number of factors triggered the mass movement of the population from rural to urban areas. While certainly creating a great deal of social disruption in the social order, in some ways urbanization proved to be beneficial for older persons. For the first time they became concentrated in small areas, which increased their visibility and made their social problems more apparent. This visibility in turn led to the development of specialized social and health services, which eventually blossomed into the modern system of governmental aid for older persons.

Stigma of Old Age

Perhaps another reason why older persons have been neglected in the literature is the stigma that has frequently been associated with old age. An increasing rate of technical and social change in western society created a way of life that emphasized youth. A rapidly changing technology and system of social values made the technical knowledge and social values of many older persons seem "out of date" or "old fashioned." Researchers are influenced by the culture in which they are socialized, and many of them were raised with negative values about old age. A negative attitude about a group is not conducive to generating interest in that group.

Although the stigma surrounding old age may have originally stifled research on aging and the aged, it was probably eventually responsible for actually generating research. During the 1950s and 1960s many minority groups began to rebel against the negative stereotypes society had placed on them. Many minority groups were no longer content merely with the fact that society was aware of their problems: they wanted society to do something about their problems. As the groups became more vocal, larger, and gained political support, they accumulated a larger audience and slowly conditions began to change.

One of the minority groups that grew out of this "minority movement" was that of the aged (see Streib, 1965). Numerous groups composed of older persons or of those who represented the interests of older persons were created. Their problems began to receive much greater attention. More researchers began to take notice of them and more studies on the social problems as well as on the social movement of the aged began to appear.

THE AGED IN PRELITERATE SOCIETIES AND IN EARLY AMERICAN SOCIETY

The majority of this book is concerned with older persons in contemporary American society. This section, however, is different. Here we will examine older persons in preliterate or nonindustrial societies and older persons in early American society.

Older Persons in Preliterate Societies

Many terms have been used to refer to preliterate societies, such as "primitive" and "nonindustrial." The term **primitive** is more of a value statement than a meaningful, empirical description of the society under study. What is primitive by one set of values may be cultured or sophisticated by another. However, the term **nonindustrial** is a generally accepted alternative to preliterate.

Most of our information about older persons in preliterate societies has come from anthropologists. Unfortunately, however, anthropology was a relative latecomer to the field of aging (see Fry, 1980, 1981; Keith, 1985). Although anthropological works on preliterate societies have often contained material about older persons, the studies have generally been fragmentary and incomplete. Interest in older persons is currently growing in anthropology (Nydegger, 1981), although at a time when preliterate societies are rapidly disappearing. However, anthropologists can also study individuals in contemporary society. For example, a number of excellent anthropological studies have appeared on older persons living in inner-city hotels.

The anthropology of aging and the aged is concerned with how the aged are viewed and treated by their societies. That is, "What statuses, privileges, rights, or duties are given or taken away because of advanced age?"

There is a dichotomous view among many individuals in contemporary American society about the ways in which preliterate societies have treated their older persons. The first view is that older persons were treated very well because the extended family could adequately care for them, and because as repositories of skills and knowledge they were needed by the society. The second view is that in preliterate societies older persons were treated very poorly and in fact often killed, because they were economically a burden. The Eskimo practice of killing or deserting older persons is generally used here as an example (see Nydegger, 1981). Later in this section we will examine some of the factors that produced both forms of treatment.

Both Simmons (1945, 1946, 1960) and Beauvoir (1973) have noted that nature has never been very kind to the aged of any species. Among primates in the "wild," few live beyond their reproductive years (Katz, 1978). In fact, about the only old animals are either domesticated pets or animals maintained in zoos. As animals age, they are likely to be killed by predators, accidents, or disease. It is interesting that although "lower animals" have an inborn propensity to care for their dependent young, they have no such propensity to care for their dependent aged.

Men and women are unique in that they have no instincts, no predetermined ways of dealing with or treating older persons; rather, the treatment of older persons is determined by the culture of the society. The culture of a society is its beliefs, values, skills, language, concepts, symbols, and artifacts; in essence, culture determines the way in which individuals act and behave toward one another. The culture of a society will determine if aging is to be viewed and treated as a positive achievement or as a repugnant and repulsive state of existence. Simmons (1960) has pointed out that if a satisfactory old age is desired, both the culture and the environment must provide for it. That is, the culture must state that aging is a positive achievement and that the aged are valuable individuals. Also, the environment must provide enough food and necessary care for older persons, who are generally a dependent segment of the society.

Research in Anthropology   Chapter 4, "Research and Theory in Gerontology," will examine research in gerontology from a broad perspective. In this section we are going to briefly examine research in anthropology.

Reports on preliterate societies have been accumulating ever since the first traders, explorers, adventurers, and missionaries visited other lands and learned of other societies. Most of the early reports were flawed in that they were more of an indictment against the "primitive" societies than objective, scholarly reports. Many early anthropologists were biased or ethnocentric in their reporting. Individuals are ethnocentric when they use their culture as a yardstick to evaluate other cultures. Thus if the anthropologists' society was monogamous (having one spouse) and monotheistic (believing in one God), they were generally critical of societies that were polygamous (having more than one spouse) or polytheistic (believing in more than one God). Ethnocentric observations of other cultures were frequented by terms such as "primitive," "barbaric," or "savage." Currently, anthropologists are interested in understanding how the culture of the society under study contributes to certain behavioral patterns. The principle of understanding the behavior of a society in light of its culture is known as cultural relativity.

Most anthropological studies are field-based. That is, the anthropologists live in the society they are studying. Thus, the anthropologists can observe and participate in the society to better understand it. This method has a number of advantages in that the anthropologists can actually experience, to an extent, what it is like to be a member of the society.

As with all types of research, there are also problems in conducting an anthropological study in preliterate societies. Some of the problems are discussed below.

1 Anthropologists are allowed to see only certain aspects of the societies that they are studying. Many of the ceremonies and rituals, as well as certain transactions of everyday life, may be hidden from the "outsiders." The sex or age of the anthropologists is often a factor in determining what they are allowed to see or not see.

2 Anthropologists have also noted that their presence tends to alter or change the behavior of those whom they are observing. In sociology and psychology this phenomenon is called the Hawthorne effect (i.e., individuals alter their behavior because they are being observed). Because of the Hawthorne effect, anthropologists cannot be certain that what they are observing is truly representative behavior of the society or simply behavior contrived for their benefit.

3 Anthropologists face a language problem. It is often difficult to understand and to learn the language of a preliterate society since the language is not in written form. It is even more difficult to comprehend the humor, idiosyncrasies, body language, slang, puns, and silent language of the society under study. Thus anthropologists may misinterpret information because of their lack of knowledge about the language of the society.

4 Anthropologists are also faced with relatively few aged individuals in preliterate societies. Without current medical, health, and sanitation knowledge, disease, illness, and infections, as well as accidents and warfare, have killed most individuals long before old age. An additional problem is that the harshness of the environment often prematurely ages individuals (see Simmons, 1945). Since most preliterate societies have no accurate way to keep track of time, the anthropologist may think that someone who is chronologically 30 years of age is 50 to 60 years of age. Goody (1976) has pointed out that anthropologists can often become very frustrated trying to ascertain actual chronological age. They may be told that "I am older than he" or "I was born after the great war." This may narrow down the individual's age but it is by no means an accurate measurement.

5 Anthropologists have recently noted that very often what individuals say they believe is in conflict with their actual beliefs and behavior (see Harlan, 1964; Koller, 1968; Lipman, 1970). To explain the difference between what individuals claimed they believed and what they actually did believe, Lipman (1970) created two terms: ritualistic deference and realistic appraisal. In essence, ritualistic deference is the repetition of an outdated cultural belief. For example, ritualistic deference may have called for the older person to be honored and sought for advice and wisdom. Thus when younger individuals were asked questions about older persons, they responded with ritualistic deference (e.g., "I will seek my grandfather's advice before getting married because he is a wise old man," or "Old people are to be respected because of their importance to the society"). However, it was found that the verbal responses were often in conflict with the actual beliefs and treatment of older persons. This type of behavior represents realistic appraisal. For example, the young man would not ask his grandfather's advice about getting married; rather he would ask the advice of his peer group.

Even though research on preliterate societies is often difficult, there have nevertheless been a number of excellent studies. The remainder of this section will utilize some of these studies in examining, first, modernization theory, and second, the treatment of older persons in preliterate societies.

Modernization Theory   In his classic work *The Role of the Aged in Primitive Society,* Simmons (1945) noted that older persons in stable preliterate societies had higher status and more power than older persons in changing preliterate societies. Although Simmons did not elaborate on this idea, he noted an inverse relationship between the status of older persons and the extent of modernization in the society. He was one of the first to espouse what has become known as modernization theory.

Cowgill has been the major proponent of modernization theory (Cowgill, 1972, 1974, 1986; Cowgill & Holmes, 1972). Essentially, the theory states that modernization brings about a total and unidirectional societal transformation which produces a decline in the status of older persons for four reasons.

First, the development of health technology. Health technology, in a variety of forms, leads initially to a higher birth rate as well as a higher survival rate of the young; this contributes to a "younging" of the population. However, the health technology eventually leads to an increase in life expectancy as well as methods of birth control, which leads to an aging of the population. This brings about intergenerational competition for jobs. One way of dealing with the competition is to force older persons into retirement. However, in work-oriented societies retirement is seen as a low-status role, and as a result older persons lose status.

Second, what Cowgill called "economic modernization" or "development," is, essentially, the application of increased knowledge in the workplace. It can also be conceptualized as industrialization. With economic modernization comes the obsolescence as well as the specialization of many traditional occupations. Additionally, with industrialization many of the high-status specialized occupations are centered in urban areas. Those who are the most mobile are generally the younger individuals in a society. Thus, it is the younger individuals who move to urban areas and obtain the high-status specialized occupations; older persons are left in rural areas with obsolete, low-status jobs and knowledge. As a result, younger individuals surpass their parents in terms of income, knowledge, and status.

Third is urbanization, which was briefly discussed above. As mentioned, older persons are left in rural areas when younger persons move to the urban areas; this virtually eliminates the extended family as well as the traditional power base of the oldest male in the extended family. As current research has indicated, this does not mean that older persons are isolated from their adult children, only that the generations become independent from each other.

The last factor in modernization is education. With modernization comes the mass education of the young. The young are also easier to educate when they are concentrated in urban areas. Older persons become dependent on younger persons for knowledge of current events and for basic tasks such as reading letters from relatives. As a result of their increase in knowledge, young adults acquire positions of power and authority, formerly held by their parents and grandparents, thus alienating them from their parents and grandparents. Thus, there is an inversion of status with younger persons having higher status.

To summarize, the basic belief of modernization theory is that with increasing modernization the status of older persons declines. To test modernization theory Cowgill and Holmes (1972) examined thirty propositions concerning the aged cross-culturally and found that there were eight universal principles:

1 Older persons represent a numerical minority in the society.
2 Aged women outnumber aged men.
3 There is a high proportion of widows in the aged population.
4 Aged individuals have age-specific roles ascribed to them that result in different treatment because of these roles.
5 With increasing age older persons leave the work force and enter advisory or supervisory roles that require less physical energy.
6 Older persons continue in political, judicial, and civic roles.
7 Norms exist that specify that the adult children of older persons have certain responsibilities to their aged parents.
8 Life, even in old age, is valued and methods are sought to prolong it.

They also reported that many of their propositions were NOT supported by their research, some of which are presented below.

1 Longevity is always related to the extent of modernization.
2 The status of older persons is always high in preliterate societies and low in "modern" societies.
3 The status of older persons is always high in societies with ancestor worship.
4 The status of older persons goes down in societies with rapid social change.
5 The status of older persons decreases in societies that have increasing literacy.
6 Retirement is only found in societies that have a surplus of food.

Several studies have found support for this theory (Palmore & Manton, 1974; Palmore & Whittington, 1971; Watson & Maxwell, 1977), while other studies have not supported the theory (Achenbaum, 1978; Dowd, 1984; Fischer, 1978; Glascock & Feinman, 1981, 1986). Fischer (1978), for example, found that the status of older persons had started to change before urbanization, industrialization, and mass education (i.e., modernization). It has been suggested that part of the conflict in research may stem from the immaturity of the theory (see Achenbaum & Stearns, 1978), and that further thought will demonstrate that the theory is correct but in need of refinement (see Achenbaum, 1978; Fry, 1988; Palmore & Manton, 1974).

Cowgill (1974), for example, has noted that in the later stages of modernization several factors may improve the status of older persons. The first is a "softening" of the work ethic, which would make retirement more acceptable. Second, with increasing modernization, societies become more affluent and thus more capable and willing to provide for dependent older persons. Thus, dependency is no longer seen negatively, but as an earned right. Third, the percentage of illiteracy will start to decrease thus reducing the distance between the generations. Fourth, the increasing segregation of older persons and their lower status may contribute to an increasing self-awareness of some of their common problems and the formation of groups to reverse the problems.

Treatment of Older Persons   The treatment of older persons varies from society to society and is often determined by a myriad of variables. It should also be remembered that these variables do not act independently of one another but interact with one another. For example, the family structure may call for an older person to be treated with respect, but the economic base may be insufficient to provide for older persons. This may bring about neglect or disrespectful treatment of older persons.

Below we will examine some of the variables that determine how older persons were treated in preliterate societies (see Rosow, 1974).

Property Ownership   Property ownership was an important variable in the treatment of older persons. Essentially, older persons who owned property could generally expect better treatment than those who did not own property. In agricultural societies, where individuals owned land, the economic livelihood of younger individuals was dependent on how much land they would be given by their parents (see Lee, 1984). Treatment also depended on the amount of property owned, with older persons owning larger more productive segments of land warranting the best treatment. How and when the property was divided had a significant influence on the future power and economic status of the young. By controlling the property, older persons also controlled the way the young treated them.

In some societies young adults were not allowed to marry until they owned land. Older persons often gave land away in exchange for a certain amount of food or other goods per year. Essentially, their land became the source of their retirement income (Quadagno, 1982).

Strategic Knowledge and/or Skills   In preliterate societies there were few ways to keep track of knowledge. As a result, older persons were often valued because of their accumulated knowledge, information, and experience. Over time they acquired information that the society needed to survive. The information may have concerned when or how to plant crops or when and in what direction to move in order to intercept an animal migration. Because the society had few ways to record this information, it had to rely on the memories of older persons; thus, they were important sources of knowledge. As such they were also frequently the teachers in the society. The knowledge they possessed was acquired gradually, through experience and as apprentices. This knowledge was often guarded since its dissemination would have reduced their status and treatment.

Older persons were not only responsible for information relating to the physical survival of the society but also for its myths, legends, and history. Older persons related these tales to the entire society through songs, stories, games, and dances. Maxwell and Silverman (1970) found that even with increasing literacy, older persons were not immediately replaced as information storage cells. This retention of older persons as sources of knowledge occurred because the literacy rate was initially low and the literate segment of the society acted primarily to supplement the information of older persons. Moreover, very often it was older persons who controlled the literacy system; they were the ones who determined who became literate or what types of information was transmitted to the rest of the society.

Often the knowledge that older persons possessed was passed on to younger individuals. This did not, however, necessarily make older persons obsolete or useless to the society. Very often older persons were assigned new roles that required learning new knowledge. The assignment of new roles was made possible because the beliefs of the society made these roles dangerous for younger individuals. In many preliterate societies there was a belief that certain "types" of individuals represented a danger to the entire society. Examples of "taboo or dangerous individuals" were girls at menarche, menstruating women, women giving birth, warriors going or returning from battle, or the dying or dead. Because of their advanced age, and perhaps closeness to the spirit world, it was believed that it was safe for older persons to be with "taboo" individuals (see Amoss, 1981).

There were some instances where the strategic knowledge possessed by older persons contributed to detrimental treatment. This was found in societies that were dependent on older persons for certain knowledge that could determine the survival or extinction of the society. Once older persons started to lose certain mental abilities, and were likely to give erroneous knowledge, they became a threat to the society. In these instances, the older persons were generally dealt with very harshly; in fact, there was little tolerance of these individuals and they were often killed.

In addition to strategic knowledge, many also possessed important skills. The skills might be in a number of areas that were important for the survival of the society.

Productivity Many preliterate societies had marginal existences. They survived by hunting and gathering and the contributions of all members were important to the society. Work was often assigned based on ability, with the most physically able harvesting food the furthest from the camp, and the least physically able, such as older persons, harvesting food nearest to the camp. Although often not as physically able, the experience of older persons in finding food still made them valuable contributors to the society.

Older individuals served important roles in the society. For example, when Eskimo women became too weak to care for children, prepare food, or perform other daily tasks, they were given the task of chewing animal skins to make them soft. When loss of teeth or other factors made this task too difficult, the women were used for other less demanding tasks such as staying awake at night to maintain the fire. Among the Incas, older persons with limited physical abilities were placed on platforms in corn fields to act as living scarecrows (Simmons, 1960). Also, older males who were no longer capable of hunting stayed in the village and repaired or made weapons. Some were also assigned tasks that were traditionally considered "women's work," such as working in the fields or preparing food.

However, although important and productive roles were often found for older persons, in some societies, especially nomadic food-gathering societies where there was little or no surplus of food, older persons could pose a threat. Many nomadic societies moved from area to area harvesting what there was to eat. They often exhausted the food in an area in a short time and thus had to keep moving to new areas to survive. When age, accidents, disease, or other factors limited the ability of individuals to produce, or keep up with the group, they were left behind. This was true for individuals in all age groups, not just the aged. That is, when individuals in other age groups, with the exception of very young children, became incapacitated and unable to keep up with the group, they too were left behind (see Halperin, 1987).

There is a need for further explanation concerning societies that either killed or abandoned their elderly. Many of the stories about aged gerontocide were misinterpretations by observers. In some societies older persons specifically requested to be killed or committed suicide. For example, in the Fiji Islands the old men killed themselves of their own "free will." Their religious beliefs stated that after death individuals lived through eternity in the same condition they were in shortly before death; thus premature death was better than living through eternity in an incapacitated, frail, decrepit state. A similar phenomenon was found among the Dinka of the Sudan. Here older persons requested that they be buried alive. They believed that if they died "naturally," the breath of life would leave their bodies and the entire community would die (Beauvoir, 1973; Simmons, 1945). Peter Freuchen (1931) noted in his book *Eskimo* that the close relationships that existed among members of Eskimo families often forced older persons to demand that they be allowed to die so that the entire family would not be put in jeopardy by their dependency. Among the Eskimo, older persons were generally placed in a hut or out in the open and allowed to freeze to death. They were also placed on ice floes and set drifting out to sea or allowed to paddle kayaks into the open sea (see Lee, 1984).

Although difficult to conceptualize in western society, among some preliterate societies it was necessary for some to die so that others could live. This was dictated by the harshness of the environment. To survive, societies created customs that distinguished between the useful and the useless. When an individual went from one stage to another, the values and beliefs of the society dictated, both to the individual and the society, that the individual should either be allowed to die or should be killed. This decision was not necessarily based on hatred or hostility but necessity. In reporting on the Lapps of northern Europe, Simmons (1960) noted that aged parents were often left to die by their adult children. The aged did not consider this action to be one of cruelty or ingratitude, but rather a necessary action based on their physical condition. It was also probably an action that the aged had earlier taken with their own parents.

It should also be noted that many societies that killed or abandoned their aged did so only after long periods of care and respect. The killing or abandonment of older persons came about not from disrespect, hatred, contempt, or neglect, but because the culture dictated that death had become appropriate, owing to a change in the aged individual's physical or mental state.

Religious Beliefs   Religious beliefs frequently stated how older persons were to be treated. With older persons generally controlling the formation and transmission of religious beliefs, these beliefs frequently had components that benefited them. As a result, the thought of offending the gods or spirits by improperly treating older persons was often enough to provide them with good treatment. Also, in many societies older persons served as mediators between the living and the dead. Communication with the spirit world by older persons was thought possible since they were so close to death themselves. Additionally, it was believed that to have lived so long older persons must have spirits that had helped them, and to offend or hurt the older person would bring the wrath of these spirits. There was also the fear that after death the spirits of older persons would return to punish those who had offended or hurt them in life.

As was noted in an earlier section, many societies had roles that only older persons could hold. In many preliterate societies there were religious groups that administered the rites-of-passage ceremony. These groups were generally composed of older persons since the ceremonial procedures were passed down from the aged to the aging. This practice gave older persons a great deal of power within the society since they were able to regulate the status of the younger community members by awarding or denying them important positions. These rewards and punishments often depended on the treatment of the old by the young.

Kinship and Family   The family was another important factor in the treatment of older persons. In many preliterate societies support came from the family, with many forms of support from the extended family. Family ties, often through arranged marriages, were carefully maintained and preserved with the knowledge that at some point certain segments of the extended family would be called on for assistance. In many preliterate societies the extended family was very large and thus providing for aged relatives was a shared burden.

Although the extended family was important, having several older persons decreased the status of these people, since they were no longer unique. Large extended families produced several "elders," thus making the lines of authority vague and unclear. Such families also meant that there would be many young members, the sheer number prohibiting their control by older persons (Lee, 1984).

In some cases the conduct of the family proved to be detrimental to older persons. For example, certain societies had harsh childrearing practices. As a result, little affection developed between parents and their children. The parents ruled on the basis of physical strength. As the physical strength of the parents began to wane the adult children abused, killed, expelled, or even sold their parents into slavery to gain their possessions (Beauvoir, 1973).

Political Power   Politically, older persons often worked themselves into powerful positions. Land ownership, strategic skills and knowledge, as well as other variables have assisted them in this area. The political power older persons possessed often placed them in a position to demand and receive beneficial treatment from younger individuals.

There were some societies where political power eventually became a liability. In these societies leaders were seen as having God-like powers. The people in the society believed that these powers represented a certain quantitative amount and were capable of being transferred intact from one leader to another. With these powers the leader was supposed to prevent evil forces from harming the society. However, these societies also believed that as the physical powers of the leader declined, so did the God-like powers and the leader's ability to protect the community from evil forces. To prevent these powers from gradually diminishing, the members of the community killed their leaders at the first sign of physical weakness.

Complexity of Society   The complexity of a society had several impacts on older persons. On the one hand, the more complex the society, the more likely it was to have specialized roles for older persons. For example, in a complex society religion was most likely to be found, which created roles for older persons. Also, in a complex society older persons were more likely to have specialized knowledge needed by the society. In a simple society, almost everyone, even young children, soon learned what was edible and hunted for grubs, worms, insects, rodents, fruits, grasses, barks, reptiles, birds, roots, fish, eggs, carrion, and other sources of food. Thus, older persons did not possess unique knowledge needed for the society to survive.

One last comment deals with the beliefs that some preliterate societies possessed. As was mentioned at the beginning of this section, the treatment of older persons was determined largely by the culture of a society. Generally, the more complex the society the more complex its culture. Certain societies evolved beliefs that influenced the treatment of older persons. For example, some societies developed beliefs surrounding certain types of foods, and certain types of foods were taboo for certain age groups. In one society ostrich eggs were taboo for all individuals except the very young and the very old. It was believed that their consumption by others would cause insanity. These eggs were easy to chew for young individuals who had no teeth or the old who had often lost their teeth. They were also an excellent source of nutrition. Thus, what evolved in many societies were beliefs that benefited the survival of older persons.

Older Persons in Early American Society

The history of the aged has been largely ignored by historians (Fischer, 1978). It was not until the mid-1970s that historians and gerontologists started to reconstruct what it was like to be old in the past (see Achenbaum, 1978; Fischer, 1978; Stearns & Van Tassel, 1986). This is not because of a lack of information; as Kebric (1983, 1988) has pointed out, there is an abundance of material yet to be examined in this area. Thus, it is probably out of a lack of interest.

As with most emerging areas, we are finding two trends. The first is that certain assumptions are being dispelled. The second is that a certain amount of controversy is created over the new findings.

The dominant cultural beliefs and attitudes about aging and the aged largely determine how older persons are treated. The beliefs that a society has about aging and the aged are not formed in a vacuum. They are often survivals from the past, at times vestiges of ancient or dead civilizations. Historical research allows us to trace some of our current beliefs about older persons.

In this section, I do not intend to provide a complete chronology of the development of contemporary western attitudes and beliefs toward older persons. Instead, I will provide the reader with a view of the aged in early American societies.

Research in History In the earlier section, "Research in Anthropology," it was pointed out that conducting research in anthropology has many strengths but also some problems. The same is true of historical research. History can tell us about the past and hopefully provide insight into the present and the future. However, there are methodological problems associated with historical research.

1 There is relatively little written on what it was like to be old in the past, since older persons constituted such a small segment of the population and old age was not seen as a distinctive life period.

2 The validity of much of what does exist is often questionable. For example, it is difficult to ascertain if the books or records from the society under examination portray the situation as it existed, as the author wanted it to exist, or as the author wanted readers to believe it existed. In other words, is the work an accurate historical account or is it fiction or philosophy? Moreover, the writer may have been unique regarding certain factors such as health, social class, power, wealth, education, prestige, and perceived aging and the aged from a unique and privileged perspective.

3 Much of the writing that does exist deals only with wealthy, powerful, or influential males and does not generally convey what it was like to be old, poor, powerless, or female.

4 It is difficult not only to judge the validity of the records but also to ascertain if the records are representative of all the aged or of only a small proportion. Two factors that could alter the representativeness of the surviving records are the concept of selected survival and the quality of the translation. The concept of selected survival is a simple one. It means that the present and future concept of the past can be distorted if selected documents, records, and books are destroyed while others are preserved. An incorrect translation can also distort the past, since in translation it is often difficult to find words that mean exactly the same thing in two languages. After numerous translations the original meaning may have been lost.

5 Many of the societies examined in this section existed for several centuries. During their existence all of them underwent numerous changes. Thus the task of analyzing the treatment of older persons is more difficult because this treatment probably varied according to the economic, political, social, and religious conditions prevalent at a given period of time.

6 Often the information needed is simply missing. Sometimes the information was never recorded; other times it was destroyed (see Achenbaum, 1978; Achenbaum & Stearns, 1978).

Even though there are some methodological limitations, we will piece together what it was like to be old in early American society.

Early American Society Two excellent books on the history of old age in America have been written: *Growing Old in America* by David H. Fischer (1978) and *Old Age in the New Land: The American Experience Since 1790* by W. Andrew Achenbaum

(1978). Both of the books have similar themes: The aged were respected in early America and this respect has declined. Both of the books reject that it was industrialization, urbanization, and mass education—or modernization—that changed the status of the aged. However, the books differ on when the devaluation of old age took place, with Fischer claiming an earlier date than Achenbaum.

It appears that until about 1790 older persons, who composed 2 percent of the population, were generally highly respected in early America. In fact, not only were most older persons respected but they were also honored, exalted, given reverence, and venerated. To an extent the image of older persons can be seen in the symbol selected to represent the country, Uncle Sam, who was a well-established national figure by 1830 (Achenbaum, 1978). Respect for older persons probably arose from several sources.

One of the primary sources was religion. The highly religious early Puritans noted that older persons were honored in both the Old and New Testaments. Many of them believed that older persons, who were few in number, had been given a special gift of long life by God. Moreover, they pictured both God and Christ as old, bearded, white-haired men. Thus, in some ways older persons in early America were equated with holiness.

Religion was not the only source of respect for older persons. Many of the aged maintained control of their financial assets as a mechanism for obtaining obedience and respect from their children. Children who refused to give the proper amount of respect were cut off financially from the family.

There is a fairly substantial amount of evidence indicating that respect for older persons was a fact in early America and not simply an example of ritualistic deference. For example, records of the seating arrangements in town meetings indicate that older persons were assigned the more prestigious seats. Thus it appears that prestige in early America was determined by age and not wealth. As in most societies there were some exceptions. Old women and slaves were not respected as much as old white men; also, the elderly poor seldom received any respect at all. In fact, as Fischer points out, often the poor of a town, no matter what their ages, were driven out so that taxes for their upkeep would not have to be raised.

The position of older persons began to change in the late 1700s. At least part of the change came about because of the French and American revolutions, both of which brought about a severance with the past. Both revolutions also spawned the concept of equality. The new equality could be seen in the seating arrangements at town halls; now the more prestigious positions went to those who had the greatest amount of money or to those who were the most useful to the community.

The change in the attitude toward older persons could also be seen in the enactment of mandatory retirement laws for public officials. The records now showed that individuals were systematically lopping off years from their ages rather than adding them on as they had done in the past when old age was more prestigious.

There were other factors indicating that a change had taken place. For example, before 1790 clothing had been flattering to older persons; after 1790 styles emerged that were flattering to the young. Gone were the powdered white wigs that covered bald heads and gray hair, and the large bulky coats for men that covered stooped shoulders, curved spines, and large stomachs. Also gone were the large skirts and blouses that hid the larger figures of many older women. In their place were more tailored clothing that emphasized the slim waistlines of youth.

The language also began to change. New words began to creep into the language and old words lost their original meaning. An example of the changing nature of language can be seen in the term "fogy." Prior to 1790 the term had been used to refer to a wounded military veteran. However, by 1830 the term "old fogy" was a derogatory term applied to older persons. Other terms such as "codger," "geezer," "pop," and "old-timer" also came into use.

Another change can be seen in family portraits. Once again, prior to 1790 most family portraits showed the oldest male in a position of power, authority, and respect; generally, he hovered above the rest of the family. After 1790 there was a tendency to depict the entire family at the same level. No individual family member emerged as a dominant figure.

Fischer found that until 1790 there was a widespread tradition to name grandchildren after grandparents—a practice that also decreased after 1790.

As we discussed above, one of the reasons for these changes was the American Revolution, which abolished the old order and replaced it with the concept of equality. Although mass education, industrialization, and urbanization are often listed as the causes, and unquestionably they did eventually contribute to the process, Fischer rejected them as primary causes. He instead concluded that the changes occurred prior to the time these factors could have had an effect.

In addition to the French and American revolutions, westward expansion may also have helped to bring about changes in the position of older persons. Although massive movement into the far west would not start for some time after the Revolutionary War, movement into the midwest did start on a large scale after the war. At that time, the English laws that prevented inward migration no longer existed. Also, many of the Native American tribes that had slowed inward migration had been decimated during the war. Thus many new lands became available for settlers. The young were no longer dependent on older persons for gifts of land.

Also, with the migration westward many of the aged lost their roles as information sources. Although the knowledge and experience of older persons may have been accurate and useful for farming in Virginia, it was not necessarily accurate or useful for farming in Ohio. In addition, professionals in numerous areas replaced older persons as sources of knowledge and can be seen in the composition of the changing work force. In 1820, 71.9 percent of the work force was engaged in agriculture. By 1890 it had dropped to 41.9 percent. Corresponding figures for manufacturing are 12.2 percent and 25.6 percent. The figures for trade and transportation are 2.5 percent and 15.7 percent (Achenbaum, 1978).

With the changing values came gerontophobia. Older persons were no longer automatically respected or venerated, but were instead more often treated with contempt and disgust. Mandatory retirement laws became more common and created rampant poverty among older persons. This situation in turn intensified the feelings of disgust toward older persons as young families were forced to care for their elderly members or pay taxes for the poor to the county or church. By 1900 the problems of aging and the aged in America were recognized as significant social problems. A study in Massachusetts in 1910 found that 92 percent of those in mental institutions were 65+ years of age, generally not because of mental or physical conditions but because there were no other public facilities for the aged poor.

To help correct the situation, literally hundreds of old-age pension and insurance bills were introduced at both the state and federal levels. Most were defeated and those that did pass were generally not very good. Although a few companies, such as American Express, provided their employees with pension plans, most older retired workers were dependent on what they had been able to save, on their families, or on charity. States that attempted to enact old-age insurance plans were generally unsuccessful because the plans were labeled as un-American, unconstitutional, or socialistic. It was also claimed that they worked against the American values of thrift, hard work, and independence.

Fischer pointed out that although the arguments against old-age pension plans sounded noble, they did not take into account the fact that the percentage of aged who were financially dependent on others was increasing because of mandatory retirement, a recession, and finally the depression. The percentage of dependent older persons spiraled from 23 percent in 1910 to 33 percent in 1922 to 40 percent in 1930 to 50 percent in 1935 and to 66 percent in 1940.

By the early 1930s, the plight of older persons began to cause common concern in several different and generally ideologically opposed segments of society. Furthermore, many organized efforts on behalf of older persons created pressure at the federal level to enact old-age insurance and pension plans, and in 1935 the Social Security Act was passed.

SUMMARY

It is only recently that older persons have received much attention from either academic or nonacademic segments of society. In the past, a variety of factors—such as a comparatively low life expectancy, low visibility of older persons, the lack of a separate life period for older persons, and a stigma being placed on being old—created conditions that allowed older persons to be largely ignored as a separate and distinctive segment of society. As a result, much of what we know about aging in the past is fragmentary and incomplete.

Anthropologists have produced some excellent studies on the aged in preliterate societies. One theory that anthropology has produced is "modernization theory," which states that with increasing modernization the status of older persons declines. This is for four reasons. First, in preliterate societies few survive to old age; as a result of modernization life expectancy increases and older persons are no longer unique or have special status. Second, with modernization the aged are obsolete in the work force. Third, with modernization comes industrialization; with industrialization comes urbanization with the young moving to urban areas, leaving older persons behind in rural areas. With the move to urban areas the young often surpass their parents and grandparents in terms of income and status, thus eroding the status of older persons. Fourth, with modernization the young will become more highly educated than the old. This will often make the knowledge of the old obsolete, and will make the old dependent on the young for information.

A major concern of anthropologists who have studied older persons in preliterate societies is the treatment of older persons. There have been two contradictory beliefs. The first is that older persons were treated very well, often because of their accumulated knowledge. The second is that they were treated very harshly, in fact often killed, because they were not valuable members of society. Both forms of treatment could be found and depended on a variety of factors.

Property ownership was one factor determining the treatment of older persons. Basically, if the property owned by older persons was valuable, they could often enjoy high status and good treatment because they controlled the distribution of the property to the young.

Strategic knowledge and/or skills is another area that determines how older persons are treated. The aged are often repositories of knowledge. Experience has provided them with information that the rest of society needs to survive. As a result, they are often treated well.

A third factor determining the treatment of older persons concerns their productivity. Older persons are often capable of producing more than they consume. Thus, they are valuable members of society. Even if physical problems prevent them from engaging in traditional forms of productivity, other less demanding, essential tasks can be found for them to do.

The religious beliefs of a society also have a bearing on how older persons are treated. Often older persons are assumed to be close to the spirit world, since they will soon be dying. Because of this proximity they are treated well.

Family and kinship ties are also important. The larger the family the more relatives there are to provide care.

Political power is another factor. Often through their lives older persons accumulate political power; they are treated well, not because of their age but because of the power they wield.

The last factor that influences the treatment of older persons is the complexity of the society. As the society achieves some degree of complexity there can often be specialized roles for older persons.

In addition to examining older persons in preliterate society, this chapter also examined the aged in early American society.

More information is starting to emerge on aging and the aged in early American society. Prior to 1790 it appears that older persons had high status in large part because they were old. After 1790 old age as a criterion for status began to wane. This decline appears to be due largely to major societal changes caused by the American and French revolutions which emphasized the concept of equality.

REFERENCES

Achenbaum, W. A. (1978). *Old age in the new land: The American experience since 1790.* Baltimore: Johns Hopkins University Press.

Achenbaum, W. A. (1987). Modernization theory. In G. L. Maddox (Ed.), *The encyclopedia of aging* (pp. 453–454). New York: Springer.

Achenbaum, W. A., & Stearns, P. N. (1978). Essay: Old age and modernization. *The Gerontologist,* **18**(3): 307–312.

Amoss, P. T. (1981). Cultural centrality and prestige for the elderly: The coast Salish case. In C. L. Fry (Ed.), *Dimensions: Aging, culture, and health* (pp. 47–64). New York: Praeger Publishers.

Aries, P. (1965). *Centuries of childhood: A social history of family life.* New York: McGraw-Hill.

Arth, M. (1972). Aging: A cross-cultural perspective. In R. Kastenbaum & S. Sherwood (Eds.), *Research planning and action for the elderly* (pp. 352–364). New York: Behavioral Publications.

Beauvoir, S. (1973). *The coming of age.* New York: Warner Communications.

Brody, E. M. (1971). Aging. In J. Turner (Ed.), *Encyclopedia of social work* (pp. 51–74). New York: National Association of Social Workers.

Carp, F. (Ed.) (1972). *Retirement.* New York: Behavioral Publications.

Clark, M. (1967). The anthropology of aging. *The Gerontologist,* **7**(1): 53–65.

Cowgill, D. O. (1970). The demography of aging. In A. M. Hoffman (Ed.), *The daily needs and interests of older people* (pp. 27–69). Springfield: Thomas.

Cowgill, D. O. (1972). A theory of aging in cross-cultural perspective. In D. O. Cowgill & L. D. Holmes (Eds.), *Aging and modernization* (pp. 1–14). New York: Appleton-Century-Crofts.

Cowgill, D. O. (1974). Aging and modernization: A revision on the theory. In J. F. Gubrium (Ed.), *Late life: Communities and environmental policy* (pp. 123–146). Springfield: Thomas.

Cowgill, D. O. (1986). *Aging Around the World.* Belmont, CA: Wadsworth.

Cowgill, D. O., & Holmes, L. D. (Eds.) (1972). *Aging and Modernization.* New York: Appleton-Century-Crofts.

Cutler, N. E., & Harootyan, R. A. (1975). Demography of the aged. In D. S. Woodruff & J. E. Birren (Eds.), *Aging: Scientific perspectives and social issues* (pp. 31–69). New York: Van Nostrand.

Dowd, J. J. (1984). Beneficence and the aged. *Journal of Gerontology,* **39**(1): 102–108.

Fischer, D. H. (1978). *Growing old in America.* New York: Oxford University Press.

Freeman, J. T. (1979). *Aging: Its history and literature.* New York: Human Sciences Press.

Freuchen, P. (1931). *Eskimo.* New York: Liveright.

Fry, C. L. (Ed.) (1980). *Aging in culture and society: Comparative viewpoints and strategies.* Brooklyn: Bergin.

Fry, C. L. (Ed.) (1981). *Dimensions: Aging, culture, and health.* Brooklyn: Bergin.

Fry, C. L. (1985). Culture, behavior, and aging in the comparative perspective. In J. E. Birren & K. W. Schaie (Eds.), *Handbook of the psychology of aging* (second edition) (pp. 216–244). New York: Van Nostrand Reinhold.

Fry, C. L. (1988). Theories of age and culture. In J. E. Birren & V. L. Bengtson (Eds.), *Emergent theories of aging* (pp. 447–481). New York: Springer.

Glascock, A. P., & Feinman, S. L. (1981). Social asset or social burden: Treatment of the aged in nonindustrial societies. In C. L. Fry (Ed.), *Dimensions: Aging, culture, and health* (pp. 13–31). New York: Praeger. Copyright 1981 by J. F. Bergin Publishers, Inc.

Glascock, A., & Feinman, S. (1986). Treatment of the aged in nonindustrial societies. In C. Fry & J. Keith (Eds.), *New methods for old age research: Strategies for studying diversity* (pp. 24–36). South Hadley, MA: Bergin and Garvey.

Goody, J. (1976). Aging in nonindustrial societies. In R. H. Binstock & E. Shanas (Eds.), *Handbook of aging and the social sciences* (pp. 117–129). New York: Van Nostrand Reinhold.

Gratton, B. (1986). The new history of the aged: A critique. In D. Van Tassel & P. N. Stearns (Eds.), *Old age in a bureaucratic society* (pp. 3–29). Westport, CT: Greenwood.

Halperin, R. H. (1987). Age in cross-cultural perspective: An evolutionary approach. In
P. Silverman (Ed.), *The elderly as modern pioneers* (pp. 283–311). Bloomington: Indiana
University Press.

Harlan, W. H. (1964). Social status of the aged in three Indian villages. *Vita Humane,* **7**(4):
239–252.

Katz, S. H. (1978). Anthropological perspectives on aging. *Annals of the American Academy
of Political and Social Science,* **438**(July): 1–12.

Kebric, R. B. (1983). Aging in Pliny's letters: A view from the second century A.D. *The
Gerontologist,* **23**(5): 538–545.

Kebric, R. B. (1988). Old age, the ancient military, and Alexander's army: Positive examples
for a graying America. *The Gerontologist,* **28**(3): 298–302.

Keith, J. (1985). Age in anthropological research. In R. H. Binstock & E. Shanas (Eds.),
Handbook of aging and the social sciences (second edition) (pp. 231–263). New York:
Van Nostrand Reinhold.

Koller, M. R. (1968). *Social gerontology.* New York: Random House.

Lee, G. R. (1984). Status of the elderly: Economic and familial antecedents. *Journal of Marriage
and the Family,* **46**(2): 267–275.

Lerner, M. (1970). When, why and where people die. In O. G. Brim, H. E. Freeman, &
S. Levine (Eds.), *The dying patient* (pp. 5–29). New York: Russell Sage Foundation.

Lipman, A. (1970). Prestige of the aged in Portugal: Realistic appraisal and ritualistic deference.
Aging and Human Development, **1**(2): 127–135.

Maxwell, R. J., & Silverman, P. (1970). Information and esteem: Cultural considerations in
the treatment of the aged. *Aging and Human Development,* **1**(4): 365–382.

Meyers, G. C. (1987). Demography. In G. L. Maddox (Ed.), *The encyclopedia of aging*
(pp. 164–167). New York: Springer.

Nydegger, C. N. (1981). Gerontology and anthropology: Challenge and opportunity. In
C. L. Fry (Ed.), *Dimensions: Aging, culture, and health* (pp. 293–302). Brooklyn: Bergin.

Palmore, E., & Manton, K. (1974). Modernization and the status of the aged: International
correlations. *Journal of Gerontology,* **29**(2): 205–210.

Palmore, E., & Whittington, F. (1971). Trends in the relative status of the aged. *Social
Forces,* **50**(1): 84–91.

Quadagno, J. (1982). *Aging in early industrial society.* New York: Academic Press.

Rosow, I. (1974). *Socialization to old age.* Berkeley: University of California.

Simmons, L. W. (1945). *The role of the aged in primitive society.* New Haven: Yale University
Press.

Simmons, L. W. (1946). Attitudes toward aging and the aged: Primitive societies. *Journal of
Gerontology,* **1**(1): 72–93.

Simmons, L. W. (1960). Aging in preindustrial societies. In C. Tibbitts (Ed.), *Handbook of
social gerontology* (pp. 62–91). Chicago: University of Chicago Press.

Stearns, P. N., & Van Tassel, D. (1986). Introduction: Themes and prospects in old age
history. In D. D. Van Tassel & P. N. Stearns (Eds.), *Old age in a bureaucratic society*
(pp. ix–xx). Westport, CT: Greenwood.

Streib, G. F. (1965). Are the aged a minority group? In A. Gouldner (Ed.), *Applied sociology*
(pp. 311–328). New York: The Free Press.

U.S. Bureau of the Census (1975). *Historical statistics of the United States, colonial times to
1970.* Washington, DC: U.S. Government Printing Office.

U.S. Bureau of the Census (1990). *Statistical abstracts of the United States: 1989.* Washington,
DC: U.S. Government Printing Office.

Watson, W. H., & Maxwell, R. J. (Eds.) (1977). *Human aging and dying: A study in sociocul-
tural gerontology.* New York: St. Martin's.

CHAPTER 4

RESEARCH AND THEORY IN GERONTOLOGY

Marshall Henrichs

INTRODUCTION

This chapter is separated into two sections, gerontological research and gerontological theory.

GERONTOLOGICAL RESEARCH

Almost all of our knowledge in gerontology is based on research. Many social policy decisions and programs that provide care and services are based on research. It is the cornerstone of all disciplines and allows one to answer questions, make decisions, and provide better care for older persons.

Courses dealing with the research process and research techniques are important for two reasons. First, to provide students with the skills that will make them capable of conducting their own research, if, for example, they want to evaluate the impact that a program is having on older persons. It is through research that they can determine which aspects of the program are "working" and which are not, thereby allowing them to modify the program so that older persons receive the maximum benefits. Second, students need the ability to analyze the research of others, which will allow them to determine which reports make a significant contribution to gerontology and which ones have limitations, or perhaps conclusions that are specific only to a small group of older persons.

This section is separated into four subsections. In the first we will discuss the functions of research. The second will examine the research process and its various stages. We will then, in the third subsection, briefly examine some major research projects in gerontology. Students will frequently read studies that have used data from these projects. Fourth, and last, we will examine the current status of research in gerontology.

The Functions of Research

There are five basic functions of research: explanation, prediction, evaluation, description, and control. I will add a sixth not commonly mentioned: care. Although they will be discussed separately, there is often considerable overlap among the functions.

The first two functions of research, explanation and prediction, are self-explanatory. Through research we seek to explain why something occurs. Often if we know the "why" we can then make predictions. Once we can explain and predict we can then create effective intervention programs that will benefit older persons.

The third function of research, and perhaps the one that will be used by most gerontologists, is evaluation. Although certainly related to the other functions, evaluation deserves special mention. As most gerontologists know, there are many programs designed to improve the lives of older persons. The evaluation of programs, through research, allows us to determine which programs are the most effective in meeting the needs of older persons.

The fourth function is description. Through research we want to be able to describe what we have studied. The description might be in terms of demographic variables such as those mentioned in Chapter 2, "Demography," or in terms of values or beliefs.

Control is the fifth function of research. For example, through research in the natural sciences we seek to control the spread of contagious diseases. In the social sciences we may want to control the negative consequences of widowhood through grief counseling programs.

There is another function of research that you don't usually find in most textbooks. This function is care. Dr. T. Franklin Williams, Director of the National Institute on Aging, has noted the close connection between research and care (1988). Basically the quality of care that older persons receive is dependent on the quality of research. Research can improve the quality of care in at least two ways. First, by documenting the existence, or extent, of an area where care is needed. Second, by improving the techniques of providing care, either in a technical sense, such as a new drug to relieve pain, or in an interpersonal sense, such as ways to interact with the bereaved, senile, or dying. A discussion of the research process and some of its components follows.

The Research Process

Through the research process one systematically tries to answer a question for which there is either no answer or no consistent or widely accepted answer. From the researchers' initial curiosity to the final presentation of the findings, one will pass through eight stages (Lastrucci, 1967).

Stage 1: The Formation of a Question or Hypothesis The research process starts when a question is raised in the minds of researchers. The question is formulated into a scientifically testable hypothesis, which is a tentative answer to the researchers' question. It is an educated guess about the outcome of the study. The purpose is to answer the question or test the hypothesis.

The key component of the question or hypothesis is that an answer should be obtainable with the use of scientific techniques. It is important to realize that science cannot answer all questions or test all hypotheses.

Research can answer questions of fact but not questions of value. A value is an opinion about the world. As such, they do not have correct or incorrect answers. Researchers can ascertain how many individuals hold certain values, why they hold these values, or the consequences of holding certain values, but they cannot conclude if the values are good or bad, moral or immoral.

There is one other consideration that must be taken into account during stage 1 of the research process: ethical issues. Until recently ethical issues have not been major issues in research; researchers simply did their research, often with little thought about the ethical issues involved.

The publicity of several "questionable" studies in the 1960s and 1970s made it impossible to continue to ignore ethical issues. As a result, most organizations, such as colleges and universities where research projects take place, have ethics committees that consider the ethical issues involved. These committees are especially active when the research involves human or animal subjects. Most scientific journals also examine the ethical issues in reports submitted for publication. Any that violate standard ethical guidelines are generally not published.

There are four general guidelines for conducting ethical research involving human beings (see Babbie, 1988). The first is that participation should be voluntary. Thus, participants should not be coerced, tricked, or forced to take part in the research. Inherent in the first guideline is also the issue of informed consent. This is a very complex and controversial issue. Essentially, informed consent means that the participants have been informed and understand the purpose of the research as well as the procedures and risks. There is the assumption that the participants are competent to give informed consent (see Berkowitz, 1978). The second guideline is that participants should not be harmed—physically, psychologically, socially, economically, or in other ways. Third, in the presentation of the results the participants should be anonymous. In research projects subjects are often required to reveal certain aspects about themselves that are generally private, such as income or certain forms of behavior considered deviant by the community. The basic principle is that others who read the research report will not be able to identify the participants. The fourth and last guideline deals with not deceiving the participants. Researchers can deceive participants about their identity or the true nature of the study.

In theory the guidelines are easy to state and justify. In practice they are sometimes difficult to follow. Some researchers claim that if the guidelines were followed their research would be invalid. For example, informing participants of the true nature of the study would alter the participants' behavior and distort the results of the study. It is recognized that there will be exceptions to the guidelines. It is up to the researchers to explain why an exception to a particular guideline is necessary. It is up to an ethics committee to determine if the exception is justified and if the research should be permitted.

Some of the unique ethical issues encountered by gerontologists have been noted. Strain and Chappell (1982) pointed out that many older persons "volunteer" to participate in research projects out of fear of losing certain services or benefits if they do not participate. Although researchers may not use any coercion or threats, some older persons may still believe that their participation is mandatory. Reich (1978) has discussed the problem of voluntary participation and noted that many older persons have reduced levels of competence, which makes following the voluntary participation or informed consent guideline difficult. This is especially true in nursing homes where the percentage with hearing or cognitive problems is high (see Annas & Glantz, 1986; Cohen-Mansfield et al., 1988; Makarushka & McDonald, 1979; Ratzan, 1986; Warren et al., 1986).

One additional ethical concern is that research should not harm participants. Many older persons have physical problems and involvement in research projects, even if only an interview, may jeopardize their health (see Yordi et al., 1982).

In addition to encountering some fairly unique ethical issues, gerontologists may find themselves in unusual ethical situations. For example, if during an interview a researcher discovers that an older person is being abused, should the abuse be reported? Assume that the research project does not involve abuse and that the researcher is not connected with any type of social service agency. Does the researcher ignore or report the abuse? If the abuse is reported there is the possibility that the abuser will become angry at the older person and perhaps more abusive, but in a more concealed way. If the abuse is reported there is also the possibility that the older person will be removed from his or her home, perhaps to a facility that is "worse" than episodes of occasional abuse. If not reported there is, of course, the possibility that the older person will be seriously harmed or killed. Currently, most states have laws requiring that abuse be reported.

Another potential ethical problem is that older persons may have unrealistic expectations about their participation in the research. They may assume, for example, that as a result of their participation in the research project certain services will be started or increased. Others may make demands on the researchers, such as requesting them to mail bills or purchase and deliver items from a store before their visit (see Strain & Chappell, 1982).

Stage 2: Review of the Related Literature   An important part of the research process is an examination of the related literature. This review is done early in the research process to see whether the question or hypothesis has been adequately answered or tested. If the answer is "yes," there is no need to pursue research. If further research is needed, researchers can use existing research to study different avenues or approaches that have been used. Researchers can also note some of the problems that others have encountered and design a research project that will circumvent the problem areas. The literature can also provide new concepts, sources of information, different measurement devices, different theories, and different scholars in the field who might be of assistance.

Stage 3: Writing the Research Proposal   The research process follows what is known as a research proposal—a written plan, outline, or step-by-step proposal of how to answer the question or how to test the hypothesis.

One aspect of the research proposal is the type of research design that will be used. There are two basic designs possible in scientific research: cross-sectional and longitudinal. These will help to determine if the differences between cohorts are a result of age changes or age differences. For example, are those 20 to 24 years of age different in certain areas from those 65+ years of age because of biological aging (age change), or are they different because they belong to different generations (age differences). If we note that intelligence scores are higher for those 20 to 24 years of age than for those 65+ years of age we often assume it is because of age changes. That is, we assume that at one time those 65+ years of age had intelligence levels similar to those now 20 to 24 years of age and that age changes have lowered the intelligence scores of those 65+ years of age. However, the distinctions may be because of age differences not age changes. That is, perhaps by being exposed to better health and educational opportunities, younger individuals have higher intelligence scores than older cohorts. Thus, the distinctions in intelligence scores is not because of age changes but because the cohorts have always been different because they have been exposed to different options and opportunities.

There is probably a tendency to see distinctions among cohorts more as a result of age changes than age differences. The need to consider both becomes obvious if we examine something like education. If we compare young adults with the aged we will find that young adults have more years of education. If one takes an "age change" perspective one has to assume that with increasing age individuals lose years of education. Obviously the distinction here is due to age differences not age changes.

A cross-sectional design describes and compares information on individuals from two or more age groups at a given period of time. In cross-sectional designs information on certain characteristics of individuals in different age groups is collected and compared. For example, a cross-sectional design may compare the health status of those 55 years of age with those 75 years of age. Cross-sectional designs are important in noting differences between age groups.

In contrast, a longitudinal design would be concerned with changes that take place in the psychological, socioeconomic, or health characteristics over time. In longitudinal designs there are certain variables that, according to the researchers, will cause a change to take place in other variables. For example, the researchers may administer a self-concept test to a group of individuals who will be retiring within a year. The same test will again be administered to the group 1 year after retirement. If a significant change has taken place in the scores, the researchers may speculate that retirement brings about a change in self-concept. It should be noted that retirement in and of itself may not bring about the observed change in self-concept. Rather the cause may be in events triggered by retirement, such as loss of income, loss of friends, loss of occupational identity, or by certain life events that have an increasing likelihood of occurring about the age of retirement, such as declining health or the death of a spouse.

As a purely descriptive statement of a particular group, a cross-sectional design is appropriate. However, cross-sectional designs should not be used to ascertain why differences exist between age groups. In his book, *Aging and Behavior,* Jack Botwinick quoted part of an address by Robert Kastenbaum:

> Occasionally I have the opportunity to chat with elderly people who live in the communities nearby Cushing Hospital. I cannot help but observe that many of these people speak with an Italian accent. I also chat with young adults who live in these same communities. They do not speak with an Italian accent. As a student of human behavior and development, I am interested in this discrepancy. I indulge in some deep thinking and come up with the following conclusion: as people grow older they develop Italian accents. (Reprinted from Jack Botwinick, Ph.D., *Aging and Behavior* (third edition) p. 381. Copyright 1984 by Springer Publishing Company, Inc., New York 10012. Used by permission of the publisher.)

Obviously, Kastenbaum's remark was not serious but merely a demonstration of the dangers of using a cross-sectional design when a longitudinal design was appropriate. Frequently in gerontology differences between the young and the old have been ascribed to the aging process when in fact other variables have been responsible, as in the above example, country of origin. This is sometimes referred to as the "life course fallacy" (Riley, 1988*b*). This example is interesting in that students laugh and claim that the point is obvious. However, if we had substituted declines in memory, physical ability, or intelligence for Italian accent, most students would not have laughed but nodded with acceptance.

In a longitudinal design one makes the same set of observations two or more times (Rogosa, 1988). This allows researchers to ascertain the amount and direction of change (see Campbell et al., 1986; Hatch & Borgatta, 1987).

While longitudinal studies have many strengths there are certain problems. Many longitudinal studies use the same subjects over the course of the study. This is called a panel longitudinal study and is different from a cohort longitudinal study which uses individuals from the same cohort but not the same individuals in subsequent observations. One problem with panel studies is that there is an attrition of subjects through death, disability, lack of interest, or other factors. The tendency is for those in the "best" physical and mental health to continue in the studies while those who suffer the greatest amount of decline are more likely to drop out. This can contribute to results that are difficult to generalize because the sample is no longer representative of the population (see Cooney et al., 1988; Norris, 1985).

Most designs in gerontology are cross sectional. Cross-sectional designs are generally easier, faster, and less expensive to complete than longitudinal designs. One design is not necessarily "better" than another. The key issue is whether the design being used is relevant for the research question (Schaie, 1987, 1988). While cross-sectional and longitudinal designs are the most frequently used, there are other designs, such as sequential designs (see Schaie, 1967, 1973, 1977, 1983*a*), that have also been used.

The researchers will decide on the research design and the techniques they are going to use. Only a few of the most commonly used research techniques will be mentioned here. One design or technique is not better than another. Each has advantages and disadvantages. The researcher has to determine which is best suited to answer the research question.

Survey research is one of the most widely used forms of data gathering in the social sciences. It consists primarily of obtaining information through an interview or questionnaire. In an interview one asks individuals questions and records their responses. A questionnaire consists of a series of written questions which the researcher gives to participants and then allows them to complete or answer.

There are problems associated with both interviews and questionnaires as data-gathering devices. Generally speaking, the problems can be classified into three categories. First, the participants may not understand the question. This can occur because of cognitive, visual, or hearing declines or because the question was poorly worded. Second, participants may distort their answers. In other words, they may lie. They may be trying to impress the researcher or may be simply unwilling to divulge certain values, facts, opinions, feelings, or predispositions. Some older person may believe that telling the truth will result in loss of certain social programs or perhaps result in institutionalization. Third, participants may give an answer to a question even though they do not have an opinion on the matter. In other words, participants may answer a question "off the top of their heads." The answers may be constructed to impress or please the researchers.

The belief has been that older persons, because of cognitive and physical health declines and increasing distance from events, as well as possible resistance to answer sensitive questions, provide less accurate answers than younger adults. Three studies have analyzed these beliefs and have reported that accuracy among older respondents is no more of a problem than among younger adults; in fact, it may be less problematic among older persons (Herzog & Dielman, 1985; Rodgers & Herzog, 1987). Gibson and Aitkenhead (1983) did not find that older persons were more reluctant to answer sensitive questions.

Because of the low cost, many interviews are now being conducted by telephone. It has been assumed that because of hearing problems, and perhaps less acceptance of the telephone, responses of older persons would be less accurate than those of other age groups. One study recently addressed this assumption and reported that although older persons gave more "don't know" answers and required more researcher assistance, telephone interviews are an acceptable way to interview older persons (Herzog & Rodgers, 1988a, 1988b; Leinbach, 1982).

One advantage of telephone interviews is that they may be less threatening to older persons. Many older persons live alone and fear crime or exploitation, especially when being interviewed by strangers. Others may be embarrassed by having researchers see their homes or their declining physical conditions. Telephone interviews avoid these problems (Covey, 1985).

A major disadvantage of telephone surveys is that a significant percentage of older persons do not own phones. Among those who rent, 8 percent of whites and 19 percent of blacks do not have phones. For homeowners the figures are 3 percent for whites and 8 percent for blacks (U.S. Senate, 1987–1988). Thus, telephone surveys could significantly underrepresent the views of low income, minority aged.

Another type of research in gerontology is called statistical comparative research or secondary analysis, which, essentially, makes use of the data obtained through interviews and questionnaires. This type of research consists of using the results of existing research and then drawing conclusions. For example, researchers might want to ascertain some of the causes of mental disorders in older persons. First, they would obtain information from mental hospitals on individuals 65+ years of age who had been admitted and diagnosed as having a mental disorder. The researchers would also obtain each patient's last address prior to admission. Utilizing the patients' addresses, the researchers would then, using other published statistics, ascertain certain aspects about the neighborhoods in which the patients had lived: crime rates, housing costs, population density, and unemployment. They might discover that most of the older persons who were diagnosed as having mental disorders came from neighborhoods that were high in crime, unemployment, population density, and substandard housing. They might conclude that the above variables are causal factors in producing mental disorders in older persons.

There are two basic problems in statistical comparative studies. The first problem is that the statistics may be inaccurate. For example, in the past mental institutions were often repositories for older persons who were poor, homeless, unable to take care of themselves, or deserted by their families, rather than those with mental disorders. Additionally, the researchers using the different statistical reports did not generate the statistics and may not know some of their limitations. The second major problem is that statistics do not deal directly with people, but with books of facts and figures. Although statistical comparative studies can be valuable, caution must be exercised in that there is a layer between the individuals being studied and those drawing conclusions.

The last type of research that we will mention is the experiment which is different from the other forms of research. Rather than simply trying to find out what exists, the researchers are manipulating certain variables. By holding some variables constant and by changing the type or amount of other variables, researchers can often determine the interrelationships among certain variables or the impact they have on one another. For example, in ascertaining the impact of a "death anxiety reduction program" on older persons, researchers would study two groups: a control group and an experimental group. The experimental group would be exposed to the experimental variable, in this case the death anxiety reduction program. The control group would not be exposed to the experimental variable. Both groups would initially be tested for death anxiety and then the experimental group would be administered the program to reduce death anxiety. At the completion of the program both groups would be retested for death anxiety. If the experimental group has a reduction in death anxiety while the control group remained the same, it would probably be assumed that the program reduced death anxiety.

Another component of the third stage in the research process is a section that defines all important or ambiguous terminology. For example, does "old" refer to someone above the age of 25, 55, 65, 75, or 85? Or will "old" be defined by physiological, biological, social, or psychological characteristics? In science, terms should be operationally defined. An operational definition is one in which something is defined with reference to a measurable criterion. For example, "poverty" is defined as having less than a certain yearly income, or "isolation" is defined as having less than a certain number of social contacts in a specified period of time.

Stage 4: The Sample   In the fourth stage researchers select an appropriate group of individuals to study. This group is referred to as the sample. The sample is selected from the population, the entire group about which the researchers wish to make observations and conclusions. Because the population is generally too large to study, researchers must measure and study a small segment of it, or a sample. For example, the population of those 65+ years of age is almost 30 million individuals. Obviously studying 30 million individuals is not practical, therefore a sample is studied. It is important that the sample be representative of the population from which it is drawn. This simply means that the characteristics of the population are represented in the sample in terms of variables such as sex, race, income, or health. If the sample is not representative of the population, then the conclusions will probably not be accurate.

There has been concern over the representativeness of many samples in gerontological research because older persons have a lower response rate than other adult age groups (see Covey, 1985; Herzog & Rodgers, 1988b) because of their poorer health, suspiciousness of researchers, lack of interest in the research, or caregivers who deny researchers access. A last reason is that researchers are often not adequately skilled in dealing with older persons, and thus unable to enlist them as participants.

There is also concern that the frail elderly are underrepresented in research because of the difficulty in locating and interviewing them (Streib, 1983). Thus, their percentage of the total aged population and needs go largely unreported.

In the past, most samples in gerontology were "convenience samples." That is, samples were based on individuals who were easy or convenient for researchers to obtain rather than on their representativeness. Institutionalized older persons were "overrepresented" because of the convenience of having a large number of individuals present in one area, which reduced the time and cost associated with the research. Additionally, institutionalized older persons were generally compliant with researchers' requests (see Covey, 1985).

Stage 5: Data Collection   In the fifth stage of the research process, researchers make observations. Depending on the specific methods, different types of observations can be made. In a participant-observer study researchers may simply watch and record what they see. In other types of studies observations may be obtained from various instruments or tests such as self-concept scales, questionnaires, or intelligence tests.

Certain measurement devices are important in research since they allow researchers to work with many concepts that cannot be readily observed. Intelligence and morale are two such concepts. When dealing with measuring devices there are two important terms to remember: validity and reliability. If a measuring device is valid, then it measures what it is supposed to measure. If a measuring device is reliable, then it measures consistently from one test period to another. A test can be reliable but not valid; however, a valid test will be reliable.

Stage 6: Categorization, Analysis, and Interpretation   The data that has been collected by means of observation are categorized, analyzed, and interpreted. Categorizing the data simply means organizing the data for analysis. Generally, the analysis refers to statistical analysis. Statistics can convert a large mass of meaningless and confusing observations into an organized and coherent body of information. Furthermore, the use of statistics allows researchers to make inferences and draw conclusions about their data. It is during the sixth stage of the research process that the original questions of the research are answered and the hypotheses either accepted or rejected (see Levenson, 1980).

The most difficult and important aspect of stage 6 is interpreting the data. Facts do not speak for themselves. Rather, individuals interpret and speak for the facts. The same set of facts can be interpreted in different ways. For example, if older persons score lower on intelligence tests than other age groups, this fact can be interpreted as an indication that older persons are less intelligent than other age groups or as an indication that intelligence tests are biased against older persons. Theories which assist in the interpretation process will be discussed in the next section.

We need to examine one other variable in this section, causation. For a variable to cause an effect, two factors must be present. First it is necessary for a particular causal variable to be present. Second, the causal variable in and of itself must be sufficient to produce the effect; the effect will not occur without the presence of the causal variable. For example, does old age cause self-concept to decline? The answer is "no." There are many older individuals who have positive self-concepts and there are also many younger individuals who have negative self-concepts. Therefore old age in and of itself is not a sufficient causal variable. Causation is not usually the result of one variable, but rather of a combination of several variables.

Determining causation can also be exceptionally difficult because of the interaction among age, period, and cohort effects. All of these effects (defined below) interact and make it difficult for the gerontologist to distinguish or to isolate the causal variable. To an extent we are back at the issue of the distinction between cohorts as a result of "age changes" or "age differences." Because of their importance in gerontological research, these three effects will be briefly examined (see Riley et al., 1972).

The first is the birth-cohort effect. A birth cohort is a group of individuals born in the same year (e.g., 1910) or the same grouping of years (e.g., 1905–1909). Researchers believe that by being born in a certain time period and by being exposed at a certain age to the values, beliefs, and experiences prevalent during the time period, each birth cohort will be different from other birth cohorts. The further removed in time they are from one another, the greater the differences among birth cohorts (sometimes called the generation gap).

The second effect is the period effect. Individuals live through different periods such as depressions, wars, or movements—ecology, civil rights, women's rights— which simultaneously affect all living birth cohorts, however, at different ages. For example, World War II affected different birth cohorts very differently. For young men it often meant delaying careers and education and going to war. For many young women it meant becoming a single parent. For children, it often meant the absence of a father figure. The same period effect can have a different impact on different birth cohorts. The researchers might therefore ask if the behavior of older persons is caused by period effects.

The third effect is aging. Each cohort can expect to undergo certain biological changes. Younger cohorts can expect maturational changes, such as menstruation in women or the growth of facial hair in men. Older cohorts can expect changes such as menopause in women or baldness in men. Researchers might ask if the behavior of older persons is caused by the aging effect.

In gerontology, researchers face the problem of separating these three effects from one another in order to determine causation. For example, they may find that older persons do not engage in sexual activity as frequently as do individuals in other adult age cohorts. Is this difference a result of the aging effect? In other words, are there age-associated biological or physical changes that make sexual activity less frequent? Or is the difference in the frequency of sexual activity a result of cohort effect? Older persons were raised in a Victorian era where sexual values may have created a lower frequency of sexual activity than that of subsequent birth cohorts. Or is the difference in rates of sexual activity a result of a period effect, such as the sexual revolution, which might have "turned off" older individuals while younger adults were "turned on." Researchers have devised various ways to isolate age and cohort effects (see Kosloski, 1986).

Stage 7: Evaluation of the Research Process   The seventh stage in the research process involves a critical evaluation of the entire research process. The researchers examine the design, measurement devices, sample, and other factors that were important in the creation of data or its interpretation. Evaluation, not acceptance, is a basic premise among researchers.

Stage 8: Presentation of the Research Report   The last stage of the research process is the presentation of the research report. This presentation consists of writing a detailed report that includes all the important steps in and the findings of the research process. The research report is then distributed to the appropriate scientific communities where the information is evaluated and perhaps utilized.

Research Projects

We have just examined the research process. Although most research in gerontology is based on one individual's research and sample, many studies have been based on larger research projects. Below are some of the major research projects that have contributed to the growth of gerontology. The projects are listed in chronological order.

Framingham Studies of Heart Disease   These longitudinal studies were started in 1948 by the U.S. Public Health Service to examine factors that contributed to the development of cardiovascular diseases. The studies used a probability sample of residents of Framingham, Massachusetts. The initial sample consisted of over 5000 men and women between the ages of 30 and 59. The study included individuals who were free of heart disease at the start of the study. Participants were periodically examined to assess the development of heart disease as well as factors that contributed to the disease. The numerous articles of the study are widely cited and it has contributed significantly to our knowledge of the risk factors involved in the development of cardiovascular disease (Heidrick, 1987).

Cornell Study of Occupational Retirement   The study was conducted between 1952 and 1962 to longitudinally measure the impact of retirement and initially involved over 3700 participants. This study was one of the first to dispel the widely held belief that retirement is detrimental to health (Streib, 1987).

Kansas City Studies of Adult Life   It is difficult to describe the importance of these studies. For gerontologists in the 1960s and early 1970s the research generated by the Kansas City studies composed a significant part of the gerontology literature; the research gave impetus and shaped the direction of future research. These studies were started in 1952 and completed in 1962. Two studies were completed: The first study was a cross-sectional study that had a stratified sample of 750 individuals 40 to 70 years of age. The second was longitudinal and composed of 280 individuals. The researchers were from several disciplines and the sample more representative than generally found.

One of the major contributions was the presentation of disengagement theory in Cumming and Henry's 1961 book *Growing Old,* which went contrary to the generally held belief of an "activity theory" of aging. The belief at the time was that middle aged and aged individuals generally had the same social-psychological needs. However, against the needs of older individuals, society gradually withdrew roles from the individual. Those who aged successfully were those who prevented or delayed this role withdrawal.

The early Kansas City studies reported the opposite and found that the withdrawal was not unilateral but mutual; that is, both society and the individual willingly participated in the withdrawal. In fact, the social-psychological needs of older persons, in areas such as life satisfaction, were satisfied through the withdrawal process.

The data was later reexamined by different researchers using different measures and some support was found for a theory that is opposite of disengagement theory, activity theory. Both activity theory and disengagement theory will be discussed in the next section.

National Institute of Mental Health (NIMH) Aging Study   From 1955 to 1966 the NIMH began a multidisciplinary, longitudinal study of community-dwelling, healthy men between the ages of 65 and 92. The study separated the process of aging from disease, and noted that much of what has been called "aging" is in actuality "disease." The study noted that older healthy individuals function in many ways, such as intellectually, in a manner similar to younger individuals. The study also reported that rates and causes of psychiatric disorders were similar for both younger and older individuals (Butler, 1987). The results of this research were published in *Human Aging* by Birren and associates (1963).

Duke Longitudinal Studies   The Duke Longitudinal Studies of Aging consisted of three studies. The first was started in 1955 after 5 years of preliminary research; it was a longitudinal study of 267 men and women between the ages of 60 and 90 and ran until 1976. The purpose of the study was to examine ". . . the basic physical, mental, and social processes of normal aging" and to ". . . account for variations in these processes . . ." (Shock et al., 1984). The study was called, "Effect of Aging upon the Nervous System—A Physiological, Psychological, and Sociological Study of Aging."

The second study, sometimes referred to as the "Duke adaptation study," was also a longitudinal study. It started in 1968 with 502 individuals between the ages of 46 and 70, and ended in 1976. The purpose of this study was to examine the impact of a stressful event, such as the death of a spouse or retirement.

The third study, known as the "old-old study," started in 1972 and the last data was gathered in 1983. The study had 1000 individuals 65+ years of age.

The Duke studies were somewhat unique in that the interest was "normal aging." In a time when the pathological aspects of aging held great interest and many studies used institutionalized populations as samples, the Duke studies started by studying noninstitutionalized, healthy, older individuals. In all of the studies participants went to the Duke Medical Center for a series of tests over a 1 to 3 day period every 2 to 3 years. Generally, the tests consisted of a medical and psychological evaluation as well as a social profile.

Literally hundreds, perhaps thousands, of articles have been generated from this research (see Palmore, 1970, 1974, 1981; Palmore et al., 1985). Four of the major findings are as follows (Palmore, 1987):

1 With increasing age, health and physical functioning generally decline.

2 While physical decline may be the norm, there are some exceptions; some individuals may show no decline and others improvement in certain functions.

3 There is little or no decline in social and psychological functioning.

4 The aged are a heterogeneous group and there are wide variations in the process of growing old.

Baltimore Longitudinal Study of Aging   Started in 1958, the Baltimore Longitudinal Study of Aging is still in progress. The study started by examining certain psychological and physiological characteristics of independent men between the ages of 18 and 96 years of age. Some of the men have been examined 21 times. The study used self-selection for its sample, with one sample participant often referring friends to the study. In 1978 the study enrolled women. By examining the participants every 18 to 24 months the study has accumulated a wealth of information on the aging process (Shock, 1987). A major purpose of the study was to distinguish the aging process from other processes, such as the consequences of disease or poverty. The results of the study have been published in numerous articles, and recently in the book *Normal Human Aging: The Baltimore Longitudinal Study of Aging* (Shock et al., 1984).

Longitudinal Retirement History Survey   This survey was conducted by the Social Security Administration. The studies started in 1969 and surveyed 11,153 individuals between the ages of 58 and 63. By the time the studies ended in 1979 there were still 7352 participants, some of them widowed women whose husbands had originally been part of the studies. Information was gathered every 2 years (e.g., 1969, 1971, 1973, 1975, 1977, 1979). At the beginning of the studies 16 percent of the participants reported that they were completely retired. At the end the figure was 76 percent. The first study accessed the impact of retirement. Studies conducted during other years often examined other aspects such as plans for retirement or future work plans. Information on widowhood was gathered during the last three studies.

This survey has provided researchers with a tremendous amount of information on the aging process and older persons; much of the information has not been analyzed. Data tapes are available for researchers (Fillenbaum, 1987).

Normative Aging Study   Between 1958 and 1963 the VA outpatient clinic in Boston conducted a study on 150 octogenarians of the Spanish American War. This study made it apparent to the VA that more information was needed on geriatric health, especially since this segment of the population would be increasing substantially in the next few decades.

As a result, in 1963 it created the Normative Aging Study, which was a multidisciplinary, longitudinal study of 2280 healthy, community-dwelling men between the ages of 25 and 75. The study sought to ascertain the causes of certain prevalent age-related diseases as well as the impact of these diseases on the aging process. Unlike many longitudinal studies, this study retained the vast majority of its subjects (84 percent in 1985). The research from the Normative Aging Study has made a number of important contributions to medicine, dentistry, psychology, and sociology (Ekerdt, 1987).

Additional Longitudinal Studies   The reader should be aware that there are other excellent longitudinal studies (see Schaie, 1983*a*). Some are the Seattle Longitudinal Study (see Cooney et al., 1988; Schaie, 1983*b*), the intergenerational studies from the Institute of Human Development in Berkeley, California (Sands & Meredith, 1989), and the Iowa State studies (Cummingham & Owens, 1983).

Cross-Sectional Studies   There have been a number of excellent cross-sectional studies. We will mention two, both done by Harris and associates (1975, 1981). Both studies involved large random samples, and had two purposes. First, they obtained some basic demographic information, such as employment or marital status. Second, the studies were interested in examining attitudes about aging, both from the aged as well as other age groups. Questions were asked such as "What are the worst things about being over 65 years of age," or "What are the serious problems of those 65+ years of age?"

Both studies provided a wealth of information that had not been readily available to gerontologists. In addition to some needed demographic information, the studies also provided a comparison of how different age groups viewed old age.

Databases for Research   In addition to the studies mentioned above there are several databases available for researchers to use. Zimmerman (1989) has pointed to two available types of databases. The first is the bibliographic database which allows students or researchers to search for references. The bibliographic databases are similar to the periodicals *Psychological Abstracts, Sociological Abstracts,* or the *Reader's Guide to Periodical Literature,* which you use to find references. Computer technology has made these actual periodicals somewhat obsolete. Most libraries now have on site computer databases with the information from these periodicals. Rather than examining several of these periodicals and copying down the references that seem relevant to your research, all that is needed is to go to the computer terminal with the relevant database, type in certain key words, and within minutes you can have a printed list of references.

The second type of database is called "archival storage of numeric data." Research projects often gather more data than they can analyze. Many of these databases are made available to other researchers for analysis. The data are generally provided on computer disks or tapes, although some research projects will also provide a printed copy of the results. Thus, a researcher who does not have the time or funding to conduct a large-scale study, can have access to one. This can save a tremendous amount of time and expense. Patrick and Borgatta (1981) and Zimmerman (1989) have reviewed some databases.

Current Status of Research in Gerontology

We have examined the research process and some research projects. On paper the research process looks simple and straightforward. However, all research is plagued by problems and this section will examine some that exist in gerontological research. These problems are not unique to gerontology; they can be found in all research.

As noted in Chapter 1, there has been a tremendous increase in recent years in the number of gerontology books and journals. One result of this is that many widely held beliefs, facts, and theories about older persons have been challenged and often replaced by new beliefs, facts, and theories. Often the explanation for the conflicts between early and current research results has been that early gerontological research generated inaccurate beliefs, facts, and theories because researchers did not follow accepted research procedures (see Montgomery & Borgatta, 1986).

There is an excellent chance that the above explanation is correct. For example, two articles that reviewed the characteristics of research published in "psychological gerontology" between 1963 and 1974 noted numerous deficiencies in the research and made recommendations for future research (Abrahams et al., 1975; Seltzer, 1975). Matilda White Riley (1987) noted in her presidential address to the American Sociological Association that when compiling material for *Aging and Society* (1972) a great deal of "research" had to be discarded because it was "scientifically invalid" (see Riley, 1988a). Edgar F. Borgatta and Christopher Hertzog noted in the introduction of a 1985 issue of *Research on Aging,* dedicated to research methods and research in aging, that the "quality of research on aging has not been stellar." Beth Hess (1982) summed up the feelings of some gerontologists when she stated in *Gerontology News,* "I don't think you've missed much if you stopped reading the journals 5 years ago."

If current research in gerontology has not improved then contemporary gerontologists may merely be substituting one set of inaccurate beliefs, facts, and theories for another. There are at least two ways to prevent this continual cycle of discrediting and replacing data. The first is to have a set of guidelines by which research is evaluated. The second is to evaluate colleagues' work more critically. Admittedly, these ideas are hardly new. In fact, more than a decade ago Robert Binstock (see Cohen, 1980) pointed out that what gerontology needed was ". . . more scholarly muckraking, the exposure of shoddy research, the unmasking of investigators concentrating on old data over and over again, and some deliberate disclosure of superficiality which creeps into research from time to time. . . ." It was pointed out by Cohen (1980) that this was a "courageous if little noticed statement."

We now need to examine problems in gerontological research. In discussing these problems, students will be provided with guidelines to critically evaluate gerontological research. The first problem is with terminology. Terminology is, of course, important in all fields and disciplines. If terms are used in a consistent manner, researchers are better able to compare and contrast the results of similar but different research projects. In gerontology there are many important terms that are frequently used but which have no consistent definition: aged, retirement, nursing home, isolation, poverty. We need to examine who gerontologists study and what their age range is.

There are two problems with the use of terms to describe older persons. The first deals with the number of terms, the second with the age ranges associated with the terms; both problems are illustrated in Table 4-1. In the left-hand column are some of the terms frequently used to describe older persons; the right-hand column gives age ranges associated with the terms.

As can be seen, not only have a wide range of terms been used, but different age ranges for the same term. A sample of individuals 55 years of age could be classified as old, older, aged, elderly, geriatric, older adults, in senior adulthood, young-old, in late adulthood, in late middle age, in midlife, middle aged, or young!

Abrahams and his associates (1975) noted in an analysis of published research that "old" subjects were from 35 to 100 years, middle aged from 40 to 70, and young from 15 to 49. A replication of this study (see Hoyer et al., 1984) found

TABLE 4-1
TERMINOLOGY AND AGE RANGES*

Term	Examples of age ranges
Aged	47–92, 52–74, 53–96, 55–97, 60+, 65+
Elderly	46–79, 50+, 52–86, 54–83, 55+, 60–89, 65–84, 67–95
Old	50–70, 53–71, 55–80, 60–79, 65–76
Older	45–82, 50+, 50–90, 51–57, 53–72, 55–77, 65+
Geriatric	45+, 48–94, 50–77, 53–91, 55–70, 65+
Senior	60+, 64–79
Older adult	45–65, 55+
Older person	58–60
Older American	55–102
Later adulthood	46–86
Late adulthood	65+
Senior adulthood	46–86
Young-old	55–70, 55–74, 65–79
Old-old	71–85, 75+, 80+
Very old	80–94
Old middle age	50–64
Late middle age	45–64
Midlife	25–64
Middle age	30–59, 35–49, 35–54, 40–59, 39–51, 45–51, 45–54
Early middle age	35–44
Young adult	31–47, 21–39
Younger	<7, 18–30, 18–39, 20–50, 30–65
Young	18–60, 18–25, 20–58, 21–49, 17–38, 18–24, 17–25, 21–49, 24–34
Respondents	60–80
Adults	21–55

* Compiled by author.

considerable improvement, but still room for further change. In a similar study Ashbaugh and Fay (1987) found little agreement among researchers as to when workers became "old" and noted that the age range went from 30 to 65. They also noted that few researchers justified the age ranges used.

It is clearly time that gerontologists, journal editors, and journal referees decide whom they are studying (e.g., aged, elderly, seniors, etc.) and the chronological age or other salient characteristic(s) of this group. Admittedly, there are valid reasons for having flexibility in this area. For example, many researchers have noted the existence of "social age" (i.e., age based on social characteristics such as retirement or widowhood), "biological age" (i.e., age based on physiological functioning), or have asked for a classification based on a combination of chronological age, social age, and biological age. The issue is complex and ignoring it only compounds the problem. With one study using "old" subjects who are in their forties and fifties and another similar study using "old" subjects who are in their seventies and eighties it is little wonder that research results often differ.

If researchers need flexibility in terminology and age range, they should be able to justify why a standard term and age range is not appropriate. Many of the problems and conflicts in research results are based on this practice.

A second major concern deals with samples, and again there are two problems. The first is that many articles do not provide a description of their samples or sampling procedures which involve a number of potentially confounding variables. While an age range is generally reported (e.g., 65–84) even this is incomplete since one sample might have individuals with a median age of 65, while another a sample with a median age of 80; thus, the studies yield different results because of age differences. Sex (i.e., male or female), an obviously important variable, is still not reported in about 25 percent of studies (see Abrahams et al., 1975; Gentry & Shulman, 1985; Hoyer et al., 1984; Seltzer, 1975).

Although specific studies will determine the variables that need to be reported, some of the following need to be reported with much greater frequency: sex, marital status, socioeconomic status, race, ethnic group, retirement status, income, educational level, health (both physical and psychological), place of residence (e.g., home or institution). Readers have the need and the right to know if the members of the sample are male or female, black or white, retired or working, in good health or poor health, or living independently in the community or dependently in a nursing home. It takes little space to report these characteristics and there is the nagging curiosity, "Why weren't they reported?" An undergraduate suggested that perhaps journal editors were responsible for the deletion to save space, since the inclusion seemed so obvious even to a neophyte researcher.

The inclusion of sample characteristics is even more important if we believe that older persons are a heterogeneous group. If this is true then certainly the purpose of gerontology is not simply to report on a nondescript group of "old" individuals but to try to ascertain differences based on certain sample characteristics.

The second problem with sampling is the lack of random or representative samples. In the last subsection on the research process it was pointed out that too many samples are convenience samples. While there are many valid reasons not to use random or representative samples, clearly the time has arrived for a greater percentage of research based on better samples.

The third problem in gerontological research is the lack of research on minority and ethnic groups. The bulk of research appears to be on white males. More research is needed on women, Native Americans, blacks, Hispanics as well as others. This is a difficult area because of the diversity. For example, because of differences Hispanics need to be separated, at a minimum, into Cuban, Puerto Rican, and Mexican. Because of language and cultural differences, Native Americans should be separated by tribe. Vietnamese should be separated into foreign versus native born. Chinese should be separated into those born in mainland China, Taiwan, or the United States. The list could go on. The major point is simply that more research is needed in this complex area (see Jackson, 1989).

Fourth, more longitudinal studies are needed. The number of studies comparing young and old groups clearly suggests that many researchers are using cross-sectional designs when a longitudinal design would have been more appropriate (see Campbell et al., 1986).

Fifth, researchers should be required to report the time period the data was collected. Readers have the right to know if the article is based on current observations or observations left over from a 1970 master's thesis.

Sixth, more research instruments need to be designed for older persons. Many of those that have been designed are questionable in validity and reliability (see Bloom, 1975). Some research instruments appropriate for older persons have small print that is difficult to read. Another concern is the use of different instruments by researchers to measure the same variable, such as intelligence or self-esteem; this makes replication of the results difficult since different instruments may yield slightly different measurements.

In concluding this section two points need to be made. First, these are only some of the guidelines to help you evaluate research (see Birren, 1959; Maddox & Campbell, 1985; Maddox & Wiley, 1976). Second, these problems are *not* unique to gerontology. There have been tremendous strides in recent years in the quality of gerontological research. This trend can be seen in the National Institute on Aging which has placed emphasis on "methodological excellence" (Riley, 1988*b*; Schaie et al., 1988).

GERONTOLOGICAL THEORY

In the last section we discussed the functions of research, examined the research process and some research projects in gerontology, and noted some problems with current research. In this section we will examine some of the social theories that have either been developed or used by gerontologists. A social theory is basically an attempt to explain, predict, and understand behavior from the perspective of a sociologist or psychologist. It attempts to integrate several sets of observations into one logically contrived set of statements.

Theories have been widely used in many disciplines. In the natural sciences there are many theories, or higher-order explanations such as laws, that are used to explain, predict, or understand events. For example, if a researcher held up and then individually dropped hundreds of different objects, obviously a theory concerning gravity could be developed and used to explain, predict, and understand the separate observations, as well as explain any exceptions, such as a helium-filled balloon rising when released.

Thus, the above theory would need to account for why most objects fell, why some objects fall at different speeds, and why some objects rise. The development of the law of gravity was based on an explanation of individual observations that were probably very confusing to early observers (i.e., some objects falling at different rates, while other objects were rising at different rates). It also allowed for accurate prediction based on certain characteristics of an object.

As early natural scientists began to discover theories and laws that explained the natural world, social and behavioral scientists searched for social theories and laws that governed human behavior.

A "good" theory about human behavior should explain and predict all of the behavior it claims to cover. As a result, some theories are quite complex and consist of numerous theorems, statements, and propositions.

Research is often conducted to test a theory. Repeated confirmation will increase the confidence that a theory is correct. Even if research continually supports a theory, it is *never* proved to be true. Scientific knowledge is never absolute; it is always open to change in light of new evidence. If the results of several thorough and properly conducted research projects do not support the theory, it needs to be rejected or revised.

Although theory has guided a great deal of research in gerontology, and has been implicit in many interpretations of research projects, to date there has not been much theorizing in gerontology. In fact, a recent book on gerontological theory, *Emergent Theories of Aging* (Birren & Bengtson, 1988), noted that gerontology is "data-rich" but "theory poor." Also, to date, most theories in gerontology have had a relatively short period of acceptance. The lack of "good," consistent theories in gerontology is not a feature of just gerontology, but of the social and behavioral sciences as well. This is a result of the complexity of human behavior, the relatively short period of time human behavior has been studied using "scientific" methods, and the interdisciplinary nature of gerontology.

The remainder of this chapter will examine eight theories that have been frequently used in gerontology: disengagement theory, activity theory, personality theory, subculture theory, labeling theory, exchange theory, the age-stratification model, and phenomenological theory.

Disengagement Theory

The development of theory in gerontology started with the formulation of disengagement theory (see Cumming et al., 1960). To fully understand the impact of disengagement theory one must first understand the beliefs held by most gerontologists at the time the theory appeared.

Prior to the presentation of disengagement theory most gerontologists ascribed to an "activity theory" of aging, even though this theory had not been formally named or developed. The activity theory of aging held that the greater an individual's level of activity the greater an individuals physical, psychological, and social adjustment (Havighurst & Albrecht, 1953). The activity theory concept was also expressed by Ernest Burgess, a central figure in gerontology from the 1940s through the 1960s, who noted in the lead article in *Aging in Western Societies* (1960) that one of the most difficult challenges of future generations would be to find new meaningful, valuable roles for older persons.

The basic belief was that successful aging consisted of retaining middle-aged levels of activity and involvement for as long as possible. This meant that as old roles were reduced or severed, new roles had to be found.

Disengagement theory was the antithesis of activity theory. After presenting it as a "tentative theory" in 1960 it was more formally stated in what is probably the most famous book in gerontology, *Growing Old* by Elaine Cumming and William Henry (1961). Disengagement theory was one of the theories that grew out of the Kansas City studies. The theory had two parts. The first concerned the disengagement of the individual from society. The proponents of the theory believed that with increasing age individuals would recognize their limitations, in terms of knowledge and energy, and realize that there were younger individuals who were more qualified for the roles they held. Thus, older persons would seek to disengage from society. The second part of the theory dealt with the disengagement of the society from individuals. Not only would older individuals seek to disengage from society, but society, through the development of norms, rules, and laws, would "push" older individuals to disengage. This happened so that younger individuals, with more knowledge and energy, could be placed in roles. Also, the deaths of older individuals would be less disruptive to the society. In other words, there was a mutual, inevitable process of disengagement which benefited both the individual and the society.

Disengagement theorists believed that high levels of life satisfaction were associated with older persons reducing both the number and importance of their roles. Thus happiness, success, or adjustment in old age consisted of older individuals recognizing that they were no longer young and that there were more competent younger individuals capable of filling their roles.

The authors noted that their findings were unexpected, especially given the current beliefs in gerontology, but that in some ways they were also common sense. They went on to say that attempting to remain middle-aged ". . . seems to require much swimming against the stream for the old person to overcome the natural tendency for the world around him to withdraw its support, leaving him deserted." They also pointed out that writers dealing with maturation or other age periods, such as childhood, did not suggest that as one progressed into adolescence, one should try and remain as childish as possible. They were noting that while the transition from childhood to adolescence or from adolescence to adulthood was seen as natural, normal, and perhaps desirable, the transition from middle age to old age was viewed very differently.

To summarize, disengagement was distinguished by four characteristics:

1 Disengagement is a gradual process. That is, it does not suddenly happen but rather is a series of events. For example, with increasing age parental roles begin to lessen in time and responsibility, work roles wind down before retirement, and community and religious roles are gradually reduced and abandoned. Thus, with increasing age the number, importance, and intensity of roles declines.

2 Disengagement is inevitable and universal since both the concept of disengagement and the process for bringing it about are part of the social structure of the society. Individuals completing the life periods will experience it.

3 Disengagement is a mutually satisfying process for both the society and the individual; it is desired by both the individual and the society. It is not functional for society to fill the roles of those aged who have suddenly died with inadequately trained personnel. Thus society is happy to see the aged disengage. Correspondingly, the aged are happy to disengage since the demands being placed on them create anxieties and pressures and make roles easy to relinquish.

4 Disengagement is the norm. This fact is demonstrated by the fact that most individuals retire.

In conducting their research Cumming and Henry examined factors such as the amount of social interaction, the number of current roles, and the amount of ego involvement in current roles. They felt that the declines noted above were logical, since they brought about a natural, normal, satisfying process called disengagement.

Upon publication the theory was almost immediately attacked (Brehm, 1968; Butler, 1976; Carp, 1968; Granick & Patterson, 1971; Havighurst et al., 1969; Hochschild, 1975, 1976; Lowenthal & Haven, 1968; Maddox, 1963, 1964, 1965, 1968, 1970; Palmore, 1968; Prasad, 1964; Reichard & Peterson, 1962; Rose, 1964; Rosow, 1967; Tallmer, 1973; Tallmer & Kutner, 1970; Tobin & Neugarten, 1961; Youmans, 1967), and both Cumming (1963, 1975) and Henry (1965) published modifications of the theory. Cumming, for example, noted that "in its original form the theory was too simple" (1963). In her modification Cumming allowed personality more importance and noted that not everyone disengages.

To date, there have been numerous attempts to test the theory; the findings are contradictory. A number of studies, especially by the proponents of activity theory, have found little support for disengagement theory. The major criticism of the theory is that it is too simple. There are many older persons who do not disengage and who do not appear to suffer from their engagement. There is also the contradictory literature of the activity theorists to contend with. For example, activity theorists claim that disengagement is largely a result of lack of opportunities for older persons rather than a result of a desire to disengage on the part of the individual. Other studies have found that it is not age in and of itself that brings about disengagement but rather the correlates of increasing age such as poor health, death of friends, or reduced finances. To explain older persons who had not disengaged, disengagement theorists would have originally said that they were off in their timing, that they were "unsuccessful disengagers," or that they constituted an elite.

There are other criticisms of disengagement. One is that it certainly cannot be applied universally since in many other societies increasing age brings with it new, powerful, and important positions. Another criticism is that there is no guarantee that the performance, enthusiasm, knowledge, or vigor of those replacing the disengagers will be of a higher quality. In fact, it may be less since decades of skills and knowledge are lost. A last criticism is that disengagement is placing a strain on many pension systems.

Although no studies have offered universal support for disengagement theory, several studies have offered limited support for certain aspects of the theory (Brown, 1974; Cumming, 1975; Streib & Schneider, 1971; Tallmer & Kutner, 1970; Williams & Wirths, 1965).

Activity Theory

As mentioned above, activity theory was the first and certainly the most dominant theoretical approach in gerontology. However, the theory was not stated explicitly; rather, there was an implicit understanding of the theory (see Cavan, 1962; Cavan et al., 1949; Havighurst & Albrecht, 1953). Disengagement theory was presented first in this text simply because it was developed and tested first. Although researchers were quick to attack disengagement theory, there was no "formal and explicit" statement of activity theory until 1972, more than a decade after Cumming and Henry's book.

There is little doubt that in the 1950s and early 1960s activity theory was the preferred theory. In his presidential address before the Division of Maturity and Old Age at the American Psychological Association in 1960, Dr. Robert J. Havighurst noted that ". . . activity theory is favored by most of the practical workers in the field of gerontology" (Havighurst, 1961).

The first formal and explicit statement of activity theory appeared in 1972 (Lemon et al., 1972). In the article the authors defined several terms, such as self-concept, role loss, and life satisfaction, and stated four postulates and six theorems that related to life satisfaction and activity. Because of limitations in their data they concentrated on the fifth theorem, the greater the activity the greater the life satisfaction. From this theorem seven hypotheses were generated which dealt with the frequency and type of activity and role changes. The authors concluded that ". . . the data provide surprising little support for the implicit activity theory of aging which has served as the theoretical base for practice as well as research in gerontology for decades." The researchers pointed out that the lack of support may have been because they used secondary data.

A formal replication of this study did not appear until 1982 (Longino & Kart, 1982). This study was specifically designed to test activity theory. The sample consisted of individuals in three different types of retirement communities. Basically the study provided "strong" support for activity theory.

The study separated the type of activity from the frequency of activity. It noted that it is not just activity that is important but rather the type of activity. As a result the researchers distinguished three types of activity: informal, formal, and solitary. Essentially, more "intimate" activity produced greater life satisfaction. Informal activity was the most intimate and consisted of activity generally found in primary relationships such as those with family, friends, or neighbors. It was predicted, and found by Longino and Kart (1982), that the greater the amount of informal activity the greater the life satisfaction. Formal activity, which consisted of activity in a setting such as a voluntary organization, was found to have a negative impact on life satisfaction. It was predicted and found that solitary activity, which consisted of watching television or walking alone, would also have little impact on life satisfaction.

Frequency of activity is the second variable. Basically, individuals who engage in informal activity on a frequent basis will have higher life satisfaction than individuals who engage in informal activity on an infrequent basis.

The basic belief behind informal activity for high life satisfaction is that with increasing age there are frequently many losses. These losses can lower self-concept. Informal activity with others can provide some support to lessen the impact these losses have. The more intimate and frequent the activity the greater the likelihood of support. The greater the support, the more self-concept is maintained and the greater one's life satisfaction.

There are numerous criticisms of activity theory. One of the major criticisms is that it may not be the type or frequency of activity that determines life satisfaction, but that those with high life satisfaction have a greater probability of forming and interacting in informal activities.

Personality Theory

Over the years there have been many studies that have supported disengagement theory and rejected activity theory; there have been many other studies that supported the reverse. A theory that attempted to explain the contradictions in the research emerged in the early 1960s and can loosely be called personality theory. Some of the major proponents of personality theory obtained their information from the Kansas City studies. While disengagement theory emerged from some of the early sets of data, personality theory emerged after a more thorough analysis of the completed study.

Personality theorists do not believe that either disengagement theory or activity theory is adequate. They believe that it is not the type or frequency of activity but personality that is the pivotal variable in determining life satisfaction. Havighurst, Neugarten, and Tobin (1968) found eight personality types, two of which can be used to explain the theory. The "reorganizers" try to remain middle-aged by finding new roles to replace lost roles. In doing so they maintain high activity and high life-satisfaction levels. Thus, the reorganizers support the arguments of activity theory. The "disengaged" have voluntarily given up most of their roles and prefer the "rocking-chair" approach to life. While they have low levels of activity they have high levels of life satisfaction, which supports the disengagement theory of aging.

Subculture Theory

A subculture is a group within the general society which, while exhibiting many of the characteristics of the general society, exhibits certain characteristics that are generally not found in other segments of the society. Some of these characteristics may be obvious such as style of clothing or hair, or more subtle such as beliefs and values. A subculture may be formed on the basis of such variables as age, sex, race, ethnicity, religion, or social class (see Longino, 1987).

A theory that emerged during the 1960s was the subculture theory (Rose, 1962, 1964, 1965) which has some of the same general concepts as disengagement theory and activity theory. Subculture theory substituted the term self-concept for life satisfaction and interaction for activity. Essentially the theory stated that an individual's self-concept is determined largely through interpersonal interaction. If the interactions are positive, self-concept is positive; if the interactions are negative, self-concept is negative. Because of variables, such as segregation and discrimination, older persons will interact more frequently with other older persons, thus forming an aged subculture. The aged subculture creates new norms and values surrounding old age that allow older persons to create a group consciousness and maintain a positive self-concept.

Several variables, according to Rose, have contributed to the formation of a subculture of older persons. First, a larger percentage of the population is now aged, which provides more older persons to form a subculture with separate ideas, beliefs, values, and behaviors. Second, the physical and social segregation of the aged has contributed to the formation of an aged subculture. Physically older persons are often concentrated in certain sections of a city or in age-segregated communities. Socially older persons can also be excluded from full participation in certain aspects of society, such as work. The increased percentage of older persons along with the fact that they are often excluded from society has led to the third variable, namely, an enhanced age consciousness. The aged can now recognize that they are "different" from the rest of society in areas such as their values, life-styles, interests, needs, and behaviors. Age consciousness is intensified by age segregation and a commonality of interests and needs which, in turn, has united the aged as a social group. Out of this unity an esprit de corps or group pride has emerged.

The proponents of subculture theory recognize that many of the distinctive behaviors of older persons result from factors other than the aged subculture. For example, biological changes, social norms, and generational differences all have an effect. However, subculture theorists generally believe that of all the subcultures to which an older person belongs, the aged subculture is the most powerful. In other words, the ethnic, religious, sex, social class, or occupational subcultures are overridden by the aged subculture.

The subculture theorists also recognize the fact that vast differences exist among segments of the aged population and thus have drawn two conclusions. First, all aged subcultures are not homogeneous; that is, just as the aged differ, so do their subcultures. For example, an aged subculture formed by wealthy individuals is likely to be very different from one formed by destitute older individuals. The wealthy aged subculture is probably based on social needs while the destitute aged subculture will probably be based on financial needs. Second, subculture theorists have concluded that because the aged are heterogeneous, the aged subculture does not have a universal impact. There are many aged in our society who because of position, wealth, power, or other characteristics are excluded from the aged subculture. For example, older persons who are employed or wealthy are less likely to be excluded from general society and therefore will probably not participate in or be influenced by the aged subculture. The proponents of an aged subculture theory note that there are several factors that keep all older persons in contact with general society and away from the subculture of the aged. These factors include family contact, the mass media, employment, welfare organizations, and resentment toward growing old.

The theory is complex and has been difficult to empirically test. Several studies in age-segregated settings that were not specifically designed to test the theory have found evidence that appears to support it (Bultena & Wood, 1969; Hochschild, 1973; Rosow, 1967; Sherman, 1975a, 1975b).

The theory was formally tested by Longino, McClelland, and Peterson (1980), who used the residents of eight age-segregated retirement communities as well as a sample of age-integrated nonretirement community dwellers. They found partial support for the theory. The age-segregated residents appeared to find participation in an aged subculture more satisfying than those in age-integrated communities. For them there was less loneliness, boredom, and feelings of not being needed. Additionally, they had more positive self-concepts. The theory hypothesized that the subculture would contribute to a political consciousness and activism since the older persons would resent the devalued societal image of older persons. This group consciousness and activism was not found. In fact, the study found the opposite and noted that those in age-segregated settings appeared to represent a "retreatist rather than an activist" life-style. Based on their findings, the researchers recommended a modification of the theory that would take into account the retreatist nature of individuals living in retirement communities.

Labeling Theory

Labeling theory has traditionally been used by sociologists to explain the behavior of, for example, the mentally ill and criminals. Bengtson (1973) suggested that this theory be used to explain some of the behavior of older persons.

Labeling theory suggests that when we are given a label such as "senile" or "old," this label has a significant impact on the way we will be treated and perceived by others. As labeled individuals we thus take on new identities, positions, and roles. Often the new identity becomes what is called a "master status." The master status is simply the status that overrides all others. It is the status that others are quick to notice and respond to. For example, once an individual is given the status of "senile," it is this status to which others will respond first. Once labeled, it is difficult for us to change the label because our behavior is interpreted in light of the new identity. Often behavior that is contradictory to the label will be ignored and behavior that supports the new identity will be emphasized. For example, if an older person who has been labeled "senile" exhibits coherent behavior, this behavior will be ignored or minimized by the belief that the person is having a "good day." However, slips of the tongue, the forgetting of a date, or any change in habits or appearance will reinforce the "fact" of senility. Those who try and change the label of senility only reinforce the label. Those who protest that there is nothing wrong with them only reinforce the fact that there is something wrong.

Initially, individuals may not accept the label they have been assigned. However, it is generally only a matter of time before the label is accepted. This situation occurs for three reasons. First, other people respond to the label as if it were valid. Second, individuals will receive positive sanctions for behaving in a manner consistent with their label and negative sanctions for behaving in an inconsistent manner. Third, individuals are often placed with others who have the same label, or ostracized so that they can only associate with those who have the same label.

The theory points out that labels can have a tremendous impact on the way we interpret and respond to others. An older person who is labeled as "normal" and tries to be independent will be admired; someone who is labeled as "senile" will be seen as incapable of living independently. Once labeled as old, sick, senile, dependent, or dying, individuals will experience a marked reduction in the number and type of available roles. Furthermore, the labeled individual will enter into largely predetermined groups and organizations. It should be pointed out, however, that individuals can respond differently to the same label. The label "old" may cause severe depression in one individual and senior pride in another. Although labeling theory is an important theory, one must recognize that it is a very general theory.

Exchange Theory

Exchange theory has a long history in sociology (Max Weber, Simmel, Durkheim), anthropology (Levi-Straus, Maus, Malinowski), and economics (Adam Smith, Bentham, Ricardo, J. S. Mill). Sociologists Homans (1961) and Blau (1964) provided an early formulation of the theory. According to the theory, in all social interaction there is an exchange of resources (e.g., money, knowledge, power) between individuals. Thus, there is a "cost" or exchange in all social interaction. The exchange can be material, such as the exchange of money or some other tangible resource, or nonmaterial, such as an exchange of love, knowledge, respect, or power.

The theory also states that individuals act rationally and seek personal gain or profit in the exchanges that occur in social interaction. Social interactions in which the exchange yields gain or profit are continued whenever possible. Those from which an individual does not gain or profit are truncated whenever possible.

Another concept in exchange theory is that of power. If individuals have "equal" resources to exchange, the relationship is said to be balanced. However, if one individual has more resources, or resources of greater value than a second individual, and the second individual needs the resources of the first, the relationship is said to be unbalanced. This can place the individual with the most valuable resources in a position of power to establish the exchange rate, which will probably be favorable in his or her direction.

Dowd (1975) was one of the first to apply exchange theory to gerontology. Dowd noted that there was one central similarity between activity and disengagement theory: a decline in social interaction with increasing age. Both of the above theories, he stated, were inadequate to explain the decline in social interaction. He noted that with increasing age there is generally a decline in power because of a decline in resources and in the value of remaining resources. For example, the skills and knowledge of older individuals have often become outdated by technological changes.

Additionally, younger individuals, who often have more recent skills and knowledge, can fulfill the same occupational roles as older persons at a lower cost and with greater efficiency. Other sources of power can be variables such as influential friends, an attractive appearance, physical strength, or respect. Often with increasing age one's influential friends have died or retired, one's appearance—as defined by society— has declined, as has one's physical strength and respect. Older persons need and want resources such as a retirement income, medical insurance, and other benefits. One of the only resources older persons have left to exchange is compliance with the demands of those in power. One demand often made is the truncation of certain roles. As a result, they disengage from roles in exchange for certain benefits.

Dowd recognized that there were individual differences based on factors such as socioeconomic status. A wealthy older person could control power resources more effectively and for a longer period of time than someone who was not wealthy.

Age-Stratification Model

Age stratification has been set forth as a model to explain the behavior of older persons (see Foner, 1975; Riley, 1971, 1977; Riley et al., 1972). Since the authors noted that their conceptualizations were at an early stage of development and needed further debate and revision, they set forth their concepts as a model, not a theory. Because the age-stratification model has received considerable attention and support from gerontologists, it is important to include a discussion of it here.

Basically the model attempts to explain the inequality found in society. Generally sociologists have explained inequality via social class. That is, society is divided into social classes, or strata, each having assigned rights and roles, which impact on behavior. The age stratification model claims that there is another variable that needs to be considered, namely age.

The age-stratification model perceives age as an important determinant of behavior for two reasons. First, age may limit the ability of the individual to perform in certain roles. Second, society differentially allocates rights, roles, privileges, and opportunities on the basis of age.

Age is a variable that determines rights, roles, and behaviors available to individuals. Chronological age can also influence role performance because of biological, legal, or social restrictions. For example, men cannot sire children or women bear children until certain stages of biological development take place; increasing age may prevent older individuals from performing at certain levels in athletic events. Age also determines role alternatives because of legal requirements. Legally, there are age requirements for certain roles such as driving an automobile, drinking alcoholic beverages, voting in elections, or holding certain offices. There are also social expectations related to certain roles. Many individuals would probably not feel very comfortable around a professor who was a 13-year-old "whiz kid."

In essence, chronological age separates or stratifies the population into age strata. Each age stratum has a set of rights, roles, obligations, and opportunities associated with it. As individuals move from one age stratum to the next, they acquire the roles of that stratum. Individual's abilities can sometimes modify the impact of age strata.

In each age stratum there are age-related role expectations, such as in modes of dress, styles of hair, or language. For example, an adolescent would be expected to have a certain type of dress, language, and hairstyle that would probably be different from that of someone 85 years of age.

In order to enforce role expectations there are sanctions, or rewards for behavior that conforms to social expectations, and punishments for behavior that deviates from social expectations.

Another mechanism used to reinforce social expectations in regard to role performance is socialization. Socialization is simply the process of learning the beliefs, values, and norms of the society in which we live. In the past, socialization was considered to be a process in which only the young engaged. Socialization is a process that ends with death. Because there are different role expectations for different age strata, socialization is a necessary process to prevent us from behaving in an unacceptable manner. Through a number of different social agencies, we learn that many forms of behavior are age specific.

Socialization is a necessary process for a smooth transition from one age stratum or one life period to another. If older persons were to keep the values, beliefs, and norms of youth, there would probably be a conflict between what was desired and what was possible. For example, if older persons were athletic when younger and regularly ran ten 5-minute miles, this activity would probably have to be modified in order to prevent internal conflict between aspirations and capabilities; they would have to learn to value a different program of physical activity. As we move from one age stratum to another, we carry with us preconceived ideas about the role expectations in the next age stratum. We acquire these ideas from a process known as anticipatory socialization.

As the individual moves from one age stratum to another, the expectations associated with a particular role can change. For example, there are different expectations for the father who has young children than there are for the father who has adult children living independent lives. Initially, the father is expected to provide his children with food, shelter, clothing, and love. By the time his children are adults, the only expectation may be to provide them with love.

The concept of birth cohort is also important in the age-stratification model. As we have seen, a cohort is a group of individuals who were born at about the same time and who experienced certain historical events at about the same age. Because of the difference in the experiences of birth cohorts, each tends to see the world from a unique perspective. Concepts of sexuality, morality, racial integration, socialized medicine, desirability of children, and couples living together prior to marriage will be perceived and evaluated very differently. Different birth cohorts will also ascribe different expectations to the same role. For example, young males today seem to have very different concepts of the role of father from that of previous birth cohorts. In the past the role of father was seen as a passive role; fathers were not involved as much in caring for and raising their children. Today fathers are often very involved in caring for and raising their children and often acquire a number of other roles that were not part of the role expectations of fathers in the past.

Although the age-stratification model has been well-received by researchers, it has some problems that must be corrected. One problem is that the theory does not take into account different social classes or racial or ethnic groups and their perceptions and expectations. Society is stratified not only on the basis of age but also on the basis of race, ethnicity, and other variables. The theory must be able to account for behavior in regard to some of these variables.

Phenomenological Theory

A very old theory in the social and behavioral sciences that has undergone a recent revival is phenomenological theory. In contemporary usage, phenomenology is considered to be a movement started in Germany by Edmund Husserl and continued through individuals such as Alfred Schutz, Max Scheler, Nicolai Hartman, Martin Heidegger, and Edith Stein (Caponigri, 1971).

Phenomenological theory first appeared in American social and behavioral sciences in an article by Donald Snygg (1941) and was later elaborated on by Combs and Snygg (1959). The basic idea behind phenomenological theory is that to understand human behavior one must understand the individual's perceptual world. It has long been recognized that individuals see the world very differently from one another. For example, the newspaper columnist Walter Lippmann talked of "stereotypes" and "pictures in our heads"; the sociologist W. I. Thomas talked about "varying definitions of the situation"; the psychologist Hadley Cantril spoke of individuals living in different "reality worlds."

The major idea is that through life experiences and socialization we develop a perceptual framework through which we selectively perceive and interpret the world. Thus individuals can perceive the same phenomena very differently. For example, older persons may respond differently to such phenomena as retirement, health changes, or widowhood. The differences in their responses are due not to the phenomenon in and of itself, but to their interpretation or perception of the phenomenon.

It is perhaps apparent that phenomenological theory draws from the age-stratification model and from the concept of socialization. However, unlike the age stratification model, phenomenological theory does not see age as the prime determinant of behavior. If one wishes to explain behavior, one does so not by age but by perceptual frameworks. Nor is the age at which an event is experienced considered of primary importance. Once again, it is not the event in and of itself that is important but the individual's interpretation of the event. According to phenomenological theory, all the members of a birth cohort may have been 20 years of age when the depression struck. However, at the time they were a heterogeneous group in regard to such variables as social class, race, or family ties, and were thus affected differently by the depression. For some it became a life-and-death struggle. For others there may have been little change in life-style. For still others the depression may have provided companionship or some other variables that made it a rewarding experience.

Phenomenological theory attempts to ascertain the individual's perceptual framework. If this can be done, it becomes simple to predict and to explain the individual's behavior. In many ways the theory is complete because there are few, if any, exceptions. In other theories, researchers talk about the "majority of individuals" or "exceptions to the rule." Phenomenological theory attempts to be a complete theory, that is, one without exceptions. It claims that if you can understand the individual's perceptual framework, you can understand and predict behavior.

The perceptual framework is based largely on socialization experiences. Through socialization individuals learn to selectively perceive the environment and discover how to interpret their perceptions. In other words, the socialization process helps to form the perceptual framework. Socialization is a process that takes place during social interaction and depending on our impressions or reactions, our socialization will vary. A person may have a significant or a neutral impact on our behavior and beliefs.

Phenomenological theory is perhaps the most comprehensive and complete theory of human behavior offered in this section. It is also the theory that has received the least amount of empirical support from researchers, but not necessarily because the theory has been rejected. Rather, this is a highly abstract theory, and it is difficult for researchers to conduct appropriate scientific studies. Phenomenological theory is a promising theory that will probably receive a great deal of attention in the future.

SUMMARY

Gerontology is founded on scientific research. It is only through research that we will be able to separate fact from ignorance, superstition, and fear. It is through research that we will be capable of designing and offering effective programs and services to benefit older persons. Theory is an attempt to provide a systematic framework for understanding research results. A theory can often explain what appears to be inexplicable, or organize what appears to be unrelated. This chapter was separated into two sections: research and theory.

There are five generally recognized functions of research: explanation, prediction, evaluation, description, and control. A sixth function, care, was also discussed.

From the initial curiosity of the researcher to the final presentation of a research report there are eight stages through which most research will pass. Stage one is the formation of a question to be answered or a hypothesis to be tested. Only questions that can be answered or hypotheses that can be tested scientifically are appropriate. In this first stage researchers should become aware of their values, so that their values do not distort their research. It is also important that researchers consider certain ethical issues. There are four general ethical guidelines that must be followed when conducting research on humans: participation is voluntary, participants are not injured, the identity of participants is anonymous, and participants are not deceived. It was pointed out that researchers in gerontology confront some unique ethical situations.

The second stage is the review of related literature. By reviewing the literature the researchers can see what research has been done, and if there is a need for further research in a certain area. If there is a need, by reviewing the literature the researchers can learn how best to conduct their research.

The third stage is writing the research proposal. Initially the researchers will have to determine what type of design to use. Generally, either a cross-sectional or longitudinal design will be used. A cross-sectional design describes and compares information on individuals generally from two or more age groups, at a given time. A longitudinal design is concerned with noting changes that take place over time. Both designs have strengths and weaknesses. The researchers will also have to determine what techniques will be used to obtain data. There are a variety of techniques, each having advantages and disadvantages depending on what type of study and what data the researchers want to obtain.

Survey research is one technique that consists of obtaining information through interviews or questionnaires. Often survey research is conducted by telephone. Statistical comparative studies are a second technique. Essentially researchers use existing data to draw conclusions. Participant observation is a third technique. This is going to the environment and observing what happens. The last technique that was mentioned was the experiment. In experiments researchers manipulate variables.

In the fourth stage the sample is selected. It is important that the sample be representative of the population. Data collection actually takes place in the fifth stage. Here researchers make and record observations, conduct interviews, or complete experiments. In the sixth stage the researchers categorize, analyze, and interpret the data they have collected. It is in this stage that they will try to determine causation.

In the seventh stage the researchers review and evaluate the research process. Evaluation, not acceptance, is the basic premise of researchers. The eighth and last stage is the presentation of the research report. Here the results of the research are disseminated, evaluated, and perhaps utilized by others.

There have been literally thousands of research projects in gerontology. Several major research projects were discussed. These projects made a significant contribution to gerontological research. Although most of the research in gerontology is very good, there are some problems. The problems in gerontological research are no different from the problems in other areas. Some of the problems mentioned were in areas such as confusing terminology, poor samples, lack of research on minority/ethnic aged, and lack of longitudinal studies.

The second part of the chapter dealt with theory in gerontology, and several theories were discussed. The first was disengagement theory. According to this theory, as individuals approach old age they gradually start to disengage from society. They start to decrease both the number of roles as well as the intensity of their remaining roles. It was believed that disengagement was inevitable and universal. It was only through disengagement that older persons could be happy.

Activity theory is the antithesis of disengagement theory. According to this theory the greater the activity of older persons, the greater their life satisfaction. Being happy in old age meant maintaining a middle-age existence.

Personality theory seemed to resolve the differences between disengagement theory and activity theory. This theory noted that there were several personality types, and that it was the type of personality, not the level of activity, that determined life satisfaction.

The next theory discussed was subculture theory. A subculture is a group within the general society that, while exhibiting many of the characteristics of the general society, exhibits certain characteristics that are not found in other segments of the society. Just as perhaps ghetto youth-gang behavior can be explained by its subculture, some have hypothesized that the aged are a subculture and that the subculture can be used to explain their behavior.

Another theory that needs to be examined is labeling theory, which has traditionally been used to explain the behavior of criminals or the mentally ill. The basic premise is that the labels we are given have a significant bearing on our behavior. Once labeled "old," or "senile," others react to the label. If an older person is labeled "senile," that person will be treated and reacted to as if he or she were senile.

Exchange theory notes that in all social interaction there is an exchange. The exchange may be in a variety of areas such as knowledge or money. A basic premise of exchange theorists is that in social interaction, individuals seek to profit from the exchange. That is, individuals seek to receive more money or knowledge than they give. Because old age often brings a decline in what individuals have to exchange, it has been noted that older persons are at a disadvantage in social interactions. As a result, they may disengage.

Age stratification is referred to as a model, not a theory, but it still needs to be discussed. Essentially, age is seen as an important determinant of behavior since it can limit individuals' abilities to perform certain roles, and because society allocated certain roles based on age. Thus, chronological age stratifies the society into age strata, each with its own set of rights, roles, obligations, and opportunities.

The last theory that attempts to explain the behavior of older persons is phenomenological theory. The basic premise is that to understand human behavior the researchers must understand how those being studied perceive their environment. Do they see retirement as a threat or a blessing?

REFERENCES

Abrahams, J. P., Hoger, W. J., Elias, M. F., & Bradigan, B. (1975). Gerontological research in psychology published in the *Journal of Gerontology* 1963–1974: Perspectives and progress. *Journal of Gerontology,* **30**(6): 668–673.

Annas, G., & Glantz, L. (1986). Rules for research in nursing homes. *New England Journal of Medicine,* **315**(18): 237–243.

Ashbaugh, D. L., & Fay, C. H. (1987). The threshold for aging in the workplace. *Research in Aging,* **9**(3): 417–427.

Babbie, E. R. (1988). *The practice of social research* (Fifth edition). Belmont, CA: Wadsworth.

Back, K. W. (1976). Personal characteristics and social behavior: Theory and method. In R. H. Binstock & E. Shanas (Eds.), *Handbook of aging and the social sciences* (pp. 403–431). New York: Van Nostrand Reinhold.

Bengtson, V. L. (1973). *The social psychology of aging.* New York: Bobbs-Merrill.

Bengtson, V. L., & Dowd, J. J. (1980–1981). Sociological functionalism, exchange theory and life-cycle analysis: A call for more explicit theoretical bridges. *International Journal of Aging and Human Development,* **12**(1): 55–73.

Berkowitz, S. (1978). Informed consent, research, and the elderly. *The Gerontologist,* **18**(3): 237–243.

Birren, J. E. (1959). Principles of research on aging. In J. E. Birren (Ed.), Handbook of aging and the individual (pp. 3–42). Chicago: The University of Chicago Press.

Birren, J. E., & Bengtson V. L. (Eds.) (1988). *Emergent theories of aging.* New York: Springer.

Birren, J. E., Butler, R. N., Greenhouse, S. W., Sokoloff, L., & Yarrow, M. R. (1963). *Human aging: A biological and behavioral study.* Washington, DC: U.S. Government Printing Office.

Blau, P. (1964). *Exchange in power in social life.* New York: Wiley.

Bloom, M. (1975). Discontent with contentment scales. *The Gerontologist,* **15**(2): 99.

Borgatta, E. F., & Hertzog, C. (1985). Introduction: Methodology and aging research. *Research on Aging,* **7**(1): 3–6.

Botwinick, J. (1984). *Aging and behavior: A comprehensive integration of research findings* (third edition). New York: Springer.

Brehm, H. P. (1968). Sociology and aging: Orientation and research. *The Gerontologist,* **8**(Spring): 20–23.

Brown, A. S. (1974). Satisfying relationships for elderly and their patterns of disengagement, *The Gerontologist,* **14**(3): 258–262.

Bultena, G. L., & Wood, V. (1969). The American retirement community: Bane or blessing? *Journal of Gerontology,* **24**(2): 209–217.

Burgess, E. W. (1960). *Aging in western societies.* Chicago: University of Chicago Press.

Butler, R. N. (1976). *Why survive? Being old in America.* New York: Harper and Row.

Butler, R. N. (1987). National Institute on Aging. In G. L. Maddox (Ed.), *The encyclopedia of aging* (pp. 468–470). New York: Springer.

Campbell, R. T., Mutran, E., & Parker, R. N. (1986). Longitudinal design and longitudinal analysis. *Research on Aging,* **8**(4): 480–502.

Caponigri, A. R. (1971). *Philosophy from the age of positivism to the age of analysis.* Notre Dame: University of Notre Dame Press.

Carp, F. M. (1968). Some components of disengagement. *Journal of Gerontology,* **23**(3): 382–386.

Cavan, R. S. (1962). Self and role in adjustment during old age. In A. M. Rose (Ed.), *Human behavior and social processes* (pp. 526–534). Boston: Houghton Mifflin.

Cavan, R. S., Burgess, E. W., Havighurst, R. J., & Goldhammer, H. (1949). *Personal adjustment in old age.* Chicago: Science Research Associates.

Cohen, E. S. (1980). Editorial: Scholarly muckraking. *The Gerontologist,* **20**(3): 226–227.

Cohen-Mansfield, J., Kerin, P., Pawlson, G., Lipson, S., & Holdridge, K. (1988). Informed consent for research in a nursing home: Process and issues. *The Gerontologist,* **28**(3): 355–359.

Combs, A. W., & Snygg, D. (1959). *Individual behavior: A perceptual approach to behavior.* New York: Harper and Row.

Cooney, T. M., Schaie, K. W., & Willis, S. L. (1988). The relationship between prior functioning on cognitive and personality dimensions and subject attrition in longitudinal research. *Journal of Gerontology: Psychological Sciences,* **43**(1): 12–17.

Covey, H. C. (1985). Qualitative research of older people: Some considerations. *Gerontology and Geriatrics Education,* **5**(3): 41–51.

Cumming, E. (1963). Further thought on the theory of disengagement. *International Social Science Journal,* **15**(3): 377–393.

Cumming, E. (1975). Engagement with an old theory. *Aging and Human Development,* **6**(3): 187–191.

Cumming, E., Dean, L. R., Newell, D. S., & McCaffrey, I. (1960). Disengagement, a tentative theory of aging. *Sociometry,* **23**(1): 23.

Cumming, E., & Henry, W. E. (1961). *Growing old: The process of disengagement.* New York: Basic Books.

Cunningham, W. R., & Owens, W. A. (1983). The Iowa State Study of the adult development of intellectual abilities. In K. W. Schaie (Ed.), *Longitudinal studies of adult psychological development* (pp. 20–39). New York: Guilford Press.

Dowd, J. J. (1975). Aging as exchange: A preface to theory. *Journal of Gerontology,* **30**(5): 584–594.

Ekerdt, D. J. (1987). Normative aging study. In G. L. Maddox (Ed.), *The encyclopedia of aging* (pp. 485–487). New York: Springer.

Fillenbaum, G. G. (1987). Longitudinal retirement survey. In G. L. Maddox (Ed.), *The encyclopedia of aging* (pp. 413–414). New York: Springer.

Foner, A. (1975). Age in society: Structure and change. *American Behavioral Scientist,* **19**(2): 144–165.

Gentry, M., & Shulman, A. D. (1985). Survey of sampling techniques in widowhood research, 1973–1983. *Journal of Gerontology,* **40**(5): 641–643.

Gibson, D. M., & Aitkenhead, W. (1983). The elderly respondent. *Research on Aging,* **5**(2): 283–296.

Granick, S., & Patterson, R. D. (1971). *Human aging II: Age 11–up followup biomedical and behavioral study.* Rockville, MD: Public Health Service.

Harris, L., & Associates (1975). *The myth and reality of aging in America.* Washington, DC: National Council on the Aging.

Harris, L., & Associates (1981). *Aging in the eighties: America in transition.* Washington, DC: National Council on the Aging.

Hatch, L. R., & Borgatta, E. F. (1987). A note on longitudinal data presentation. *Research on Aging,* **9**(4): 572–581.

Havighurst, R. J. (1961). Successful aging. *The Gerontologist,* **1**(March): 4–7.

Havighurst, R. J., & Albrecht, R. (1953). *Older people.* New York: Longmans, Green.

Havighurst, R. J., Neugarten, B. L., Munnichs, J. M. A., & Thomae, H. (Eds.) (1969). *Adjustment to retirement: A cross-national study.* Netherlands: Van Gorkum.

Havighurst, R. J., Neugarten, B. L., & Tobin, S. S. (1968). Personality and patterns of aging. In B. L. Neugarten (Ed.), *Middle age and aging: A reader in social psychology* (pp. 173–177). Chicago: University of Chicago Press.

Heidrick, M. L. (1987). Framingham studies of heart disease. In G. L. Maddox (Ed.), *The encyclopedia of aging* (pp. 260–262). New York: Springer.

Henry, W. E. (1965). Engagement and disengagement: Toward a theory of adult development. In R. Kastenbaum (Ed.), *Contributions to the psychobiology of aging* (pp. 19–35). New York: Springer.

Herzog, A. R., & Dielman, L. (1985). Age differences in response accuracy for factual survey questions. *Journal of Gerontology,* **40**(3): 350–357.

Herzog, A. R., & Rodgers, W. L. (1988*a*). Interviewing older adults: Mode comparison using data from a face-to-face survey and a telephone resurvey. *Public Opinion Quarterly,* **52**(1): 84–99.

Herzog, A. R., & Rodgers, W. L. (1988*b*). Age and response rates to interview sample surveys. *Journal of Gerontology,* **43**(6): 200–205.

Hess, B. (1982). Research in gerontology: State of the art. *Gerontology News,* May.

Hochschild, A. R. (1973). *The unexpected community.* Englewood Cliffs: Prentice-Hall.

Hochschild, A. R. (1975). Disengagement theory: A critique and proposal. *American Sociological Review,* **40**(5): 553–569.

Hochschild, A. R. (1976). Disengagement theory: A logical, empirical, and phenomenological critique. In J. F. Gubrium (Ed.), *Time, roles, and self in old age* (pp. 53–87). New York: Human Sciences Press.

Homans, G. (1961). *Social behavior: Its elementary forms.* New York: Harcourt, Brace and World.

Hoyer, W. J., Raskind, C. L., & Abrahams, J. P. (1984). Research practices in the psychology of aging: A survey of research published in the *Journal of Gerontology*, 1975–1982. *Journal of Gerontology*, **39**(1): 44–48.

Jackson, J. S. (1989). Race ethnicity, and psychological theory and research. *Journal of Gerontology: Psychological Sciences*, **44**(1): 1–2.

Keith, J. (1988). Participant observation. In K. W. Schaie, R. T. Campbell, W. Meredith & S. C. Rawlings (Eds.), *Methodological issues in aging research* (pp. 211–230). New York: Springer.

Kosloski, K. (1986). Isolating age, period, and cohort effect in developmental research. *Research on Aging*, **8**(4): 459–469.

Lastrucci, C. L. (1967). *The scientific approach: Basic principles of the scientific method.* Cambridge, MA: Schenkman Publishing.

Leinbach, R. M. (1982). Alteration to the face-to-face interview for collecting gerontological needs assessment data. *The Gerontologist*, **22**(11): 78–92.

Lemon, B. W., Bengtson, V. L., & Peterson, J. A. (1972). An exploration of the activity theory of aging: Activity types and life satisfaction among in-movers to a retirement community. *Journal of Gerontology*, **27**(4): 511–523.

Levenson, R. L. (1980). Statistical power analysis: Implications for researchers, planners, and practitioners in gerontology. *The Gerontologist*, **20**(4): 494–498.

Longino, C. F. (1987). Subcultures. In G. L. Maddox (Ed.), *The encyclopedia of aging* (pp. 649–650). New York: Springer.

Longino, C. F., & Kart, C. S. (1982). Explicating activity theory: A formal replication. *Journal of Gerontology*, **37**(6): 713–722.

Longino, C. F., McClelland, K. A., & Peterson, W. A. (1980). The aged subculture hypothesis: Social integration, gerontophilia and self-conception. *Journal of Gerontology*, **35**(5): 758–767.

Lowenthal, M. F., & Haven, C. (1968). Interaction and adaptation: Intimacy as a critical variable. *American Sociological Review*, **33**(1): 20–30.

McCaslin, R. (1988). Reframing research on service use among the elderly: An analysis of recent findings. *The Gerontologist*, **28**(5): 592–599.

Maddox, G. L. (1963). Activity and morale: A longitudinal study of selected elderly subjects. *Social Forces*, **42**(2): 195–204.

Maddox, G. L. (1964). Disengagement theory: A critical evaluation. *The Gerontologist*, **4**(2): 80–82.

Maddox, G. L. (1965). Fact and artifact: Evidence bearing on disengagement theory from the Duke Geriatric Project. *Human Development*, **8**(2–3): 117–130.

Maddox, G. L. (1968). A current theoretical issue in gerontology. In B. L. Neugarten (Ed.), *Middle age and aging: A reader in social psychology* (pp. 184–192). Chicago: University of Chicago Press.

Maddox, G. L. (1970). Themes and issues in sociological theories of human aging. *Human Development*, **13**(1): 17–27.

Maddox, G. L., & Campbell, R. T. (1985). Scope, concepts, and methods in the study of aging. In R. H. Binstock & E. Shanas (Eds.), *Handbook of aging and the social sciences* (pp. 3–31). New York: Van Nostrand Reinhold.

Maddox, G. L., & Wiley, J. (1976). Scope, concepts and methods in the study of aging. In R. H. Binstock & E. Shanas (Eds.), *Handbook of aging and the social sciences* (pp. 3–34). New York: Van Nostrand Reinhold.

Makarushka, J. L., & McDonald, R. D. (1979). Informed consent, research, and geriatric patients: The responsibility of institutional review committees. *The Gerontologist,* **19**(1): 61–66.

Montgomery, R. V., & Borgatta, E. F. (1986). Plausible theories and the development of scientific theory. *Research on Aging,* **8**(4): 586–608.

Norris, F. H. (1985). Characteristics of older nonrespondents over five waves of a panel study. *Journal of Gerontology,* **40**(5): 627–636.

Palmore, E. (1968). The effects of aging on activities and attitudes. *The Gerontologist,* **8**(3): 259–263.

Palmore, E. (Ed.) (1970). *Normal aging.* Durham, NC: Duke University Press.

Palmore, E. (Ed.) (1974). *Normal aging II.* Durham, NC: Duke University Press.

Palmore, E. (1981). *Social patterns in normal aging: Findings from the Duke longitudinal study.* Durham, NC: Duke University Press.

Palmore, E. (1987). Duke longitudinal studies. In G. L. Maddox (Ed.), *The encyclopedia of aging* (pp. 197–198). New York: Springer.

Palmore, E., Busse, E. W., Maddox, G. L., Nowlin, J. B., & Siegler, I. C. (Eds.) (1985). *Normal aging III.* Durham, NC: Duke University Press.

Patrick, C. H., & Borgatta, E. F. (1981). Special issue: Available data bases for aging research. *Research on Aging,* **3**(4): 371–501.

Prasad, S. B. (1964). The retirement postulate of the disengagement theory. *The Gerontologist,* **4**(1): 20–23.

Ratzan, R. M. (1986). Communication and informed consent in clinical geriatrics. *International Journal of Aging and Human Development,* **23**(1): 17–26.

Reich, W. T. (1978). Ethical issues related to research involving elderly subjects. *The Gerontologist,* **18**(4): 326–337.

Reichard, S. F., & Peterson, P. (1962). *Aging and personality.* New York, Wiley.

Riley, M. W. (1971). Social gerontology and the age stratification of society. *The Gerontologist,* **11**(1, Part 1): 79–87.

Riley, M. W. (1977). Age strata in social systems. In R. H. Binstock & E. Shanas (Eds.), *Handbook of aging and the social sciences* (pp. 189–217). New York: Van Nostrand Reinhold.

Riley, M. W. (1987). On the significance of age in sociology. *American Sociological Review,* **52**(1): 1–14.

Riley, M. W. (1988*a*). On the significance of age in sociology. In M. W. Riley (Ed.), *Social structure and human lives* (pp. 24–45). Newbury Park, CA: Sage.

Riley, M. W. (1988*b*). Forward. In K. W. Schaie, R. T. Campbell, W. Meredith, & S. C. Rawlings (Eds.), *Methodological issues in aging research* (pp. vii–x). New York: Springer.

Riley, M. W., Johnson, M., & Foner, A. (1972). Elements in a model of age stratification. In M. W. Riley, M. Johnson & A. Foner (Eds.), *Aging and society, Volume Three: A sociology of age stratification* (pp. 3–26). New York: Russell Sage Foundation.

Rodgers, W. L., & Herzog, A. R. (1987). Interviewing older adults: The accuracy of factual information. *Journal of Gerontology,* **42**(4): 387–394.

Rogosa, D. (1988). Myths about longitudinal research. In K. W. Schaie, R. T. Campbell, W. Meredith & S. C. Rawlings (Eds.), *Methodological issues in aging research* (pp. 171–210). New York: Springer.

Roman, P., & Taietz, P. (1967). Organizational structure and disengagement: The emeritus professor. *The Gerontologist,* **7**(2): 147–152.

Rose, A. M. (1962). The subculture of the aging: A topic for sociological research. *The Gerontologist,* **2**(2): 123–127.

Rose, A. M. (1964). A current theoretical issue in social gerontology. *The Gerontologist,* **4**(1): 46–50.

Rose, A. M. (1965). The subculture of the aging: A framework for research in social gerontology. In A. M. Rose & W. Peterson (Eds.), *Older people and their social worlds* (pp. 3–16). Philadelphia: F. A. Davis.

Rosow, I. (1967). *Social integration of the aged.* New York: Free Press.

Salthouse, T. A. (1987). Research methods in psychology. In G. L. Maddox (Ed.), *The encyclopedia of aging* (pp. 573–574). New York: Springer.

Sands, L. P., & Meredith, W. (1989). Effects of sensory and motor functioning on adult intellectual performance. *Journal of Gerontology: Psychological Sciences,* **44**(2): 56–58.

Schaie, K. W. (1967). Age changes and age differences. *The Gerontologist,* **7**(2): 128–132.

Schaie, K. W. (1973). Methodological problems in descriptive developmental research on adulthood and aging. In J. R. Nesselroade & H. W. Reese (Eds.), *Life-span developmental psychology: Methodological issues* (pp. 253–280). New York: Academic Press.

Schaie, K. W. (1977). Quasi-experimental research designs in the psychology of aging. In J. E. Birren & K. W. Schaie (Eds.), *Handbook of the psychology of aging* (pp. 39–58). New York: Van Nostrand Reinhold.

Schaie, K. W. (Ed.) (1983*a*). *Longitudinal studies of adult psychological development.* New York. Guilford.

Schaie, K. W. (1983*b*). The Seattle longitudinal study: A 21-year exploration of psychometric intelligence in adulthood. In K. W. Schaie (Ed.), *Longitudinal studies of adult psychological development* (pp. 64–135). New York: Guilford.

Schaie, K. W. (1987). Research methods in gerontology. In G. L. Maddox (Ed.), *The encyclopedia of aging* (pp. 570–573). New York: Springer.

Schaie, K. W. (1988). Methodological issues in aging research: An introduction. In K. W. Schaie, R. T. Campbell, W. Meredith, & S. C. Rawlings (Eds.), *Methodological issues in aging research* (pp. 1–12). New York: Springer.

Schaie, K. W., Campbell, R. T., Meredith, W., & Rawlings, S. C. (Eds.) (1988). *Methodological issues in aging research.* New York: Springer.

Seltzer, M. M. (1975). The quality of research is strained. *The Gerontologist,* **15**(6): 503–507.

Sherman, S. R. (1975*a*) Patterns of contacts for residents of age-segregated and age-integrated housing. *Journal of Gerontology,* **30**(1): 103–107.

Sherman, S. R. (1975*b*). Mutual assistance and support in retirement. *Journal of Gerontology,* **30**(4): 479–483.

Shock, N. W. (1987). Baltimore longitudinal study of aging. In G. L. Maddox (Ed.), *The encyclopedia of aging* (pp. 52–54). New York: Springer.

Shock, N. W., Greulich, R. C., Andres, R., Arenberg, D., Costa, P. T., Lakatta, E. G., & Tobin, J. D. (1984). *Normal human aging: The Baltimore longitudinal study of aging.* Washington, DC: U.S. Government Printing Office.

Snygg, D. (1941). The need for a phenomenological system of psychology. *Psychological Review,* **48**(4): 404–434.

Strain, L. A., & Chappell, N. L. (1982). Problems and strategies: Ethical concerns in survey research with the elderly. *The Gerontologist,* **22**(6): 526–531.

Streib, G. F. (1983). The frail elderly: Research dilemmas and research opportunities. *The Gerontologist,* **23**(1): 40–44.

Streib, G. F. (1987). Cornell study of occupational retirement. In G. L. Maddox (Ed.), *The encyclopedia of aging* (pp. 148–150). New York: Springer.

Streib, G. F., & Schneider, C. J. (1971). *Retirement in American society.* Ithaca, NY: Cornell University Press.

Tallmer, M. (1973). A current issue in social gerontology. *Journal of Geriatric Psychiatry,* **6**(1): 99–108.

Tallmer, M., & Kutner, B. (1970). Disengagement and morale. *The Gerontologist,* **10**(4, Part 1): 317–320.

Tobin, S. S., & Neugarten, B. L. (1961). Life satisfaction and social interaction in the aging. *Journal of Gerontology,* **16**(4): 344–346.

U.S. Senate, Special Committee on Aging (1987–1988). *Aging America: Trends and projections.* Washington, DC: U.S. Government Printing Office.

Warren, J. W., Sobol, J., Hoopes, J. M., Damron, D., Levenson, S., DeForge, B. R., & Muncie H. L. (1986). Informed consent by proxy: An issue in research with elderly patients. *New England Journal of Medicine,* **315**(18): 1124–1126.

Williams, R. H., & Wirths, C. G. (1965). *Lives through the years.* New York: Atherton.

Williams, T. F. (1988). Research and care: Essential partners in aging. *The Gerontologist,* **28**(5): 579–585.

Yordi, C. L., Chu, A. S., Ross, K. M., & Wong, S. J. (1982). Research and the frail elderly: Ethical and methodological issues in controlled social experiments. *The Gerontologist,* **22**(1): 72–77.

Youmans, E. G. (1967). Disengagement among older rural and urban men. In E. G. Youmans (Ed.), *Older rural Americans* (pp. 27–42). Lexington, KY: University of Kentucky Press.

Zimmerman, B. L. (1989). Databases on aging: A researcher's guide. *The Aging Connection,* **10**(6): 12.

PHYSICAL AND PSYCHOLOGICAL ASPECTS

Jim Harrison/Stock, Boston

CHAPTER **5**

BIOLOGY AND PHYSIOLOGY

Sam Sweezy/Stock, Boston

INTRODUCTION

Increasing age brings about many changes. The changes that are often the most noticeable and the most feared are biological and physiological changes. While there is an enormous interest in this area there has not been a corresponding amount of research.

Four reasons probably account for the lack of research. First, this "area" has attracted a tremendous number of charlatans, frauds, witchdoctors, and quacks, most with prestigious sounding titles, and all with creams, lotions, elixirs, or potions that are guaranteed—for a price—to stop or reverse the aging process. As a result, this area has had a lower status in the scientific community than others, and until recently did not attract scientists or funding for adequate research. Second, some individuals for a variety of personal, religious, or philosophical reasons do not believe that it is proper or desirable to investigate areas that could have an influence on the life span, and they discourage this type of research (see Hayflick, 1974). Third, because the study of gerontology is relatively immature there were few organizations willing to sponsor, plan, and fund research in this area until 1974. For example, the National Institute of Aging, which is a major sponsor of research in the area of the biological and physiological aspects of aging, was not founded until then (see Mayer, 1987). The fourth, and last reason deals with the value society has placed on older persons. In the past, and to a significant extent the present, there has been more value placed on the young, and this has contributed to more funding, and hence research, on the first decades of life rather than on the last decades.

In addition to a lack of research on senescence, much of the research that does exist deals with the aging of nonhuman organisms in artificial laboratory environments; additionally, many of the studies on humans deals with pathological aging changes, rather than "normal" aging changes.

In this chapter we will examine some of the biological and physiological changes that take place with increasing age. The chapter is separated into three sections. In the first we will examine the term "senescence" or "biological aging." Here we will examine some of the consequences of senescence and will differentiate senescence from other biological processes. In the second section we will look at some of the theories dealing with the cause of senescence. In the third and longest section, we will examine the consequences of biological and physiological aging in contemporary American society.

DEFINITION OF SENESCENCE

The term senescence means biological aging. Since all human beings are mortal, senescence is a process through which all individuals, unless they die young, will eventually pass. However, it should be pointed out that not all organisms age. There are certain unicellular organisms that appear to have the ability to exist "endlessly," or at least until killed by accidents, disease, or predators. Examples of such organisms are protozoa and paramecia. There may also be certain forms of fish and amphibians that have an "indeterminate life span" (Hayflick, 1987).

At the human level it is difficult to write about or to conduct research on senescence

124

for three reasons. First, individuals age at different rates; that is, there is not a single defined process that all individuals uniformly follow. Second, within each individual parts of the body age at different rates. For example, a physician may find that a 70 year old has the heart of a 50 year old but the lungs of an 80 year old. Thus, although senescence is inevitable for humans beings, it affects individuals in varying degrees of severity and may affect some parts of the body more than others. Third, it is frequently difficult to distinguish the results of ''normal'' aging from ''pathological'' aging. There can be certain conditions, perhaps caused by lifestyle, which occur on such a regular basis that they are considered part of senescence rather than disease.

Senescence is a continual process, with some believing that it starts before birth and others believing that it starts at birth and that we spend the first one-fourth of our lives growing and maturing and the following three-fourths aging or declining. The literature seems to indicate that most bodily functions reach their peak in terms of optimum ability to develop, perform, or function between the ages of 3 and 20 (Bafitis & Sargent, 1977). After this, development ceases and a period of decline takes place. With increasing age there are declines in many functions and tissues. However, for most of us the declines are not noticeable for three reasons. First, the declines are very gradual, they do not occur in a matter of weeks or months but rather over several decades. Second, most of the affected parts of the body are structured so that there is a reserve capacity. Thus, the decline is not at first apparent. For example, a human being can live with 20 percent of a liver, a small portion of stomach and intestines, and one lung and kidney. Therefore, although a decline is taking place it is not having an impact on functioning and is not noticeable. Third, some parts of the body are duplicated in function by other parts so that when one area begins to decline another area can compensate.

Senescence or biological aging can be distinguished from other biological processes in five ways (Kart, 1976; Mayer, 1987; Strehler, 1962, 1973, 1982):

1 The condition must be universal; that is, it must happen to all aging individuals. For example, for cancer to be considered a part of senescence it would have to be a characteristic of all older persons. Since cancer is not an inevitable consequence of aging, it is not considered to be part of the process of senescence.

2 Senescence is a process that comes from within the individual; that is, it is a ''natural'' process, not one caused by external factors such as exposure to radiation.

3 The onset, or occurrence, of senescence takes place gradually rather than suddenly. Thus a rapid change to an individual caused by an accident or surgery would not be considered part of the process of senescence.

4 The effects of senescence have a deleterious effect on the individual. Senescence leads to a decline in the functioning and performance of the individual.

5 The process of senescence is unidirectional; that is, the effects of senescence are in the direction of decline and cannot be reversed by normal body process.

It should be pointed out that senescence is more than one process: it is many. It should also be noted that as yet there is no universally accepted theory of the cause of senescence.

THEORIES ABOUT THE CAUSE OF SENESCENCE

There are currently a number of theories about how and why the body ages. In fact, as Mayer (1987) has noted, some believe that there are almost as many theories about the cause of senescence as there are biogerontologists. Currently, no one theory has received what could be considered a majority of support. This shows the complexity of the aging process as well as its interdisciplinary nature.

There are different ways to conceptualize and organize theories of senescence. For example, some writers organize the theories according to the factors that are causing aging. Thus, specific theories would be listed under headings such as "program theories" or "wear-and-tear theories." Other writers organize the theories according to the level at which aging is taking place. Using this organization, theories would be grouped under headings such as "genetic level," "cellular level," and "tissue and organ level." Be aware that there are different ways of conceptualizing and organizing these theories. For this book the theories will be considered alphabetically. You will note that many of theories are connected and overlap.

Autoimmunity Theory

The body has an immune system which is designed to protect the body from the invasion of foreign matter such as bacteria or viruses. In normal individuals, the body can distinguish between its own matter and foreign matter. When foreign matter enters the body the immune system produces antibodies which attack the foreign matter. The autoimmunity theory of senescence holds that with increasing age two important changes take place which produce aging. First, the ability of the immune system to distinguish between the body's own matter and foreign matter is diminished. As a result, the immune system ends up attacking "normal" body matter. Second, for a variety of reasons, with increasing age there are more mutations in cell divisions. The consequence is that the body responds to these mutant cells as "foreign matter." The interaction of antibodies on the body's own matter is called an autoimmune response, in which the body is essentially attacking and destroying itself (see Adler, 1974; Mayer, 1987; Rockstein & Sussman, 1979; Walford, 1969).

This is an important theory, although it explains only what happens not why it happens. Other theories consider why, with increasing age, the immune system declines or why mutations in cell divisions increase (Rockstein & Sussman, 1979).

Collagen Theory

This is also referred to as the cross-linkage theory. Collagen is a substance that is found in the connective tissues of the body. The connective tissues bind the body together and give it support (Tonna, 1987). Collagen, for example, is important in providing a structural framework for the skin, heart, and lungs. It is also important to muscle and the lining of blood vessel walls. According to Rockstein and Sussman (1979), collagen literally holds the cells of these body tissues together. In human beings more than half of the body is composed of connective tissue.

With increasing age, the collagen in the connective tissue becomes more rigid. This can have several consequences. For example, some researchers have speculated that this rigidity may make the transmission of nutrients and the expulsion of waste products more difficult, which has a deleterious impact on the individual (see Bjorksten, 1974). Less elasticity in the blood vessels can increase blood pressure; in the skin it can cause wrinkles and sagging. It can also have consequences for the heart and lungs. For both there is a lower level of functioning. For example, the capacity of lungs to expand and take in new air, or to contract and expel old air, is reduced. The heart will also have a lower capacity to expand and contract.

The change in collagen results from what is called cross linking. Essentially in cross linking certain proteins in the body, such as collagen, bind or link together. This linking changes both the structure and function of the proteins (Mayer, 1987). This is an important theory but does not explain why cross linking takes place.

Error Theory

Small cells are incredibly complex. For example, within most, if not all, body cells there are DNA molecules which determine the identity, function, and reproduction of the cell. Thus, some cells function in one way, others in a very different way. The error theory considers problems that can occur with DNA molecules within cells. For example, something may change the DNA within a cell, thereby altering the cell's identity, function, or rate of reproduction. For cells that reproduce, the new cells have the error. For cells that do not reproduce, the theory holds that over time more and more cells in a certain organ or area are damaged. Although initially the impact on the organism is small, the damage to an organ or area is cumulative, which brings about aging.

Free Radical Theory

An example of a "special case" of the cross-linking theory is the free radical theory (Rockstein & Sussman, 1979). According to this theory aging is caused by free radicals.

In the process of normal cell metabolism, free radicals are produced. Free radicals are highly unstable chemical compounds. Because they are unstable they are highly reactive chemically and thus interact with other nearby molecules, often cell membranes. This interaction changes or damages the structure and function of these nearby molecules. When they interact with nearby cells, free radicals are also capable of damaging the genetic material in these cells. Although the damage caused by free radicals at any time is small, it is cumulative, and this theory holds that the cumulative damage causes senescence. Antioxidants, also called free radical scavengers since they stabilize free radicals, have been recommended as a way of combating free radicals (see Ames, 1983; Harman, 1968; Mayer, 1987; Rockstein & Sussman, 1979).

Hormone Theory

There are several theories involving hormones. The hormones that have been examined the most closely are the "sex" hormones. The basis for the hormone theory comes from the drop in hormone levels that accompanies menopause. After menopause, the aging process is accelerated in several areas. Thus, hormones have been seen as controlling senescence. Additional support is provided by research on hormone replacement therapy (HRT), which has been found to relieve some of the symptoms of menopause.

Another hormone theory deals with the impact of the thyroid gland. It is known, for example, that individuals with hypothyroidism exhibit symptoms of premature aging; when given thyroid injections the thyroid gland starts to work "normally" and some of the symptoms disappear.

The hypothalamus and pituitary glands have also been examined, since they regulate the endocrine glands (Mayer, 1987). These are sometimes considered the master glands, since they regulate the hormone production of other glands. More research on these glands and their impact on senescence is needed (Mayer, 1987).

Immune System Theory

Earlier we briefly examined the autoimmunity theory; another theory that deals with the immune response is the immune system theory. This theory states that with increasing age the immune system declines thus making organisms more receptive to a variety of degenerative conditions, such as heart disease or cancer. Much of this theory is linked to the decline in the functioning of the thymus gland. It has been suggested that the decline in the immune system is a natural, normal part of the aging process. In fact, the decline is needed to protect the individual from the autoimmune response (Schneider & Reed, 1985). Although an interesting theory, it appears to account more for age-related diseases than age-related changes.

Program Theory

There are several variations on the program theory. We will look at one called cellular programming. At one time it was believed that most cells had an infinite ability to divide. That is, if cells were allowed to grow and divide in a laboratory culture, divisions would continue as long as the culture was maintained. This was based on research during the early part of this century that kept a culture of cells alive and dividing for 34 years (see Hayflick, 1974, 1977). This belief was challenged during the early 1960s by Leonard Hayflick and Paul Moorehead (1961) who found that when human tissue cells were placed in a cultured medium, they only divided approximately 50 times before dying. It is now believed that the earlier work, which showed infinitive divisions, was flawed because it used contaminated cultures.

Hayflick and Moorehead took human lung cells and placed them in a medium that allowed them to grow. Once the cells covered the bottom of the laboratory glassware they were divided between two cultured glassware containers (subcultivation). Once the cells in the second container had doubled another subcultivation took place. This process was repeated until the cells stopped dividing and died. In addition to finding that normal cells have a finite number of divisions, Hayflick and Moorehead also noted that as the cells aged, the amount of time that it took to divide increased. They found, for example, that initially the cultured cells took a week to reach confluence, or to double enough times to cover the bottom of the laboratory glassware; the first signs of aging were that it took 10 days for confluence rather than 7 days.

They also took tissue cells from human subjects 20 to 87 years of age and cultured the cells. While they did not find a perfect correlation between the age of the individual the cells were taken from and the number of doubling before cell death, they did find that the number of doubling was far less for cells from older individuals than for cells taken from younger individuals (Hayflick, 1974).

Although an attractive theory, and one supported by considerable laboratory evidence, it does not take into account the impact of environmental factors. For example, if cells are preprogrammed to age and die then factors such as nutrition, smoking, and exercise should have little or no effect on the programming. Obviously, this is not what epidemiological studies have found.

After further studies Hayflick (1980) noted that all *normal* cells can only divide a limited number of times. Cancer cells, which are not *normal,* appear to have an infinitive ability to divide.

Somatic Mutation Theory

There are several variations of this theory, which was popular in the 1950s and 1960s and which ties in with some of the other theories mentioned earlier, especially the autoimmunity and error theories. The basic concept is that with increasing age there are more cell mutations due to factors such as the radiation produced by the sun. The cumulative cell mutations contribute to decreased functioning and bring about the aging of the organism.

Wear-and-Tear Theory

The wear-and-tear theory of senescence states simply that the body is similar to a machine and that over time the parts wear out. This theory falls short on three counts. First, it does not fit the universality criterion. For example, although the hearts or lungs of some individuals "wear out," their kidneys do not; yet the reverse situation takes place in other individuals. Second, the theory does not take into account the ability of the body to repair itself. Third, the theory does not consider the fact that continued or chronic use of the body can actually improve its functioning. Exercise is an example of how the continued use of the body can improve performance and functioning.

THE RESULTS OF AGING

In this section we are going to examine the physiological and biological effects of aging in contemporary American society. The physical and biological changes that accompany old age are caused by at least two factors. The first is senescence; the second life-style.

Some of the changes that we will be discussing are the result of senescence; thus they are inevitable and all will experience them. It is important to remember that although everyone may experience the changes brought about by senescence, these changes may occur in varying degrees and at different ages. Also, the impact of senescence will depend on a variety of factors, such as the presence or absence of disease. An individual without heart disease will not be affected by senescence of the heart nearly as much as someone who has extensive heart disease.

Other biological and physiological changes accompanying old age are the results of life-style. These changes are not universal and thus not part of the senescence process. Because many Americans share the same life-style, these changes are found so frequently among the contemporary aged population that they are assumed to be a natural, normal part of the senescence process. Changes caused by life-style are not inevitable with increasing age but rather are the results of such factors as poor or negligent medical care, stress, inadequate nutrition, lack of exercise, or smoking.

Because most studies have not adequately separated the consequences of senescence from life-style, this section will be discussing the consequences of both on biological and physiological aging in western society. Thus, we will be examining the "aging process" that most individuals will experience.

Quite frankly, most students will find the following discussion gloomy and depressing since the emphasis is on decline. However, there are three positive aspects that must be remembered. First, the declines are generally gradual and in many cases not significant since they do not have much of an impact on the individual in terms of functioning. Second, many of the declines are caused by life-style and excellent information exists on the consequences of certain life-styles, such as smoking, lack of exercise, and nutrition. Thus, through the selection of life-styles we can generally determine the rate and extent of our aging process. Third, recent research has separated many of the effects of senescence from life-style, and it indicates that, until very old age, many of the common undesirable changes are more a result of life-style than senescence. That is, the changes produced by senescence do not occur as early and are not as extensive as earlier research had indicated.

The following will discuss the consequences of senescence on the body systems: cardiovascular, endocrine, gastrointestinal, integumentary, muscular, neurosensory, reproductive, respiratory, skeletal, urinary. At the end of some sections, certain disorders related to that system will be discussed.

Cardiovascular System

There is probably more written about the heart than any other organ in the human body. The heart is not only conceptualized from a biological or medical viewpoint but also from that of poetry and literature. The heart is a relatively small organ, about the size of a fist; its weight is about 1 pound. It is the one muscle that can work continually without tiring; in a normal lifetime the heart will beat two to three billion times and pump 80 to 90 million gallons of blood.

Numerous studies have been performed on the heart to ascertain the impact of aging on heart function. However, many of the studies are flawed in that they utilized individuals with cardiovascular disease. Thus, many of the studies reported large declines in heart function as a consequence of senescence when they should have attributed the declines to disease (see Lakatta, 1985).

The heart consists of four chambers, which can be conceptualized as two separate pumps. The right side of the heart receives deoxygenated blood and waste that is returning from circulating through the body. From here the blood is pumped into the lungs where oxygen is added and carbon dioxide removed. The oxygen-rich blood then goes to the left side of the heart where it is pumped out through the vascular system of the body. As the blood circulates through the body it leaves oxygen and accumulates waste products and nutrients for transportation to other organs. The blood then returns to the right side of the heart to start the cycle again.

There are numerous changes that take place in the cardiovascular system with increasing age. Some of the changes are normal age-related changes. Others that occur very frequently, and are major causes of death and disability in contemporary American society, are pathological and result primarily from life-styles frequently found in contemporary American society.

Changes take place in areas such as the heart muscle, the heart valves, and the heart's vascular system. In the aged heart muscle there are fewer muscle cells than in a younger heart. This is because heart muscle cells do not replace themselves once they die. As a result, older hearts have less muscle tissue. Heart valves, which prevent blood from flowing in the wrong direction, also change with increasing age. They tend to become larger which makes them more rigid, creating two consequences. First, the rigid valves can prevent blood from being pumped out of a heart chamber, or second, can allow a backflow of blood; that is, rather than a contraction of the heart forcing the blood forward, a faulty valve allows some of the blood to be forced backward. The walls of the heart's vascular system also acquire deposits which make them more rigid and less elastic.

We will now examine the impact of these changes on heart function. There are several ways to measure the functioning of the cardiovascular system; the most common is to measure blood pressure. Blood pressure consists of two readings: the pressure in the arteries when the heart has contracted and when it has relaxed. It is basically measuring the elasticity of the vascular system. Generally speaking, blood pressure goes up with increasing age because the arteries tend to become less elastic. Part of the change in the arteries is "normal." However, what is generally seen is pathological and will be discussed in the next subsection.

Other measures of the functioning of the cardiovascular system are maximum heart rate, stroke volume, and electrocardiographic readings.

Maximum heart rate is the number of times the heart is capable of beating per minute. The simple formula for determining maximum heart rate is to subtract an individual's age from 220. Thus, someone 60 years of age would have a maximum heart rate of approximately 160; someone 20 years of age a maximum heart rate of 200. Although there are "normal" variations (see the section on exercise in the next chapter) the trend is universal: with increasing age maximum heart rate decreases.

Stroke volume is another way of measuring the impact of aging on the cardiovascular system. Stroke volume is the amount of blood pumped out of the heart (left ventricle) with each contraction. A diseased or weak heart would have a less forceful contraction and thus pump less blood than the heart of a normal individual. After about age 20, stroke volume decreases about 0.7 percent per year (Rockstein & Sussman, 1979; Whitbourne, 1985).

Electrocardiographic (ECG or EKG) readings are another way of measuring the functioning of the cardiovascular system. The heart is a pump that is regulated by electrical activity. Essentially, there are small electrical charges that trigger the contractions of the heart. With four chambers, the electrical charges must either work in sequence or the functioning of the heart is going to be reduced contributing to poorer performance or death. This is known as an "irregular heartbeat" or an arrhythmia. The percent of the population that has "abnormal" ECG readings increases with increasing age although the percentage due to "normal" aging and pathological conditions is not clear.

Conditions Affecting the Cardiovascular System   Diseases of the cardiovascular system are the major causes of death and disability in contemporary American society. In this section we will be examining two different areas: disease and symptoms of disease. For example, high blood pressure is generally considered a disease when it should be considered the symptom of a disease.

High blood pressure (HBP) or hypertension is often a "silent" disease. That is, individuals with HBP are often not aware of the existence of the disease until the disease has caused damage to organs such as the kidneys, heart, or eyes. When the organs affected by HBP start to produce symptoms, it is then that the HBP is detected. Because HBP does not generally produce symptoms, many individuals with diagnosed HBP ignore their physicians' advice and do not take their medications. HBP can generally be controlled through diet, exercise, and medication. The consequences of untreated HBP can be numerous and include stroke, heart failure, kidney damage, and death. The causes of HBP can be varied with one frequent cause being "hardening of the arteries," which means that the arteries have become less elastic; thus when the heart contracts there is less "give," which creates more pressure.

There are so many diseases that can affect the heart. The area is complex for the layperson because of the number of terms that are used to describe heart disease. Basically, for discussion in this text, we will conceptualize two types of heart disease: disease that affects the vascular system of the heart and disease that affects the heart muscle. As we will see shortly, one type of disease can often cause the other.

Disease that affects the vascular system of the heart is often referred to as cardiovascular disease, coronary heart disease, ischemic heart disease, or coronary artery disease. Essentially similar, they describe conditions of the arteries that supply blood to the heart. Remember, the heart is a muscle that is continually working and thus needs a continual supply of oxygen-rich blood.

Two diseases that occur in the heart's vascular system are atherosclerosis and arteriosclerosis. Arteriosclerosis is sometimes called "hardening of the arteries," and refers to the loss of elasticity in the vascular system. Atherosclerosis is when there is a buildup inside the walls of the blood vessels.

Numerous epidemiological studies have been done to determine the causes of atherosclerosis. The studies have consistently reported that the causes are high cholesterol level, smoking, lack of exercise, and HBP. Fatty deposits accumulate on the inner walls of the heart arteries making the arteries less elastic and reducing the opening for blood flow to the heart muscle. The lack of blood to the heart muscle can precipitate a "heart attack," which is a general term meaning that part of the heart has been deprived of oxygen and has died. This results in the second type of disease where the heart muscle is damaged. A more specific term would be myocardial infarction (MI). The "myo" refers to muscle, the "cardial" to the heart. An infarction means that tissue has died because of lack of oxygen. For those who survive myocardial infarctions the dead heart tissue is replaced with scar tissue. Very often individuals are warned of the extent of atherosclerosis by chest pain or angina pectoris, which is a symptom of the cardiovascular disease.

There are a variety of ways to correct or minimize the consequences of cardiovascular disease. There are drugs, for example, to control HBP. Additionally, surgical techniques such as by-pass surgery or valve replacement are used to replace clogged arteries and defective valves. Pacemakers are used to regulate the heartbeat.

Endocrine System

The endocrine system consists of ductless glands which release hormones into the blood stream to transport to other parts of the body to regulate tissues and organs. The endocrine system is a very complex system, involving many aspects of daily functioning. The system involves "feedback loops" through which the functioning of the body is monitored and, based on this monitoring, appropriate hormones secreted. Some of the endocrine glands are adrenal, hypothalamus, ovaries, pancreas, parathyroids, pineal, pituitary, testes, thymus, and thyroid.

In general the endocrine system shows relatively little age-related change, the ovaries being an exception. Most of the disorders of the endocrine system, such as diabetes or thyroid problems, occur early in life. Disorders, when they do occur, are more likely to be a result of disease than age. Originally it was believed that significant declines took place in several areas. For example, it has been noted that the basal metabolic rate declines with increasing age. This was originally attributed to declines in the thyroid gland. It is now believed to be a result of the loss of lean body mass that frequently accompanies old age (Lyles, 1987).

Relatively minor changes in some of the endocrine glands have been reported: less coordination and higher hormone threshold levels to be activated. For example, the blood-sugar level has to be higher in an older person before the pancreas will release insulin (Bromley, 1974; Finch, 1976; Weg, 1975; Whitbourne, 1985).

Gastrointestinal System

The gastrointestinal system is essentially a large tube through which food is processed so that the nutrients from the food can be utilized by the body. The tube starts with the mouth and ends with the anus. For the body to be able to use the nutrients the food must be broken down, through the process of digestion, into small molecules that the body can absorb. Digestion starts in the mouth and involves other systems of the body such as the teeth, which are part of the skeletal system, and ends with the excretion of waste material and unprocessed food.

The first part of the system consists of the mouth, esophagus, and stomach. The mouth plays two roles in digestion. First, the teeth chew or masticate food breaking the food down for the digestive process; second, the salivary glands secrete saliva which has enzymes to start digesting the food. From the mouth the food travels through the throat (pharynx) into the esophagus and then into the stomach. The muscular action of the stomach and certain digestive juices, such as pepsin, continue breaking down or digesting the food. The food then goes to the small intestine where the gall bladder, pancreas, and liver secrete juices to further aid digestion. Many nutrients are absorbed along the 22– to 25–foot small intestine. After 4 to 8 hours the material is transferred to the large intestine where further absorption takes place, primarily of water and vitamins. The material becomes more solid and is excreted as feces.

There are numerous age-related changes in the gastrointestinal system: some caused by the aging of the system itself and some related to other areas, such as the vascular system.

In the mouth there are some major changes that impact on digestion. First, there are frequently problems with teeth (which will be discussed in more detail in the section on the skeletal system), such as missing teeth, poorly fitting dentures, or sore gums. Second, there is less saliva secreted, which has three implications: (1) less saliva will reduce the digestive process that occurs in the mouth; (2) the reduction in saliva diminishes taste, since taste buds must be in a solution to work; (3) the reduction of saliva will make food more difficult to chew and swallow. The reduction in saliva creates a "dry mouth," as does the tendency in older persons to breathe through their mouths due to chronic sinus conditions. A third major change in the mouth is that the chewing force is reduced, thus affecting the extent food is chewed before swallowing (Groth, 1988).

In the esophagus, food is transported via peristaltic movements, which are a series of muscular contractions that move the food down to the stomach. These movements decrease with increasing age; additionally, the nerves controlling the contractions become less coordinated. The end result is that swallowing becomes more difficult, with many individuals reporting the sensation of food "sticking" in the esophagus. Additionally, at the lower end of the esophagus, just before the stomach, there is muscle that closes off the esophagus from the stomach, preventing some of the stomach juices from getting into and irritating the esophagus. With increasing age this muscle does not close as well as in younger individuals and often results in "heartburn."

In the stomach, digestive juices are in smaller quantities and the muscular contractions of the stomach decrease. Although studies are limited, it appears that the absorptive capability of the small intestine also declines with increasing age, although it is difficult to determine if the absorption decreases because of changes in the intestine itself or in other areas such as the vascular supply to the intestine. In the large intestine there are also age-related changes which may slow the elimination of waste material.

The impact of senescence on the liver, which makes bile to aid in the digestion of fat, is unclear. Some studies claim that significant declines in size, weight, and liver chemistry take place while others state that there is little or no change (Berman et al., 1988; Whitbourne, 1985).

Conditions Affecting the Gastrointestinal System   One of the most frequent problems is constipation. This occurs in part because of age-related changes such as slower transport time due to decreased muscle tone to induce peristaltic movement (i.e., muscular contractions that move waste through the intestines), as well as lack of exercise, inadequate fluid intake, poor nutritional habits (i.e., lack of fiber in diet), consumption of certain drugs, and overreliance on laxatives which can create a "lazy" colon.

Another major problem is cancer. In those age 65–74, cancer of the digestive organs is the second leading cause of cancer deaths for men and the first for women. For the age group 75–84, it is the leading cause of cancer deaths for both males and females.

Integumentary System

The integumentary system consists of the skin, including the glands in the skin, the nails, and hair. Skin serves as a barrier to maintain the internal environment of the body and contain that environment to keep external factors, such as bacteria, from entering the body. The skin can also act as a sense organ notifying the individual of temperature, pressure, pain, or touch. The sweat glands help to maintain body temperature.

In comparison with other major organs of the body, there has been relatively little research done on the aging skin. This may be because skin is not seen as an organ that fails, resulting in death (Kligman et al., 1985)

Some of the most noticeable changes of increasing age occur in the skin. With increasing age the skin can be expected to wrinkle, become paler and thinner, exhibit "liver spots," sag, lose much of its hair, damage more easily, heal more slowly, become dryer, lose its elasticity, and lose much of its capability as a regulator of body temperature.

The skin consists of two layers plus an additional layer of subcutaneous fat. As one becomes older, the outer skin or epidermis and the inner skin, the dermis, will become thinner, as does the subcutaneous fatty layer—a process that contributes to many of the common skin conditions of old age such as loose skin on the arms. This thinning of the skin can most easily be seen in the hands of older persons, which will often have prominent knuckles, blood vessels, and tendons. Furthermore, the loss of the subcutaneous fat can increase the probability of pressure sores.

Of all of the changes that take place in the skin, the most serious is the loss of its ability to regulate body temperature. With increasing age, individuals become susceptible to the development of heat- or cold-related disorders because of the inability of the body to respond adequately to external temperatures. Because of a marked reduction in the number of sweat glands as well as the amount of sweat produced in remaining glands, there is an inability to sweat freely which can lead to an increased probability of heat-related problems, such as heat stroke or heat exhaustion. The loss of the insulating layer of subcutaneous fat along with a decline in the circulatory system can make older persons more susceptible to the cold (Bromley, 1974; Rossman, 1977). In fact, 40 percent of all accidental deaths from hypothermia (i.e., the lowering of the core body temperature) are of older persons (Rango, 1985). Poverty, not just age, plays an important role here since many older persons live in substandard, poorly heated housing, or do not have the economic resources to maintain adequate levels of heat within their homes.

Along with the changes noted above, there are several other changes in the skin that take place with the onset of senescence. There is generally a "loss of bloom" among older persons; this occurs because the cells contributing to pigmentation have been lost and because many blood vessels near the surface of the skin have ceased to function. Wrinkles come from the repetition of facial expressions, such as laughing or frowning. Sagging skin is the result of the loss of elasticity and fatty tissue, the force of gravity, and the loss of muscle mass (see Kligman et al., 1985; Selmanowitz et al., 1977).

Hair has minimum biological or physiological function in humans, since it is too sparse to provide warmth or protection; however it does have a number of social characteristics connected with it. Individuals are often judged by the amount, color, or style of hair. With increasing age, baldness or thinning of scalp and body hair is almost inevitable, although there are some variations by race, ethnic group, and sex. For example, Asians and Native Americans rarely experience baldness. Men tend to become increasingly bald by hair loss starting at the front of the scalp and progressing to the back; women tend to have a decrease in the density of hair on the top of the scalp. Hair loss on most parts of the body, such as the arms and legs, can be extensive. In men the beard may become sparse. There is often increased hair growth in men in the ears, eyebrows, and nose. In women the change in the androgen/estrogen ratio may produce darker and coarser facial hair, especially on the upper lip and chin. The follicles of remaining hair become thinner and the hair grows slower. Furthermore, the loss of pigmentary cells will first lead to graying of the hair and eventually to white hair, which starts with the scalp and eventually progresses to other areas (see Selmanowitz et al., 1977).

There are also changes in the nails with increasing age. They tend to become thicker, and grow more slowly.

Conditions Affecting the Integumentary System   Although skin conditions rarely result in death they do occur frequently in older persons. One study found that about 66 percent of the older persons examined had skin conditions that needed medical intervention (Kligman et al., 1985). Although these conditions were generally not life-threatening, many interfered with the quality of life. Two frequent conditions that affect older persons are itching and pressure sores.

Itching, or pruritus, is a common skin condition (Carter & Balin, 1983) and can be caused by factors such as dry skin, due to a decrease in oil production, certain drugs, or a dry environment. Although the condition may appear to be relatively minor, it can in fact cause significant distress.

Pressure sores occur frequently in older persons who are immobile. One study reported that 3 to 11 percent of older persons in acute care hospitals or nursing homes had pressure sores (Allman, 1989). These are sometimes referred to as "bed sores," although technically, since they can occur in nonbed situations, such as prolonged sitting in a chair or wheelchair, pressure sore or pressure ulcer are better terms. Pressure sores generally occur in areas of the body where there is relatively little tissue between a bone and the skin. When pressure is placed on this area the bone presses against the stationary object, such as a chair seat, reducing or stopping the flow of blood to the area. Ultimately this reduced or severed blood supply causes tissue to die thus producing a ''wound'' or sore. The health status of the individual, the time the blood flow is reduced, and the applied pressure determine the amount of damage. Once they develop, the treatment of pressure sores is generally difficult, prolonged, and expensive. The best approach is to prevent them from occurring. Older persons with pressure sores are at an increased risk of death (Allman, 1989).

Muscular System

The muscular system functions with two other systems: the skeletal system and the cardiovascular system. It is the muscular system that provides movement for the skeletal system; the cardiovascular system consists of cardiac muscle as well as muscle in the walls of blood vessels.

For this section we will concentrate on the voluntary skeletal muscles. The voluntary muscles are those over which we normally have control; they are found in the arms and legs as well as other parts of the body. Most of the literature claims that our muscles reach their maximum strength, power, and ability to rapidly respond by age 30. After that the above qualities decline, along with muscle mass (a 30 percent loss by age 80), elasticity, and stamina, although the losses due to senescence are minimal until the late sixties or early seventies. It has also been found that older individuals are not as coordinated as younger individuals in tasks requiring muscular work primarily due to atrophy from nonuse since by age 30, most individuals no longer exercise regularly. There is less decline in muscle mass and function among those who stay active than among those who become sedentary (Bromley, 1974; Shanck, 1976; Shock, 1974; Weg, 1975; Whitbourne, 1985).

Neurosensory System

The neurosensory system is a large and complex system. It is also a system in which certain areas, such as the brain, are very difficult to study, especially in normal individuals. Perhaps because of this it is the least understood system. It has two primary purposes. First, it is the individual's link to the outside environment. Through the senses, such as vision, touch, and hearing, the individual can be aware of what is happening externally. Second, the internal environment, such as heart beat and respiration, is controlled and regulated by the brain and nervous system. First we will discuss the central nervous system, which consists of the brain and nervous system; second we will discuss the senses.

As was noted earlier, the brain controls many functions within the body such as the heart and respiration. The brain is also responsible for our thinking and personality and it controls our senses. With increasing age several age-related changes occur. The most dramatic, and frequently reported, is the decline in brain weight. Older persons can expect about a 20 percent decline in brain weight because of the loss in brain cells and extracellular fluid (Berman et al., 1988; Brody, 1987; Rockstein & Sussman, 1979). The impact this has on mental functions such as memory and intelligence will be discussed in Chapter 8, dealing with the psychological aspects of aging. There are four readily identifiable brain rhythms that can be measured by the electroencephalogram (EEG). Generally, the faster brain waves indicate alertness and the slower brain waves drowsiness or sleepiness or brain dysfunctioning. With increasing age there is a slowing of brain waves (electrical activity) and a reduction in blood flow to the brain. The nerve pathways that transmit messages to and from parts of the body also lose cells. Thus, it takes older persons longer to transmit information via nerves since they travel at a slower rate (Bromley, 1974; Kart et al., 1988; Shock, 1962, 1974; Solomon et al., 1970; Weg, 1973, 1975, 1976, 1983; Woodruff, 1975).

Vision accuracy, for both near and far perception, adaptation to light and dark, color discrimination, ability to adapt to glare, visual field, and visual acuity all diminish with increasing age. About 7 percent of those 65 to 74 and 16 percent of those 75+ are blind or are seriously impaired. Generally the decline will become more rapid after age 45. The fluid that lubricates and cleanses the eyes also diminishes, frequently causing "dry eyes," which can be a source of discomfort, often resulting in rubbing which may cause a secondary infection.

The decline in vision comes about because of physical changes in the eye. The optical nerves atrophy; the lens yellows and thus filters out violet, blue, and green light; the lens loses its elasticity; the pupils become smaller and irregular in shape; and the eye does not admit as much light. Also, the eyelids may sag, often enough to interfere with vision. For many older persons the changes noted above are intensified by diseases such as cataracts and glaucoma. Vision impairments are important since they can curtail everyday activities, decrease mobility, and cause a poor orientation to one's environment. To an extent, many visual impairments can be corrected with glasses and contact lenses. Magnifying glasses, talking books, large-print books, proper lights, or color coding assist the visually impaired (Bromley, 1974; Burnside, 1976; Ernst & Shore, 1975; Kart, 1976; Plude, 1987).

The ability to hear also diminishes with increasing age. Approximately 13 percent of those 65 to 74 and 26 percent of those 75+ have serious hearing problems. Generally, the decline in hearing starts at about age 25. Some of the hearing loss is due to the atrophy of the nerve tissue in the ear. This degeneration occurs in part because the blood flow to the auditory nerves is reduced with hardening of the arteries; thus, the nerves die. Hearing loss is also a result of calcification of the bones in the inner ear. Normal age-related hearing loss is called presbycusis. Disease and acoustical accidents or abuse, through such factors as loud music or a noisy work environment, also account for hearing loss. Wax buildup accounts for some acute hearing loss.

Hearing loss can be of two types: loss of volume or loss of pitch. Volume simply refers to the intensity of a sound, whereas pitch refers to the level of a sound. A soprano has a high-pitched voice and a basso a low-pitched voice. Although most people assume that hearing losses are the loss-of-volume type, most older persons in fact suffer from a loss of ability to hear high-pitched sounds. Thus many older persons prefer low-pitched organ music to other types of music. It should be noted that if a person suffers from loss of ability to hear high-pitched sounds, it will not increase that individual's ability to hear by raising the volume of one's voice. Increasing the volume of one's voice also increases the pitch. The louder one shouts, the less likely the afflicted individual is to hear. Ironically, whispering may enable the individual to hear better, because it decreases the pitch of the voice.

Three additional factors often intensify the decline in hearing when older persons are talking with each other. First, the pitch of the voice generally increases, meaning that if two older persons are talking with each other they may have difficulty in understanding each other. Second, visual impairments may nullify the potential benefits of face-to-face communication. Third, other changes, such as dentures, may cause words to be slurred.

It has frequently been noted that those older persons who are hard-of-hearing exhibit many characteristics of "senile" individuals, such as not responding or incorrectly responding to a question. It has also been reported that hearing problems can cause depression, paranoia, and disturbances in the sense of balance. Thus, hearing disorders are sometimes incorrectly interpreted to be symptoms of senility. The loss of the ability to hear can also create problems in social interaction. Many older persons avoid social interaction because they are afraid that their verbal responses or behavior will be inappropriate.

Hearing problems can lead to other problems because individuals may misinterpret many "normal" sounds in their environment and become fearful. They also may not be able to distinguish noises that require some type of action, creating a situation in which they may not be aware of certain dangers. For example, a person with impaired hearing may not be able to hear a fire alarm or the directions of a physician concerning medication.

Hearing problems can often be improved by a hearing aid, a quiet environment, simple verbal communication, or face-to-face interaction (Burnside, 1976; Corso, 1977; Ernst & Shore, 1975).

It has generally been believed that the ability to taste declines with increasing age (Burnside, 1976; Ernst & Shore, 1975; Herr, 1976) although some researchers disagree (Engen, 1977). This decline can result in loss of appetite or overreliance on spicy or heavily seasoned foods. Recent evidence has suggested that the decline, although prevalent, is less a result of the aging process and more a result of either pathological conditions or other factors that destroy taste buds such as smoking, certain drugs, or dentures. Two negative consequences of a decline in the ability to taste are that many individuals lose their appetites and become malnourished; others are unable to detect spoiled food.

Like the studies on the sense of taste, the studies on the sense of smell do not set forth any definite conclusions. In the past it was believed that with increasing age, most individuals lost the ability to identify common odors (see Schiffman & Pasternak, 1979). If this were true, the loss of smell would create two problems. First, individuals would not be able to recognize certain danger signals, such as the smoke from a fire, and second, many of the pleasures of life, such as the fragrance of a flower or perfume, would be lost (see Burnside, 1976; Ernst & Shore, 1975).

Again, recent evidence is challenging the belief that the sense of smell declines as a result of the aging process. Although most studies have found a diminished sense of smell in older persons, the decline is for pathological reasons, not from senescence (Engen, 1977; Whitbourne, 1985).

The sense of touch places individuals in contact with both external and internal events. It informs individuals of changes in temperature and of pain or pressure on the skin. For most individuals the ability to feel sensations on the skin will begin to diminish at about age 55. They will generally become less sensitive to temperature changes, touch, and pain. The loss of sensitivity generally starts in the lower half of the body and works upward. There are several possible consequences. First, individuals may not be aware of bruises or cuts, which might contribute to the development of a serious condition because a minor condition was not treated. Second, the individual with a chronic condition, such as arthritis, may be released from at least some of the discomfort associated with the disorder (Burnside, 1976; Ernst & Shore, 1975; Kenshalo, 1977).

Conditions Affecting the Neurosensory System   First we will discuss one disease of the central nervous system (CNS): stroke. Second, we will examine two frequent conditions of the eyes: cataracts and glaucoma.

Stroke, or cerebrovascular accident (CVA), is the third leading cause of death among older persons. In a stroke the blood supply to part of the brain is suddenly disrupted, causing death or damage to brain cells. The amount, location, and duration of the disruption will determine the impact. Strokes can be caused by atherosclerosis, blood clots which plug arteries and restrict blood flow, or a ruptured blood vessel. The hemisphere of the brain, the area affected within that hemisphere, as well as the extent of damage will determine the consequences. Very often the symptoms are initially modest, such as lapses in memory or impaired physical functioning, which are often dismissed as normal consequences of aging. If the damage is significant, the individual may have paralysis, be unable to speak or understand others, and may have visual impairments. The prognosis depends on the extent of damage as well as the area damaged. For those who have suffered mostly losses of motor functions, the prognosis is generally fairly good; those suffering motor and sensory losses do not have as good a prognosis. Frequently there is warning of an impending stroke by transient ischemic attacks, where there is a temporary reduction in the blood supply. These cause temporary symptoms such as weakness in arms or legs, dizziness, impairment of judgment, and difficulty with speech.

The next two conditions, cataracts and glaucoma, have the ability to cause blindness. According to a study cited by Plude (1987), blindness is second to cancer as the most feared aspect of aging.

Cataracts are very frequent after age 65, with Roberts (1987) reporting their presence in 46 percent of those 75 to 85 years of age; the extent of their growth and their placement will determine the amount of visual distortion. About 5 percent of those with cataracts will need cataract surgery (Stengel, 1986), which accounts for many eye-related hospitalizations. With cataracts the lens of the eye becomes cloudy or opaque. Generally, cataracts grow slowly. Several surgical techniques exist to remove cataracts and replace the lens with an artificial surgically implanted lens, or by having the individual wear glasses or contact lenses (Stengel, 1986). Some of the reported risk factors for cataracts are advanced age, female gender, diabetes, high blood pressure, exposure to certain drugs, myopia, glaucoma, and steroid use (White et al., 1986).

Glaucoma is another frequent visual problem of older persons. It is present in about 1.2 percent of those under age 65, 2.3 percent of those age 65 to 74, and 3.5 percent of those 75+ (White et al., 1986). Although there are different forms of glaucoma, generally the fluid pressure within the eye increases and causes optic nerve damage. It is quite painless, and thus it is referred to as a "silent disease." Often the disease is not noticed until substantial damage has occurred. Some of the symptoms are blurry vision, the occurrence of halos or rainbows around lights, and the loss of field or side vision. If it is not controlled medically, vision will continue to deteriorate. Medication and surgery can often check the disease.

Reproductive System

The reproductive system will also be discussed in Chapter 7, "Sexuality." Every system in the body exists for a purpose; the purpose of the reproductive system is to perpetuate the species. In males the system consists of paired testes, paired tubes (vas deferens) leading from the testes through the prostate gland, and the urethra which is located in the penis. As will be seen in a later section, the urethra in the male functions as part of two systems: reproduction and urinary. In the female the system consists of paired ovaries, paired fallopian tubes leading from the ovaries to the uterus, the vagina, and the breasts. In both men and women the reproductive system produces hormones that have an influence on reproductive capability as well as secondary sex characteristics (see Harman & Talbert, 1985).

With increasing age, males do not experience one definitive event, such as menopause in women, that indicates that a change is taking place in the reproductive system. Rather, declines are gradual. Changes in the amount of testosterone produced by the testicles, which was responsible in adolescence for the development of secondary sex characteristics such as the development of facial hair, body hair and a deeper voice, declines with increasing age, with significant declines being reported by age 60. Although the testicles shrink in size and sperm production decreases with increasing age, men as old as 94 have fathered children (Rockstein & Sussman, 1979).

The prostate gland undergoes dramatic change with increasing age and is a frequent source of problems for many older men. It generally increases in size and weight, doubling by the time an individual is 70 to 80 years of age (Rockstein & Sussman, 1979). This can result in a variety of problems, several related to urination. The amount of fluid secreted by the prostate gland with each ejaculation is also reduced. Additionally, the prostate is a frequent source of cancer in older men. The penis also undergoes some changes with increasing age. The vascular capability generally decreases; the tissue that becomes engorged with blood to cause an erection also changes. The results generally mean a slower erection and a penis that is less rigid.

In women one major indicator of the aging process is menopause, which generally occurs anywhere from the early 40s to the mid-fifties. Unlike males who generally remain fertile throughout life, menopause indicates an end of the ability to reproduce. The most dramatic change is in the ovaries which reduce or stop estrogen and progesterone production. This brings on menopause as well as changes in other areas. In the vagina the elasticity of the walls is reduced as is the amount of fluid secreted on sexual stimulation. The breasts tend to lose tone as mammary tissue is replaced with fat, which is less firm, and because of a decrease in the elasticity of the skin. The uterus also shrinks in size.

Conditions Affecting the Reproductive System   In males an almost universal problem after 40 years of age is benign prostatic hypertrophy (Riehle & Vaughan, 1983). Essentially, this is a noncancerous enlargement of the prostate gland. The enlarged gland frequently interferes with urination, causing an urge to urinate frequently, dribbling of urine after urination, a decreased force while urinating, and the sensation of still needing to urinate immediately after urination. It can also cause the retention of a pool of urine in the bladder. Some of these problems can increase the likelihood of a urinary tract infection.

Although it has been estimated that as many as 50 percent of older males have cancerous prostate tissue, in some men the disease spreads so slowly that they die from other conditions before the cancer spreads. Nonetheless, prostate cancer is the third leading cause of cancer deaths in older men (Riehle & Vaughan, 1983). There are a variety of treatments for both benign prostatic hypertrophy and cancer of the prostate. The treatments can include drugs, radiation, and several types of surgical procedures.

One frequent disorder for females is breast cancer. Many older women falsely believe that after menopause the risk of breast cancer decreases; as a result many no longer conduct breast self-examinations. For many this leads to the discovery of cancer at a later stage, which makes the survival rate lower.

Respiratory System

The respiratory system consists of the lungs and air passageways to the lungs such as the nasal cavity, throat, and trachea. Its purpose is to supply oxygen to the body and eliminate carbon dioxide. The oxygen for metabolism is obtained from the inhalation of oxygen into the lungs. The oxygen is absorbed by the lungs and carried through the bloodstream to various parts of the body. Lack of oxygen can cause muscular weakness, sleepiness, confusion, and poor motor coordination. With increasing age the respiratory system becomes less efficient. The lung capacity becomes smaller, and scarring has made the lung tissue more rigid, thus reducing the expansive capacity of the lungs, as well as the ability of the lungs to absorb oxygen. Thus the lungs of older persons inhale less new oxygen and are less capable of absorbing the oxygen that has been inhaled than are the lungs of younger individuals. This brings about a lowered metabolic rate (Bromley, 1974; Roberts, 1976a; Shock, 1962, 1974; Weg, 1973, 1975, 1976).

Skeletal System

Bones give shape and form to the body, protect internal organs, serve as areas onto which muscles—via tendons—can be attached, allowing the body to be mobile, and serve as a repository for certain chemicals such as calcium. Generally the bones reach their maximum size by the late teens, although the bone mass continues to develop until the mid-thirties when the greatest density is reached. After age 35 women start to lose bone mass at the rate of 0.75 to 1.0 percent per year. Men generally do not start to lose bone mass until about 50 to 55 years of age and then the loss is about 0.40 percent a year (Smith et al., 1981). This decrease in bone mass affects both the size and strength of the bones, with the result that bones become brittle and weak, more prone to fracture, and slower to heal.

Increasing age also has an effect on the individual's overall stature. Both the invertebral discs in the spine and the cartilage between the discs decrease in size and strength. As the discs and cartilage collapse, older persons become shorter in stature. An average loss in height is 2 to 3 inches but losses as great as 12 inches have been reported (see Miller, 1985). Three other factors intensify the impression that older persons are shorter than younger persons. First, the lack of good muscle tone causes many aged individuals to stoop. Second, those born before 1900 are on the average 2 inches shorter than those born after 1900. Third, the vertebral column in many older people will become bowed in the thoracic region. Because of the "shrinkage" in the trunk area, many appear to have unusually long arms or legs (see Bromley, 1974; Rossman, 1977; Shanck, 1976; Weg, 1973, 1975).

With increasing age, calcification can also occur around the joints. This hardening can restrict movement and cause pain. With senescence, the layer of cartilage between joints becomes thinner and more likely to splinter and fragment. In addition, the lubrication of the joints decreases, a phenomenon that can cause dryness and eventually crumbling of the joints.

Teeth are another part of the bone structure affected by increasing age. They are an important part of the body for two reasons. First, they grind and crush certain foods for proper digestion. When left untreated and unrepaired, teeth can make eating a painful and unpleasant experience, and can result in the selection of only certain types of food that are not painful to chew. The result is a restricted diet producing nutritional problems. Second, teeth contribute to the individual's overall appearance. Individuals are continually reminded of the loss, discoloration, or damage to their teeth in both eating and social interaction. If they have missing or damaged teeth, they often must be careful of what and how they eat. In terms of social interaction, they may be embarrassed about the condition of their teeth and thus avoid smiling or looking directly at others. Others may avoid social interaction.

Diet, frequency of repair, chewing or masticatory habits, and care of mouth and teeth are, of course, factors involved in the condition of one's teeth. With increasing age teeth generally become more of a problem. Reduction in the amount of saliva increases the risk of tooth decay and some drugs cause a decrease in saliva. Periodontal disease frequently occurs in the aged and makes tooth extraction necessary. Years of chewing food and grinding the teeth produce a flattened, worn tooth surface.

Smoking can also increase tooth loss (Daniell, 1983). Poor mouth care is another factor (see Pettigrew, 1989). A variety of conditions, such as arthritis, which can make it difficult to hold a toothbrush, or "forgetfulness" can contribute to problems such as cavities or periodontal disease. Some conditions, such as arthritis, can be compensated for by such devices as an electric toothbrush. Today many older persons have lost all or most of their teeth. It should be emphasized that most individuals lose their teeth because of poor or negligent care, not as a result of senescence. Most dentists now emphasize preventive dentistry, which will allow most older persons to maintain their teeth.

Dentures are an alternative faced by many older individuals. Often dentures are uncomfortable, limit the types of foods that can be eaten, do not fit well or look natural, and can take on a "denture odor." Social interaction may be avoided because of the fear that the dentures may slip or become loose during conversation. It should also be noted that with the extraction of the teeth, osteoporosis, or the loss of bone mass, proceeds at an accelerated rate in the jaw. This deterioration can lead to a change in physical appearance and cause some medical problems in the mouth (see Tonna, 1977).

Conditions Affecting the Skeletal System   The most frequently discussed condition of bones is osteoporosis. Although a term frequently used, it is a term that is difficult to define because it is not one disease but several diseases. The problem in defining the term can be seen in two ways. First, if one looks at articles on osteoporosis very seldom is a definition provided. It is almost as though "everyone" knows what it is therefore we don't need to define it. The second problem can be seen in the variety of definitions that have been offered. An early definition (Albright et al., 1941) defined osteoporosis as too little normal bone. There are two problems with this definition; the first is that there is not an empirical indicator for "too little"; the second is that current research suggests that the remaining bone may not be "normal" (see Exton-Smith, 1985). For some writers osteoporosis is defined as a loss of bone mass that is greater for an individual than normally seen for that individual's age category. For other writers it is when the loss is so great that the likelihood of fracture is present (White et al., 1986).

Osteoporosis is a "silent," gradual, progressive disease that can exist for decades before any consequences or symptoms are noticed (Sobel, 1986). It can be a painful, disfiguring disease that frequently leads to the loss of independence (Roberto, 1988). It is also a disease that affects females four times more frequently than males (Weg, 1983). It is estimated that 10 percent of females 50+ years of age have osteoporosis severe enough to cause fracture (Steinberg, 1986). By age 65, one-third of females have suffered a compression fracture of the spine; by age 75 it is 50 percent (Hallal, 1985; Scileppi, 1983). One-third of females and one-sixth of males will have a hip fracture during old age (Miller, 1985; Rowe & Kahn, 1987).

Females are more affected by osteoporosis for two reasons. First, they have less bone mass than men. For example, at age 18 females have about 20 percent less bone mass than men of comparable weight. Second, the loss of bone mass starts earlier in females and progresses at a more rapid rate. It is believed that this is because of menopause (see Exton-Smith, 1985).

In advanced osteoporosis, fractures can occur even under ordinary stress such as walking. These are often said to be "spontaneous fractures" and occur under minimum stress. In fact, it is speculated that many spontaneous fractures occur while walking and cause the individual to fall, often blurring the cause of the fracture. Other fractures occur under more pronounced stress, such as falls. The most likely sites of fracture are the spine, hip, or wrist (Barzel, 1987). Osteoporosis in the spine can cause compression and significant pain. Hip fracture can cause not only permanent disability but is also associated with a mortality rate as high as 20 percent (Jensen & Tondevold, 1979). The economic cost of osteoporosis has been estimated at $6.1 billion dollars per year (Steinberg, 1986).

Osteoporosis is difficult to diagnose using traditional x-rays, especially in certain high risk areas such as the spine (Steinberg, 1986). In fact, osteoporosis cannot be detected with x-rays until 30 to 50 percent of the bone has been lost (Hallal, 1985; Raisz, 1988; Scileppi, 1983; Sobel, 1986). Other techniques such as computed tomography is being used (see Blechman et al., 1988; Weissman, 1986). Because it is difficult to diagnose, it is often mistaken for rheumatoid arthritis.

Studies on bone replacement have generally indicated that once lost, bone cannot be replaced, although some studies have indicated the opposite. A conservative stance at this time would be to say that further research is needed in this area.

The causes of osteoporosis are varied and can include some of the following nine variables (factors) (see Steinberg, 1986):

1 Disease: There are certain diseases that place the older person at an increased risk and rate of osteoporosis: hyperparathyroidism, hyperthyroidism, alcoholism, cirrhosis of the liver, diabetes mellitus.

2 Drugs: Certain drugs that older persons consume can also increase the risk and rate of osteoporosis. These drugs interfere with calcium absorption.

3 Gender: Women are more likely to have osteoporosis than men. In women it occurs earlier than in men.

4 Hormones: After menopause the rate and risk of osteoporosis increases substantially because of a lack of estrogen.

5 Inactivity: Inactivity has been found to produce significant demineralization of the bones.

6 Nutrition: Bones contain about 99 percent of the calcium of the body (Rivlin, 1986). Calcium is used in several ways by the body. Thus, if calcium is in short supply, the body will use the calcium in the bones. Women have lower calcium intakes than men throughout life, with further declines taking place with increasing age. However, the need for calcium often increases in older persons because of decreased intestinal absorption. (Note: There are other nutritional factors that interfere with calcium that older persons obtain. Many individuals believe that by consuming certain foods or by taking certain calcium supplements they are obtaining sufficient calcium. However, it is not the amount of calcium consumed but the amount absorbed by the body. There are several factors that influence whether calcium is absorbed. For example, Vitamin D is needed for calcium absorption. Individuals low in Vitamin D will have a lower rate of calcium absorption. Other factors, such as high amount of fat, zinc, Vitamin A, caffeine, iron, or alcohol can all interfere with the absorption of calcium. A diet high in protein can increase calcium excretion [Rivlin, 1986].)

7 Physique: Small, slender females appear to have an increased risk of osteoporosis than larger women.

8 Race: Whites and Asians appear to be more susceptible than blacks. In whites, those of northwestern European descent are at greater risk than those of Mediterranean descent. It is very rare in black males.

9 Smoking: Smoking has been shown to increase the rate of osteoporosis (Daniell, 1976). This could be because female smokers appear to experience menopause earlier than nonsmokers (Linquist & Bengtsson, 1979) although male smokers are also at an increased risk of osteoporosis (Seeman et al., 1983).

Now that we have examined some of the causes we should look at some of the treatments. As noted earlier, the conservative belief is that osteoporosis cannot be reversed. Thus, the current trend is to treat osteoporosis before it occurs. One way of doing this in postmenopausal women is with hormone replacement therapy. Studies indicate that women who take estrogen have fewer fractures than nontreated women, although estrogen does not stabilize all individuals. Hormone replacement therapy is controversial because some studies have noted an increased risk of cancer.

Other treatments include calcitonin, which is a naturally occurring hormone. Calcitonin is often recommended when estrogen cannot be used. Calcitonin has some undesirable side effects, is expensive, and at this point must be injected daily (Sobel, 1986).

Fluoride is also being used. While estrogen and calcitonin reduce the rate of bone loss, fluoride appears to increase bone growth. There are some undesirable side effects of fluoride therapy such as nausea and bone pain (Bush, 1987).

Calcium, either as a supplement or in calcium-rich foods, has also been recommended. Again, studies here are contradictory.

Arthritis is another frequent condition of older persons. Arthritis is an inflammation of a joint. There are two major types, but over 100 different arthritic conditions. The first major type is rheumatoid arthritis which refers to the inflammation of a joint membrane. This is a severely crippling form of arthritis affecting three times more females than males. This most often affects the fingers, wrists, elbows, hip, and knees. The second major type is osteoarthritis. This is so frequent that some have said that it is universal with increasing age. Generally, this is a more mild form of arthritis, sometimes also called degenerative joint disease. The weight-bearing joints are the most frequently affected, and sometimes prior injury appears to determine the age at onset and the severity.

Urinary System

It is this system that probably causes older persons more concern and distress than any other. Disorders of the urinary system are a major cause of death and illness among older persons. While many diseases are "silent" with little or no discomfort, disorders in the urinary system often cause distressing symptoms.

The urinary system typically consists of two kidneys, one on each side of the midbody, each of which has a tube called a ureter connected to the bladder. The tube leaving the bladder for the excretion of urine is the urethra.

The kidneys filter waste material from blood. The kidneys are also responsible for maintaining the fluid and electrolyte balance of the body. The kidneys perform this function by regulating the amount of fluid or other substances that are excreted. Age takes a definite toll on the functioning of the kidneys, with almost any measure indicating a decline. The weight of the kidneys declines from a maximum between the ages of 30 and 40 of 270 grams each to 190 grams by 80 years of age. The filtration rate of the blood declines about 0.7 percent per year (see Rockstein & Sussman, 1979). Additionally the blood flow to the kidneys declines by as much as 10 percent per decade (see Kart et al., 1988).

The ureters, tubes approximately 10 inches long, transport urine from the kidneys to the bladder via peristaltic contractions. There are a few age-related changes that are significant for this discussion.

The bladder is a muscular sac which stores the urine prior to excretion. Bladders of young adults can normally hold between 500 and 600 milliliters of urine. Urine is released through the urethra. The major change in the bladder with increasing age is that it has a capacity about one-half that of a young adult, thus causing the need for more frequent urination.

Conditions Affecting the Urinary System   There are numerous problems associated with the urinary system, three of which will be discussed below: incontinence, frequent urination, and urinary tract infections (UTIs).

Urinary incontinence is the involuntary loss of urine through the urethra, which causes both social and hygienic problems (Herzog et al., 1989). Urinary incontinence is a major problem in older persons; its symptoms can cause tremendous distress (Krane & Siroky, 1981). The percentage of older persons affected by urinary incontinence will vary according to the type of study. Studies that include all older persons affected by any degree of urinary incontinence will have higher figures than studies that include only those who have a severe problem. About 25 percent of aged males and 42 percent of females are affected by urinary incontinence to some extent (Mitteness, 1987; Reaching consensus on incontinence, 1989; Specht, 1986). Urinary incontinence is a major cause of institutionalization (Resnick et al., 1989); it is also a major caregiver burden (Palmer, 1988). Incontinence is not caused by senescence but some underlying factor (Herzog et al., 1989). Incontinence is not a disease or disorder but symptomatic of a disease or disorder. There are medical, social, and psychological consequences to urinary incontinence. A major medical consequence is that continually urine-soaked individuals will develop a variety of skin disorders, such as decubitus ulcers, which if left untreated can cause serious infections. Another medical consequence is the $10 billion in direct costs of managing incontinent individuals (Reaching consensus on incontinence, 1989). Incontinence also increases the risk of urinary tract infections. Social consequences of incontinence are that the individual will be embarrassed in social situations and withdraw from social interaction. The psychological consequences can also be dramatic. In American society there are a variety of taboos concerning excretion. The individual who has lost control of this function may feel a loss of self-worth and become depressed (see Noelker, 1988; Tulloch, 1989).

The causes of urinary incontinence are varied, and there are many new techniques for its diagnosis and treatment (see Krane & Siroky, 1981). For some it may be the result of neurological conditions or disease. Some individuals suffer urinary incontinence as a result of surgical procedures which have damaged nerves or other areas that control voluntary urination. Certain drugs can increase fluid loss to the point where the individual can no longer control the urine flow while other drugs can make an individual sleep so deeply that the urge to urinate is not noticed and the bladder empties itself. Infection can also cause incontinence. Older persons generally do not completely empty their bladders during urination but retain a pool of urine. This pool is likely to host organisms that can cause urinary tract infections. In the male the organisms are frequently from prostate infections; in females the organisms are frequently from the vagina (Riehle & Vaughan, 1983). Additionally, individuals who have had chronic urinary incontinence undergo a decrease in bladder size, thus making methods to restore continence difficult. Also, the urge to urinate is sensed by younger individuals when the bladder is about half full; in older persons the urge is not sensed until the bladder is almost full. This can create problems if an appropriate place to urinate is not available (see Reaching consensus on incontinence, 1989).

Many older persons use various strategies to manage and disguise their incontinence. These individuals have often accepted incontinence as a part of the aging process and have decided not to seek professional help. Some of the ways it is managed is through the use of urine-collection devices such as pads or towels, frequently washing and changing clothing, and reorganizing daily life to minimize the chance of "accidents" in public (Mitteness, 1987).

There are several ways that have been used to correct urinary incontinence. Depending on the cause, surgery, drugs, catheters, and appliances such as bedside urinals have been used. When the urinary incontinence was believed to be psychological in origin various therapies were attempted. For example, one study of individuals in an institution substituted personal pajamas for institutional pajamas and found that the rate of urinary incontinence decreased significantly. Biofeedback has also been attempted with varying degrees of success. Removing environmental barriers to the individual's access to the bathroom has also been found to be successful (see McCormick et al., 1988).

One recent study employed pelvic exercise (Kegel exercise) and biofeedback which resulted in a significant decline in urinary incontinence. The study also reported that individuals spent less money on supplies for incontinence, and that there was an improvement in the quality of their lives (see Baigis-Smith et al., 1989; Heller et al., 1989).

A major point is that urinary incontinence is no longer seen as an inevitable or unfortunate aspect of aging, but as a condition that has an underlying, treatable cause (Herzog et al., 1989).

The need to urinate frequently is a problem for many older persons. The decrease in bladder size is one major factor. The need is especially apparent after going to bed. One study reported that 72 percent of older persons rose to urinate at least once after going to bed. Of this 72 percent, 73 percent rose more than once. This can cause sleep deprivation and result in fatigue. Getting out of bed at night, when the individual is sleepy and it is dark, increases the risk of stumbling or falling and of injury (Barker & Mitteness, 1988; Palmer, 1988). In fact, one study reported that 44 percent of the falls experienced by older persons happened while going to or returning from the bathroom (Herzog et al., 1989).

As was noted above, UTIs can cause incontinence. The frequency of UTIs increases with increasing age, especially for females. There are a number of factors responsible for UTIs: low fluid intake, poor hygiene, holding urine, existing diseases (e.g., diabetes, HBP) (Specht, 1986).

SUMMARY

The biological and physiological changes that accompany old age are among the most feared changes associated with the aging process. Although there is concern in this area, there has not been a corresponding amount of research, and much of the research that exists has been conducted on nonhumans.

Senescence is a general term for biological/physiological aging. Senescence is a process that all human beings will experience—unless they die young. Although senescence is universal, the rate and extent of aging is somewhat individual in many areas. For some individuals one area of the body may age very rapidly and another very slowly, while for another individual the reverse is true. It is often difficult to separate the result of senescence from the results to life-style, and many studies have incorrectly assumed that changes brought about by life-style were consequences of senescence.

There are many theories about why we age. The autoimmunity theory claims that with increasing age the immune system of the body has difficulty distinguishing between foreign matter and the matter of the body. Essentially, the immune system attacks and destroys the body. Collagen theory is another important theory. Collagen is found in the connective tissues of the body; it provides structure and support for the body by holding tissues together. With increasing age the collagen becomes more rigid, as a result of cross linking. This rigidity prevents the transmission of nutrients or the expulsion of waste materials. It also affects the organs. For example, the lungs become less capable of contracting and expanding. The error theory states that aging is caused by minor but continual changes in the DNA molecules in cells. A variety of factors cause damage to the DNA which determines the identity, function, and reproduction of cells. The free radical theory is another important theory. Free radicals are highly unstable compounds that are produced by normal cell metabolism. Because they are unstable, the free radicals interact with other nearby molecules, which damage them. Although the damage is small, it is cumulative, thus producing aging. There are many hormone theories of aging. Hormone theories have their basis in the "sex" hormones, since changes in hormone levels in females produce menopause and the acceleration of "aging" in certain areas. Several hormones have been examined but more research is needed. Earlier we examined the autoimmunity theory. There is also an immune system theory of aging. This theory states that with increasing age the immune system declines thus making the individual more receptive to a variety of degenerative conditions. A theory that has received considerable attention is the program theory of aging. This theory claims that the body is programmed to age. A theory similar to the error theory is the somatic mutation theory. This theory believes that the body sustains damage on a regular basis from a variety of factors which results in cell mutations. The cell mutations contribute to a decreased level of functioning. The last theory discussed was the wear-and-tear theory. This theory perceives the body as a machine that wears out with use and does not consider that use may strengthen the body.

Although we do not know why the body ages, we do know some of the consequences of aging. Again, however, it needs to be pointed out that in some areas there is still confusion between declines that are produced by senescence and declines that are produced by life-style.

In the cardiovascular system we see age-related changes in the heart's muscle, valves, and vascular system. Since heart cells do not replace themselves we see less heart muscle. The valves of the heart tend to become larger and more rigid. The heart's vascular system becomes less elastic. The maximum heart rate of older persons is not as great as in younger persons. Also, with increasing age, the amount of blood the heart pumps with each contraction is reduced. There are also some changes in the electrical activity of the heart. With increasing age there are some conditions such as high blood pressure, cardiovascular disease, and heart attacks, that occur frequently.

The endocrine system releases hormones into the blood stream which regulate body tissues and organs. There are relatively few age-related changes in this system.

In the gastrointestinal system there are numerous age-related changes. There are often problems in the mouth, with a loss of teeth and a reduction in saliva, which is essential for the digestion of certain foods. The muscular contractions in the esophagus, which move food from the mouth to the stomach, are reduced. The amount of digestive juices in the stomach is reduced. The absorption of nutrients by the intestines appears to be diminished; the elimination of waste material is slower.

One frequent problem with the gastrointestinal system is constipation. This is generally related to age (i.e., weaker muscular contractions moving the waste through the system) and life-style (i.e., poor nutritional habits).

The integumentary system consists of the skin, including the nails and hair. There are numerous age-related changes in the skin, although much of what we see is related to life-style (i.e., too much sun prematurely ages the skin). The skin will generally become dryer and thinner. It has a diminished capacity to regulate body temperature. There are also changes in the hair and nails. The hair generally becomes thinner and loses its pigmentation. Nails grow slower. Itching and pressure sores are two frequent conditions affecting the integumentary system.

The muscular system appears to undergo age-related changes, but most of what we actually witness is a result of life-style. Generally, there is a reduction in muscle tissue and an increase in fatty tissue with increasing age. Part of this is age-related; most is due to more sedentary life-styles with increasing age.

The neurosensory system is very complex and includes the brain, nervous system, and senses. There appear to be age-related changes in the brain in terms of a reduction in weight, blood flow, and electrical activity. There are also age-related changes in the senses, with declines taking place in vision and hearing. Although taste and smell generally decline with increasing age, the cause has not been established. Stroke is one of the major conditions affecting the neurosensory system. Cataracts and glaucoma are two conditions that affect the eyes of older persons.

The reproductive system is also discussed in Chapter 7, "Sexuality." There are changes for both males and females. For females the most noticeable change is generally menopause. For both males and females the sex organs undergo age-related changes. A common problem in the reproductive system for men involves the prostate. It often enlarges with increasing age causing problems. For women, breast cancer is a frequent disorder.

The respiratory system undergoes age-related changes which are often exacerbated by certain life-styles, such as smoking. Generally we see declines in the capability of the lungs to expand and contract, as well as in the ability of the lungs to absorb oxygen.

The skeletal system gives shape, support, and protection to the body. There are many age-related changes. Bones, generally, lose density with increasing age. Part of the skeletal system is the teeth. Although most current older persons have lost some or all of their teeth, this is most likely a result of life-style, not aging. Osteoporosis is a condition that affects the bones. It is a loss of bone mass. This is a silent, progressive disease that often leads to bone fractures.

The urinary system undergoes several age-related changes. In the kidneys there is a reduction in the filtration rate. The bladder's capacity is reduced. Urinary incontinence is the involuntary loss of urine. This is a problem that can have devastating effects on older persons, since it often reduces their social contacts. Frequently it is a manageable problem.

REFERENCES

Adler, W. H. (1974). An "autoimmune" theory of aging. In M. Rockstein, M. L. Sussman, & J. Chesky (Eds.), *Theoretical aspects of aging* (pp. 33–42). New York: Academic Press.

Albright, F., Smith, P. H., & Richardson, A. M. (1941). Postmenopausal osteoporosis. *Journal of the American Medical Association,* **116**(22): 2465–2474.

Allman, R. M. (1989). Pressure ulcers among the elderly. *New England Journal of Medicine,* **320**(13): 850–853.

Ames, B. N. (1983). Dietary carcinogens and anticarcinogens: Oxygen radicals and degenerative disease. *Science,* **221**(4617): 1256–1264.

Bafitis, H., & Sargent, F. (1977). Human physiological adaptability through the life sequence. *Journal of Gerontology,* **32**(4): 402–410.

Baigis-Smith, Jr., Smith, D. A. J., Rose, M., & Newman, D. K. (1989). Managing urinary incontinence in community-residing elderly persons. *The Gerontologist,* **29**(2): 229–233.

Bales, C. W. (1989). Nutritional aspects of osteoporosis: Recommendations for the elderly at risk. In M. P. Lawton (Ed.), *Annual review of gerontology and geriatrics* (pp. 7–34). New York: Springer.

Barker, J. C., & Mitteness, L. S. (1988). Nocturia in the elderly. *The Gerontologist,* **28**(1): 99–104.

Barzel, M. S. (1987). Osteoporosis. In G. L. Maddox (Ed.), *The encyclopedia of aging* (pp. 506–508). New York: Springer.

Berman, R., Haxby, J. V., & Pomerantz, R. S. (1988). Physiology of aging, Part 1: Normal changes. *Patient Care,* **22**(1): 20–36.

Bjorksten, J. (1974). Crosslinkage and the aging process. In M. Rockstein, M. L. Sussman, & J. Chesky (Eds.), *Theoretical aspects of aging* (pp. 43–59). New York: Academic Press.

Blechman, W. J., Roth, S. H., & Wilske, K. R. (1988). Are you up to date on osteoarthritis? *Patient Care,* **22**(6): 57–85.

Brody, H. (1987). Central nervous system. In G. L. Maddox (Ed.), *The encyclopedia of aging* (pp. 108–112). New York: Springer.

Bromley, D. B. (1974). *The psychology of human ageing* (second edition). Baltimore: Penguin Books.

Burnside, I. M. (1976). The special senses and sensory deprivation. In I. M. Burnside (Ed.), *Nursing and the aged* (pp. 380–397). New York: McGraw-Hill.

Bush, J. F. (1987). Osteoporosis: When first-line treatment fails. *Medical Aspects of Human Sexuality,* **21**(10): 28–34.

Carter, D. M., & Balin, A. K. (1983). Dermatological aspects of aging. *Medical Clinics of North America,* **67**(2): 531–543.

Corso, J. F. (1977). Auditory perception and communication. In J. E. Birren & K. W. Schaie (Eds.), *Handbook of the psychology of aging* (pp. 535–553). New York: Van Nostrand Reinhold.

Daniell, H. W. (1976). Osteoporosis of the slender smoker. *Archives of Internal Medicine,* **136**(3): 298–304.

Daniell, H. W. (1983). Postmenopausal tooth loss: Contributions to edentulism by osteoporosis and cigarette smoking. *Archives of Internal Medicine,* **143**(9): 1678–1682.

Engen, T. (1977). Taste and smell. In J. E. Birren & K. W. Schaie (Eds.), *Handbook of psychology of aging* (pp. 554–561). New York: Van Nostrand Reinhold.

Epstein, M. (1985). Aging and the kidney: Clinical implications. *American Family Practice,* **31**(4): 123–138.

Ernst, M., & Shore, H. (1975). *Sensitizing people to the processes of aging: The in-service educator's guide.* Dallas: Dallas Geriatric Research Institute.

Exton-Smith, A. N. (1985). Mineral metabolism. In C. E. Finch & E. L. Schneider (Eds.), *Handbook of the biology of aging* (second edition) (pp. 511–539). New York: Van Nostrand Reinhold.

Finch, C. B. (1976). Biological theories of aging. In I. M. Burnside (Ed.), *Nursing and the aged* (pp. 92–98). New York: McGraw-Hill.

Groth, K. (1988). Age-related changes in the gastrointestinal tract. *Geriatric Nursing,* **9**(5): 278–280.

Hallal, J. C. (1985). Osteoporotic fractures exact a toll. *Journal of Gerontological Nursing,* **11**(8): 13–19.

Harman, D. (1968). Prolongation of the normal lifespan and inhibition of spontaneous cancer by antioxidants. *Journal of Gerontology,* **23**(4): 298–300.

Harman, S. M., & Talbert, G. B. (1985). Reproductive aging. In C. E. Finch & E. L. Schneider (Eds.), *Handbook of the biology of aging* (pp. 457–510). New York: Van Nostrand Reinhold.

Hayflick, L. (1974). The longevity of cultured human cells. *Journal of the American Geriatrics Society,* **22**(1): 1–12.

Hayflick, L. (1977). The cellular basis for biological aging. In C. E. Finch & L. Hayflick (Eds.), *Handbook of the biology of aging* (pp. 159–188). New York: Van Nostrand Reinhold.

Hayflick, L. (1980). The cell biology of human aging. *Scientific American,* **242**(1): 58–65.

Hayflick, L. (1985). Theories of biological aging. *Experimental Gerontology,* **20**(2): 145–159.

Hayflick, L. (1987). Biological aging theories. In G. L. Maddox (Ed.), *The encyclopedia of aging* (pp. 64–68). New York: Springer.

Hayflick, L., & Moorehead, M. (1961). The serial cultivation of human diploid cell strains. *Experimental Cell Research,* **25**(6): 585–621.

Heitkemper, M., & Bartol, M. A. (1987). Gastrointestinal problems. In D. L. Carnevali & M. Patrick (Eds.), *Nursing management for the elderly* (second edition) (pp. 423–446). New York: Lippincott.

Heller, B. R., Whitehead, W. E., & Johnson, L. D. (1989). Incontinence. *Journal of Geriatric Nursing,* **15**(5): 16–23.

Herr, J. J. (1976). Psychology of aging: An overview. In I. M. Burnside (Ed.), *Nursing and the aged* (pp. 36–44). New York: McGraw-Hill.

Herzog, A. R., Diokno, A. C., & Fultz, N. H. (1989). Urinary incontinence: Medical and psychosocial aspects. In M. P. Lawton (Ed.), *Annual review of gerontology and geriatrics: Volume Nine* (pp. 74–119). New York: Springer.

Jensen, J., & Tondevold, E. (1979). Mortality after hip fracture. *Acta Orthopedica Scandinavia,* **50**(2):161.

Kart, C. S. (1976). Some biological aspects of aging. In C. S. Kart & B. B. Manard (Eds.), *Aging in America* (pp. 179–183). Port Washington, NY: Alfred Publishing.

Kart, C. S., Metress, E. K., & Metress, S. P. (1988). *Aging, health, and society.* Boston: Jones and Bartlett.

Kenshalo, D. R. (1977). Age changes in touch, vibration, temperature, kinesthesis, and pain. In J. E. Birren & K. W. Schaie (Eds.), *Handbook of the psychology of aging* (pp. 562–579). New York: Van Nostrand Reinhold.

Kligman, A. M., Grove, G. L., & Balin, A. K. (1985). Aging of human skin. In C. E. Finch & E. L. Schneider (Eds.), *Handbook of the biology of aging* (second edition) (pp. 820–841). New York: Van Nostrand Reinhold.

Krane, R. J., & Siroky, M. B. (1981). Diagnosis and treatment of urinary incontinence. In C. Eisdorfer (Ed.), *Annual review of gerontology and geriatrics* (pp. 385–402). New York: Springer.

Lakatta, E. G. (1985). Heart and circulation. In C. E. Finch & E. L. Schneider (Eds.), *Handbook of the biology of aging* (second edition) (pp. 377–413). New York: Van Nostrand Reinhold.

Linde, M. (1986). Cerebrovascular accidents. In D. L. Carnevali & M. Patrick (Eds.), *Nursing management for the elderly* (second edition) (pp. 379–402). New York: Lippincott.

Lindquist, O., & Bengtsson, C. (1979). The effect of smoking on menopausal age. *Maturitas,* **1**(1): 141.

Lyles, K. W. (1987). Endocrine system. In G. L. Maddox (Ed.), *The encyclopedia of aging* (pp. 208–211). New York: Springer.

McCormick, K. A., Scheve, A. S. S., & Leahy, E. (1988). Nursing management of urinary incontinence in geriatric inpatients. *Nursing Clinics of North America,* **23**(1): 231–264.

Mayer, P. J. (1987). Biological theories of aging. In P. Silverman (Ed.), *The elderly as pioneers* (pp. 17–53). Bloomington: Indiana University Press.

Miller, G. (1985). Osteoporosis: Is it inevitable? *Journal of Gerontological Nursing,* **11**(3): 10–15.

Mitteness, L. S. (1987). The management of urinary incontinence by community-living elderly. *The Gerontologist,* **27**(2): 185–193.

Noelker, L. S. (1988). Incontinence in elderly cared for by family. *Nursing Clinics of North America,* **23**(1): 139–157.

Palmer, M. H. (1988). Incontinence: The magnitude of the problem. *Nursing Clinics of North America,* **23**(1): 139–157.

Pettigrew, D. (1989). Investing in mouth care. *Geriatric Nursing,* **10**(1): 22–24.

Plude, D. J. (1987). Sensory, perceptual, and motor function in human aging. In P. Silverman (Ed.), *The elderly as modern pioneers* (pp. 94–113). Bloomington: Indiana University Press.

Raisz, L. G. (1988). Local and systemic factors in the pathogenesis of osteoporosis. *New England Journal of Medicine,* **318**(13): 818–825.

Rango, N. (1985). The social epidemiology of accidental hypothermia among the aged. *The Gerontologist,* **25**(4): 424–430.

Reaching consensus on incontinence (1989). *Geriatric Nursing,* **10**(2): 78–80.

Resnick, N. M., Yalla, S. V., & Laurino, E. (1989). The pathophysiology of urinary incontinence among institutionalized elderly persons. *New England Journal of Medicine,* **320**(1): 1–7.

Riehle, R. A., & Vaughan, E. D. (1983). Genitourinary disease in the elderly. *Medical Clinics of North America,* **76**(2): 445–461.

Rivlin, R. S. (1986). Osteoporosis: Nutrition. *Public Health Reports,* **104**(4 Supplement): 131–136.

Roberto, K. A. (1988). Women with osteoporosis: The role of the family and service community. *The Gerontologist,* **28**(2): 224–228.

Roberts, J. C. (1987). Eye: Structure and function. In G. L. Maddox (Ed.), *The encyclopedia of aging* (pp. 245–247). New York: Springer.

Roberts, S. L. (1976a). Cardiopulmonary abnormalities in aging. In I. M. Burnside (Ed.), *Nursing and the aged* (pp. 286–316). New York: McGraw-Hill.

Roberts, S. L. (1976b). Renal abnormalities in aging. In I. M. Burnside (Ed.), *Nursing and the aged* (pp. 316–345). New York: McGraw-Hill.

Rockstein, M., & Sussman, M. (1979). *Biology of aging.* Belmont, CA: Wadsworth.

Rossman, I. (1975). Human aging changes. In I. M. Burnside (Ed.), *Nursing and the aged* (pp. 92–98). New York: McGraw-Hill.

Rossman, I. (1977). Anatomic and body composition changes with aging. In C. E. Finch & L. Hayflick (Eds.), *The handbook of the biology of aging* (pp. 189–221). New York: Van Nostrand Reinhold.

Rowe, J. W., & Kahn, R. L. (1987). Human aging: Usual and successful. *Science,* **237**(4811): 143–149.

Schiffman, S. S. (1987). Taste. In G. L. Maddox (Ed.), *The encyclopedia of aging* (pp. 655–658). New York: Springer.

Schiffman, S. S., & Pasternak, M. (1979). Decreased discrimination of food odors in the elderly. *Journal of Gerontology,* **34**(1): 73–79.

Schneider, E., & Reed, J. (1985). Life extension. *New England Journal of Medicine,* **312**(18): 1159–1168.

Scileppi, K. P. (1983). Bone and joint disease in the elderly. *Medical Clinics of North America,* **67**(2): 517–530.

Seeman, E., Melton, L. J., O'Fallon, W. M., & Riggs, B. L. (1983). Risk factors for spinal osteoporosis in men. *American Journal of Medicine,* **75**(6): 977–983.

Selmanowitz, V. J., Rizer, R. L., & Orentreich, N. (1977). Aging of the skin and its appendages.

In C. E. Finch & L. Hayflick (Eds.), *Handbook of the biology of aging,* (pp. 496–512). New York: Van Nostrand Reinhold.

Shanck, A. H. (1976). Musculoskeletal problems in aging. In I. M. Burnside (Ed.), *Nursing and the aged* (pp. 365–379). New York: McGraw-Hill.

Shock, N. W. (1962). The physiology of aging. *Scientific American,* **206**(1): 100–110.

Shock, N. W. (1974). Physiology of aging. In W. C. Bier (Ed.), *Aging: Its challenge to the individual and to the society* (pp. 47–60). New York: Fordham University Press.

Shock, N. W. (1977). Physiological aspects of aging in man. In J. E. Birren & K. W. Schaie (Eds.), *Handbook of the psychology of aging* (pp. 97–122). New York: Van Nostrand Reinhold.

Smith, E. L., Sempos, C. T., & Purvis, R. W. (1981). Bone mass and strength decline with age. In E. L. Smith & R. C. Serfass (Eds.), *Exercise and aging: The scientific basis* (pp. 59–88). Hillside, NJ: Enslow.

Sobel, S. (1986). Osteoporosis: Regulatory view. *Public Health Reports,* **104**(4 Supplement): 136–139.

Solomen, N., Shock, N. W., & Aughenbaugh, P. S. (1970). The biology of aging. In A. M. Hoffman (Ed.), *The daily needs and interests of older people* (pp. 195–208). Springfield, IL: Thomas.

Specht, J. (1986). Genitourinary problems. In D. L. Carnevali & M. Patrick (Eds.), *Nursing management for the elderly* (second edition) (pp. 447–464). New York: Lippincott.

Steinberg, K. K. (1986). Introductory remarks. *Public Health Reports,* **104**(4 Supplement): 125–127.

Stengel, G. B. (1986). Vision problems. In D. L. Carnevali & M. Patrick (Eds.), *Nursing management for the elderly* (second edition) (pp. 586–600). New York: Lippincott.

Strehler, B. L. (1962). *Time cells and aging.* New York: Academic Press.

Strehler, B. L. (1973). A new age for aging. *Natural History,* **82**(2): 9–18, 82–85.

Strehler, B. L. (1982). Aging: Concepts and theories. In A. Viidik (Ed.), *Lectures on gerontology, Volume One* (pp. 1–56). New York: Academic Press.

Thompson, J. S., Wekstein, D. R., Rhoades, J. L., Kirkpatrick, C., Brown, S. A., Roszman, T., Straus, R., & Tietz, N. (1984). The immune status of healthy centenarians. *Journal of the American Geriatric Society,* **32**(4): 274–281.

Tonna, E. A. (1977). Aging of the skeletal-dental systems and supporting tissues. In C. E. Finch & L. Hayflick (Eds.), *Handbook of the biology of aging* (pp. 470–495). New York: Van Nostrand Reinhold.

Tonna, E. A. (1987). Collagen. In G. L. Maddox (Ed.), *The encyclopedia of aging* (pp. 129–130). New York: Springer.

Tulloch, G. J. (1989). The incontinency taboo. *Geriatric Nursing,* **10**(1):19.

Walford, R. L. (1969). *The immunological theory of aging.* Baltimore: Williams and Wilkins.

Weg, R. B. (1973). Changing physiology of aging: Normal and pathological. In R. H. Davis (Ed.), *Aging: Prospects and issues* (pp. 43–56). Los Angeles: Ethel Percy Andrus Gerontology Center, University of Southern California.

Weg, R. B. (1975). The physiology of aging: Normal and pathological. In D. S. Woodruff & J. E. Birren (Eds.), *Aging: Scientific perspectives and social issues* (pp. 229–256). New York: Van Nostrand.

Weg, R. B. (1976). Changing physiology of aging. In D. S. Woodruff & J. E. Birren (Eds.), *Aging: Scientific perspectives and social issues* (pp. 99–112). New York: McGraw-Hill.

Weg, R. B. (1983). Changing physiology of aging. In D. S. Woodruff & J. E. Birren (Eds.), *Aging: Scientific perspectives and social issues* (second edition) (pp. 242–284). Monterey, CA: Brooks/Cole.

Weissman, B. N. (1986). Osteoporosis: Radiologic and nuclear medicine procedures. *Public Health Reports,* **104**(4 Supplement): 127–131.

Whitbourne, S. K. (1985). *The aging body: Physiological changes and psychological consequences.* New York: Springer.

White, L. R., Cartwright, W. S., Cornoni-Huntley, J., & Brock, D. B. (1986). Geriatric epidemiology. In C. Eisdorfer (Ed.), *Annual review of gerontology and geriatrics: Volume Six* (pp. 215–312). New York: Springer.

Wild, L. (1986). Cardiovascular problems. In D. L. Carnevali & M. Patrick (Eds.), *Nursing management for the elderly* (second edition) (pp. 361–378). New York: Lippincott.

Woodruff, D. S. (1975). A physiological perspective on the psychology of aging. In D. S. Woodruff & J. E. Birren (Eds.), *Aging: Scientific perspectives and social issues* (pp. 179–200). New York: Van Nostrand.

CHAPTER 6

PHYSICAL HEALTH

George Bellrose/Stock, Boston

INTRODUCTION

Health is a complex term to define (see Kovar, 1987). The World Health Organization has defined health as "a state of complete physical, mental, and social well-being and not merely the absence of disease and infirmity" (World Health Organization, 1946). What constitutes "good" health for individuals in one life period may constitute poor health in a different life period. Also, what constitutes "good" health for some may constitute "poor" health for others (see Levkoff et al., 1987). Individuals are willing to accept different health states as "normal," depending on past health and current demands and expectations. At best, the term health is a subjective one. The hypochondriac can be declared medically in "good" health and yet voice many physical complaints. On the other hand, individuals who have recuperated from major illnesses, injuries, or surgical procedures may claim that their health, even though markedly reduced from that of previous levels, is very good in comparison to what it was when they were incapacitated.

This chapter will examine the physical health of older persons in contemporary American society (Chapter 8, "Psychological Aspects," will examine mental health). This chapter is divided into six sections that discuss the following topics: the importance of health, health characteristics, hospitalization, the current health status, factors that determine physical health, and medical swindles.

IMPORTANCE OF HEALTH

Health is obviously an important factor in the lives of older persons. Health status can determine not only the activities individuals can engage in but the extent of their participation. The presence or absence of good health also has a bearing on an individual's ability to successfully complete certain tasks or activities. Poor health can make individuals dependent on others for some of the basic necessities of life and can force them to deplete decades of savings in a relatively short period of time on health care. Self-assessed health is one of the most important variables influencing life satisfaction (see Cockerham et al., 1983). In essence, health is one of the most important aspects in old age for determining quality of life.

HEALTH CHARACTERISTICS OF OLDER PERSONS

In the previous chapter it was pointed out that with increasing age biological and physiological declines generally take place. This fact is well known; therefore it becomes relatively easy to perceive older persons as frail, sick, and decrepit individuals near death. In actuality the majority of older persons present a far different picture. Although there are physical declines in most older persons, this does not necessarily mean that they are incapacitated. It should be remembered that although declines generally take place, most physiological systems of younger individuals have a reserve capacity and are capable of performing at levels above need. Thus, there can be a dramatic decline in a particular area without a significant impact on the functioning of the individual and declines may not be apparent or cause limitations for decades.

The literature also indicates that although physical changes may bring about limitations, older persons can often regain lost functioning through surgery, drug therapy, rehabilitation, life-style modifications, or prosthetic environments.

We will now examine some health characteristics of older persons. Specifically we will examine acute and chronic conditions, and self-assessed health.

Acute Conditions

Acute conditions are those that are temporary such as a cut, the flu, or a cold. As is shown by Table 6-1, with one or two exceptions, the rates of acute conditions decrease with increasing age.

However, when acute conditions occur in older persons their impact can often be more severe than for younger individuals. This fact is readily apparent from an examination of the duration of illness in the aged population. Although individuals 65+ have fewer acute conditions, they spend three times as many days in restricted activity because of acute conditions than do younger individuals (National Center for Health Statistics, 1984b). The reasons for the increased severity can vary. One reason deals with declines in circulation and immune reaction. Because of declines in these areas older persons with wounds (i.e., surgical incisions, pressure sores, cuts, blisters, etc.) will have a slower healing time and a greater opportunity for infection to occur. A second reason that an acute disorder, such as the flu, can often be more severe, even lethal, is that many older persons are not physiologically strong enough to fight the infection, or they may have other disorders and conditions that interact with the flu to have deleterious consequences.

As was noted earlier, generally there is a tapering off of acute conditions through life; this decline is explained partly by the fact that many acute disorders are "childhood diseases," such as mumps and measles, to which most older persons have acquired immunity. It is also partly explained by the fact that most older persons are not in contact with as many people from whom they might acquire an acute condition,

TABLE 6-1
ACUTE CONDITIONS BY TYPE AND SELECTED CHARACTERISTICS
Rate Per 100 Population, 1987

	Infective and parasitic	Respiratory		Digestive system	Injuries
		upper	other		
1987 total	23.2	35.5	44.6	6.3	27.0
Under 5 years	57.0	97.5	62.7	10.7	25.9
5–17 years	44.8	53.3	58.1	8.4	33.5
18–24 years	22.5	29.8	58.3	7.9	33.3
25–44 years	18.2	28.2	46.0	5.0	28.5
45–64 years	7.8	21.4	28.3	3.3	18.2
65+ years	5.5	14.3	20.4	6.8	21.7

Source: U.S. Bureau of the Census, 1990.

such as the flu. Additionally, their activity levels are also generally less physical, thus reducing the likelihood of injuries such as cuts, sprains, or broken bones.

Chronic Conditions

Older persons are more affected by chronic conditions than are younger age groups. A chronic condition is defined as one that the individual has had for at least 3 months or one that belongs to a specific group of conditions (e.g., arthritis). Many chronic conditions are permanent or will affect the individual for a significant period of time. The chronic conditions that most frequently affect those in contemporary American society are presented in Table 6-2.

As can be seen the four leading chronic conditions for older persons are arthritis, high blood pressure, hearing impairments, and heart conditions. As would be expected, the major chronic conditions differ for each age group as do the rates. For example, for those under 18 years of age the four leading chronic conditions are hay fever,

TABLE 6-2
PERSONS WITH SELECTED CHRONIC CONDITIONS BY AGE AND SEX: 1987
Rate per 1000 Persons

	Under 18 years	18–44 years	45–64 years	65–74 years	75+ years
Heart conditions	22.2	40.7	126.1	284.7	322.2
High blood pressure	3.2	61.8	252.0	392.4	337.0
Varicose veins of lower extremities	.7	26.8	54.1	82.5	64.8
Hemorrhoids	.6	46.9	79.7	74.1	73.1
Chronic bronchitis	62.1	40.4	56.9	86.9	58.2
Asthma	52.5	34.5	36.3	39.0	37.8
Chronic sinusitis	57.6	149.5	192.1	154.0	131.4
Hay fever, allergic rhinitis without asthma	64.0	121.2	93.8	89.8	44.9
Dermatitis, including eczema	32.1	38.3	41.8	25.8	39.4
Disease of sebaceous glands	28.0	35.5	9.0	6.7	6.6
Arthritis	2.8	52.8	273.3	463.6	511.9
Diabetes	2.0	11.9	56.4	98.3	98.2
Migraine	8.4	54.0	45.7	18.8	10.5
Diseases of urinary system	7.3	27.8	39.6	54.8	67.7
Visual impairments	10.1	29.3	47.3	56.3	111.2
Cataracts	.2	1.7	18.6	105.2	252.0
Hearing impairments	16.0	54.1	135.6	264.7	348.0
Deformities or orthopedic impairments	35.8	135.4	155.0	154.9	182.0
Frequent indigestion	2.6	28.0	40.5	45.6	40.9
Frequent constipation	7.6	14.4	18.2	50.4	97.9

Source: U.S. Bureau of the Census, 1990.

chronic bronchitis, chronic sinusitis, and asthma. Additionally, the percentage of each age group with one or more chronic conditions increases with increasing age. For the age group 45–65 it is 72 percent. For the age group 65+ years of age it is 86 percent. Those in the age group 65+ are more likely to have multiple chronic conditions.

Studies have indicated that as income goes up, the rate of chronic conditions goes down. The reverse is also true; that is, as income goes down, the rate of chronic conditions goes up. Race is also a factor in restrictive chronic conditions. The data indicates that whites have a lower rate of incapacitating chronic conditions than other races. Education also relates to restrictive chronic conditions. With increasing levels of education, incapacitating chronic conditions go down. The reverse is also true (Wilder, 1973).

Although most older persons have chronic conditions, a more important question deals with how these chronic conditions influence activity levels. Table 6-3 indicates the leading chronic conditions causing activity limitations. Activity limitations are defined as the "inability to carry on the major activity of one's age-sex group, such as working, keeping house, or going to school; restriction in the amount or kind of major activity; or restriction in relation to other activities, such as recreational, church, or civic interest" (National Center for Health Statistics, 1985). The table shows that the two leading chronic conditions limiting activities in older persons are arthritis/rheumatism and heart disease (see Weg, 1975b). The older conditions, in order of frequency of activity limitation, are hypertension, impairment of the lower extremities and hips, and impairment of the back and spine.

Another important question deals with how older persons with chronic conditions view the quality of their lives. Pearlman and Uhlmann (1988) examined the perception of life assessment of older persons who had at least one chronic disease. Generally, they viewed their quality of life as such that they had "no major complaints." When the researchers compared the ratings of older persons on the quality of their lives and the rating made by their physicians, the ratings of the physicians consistently

TABLE 6-3
PERSONS WITH ACTIVITY LIMITATIONS BY SELECTED CHRONIC CONDITIONS, 1985

	Under 45 years	45–64 years	65+ years
Percent limited by:			
Heart conditions	4.7	21.5	27.1
Arthritis and rheumatism	5.4	22.8	29.7
Hypertension	2.9	15.2	14.2
Impairment of back/spine	12.5	10.4	4.4
Impairment of lower extremities and hips	10.7	8.2	7.8
Percent of all persons with:			
No activity limitation	92.8	76.6	60.4
Activity limitation	7.2	23.4	39.6
In a major activity	4.9	17.5	24.1

Source: U.S. Bureau of the Census, 1990.

fell below those of the older persons. The researchers observed that there are many variables that determine quality of life for older persons and that physicians consistently underestimated quality of life for older persons.

Self-Assessed Health

Although we can note that older persons have more chronic conditions and activity limitations, this information does not tell us how older persons conceptualize their health. One study by the National Center for Health Statistics (1987a) had individuals subjectively rate their health. The results are in Table 6-4.

As can be seen, the figures remain fairly constant after age 65. The constancy of the figures is caused by two factors. First, those with the most serious conditions have died leaving those in the "excellent or very good" and "good" categories as survivors. Second, older persons may be willing to accept lower health status as "excellent or very good." It can also be seen that a significant percentage in all age categories define their health as excellent or very good, even though they are affected with a variety of chronic conditions. Thus, many chronic conditions, even though they may produce activity limitations, do not negatively influence subjective assessment of health status. Chronic conditions and limitations need to be viewed from the perspective of the individual and that individual's assessment of how the condition impacts on his or her life.

HOSPITALIZATION

Older persons are more likely than those in other age groups to require short-term hospitalization. Table 6-5 presents the days of care per 1000 persons by age category and the average stay in days.

As can be seen, after infancy there is a drop in hospital utilization rate. The increase starts in early adulthood and by ages 45–64 significant increases have taken place. We see increases for each successive age category. The average stay in length of days is also highest for those 65+ years of age, reflecting the seriousness of the condition, the weakened state of the individual, and the interaction of several conditions

TABLE 6-4
RESPONDENT-ASSESSED HEALTH STATUS

	Excellent or very good, %	Good, %	Fair or poor, %
55–64 years	44.8	30.4	24.2
65–74 years	36.2	31.7	31.7
75–84 years	35.2	30.5	33.6
85+ years	35.5	27.8	36.2

Source: Adapted from National Center for Health Statistics, 1987a.

TABLE 6-5
HOSPITAL UTILIZATION RATE, 1987

	Days of care per 1000 persons		Average stay (days)	
Age	Male	Female	Male	Female
Under 1 year	1240	1004	5.8	6.0
1–4 years	223	178	3.5	3.9
5–14 years	182	136	5.0	4.4
15–24 years	351	595	6.3	3.7
25–34 years	442	783	6.6	4.1
35–44 years	542	611	6.4	5.2
45–64 years	1099	1041	6.7	6.9
65–74 years	2445	2174	7.9	8.4
75+ years	4471	3894	8.7	9.3

Source: U.S. Bureau of the Census, 1990.

which increase the need for a longer period of hospitalization. The major reasons for hospitalization are shown in Table 6-6.

Table 6-6 indicates that the major reasons for hospitalization are diseases of the circulatory system, digestive system, and respiratory system, and neoplasms (92 percent are malignant), injury and poisoning, diseases of the genitourinary system, and diseases of the musculoskeletal system.

With efforts to contain hospital costs, there is an increasing emphasis being placed on day hospitals. Geriatric day hospitals provide for medical care, assessment, and rehabilitation. Patients go to the hospital during the day, generally three to four times per week, and then go home at night. Day hospitals allow for early discharge from a hospital or are used as an alternative to hospitalization; both ideally result in

TABLE 6-6
MAJOR REASONS FOR HOSPITALIZATION
Rate per 10,000 population

Diagnosis	45–64 years	65+ years
All conditions	1622.2	3673.1
Diseases of the circulatory system	381.5	1145.3
Diseases of the digestive system	217.1	441.7
Diseases of the respiratory system	130.0	407.6
Neoplasms (i.e., tumors)	171.9	359.6
Injury and poisoning	124.6	279.8
Diseases of the genitourinary system	136.2	257.4
Diseases of the musculoskeletal system	142.0	189.1

Source: National Center for Health Statistics, 1987a.

equal or greater care at a lower cost. A summary of day hospitals found them to be very effective in terms of care; however it was also reported that the costs were greater than for hospitalization since the length of utilization was somewhat greater, and because there were transportation costs to and from the hospital (Eagle et al., 1987).

Early or more efficient discharge of patients is also becoming a reality under certain medical insurance systems where the amount that will be paid to care providers (e.g., physicians, hospitals) is fixed for specific medical conditions. This can mean that patients are discharged with more posthospitalization medical needs.

CURRENT HEALTH STATUS OF OLDER PERSONS

Many gerontologists have been asking, "Is the health status of older persons, as a group, getting better, remaining constant, or becoming worse?" In trying to answer this question gerontologists have come up with two very different answers.

The first answer is that the health status of those 65+ years of age is getting worse and will continue to do so. The explanation is that the aged population is itself aging. Thus because the aged population is getting older, gerontologists have theorized that the health status of older persons is and will continue to decline over the next several decades.

However, in the second answer, gerontologists have said that the health status of those 65+ years of age is improving and will continue to do so. This improvement is explained by intervening factors that offset the aging influence. For example, individuals currently reaching old age have generally been subjected to better nutritional, environmental, medical, and health standards than previous generations. Thus, they are in better health when they reach old age. Also, medical insurance, such as medicare and medicaid, has and will continue to provide for access to more and better health care. There are also more programs that assist older persons in maintaining health (see Bender & Hart, 1987). For example, there are numerous nutritional programs, such as meals-on-wheels, as well as financial programs, such as Supplemental Security Income, that assist older persons, either directly or indirectly in maintaining health. Last, nursing homes and other long-term care facilities have increased substantially in numbers thus removing a greater percentage of the aged from the community, leaving a "healthier" segment for gerontologists to study (see Palmore, 1976, 1986). For example, one major source of information on the health of older persons has come from the National Health Interview Survey, which *only* examined noninstitutionalized individuals; thus the data from this survey will make older persons appear "healthier" than if a sample from the total population had been used (National Center for Health Statistics, 1986*a*, 1986*b*, 1986*c*).

Palmore (1976, 1986) examined data from the National Center for Health Statistics from 1961 to 1981 that sheds light on the question and the answers presented above. Palmore examined seven categories of illness and disability.

1 Days of restricted activity. Restricted activity days referred to days when individuals reduced their usual activities because of an illness of injury.

2 Days of bed disability. This category referred to days when individuals were in bed because of an injury or illness.

3 Injuries. Injuries consisted of the number of injuries per 100 individuals on a yearly basis.

4 Acute conditions. An acute condition was defined as one lasting less than 6 months and which required medical attention or restricted activity.

5 Visual impairments. For a visual impairment an individual had to have vision problems even with glasses.

6 Severe visual impairment. Severe visual impairment was defined as the inability to read newspaper print even when wearing glasses.

7 Hearing impairments. Individuals in this category were deaf (in one or both ears), heard a ringing noise, used a hearing aid, or had other hearing problems.

Palmore concluded that all the measures indicated an increase in the health of older persons between 1961 to 1981.

Where do we go from here? In the future, will the health of older persons become better or worse? As might be expected, there are different projections. The projections are more than idle thoughts about the future. If society can make accurate projections, and then plan and implement a health care system based on these projections, future members of society are more likely to receive the health care that they need.

A pessimistic projection makes two assumptions. First, that life expectancy will continue to increase, and second that chronic disorders will continue to occur at about the same age and with the same frequency. If this occurs then the percentage of older persons, and the very old, will increase, and this segment of the population will have chronic disorders that require medical care for longer periods of time, thus increasing the health care needs and costs of older persons (see Schneider & Brody, 1983). With this projection it is sometimes said that the period of chronic illness is "telescoped" or increased.

The optimistic projection also makes certain assumptions. The first is that life expectancy has more or less reached its biological maximum; future medical advances and changes in life-style will not increase it significantly. Second, changes in several areas have made it so that a maximum percentage of the population now reaches old age. That is, premature death, due to factors such as infectious disease and accidents, have been largely eliminated, and future advances will not alter this very much. Third, advances in several areas will delay the onset of chronic diseases. This means that the percentage of older persons will not increase significantly, that the aged population will not continue to grow older, and that the onset of chronic disease and disability will occur later. This will contribute to a shorter period of illness and disability which will occur near the end of life. Health care costs will be reduced because the period of illness and disability will be compressed, and also because most individuals will not be dying from diseases where a "cure" is possible and expensive medical care needed, but from aging where a "cure" is not possible and less expensive medical intervention is needed (see Fries, 1980, 1984). With this projection the period of chronic illness is compressed, and articles refer to the "compression of morbidity."

FACTORS THAT DETERMINE PHYSICAL HEALTH

There are many factors that influence health. If there is one conclusion that can be made about the health of older persons it is that many health problems are not inevitable consequences of aging but the result of life-styles. Factors such as exercise, nutrition, smoking, and body weight are all related to health. With increasing knowledge about the causes of health problems in older persons, individuals will have a greater capability of controlling the onset and the severity of certain health problems. This section will alphabetically examine variables that, depending on the type and amount, can influence health. Specifically this section will examine the impact of alcoholism, drugs, education, exercise, income, medical care, nutrition, race, sex, and smoking on health.

Alcoholism

The consequences of alcoholism in the United States are enormous. Many writers have quantified the economic cost of alcoholism in terms of cost of prevention and treatment programs, or the cost of workdays lost. Although the figures vary, the cost is always in the billions of dollars. The cost in terms of lost careers and opportunities, and dissolved families is more difficult to quantify, but no less significant. Alcohol is a unique drug in that it has acquired legal status while many other ''drugs'' are considered illegal. Given the scientific knowledge on alcohol and its potentially devastating physical consequences, as well as the extent of abuse, it is interesting that more restrictive legislation has been so slow in developing. This is primarily because powerful lobbies have protected alcoholics' privileged status. This can clearly be seen in several areas but none so clearly as drunken driving laws which have traditionally been very lax, even for drunken drivers who kill and maim others, sometimes repeatedly. Fortunately, the laws in this area are being strengthened. Unfortunately, the inadequacy of the laws and the demands for tougher laws have come about only after highly publicized tragedies could no longer be ignored.

Alcohol use is and will continue to be a controversial issue in contemporary American society. Even the terminology is controversial. For example, some believe that the term ''alcoholism'' is inappropriate in part because it has acquired a negative meaning, like social*ism* or commun*ism,* and in part because some believe that more descriptive terminology such as ''alcohol dependence'' or ''alcohol abuse'' are needed. There is also controversy over the classification of alcoholism. Many believe that it is a disease and should be treated like other diseases. Others believe that it is a voluntary life-style selection. Both the definition and classification of alcoholism are important issues but further elaboration is beyond the scope or purpose of this book. This book will use the term alcoholism.

Alcoholism is a problem for all age groups. This section will describe alcoholism for older persons. This is a relatively recent research area, with little research before 1959 and no major studies appearing until the 1970s and 1980s (see Gottheil et al., 1985; Hartford & Samorajski, 1982; Kola & Kosberg, 1981; Maddox et al., 1985; Mishara & Kastenbaum, 1980; Wood & Elias, 1982). Alcoholism is a significant problem that has the potential of accelerating the aging process, disability, and death. In examining alcoholism this subsection will discuss the definition of alcoholism, the percentage of older persons afflicted with alcoholism, its causes, consequences, treatment, and other consequences of alcohol use.

Definition of Alcoholism   There are many definitions of alcoholism. Existing definitions are based on a variety of standards that range from moral beliefs to frequency of use. The American Psychiatric Association's *Diagnostic and Statistical Manual of Mental Disorders* (DSM-III) lists two types of alcoholism: alcohol abuse and alcohol dependency. Alcohol abuse is present when the individual needs alcohol on a daily basis to adequately function, has repeatedly attempted and failed to control his or her drinking behavior, has blackouts, cannot stop drinking, and has alcohol-related social or legal problems (such as work absences, marital problems, drunken driving charges, etc.). Alcohol dependence consists of all of the above plus an increased tolerance for alcohol, meaning that the individual will have to consume more alcohol to achieve the desired effect, and will develop a physical dependency on alcohol which will manifest itself after a reduction or cessation of alcohol consumption in physical symptoms such as "morning shakes."

Older Persons Who Are Alcoholic   As noted above, there have been relatively few studies on older persons who are alcoholic. This is probably for three reasons. First, the percentage of older persons who are alcoholic is lower than for other adult age categories. This may be because the percentage of older persons who drink is lower than for other adult age groups, thus the pool of potential alcoholics is lower, because many younger alcoholics die before they reach old age from alcohol-related diseases or from accidents or suicide, or because older alcoholics have become "nondrinkers," probably because of health concerns associated with drinking. Second, older persons who are alcoholic are less likely to come to the attention of human service agencies. This is largely because they have lower visibility because a greater percentage are retired, widowed, or more socially isolated than other age groups (see Johnson, 1989). Third, there is limited knowledge and concern about older persons who are alcoholic because many older alcoholics are incorrectly diagnosed or not diagnosed by health professionals.

The percentage defined as alcoholic will obviously depend on the definition being utilized as well as the sample being surveyed. A survey of the general older population would find that between 2 and 10 percent are alcoholic. Higher rates are found among males, the widowed, and the never-married (LaGreca et al., 1988; Stern & Kastenbaum, 1984). Those in nursing homes have a rate that is about 20 percent; about 10 percent of those receiving treatment for alcoholism are 60+ years of age (see Atkinson & Schuckit, 1981; Heinemann & Hoffman, 1986).

Causes of Alcoholism   The causes of alcoholism have been debated for decades. The causes will depend on the type of alcoholic that is being examined. Many believe that there are different types of older alcoholics, with early onset and late onset being the most common general categories mentioned. Early onset refers to someone who became an alcoholic before reaching old age. Late onset refers to someone who became an alcoholic after reaching old age. Studies indicate that each category has about 50 percent of older persons who are alcoholic (Dupree et al., 1984; Wood, 1987).

The causes are elusive and will, of course, often differ depending on the type of alcoholism (early or late onset). This section will examine some of the suspected variables related to late onset alcoholism, sometimes called stress induced alcoholism. These variables can also have other consequences, such as depression or suicide. Not all studies have reported that stressful life events precipitate alcoholism (see LaGreca et al., 1988).

Bereavement   In Chapter 17, "Dying and Death," we will find that although difficult, most older persons adjust to the death of a significant other. However, some individuals are unable to adjust. Some of these individuals turn to support groups, religion, or other sources for strength; others turn to alcohol. The death of a significant other can be stressful because of the interpersonal relationship that was severed; the death can also remind the individual of his or her own mortality.

Drinking is often a social activity, where one individual monitors and regulates the drinking behavior of the other. For example, if the drinking of one spouse becomes excessive the other spouse can apply social sanctions to reduce the problem. With bereavement there is frequently no one to monitor the individual's drinking. This can lead to an increased probability of alcoholism. There is also the issue of loneliness. Often after decades of marriage, the death of a spouse or significant other can produce a state of loneliness which may precipitate alcoholism. The treatment of alcoholism in this case can be difficult since the alcoholism can "mask" or hide the loneliness. As a result, alcoholism, not loneliness, is seen as the problem.

Retirement   As we will see in Chapter 13, "Work, Retirement, and Leisure," retirement is an opportunity for most older persons. However, for some it is an endless burden. The second type of individual is likely to seek relief with alcohol. There are several ways retirement can, for some older persons, contribute to alcoholism.

Some individuals are upset with the loss of occupational identity, income, or the work. For others, filling in the excess time is difficult. Many older persons were raised during an era when the workday was 10 to 12 hours and the workweek was 6 days. Consequently, many of them did not develop hobbies or other leisure-time activities. Many others find that the people or things that filled their spare time when they were younger are no longer present in old age. For example, many found that owning a home was time-consuming with maintenance and repairs. However, in old age they may have moved into an apartment, senior high rise, or nursing home where these activities are no longer available to them. Others may find that the activities they engaged in prior to retirement are too expensive to continue in retirement. Still others find that physical limitations prevent them from engaging in a variety of activities that were previously time-consuming. Thus, many older persons find that they have excessive amounts of time that they do not know how to utilize.

Most older persons find ways to fill the time blocks created by retirement. Some go back to school and obtain high school, college, or even graduate degrees. Others start hobbies or expand existing hobbies. Still others develop an interest in reading, writing, or traveling. However, some find that the ways they had planned to use the excess time are not practical. They find that they do not have the skills or patience to write a novel or go back to school, or that travel plans are not practical because of financial or physical limitations.

Older persons thus start to look for ways to fill in the time blocks. Many find that with fewer obligations it is easier to gradually start drinking earlier in the day. Drinking as a social activity can fill in time; the consequences of heavy drinking, such as passing out from drunkenness, can also fill in time.

There is one other way retirement can trigger alcoholism. Earlier we saw that the death of a spouse, or significant other, can trigger alcoholism. So can marriage. Many couples find that marriages that ''worked'' when the partners were apart 8 to 10 hours a day, experience conflict after retirement when the partners are thrown together for an additional 8 to 10 hours per day. Wives find that husbands interfere with and often suggest ways to modify well-established household routines. This can cause conflicts which may lead a partner to seek solitude in a bar, lodge, club, or other facility where drinking is not only a legitimate but an expected behavior, or to seek solace from alcohol at home or in the home of a friend. Fighting between the couple may increase for two reasons. First, the drinking may make the alcoholic aggressive, quarrelsome, and irrational. Second, the nonalcoholic spouse may see the drinking as a waste of time and money and confront the alcoholic.

Physical Illness   The increased frequency of illness and disease that accompanies increasing age is also associated with alcoholism. These problems can restrict mobility, cause pain, force dependency on others, and rapidly deplete decades of savings.

For many individuals there are no medical cures for their problems. Physicians tell them to ''learn to live with their conditions.'' Alcohol, often in ever-increasing amounts, provides some individuals with a ''socially acceptable'' way of dealing with their physical illness. Alcohol may help to deaden chronic pain or produce a semiconscious state where the individual's physical problems are no longer a cause of concern.

There are three problems associated with alcohol use as a source of treatment for medical problems. First, the individual may not seek other medically approved modes of treatment that might help or even eliminate the condition. Second, by using alcohol as an escape from reality, the individual does not have the mental capacity to understand that the condition may eventually lead to a different but satisfactory life. Third, the alcohol may exacerbate the existing condition or create new conditions.

Consequences of Alcoholism   The consequences of alcoholism can be substantial in terms of economic, physical, or social costs. This subsection will examine two of the consequences of alcoholism.

Physical Consequences   The physical consequences of alcoholism are well known and include an increased risk of liver and pancreas damage; mouth, pharynx, larynx, esophagus, and liver cancer; infection; sleep disturbances; heart disease; pneumonia; and osteoporosis. Other consequences are lower rates of androgen production and increased estrogen production in males, anemia, and slower wound healing.

Four additional physical consequences need to be specifically mentioned. The first is drug interaction. As will be mentioned in the next section, older persons consume more over-the-counter (OTC) and prescription drugs than any other age group. Alcohol and drugs can interact in a variety of ways, almost all of them with negative consequences for the individual. Alcohol can nullify the effects of certain drugs while intensifying others to lethal levels. The combination of certain drugs and alcohol can also produce low blood pressure or gastrointestinal bleeding.

The second physical consequence that needs to be mentioned is malnutrition. This can occur because alcohol is substituted for food. Also, when there is not enough money to purchase both alcohol and food, food generally loses out.

The third physical consequence is that alcohol may mask or hide the symptoms of certain physical conditions while the conditions are more amenable to treatment. By the time the alcoholic notices the symptoms and seeks medical assistance, the prognosis may have deteriorated.

The fourth physical consequence is that alcohol may exacerbate existing physical conditions, such as liver disease, or create new illnesses or disabilities.

Social Consequences   A major social consequence is the withdrawal of family and friends. Thus, those most in a position to help the individual are also those who are most affected and who pull away from the alcoholic, often after repeated attempts to help. In fact, it has been reported that older alcoholics do not have large, well-established social networks, although it is not known if this condition existed prior to the alcoholism (Dupree et al., 1984). Other social consequences can be economic, legal problems (such as drunken driving convictions), or work-related problems.

Treatment of Older Alcoholics   There are many types of alcohol treatment programs and their goals can vary tremendously. Treatment programs can consist of in-patient or out-patient programs that can include individual or group therapy, drug therapy, and alcohol education. The goals of the programs can include anything from alcohol abstinence to sobriety to less frequent alcohol use.

Until recently, many older alcoholics were not categorized as having an alcohol-related problem and even if diagnosed were less likely to receive treatment. This has changed somewhat. In the human service field there is an increasing trend to compartmentalize services on the basis of age or some other characteristic, such as financial status or race. The same trend is being seen in treatment programs for alcoholics, namely a specialization of services to specific groups; in this case, late-onset aged alcoholics (see Dupree et al., 1984).

Janik and Dunham (1983) have noted that there are several ''common sense'' reasons to have specific treatment programs for older persons. The reasons include greater difficulty with psychotherapy (especially if it involves confrontation methods), physical limitations that restrict the use of certain drug therapy techniques, lower levels of motivation because of a more advanced age and less optimism about future prospects, transportation problems in attending out-patient treatment programs, and problems in relating to therapists who are often considerably younger than themselves.

To ascertain if treatment programs for older persons were more effective than treatment programs that dealt with a spectrum of ages, Janik and Dunham (1983) examined data from the National Alcoholism Program Information System, which included information on 550 treatment programs. They concluded that there was little support for treatment programs specifically for older persons (see Atkinson & Schuckit, 1981). However, Kofoed and his associates (1987), offered preliminary data indicating that treatment programs for the aged may be more beneficial in bringing about increased compliance with therapy and increased likelihood of completing the treatment program. They believe that further research is needed before any definitive conclusions can be reached.

The major limitation to effective treatment of older alcoholics is that many professionals do not see alcoholism as a problem in the older segment of the population and that many of those who do recognize it as a problem have a limited knowledge base from which to design effective programs (see Brown, 1982; Kola et al., 1984).

Other Consequences of Alcohol Use   This section has addressed alcoholism and examined the negative consequences of alcohol use. Several studies have suggested that there may be some "beneficial" uses of alcohol for older persons. In a summary of studies on older persons Mishara and Kastenbaum (1980) reported that establishing a "cocktail hour" for older persons in institutions decreased the use of certain prescription drugs and reduced sleep problems. Alcohol use was found to increase socialization, friendliness, and make individuals "happier."

The studies did not report any episodes of drunkenness or alcohol abuse. The major problems encountered were not with the patients but with staff members who had personal views on alcohol use and found its use inappropriate in an institution. Although further studies are needed, these preliminary studies indicate some positive consequence of moderate alcohol use.

One additional study on what might be called "social drinking" among healthy older persons living independently in the community did not find any significant differences between the cognitive, psychological, or social functioning of drinkers and nondrinkers (Goodwin et al., 1987).

Drugs

This section will deal with the use of "legal drugs" among older persons. Legal drugs include both prescription and over-the-counter (OTC) drugs.

It has already been pointed out that older persons suffer from more chronic disorders than do other age groups. Consequently, older persons are more likely to use drugs. Drugs can have three effects. First, they can bring about the intended result such as relief from pain, reduction of anxiety, elimination of an infection, or retardation or amelioration of disease. Second, although they often achieve the desired results, drugs can also bring about a number of undesired side effects such as loss of hair or impotence. Third, drug misuse or abuse through both overutilization and underutilization can lead to serious medical complications, sometimes resulting in death (see Brady, 1975; Briganti, 1975; Engel, 1986; Lamy, 1986; Silverstone et al., 1986; Simonson, 1986).

This section is separated into five subsections: drug use, how the aged body handles drugs, drug-related problems, reasons for drug-related problems, programs to reduce drug-related problems.

Drug Use among the Aged   Although the figures vary, studies indicate that older persons use 20 to 25 percent of all prescription drugs (see Krupka & Vener, 1979; Vestal & Dawson, 1985). Krupka and Vener (1979) reported in their study of noninstitutionalized older persons that on a daily basis 67 percent used one or more prescription drugs, 65 percent took one or more OTC drugs, and 98 percent consumed one or more social drugs (e.g., alcohol, caffeine, and nicotine). A further analysis of drug users found that 24 percent took up to two drugs per day, 55 percent took three to five drugs per day, and 22 percent took six or more drugs per day. For those who took drugs, the average number of drugs was prescription 2.0, OTC 1.8, social 1.8.

The most frequently used prescription and nonprescription drugs are analgesics (67 percent), cardiovascular medications (34 percent), laxatives (31 percent), vitamins (29 percent), antacids (26 percent), and antianxiety medications (22 percent) (Vestal & Dawson, 1985).

Drugs and the Aged Body   There are important age-related changes that influence the way the body handles drugs. Remember that the aged population is heterogeneous, and that we need to generalize in this section. In examining how the aged body handles drugs we need to examine absorption, distribution, metabolism, and excretion (see German & Burton, 1989; Omenn, 1982; Weg, 1975b).

Absorption   Drugs can enter the body via intravenous or subcutaneous injection, inhalation, absorption through the skin, orally, from the eye as well as through other means. Most drugs are administered orally. Absorption is concerned with how the drugs circulate within the body.

There are assumed to be some age-related changes that may interfere slightly with the absorption of drugs, although further research is needed in this area. For example, because of the decline in the number of cells and blood flow in the gastrointestinal tract, the absorption of the drug is assumed to be reduced (see Montamat et al., 1989; Santo-Novak & Edwards, 1989).

Distribution   Once absorbed into the bloodstream, drugs circulate to other parts of the body where they can be active, stored, metabolized, or excreted. Changes in body composition with increasing age, such as more body fat and less body water, means that the drug concentration is higher for water-soluble drugs, while for fat-soluble drugs the concentration is reduced. A higher drug concentration can lead to a "drug overdose," while a lower concentration may mean that the drug is too diluted to accomplish its mission.

Metabolism   Drugs are often changed in the body by various metabolic processes that generally take place in the liver. For some drugs this ends their effectiveness; for others the resulting compound is still active, although generally at a reduced level. Those with disorders that contribute to a decline in liver functioning often have a lower rate of drug metabolism.

Excretion   The body can excrete drugs in a variety of ways, such as through urine, feces, or sweat. Kidney functioning, excretion via the intestinal tract, and sweating all decline with increasing age. Thus, in older persons many drugs will be excreted at a slower rate than for younger individuals. This will result in a higher concentration of drugs within the body and can lead to drug-related problems.

Drug-Related Problems   As was noted above, prescription and OTC drug usage increases with increasing age. This increases the probability of drug interactions that will cause detrimental reactions. Older persons have detrimental reactions to drugs three to seven times more frequently than younger age groups (see Goldberg & Roberts, 1983; Montamat et al., 1989), and 12 to 17 percent of all acute hospital admissions of older persons are for adverse drug reactions (Santo-Novak & Edwards, 1989).

Reasons for Drug-Related Problems   There are several reasons for the higher incidence of drug-related problems among older persons which will be discussed in alphabetical order below (see Gaitz & Wilson, 1986).

Chronic Problems   Because older persons often have more than one chronic condition, they frequently take more than one drug. This increases the risk of drug interactions and of having drug-related problems. Additionally, certain chronic conditions can have an impact on physiological functioning which can increase the concentration of a drug and the probability of a drug-related problem. For example, kidney or liver disease can reduce the excretion or metabolism of a drug thus increasing its concentration in the body and increasing the probability of a problem.

Economic Problems   Even with financial assistance through various types of insurance, drugs can be expensive. As a result, older persons may not purchase prescribed drugs or they may modify the drug schedule so that their drugs will last longer. In fact, underutilization is the most common noncompliance error (German & Burton, 1989). Additionally, individuals may not have the money to pay for transportation to and from a pharmacy.

Memory Problem   The individual may forget to take a drug, either as a result of a mental condition or simple "forgetfulness" (see Morrell et al., 1989). Certain drugs may induce confusion or drowsiness thus increasing the risk of memory problems (see Rost & Roter, 1987).

Polypharmacy/Polymedicine   The terms polypharmacy and polymedicine are frequently used to describe "overmedication." Although the term polypharmacy has traditionally been used, pharmacists have objected to this term claiming that it is really an example of polymedicine.

As has been noted, older persons are more likely to use more drugs than other age groups. With greater drug utilization there is a greater likelihood of toxic or adverse drug interactions taking place. The drug interactions are likely to occur especially when individuals are using different physicians for different conditions, with each prescribing drugs that have the potential of interacting in a toxic or adverse manner. Additionally, some physicians prescribe more than one drug and are not aware of the possible toxic or adverse drug interactions.

Some pharmacists may also have limited knowledge of geriatric pharmacy. In fact, when one study asked practicing pharmacists about the "most difficult aspect of geriatric pharmacy," the pharmacists reported that it was "inadequate professional skills or knowledge" (Pratt et al., 1982). This same study reported that when asked to calculate the correct dosage of a commonly prescribed drug for older persons only 20 percent determined the correct dosage.

Scheduling Problems   In a medical facility, such as a nursing home, drugs are administered according to a set schedule. For those living independently in the community, they have to remember to take a drug at a certain time. Scheduling problems can include omission, consuming an incorrect dosage, or the improper timing or sequencing of dosages.

For those living in the community "life events" can frequently create scheduling problems. Individuals may be away from their homes and drugs for longer than expected. They may find themselves at events where certain types of food are being served that will interfere with the absorption of their drugs. Or, because certain drugs need to be taken with or without food, those at social events may find that scheduling a drug in conjunction with the host's schedule is difficult.

Self-Administration   Because most older persons live independently in the community, and their drugs are self-administered, the self-administration of drugs can be a problem. The problems associated with the self-administration of drugs are covered in sections on memory problems and scheduling problems.

Self-Medication   As is noted in the section on nutrition, many older persons take nutritional supplements. Others use OTC drugs to self-medicate certain conditions. Often older persons self-medicate with "leftover" drugs from previous illnesses or friends' previous illnesses. This often results from "self-diagnosis," which obviously has inherent problems. The self-medication can also result in not only drug-related problems but the risk of not treating the disease or disorder at an early stage in its development when it is more amenable to treatment. The individual may also be using outdated drugs that are either not effective or dangerous.

The greatest area of self-medication is with OTC drugs. We are bombarded with advertisements from drug manufacturers about the effectiveness of OTC drugs for any and all physical complaints or symptoms. Older persons, as others, often do not see OTC drugs as "real" drugs. The OTC drugs are often considered "low" power drugs while prescription drugs are considered more powerful drugs. There are many OTC drugs that are very powerful pharmacologically. Additionally, these drugs are often self-prescribed in conjunction with prescription drugs, which can cause a variety of drug-interactions (see Bachur, 1986; Trainor, 1988).

Side Effects of Drugs   Many drugs have undesirable side effects such as constipation, confusion, dizziness, impotence, or diarrhea. Some patients may not take the drugs, or take the drugs on an irregular basis, because of these side effects.

Transportation Problems   Transportation to and from a pharmacy may be a problem because of cost, physical limitations, or fear of crime.

Understanding/Knowledge   Often older persons are given prescriptions with little or no explanation of the purpose of the drug, the scheduling of the drug, the cost of the drug, or the consequences of the drug. For example, certain drugs can have their potency enhanced or reduced depending on whether the drug is taken with or without certain foods (see Alford, 1986; Morrell et al., 1989).

Programs to Reduce Drug-Related Problems   Drug-related problems are now recognized as a major problem for older persons and numerous attempts have been made to reduce the incidence of drug-related problems.

Ostrom (1986) has listed several guidelines for drug compliance in the aged:

1 Make certain that the patient understands the purpose, scheduling, and consequence of the drug. Depending on the patient, the physician might want to ask the patient questions to ascertain the level of patient understanding.

2 Inform the patient of the symptoms of adverse or toxic drug reactions. The patient should be encouraged to carefully monitor his or her condition and report any symptoms.

3 If possible, the scheduling of drugs should be simplified in terms of the number of drugs and the scheduling of drugs (e.g., if medically possible, reduce scheduling from four times a day to twice a day).

4 If necessary, check the cost of the drug being prescribed and ascertain the patient's ability to pay for the drug. Provide a lower-cost drug if possible. If the drug is going to be taken for a long period find out if there is a lower price for a large supply.

5 Provide an aid to assist the patient in drug compliance. This might be a piece of paper listing each drug and when and how it is to be taken. There might also be a form for the patient to note when a drug was taken.

Essentially, there should be a "drug history" provided for each patient. This should include information on drug allergies, past and current drug usage, as well as compliance with drug scheduling. Each existing medication needs to be reevaluated in terms of need and dose. Factors that might influence drugs such as OTC drug usage and nutritional status should also be examined.

A pilot program has been developed using a computer program that analyzed the side effects of medications as well as other physical problems. It was noted that the frequency of drug use and drug changes for older persons as well as the length of time between physician visits could make a readily available monitoring system useful. An easy-to-use computer program was written so that individuals with no computer experience could operate it. The program had the ability to ask up to 400 questions, but based on input most individuals were asked fewer than 20 questions. The computer program was designed to notify users if the symptoms they were experiencing needed to be further analyzed by a physician. The study found that most individuals had little difficulty operating the "user friendly" program. The study concluded that a computer with the above program located in a senior center would be used by older persons and could lead to successful early intervention of medication error or other physical problems (Holmes et al., 1988).

"Shopping-bag days" is another program aimed at reducing drug-related problems. In this program individuals can bring in all their prescriptions (often in shopping bags) so pharmacists can review the purpose, side effects, dangers, and scheduling of each drug, and outdated drugs can be discarded. For many drug stores this is done on a regular basis.

Education

The tendency is for those with higher levels of education to have higher levels of health. Higher levels of education correlate with higher socio-economic status. Those with higher socio-economic status are more likely to have regular, high quality health care (Harris et al., 1989).

Exercise

There is little doubt that we are becoming an exercise-conscious society. The major reason for this is the epidemiological studies that have, since the early 1950s, consistently reported that those who exercise have lower rates of coronary heart disease than those who do not exercise (see Crandall, 1986).

Until recently, using the terms "exercise" and "older persons" in the same sentence would have seemed out of place. Old age was seen as a delicate and precarious time of life. It was widely believed, by both the young and the old, that older persons should lead sedentary, quiet, nonphysical lives. Because of this, senior centers were generally repositories of passive, nonphysical activities such as card games, billiards, knitting, crafts, and shuffleboard. Physical exercise was viewed as an activity that would place too much strain on various parts of the body and cause something to rip, tear, break, or burst.

Changes in the beliefs about older persons and exercise came about because many older persons who exercised found that they not only enjoyed the health benefits, such as weight control and fitness, but also the activity. As a result they started asking about the consequences of exercise on an aging body. Although very little "good" research existed, there were many myths or "common sense" beliefs, most of which said that exercise was harmful, even dangerous, for older persons. Some of the myths were that bones would break, hearts would stop, and muscles would rip. In other words, the consequences of exercise were more dangerous than the consequences of a sedentary life-style.

Gradually some of the myths started to lose their credibility because of expanded research on the number of older persons who were exercising. In the running community Larry Lewis was still running at 104 years of age (Anonymous, 1971). Johnny Kelley at 73 gained international attention when he ran his fiftieth Boston marathon. Jack Foster at 44 placed seventeenth out of 67 in the 1976 Olympic marathon. Dr. Paul Spangler at 84 ran marathons in approximately 5 hours. The list could go on. Basically runners were delighted to find that they did not "hit the wall" at 40, 50, 60, 70, or even 80 (see Dressendorfer, 1980; Maud et al., 1981; Pollock, et al., 1971; Pollock et al., 1974; Pollock, & Ribisl, 1978; Pollock & Willmore, 1974; Shephard & Montelpare, 1988; Webb et al., 1977).

Although the majority of articles on older persons who exercise have been on joggers or runners, there have also been articles on other types of exercise, such as swimming and walking (Moore, 1989; Pollock et al., 1971). Additionally, although many articles have been written on older persons who train and frequently compete in athletic events, there have also been numerous articles on older persons who simply want to exercise.

This section will examine the consequences of exercise, primarily for those who jog or run. The first section will examine the physiological consequences of exercise on older persons. The second will examine the consequences of exercise on the aging process. The third section will examine some of the potential dangers in exercise, and the last section will examine exercise programs for older persons.

Consequences of Exercise   The theories of aging were examined in the previous chapter. Although there is controversy as to why we age, there is less controversy over the reason why many individuals age very rapidly in contemporary American society. The major reason is life-style. Factors such as lack of exercise, smoking, alcohol abuse, inadequate medical care, or nutritional inadequacy can all escalate the aging process. The question becomes, "How much of the aging process is due to a natural aging process and how much is due to life-style?"

The remainder of this section will examine several physiological parameters for those who exercise and the general older population.

Blood Pressure   Blood pressure increases would be expected with increasing age due to an increasing incidence of cardiovascular disease and obesity. In fact, this is what is found: Blood pressure levels generally increase with increasing age. For example, the average reading for a male 18–24 is 124/76. For a male 65–74 the average reading is 142/83. For women the readings are 111/70 and 146/81 (National Center for Health Statistics, 1986c). Thus, we can see that there tends to be an increase in blood pressure with aging. Table 6-7 reports the percentage of the population that has high blood pressure.

The next area that needs to be examined are the blood pressure levels of older persons who exercise. There have been numerous studies in this area (see Crandall, 1986) with the finding that most older persons who exercise have substantially lower blood pressure levels than age peers who do not exercise.

TABLE 6-7
PERCENTAGE OF THE POPULATION WITH
HIGH BLOOD PRESSURE

Age	Men	Women
18–24	16.0	2.0
25–34	20.6	4.4
35–44	25.3	14.9
45–54	40.0	29.1
55–64	46.0	41.3
65–74	53.0	56.2

Source: U.S. Bureau of the Census, 1987a.

Bones The consequences of the aging process on bones was discussed in the last chapter. The question becomes, "Is osteoporosis an inevitable part of the aging process, or is it a result of life-style selections such as sedentary behavior, nutritional problems, and smoking?" As noted in the last chapter, the causes of osteoporosis are varied and include factors such as lack of exercise and calcium, smoking, and bone damage.

It is now believed that bones respond much like other body parts to stress: they strengthen. Basically, if something is not used it tends to atrophy or grow weaker and smaller; if it is used it tends to strengthen. In one 3-year study of older women in a nursing home the nonexercise group was found to have a bone mineral loss of 3.3 percent with the exercise group having a bone mineral gain of 2.3 percent (Smith, 1982). The exercises developed for this group were done for 30 minutes a day, 3 days a week. The exercises were all activities that could be performed while sitting (see Smith, 1981; Smith et al., 1981).

A study on older long-distance runners between the ages of 50 and 72 reported that runners had a bone mineral content that was 40 percent greater than a comparison group of nonrunners (Lane et al., 1986). Increases in bone mineral have also been found among those enrolled in a 4-month exercise program that included an exercise bicycle combined with walking/jogging (Blumenthal et al., 1989).

Cholesterol Cholesterol is a widely discussed topic in contemporary American society. Like blood pressure, cholesterol generally increases with increasing age. Again, this has been assumed to be an inevitable consequence of the aging process. For example, for men 20–24 the average total cholesterol level is 180. By age 65–74 it had increased to 221. For women the corresponding figures are 184 and 246 (National Center for Health Statistics, 1986*b*).

Again, there are numerous studies in this area generally indicating that those who exercise and follow proper dietary guidelines have significantly lower cholesterol levels than those who do not (Hartung & Farge, 1977; Pollock, 1974; Pollock et al., 1974; Tami et al., 1988).

Fat With increasing age lean tissue generally decreases and body fat increases. Young men generally have body fat levels of 10 to 17 percent. For older men the level is 18 to 27 percent. For women the figures are 22 to 34 percent and 29 to 38 percent (see Crandall, 1986). Again the question becomes, "Is it the aging process that produces the increase in body fat or life-style?" Studies by Pollock and his associates (1971, 1974) on older runners, reported body fat levels of 13.6 percent in men 70 to 75 years of age. A study on two female swimmers 70 years of age found body fat levels of 20.3 percent and 26.8 percent (Vaccaro et al., 1981).

Heart One of the primary reasons people exercise is because of benefits to the heart. The consequences of exercise on the heart can be examined by looking at three variables: resting heart rate, maximum heart rate, stroke volume.

After infancy the resting heart rate remains fairly constant throughout the life span of most individuals. For those 20–29 the average resting heart rate for males is 76; for females 78. At ages 70–79 the rates are 77 for both males and females. Thus, the aging process has little impact on resting heart rate.

One aspect of resting heart rate that we might examine is low resting heart rate.

Although at one time seen as a pathological condition, a low resting heart rate is now generally seen as a condition of a healthy heart. The lower heart rate is simply an indicator that the heart needs to pump fewer times to supply the body with blood. Trained endurance athletes frequently have resting heart rates in the thirties or forties. The question for this section is, "Can older runners maintain low resting heart rates?"

The answer is "yes." Studies on older runners have consistently found resting heart rates in the forties, fifties, and sixties (Pollock et al., 1974).

Maximum heart rate is the number of times the heart is capable of beating per minute. The more beats per minute the greater the athletic potential of the individual. It is known that maximum heart rate declines with increasing age. One frequently used way to determine maximum heart rate is to subtract one's age from 220. For example, someone 60 years of age would have a maximum heart rate of 220 minus 60 which equals 160. Studies on the impact of aging on the maximum heart rate indicate that chronic exercise will delay the decline (see Crandall, 1986).

The last area that needs to be examined concerning the heart is stroke volume, which is the amount of blood pumped by the left ventricle with one heart beat. Because this is more complex to measure than the other heart-related variables we have examined, fewer studies exist. During strenuous exercise young untrained men can pump 103 milliliters of blood per beat; highly trained young men can pump up to 210 milliliters per beat. One study on a 71-year-old runner found that his heart pumped 141 milliliters per beat (Dressendorfer, 1980).

Joints   Many individuals have a "wear-and-tear" philosophy concerning exercise. As a result they believe that exercise will literally wear out certain parts of the body. Joints are frequently mentioned. The myths that surround exercise often state that joints frequently used in certain sports are likely to cause individuals problems in later life. Studies of older runners have not found this to be true (Ryan, 1981). The "use it or lose it" rule applies. Exercise generally strengthens joints, it doesn't harm them.

Muscle   As we saw in the last chapter, with increasing age there is generally a decrease in muscle tissue and an increase in body fat. Again, "How much of this is caused by the aging process and how much is caused by the changes in life-style that generally accompany increasing age?" It is difficult to assign an absolute percentage to the amounts caused by aging and life-style. It is believed that both are responsible. Certainly those who exercise delay the amount of muscle tissue that is lost, but studies on athletes who continue to exercise at the same level of intensity over long periods of time are still found to have a decline in muscle mass (Kasch & Kulberg, 1981). What we see here is that while exercise can delay the aging process, often for decades, it cannot prevent it.

VO$_2$max   A term used frequently in exercise science is VO$_2$max. Basically, VO$_2$max is the ability of the body to use oxygen. The higher the VO$_2$max the greater one's athletic potential. VO$_2$max peaks during the early twenties and then declines dramatically with increasing age. Again we need to ask, "Is the decline caused by the aging process or life-style?" One 10-year longitudinal study on track champions 50-82 examined this question. During the 10-year study some of the runners stopped training and others reduced their level of training. About half of the runners continued to train at the same intensity level during the entire 10-year period. For those who continued to train at the same high-intensity level the loss in VO_2max over the 10-year period was 2 percent; for the men who trained at a lower intensity level the decline was 13 percent (see Legwold, 1982). Kasch and his associates (1988) conducted a 20-year longitudinal study on runners who were 45 at the start of the study. At the end of the study the VO_2max of the runners was 40 percent higher than for sedentary individuals of the same age (see Cunningham et al., 1987).

The decline in VO_2max is clearly a function of life-style until about ages 55–60 when declines will start to take place even if the same level or a greater level of exercise is utilized.

Exercise and the Aging Process   "Does exercise slow the aging process?" At the end of what has become a classic article, "Disuse and Aging," Dr. Walter M. Bortz II (1982) related a personal experience of having a leg in a cast for 6 weeks and then observing that the leg had aged 40 years when the cast was removed. He noted that although this is a common observation in medicine, physicians have been slow to accept the value of exercise (see Bortz, 1980).

There is no doubt that exercise can significantly slow the "aging process" for most individuals. How much of the slowing is due to exercise influencing senescence and how much is due to exercise influencing life-style is uncertain. What is certain is that when we examine the consequences of "normal" aging (i.e., increases in cholesterol, blood pressure, body fat; decreases in muscle, VO_2max) that a number of studies clearly indicate that those who exercise can significantly delay the aging process, at least until about 55 to 60 years of age, after which the declines will occur, but still lag far behind those who do not exercise.

Kasch and his associates (1988) conducted a 20-year longitudinal study on fifteen men. The men averaged 45 years of age at the beginning of the study and 65 at the end. The men participated in different types of exercise—walking, swimming, running, or cycling—an average of 3.6 days per week. The average number of calories utilized per week in exercise was 2104. The authors reported that during the study, body weight decreased slightly and that height remained constant. At the end of the study blood pressure averaged 120/77, a reading consistent with that at the beginning of the study (120/79).

VO_2max declined 3 percent by the eighteenth year of the study and 12 percent by the twentieth year. Two of the men had gains in VO_2max over the 20-year study suggesting that the aging process may not be producing all of the drop seen (see Kasch, 1976; Kasch & Kulberg, 1981; Kasch & Wallace, 1976).

The two major causes of death, heart disease and cancer, have even been found to be lower among those who exercise. Epidemiological studies (see Crandall, 1986) have consistently demonstrated that those who exercise have lower rates of heart disease. Recent evidence also suggests that those who exercise have lower rates of cancer (Albanes et al., 1989). In part the lower rates of heart disease and cancer for those who exercise may be attributed to the fact that these individuals are more health conscious.

An article in *Geriatrics* summarized much of the research when it stated,

". . . studies suggest that regular exercise can retard premature aging, help prevent diseases of the cardiovascular system, and slow down the functional decline of the cardiovascular system. . . ." (Kent, 1982).

Potential Dangers of Exercise for Older Persons   The myths that were prevalent one and two decades ago stated that older persons who exercised would be beset with injuries. Essentially it was believed that exercise would do them more harm than good. As stated earlier, part of this belief came from ignorance due to the lack of research. Part was probably also due to the fact that some older persons were "not acting their age." As a society we are tolerant of scantily clad young men and women running through our streets, but we are less tolerant of older men and women engaging in the same activity. Thus, one way of keeping older persons "in their place" was by stressing the hazards of exercise.

The facts today do not support the belief that exercise is dangerous for older persons. Obviously, there are some exceptions, and different types of exercise at various levels of intensity apply to different individuals. However, studies do not indicate a higher rate of injury in older athletes than in younger athletes (see Crandall, 1986; Hogan & Cape, 1984).

However, there are some potential concerns that need to be addressed. The number and level of the concerns will depend on the individual and factors such as health status and previous exercise pattern. The starting point for all older persons considering an exercise program is a thorough physical examination; ideally the physician could also provide some information that would assist the individual in starting and continuing with the exercise program.

One specific area of risk deals with the ability of the body to regulate temperature. Individuals engaged in activity that will increase body temperature, such as running, need to recognize that with increasing age the ability of the body to regulate body temperature decreases, thus increasing the risks of heat-related injuries and death. The same is true of athletes who exercise in the cold while running or skiing. They will be at greater risk of hypothermia and frostbite.

Exercise Programs for Older Persons   It is estimated that 50 percent of the physical declines older persons experience, and often attribute to aging, are caused by disuse (Smith & Gilligan, 1983). Thus, many of the declines that we normally see could be slowed with exercise programs for older persons. However, relatively few programs exist in this area. This is because many individuals, both young and old, see inactivity as a reward that older persons have earned. Others have a stereotyped image of older persons as frail and fragile.

However, the benefits of exercise on balance, coordination, endurance, flexibility, and strength should not be underestimated (see Sager, 1983, 1984). Unfortunately, because many individuals in the recreation area are afraid that exercise programs will cause massive death and destruction among older persons, too few programs exist. To help determine who is capable of participating in exercise programs, Smith and Gilligan (1983) have provided a safe way to test the physical fitness of older persons.

Some positive results are being seen. Even programs that provide low-intensity training, because the participants are at an increased risk of a coronary event, have found significant positive results (Foster et al., 1989). Also, many sports now provide an opportunity for masters (those 40+ years of age) to train and compete in events. Additionally, organizations now exist for older persons in swimming, rowing, skiing (both downhill and cross-country), softball, bicycling, tennis, and track and field (Stovas, 1984).

One problem that has been associated with exercise programs for older persons is that participants often expect dramatic changes in short periods of time. Participants need to remember that it took decades of inactivity to raise their cholesterol, blood pressure, and body fat levels, and that it will take time to lower them, perhaps months or in some cases years. The amount of change will depend on the duration and intensity of the exercise program.

Income

Income is an important variable in determining health. Income can determine the quality and frequency of health care, as well as other health-related variables such as nutritional status and selected living conditions that can influence health.

Essentially, high income is associated with good health; low income is associated with poor health. This can be seen in several ways. First, by examining how individuals in different income categories perceive their health. The percentage who classify their health as fair/poor is 26.6 percent for those earning under $5000 and 6.0 percent for those earning more than $25,000. A second way of determining the association between income and health is to examine the percent limited in activity because of a chronic condition. For those who earn under $5000 a year the percentage is 29.3; for those with incomes above $25,000 the percentage is 8.7. A third way is to examine the number of yearly bed disability days per person for different income categories. For those earning under $5000 the figure is 13.2; for those earning more than $25,000 the figure is 4.5 (National Center for Health Statistics, 1987*a*).

As we can see from the above figures, not only do a higher percentage of those in the lower income category classify themselves as being in fair/poor health, but they are more likely to be limited in an activity because of a chronic condition and have more bed disability days.

Medical Care

Evidence has emerged which suggests that health care for older Americans is "deficient" (Kane et al., 1980). There are at least three reasons for the "deficient" care. The first deals with attitudes. The attitudes of those in the medical professions reflect those of the society in general and are often negative. The second is in the area of knowledge. The knowledge of geriatrics in professionals is often limited. The third factor may be the change in reimbursement for Medicare. Each of these will be examined below.

Attitudes are frequently difficult to directly assess. One way to examine attitudes and the stereotypes produced by the attitudes is to examine patient care. One example is on the care of women with breast cancer. One study by Chu and his associates (1987) found that older women received fewer services than younger women. For example, surgical procedures, chemotherapy, and radiation were less extensive for older women than for younger women. One possible explanation is that more aggressive treatment might have placed the older women at an increased risk of death, and was therefore avoided. However, the same pattern was seen in the referral of women to support groups; that is, younger women were referred more frequently than older women. The article concluded, in a very carefully worded manner, that more information is needed on why the older women did not receive more services, such as a more extensive dissection of lymph nodes or chemotherapy. Additionally, the impact this reduced service had on survival and quality of life needed to be examined (see Greenfield et al., 1987; Samet et al., 1986; Silliman et al., 1989; Wetle et al., 1988).

Wetle (1987), in an editorial in the *Journal of the American Medical Association,* pointed out that old age has become a risk factor for inadequate treatment. Dr. Wetle said that many physicians stereotype older persons and believe that aggressive treatment will yield a poor prognosis. Wetle noted the heterogeneity of older persons and called upon physicians to examine variables, such as prognosis or functional impairment, on an individual basis, and to not make age alone the basis for treatment decisions.

The negative stereotype of older persons is unfortunate and there are now numerous examples of older persons reacting favorably to aggressive treatment. For example, surgery was an option that many physicians avoided in regard to older persons. It was believed that the risks were simply too great when compared with the possible benefits. Also, there may have been a "Why bother?" attitude among many physicians that stemmed from the belief that the older person was destined to die soon anyway. New surgical techniques, which result in a lower mortality rate and changing attitudes among some physicians, have made surgery a much more frequent option for older persons. As would be expected, the survival rate for older persons following most surgery procedures is generally somewhat lower than it is for other age groups. For example, after open-heart surgery 16.5 percent of those 70+ years of age and 9.15 percent of those under 70 years of age died in the hospital (Wisoff et al., 1976). The same trend has been found for hip fractures: a higher mortality rate for older persons (Jensen & Tondevold, 1979; see also Ford, 1989; Magaziner et al., 1989; Mossey et al., 1989). A 10-year study on cardiac valve replacement found that the in-hospital mortality rate for all ages was 14.2 percent and for those 65+ was 14.4 percent (Fishman & Roe, 1978). A recent study in the *Journal of the American Medical Association* (Hosking et al., 1989) on surgery in patients 90+ years of age noted that most patients "tolerated" the surgery very well. Thus, although older persons generally have a higher postoperative mortality rate, there are some surgical techniques that do not produce a significant difference in mortality rate.

The higher post-surgical mortality rate for older persons is to be expected for several reasons: older persons are often in a weakened physical condition prior to the surgery; they do not have the reserve capacities to draw on that younger individuals have; they are often referred to physicians only when the disorder is advanced; and they often have other problems which decrease the likelihood of survival.

While physicians have been making strides in perfecting surgical procedures for the aged, nursing may be lagging behind. A recent article in *Nursing Times* ("Surgery for Elderly Patients," 1989) noted the lack of information on surgery and the elderly and stated that more information is needed on the special needs of aged surgical patients.

Evidence also exists indicating that nurses frequently hold negative attitudes about older persons, which may influence care (see Gomez et al., 1985). One reason appears to be their lack of training in geriatrics which makes solving the problems of older patients more difficult and frustrating (Brower, 1985). Some studies have reported that courses in geriatrics and working with older persons can create more positive attitudes toward older persons (see Gomez et al., 1985).

Attitudes also lead to less rehabilitation of older persons. Becker and Kaufman (1988) have provided an excellent review of the literature dealing with rehabilitation in old age. They pointed out that rehabilitation has been associated with the young and middle-aged, not older persons. Old age has traditionally been viewed as a time of physical losses, thus rehabilitation was often not seen as needed or practical. The "cost effectiveness" of rehabilitation for older persons, in an age of "cost constraints," has also been an issue that some have mentioned. Although rehabilitation can be effective for older persons, there are still barriers to receiving it.

It has also been reported that physical therapists are "significantly less aggressive in goal setting with elderly patients" (Kvitek et al., 1986). Part of the reason may be that therapists want to "protect" older persons; other reasons could be that therapists see less value in geriatric rehabilitation and prefer to use their time on younger individuals, or else they prefer to work with younger individuals.

In examining the attitudes of health care providers to older persons, Baker (1984) found that they preferred to work with older individuals who had "disease-related symptoms" rather than those with normal "age-related symptoms." The author said that, although difficult to assess, the impact of this preference probably affected the quality of care for older persons.

A second major reason for "deficient" medical care is that many health professionals lack knowledge in geriatrics. The U.S. Congress, Office of Technology Assessment (1987) reported that this contributed to physicians misdiagnosing, mistreating, under-treating, or even "writing off" older persons (see Goodwin, 1989). Another study that asked physicians to identify their three major areas of specialization found that only 0.2 percent identified geriatrics as one of the areas. Furthermore, these individuals were less likely to be board certified or members of professional organizations, suggesting that there may be a higher incidence of less qualified physicians specializing in geriatrics (Kane et al., 1980).

Hesse and her associates (1988) asked physicians to complete a questionnaire on geriatric health policy. The questionnaire contained questions dealing with issues such as health service needs of older persons, medicare and medicaid, and other specific programs and services older persons utilized. The results found that there was a lack of knowledge about geriatric health policy. The article noted that there are severe consequences for older persons in that some may have services provided that they cannot afford and others may not have covered services provided because a physician believes that they are too expensive for the individual.

The third reason older persons often receive deficient medical care deals with the prospective payment system (PPS). PPS determines in advance how much will be paid by medical insurance organizations to health care provided for certain types of medical care. Research is emerging that suggests the PPS, implemented by medicare in 1983, may contribute to a lowering of medical care for older persons. Fitzgerald and his associates (1988) examined the care of older persons with hip fractures both before and after PPS was implemented. They reported several facts that suggest a drop in medical care: the average hospitalization went from 21.9 days to 12.6 days; the percent discharged to nursing homes went from 38 percent to 60 percent; the amount of in-hospital physical therapy declined. The researchers concluded that for patients with hip fractures, the care had deteriorated since the implementation of PPS (see Binstock, 1987).

Nutrition

From conception to death the nutrients in food are necessary to maintain health and life. A diet that is too low or too high in nutrients can have a bearing on the quality and length of life. A diet that is low in essential nutrients can result in malnutrition, a variety of health problems, a decline in the ability of the body to fight infection or recover from illness, and even death. A diet that has an excess of nutrients, such as calories or saturated fat, can also be detrimental to health and contribute to an assortment of health problems including death (see Roe, 1987; Worthington-Roberts & Hazzard, 1982; Worthington-Roberts & Karkeck, 1986; Young, 1983).

Nutrition involves more than obtaining ''enough'' nutrients; it is concerned with obtaining nutrients from the ''right'' sources. For example, protein can be obtained from certain animal sources that are high in saturated fat or from vegetable sources that have no saturated fat. Because many sources of basic nutrients contribute to diseases such as coronary heart disease, cancer, cataracts, and diabetes, simply obtaining the proper amount of essential nutrients is no longer considered sufficient. Rather, individuals should strive to obtain nutrients from sources that will contribute to their health.

With increasing age, obtaining adequate nutrition becomes more difficult because of three factors. First, there are numerous physiological, psychological, financial, and social changes, all of which can have a bearing on an individual's nutritional status. If the individual does not adapt to these changes, both the quality and the quantity of life can be affected (see Balabokin et al., 1972).

Second, the area of nutrition and older persons has received relatively little attention (Collinsworth 1989; Schneider et al., 1986). As a result, there are many conflicting research reports. As we will see later in this section, there is even controversy over the appropriate recommended dietary allowances (RDAs) of certain nutrients for older persons.

Third, gerontologists do not agree on which age-related changes are pathological and need treatment, and which changes are "normal" and should be accepted and tolerated. An example of an age-related change that is seen as pathological is the loss of calcium which can contribute to osteoporosis. This age-related change is seen as pathological and dietary increase in calcium is recommended to stop or delay the change. However, other age-related changes are seen as "normal," and a very different approach is taken. For example, with increasing age there is a decline in the basal metabolic rate (BMR) and in lean body mass. These changes are accepted as normal, and the recommendation is to decrease caloric intake. It would be just as logical to maintain caloric intake *and* to increase physical activity to preserve lean body mass and increase the BMR.

The remainder of this section is subdivided into five subsections: nutritional needs, nutritional status, nutritional problems, factors that contribute to nutritional problems, and nutritional programs.

Nutritional Needs of Older Persons   This subsection will examine the nutritional needs of older persons (see Harper, 1981). It must be remembered that "older persons" do not compose one group but many. Thus, there is technically not one set of needs but many sets of needs, depending on the characteristics of the individuals being examined. For example, the nutritional needs of a 65-year-old marathoner are very different from the nutritional needs of a 65-year-old bed-bound nursing home patient. Obviously the needs of each "type" of individual cannot be presented; thus, this section will discuss the RDAs for "older persons" as established by the National Academy of Sciences.

It is difficult to determine the nutritional needs of older persons because the RDAs are a source of controversy. The RDAs have been prepared and published by the Food and Nutrition Board of the National Research Council of the National Academy of Sciences since 1941. The ninth edition came out in 1980 with the tenth scheduled for publication in 1985. The board was initially unable to issue the tenth edition because of disagreement on how to interpret the meaning of certain studies on RDA requirements (Food and Nutrition Board, 1986). The major point that students need to remember is that RDAs are a source of controversy. What constitutes an adequate RDA for one scientist is clearly inappropriate for another. For this book we will be referring to the RDAs established by the Food and Nutrition Board.

Traditionally, the RDAs for older persons have been established based on studies conducted on young adults. The RDAs have existed for two groups of adults, those 23–50 and those 51+. These two groups are clearly inadequate. Gerontologists recognize that the age category 65+ is inadequate since it blurs the distinction between other age segments such as those 65–69 or those 80–84. With these limitations stated, we will now examine the nutritional needs of the aged in selected areas.

Calories   Calories are a way of measuring the amount of energy within a food. As is well known, if calories are not burned or expended by the body, they accumulate as body fat. Studies on animals have fairly consistently reported that a diet restricted in calories will increase life expectancy. This appears to be because the aging process develops at a slower rate which delays the beginning of aging-related disease (see Guigoz & Munro, 1985).

Generally, with increasing age the number of calories required per day declines.

This is for two reasons. First, in adulthood the BMR declines about 2 percent per decade as a result of a decline in the number of functioning cells. The BMR is simply the amount of energy necessary for the lean body mass to function. Since lean body mass generally declines with increasing age, the BMR declines. Thus, in normal functioning, the body is burning fewer calories. Second, most older persons are less active than younger individuals. An active individual requires more calories than a sedentary individual.

To prevent obesity the general guideline of the Food and Nutrition Board of the National Academy of Sciences is that with increasing age the total number of daily calories should gradually be reduced so that by age 75 the individual is consuming 75 to 80 percent that of a young adult.

For most individuals this means that a conscious change in diet must take place. When consuming 1800 to 2500 calories per day, individuals may meet their nutritional requirements with little or no planning. However, when consuming 25 percent fewer calories a day, a random selection of foods may no longer provide all the essential nutrients. Thus, older persons will have to obtain the same nutrients but from less food. This means a change to "nutrient dense" foods: foods that have high nutritional value. Six areas will be examined: protein, carbohydrates, fat, vitamins, minerals, and fluid.

1 Protein: Protein is often considered a building block of the body. Protein is essential for health. The RDA for protein is considered by many to be slightly higher for older persons than for other age groups (Guigoz & Munro, 1985; Kokkonen & Barrows, 1987), while others believe that the needs are similar (Kart et al., 1988).

2 Carbohydrates: Carbohydrates are an energy source for the body. When the body is looking for sources of energy, it first looks for carbohydrates. There are different types of carbohydrates. Refined carbohydrates often contain energy but few other nutrients. Complex carbohydrates have fewer calories and more nutrients. The needs in this area do not appear to change with increasing age.

3 Fat: Although dietary fat has achieved a "bad name" in the American diet, it is essential for life. It is not fat in and of itself that is "bad," but the amount and the type of fat that is consumed in the traditional American diet. Excessive saturated fat is responsible for coronary heart disease, certain types of cancer, and obesity. The needs in this area do not appear to change with increasing age.

4 Vitamins: Vitamins in proper amounts are essential for life and health. They help to regulate the metabolism of the body. The need for most vitamins remains essentially the same throughout life (see Hefley, 1987).

Inadequate vitamin intake can cause physical symptoms such as fatigue, poor resistance to infection, slow wound healing, as well as psychological symptoms such as loss of memory, disorientation, or intellectual impairment (see Baker et al., 1979).

Vitamin supplements are a source of controversy. Often those taking the supplements do not need them. Others spend a significant amount of money per month on needless supplements. Additionally, some supplements in large dosages can be dangerous.

5 Minerals: Minerals are also essential for the normal functioning of the body. Several specific minerals will be discussed below.

Calcium   Calcium is currently the ''in'' mineral. Numerous products now flaunt the amount of calcium they possess. The appeal of calcium is largely because of osteoporosis, or loss of bone mass, although calcium is also important in areas such as blood coagulation and heart functioning. As we saw in Chapter 5, ''Biology and Physiology,'' the loss of bone mass is a gradual, continual problem for most older persons. One of the reasons is that calcium absorption decreases with increasing age or an inadequate intake of calcium. The inadequate intake can be related to an inadequate amount of calcium in the foods consumed or the types of foods consumed. That is, while some diets are deficient in calcium, others have an adequate total amount of calcium but the foods consumed interact to prevent the calcium from being absorbed. For example, a high intake of protein or bran can interfere with calcium absorption. Many nutritionists believe that there is a need for the aged to increase their calcium intake from 800 mg per day, to 1200 to 1500 mg per day.

Iron   Iron is essential for healthy blood cells. The iron combines with oxygen in cells, which is then carried to other parts of the body. Iron deficiency is a common problem for many groups in American society, including older persons. Although women have been made more iron conscious than men, because of loss of iron through menstruation, after menopause this consciousness may diminish. Older persons need to be concerned with iron intake since blood loss may occur through conditions such as hemorrhoids, gastrointestinal bleeding, or ulcers. Additionally, iron stores are generally low and iron utilization is not as efficient in older persons.

Sodium   Sodium, like fat, has achieved a negative image in modern society. As with fat, sodium is essential for life. It is not sodium that is bad for the body, but the amount of sodium consumed in the typical American diet. In younger individuals the kidneys excrete excessive sodium. In older persons with decreased kidney functioning, the sodium may accumulate in the body causing conditions such as high blood pressure.

Potassium   Potassium deficiencies are uncommon in older persons. It is most likely to occur in those who have suffered a major fluid loss through vomiting, diarrhea, or alcohol abuse.

6 Fluid: Water is something taken for granted in American society. Yet water is the basic building block of life, and composes about 66 percent of our body weight. Although an individual can live for many weeks without food, without water an individual will die within a week.

Water is important in such areas as aiding digestion and regulating body temperature.

Normally, if the body needs water the individual feels thirsty and consumes water. An older individual may have more of a need for water because of chronic illness or certain drugs that produce excessive water loss. Many older individuals, especially those with mental impairments, are often found upon medical examination to be dehydrated.

Nutritional Status of Older Persons   There have been numerous studies on the nutritional status of older persons, with the majority using RDAs as the basis for their conclusions (see Omdahl et al., 1982). The results have been mixed and have depended on the characteristics of the sample. One study found that for those 70 to 80 years of age 6 percent of the men and 5 percent of the women were malnourished. For those 80+ years of age the figures increased to 12 percent for men and 8 percent for women (see Guigoz & Munro, 1985).

A study of 100 noninstitutionalized aged men and women (Yearick et al., 1980) reported that calcium, vitamin A, and thiamine were most likely to be deficient, mainly with women. Energy came from the following sources: protein 17 percent, carbohydrates, 47 percent, fat 36 percent. The study also reported that most of those taking vitamin supplements did not need them, and that many who needed vitamin supplements did not take them (see Garry et al., 1983, 1984; Garry et al., 1982; Sobal et al., 1986).

A study on 2653 older persons (Murphy et al., 1989) concluded that the elderly were in need of nutrition education programs that stressed the importance of increasing daily intake in certain areas (e.g., grains and dairy products) and decreasing intake in other areas (e.g., fats, sweets, and alcohol).

It has also been reported that nutritional problems are most likely to be found in minority groups, such as blacks and Hispanics, and among the socially isolated, frail, and poor (Akin et al., 1987; Ludman & Newman, 1986).

Nutritional Problems of Older Persons   Older persons can suffer from several common nutritional problems. Some of these are listed and described alphabetically below (see McCall, 1986).

Anemia   A common problem for many age groups is iron-deficiency anemia. Many individuals are anemic throughout life due to an inadequate diet. As mentioned earlier, many incorrectly assume that iron is only necessary for growing children or menstruating women and thus become less iron conscious with increasing age.

Constipation   Constipation in older persons is related primarily to an inadequate intake of fiber and fluid. Other factors that can increase the probability of constipation are abuse of laxatives, lack of exercise, a decrease in the contractions in the intestines, and certain drug use.

Mental Functioning Impairment   Studies have also reported that mild or "subclinical" malnutrition may contribute to impaired mental functioning (Goodwin et al., 1983). In a study of healthy, noninstitutionalized older persons, it was reported that those with low blood levels of vitamin C, vitamin B_{12}, riboflavin, or folic acid scored lower on certain tests of cognitive functioning (see Raskind, 1983).

Obesity   There is little doubt that obesity is a major problem in old age. One study on 3600 individuals 60+ years of age found that 50 percent of the women and 18 percent of the men were "significantly" overweight (see Worthington-Roberts & Karkeck, 1986). Other studies have indicated that between 30 and 60 percent of older persons are overweight (Howell, 1974; Osborn, 1970; Sherwood, 1970; Yearick et al., 1980). Generally the pattern is to add 2 to 3 pounds per decade throughout adulthood; thus by age 65 the individual's weight has increased 40 to 60 pounds. Some studies have reported that at about age 65 weight levels stabilize. Rather than indicating a weight stabilization, this probably reflects the 30 to 40 percent higher mortality rate of the obese. Thus, the more obese are dying, which lowers the average weight figures, giving the appearance that weight stabilizes about age 65. The figures are also lowered because of an increase in individuals with diseases that cause weight loss.

Generally, the weight gain does not occur because of an increase in food consumption; rather, it is through continuation of previous eating patterns. Remember, as most individuals age, their need for energy decreases. If they maintain the same caloric intake, what was an adequate diet to maintain weight in the past will become a diet with excessive calories (see Berger, 1976).

Obesity may also occur because of the consumption of foods high in sugar. The taste buds apparently remain receptive to sweet taste longer than to other tastes (Berger, 1976) and the group of foods that older persons favor is that of sweets (Brogdon & Alford, 1973).

As would be expected, obesity is not randomly distributed throughout the population but is more prevalent in certain groups. For example, women are more likely to be overweight than men, and individuals in the lower socioeconomic classes tend to be overweight more often than individuals in other socioeconomic classes.

Being old and overweight can cause several problems, including mobility limitations (Harris et al., 1989) and death. It also appears that the location of fat is a risk factor in death, with fat in the abdomen posing a greater risk than fat in the hips or buttocks (Maddox, 1987).

Being overweight can also cause health-related problems. For example, diabetes mellitus, arteriosclerosis, varicose veins, hernias, cardiovascular disease, peptic ulcers, hypertension, respiratory difficultly, and slowing of wound healing after surgery all occur with greater frequency in overweight individuals (see National Center for Health Statistics, 1987b; Weg, 1975b).

Obesity can exacerbate other problems. For example, many older persons are restricted by arthritis. Excessive weight can further decrease mobility. It can also fatigue the individual faster and will probably have a bearing on life satisfaction. Many older individuals also have balance problems. Increased weight and decreased agility may make them more prone to falling and injury.

It should be noted that an overweight person is not necessarily getting adequate nutrition. The excess bulk may be a result of empty calories, that is, of foods with little or no nutritional value.

Weight Loss   Although obesity is a frequent nutritional problem in older persons, so is weight loss. Weight loss can result from a variety of factors such as inadequate nutritional intake or disease.

Factors That Contribute to Nutritional Problems   We have examined the nutritional status of older persons as well as some of their nutritional problems. It is now time to look at the cause of many of the problems in alphabetical order (see Calasanti & Hendricks, 1986).

Aging Process   There are aging changes that may contribute to nutritional problems in older persons. For example, with increasing age the skin has a decreased ability to synthesize vitamin D. Additionally, there are changes in the alimentary canal, from the mouth through the gastrointestinal tract. In the mouth the number of taste buds decreases dramatically. The loss of taste can cause individuals to lose interest in food. Tooth and gum problems, which will be discussed separately, are also factors. The salivary glands decrease the amount of saliva secreted, and thus, the digestive enzymes (by causing irritation of the mouth and tongue) can make chewing and swallowing more difficult and impair the digestion of food. Other aging-related changes that can cause nutritional problems are in the reduction of digestive enzymes in the stomach and in the decrease of absorption of nutrients in the gastrointestinal tract. The peristaltic movement is also slower.

Alcohol Abuse   Alcohol abuse can also cause nutritional problems. Alcohol may be substituted for other needed foods. Thus, the individual consumes empty calories with little or no nutritional benefit. Those on a limited income may spend their money on alcohol rather than food. Alcohol may also inhibit the absorption of certain nutrients, such as thiamine.

Drug Interaction   Older persons frequently take prescription and nonprescription drugs. Most are not aware of the consequences of drug use on nutritional status; drugs can interfere with the absorption, utilization, and rate of excretion of nutrients. For example, some drugs taken for high blood pressure can cause calcium depletion. Some drugs can cause overeating. Other drugs can cause constipation or diarrhea. Some can cause vitamin deficiencies. Others may cause intestinal bleeding or ulcers. Drugs can also influence the sense of taste and smell, thus affecting appetite.

Education   Some studies indicate that education plays an important role in diet. The higher the level of education, the ''better'' the diet, since higher levels of education are generally associated with higher levels of income and knowledge of nutrition. It has been reported that much of the nutritional information available to older persons is not very reliable (Kivela & Nissineh, 1987). This may make them more susceptible to ''food fads'' (see Lank & Vickery, 1987).

Food Interaction   The interaction of certain foods interferes with the proper absorption of certain nutrients. Tea, for example, interferes with iron absorption.

Illness and Disease   Nutritional problems can also occur in older persons because of an increase in chronic and acute conditions. Preparing a meal can be very difficult for someone with failing eyesight who cannot read a recipe or see the dials on the stove, or someone with arthritis who cannot hold a kitchen utensil. The kitchen with knives, and hot burners, can be a dangerous place if one's senses are not alert to potential dangers. Additionally, an illness or disease that affects mobility may make food preparation difficult, and restrict shopping for food.

Certain illness may also decrease appetite, or make it so that only certain foods ''taste good'' or can be consumed without nausea. Certain conditions may also affect the absorption of nutrients.

Income   Generally speaking, the lower the income, the worse the diet. Studies indicate that as income goes down, the likelihood of maintaining an adequate diet also goes down (Akin et al., 1987; Davis et al., 1985; Sherwood, 1970).

Mental Problems   Individuals with certain mental disorders may not be able to prepare nutritious meals. These individuals may even forget if they have eaten.

Race   Being a member of a minority racial group has been reported to contribute to lower nutritional status (Akin et al., 1987; Harel, 1985). Obviously, income plays a role here, with minority elderly generally having less income. The role of ethnicity in nutritional status has not been examined (see Calasanti & Hendricks, 1986).

Social Isolation   There is a social aspect often connected with food. Holidays, for example, are often structured around the preparation and consumption of food. The preparation and consumption of food is also a social event which gives pleasure to many individuals and provides them with important roles. Eating can also be pleasurable in terms of the taste, texture, and odors of the food. Social isolation can cause individuals to lose interest in the preparation and consumption of food (see Roundtree & Tinklin, 1975; Troll, 1976).

Generally speaking, the greater the social interaction, the greater and more varied the nutritional intake (Sherwood, 1970). Social isolation may make the individual more prone to eat foods that require little or no preparation and that have little or no nutritional value. Some authors believe that social isolation can upset the digestive process, particularly in terms of the nitrogen balance of the body (Sherwood, 1970). Studies have found that those living with a spouse have better diets than those living alone (Axelson & Penfield, 1983; Davis et al., 1985).

Tooth and Mouth Problems   As we saw in the last chapter, many older individual have had extensive tooth loss. This can contribute to nutritional problems in several ways. First, loose or poorly fitting dentures can make eating painful and difficult. Consequently, many older persons restrict their diets to certain types of soft foods. They may avoid salads, raw vegetables, and meats (Osborn, 1970). Yet basic nutritional knowledge suggests that all of these are important in a good diet. Second, with loose or poorly fitting dentures, the individual may not be able to properly chew foods or it may take significantly longer to properly masticate food (see Kart et al., 1988; Wayler et al., 1984). Masticatory ability is related to dental integrity; generally, those with more teeth have better masticatory ability than those with dentures or missing teeth. As a result, foods will not be properly prepared for the action of the digestive juices. Poorly masticated foods can lead to gastrointestinal complaints such as constipation (see Osborn, 1970). Third, dentures can be a source of embarrassment that may restrict the consumption of certain foods, especially when eating with others.

Widowhood   Widowhood can affect nutritional status in three ways. First, widowhood may produce social isolation. The consequences of this have been discussed. Second, income may decline with widowhood, thus limiting the individual's ability to purchase food. Third, the individual may not have the ability or knowledge to prepare nutritious meals. A woman may have depended on her husband to do the shopping, or a male may have depended for decades on his wife to prepare meals (see Davis et al., 1985).

Nutritional Programs for the Aged   It has been recognized that the nutrition of older persons is often substandard. This condition can create unnecessary health problems as well as health costs. Because of this a variety of nutritional programs have been established to try and meet the needs of older persons. This section will describe some of the programs that exist (see Fanelli & Abernethy, 1986; Lank & Vickery, 1987).

The largest nutrition programs for older persons are those of the federal government. The 1965 Older Americans Act had Title IV, which created a pilot nutrition program.

In 1972 an amendment to the act added Title VII, which among other developments created the National Nutrition Program for the Elderly. In 1978 amendments to the Comprehensive Older Americans Act made area agencies on aging responsible for nutrition programs and established a home-delivered meals program (Austin, 1987; Calasanti & Hendricks, 1986).

There are numerous examples of other nutrition programs, at a less extensive level. Shannon and her associates (1983) trained aged individuals to conduct nutrition workshops and be a resource on nutrition in senior centers. The researchers believed that "peer educators" would be better received by older persons. The "peer educators" appear to have fulfilled their function of increasing nutritional awareness among the aged.

Glanz and Scharf (1985) described an innovative and comprehensive nutrition training program for social workers dealing with homebound aged. The goal of the program was to keep older persons in their homes as long as possible through self-care, caregiver support, and social services programs such as meals-on-wheels. The homebound are a unique group in that they have health problems that may limit food shopping, food preparation, or food consumption. It was recognized that poor nutrition could contribute to health problems which might mandate institutionalization. A nutrition program had the potential to prevent and discover nutritional problems. In this program, social workers, who were already seeing the aged on a regular basis, were trained to "influence" nutrition among older persons. There were six areas they were trained to deal with:

1 Nutrition services: They made clients aware of services such as meals-on-wheels and homemaker services for shopping or meal preparation.

2 Nutrition advocacy: They assisted their clients in obtaining food stamps and free food supplies.

3 Nutrition intervention/education skills facilitation: They instructed their clients in areas such as food preparation (easy recipes or inexpensive recipes) and shopping.

4 Information: They provided clients with information on the nutritional content of various foods.

5 Medical intervention: Medical intervention was sought if nutritional problems were suspected.

6 Behavior change: Clients were assisted in changing their behavior to follow diets or exercise.

This was found to be a comprehensive approach that had the potential to allow individuals to remain self-sufficient for a longer period of time.

Fishman and her associates (1987) also developed a nutrition program for homebound older persons. This program used master's level students enrolled in a nutrition program to provide nutrition counseling services for homebound aged. The students had an initial visit with a client and gathered information on health status and diet. The diet of each client was analyzed via a computer program. Students then assessed each diet, planned any dietary changes, and implemented the changes via contact with the client. The program was evaluated to be an efficient and cost-effective way of maintaining nutritional adequacy in homebound older persons.

A local cable television station created a game show for the aged called *Let's*

Make a Meal, which was similar in nature to the national television program *Let's Make a Deal.* The local program had a wheel divided into categories: bread, dessert, vegetable/salad, and main dish. Contestants were selected from the audience and, after spinning the wheel, were asked to answer questions about nutrition. Contestants were awarded small prizes and gifts (Balsam & Poe, 1987).

Race

Before starting this section it must be mentioned that relatively little data exists in this area. Most of what exists has reported on "whites" and "nonwhites," or whites and blacks. In 1976 the Bureau of the Census started to keep some data on Hispanics, although it is only recently that distinctions between Puerto Ricans, Mexicans, and Cubans was made. Data on other racial groups is either lacking or incomplete. It should also be mentioned that it is difficult with the existing information to determine if the differences in health are caused by genetic factors or other factors such as income or education.

For blacks the major chronic conditions are high blood pressure, arthritis, chronic sinusitis, orthopedic impairments (for the general population the leading four chronic conditions are arthritis, high blood pressure, hearing impairments, and heart conditions). What is striking is the high rate of hypertensive disease. The percentage of aged blacks with activity limitations due to hypertension is 24.4 percent; the figure for whites is 10.3 percent (U.S. Bureau of the Census, 1987). Table 6-8 examines the percentage of individuals according to health status for those 65+ years of age by sex and race.

As can be seen, whites are more likely to declare their health as excellent or very good than blacks. Blacks, especially females, are more likely to define their health as fair or poor than whites. Again, much of the difference is probably due to income.

The National Center for Health Statistics (1984*b*) has provided three additional indicators of the differences in the health of older Americans by ethnicity and race: days of restricted activity per year, bed disability days per year, and percentage

TABLE 6-8
HEALTH STATUS FOR THOSE 65+ YEARS OF AGE BY SEX
AND RACE

	Health status		
	Excellent or very good	Good	Fair or poor
White male	36.7	30.6	32.3
Black male	26.6	25.1	47.7
White female	36.8	32.5	30.1
Black female	24.1	21.2	53.0

Source: National Center for Health Statistics, 1987a.

TABLE 6-9
SELECTED INDICATORS OF HEALTH BY RACE AND ETHNICITY

	Days of restricted activity	Bed disability days	% with activity limitations
White	38.7	12.9	44.3
Black	56.9	22.9	57.2
Hispanic	46.5	20.7	47.5
Mexican-American	52.8	26.1	52.4
Puerto Rican	61.4	35.7	52.6
Cuban	43.6	17.6	42.1

Source: National Center for Health Statistics, 1984*b*.

with activity limitations. This information is presented in Table 6-9 for whites, blacks, Hispanics in general, and three subcategories of Hispanics.

With one or two exceptions, whites have better health than any of the other groups. It also becomes apparent that Hispanics are not one group about which generalizations can be made but at least three distinctive groups with different levels of health. Puerto Ricans, for example, have more restricted days of activity, more bed disability days, and a higher percentage of activity limitations. Cubans have the lowest.

One study on Puerto Ricans found that aged Puerto Ricans were admitted to nursing homes about 7 years younger than whites. Additionally, those admitted had more disabilities than whites (Espino et al., 1988).

Relatively little information exists on aged Native Americans although it has been suggested that of all the aged groups in contemporary American society their health is the poorest (see Seccombe, 1989).

There are a variety of factors that have been used to explain why ethnic and racial minority groups have poorer health than whites. One factor is genetics. Genetics for blacks account for sickle cell anemia, and possibly hypertension. A second possible explanation is cultural. That is, a certain ethnic or minority racial group may have a certain diet that influences health. A third possible explanation deals with health care. Many minority older persons do not speak English, making communication with health professionals difficult. Additionally, many were raised to believe in nontraditional forms of medicine, which in many cases will be detrimental to their health. Also, many do not have health insurance or understand the various programs that are available (see Petchers & Milligan, 1988; Siddharthan & Sowers-Hoag, 1989). A fourth explanation is that ethnic and racial minority groups are overrepresented in the lower social classes, and it is socioeconomic factors rather than ethnicity or race that is accounting for the health differences.

The socioeconomic factor has received the greatest amount of attention. One way of investigating this is to control for socioeconomic variables, which is done by comparing those in similar circumstances and then seeing if health differs by ethnicity or race. When controlling for socioeconomic factors several researchers have found health differences, suggesting that the health differences are caused by ethnicity or race (see Dowd & Bengtson, 1978; Ferraro, 1987; Krause, 1987). However, in a sample of aged Alaskan Native Americans and whites Seccombe (1989) did not find that ethnicity was an important variable. As in many areas the results are mixed and from a limited number of studies, many with methodological limitations. Further studies are needed to demonstrate that ethnicity and race are important for determining health status in some minority groups but not others.

So far we have discussed minority groups that have a lower health status than whites. Some studies have indicated that the health of aged Chinese Americans (Yu, 1986) and Japanese Americans (Liu, 1986) is better than that of white Americans (Yu, 1989). Although further studies are needed this may be related to higher levels of income and education for Chinese and Japanese Americans.

Sex

In Chapter 17, "Dying and Death," we will briefly examine longevity. In that chapter we will find that women live longer than men. In this chapter we will find that just as there are differences in life expectancy, there are also differences in health, although initially not in the hypothesized direction.

Given the difference in life expectancy one would expect that overall the health of women would be better than the health of men. In fact, we find the reverse; women have higher rates of illness and disability, physician visits, and hospitalization.

The lower life expectancy for men can be explained by the fact that men have several risk factors in greater proportion than women: smoking, alcohol use, high blood pressure, and occupational risks. There is only one factor where more women have a higher rate than men: obesity. One other risk factor favors women through about the mid-forties and then favors men: serum cholesterol. Serum cholesterol levels are lower for women until the mid-forties for two reasons. First, the female reproductive period appears to protect women. With menopause this protection ceases. Second, by the mid-forties many men with high serum cholesterol levels have died.

Women have also been found to have more acute conditions. Women in general report 228 conditions per 100 women; for men the rate is 202. Even if conditions related to reproduction, such as acute conditions due to delivery, are excluded the acute condition rate for females is still 11 percent higher.

It was also found that women tended to "slow down" more as a result of acute conditions. This can be seen in a higher rate of bed-disability days and restricted activity days as a result of acute conditions.

Women are more likely to have chronic conditions that are less likely to contribute to death. For example, heart disease, with coronary heart disease being the more likely cause of death, is the major cause of death in contemporary American society. The rate per 1000 for men is 30.9; for women the figure is 16.7. In the second leading cause of death, cancer, men have rates that are 25 percent higher than women and they are likely to have cancers that have lower 5-year survival rates. For example, 26 percent of male cancer is lung cancer which has a relatively low 5-year survival rate, while 32 percent of the cancer in women is breast cancer which has a relatively high 5-year survival rate. For some chronic conditions that have high death rates, the level of males and females are almost even. For example the extent of cerebrovascular diseases is similar. However, the incidence of stroke is 18 percent higher in men than women and men are 19 percent more likely to die from cerebrovascular disease than women (National Center for Health Statistics, 1983).

Some additional factors are needed to help explain why women live longer than men but have a higher morbidity or illness rate. One factor is that females appear to be more knowledgeable about the status of their health. One study reported that during medical examinations 59 percent of white males but 75 percent of white females who were found to have high blood pressure were aware of their condition. This probably means greater medical monitoring and control over certain conditions. This also probably means that females report health problems more frequently than males. Females also tend to utilize medical services more than males. This may be because of such factors as pregnancy or the greater emphasis on yearly physical exams. This could allow for conditions to be diagnosed and treated at an earlier and more amenable stage of development. One additional reason women have more health problems is that they live longer and have more time to develop problems.

Thus, while women have a higher incidence of chronic conditions, which contributes to more bed disability and activity limitations, the conditions are less likely to contribute to death (Verbrugge, 1984, 1987). Males, on the other hand, are less likely to be bothered on a daily basis by chronic conditions, but tend to have conditions that are less likely to contribute to disability, diagnosis, or treatment but more likely to contribute to death.

Smoking

Currently about 35 percent of males and 29.4 percent of females smoke cigarettes (U.S. Bureau of the Census, 1987). For those 65+ years of age the percentage for males is 19.6; for females it is 13.5. The difference is that with increasing age many smokers stop smoking for health-related reasons and because smokers die earlier than nonsmokers. A longitudinal study of U.S. veterans (Rogot, 1978) reported that at age 35 a nonsmoker had a life expectancy of 43.5 years; a heavy smoker 34.8 years.

There is no doubt that smoking is a major health risk (Wynder, 1988). The risks from smoking are dose-related; that is, the more one smokes the greater the risk. What older smokers face are the health consequences of decades of smoking. This can be seen in the increased rates of lung cancer for each successive age group. We can also see increases in other smoking-related health consequences such as heart disease and emphysema. In an examination of health practices it was found that smoking was highly correlated with hospital use (Lubben et al., 1989).

Once they stop smoking, older persons can see rapid improvement in health in declines in heart rate, blood pressure, bronchial irritation, and coughing (Minkler, 1987).

MEDICAL SWINDLES

In almost all societies there are individuals who exploit others. Contemporary American society is no exception. Older persons are particularly vulnerable to exploitation by con artists for four reasons. First, older persons very often live alone or in some kind of isolation from the rest of society—a fact that can make them vulnerable and naive. The attention of the "friendly" con artist can be a form of flattery that will set them up for a swindle. Second, the visual and hearing impairment of older persons may make the small print in a contract or a verbal guarantee difficult to understand. Third, ignorance can contribute to exploitation. For example, an older person may know that he or she has a serious disease but not know much about the disease. The con artist can capitalize on the individual's ignorance by recommending "miracle" cures. Fourth, desperation often contributes to medical swindles. Individuals who have been told that there is no cure or that nothing more can be done to alleviate the symptoms of their condition or disease may turn to a con artist out of desperation. The National Institute on Aging (1985) has estimated that 60 percent of all health care swindle victims are 65+ years of age.

Although some medical swindles may actually have a positive placebo effect, the majority are harmful. They are harmful financially since the "cure" will probably be expensive. For many older persons the money they spend on useless cures is money that could have gone to legitimate physicians or to other health-related items. At the national level it is estimated by the U.S. House of Representatives Subcommittee on Health and Long-Term Care that $10 billion is spent every year on medical quackery (Edsall, 1988; National Institute on Aging, 1985). Medical swindles are harmful since the older person may stop taking or not start taking prescribed medication. For example, the diabetic may decide to stop using insulin in preference for a "miracle drug." A cancer patient may decide not to undergo surgery or radiation because of a con artist's promises. While individuals have the right to select the amount and type of treatment, they need to have facts, not false promises. The results here can be illness or death. Individuals who are conned into medical swindles may delay legitimate medical treatment. By the time they finally obtain treatment from a physician, their illness or disease may have advanced from a treatable illness to a terminal illness. Because some individuals who use useless "cures" experience remission of their disease or condition, perhaps because of earlier legitimate treatment, they associate the remission with useless treatment. For example, with certain types of arthritis the symptoms may disappear for a period of time. If the individual was receiving treatment from a con artist the "cure" would be associated with the treatment, and almost certainly additional treatments would be suggested to prevent a recurrence. There is one last danger of medical swindles; namely the "cure" itself may be dangerous. Individuals who use the "miracle cures" are often exposing themselves to a variety of substances that have not been prepared or tested under proper conditions.

The National Institute on Aging (1985) reported that health quackery items generally have the following characteristics:

• A quick, painless cure for diseases/conditions that traditional science cannot cure.

• The use of a "secret" formula.

• Support for their claims is through testimonials and case histories, not scientific evidence.

- There is usually only one distributor of the product.
- The remedy is generally effective for several conditions.

SUMMARY

Health is a difficult term to define. What may constitute "good" health for one individual may constitute "poor" health for another. This chapter examined health in old age. Specifically it was divided into six sections: importance of health, health characteristics, hospitalization, health status, factors that determine health, and medical swindles.

Health determines not just the length of life but also its quality. An individual's health status will determine not only the ability to participate in certain activities, but also the length of time the individual will have to participate.

There are three health characteristics that were examined: acute conditions, chronic conditions, and self-assessed health. Acute conditions are temporary, such as a cut or cold. The incidence of acute conditions generally goes down with increasing age, because most older individuals have acquired immunity to certain infectious diseases, are infrequently in situations to contract infectious diseases, and are not as likely to engage in activities that will cause acute conditions. However, once older persons have acute conditions, these conditions are often more serious than for younger individuals. This is because of certain age-related changes, such as a lowered immune system, and because they frequently have other diseases and conditions, such as a heart condition, which will interact with the acute condition.

Chronic conditions are those lasting for at least 3 months. Many chronic conditions are permanent. The four leading chronic conditions for older persons are arthritis, high blood pressure, hearing impairments, and heart conditions. Chronic conditions tend to be higher among the very old, minority group members, and those with lower levels of income and education. Although the majority of older persons have chronic conditions, for many there is little impact on their activities or their quality of life.

Older persons are less likely to assess their health as "excellent" or "very good" than younger age groups. However, after old age there is little change by age group on self-assessed health.

Older persons are more likely to be hospitalized than younger age groups. The major reasons for hospitalization are diseases of the circulatory system and diseases of the digestive system.

Gerontologists have been asking if the health of older persons is getting "better" or "worse." Those who believe that the health of older persons is getting worse have noted that the aged population is aging. Others believe that changes in life-style, coupled with more and better health care have produced a "healthier" aged population. Studies indicate that older persons are healthier today than in the past.

There are several factors that determine physical health. This chapter examined alcoholism, drugs, education, exercise, income, medical care, nutrition, race, sex, and smoking.

Alcoholism is a controversial area of study, with even controversial terms. The study of aged alcoholics is of recent origin. Because the percentage of older alcoholics is lower than other adult age groups, older alcoholics are less likely to come to the attention of social service agencies, and many are incorrectly diagnosed by health professionals. Although the figures vary, between 2 to 10 percent of older persons are alcoholic. The causes of alcoholism are varied and are generally separated in early onset (before age 65) and late onset (from age 65+). Some of the causes for a small percentage of older persons of late onset alcoholism are bereavement, retirement, and physical illness. The consequences of alcoholism can be physical (e.g., contributing to existing or creating new physical problem) or social (e.g., forcing the withdrawal of family members or creating legal problems). There are effective treatment programs for aged alcoholics.

Drugs can also influence physical health. In this chapter we only considered ''legal'' drugs and those obtained either over the counter or by a prescription. Because older persons have more chronic disorders, they are also more likely to use drugs than younger age groups. Generally, because of age-related changes the absorption, distribution, metabolism, and excretion of drugs is different in older persons than in younger persons. This, as well as some other variables, causes a disproportionate number of drug-related problems for older persons. Some of the reasons for drug-related problems are that older persons frequently take more than one drug thus increasing the risk of drug interaction, often do not have the money to purchase drugs, may have memory problems that interfere with proper sequencing of drugs, may have been prescribed more drugs than they really need, may have scheduling problems in taking their drugs, may try to self-medicate, may not take drugs because of their side effects, may not have transportation to a pharmacy to get drugs, or may not understand the purpose of scheduling of the drug. There are a variety of programs to reduce drug-related problems.

A third factor related to health is education. Basically, the higher the level of education the better the health. It may not be education that is the important variable here but socioeconomic standing. Generally, the higher the education the higher the socioeconomic standing and those people are more likely to have regular, high-quality health care.

The fourth factor is exercise. In the past, exercise was considered an activity of the young not the aged. A variety of studies have now found that the aged can exercise safely and with the same benefit that the young obtain. Many of the changes that we now assume are age-related are more indicative of a sedentary life-style. Although exercise cannot stop the aging process, it can slow it down. Those who exercise can maintain the physiological profile of someone several decades younger. There are certain risks associated with exercise and the first step is a thorough physical examination.

Income is also related to health. This was briefly discussed in the section on education. The higher the income the better the health.

The sixth factor is medical care. Many believe that medical care for older persons is deficient in contemporary American society. In part this related to the attitudes of health professionals toward the elderly; in part it relates to a lack of knowledge about geriatrics among many health professionals; and it also involves the prospective payment system.

Nutrition, the seventh factor, is also a health factor. Nutrition is not just concerned with obtaining enough nutrients, but is also interested in the sources. Nutritional needs depend on the individual. An active 65-year-old's needs are different from someone who is inactive. Generally, we find that the need for calories decreases primarily because activity levels decrease. Protein, carbohydrate, fat, and vitamin needs are believed to remain basically the same in adulthood. The minerals calcium and iron probably need to be increased or at least closely monitored. Fluid is often deficient in older persons and needs to be watched.

In terms of nutritional status, the aged have many nutritional problems: anemia, constipation, mental functioning impairment, obesity, weight loss. These problems can be caused by the aging process, alcohol abuse, drug interactions, education, income, illness and disease, food interactions, mental problems, race, social isolation, tooth and mouth problems, and widowhood. There have been several successful nutritional programs for older persons.

Race is another variable that is related to health. Generally, the health of whites is better than for nonwhites. The cause is probably related more to income than race, with whites having higher income levels.

Sex is another variable that needs to be examined. Although women live longer than men, women appear to have more health-related problems. Although it appears to be inconsistent (i.e., those with more health problems live longer) part of the explanation is that women are more likely to report problems, and the problems they have are less life-threatening.

The last variable that we want to examine is smoking. Smoking is a major health risk. Smokers have more health problems than nonsmokers.

The last section in this chapter was medical swindles. Older persons are often vulnerable to medical swindles because they have more chronic or incurable health problems. Living alone, being desperate for a cure, and not being able to read the small print on a contract contribute to the exploitation of older persons. Most of these swindles are harmful to older persons. They may spend money on useless "cures" rather than on legitimate medical care, they may delay legitimate medical treatment, and the "cure" may be dangerous.

REFERENCES

Akin, J. S., Guilkey, D. K., Popkin, B. M., & Smith, K. M. (1987). Determinants of nutrient intake of the elderly. *Journal of Applied Gerontology*, **6**(3): 227–258.

Albanes, D., Blair, A., & Taylor, P. R. (1989). Physical activity and risk of cancer in the NHANES I population. *American Journal of Public Health*, **79**(6): 744–750.

Alford, D. M. (1986). The role of nursing. *The Gerontologist*, **26**:(6) 610–613.

Anonymous (1971). *Running after forty*. Mountain View, CA: World Publications.

Atkinson, J. H., & Schuckit, M. A. (1981). Alcoholism and over-the-counter and prescription drug misuse in the elderly. In C. Eisdorfer (Ed.), *Annual review of gerontology and geriatrics: Volume Two* (pp. 255–284). New York: Springer.

Austin, C. (1987). Nutrition programs. In G. L. Maddox (Ed.), *The encyclopedia of aging* (pp. 495–496). New York: Springer.

Axelson, M. L., & Penfield, M. P. (1983). Food- and nutrition-related attitudes of elderly persons living alone. *Journal of Nutrition Education,* **15**(1): 23–27.

Bachur, J. A. (1986). A social work perspective. *The Gerontologist,* **26**(6): 614–617.

Baker, H., Frank, O., Thind, I. S., Jaslow, S. P., & Louria, D. B. (1979). Vitamin profiles in elderly persons living at home or in a nursing home, versus profiles in healthy young subjects. *Journal of the American Geriatrics Society,* **28**(10): 444–450.

Baker, R. R. (1984). Attitudes of health care providers toward elderly patients with normal aging and disease-related symptoms. *The Gerontologist,* **24**(5): 543–545.

Balabokin, M. E., Danon, D., Gurian, B. S., Robinson, R., & Shanas, E. (1972). Health and nutrition. *The Gerontologist,* **12**(2, Part II): 21–29.

Balsam, A., & Poe, D. (1987). Game show promotes nutrition education for elders. *Journal of Nutrition Education,* **19**(4): 168d.

Becker, G., & Kaufman, S. (1988). Old age, rehabilitation, and research: A review of the issues. *The Gerontologist,* **28**(4): 459–469.

Bender, C., & Hart, J. P. (1987). A model for health promotion for the rural elderly. *The Gerontologist,* **27**(2): 139–142.

Berger, R. (1976). Nutritional needs of the aged. In I. M. Burnside (Ed.), *Nursing and the aged* (pp. 113–122). New York: McGraw-Hill.

Binstock, R. H. (1987). Health care: Organization, use, and financing. In G. L. Maddox (Ed.), *The encyclopedia of aging* (pp. 307–311). New York: Springer.

Blumenthal, J. A., Emery, C. F., Madden, D. J., George, L. K., Coleman, R. E., Riddle, M. W., McKee, D. C., Reasoner, J., & Williams, R. S. (1989). Cardiovascular and behavioral effects of aerobic exercise training in healthy older men and women. *Journal of Gerontology: Medical Sciences,* **44**(5): M147–157.

Bortz II, W. M. (1980). Effect of exercise on aging—effect of aging on exercise. *Journal of the American Geriatrics Society,* **28**(2): 49–51.

Bortz II, W. M. (1982). Disuse and aging. *Journal of the American Medical Association,* **248**(10): 1203–1208.

Brady, E. S. (1975). Drugs and the elderly. In R. H. Davis & W. K. Smith (Eds.), *Drugs and the elderly* (pp. 1–6). Los Angeles: University of Southern California Press.

Briganti, F. J. (1975). Side effects of drugs used by the elderly. In R. H. Davis & W. K. Smith (Eds.), *Drugs and the elderly* (pp. 25–32). Los Angeles: University of Southern California Press.

Brogdon, H. G., & Alford, B. A. (1973). Food preferences in relation to dietary intake and adequacy in a nursing home population. *The Gerontologist,* **13**(3, Part 1): 355–358.

Brower, H. T. (1985). Do nurses stereotype the aged? *Journal of Gerontological Nursing,* **11**(1): 17–28.

Brown, B. B. (1982). Professionals' perception of drug and alcohol abuse among the elderly. *The Gerontologist,* **22**(6): 519–524.

Calasanti, T. M., & Hendricks, J. (1986). A sociological perspective on nutrition research among the elderly: Toward conceptual development. *The Gerontologist,* **26**(3): 232–238.

Chu, J., Diehr, P., Feigl, P., Glaefke, G., Begg, C., Glicksman, A., & Ford, L. (1987). The effect of age on the care of women with breast cancer in community hospitals. *Journal of Gerontology,* **42**(2): 185–190.

Cockerham, W. C., Sharp, K., & Wilcox, J. A. (1983). Aging and perceived health status. *Journal of Gerontology,* **38**(3): 349–355.

Collinsworth, R. (1989). Nutritional assessment of the elderly. *Journal of Gerontological Nursing,* **15**(12): 17–21.

Crandall, R. (1986). *Running: The consequences.* Jefferson, NC: McFarland.

Cunningham, D. A., Rechnitzer, P. A., Howard, J. H., & Donner, A. P. (1987). Exercise training of men at retirement: A clinical trial. *Journal of Gerontology,* **42**(1): 17–23.

Davis, M. A., Randall, E., Forthofer, R. N., Lee, E. S., & Margen, S. (1985). Living arrangements and dietary patterns of older adults in the United States. *Journal of Gerontology,* **40**(4): 434–442.

Dowd, J., & Bengtson, V. (1978). Aging in minority populations: An examination of the double jeopardy hypothesis. *Journal of Gerontology,* **33**(3): 427–436.

Dressendorfer, R. H. (1980). Physiological profile of a masters runner. *Physician and Sportsmedicine,* **8**(8): 49–52.

Dupree, L. W., Broskowski, H., & Schonfeld, L. (1984). The gerontology alcohol project: A behavioral treatment program for elderly alcohol abusers. *The Gerontologist,* **24**(5): 510–516.

Eagle, D. J., Guyatt, G., Patterson, C., & Turpie, I. (1987). Day hospitals' cost and effectiveness: A summary. *The Gerontologist,* **27**(6): 735–740.

Edsall, R. L. (1988). Focusing the fight against health fraud. *Patient Care,* **22**(6):12.

Engel, P. A. (1986). Toxicity of drugs in the aged. In R. L. Judd, C. G. Warner, & M. A. Shaffer (Eds.), *Geriatric emergencies* (pp. 11–23) Rockville, MD: Aspen.

Espino, D. V., Neufeld, R. R., Mulvihill, M., & Libow, L. S. (1988). Hispanic and non-Hispanic elderly on admission to the nursing home: A pilot study. *The Gerontologist,* **28**(6): 821–824.

Fanelli, M. T., Abernethy, M. M. (1986). A nutritional questionnaire for older adults. *The Gerontologist,* **26**(2): 192–197.

Ferraro, K. F. (1987). Double jeopardy to health for black older adults? *Journal of Gerontology,* **42**(5): 528–533.

Fishman, N. H., & Roe, B. B. (1978). Cardiac valve replacement in patients over 65 during a 10–year period. *Journal of Gerontology,* **33**(5): 676–680.

Fishman, P., VanMarrelo, C., & Arthur, E. (1987). A college-based nutrition counseling service for homebound elderly persons. *Journal of Nutrition Education,* **19**(6): 273–276.

Fitzgerald, J. F., Moore, P. S., & Dittus, R. S. (1988). The care of elderly patients with hip fracture. *New England Journal of Medicine,* **319**(21): 1392–1397.

Food and Nutrition Board (1986). Recommended dietary allowances: Scientific issues and process for the future. *Journal of Nutrition Education,* **18**(2): 82–87.

Ford, A. B. (1987). Looking after the old folks. *American Journal of Public Health,* **77**(12): 1499–1500.

Ford, A. B. (1989). Reducing the threat of hip fracture. *American Journal of Public Health,* **79**(3): 269–270.

Foster, V. L., Hume, G. J. E., Byrnes, W. C., Dickinson, A. L., & Chatfield, S. J. (1989). Endurance training for elderly women: Moderate vs. low intensity. *Journal of Gerontology: Medical Sciences,* **44**(6): M184–178.

Fries, J. F., (1980). Aging, natural death, and the compression of morbidity. *New England Journal of Medicine,* **303**(3): 130–135.

Fries, J. F. (1984). The compression of morbidity: Miscellaneous comments about a theme. *The Gerontologist,* **24**(4): 354–359.

Gaitz, C. M., & Wilson, N. L. (1986). Comments by a psychiatrist and a case manager. *The Gerontologist,* **26**(6): 606–609.

Garry, P. J., Goodwin, J. S., & Hunt, W. C. (1983). Iron status and anemia in the elderly: New findings and a review of previous studies. *Journal of the American Geriatrics Society,* **31**(7): 389–399.

Garry, P. J., Goodwin, J. S., & Hunt, W. C. (1984). Folate and vitamin B_{12} status in a healthy elderly population. *Journal of the American Geriatrics Society,* **32**(10): 719–726.

Garry, P. J., Goodwin, J. S., Hunt, W. C., Hooper, E. M., & Leonard, A. G., (1982). Nutritional status in a healthy elderly population: Dietary and supplemental intakes. *American Journal of Clinical Nutrition,* **36**(8): 319–332.

German, P. S., & Burton, L. C. (1989). Medication and the elderly. *Journal of Aging and Health,* **1**(1): 4–34.

Glanz, K., & Scharf, M. (1985). A nutrition training program for social workers serving the homebound elderly. *The Gerontologist,* **25**(5): 455–459.

Goldberg, P. B., & Roberts, J. (1983). Pharmacologic basis for developing rational drug regimens for elderly patients. *Medical Clinics of North America,* **67**(2): 315–344.

Gomez, G., Otto, D., Blattstein, A., & Gomez, E. A. (1985). Beginning nursing students can change attitudes about the aged. *Journal of Gerontological Nursing,* **11**(1): 6–11.

Goodwin, J. S. (1989). Knowledge about aging among physicians. *Journal of Aging and Health,* **1**(2): 234–243.

Goodwin, J. S., & Garry, P. J. (1988). Lack of correlation between indices of nutritional status and immunologic function in elderly humans. *Journal of Gerontology,* **43**(2): M46–49.

Goodwin, J. S., Goodwin, J. M., & Garry, P. J. (1983). Association between nutritional status and cognitive functioning in a healthy elderly population. *Journal of the American Medical Association,* **249**(21): 2917–2921.

Goodwin, J. S., Sanchez, J., Thomas, P., Hunt, C., Garry, P. J., & Goodwin, J. M. (1987). Alcohol intake in a healthy elderly population. *American Journal of Public Health,* **77**(2): 173–177.

Gottheil, E., Druley, K. A., Skoloda, T. E., & Waxman, H. M. (Eds.) (1985). *The combined problems of alcoholism, drug addiction, and aging.* Springfield, IL: Thomas.

Greenfield, S., Blanco, D. M., Elashoff, R. M., & Ganz, P. A. (1987). Patterns of care related to age of breast cancer patients. *Journal of the American Medical Association,* **257**(20): 2766–2770.

Guigoz, Y., & Munro, H. N. (1985). Nutrition and aging. In C. E. Finch & E. L. Schneider (Eds.), *Handbook of the biology of aging* (second edition) (pp. 878–893). New York: Van Nostrand Reinhold.

Haber, D. (1986). Health promotion to reduce blood pressure level among older blacks. *The Gerontologist,* **26**(2): 119–121.

Harel, Z. (1985). Nutrition site service users: Does racial background make a difference. *The Gerontologist,* **25**(3): 286–291.

Harper, A. E. (1981). Dietary guidelines for the elderly. *Geriatrics,* **36**(7): 34–42.

Harris, T., Kovar, M. G., Suzman, R., Kleinman, J. C., & Feldman, J. J. (1989). Longitudinal study of physical ability in the oldest-old. *American Journal of Public Health,* **79**(6): 698–702.

Hartford, J. T., & Samorajski, T. (1982). Alcoholism in the geriatric population. *Journal of the American Geriatrics Society,* **30**(1): 18–24.

Hartung, G. H., & Farge, E. J. (1977). Personality and physiological traits in middle-aged runners and joggers. *Journal of Gerontology,* **32**(2): 541–548.

Hefley, M. L. (1987). Vitamins. In G. L. Maddox (Ed.), *The encyclopedia of aging* (pp. 684–685). New York: Springer.

Heinemann, M. E., & Hoffman, A. (1986). Alcoholism. In D. L. Carnevali & M. Patrick (Eds.), *Nursing management for the elderly* (second edition) (pp. 301–317). New York: Lippincott.

Hesse, K. A., Levkoff, S. E., & Campion, E. W. (1988). House officers' knowledge of geriatric health policy: Are the gatekeepers learning the rules. *The Gerontologist,* **28**(2): 233–236.

Hogan, D. B., & Cape, R. D. (1984). Marathoners over 60 years of age: Results of a survey. *American Geriatrics Society Journal,* **32**(2): 121–123.

Holmes, D., Holmes, M., & Teresik, J. (1988). Routine collection of medication side effect data using computer terminals located in a senior center. *The Gerontologist,* **28**(1): 105–107.

Hosking, M. P., Warner, M. A., Lobdell, C. M., Offord, K. P., & Melton, L. J. (1989). Outcome of surgery in patients 90 years of age and older. *Journal of the American Medical Association,* **261**(13): 1909–1915.

Howell, S. C. (1974). Nutrition education in relation to aging. In S. Grabowski & W. D. Mason (Eds.), *Learning for aging* (pp. 265–283). Washington, DC.: Adult Education Association.

Janik, S. W., & Dunham, R. G. (1983). A nationwide examination of the need for specific alcoholism treatment programs for the elderly. *Journal of Studies on Alcohol,* **44**(2): 307–317.

Jensen, J. S., & Tondevold, E. (1979). Mortality after hip fracture. *Acta Orthopaedica Scandinavica,* **50**(2): 161–167.

Johnson, L. K. (1989). How to diagnose and treat chemical dependency in the elderly. *Journal of Gerontological Nursing,* **15**(2): 22–26.

Kane, R., Solomon, D., Beck, J., Keller, E., & Kane, R. (1980) The future need for geriatric manpower in the U.S. *New England Journal of Medicine,* **302**(24): 1327–1332.

Kart, C. S., Metress, E. K., & Metress, S. P. (1988). *Aging, health and society.* Boston: Jones and Bartlett.

Kasch, F. W. (1976). The effects of exercise on the aging process. *Physician and Sportsmedicine,* **4**(6): 64–68.

Kasch, F. W., & Kulberg, J. (1981). Physiological variables during 15 years of endurance exercise. *Scandinavian Journal of Sports Science,* **3**(2) 59–62.

Kasch, F. W., & Wallace, J. P. (1976). Physiological variables during 10 years of endurance exercise. *Medicine and Science in Sports,* **8**(1): 59–62.

Kasch, F. W., Wallace, J. P., VanCamp, S. P., & Verity, L. (1988). A longitudinal study of cardiovascular stability in active men aged 45 to 65 years. *Physician and Sportsmedicine,* **16**(1): 117–125.

Kent, S. (1982). Exercise and aging. *Geriatrics,* **37**(6): 132–135.

Kivela, S-L., & Nissinen, A. (1987). Nutrition education and changes in nutrition behavior among the 65–74 year old population of eastern Finland. *Journal of Nutrition Education,* **19**(2): 77–82.

Kofoed, L. L., Tolson, R. L., Atkinson, R. M., Toth, R. L., & Turner, J. A. (1987). Treatment compliance of older alcoholics: An elder-specific approach is superior to "mainstreaming." *Journal of Studies on Alcohol,* **48**(1): 47–51.

Kokkonen, G. C., & Barrows, C. H., (1987). Nutrition. In G. L. Maddox (Ed.), *The encyclopedia of aging* (pp. 492–495). New York: Springer.

Kola, L. A., & Kosberg, J. I. (1981). Model to assess community services for the elderly alcoholic. *Public Health Reports,* **96**(5): 458–463.

Kola, L. A., Kosberg, J. I., & Joyce, K. (1984). The alcoholic elderly client: Assessment of policies and practices of service providers. *The Gerontologist,* **24**(5): 517–521.

Kovar, M. G. (1987). Health assessment. In G. L. Maddox (Ed.), *The encyclopedia of aging* (pp. 302–305). New York: Springer.

Krause, N. (1987). Stress in racial differences in self-reported health among the elderly. *The Gerontologist,* **27**(1): 72–76.

Krupka, L. R., & Vener, A. M. (1979). Hazards of drug use among the elderly. *The Gerontologist,* **19**(1): 90–95.

Kvitek, S. D. B., Shaver, B. J., Blood, H., & Shepard, K. F. (1986). Age bias: Physical therapists and older patients. *Journal of Gerontology,* **41**(6): 706–709.

LaGreca, A. J., Aker, R. L., & Dwyer, J. W. (1988). Life events and alcohol behavior among older adults. *The Gerontologist,* **28**(4): 552–558.

Lamy, P. P. (1986). Considerations from pharmacology. *The Gerontologist,* **26**(6): 603–605.

Lane, N. E., Bloch, D. A., Jones, H. H., Marshall, W. H., Wood, P. D., & Fries, J. F. (1986). Long-distance running, bone density, and osteoarthritis, *Journal of the American Medical Association,* **255**(9): 1147–1151.

Lank, N. H., & Vickery, C. E. (1987). Nutrition education for the elderly: Concerns, needs, and approaches. *Journal of Applied Gerontology,* **6**(3): 259–267.

Legwold, G. (1982). Masters competitors age little in 10 years. *Physician & Sportsmedicine,* **10**(10): 27.

Levkoff, S. E., Cleary, P. D., & Wetle, T. (1987). Differences in the appraisal of health between aged and middle-aged adults. *Journal of Gerontology,* **42**(1): 114–120.

Liu, W. T. (1986). Health services for Asian Americans. *Research on Aging,* **9**(1): 156–175.

Lubben, J. E., Weiler, P. G., & Chi, I. (1989). Health practices of the elderly poor. *American Journal of Public Health,* **79**(6): 731–734.

Ludman, E. K., & Newman, J. M. (1986). Frail elderly: Assessment of nutrition needs. *The Gerontologist,* **26**(2): 198–202.

McCall, P. L. (1986). Nutritional emergencies. In R. L. Judd, C. G. Warner, & M. A. Shaffer (Eds.), *Geriatric emergencies* (pp. 221–254). Rockville, MD: Aspen.

Maddox, G. L. (1987). Obesity. In G. L. Maddox (Ed.), *The encyclopedia of aging* (p. 498). New York: Springer.

Maddox, G. L., Robins, L. N., & Rosenberg, N. (Eds.) (1985). *The nature and extent of alcohol problems among the elderly.* New York: Springer.

Magaziner, J., Simonsick, E. M., Kashner, T. M., Hebel, J. R., & Kenzora, J. E. (1989). Survival experience of aged hip fracture patients. *American Journal of Public Health,* **79**(3): 274–278.

Maud, P. J., Pollock, M. L., Foster, C., Anholm, J. D., Gutten, G., Al-Nouri, M., Hellman, C., & Schmidt, D. H. (1981). Fifty years of training and competition in the marathon: Wally Hayward, age 70—a physiological profile. *South African Medical Journal,* **31**(1): 153–157.

Minkler, M. (1987). Health promotion. In G. L. Maddox (Ed.), *The encyclopedia of aging* (pp. 316–317). New York: Springer.

Mishara, B. L., & Kastenbaum, R. (1980). *Alcohol and old age.* New York: Grune and Stratton.

Montamat, S. C., Cusack, B. J., & Vestal, R. E. (1989). Management of drug therapy in the elderly. *New England Journal of Medicine,* **321**(5): 303–309.

Moore, S. R. (1989). Walking for health: A nurse-managed activity. *Journal of Gerontological Nursing,* **15**(7): 26–28.

Morrell, R. W., Park, D. C., & Poon, L. W. (1989). Quality of instructions on prescription drug labels: Effects on memory and comprehension in young and old. *The Gerontologist,* **29**(3): 345–354.

Mossey, J. M., Mutran, E., Knott, K., & Craik, R. (1989). Determinants of recovery 12 months after hip fracture: The importance of psychosocial factors. *American Journal of Public Health,* **79**(3): 279–286.

Murphy, S. P., Everett, D. F., & Dresser, C. M. (1989). Food group consumption reported by the elderly during the NHANES I epidemiologic followup study. *Journal of Nutrition Education,* **21**(5): 214–220.

National Center for Health Statistics (1983). Sex differences in health and use of medical care, United States, 1979. *Vital and Health Statistics,* Series 3, No. 24.

National Center for Health Statistics (1984*a*). Changes in mortality among the elderly. United States, 1940–1978 supplement to 1980. *Vital and Health Statistics,* Series 3.

National Center for Health Statistics (1984*b*). Health indicators for Hispanic, black, and white Americans. *Vital and Health Statistics,* Series 10, No. 148.

National Center for Health Statistics (1985). Health characteristics according to family and personal income. *Vital and Health Statistics,* Series 10, No. 147.

National Center for Health Statistics (1986*a*). Prevalence of selected chronic conditions, United States, 1979–1981. *Vital and Health Statistics,* Series 10, No. 155.

National Center for Health Statistics (1986*b*). Total serum cholesterol levels of adults 20–74 years of age, United States, 1976–1980. *Vital and Health Statistics,* Series 11, No. 236.

National Center for Health Statistics (1986*c*). Blood pressure levels in persons 18–74 years of age in 1976–1980, and trends in blood pressure from 1960 to 1980 in the United States. *Vital and Health Statistics,* Series 11, No. 234.

National Center for Health Statistics (1987*a*). Health statistics on older persons, United States, 1986. *Vital and Health Statistics,* Series 3, No. 25.

National Center for Health Statistics (1987*b*). Anthropometric reference data and prevalence of overweight, United States, 1976–1980. *Vital and Health Statistics,* Series 11, No. 238.

National Institute on Aging (1985). Health quackery. *Age Page.*

O'Hanlon, P. O., & Kohrs, M. B. (1978). Dietary studies of older Americans. *American Journal of Clinical Nutrition,* **31**(6): 1257–1267.

Omdahl, J. L., Garry, P. J., Hunsaker, L. A., Hunt, W. C., & Goodwin, J. S. (1982). Nutritional status in a healthy elderly population: Vitamin D. *American Journal of Clinical Nutrition,* **36**(12): 1125–1233.

Omenn, G. S. (1982). Pharmacogenetics. In C. Eisdorfer (Ed.), *Annual review of gerontology and geriatrics: Volume Three* (pp. 27–51). New York: Springer.

Osborn, M. O. (1970). Nutrition of the aged. In A. M. Hoffman (Ed.), *The daily needs and interests of older people* (pp. 235–257). Springfield, IL: Thomas.

Ostrom, J. (1986). Medications and the elderly. In D. L. Carnevali & M. Patrick (Eds.), *Nursing management for the elderly* (second edition) (pp. 143–163). New York: Lippincott.

Palmore, E. (1976). The future status of the aged. *The Gerontologist,* **16**(4): 297–302.

Palmore, E. (1986). Trends in the health of the aged. *The Gerontologist,* **26**(3): 298–302.

Pearlman, R. A., & Uhlmann, R. F. (1988). Quality of life in chronic diseases: Perception of elderly patients. *Journal of Gerontology,* **43**(2): M25–M30.

Petchers, M. K., & Milligan, S. E. (1988). Access to health care in a black urban elderly population. *The Gerontologist,* **28**(2): 213–217.

Pollock, M. L. (1974). Physiological characteristics of older champion track athletes. *Research Quarterly,* **45**(4): 363–373.

Pollock, M. L., Miller, H. S., Janeway, R., Linnerud, A. C., Robertson, B., & Valentino,

R. (1971). Effects of walking on body composition and cardiovascular function of middle-aged men. *Journal of Applied Physiology*, **30**(1): 126–130.

Pollock, M. L., Miller, H. S., & Wilmore, J. (1974). Physiological characteristics of champion track athletes 40 to 75 years of age. *Journal of Gerontology*, **29**(6): 645–649.

Pollock, M. L., & Ribisl, P. M. (1978). Effects of fitness on aging. *Physician and Sportsmedicine*, **6**(8): 45–49.

Pollock, M. L., & Wilmore, J. (1974). Physiological characteristics of champion track athletes 40 to 75 years of age. *Journal of Gerontology*, **29**(6): 645–649.

Pratt, C. C., Simonson, W., & Lloyd, S. (1982). Pharmacists' perceptions of major difficulties in geriatric pharmacy practice. *The Gerontologist*, **22**(3): 288–292.

Raskind, M. (1983). Nutrition and cognitive function in the elderly. *Journal of the American Medical Association*, **249**(21): 2939–2940.

Roe, D. A. (1987). *Geriatric nutrition* (second edition). Englewood Cliffs, NJ: Prentice-Hall.

Rogot, E. (1978). Smoking and life expectancy among U.S. veterans. *American Journal of Public Health*, **68**(10): 1023–1025.

Rost, K., & Roter, D. (1987). Predictors of recall of medication regimens and recommendations for lifestyle change in elderly patients. *The Gerontologist*, **27**(4): 510–515.

Roundtree, J. L., & Tinklin, G. L. (1975). Food beliefs and practices of selected senior citizens. *The Gerontologist*, **15**(6): 537–540.

Rozovski, S. J. (1984). Nutrition for older Americans. *Aging*, **344**(April–May): 49–64.

Ryan, A. J. (1981). Exercise and arthritis: An encouraging report. *Physician and Sportsmedicine*, **9**(5): 43.

Sager, K. (1983). Senior fitness—for the health of it. *Physician and Sportsmedicine*, **11**(10): 31–36.

Sager, K. (1984). Exercise to activate seniors. *Physician and Sportsmedicine*, **12**(5): 144–149.

Samet, J., Hunt, W. C., Key, C., Humble, C. G., & Goodwin, J. S. (1986). Choice of cancer therapy varies with age of patient. *Journal of the American Medical Association*, **255**(24): 3385–3390.

Santo-Novak, D., & Edwards, R. M. (1989). Rx: Take caution with drugs for elders. *Geriatric Nursing*, **10**(2): 72–75.

Schneider, E. L., & Brody, J. A. (1983). Aging, natural death, and the compression of morbidity: Another view. *New England Journal of Medicine*, **309**(14): 854–859.

Schneider, E. L., Vining, E. M., Hadley, E. C., & Farnham, S. A. (1986). Recommended dietary allowances and the health of the elderly. *New England Journal of Medicine*, **314**(3): 157–160.

Seccombe, K. (1989). Ethnicity or socioeconomic status? Health differences between elder Alaska Natives and whites. *The Gerontologist*, **29**(4): 551–556.

Shannon, B. M., Smiciklas-Wright, H., Davis, B. W., & Lewis, C. (1983). A peer educator approach to nutrition for the elderly. *The Gerontologist*, **23**(2): 123–126.

Shephard, R. J., & Montelpare, W. (1988). Geriatric benefits of exercise as an adult. *Journal of Gerontology*, **43**(4): 86–90.

Sherwood, S. (1970). Gerontology and the sociology of food and eating. *Aging and Human Development*, **1**(1): 61–68.

Siddharthan, K., & Sowers-Hoag, K. (1989). Elders' attitudes and access to health care: A comparison of Cuban immigrants and native-born Americans. *Journal of Applied Gerontology*, **8**(1): 86–96.

Silliman, R. A., Guadagnoli, E., Weitberg, A. B., & Mor, V. (1989). Age as a predictor of diagnostic and initial treatment intensity in newly diagnosed breast cancer. *Journal of Gerontology: Medical Sciences*, **44**(2): M46–50.

Silverstone, B., Whittington, F. J., & Roberts, J. (1986). A practice concepts symposium on drug misuse in the elderly: Examination of a case history. *The Gerontologist,* **26**(6): 595–598.

Simonson, W. (1986). The viewpoint of a clinical pharmacist. *The Gerontologist,* **26**(6): 599–602.

Smith, E. L. (1981). Bone changes in the exercising older adult. In E. L. Smith & R. C. Serfass (Eds.), *Exercise and aging: The scientific basis* (pp. 11–18). Hillside, NJ: Enslow.

Smith, E. L. (1982). Exercise for prevention of osteoporosis: A review. *Physician and Sportsmedicine,* **10**(3): 72–83.

Smith, E. L., & Gilligan, C. (1983). Physical activity prescription for the older adult. *Physician and Sportsmedicine,* **11**(8): 91–101.

Smith, E. L., Sempos, C. T., & Purvis, R. W. (1981). Bone mass and strength decline with age. In E. L. Smith & R. C. Serfass (Eds.), *Exercise and aging: The scientific basis* (pp. 59–88). Hillside, NJ: Enslow.

Sobal, J., Muncie, H. L., & Baker, A. S. (1986). Use of nutritional supplements in a retirement community. *The Gerontologist,* **26**(2): 187–191.

Stern, D. S., & Kastenbaum, R. (1984). Alcohol use and abuse in old age. In J. P. Abrahams & V. Crooks (Eds.), *Geriatric mental health* (pp. 154–168). New York: Grune and Stratton.

Stovas, J. (1984). Seniors walk away from sedentary life. *Physician and Sportsmedicine,* **12**(4): 144–152.

Surgery for elderly patients (1989). *Nursing Times,* **85**(29): 26–30.

Tami, T., Nakai, T., Takai, H., Fujiwaru, R., Miyabo, S., Higuchi, M., & Kobayashi, S. (1988). The effects of physical exercise on plasma lipoprotein and apolipoprotein metabolism in elderly men. *Journal of Gerontology,* **43**(4): 75–79.

Trainor, P. A. (1988). Over-the-counter drugs: Count them in. *Geriatric Nursing,* **9**(5): 298–299.

Troll, L. E. (1976). Eating and aging. *Journal of the American Dietetic Association,* **59**(November): 456–459.

U.S. Bureau of the Census (1987). *Statistical abstracts of the United States: 1987.* Washington, DC: U.S. Government Printing Office.

U.S. Bureau of the Census (1990). *Statistical abstracts of the United States: 1990.* Washington, DC: U.S. Government Printing Office.

U.S. Congress, Office of Technology Assessment (1987). *Life-sustaining technologies and the elderly.* Washington, DC: U.S. Government Printing Office.

Vaccaro, P., Dummer, G., & Clarke D. (1981). Physiological characteristics of female master swimmers. *Physician and Sportsmedicine,* **9**(12): 75–78.

Verbrugge, L. M. (1984). A health profile of older women with comparisons to older men. *Research on Aging,* **6**(3): 291–322.

Verbrugge, L. M. (1987). Sex differences in health. In G. L. Maddox (Ed.), *The encyclopedia of aging* (pp. 601–604). New York: Springer.

Vestal, R. E., & Dawson, G. W. (1985). Pharmacology and aging. In C. E. Finch & E. L. Schneider (Eds.), *Handbook of the biology of aging* (second edition) (pp. 744–819). New York: Van Nostrand Reinhold.

Vogel-Sprott, M., & Barrett, P. (1984). Age, drinking habits, and the effects of alcohol. *Journal of Studies on Alcohol,* **45**(6): 517–521.

Wayler, A. H., Muench, M. E., Kapur, K. K., & Chauncey, H. H. (1984). Masticatory performance and food acceptability in persons with removable partial dentures, full dentures, and intact natural dentition. *Journal of Gerontology,* **39**(2): 284–289.

Webb, J. L., Urner, S. C., & McDaniels, J. (1977). Physiological characteristics of a champion runner: Age 77. *Journal of Gerontology,* **32**(3): 286–290.

Weg, R. (1975*a*). Drug interaction with the changing physiology of the aged: Practice and potential. In R. H. Davis & W. K. Smith (Eds.), *Drugs and the elderly* (pp. 70–90). Los Angeles: University of Southern California Press.

Weg, R. (1975*b*). Changing physiology of aging: normal and pathological. In D. S. Woodruff & J. E. Birren (Eds.), *Aging: Scientific perspectives and social issues* (pp. 229–256). New York: Van Nostrand.

Wells-Parker, E., Miles, S., & Spencer, B. (1983). Stress experiences and drinking histories of elderly drunken-driving offenders. *Journal of Studies on Alcohol,* **44**(3): 429–437.

Wetle, T. (1987). Age as a risk factor for inadequate treatment. *Journal of the American Medical Association,* **258**(4): 516.

Wetle, T., Cwikel, J., & Levkoff, S. E. (1988). Geriatric medical decisions: Factors influencing allocation of scarce resources and the decision to withhold treatment. *The Gerontologist,* **28**(3): 336–343.

Whittington, F. J. & Maddox, G. L. (1986). A view from sociology. *The Gerontologist,* **26**(6): 618–621.

Wilder, C. A. (1973). Limitations of activity due to chronic conditions. *Vital and Health Statistics,* Series 10, Number 80.

Williams, T. F. (1986). Geriatrics: The fruition of the clinician reconsidered. *The Gerontologist,* **26**(4): 345–349.

Wisoff, B. G., Hartstein, M. L., Agop A., Aintalian, A., & Hamby, R. I. (1976). Results of open heart surgery in the septuagenarian. *Journal of Gerontology,* **31**(3): 275–277.

Wood, W. G. (1987). Alcoholism. In G. L. Maddox (Ed.), *The encyclopedia of aging* (pp. 25–27). New York: Springer.

Wood, W. G., & Elias, M. F. (Eds.) (1982). *Alcoholism and aging: Advances in research.* Boca Raton, FL: CRC Press.

World Health Organization (1946). *World Health Organization Charter.* Geneva: World Health Organization.

Worthington-Roberts, B. S., & Hazzard, W. R. (1982). Nutrition and aging. In C. Eisdorfer (Ed.), *Annual review of gerontology and geriatrics: Volume Three* (pp. 297–328). New York: Springer.

Worthington-Roberts, B. S., & Karkeck, J. M. (1986). Nutrition. In D. L. Carnevali & M. Patrick (Eds.), *Nursing management for the elderly* (second edition) (pp. 189–218). New York: Lippincott.

Wynder, E. L. (1988). Tobacco and health: A review of the history and suggestions for public health policy. *Public Health Reports,* **103**(1): 8–16.

Yearick, E. S., Wang, M-S., L., & Pisias, S. J. (1980). Nutritional status of the elderly: Dietary and biochemical findings. *Journal of Gerontology,* **35**(5): 663–671.

Young, E. A. (1983). Nutrition, aging, and the aged. *Medical Clinics of North America,* **67**(2): 295–313.

Yu, E. S. H. (1989). Health of Chinese elderly in America. *Research on Aging,* **8**(1): 84–109.

CHAPTER 7

SEXUALITY

Frank Siteman/Stock, Boston

INTRODUCTION

We have become a very sexually oriented, sexually conscious, and sexually knowledgeable society. Current concepts and views on sexuality are extremely different from 100 years ago in terms of its discussion, display, perception, and purpose. Where sexuality was seldom discussed in the past, it has currently reached a saturation level. Talk shows, movies, college and high school courses, and magazines are inundating the marketplace while it is still a "hot" topic. While the Victorian era prevented the public display of sexuality in behavior or in clothing styles, public behavior today is often blatantly sexual and clothing is often designed to enhance not hide sexuality. Where in the past sex was perceived as an abnormal drive that needed to be controlled or the individual would suffer from a variety of physical and psychological illnesses, today it is frequently seen as a life force that needs to be expressed in a myriad of forms for psychological and physical well-being. The last view that has changed deals with the purpose of sex. While in the past the purpose of sex was procreation today its function is primarily recreational.

Given the tremendous emphasis on sexuality in contemporary American society it is interesting that gerontologists have only recently started to explore the sexuality of older persons in a scientific, systematic manner. Traditionally human sexuality was viewed as an area of importance for the young, but not for older persons. It was assumed that just as the ability to have children declined with increasing age, so did all sexual activity and thought. These were supposedly the sexless years when individuals were "too old," "too fragile," "too sick," or "too tired" to think about, much less engage in, sexual activity. Besides, it was believed that older persons did not have sexual feelings or desires. To reinforce the cultural belief of a sexless old age, there were many jokes about the feeble, inept attempts of older persons to engage in sexual acts. Situations in which the sexuality of older persons was difficult to deny, such as an older man marrying and impregnating a young woman, often evoked feelings of disgust or repugnance. Older persons who did not meet the societal stereotype were seen as deviants and promptly labeled as "dirty" old men and women (see Covey, 1989; Lobsenz, 1974).

This chapter will examine the sexuality of older persons, and is divided into eight sections. The first section will examine some of the methodological problems involved in studying the sexuality of older persons. The second section is a chronological review of the history of research on aged sexuality. In addition to reviewing the work of Alfred C. Kinsey, Johnson and Masters, and other sex researchers, some of the limitations of this research will be mentioned. In the third section we will look at the importance of sexuality to older persons; here we will find that sexuality can be as important in the later life periods as the earlier life periods, and that sexuality can take many forms. In the fourth section the factors that influence sexual activity will be discussed. This section will examine the physiological and sociopsychological factors that have a bearing on rates and forms of sexual expression. The fifth section will examine three of the forms of sexual expression: heterosexual expression, masturbation, and forms of homosexuality. In the sixth section we will consider some of the factors that contribute to sexual problems among older persons. Reasons for declining or discontinuing sexual activity will be discussed as will specific factors that contribute to sexual dysfunctioning. In the seventh section ways of treating sexual dysfunctions will be discussed. It will be reported that sexual dysfunctioning in older persons can often be successfully treated. Finally, in the eighth and last section we will look at the sexual liberation of older persons. Here it will be noted that the purpose of sexual liberation is not to force sexuality on older persons but to allow them the choice of determining their own mode and frequency of sexual expression.

METHODOLOGICAL PROBLEMS IN STUDYING THE SEXUALITY OF OLDER PERSONS

Information on human sexuality has always been available in western society. Poets, writers, teachers, and ministers have frequently felt the need to acquaint others with their perspectives on sexuality. The position, tone, details, and nature of the information has, of course, varied according to the spokesperson, the time, and the place.

Although sexuality was frequently written about and discussed, there have been three major problems with what has been presented; the first two problems are relevant to all sex research, the third is relevant primarily to gerontologists interested in sex research.

The first problem is that most of what has been written was based on philosophical beliefs, not scientific research. This was noted by the late Dr. Alfred C. Kinsey in his 1948 book *Sexual Behavior in the Human Male,* where he said that until his work there had only been nineteen studies that had examined human sexual behavior from a scientific perspective, and that many of these studies had methodological limitations. Although scientific research on human sexuality has advanced, there is still a significant amount of information that is based more on personal belief and philosophy than on scientific research. This is probably because sexuality is still a "sensitive" and "touchy" area for many, and scientific research is considered an inappropriate way of gathering answers to questions.

The second problem is that researchers are inconsistent in the way they present information. There are inconsistencies in the age categories they report, in how they report information, and in the types of behavior they observe and report. Concerning the age categories, some researchers present the results of all participants 50+ years of age, which obviously blurs the distinction between a 50-year-old and a 75-year-old. Others report on those 50 to 59 years of age while another study will use the age grouping 51 to 60. There are also differences in how information is reported. For example, concerning rate of sexual intercourse, some researchers present one figure for all older persons studied, thus blurring the distinction between men and women and different age groups. Other researchers separate men and women but report only one figure for each sex, thus obviously obscuring the distinction between those who are married and those who are not married and different age groups. The terminology can also be confusing. Some studies examine the weekly rate of **sexual intercourse** while others specify the rate for **sexual behavior** or **sexual activity.**

It is important to note that the criticism of using different age categories, reporting techniques, and terminology is not directed at specific studies. Studies have different purposes and researchers certainly have the right to determine what will be studied and how the results will be reported. The major point is that the different age categories, reporting techniques, and terminology have made it difficult to form conclusions about aged sexuality. Most of the studies have not been designed to replicate or confirm earlier research, but to examine a different aspect or area of aged sexuality. Thus, there is not a large body of knowledge on aged sexuality that has extensive scientific support.

The third problem is that the sexuality of older persons was seldom discussed or researched until recently. This created two problems. First, those interested in conducting research in this area did not have much of a base to assist them. They had to discover ways to circumvent problems. The second problem was in the area of attitudes. Many believe that this is an unnecessary or inappropriate area of research. Earlier and more aggressive research in this area might have changed attitudes and allowed for more research.

The next section will provide a brief preview of the research that has been conducted on aged sexuality.

HISTORY OF RESEARCH ON THE SEXUALITY OF OLDER PERSONS

Two early studies on the sexuality of older persons by Lorand in 1913 and Pearl in 1925 (summarized in Berezin, 1969) advanced cautious and semi-Victorian statements about sex in the later years. Lorand associated sexual intercourse at a young age with premature senility (see Burnside, 1975b), and Pearl's study of men with prostatectomies noted that both psychological and physiological factors accounted for the decline in the frequency of their sexual activity (see Kinsey, Pomeroy, & Martin, 1948).

A new era of scientific research on human sexual behavior was ushered in by Dr. Alfred Kinsey and his associates in 1948 with the publication of *Sexual Behavior in the Human Male,* and then again in 1953 with *Sexual Behavior in the Human Female.* Because Kinsey's reputation as a scientist and teacher was beyond reproach, he added respectability to the study of sex. However, his research did not eliminate any of the three problems mentioned above. Although important and frequently cited, the works of Kinsey and his associates suffer from four major methodological limitations, the first two characterizing most sex research on older persons.

First, the samples were not representative of the aged population. Second, there was subject self-selection. That is, participants could elect to participate or not participate in the study. It is generally believed that those who participate in sex research are "different" from those who elect not to participate in sex research. Those who participate in sex studies are probably more sexually liberal than those who elect not to participate (see Palmore, 1952). Third, the samples of aged individuals were very small. For males aged 60+ years, Kinsey had histories on only 87 white and 39 black males, out of a total of 5300 respondents (2.4 percent). Kinsey realized the limitations of this small sample but noted that interest in the area warranted the inclusion of this information. The study on females had 5940 participants; 56 were 61+ years of age (0.9 percent) (another 80 were 56 to 60 years of age). Again, it was noted that the "older" group of females was inadequate. Fourth, the studies were cross sectional, which means that life histories were gathered at one time. Thus, researchers were often asking respondents questions about events that happened 10, 20, 30, or 40+ years prior to the interview, and which a variety of experiences had "colored" or erased.

The next major research project on aged sexuality emerged as part of the Duke Longitudinal Studies (see Busse & Maddox, 1985; Palmore, 1970, 1974, 1981; Palmore et al., 1985). The first set of studies started in 1955 with 270 participants and ended in 1976 with 44 remaining participants. The second round of studies started in 1968 with 502 participants and ended in 1976 with 375 of the original participants. The research reports and articles generated by the studies helped to dispel many of the sexual myths about older persons (Palmore, 1981). Some of the sexual myths that were dispelled follow:

- Most older persons are asexual.
- Sexual dysfunctioning in older persons is irreversible.
- On reaching old age rapid declines take place in remaining sexual capabilities.
- Sexual thought and interest in the aged is abnormal and atypical.
- Sexual activity in old age is damaging or hazardous.

The Duke Longitudinal Studies had four methodological advantages over the Kinsey research. First, the participants were studied longitudinally. That is, rather than a "one-shot" cross-sectional interview, the participants were studied several times over several years. This way information was obtained about current levels of functioning and behavior and compared with earlier periods. Second, the studies were multidisciplinary and data was acquired through the use of a variety of instruments. While Kinsey only used interviewing/questionnaires, the Duke research added psychological and physiological testing. Third, the Duke research had more aged participants. Fourth, the participants in the Duke studies probably constituted a more representative sample than those in Kinsey's research.

The Duke studies concluded that generally both sex drive and activity decline with increasing age. However, there were many individual variations and they reported that many individuals maintain earlier patterns of interest and sexual activity and that for some the level of sexual activity increases from earlier levels.

The research by William Masters and Virginia Johnson added a new dimension to the study of human sexuality: the physiological measurement of sexual response. Rather than relying on self-report and simply counting the number of times people engaged in a certain activity, this research used a variety of instruments to empirically measure what happens physiologically during sexual activity.

Their first book, *Human Sexual Response,* and their second book, *Human Sexual Inadequacy,* have separate chapters on "aging females" and "aging males." In the first book an aging female was someone 40+ years of age. For men it was 50+ years of age. In the second book someone was aging if they were 50+ years of age. There were only 20 men and 11 women over 60 years of age reported on in the first book. The book detailed the specific physiological response to sexual stimulation. Although the book noted many different physiological measurements for younger and older participants, it also stated:

• For women, there is no physiological reason that an earlier, satisfying mode and frequency of sexual activity cannot be maintained in postmenopausal years.
• For men, sexual responsiveness decreases with increasing age.
• For both men and women, the most important factor in maintaining sexual functioning is regular sexual activity.

The next major study of aged sexuality was done by Bernard D. Starr and Marcella Bakur Weiner (Starr, 1985; Starr & Weiner, 1981). This study had one important added dimension, namely that in addition to "counting" or measuring sexual acts, they decided to ask participants to "report the inner experiences of sex. . . ."

Ultimately these "inner experiences" were quantified; however, the importance of this approach cannot be underestimated. It must be remembered that until recently the sexual lives of older persons were considered to be virtually nonexistent; given the research by Johnson and Masters it appeared that whatever remained could not be as "good" as what had existed previously. Starr (1985) noted that although the sexuality of older persons could no longer be denied, the image most individuals had was of a situation that was strained, difficult, and often unpleasant for both partners, leading to the ultimate question of why do older couples even "bother" to have sex.

Thus, Starr and Weiner wanted to take the study of aged sexuality beyond counting the type and frequency of sexual behavior or the measuring of sexual response as subjective measures of sexuality. They wanted to ascertain the meaning of the experience to the individual.

To gather information they asked individuals 60+ years of age in senior centers across the United States to respond to a questionnaire containing fifty open-ended questions. In total, 800 individuals (518 women and 282 men) participated in the study. The final report was very candid about its methodological limitations, one of the greatest being a very small response rate, 14 percent. Some of the findings are reported below:

• A continued interest in sex in the later years.
• About 80 percent were sexually active.
• A weekly frequency of sexual intercourse of 1.5 for those 60–69; 1.4 for those 70–79 and 1.2 for those 80+.
• For 36 percent sex was better now than when younger; for 39 percent it was the same, and for 26 percent it was worse.
• 97 percent said that they liked sex.
• The length of the sex act was the same as when younger for 39 percent; it was shorter for 22 percent; it was longer for 39 percent.

The last major report on aged sexuality was sponsored by the Consumers Union of the United States. A notice placed in the magazine *Consumer Reports* asked readers

50+ years of age to request a questionnaire on sexuality and intimacy. In response to requests, 9800 questionnaires were distributed and 4246 usable questionnaires were returned. The results were published in 1984 in *Love, Sex, and Aging* by Brecher. The author noted the limitations of this study which included a nonrandom sample and subject self-selection. Some of the findings follow:

• Sex in marriage is more important to men than women.
• Unmarried individuals who are sexually active are happier than sexually inactive individuals.
• Some individuals in their eighties continue to engage in and enjoy sexual activity.
• Women who take estrogen are more sexually active than those who do not.
• Frequency of sex declines with increasing age for both men and women.

In summary, there have been several important studies on aged sexuality. The studies have had different goals and methodologies, and different strengths and weaknesses. Together, the studies have contributed significantly to a better understanding of the sexuality of older persons, although many questions still remain. Students need to be aware that because of the emerging interest in this area, and the scarcity of studies, some of the "better" studies have been cited so frequently that they have become accepted as fact, when in fact replication and support is needed.

The question is, "Where will research go from here?" Ideally, some of the problems noted earlier will be corrected. We may also see a change in the direction of some of the studies. In the past there has been a focus on numbers (e.g., weekly frequency of sexual activity, number of orgasms); perhaps in the future there will be more attention to some of the other dimensions of sexuality, such as the changing patterns of love, affection, and intimacy. There can also be more attention to "what is erotic" for different age groups, as well as sexual dreams, desires, and fantasies (see Weg, 1983*a*, 1983*b*).

As was noted earlier, traditionally sexuality has been viewed as an area of concern for the young, not older persons. The next section will examine the importance of sexuality for older persons.

IMPORTANCE OF SEXUALITY TO OLDER PERSONS

Sexuality has traditionally been seen as the domain of the young, not of older persons. Sexuality is seen as an important part of the adolescent maturation process. Its importance and evolution in early adulthood is the source of literally thousands of books and articles. However, the importance of sexuality for older persons is seldom mentioned and most writers cling to the illusion that older persons are sexless.

Pocs and associates (1977) noted, for example, that most college students have a difficult time conceptualizing their parents as sexual beings. Many older persons also believe that society sees them as nonsexual. Brecher's study, on over 4000 individuals 50+ years of age, found that 86 percent believed that "society thinks of older people as nonsexual." This observation has been repeated by several researchers

(Burnside, 1976; Butler & Lewis, 1976, 1982; Roff & Klemmack, 1979; Starr, 1985, 1987; Starr & Weiner, 1981).

The reasons for denying the aged a sexual role are complex and varied and there are many possible explanations. One popular explanation in gerontology has been that it is the younger generation that perpetuates the myth of aged asexuality. After all, it is the young who benefit from the myth. Young men who are just beginning careers and who have low salaries and prestige do not have to feel threatened that older men with more money and prestige will have access to the young women in the society. Similarly, young women do not have to fear that older women, with more money and status, will attract young men. Thus, by making older persons asexual, the young effectively remove potential sexual competitors. Although this explanation is certainly possible, there is no empirical research to support it. Also, on the surface this explanation does not appear to be valid.

Although sexuality has been frequently denied older persons, sexuality is an important component of life at this time (see Starr, 1985; Starr & Weiner, 1981; Weg, 1975*b*, 1983*b*). Starr and Weiner have noted that sex is a psychological as well as a physical need, and that these needs are lifelong. Masters and Johnson (1966) have also pointed out that healthy older persons generally have sex drives that "demand resolution."

Although we commonly associate sexual intercourse with sexuality, this is a limited perspective. Rather, sexuality encompasses a wide variety of different forms of behavior and expression. Holding, caressing, touching, flirting, masturbating, or even talking can all be expressions of sexuality.

While noting the importance of aged sexuality, gerontologists have also noted that there is too much emphasis on "genital sex." Perhaps this is because of the quantitative nature of science, which is more comfortable with tables and figures listing the number of orgasms per week rather than ascertaining the quality or meaning of the orgasm (see Ludeman, 1981; Weg, 1983*b*). Starr (1985, 1987) discussed the concept of "pleasuring," which he said refers to different forms of sexual behavior and arousal that give the individual or couple pleasure. Starr (1985) said that too many couples have been socialized to believe that "sex" means sexual intercourse and noted that too many couples seem more satisfied with completing "the act" rather than "experiencing the act." Many researchers have agreed with this concept, observing that if aged couples are planning to be dependent on the male erection, many are going to be disappointed with their sex lives. However, by broadening the concept of sexuality, other equally satisfying activities may be discovered.

Many gerontologists believe that older persons have a great need to give and receive sexually. For many, old age is a time of declines in health, income, friends, roles (e.g., spouse, parent, worker). It is at this time that reaffirmation of oneself as an attractive, worthwhile, and important human being is needed most.

One study investigated how sexuality influenced the self-esteem of older adults (Stimson et al., 1981). It found that sexuality was equally important to younger and older men, with the difference being that young men placed value on quantity where older men placed it on quality. Feeling attractive to the other sex and capable of performing can "sustain pride." The study noted that women are socialized to "accept youth as a prerequisite for desirability''; because of this, they use the standards of the young to evaluate themselves. For older women this can be devastating in that older women may feel "unattractive" and have a lower sense of self-worth. Sexual activity may reaffirm that she is attractive, needed, and loved.

In summary, we have seen that sexuality is an important part of the life cycle. For most there are significant changes in sexual activity, beliefs, and functioning with increasing age. However, most of the changes do not have to diminish the quality of the sexual experience. Although sexuality may be experienced in different ways, enjoyment has not changed.

The next section will examine sexual activity among older persons, including rates of sexual activity, factors that determine sexual activity, and different forms of sexual activity.

FACTORS THAT INFLUENCE SEXUAL ACTIVITY

There are, of course, numerous factors that influence sexual activity. This section examines some of the physiological, and sociopsychological factors that influence sexual activity in older persons as well as the rates of frequency of sexual activity, and the different forms it takes.

Physiological Factors

Men   Masters and Johnson (1966) reported that there are several physical changes that occur in the aging male that can affect the male's sexual behavior. Generally speaking, the aging male can expect the following changes to take place.

1 It will take the male longer to achieve an erection, with some older men requiring 30 to 40 minutes to achieve an erection (Runciman, 1975), and the erection may not be as "full" (Ludeman, 1981). In general, the older male will need more stimulation in order to achieve an erection (Comfort, 1974). However, the male will often be able to maintain the erection longer without ejaculation (Burnside, 1975*a*; Pfeiffer, 1974; Weg, 1975*a*). Because he is better able to control ejaculation, the aged male can elongate the sensual or pleasurable part of the sex act for both himself and his partner (Masters & Johnson, 1966). The older male will find that his penis will usually become flaccid immediately after ejaculation. In contrast, a young man's penis will often remain erect for minutes or hours after sexual intercourse.

2 In younger men the orgasm stage consists of two parts: first, the initial feeling the ejaculation is about to take place; and second, the feeling the ejaculation is taking place (Weg, 1976). With increasing age, these two stages blend into one. Thus, the orgasm stage is generally shorter (Ludeman, 1981).

3 The time between erections and/or orgasms will generally increase with age. Whereas a younger man may be able to have several erections and orgasms in one day, an older man may be able to have only one orgasm or one erection per day or per week.

4 In an older man there will be a lessening in the intensity of the orgasm; the ejaculation will be less forceful and the amount of fluid ejaculated smaller or even nonexistent (Burnside, 1975a; deNigola & Peruzza, 1974; Pfeiffer, 1974).

5 Although with increasing age the penis does not generally change in size, shape, or appearance, the testes do become smaller and more flaccid (Weg, 1975a).

6 The prostate gland in most older men is likely to grow larger; it can, as a result, cause a variety of problems which may necessitate medical intervention.

7 Unlike women who cease to be fertile with increasing age, men can continue to sire children indefinitely. Although the sperm count does decrease with age, it nevertheless generally remains high enough for most older men to father children.

8 Although many changes take place physically and biologically, sexual pleasure does not therefore lessen or diminish in old age. Rather, satisfactory sexual expression can and does take place even in advanced old age. The changes that take place do not necessarily negatively affect an aged male's interpretation of the sexual experience (Masters & Johnson, 1966).

It must be emphasized that there are vast differences in the sexual capabilities of aged men, which averages tend to distort. Although there are trends, which most men can expect to experience, they will occur at different ages and to different degrees. For example, we noted that most men can expect that with increasing age the refractory period will increase (i.e., the time between an orgasm and the next erection), it will take longer to obtain an erection and that the erection will be less stiff than when younger. Although these are trends, Brecher's study (1984) of men 50+ years of age found that for 35 percent the refractory period had not increased, 50 percent did not take longer to obtain an erection, and for 54 percent the erection was not less stiff than when younger.

What the studies do point out is that with increasing age there is a decline in the percentage who have a high interest in sex, and who are sexually active. Additionally, for those who are sexually active, there will be a decline in the frequency of sexual expression. Most of the studies show that the declines are more substantial for women than for men. That is, a higher percentage of men will be sexually active, and sexually active men will be more active than sexually active women of the same age.

Masters and Johnson stated, "There is no question of the fact that the human male's sexual responsiveness wanes as he ages" (1966). However, males who adjust to the changes in sexual functioning, who are "relatively" healthy, and who have a capable partner, can continue to engage in sexual activity "indefinitely." Both Brecher's and Starr and Weiner's studies reported the general pattern of a decline in male sexual activity with increasing age.

Women   Physiologically, women can expect a number of physical and biological changes to influence their sexual expression. Perhaps the most dramatic is simply the aging process per se. Some believe that societal attitudes make the aging process more difficult for women than for men. Thus, physical aging may be more damaging to the sexuality of women then men. Susan Sontag's (1972) classic article "The

Double Standard of Aging'' has clearly and succinctly summarized the consequences of societal attitudes as they affect the aging of men and women. Sontag said that ''. . . there is a double standard about aging that denounces women with special severity.'' She noted that just as men are allowed more freedom in sexual infidelities, society is also more permissive about their aging. Sontag mentioned how traditionally attractiveness has been more important in the lives of women than men, and that for aging women these standards become difficult to maintain. She also said that for men their sexual attractiveness often increases with increasing age, as they rise in power and fame. However, women who manifest similar characteristics are often seen as undesirable. Sontag noted that just as women are entering their sexual prime physically, socially they are ''being disqualified as sexually attractive persons. . . .'' She continued by saying that for men social standards of attractiveness conform to the natural aging process. For example, grey hair looks distinguished on a man, while making a woman look old. For women, however, societal standards are such that sexual attractiveness can be maintained only by covering up the natural normal aging process (Robinson, 1983; Weg, 1983*b*).

Sontag's comments have been reinforced by several writers. For example, Weg (1983*b*) has noted that societal values tell older men that they are distinguished but older women that they are ''neutered, colorless, wrinkled hags. . . .'' Ludeman (1981) stated in her study of women over 60 years of age that none saw themselves as sexually appealing.

Thus, for women many of the most devastating changes to their sexuality may be in the cosmetic physical changes that occur. In addition to these changes there are several other important biological changes that take place. Some of these changes are mentioned below.

1 The walls of the vagina become thinner in old age. The vagina also shortens in both length and width, and much of its expansive capacity is lost. The Bartholin glands that lubricate the vagina upon sexual stimulation respond more slowly and provide less lubrication with increasing age. Whereas a young woman's vagina will lubricate within 15 to 30 seconds after stimulation, an older woman's vagina may take 3 to 5 minutes to respond, and even then there will be a reduced amount of lubricant. These factors may lead to dyspareunia or painful intercourse, vaginal burning, pelvic aching, the desire to urinate, or a burning or irritating sensation at urination. It should be noted that women who have been sexually stimulated on a regular basis from adolescence suffer less loss in lubrication than those who have not (Starr, 1987).

2 The orgasmic stage is generally shorter in older women and may at times be painful. Orgasm is also affected in terms of intensity. Physiologically, orgasm does not appear to be as intense in older women as in younger women. The number of uterine contractions diminishes from three to five down to one or two (Weg, 1976). However, the decline in duration and intensity of orgasm does not affect or detract from interpreting the sexual experience as pleasurable and satisfying. Also, the capacity for multiple orgasms is still present (Weg, 1983*b*).

3 The clitoral hood diminishes in size and the pubic area loses much of its fatty deposit. Thus, the clitoris may not be protected from direct stimulation by the penis. After prolonged intercourse some women may find that the clitoris becomes irritated. The clitoris also diminishes in size with increasing age. It does not, however, appear to become less sensitive or less responsive to stimulation.

4 With increasing age menstruation and fertility will cease. This stage is generally referred to as the climacteric (or menopause). It is important to note that it is the reproductive capability that has ceased, not sexuality (Rykken, 1987). After menopause, many women become more interested in sex and sexual activity (Weg, 1983*b*, 1987).

We saw that sexual interest and activity in men develop and peak early in life with a decline occurring in the early twenties. Women follow a different pattern: potential for sexual responsiveness develops later, in the late twenties or early thirties, and sexual potential remains fairly constant from the late teens to the sixties.

While Masters and Johnson (1966, 1970) noted the decline in male responsiveness, concerning women they said, ''. . . there is not a time limit drawn by the advancing years to female sexuality'' (1966). They continued by saying that most normal, aging women have sex drives, and that there is no physical reason that these cannot be satisfactorily met by various modes of sexual expression. They concluded, ''The healthy aging woman normally has sex drives that demand resolution'' (1966).

Sociopsychological factors

In addition to physical factors, there are a variety of sociopsychological factors that have a significant influence on sexual activity. This section will examine marital status, social class, sex (male and female), and previous sexual activity.

Marital Status   In their analysis of sexuality the Duke studies focused the majority of their attention on married participants. This was because one of the early studies found that only 7 percent of the nonmarried were sexually active, while 54 percent of the married were sexually active (Newman & Nichols, 1960). The researchers concluded that among the aged, sexual activity and marital status are closely related, particularly for women.

Although they did not separate married men and women, Starr and Weiner (1981) noted that 30 percent of the women and 7 percent of the men in their study were not sexually active. Although they did not attribute this to marital status, they noted that more women than men lacked the opportunity for sexual relations.

Brecher (1984) found that for the age categories fifties, sixties, and seventies, the following percentages of married men were sexually active: 98, 93, 81 percent. For married women the percentages were: 95, 89, and 81 percent. Percentages for unmarried men were: 95, 85, and 75 percent. For unmarried women the percentages were: 88, 63, and 50 percent. Part of the difference in sexual activity between married and unmarried men and women relates to the fact that the men were socialized in an era when the ''double standard'' was more prevalent. Brecher (1984) found that when he asked, ''Is it okay for older couples who are not married to have sexual relations?'' 57 percent of the women agreed versus 72 percent of the men. The difference in attitudes may also be seen in adultery rates. After age 50, 8 percent of the women and 23 percent of the men admitted engaging in adultery (Brecher, 1984).

Social Class   Early studies found that lower classes tended to be more sexually active than those in the higher social classes. However, it is currently believed that those in the higher social classes are more sexually active. The earlier studies looked at rates of sexual intercourse; later studies have looked at sexual activity. Different patterns of sexual activity have been reported with those in the higher social classes, such as masturbating more frequently, having more nocturnal emissions, and petting to orgasms more frequently.

Sex   Differences in sexual activity by gender have been reported, with men being more active than women in the same age group. The differences have two possible explanations. First, women may be more hesitant to report sexual information. Second, women are generally married to older men, whose age increases the probability of a lower rate of sexual activity. Thus, in examining the sexual activity of 75 year old men and women, the men's activity is higher since their spouses average 70 years of age; the women's activity is lower since their spouses average 80 years of age.

The Kinsey studies supported this trend by reporting that the number of sex acts per week for those 60 years of age was 1.3 for men and 0.6 for women. However, this changed with the Duke studies, Starr-Weiner study, and the Brecher study. The Duke studies indicated that men engaged in more sexual activity than women until very old age when the figures for women became higher than for men. Starr and Weiner noted that the percentage who engaged in sex once per week at ages 60–69 was 23.4 percent of women and 18.6 percent of the men. For the ages 70–79 the figures were 21.7 percent for women and 10.7 percent for men. Brecher's figures for engaging in sex once per week were 28 percent for women and 25 percent for men.

Previous Sexual Activity   The Duke studies reported on the relationship between sexual drives and activity in early adulthood and old age. Basically, a strong drive in early adulthood correlated with a moderate drive in old age. Those who had low sex drives as young adults had little or no sex drive in old age.

A study (Pfeiffer & Davis, 1972) sought to explain the variables that impacted on sexual interest and activity. The study found that extensive sexual activity in early adulthood, and the enjoyment of that activity, generally meant continued sexual interest and activity in later life. If sex was not of much interest in early life, and there was little enjoyment of the activity, then it was likely to be terminated in midlife. They again noted that older women have their sexual lives linked to a "socially sanctioned" partner. The research noted that the decline in interest and activity on the part of women may be "defensive" in that women can expect an average of 11 years of widowhood with little opportunity for a socially sanctioned sexual partner, thus sexual feelings are inhibited.

FORMS OF SEXUAL EXPRESSION

As noted above, sexuality can be expressed in many ways. This section will examine three forms of sexual expression: heterosexual expression, solitary expression (masturbation), and homosexual expression.

Heterosexual Expression

Males   Although decline in frequency of expression is a frequent finding, the age at which it occurs varies according to the study. Some researchers have found a sharp decline in sexual activity at age 50 (Brecher, 1984); others have found the decline at age 60 (Masters & Johnson, 1966); other researchers did not note a significant decline until the seventies (Palmore, 1981). The research results are different because different aspects of sexuality were examined. Further research may find that declines take place in certain areas before others. One perspective may find earlier declines than another perspective. If we examine the percent of men who are sexually active Brecher (1984) found that for the age groups 50–59, 60–69, and 70+ they were 98, 91, 79 percent. Starr and Weiner (1981) found that for those 60–69, 70–79, and 80+ the percentages were 93, 89, and 85 percent.

As mentioned above, while the trend is toward a decline there are exceptions. For example, a man may be in an unhappy marriage where sexual intercourse with his wife is infrequent. Or, a man may have a wife who has a chronic illness which limits their sexual activity. After divorce or the death of his wife, a man may remarry and his sexual activity may increase. The Duke studies noted that while decline was the general pattern in 31 percent of the men studied, 20 percent of the men had an increase in sexual activity from one study period to another (Verwoerdt et al., 1969). Again, it must be remembered that averages tend to cancel out individual patterns.

Concerning weekly rates of sexual activity Kinsey found that for those in their fifties, sixties, and seventies the rates decline from 1.5 to 1.3 to 0.9. Brecher (1984) found that for married males weekly rates of sexual activity for those in their fifties, sixties, and seventies declined from 1.3 to 1.0 to 0.6. Starr and Weiner (1981) found that the frequency of sexual activity for both men and women in their sixties, seventies, and eighties went from weekly rates of 1.5 to 1.4 to 1.2. Again, although the figures vary, they indicate a decline with increasing age.

Kinsey said that the basic conclusion was that for men there is a "gradually diminishing" pattern of sexual activity, which starts at about age 16. Kinsey continued by saying that the rate of decline in old age does not exceed the rate in earlier decades. Kinsey believed that the cause was primarily physical, although "psychologic fatigue" was also mentioned. Psychologic fatigue dealt with a loss of interest because of repetitive behavior, and no new techniques, contacts, or situations.

Females   For women we see the same general pattern as for men: a decline in the percentage who are sexually active, Brecher (1984), and a decline in the frequency of sexual activity for the sexually active. The percentage of sexually active married women in their fifties, sixties, and seventies were 95, 89 and 81 percent. The percentages for women who were not married were 88, 63, and 50 percent. Percentages having orgasms while asleep or when waking up went from 26 to 24 to 17 percent. Frequency of sexual activity also declines. Brecher (1984) noted that the frequency of sex with husbands for the three age categories went from 1.3 times per week to 1.0 to 0.7.

Although there are physical changes, the changes do not necessarily hamper or detract from a sexual experience. For example, while it was noted that intercourse or an orgasm may be painful for some aged women, the Starr-Weiner survey (1981) found that 84 percent said that there was no pain associated with intercourse. While the clitoral hood diminished in size, the clitoris does not appear to lose any of its sensory receptors. In fact, the frequency of orgasm is higher in women over 60 years of age than in younger women (Starr & Weiner, 1981).

Physically, women appear to be able to maintain regular sexual activity if they are in good health, have maintained a regular sex life throughout adulthood, and have a sexually capable partner. The Duke Longitudinal Studies found that the factors associated with continued sexual activity in aged women were enjoyment of past sexual activity, marital status, younger age, good health, and previous sexual activity.

Solitary Expression (Masturbation)

The limitations of Kinsey's work on the aged have already been noted. For men he said that masturbation was the first major form of sexual activity to cease. In his data he did not have a single record of an older male masturbating to orgasm. For aged women he did not report any information on masturbation.

Masters and Johnson (1966) noted that in aging males all forms of sexual activity decline, including masturbation. For older women they noted that many who do not have a partner reverted to earlier forms of sexual behavior, such as masturbation, for relief from sexual tension.

Starr and Weiner (1981) observed that of all the sensitive topics in their research (e.g., sexual intercourse, nudity, etc.) masturbation aroused "pronounced guilt and defensiveness." It must be remembered that the sexual socialization of older persons was in an era when masturbation was condemned. Although many masturbated, many suffered guilt and were fearful of the consequences. The percentage approving of masturbation to relieve sexual tension was 82 percent of males and 85 percent of females. The percentage actually masturbating were 44 percent of males and 47 percent of females. As expected, there were differences by marital status and age. The percentage of married males and females who masturbated were 40 and 39 percent. The figures for the widowed were almost identical to the married. However, the percentages for the divorced and single were significantly higher: divorced males 57 percent, divorced females 66 percent, single males 69 percent, single females 81 percent.

For many older women masturbation may be their only sexual outlet. Butler and Lewis (1976) noted that most "experts" believe that masturbation is a "healthy" form of sexual expression, providing both physical and emotional release (see Starr, 1987).

Homosexual Expression

There is relatively little information on aged homosexuality, and much of what does exist is somewhat dated, especially given the change in societal attitudes and the appearance of the HIV-AIDS epidemic (Allen, 1961; Gray & Dressel, 1985; Harry & DeVall, 1978; Kelly, 1977; Kimmel, 1978, 1979–1980; Raphael & Robinson, 1980; Weinberg, 1970). Kinsey and associates (1948, 1953), Masters and Johnson (1966, 1970), and Starr and Weiner (1981) reported virtually nothing on the number or percentage of older persons who are homosexual. Brecher (1984) found in his study of 2402 men and 1844 women that fifty-six men (2.33 percent) and nine women (0.49 percent) were homosexual. Others have indicated that the figures may parallel the younger population, with figures of 10 percent being cited (see Teitelman, 1987). The information that has been collected would suggest two conclusions. First, that just as with heterosexuals, there are very different life-styles among homosexuals. Second, that more research is needed.

It is of course difficult to ascertain the impact that the HIV-AIDS epidemic will have on the future aged homosexual population (see Catalano & Schmidt, 1989; Catania et al., 1989). Prior to the HIV-AIDS epidemic it was speculated that homosexuality might become more prevalent in old age. Starr and Weiner (1981) found that 59 percent of men and 67 percent of women approved of homosexuality for consenting adults. With the added visibility of the gay rights community and more gays "coming out of the closet" there may be more acceptance of the life-style, which may also lead to more experimentation.

Homosexuality may become an option used more by women, for whom sexual partners are more difficult to find, than men. Just as there have been significant changes in the percentage of women in the work force and having premarital and extramarital sex, there may also be increases in the number entering into homosexual relationships. Many younger women today were raised with liberal concepts of sexuality and may be more willing to experiment with different forms of sexual expression. Traditionally, in American society, men were supposed to initiate sexual activity. This attitude may have prevented many women from seeking homosexual relationships. With changing sexual norms, there may be a change in this area.

SEXUAL PROBLEMS OF OLDER PERSONS

The section on factors influencing sexual activity noted that normal physical changes take place in both aging men and women that can affect sexual activity. Generally, if these physical changes are recognized as inevitable and "natural" results of aging, sexual activity can continue, although the mode and frequency may change. It was also noted that a variety of sociopsychological factors influence sexual activity.

This section will examine sexual problems in old age which often lead to lower frequency or even discontinuation of sexual activity. It is divided into two subsections. The first section will examine some of the reasons for discontinuing sexual activity; the second will examine specific factors contributing to the reduction or discontinuation of sexual activity.

Reasons for Discontinuing Sexual Activity

One of the Duke studies on sexuality was based on 261 men (98 percent were married) and 241 women (71 percent were married) between the ages of 46 to 71 (Pfeiffer, Verwoerdt, & Davis, 1972). Information on sexual histories was gathered through a self-administered medical history questionnaire. There are three important aspects that need to be considered from this study. The first deals with decline in sexual activity, the second with the age at cessation of sexual relations, and the third the reasons for the cessation of sexual relations.

Concerning the first aspect, the decline in sexual activity, it was reported that with each successive age group an increasing percentage reported a decline in sexual interest and activity. For example, 49 percent of the men and 58 percent of the women in the age group 46–50 reported a decline in sexual interest and activity. The percentages for the age categories 51–55, 56–60, and 61–65 for men were 71, 72, and 89. For women the percentages were 88, 79, 88. For the age group 66–71 the percentage for men was 88 and for women it was 96. As can be seen, the sharpest declines take place in the age categories 51–55 and 56–60.

The second aspect deals with the age at cessation of sexual relations. Essentially we see an earlier cessation for women than for men; the reasons will become apparent below. For example, in this study by age 46–50 none of the men had discontinued sexual intercourse, but 14 percent of the women had. For the age category 66–71 the percentages were 24 for men and 73 for women.

The third aspect deals with the reasons for the cessation of sexual activity, which are presented in Table 7-1.

Three observations can be made from Table 7-1. First, for the men who had discontinued sexual activity, 71 percent attributed the cessation to themselves through illness, loss of interest, or inability to perform. This percentage seems valid when we look at the women who have ceased having sexual relations. Seventy-eight percent attributed their cessation of sexual relations to their spouses' illness, death, loss of interest, or inability to perform. Only 10 percent of the women not having sexual relations attribute the cessation to their illnesses, loss of interest, or inability to perform. Both the men and women in this study stated that the male was the primary reason

TABLE 7-1
REASONS FOR CESSATION OF SEXUAL RELATIONS

Reason	Men, %	Women, %
Death of Spouse	—	36
Separation or divorce from spouse	—	12
Illness of spouse	14	20
Loss of interest by spouse	9	4
Spouse unable to perform sexually	6	18
Illness of self	17	2
Loss of interest by self	14	4
Self unable to perform sexually	40	4

Source: Modified from Pfeiffer, Verwoerdt & Davis, 1972).

for the discontinuation of sexual activity. Thus, the male appears to be the determining factor in the continuation or discontinuation of sexual activity in a marriage (Pfeiffer et al., 1972).

The second observation from Table 7-1 is that the major reasons are not related to interest. Only 14 percent of men and 4 percent of women discontinued sexual relations because of a lack of interest. This reinforces what has been stated previously, that even in old age sexual feelings and ''needs'' are present in most individuals.

The third observation is that in most of the cases the cessation in sexual relations was not dictated by an inevitable aging process, but more by physical illness or the death of a spouse.

The next section will examine some of the specific factors that create sexual problems for older persons.

Specific Factors Contributing to the Reduction or Discontinuation of Sexual Activity

Abstinence   For many older individuals sexual problems occur after long periods of abstinence. For example, an individual's spouse may have a debilitating chronic illness which forces him or her to cease all sexual activity. The stress of the illness on the healthy spouse may lower that individual's sexual feelings and desire. After the death of the spouse the individual may initially continue to be asexual; however, after a certain period, the individual may form a new relationship where sexual activity is desired. However, upon resumption of sexual activity, after long periods of abstinence, both men and women may find that their abilities have declined dramatically. Men may be unable to achieve an erection and women may find that penetration by the male is painful. This is sometimes referred to as ''widower's syndrome'' (Burnside, 1975a; Runciman, 1975; Travis, 1987) and can often be reversed in 2 to 3 months (Rykken, 1987).

Aging   In women, after menopause the amount of estrogen secreted by the ovaries is markedly reduced. For many women this does not cause any problems since the ovaries and adrenal gland will produce another hormone, which is converted to estrogen. However, for many other women menopause results in an estrogen deficiency which can produce changes in the vagina (e.g., thinning walls, shrinking capacity, less lubrication and elasticity), urinary tract (e.g., increased risk of infection), and bones (e.g., increased rate of osteoporosis). In addition, hot flashes and flushes will be common.

Almost all the studies have reported a decline in sexual activity with increasing age. Because increasing age brings with it many changes, for most the decline in sexual activity is multicausal. One question is how much of the decline is caused by aging per se and how much by these other factors, such as loss of spouse or a chronic health condition. Although no study has attempted to rule out most confounding variables, Brecher's (1984) study did examine sexual activity in three age periods (fifties, sixties, and seventies) for two groups: those in good health and those with health problems. What the study found was that sexual activity was lower for each successive age group, even in the group that had good health. The author concluded that at least part of the decline in the percentage engaging in sexual activity and the frequency of the activity is caused by aging.

Alcohol Abuse, Drug Abuse, Smoking   It is well known that alcoholism can interfere with male potency, both psychologically and physiologically. One study reported that 8 percent of the alcoholics it studied were impotent (Lemere & Smith, 1973). Physiologically alcohol is a depressant and can lead to male impotence (Glover, 1975). Additionally, alcohol abuse can cause neurological damage decreasing the ability to have an erection (Lemere & Smith, 1973), as well as liver damage resulting in lower testosterone levels. Women alcoholics seldom complain of sexual dysfunctioning (Solnick & Corby, 1983).

Psychologically excessive use of alcohol may also contribute to impaired sexual performance, which can perpetuate fears of impotence because of age. Future sexual episodes will be approached with fear and anxiety over failure. This fear and anxiety may create sexual dysfunctioning. For others, rather than fail again, it is less threatening to withdraw.

Drug use and abuse may also lead to sexual problems. As noted in Chapter 6, "Physical Health," older persons take more drugs than any other age group. Many of these drugs have an impact on sexual performance or desire. For example, some of the drugs taken for high blood pressure lessen sexual desire or cause impotence in men (Travis, 1987). Brecher's (1984) study of aged sexuality found that 18 percent of male and female respondents were taking antihypertensive medication. He reported that those taking the medication were not as sexually active as those not taking the medication. Furthermore, those on the medication who were sexually active were significantly less likely to be sexually active weekly and less likely to report a high enjoyment of sex. Brecher did note that some of the differences may have been because of factors other than the medication, such as age or health problems. Those experiencing sexual problems as a result of their medication should ask their physician about the possibility of a different drug or of reducing the dosage of the drug they are taking.

Some tranquilizers that are frequently prescribed can lead to a lower sexual desire and depression. It has also been reported that smoking may inhibit the sex drive (Rossman, 1975). Nicotine can affect sexual performance, since it causes the blood vessels to contract, making it more difficult for males to have an erection (Rykken, 1987).

Attitudes   Attitudes can have a significant impact on an individual's beliefs, values, and sexual expression. There are three groups whose attitudes need to be examined: older persons, their children, and professionals.

Older Persons   There are many aged who no longer believe that sexual behavior is appropriate (Butler & Lewis, 1976). Advice books for the aged have not condoned sexual expression, dating, or remarriage (Arluke et al., 1984). Most of the romantic models portrayed by the mass media have been young individuals. Although the studies by Brecher (1984) and Starr and Weiner (1981) seemed to indicate that the aged were sexually knowledgeable and liberated, the limitations of these studies, in that the participants were self-selected, have already been mentioned. A study designed to assist the aged in understanding the influence of the aging process on sexuality via a sex education class found very different results. In presenting a film and discussion on sexually explicit material the instructor found that many of the participants became disturbed over the presentation. The first session had thirty participants who completed a pretest. The second session had four returning participants. The authors noted that this demonstrated the need for more sex education programs for the aged (Brower & Tanner, 1979).

Adult Children of Older Persons   There have been empirical studies on how adult children view the sexual behavior of their parents. One study asked college students whose parents were married to provide information on what they believed about their parents' sex lives. The researchers found that most of the students were very uncomfortable with the survey. They found when comparing the students' estimates with the Kinsey data, which researchers considered low, that the students consistently underestimated the sexual behavior of their parents, with some figures being astonishing low. This indicated that even with the sexual revolution, many individuals are still uncomfortable with universal sexuality (Pocs et al., 1977). A second article was written by a gerontologist after showing a pornographic film of an aged couple engaging in a variety of sex acts. He noted that the students reacted with ''disgust'' or ''amusement'' (Thomas, 1982).

Professionals   Another factor that contributes to sexual problems in older persons is the attitude professionals have toward sexuality in the aged. Although the sex problems of the young are readily referred to sex counselors, psychologists, physicians, social workers, or ministers, the sex problems of older persons are frequently considered irreversible since it is believed that they are caused by the aging process, or ignored since sex is considered inappropriate or irrelevant for older persons.

Broderick (1975) found that when he tried to get a group of psychiatrists, social workers, psychologists, and other professionals to listen to information on the sexuality of older persons, he was met with laughter, jokes, and wisecracks. It is difficult to convince even professionals that the aged have sexual needs, and to break through preconceived beliefs and attitudes.

There is an indication that this may be changing in certain areas. For example, although they may not be seen as professional, attitudes toward aged sexuality have apparently changed in ''advice books on romance and sexuality for the aged'' (Arluke et al., 1984). In their study they separated advice books into those published before 1970 and those published after 1970. They found that in the pre-1970 books 25 percent approved of sexual activity among the aged. In the post-1970 books the figure was 60 percent. The article said that while this appears to indicate a change in attitude toward aged sexuality, it noted that other attitudes still remained relatively unchanged. For example, during each time period only 26 percent of the books approved of remarriage. Concerning dating, the figures were 10 percent and 24 percent. The authors concluded by noting that although the majority of post-1970 books stated that sexual activity was acceptable and important, those who do not have a sexually active spouse are not given the means for expressing their sexuality.

Two studies of nursing students suggest that in this area attitudes may be becoming more accepting. One study was on senior baccalaureate students (Damrosch, 1982), the other on students enrolled in a master's program (Damrosch, 1984). Students read a story about a sexually active nursing home patient or about a nursing home patient where sexual activity was not mentioned. The sexually active patient was seen as healthier, more cheerful, and more well-adjusted. Negatively, the students did not believe that the sexually active patient would be as "popular" with other staff members. Reasons for the acceptance of the sexually active patient include liberalization of sex attitudes in American society, courses in geriatric nursing, younger more sexually tolerant students, the appeal of an "atypical" patient as opposed to a "typical" patient.

A recent event suggests that the changes in nursing may not be as great as the above studies indicated. An article in *Nursing Times* (Roberts, 1989) presented information on sexuality in late life, accompanied by some drawings. An editorial (Andrews, 1989) about a month after the article appeared said that it triggered a "hornets' nest," and suggested that there are still many ageists, especially when it comes to the sexuality of older persons.

Boredom   Another factor that may cause sexual problems in the aged is boredom with one's partner. Repetition of the same act with the same individual can produce a situation that will not be very erotic or satisfying for either partner. Boredom can lead to less frequent sexual activity, which, as we have seen, can cause decline in sexual performance, and thus a reduction in sexual encounters. Also, if boredom made the male impotent during one sexual episode, he may fear that it is permanent. For the woman, she may take the male's impotency as a sign that she is no longer attractive or loved.

Illness   There are two types of illness that need to be discussed: acute and chronic.

Acute   As mentioned in Chapter 6, "Physical Health," older persons have fewer acute conditions than younger age groups. However, there are certain conditions that can significantly impact on sexual functioning. For example, in women urinary tract infections and in men an infection of the testes or urethra can cause sexual problems (see Gingrich, 1987).

Chronic   A chronic illness is one that is either permanent or which the individual has for a long period of time. Several chronic illnesses are discussed below.

Arthritis: Arthritis may limit sexual expression because of pain and forces many individuals to abstain from sexual relationships or other forms of sexual expression. According to Weg (1975a), this is unfortunate since during sexual intercourse cortisone is released from the adrenal glands and may help relieve the suffering of an arthritic individual (see Butler & Lewis, 1976).

Coronary heart disease: Years ago patients with coronary heart disease (CHD) were told to abstain from sexual intercourse because it was widely believed that the exertion would precipitate a cardiac event (i.e., heart attack). Thus, many individuals with CHD became asexual out of fear. Sudden death during or shortly after sexual activity is relatively rare, accounting for about 0.6 percent of all sudden deaths, most of which occur during illicit affairs (Rykken, 1987).

Currently, most physicians encourage their patients to resume the style of life they had before the onset of the disease, including sexual activity. Several studies have shown that for most individuals sexual intercourse is no more demanding than climbing two flights of stairs, walking briskly, or even driving home from work (Burnside, 1975a; Butler & Lewis, 1976; Glover, 1975; Rossman, 1975; Rykken, 1987; Weg, 1983b). CHD patients are often advised to wait a certain amount of time before becoming sexually active, generally 3 months. Of those who follow this advice, about 30 percent resume previous levels of sexual activity, about 60 percent reduce their sexual activity from previous levels, and about 10 percent abstain completely (Glover, 1975).

Brecher (1984) also reported on those who had a heart attack. He found that for men 86 percent were sexually active after a heart attack compared with 94 percent in the "healthy" group. There was a significant difference between those having sex weekly: 68 percent of the heart attack group compared with 82 percent of the healthy group. The enjoyment of sex was similar.

Diabetes: Diabetes is a disease that can significantly limit the sexual expression in aged men. The national rate per 1000 for those 65+ years of age is 108.3 for men and 91.1 for women (the total figures are 27.8 for men and 27.9 for women) (U.S. Bureau of the Census, 1990). About 10 percent of those in the Brecher study were diabetic. Almost 50 percent of male diabetics are impotent by age 60; they are unable to achieve an erection, with the percentage increasing with increasing age (Felstein, 1983; Kent, 1975c; Rykken, 1987; Weg, 1983b). It appears that the cause of the diminished sexual capacity is neurologically based (Solnick & Corby, 1983; Weg, 1978).

Aged diabetic women do not appear to have their sexual expression limited by the disease, although vaginal lubrication may be reduced in some (Weg, 1983b). Brecher's study found that about 4 percent of the women were diabetic. Ellenberg (1977) found that there was very little difference between a diabetic group and a nondiabetic group in terms of interest in sex and orgasmic response. Two possible explanations for the differences have been offered. Ellenberg (1977) believes that the male sex drive is mostly physical. In women, however, the sex drive is mostly psychosocial and emotional. The second explanation is that diabetes affects the male erectile response, but does not affect women sexually, or at least in ways that are measurable.

Mental health: Chapter 8, on the psychological aspects of older persons, discusses mental health. Mental impairments in relationships can have a significant impact on both the sexual activity and sexual feelings. For example, someone with depression may have lower levels of sexual desires or needs. This individual's partner may find that living with this individual is so stressful that his or her sexual feelings are blunted.

Individuals with diseases such as Alzheimer's disease may find that sexual feelings are absent or that they express them at the wrong times or with the wrong individuals. Being the caregiver of someone with Alzheimer's also presents some problems, since this individual is both a caregiver and a lover. It may be difficult for many caregivers to switch roles. Additionally, caregiving may make them too exhausted to have sexual feelings, or they may have the feeling that they are sexually exploiting the impaired spouse.

Osteoporosis As reported in Chapter 5, "Biology and Physiology," osteoporosis is a degenerative disease that results in the loss of bone mass. The disease affects far more women than men, and increases after menopause. The disease can frequently cause pain in the bones and joints (Wheeler, 1976), a collapsing of the spine, and kyphosis, which is a postural deformity that is an abnormal curving of the spine, sometimes called "humpback" or "hunchback." Thus, certain sexual activity may be painful. Additionally, there may be a diminished sexual desire because of self-image (Reyniak, 1987).

The seriousness and prevalence of the disease is just beginning to be recognized (Bachmann, 1987). The ideal treatment is prevention. For those with the disease the mode of medical intervention varies according to the physician. Whatever the treatment, it is important to recognize that the disease has an impact on more than just the bones. Thus, treatment needs to focus on the whole patient (see Bachmann, 1987; Bush, 1987).

Lack of Partner One of the major reasons for the discontinuation of sexual activity is the lack of a partner. We have seen that most older males are married, while most older females are widowed. Additionally, the "double-standard," with which current older women grew up, makes it easier and more acceptable for older males to have lovers (Starr, 1987).

Lack of Privacy Many older persons live in dependent environments, such as nursing homes, or the homes of friends or relatives. Many have also had adult children, often divorced or widowed, move back in with them. Generally, there is a lack of privacy in these environments. Sexual expression can become difficult because of this. Frustration, depression, or a hurried, unsatisfactory sexual act can result.

Obesity Obesity can also cause sexual problems. Very often with increasing age there is also an increasing weight problem. Although many studies indicate that overweight individuals engage in sexual intercourse with the same frequency as others, obesity can nevertheless cause sexual problems, especially in older persons. In a society that values slenderness, an overweight sexual partner may be physically undesirable. Obesity may also make certain modes of sexual expression difficult or impossible. The limitations imposed by obesity come at a time when other physical limitations are already limiting sexual expression.

Preoccupation with a Career Preoccupation with a career can also lessen both sexual interest and response. Many older persons are at the zenith of their careers. They have finally reached long-sought-after career goals, and the careers become their only interests. They work exceptionally long and demanding hours and become totally involved in their work. By the time they come home, they are too physically and mentally exhausted to engage in sexual behavior (Felstein, 1983).

Postmenopausal Conditions   As we noted previously, many aged women undergo changes in the sexual organs that can cause painful sexual intercourse or painful orgasms. Very often this situation can be corrected by hormone replacement therapy or the use of a lubricating cream. However, some believe that hormone replacement therapy may be dangerous and that the benefits are not worth some of the known side effects or the possible risks.

Surgery   Thousands of the aged have surgery every year. For many, the surgeries are successful and they return to their lives and families healthier than before. Many individuals undergo necessary surgical procedures that can have a significant impact on their ability to continue sexual activity. For others, the surgeries may be mutilating, and while having no impact on sexual ability, can impact on their self-image, or the image that a sexual partner has of them. Several common surgical procedures will be examined below.

Hysterectomy and Oophorectomy   Hysterectomy refers to removal of the uterus and oophorectomy refers to removal of the ovaries. Brecher reported that 34 percent of his sample of females had undergone a hysterectomy and 18 percent an oophorectomy. Studies have indicated that these surgical procedures result in from 10 to 38 percent sexual dysfunctioning (see Solnick & Corby, 1983). For many women who have had these operations, normal sexual functioning appears to be related more to psychological adjustment (Dennerstein et al., 1977). Brecher's study (1984) reported a small impact on sexual activity or enjoyment of sex.

Concerning removal of the ovaries, Brecher reported that those taking estrogen were as sexually active and enjoyed sex as much as those who had not had the surgery; those not taking estrogen had a significantly lower rate of sexual activity and enjoyment of sex.

Mastectomy   Breast cancer is a leading cause of death of women. The death rate in 1986 per 100,000 women aged 55–64, 65–74, 75–84, and 85+ were 80.9, 109.9, 136.2, and 180.0 (U.S. Bureau of the Census, 1990). Five percent of Brecher's female subjects had had a mastectomy. Traditionally, breast cancer has been treated with a radical mastectomy, which is the removal of the entire breast and the surrounding tissue and muscle, and a dissection of the area lymph nodes. More conservative surgical approaches, such as modified radical mastectomy that involves less muscle trauma (Ashikari, 1984) or a lumpectomy where primarily the tumor is removed, are now often used, especially if the disease is in an early stage. The latter two operations are less disfiguring and make breast reconstruction easier (see Dinner, 1984). Other medical intervention may also take place, such as radiation or chemotherapy (Peters, 1984).

The major issue in a mastectomy is one of image. American society has been made very "breast-oriented" by the mass media, and the loss of a breast can be psychologically devastating to a woman and her partner. As Polivy (1977) has noted, the loss of a breast to the woman and her partner is probably more sexually damaging than the removal of the uterus because breasts are an important and visible symbol of both sexuality and femininity.

A recent study on lumpectomy and mastectomy patients found significant postoperative differences. Although at 6 months both groups felt "less attractive and feminine" than before surgery, the mastectomy patients felt it to a greater extent. By 14 months the lumpectomy patients had returned to presurgery feelings of attractiveness and femininity. The mastectomy patients had not regained presurgery levels. The lumpectomy patients were more open and at ease in talking about their surgeries. The lumpectomy patients also appeared to have more emotional support from their spouses. Sexually, lumpectomy patients felt their partner's performance was enhanced; mastectomy patients felt their partner's behavior had declined (Budoff, 1984; Steinberg et al., 1985). Brecher's study found that a mastectomy had a moderate impact on sexual activity and enjoyment of sex.

Prostatectomy   As life expectancy increases, so does the likelihood that a male will have to have a prostate operation precipitated by factors such as enlargement which appears to be a natural part of the aging process, and which is almost "universal" in men 40+ years of age (Riehle & Vaughn, 1983), acute infections, and cancer. Brecher (1984) reported that 13 percent of his subjects had had a prostate operation and another 13 percent had prostate trouble. In the past, many became impotent because of the nerve damage caused by the operation, which was either through the abdomen or perianal wall. Surgical techniques that are appropriate for some prostate disorders (transurethral prostatectomy—surgery performed by inserting an instrument through the urethra) have significantly lowered the number of men who have nerve damage, although it often causes retrograde ejaculation (ejaculation into the bladder). Brecher's study found that men who had had prostate operations engaged in sex less frequently (83 to 94 percent) and were less likely to have sex weekly (64 to 82 percent). Both groups had similar levels of enjoyment of sex (Fisher, 1987; Libman & Fichten, 1987; Mandel & Schuman, 1987).

TREATING SEXUAL DYSFUNCTIONING IN OLDER PERSONS

As we have seen, many of the professionals who deal with older persons do not understand the sexual problems of older persons or have techniques to deal with these problems. However, there are both psychological and medical techniques to provide the vast majority of older persons who suffer from sexual dysfunctioning with a satisfactory sex life, if they desire it. This section will examine both medical and psychological techniques of ameliorating sexual dysfunctioning.

Medical Techniques

For men who cannot achieve an erection there are at least two medical techniques that will allow sexual intercourse to take place. The first is the surgical implantation of a prosthesis in the penis. There are two types of penile prostheses currently used. The first is a semirigid splint or rod which is surgically implanted into the penis. This procedure was first done in 1936 and has been perfected so that the actual surgery procedure is relatively short (30 minutes), and there are few postoperative complications. These early prosthetic devices made the penis rigid at all times, which proved embarrassing for some individuals. Most of the splint- or rod-type penile prostheses new being implanted have a hinge which can be engaged during intercourse, and disengaged at other times thus giving the penis a more natural appearance. Although the splint makes the penis erect, it does not add to its diameter. There are relatively few complications with this device and 1-year postsurgery results have generally been excellent.

The second type of penile prosthesis was developed in 1973 and involves the surgical implantation of an inflatable rubber cylinder in the penis and a pump filled with a fluid in the scrotum. The individual can squeeze the pump and force the fluid into the cylinder thus inflating the cylinder and causing an erection. By squeezing a release valve on the pump, the fluid will flow from the cylinder back into the pump and the penis will again become flaccid, and unobtrusive. An advantage with this prosthetic device is that during intercourse the diameter of the penis will increase, thus making the erection more "natural." Early inflatable penile prosthetic devices had a failure rate as high as 30 percent, although since 1979 it has been as low as 5 percent (Gregory, 1982; Kent, 1975c).

The second type of surgery is revascularization. An erection is caused by an increase in blood flow to the penis. If enough blood cannot reach the penis to bring about an erection because of a vascular problem, surgery may be capable of correcting the problem (see Riehle & Vaughan, 1983).

In addition to surgery, there are some other techniques to be considered. The first deals with exercise. Glover (1975) reported on a study in which physical exercise increased both the frequency and quality of sexual intercourse among cardiac patients. The exercise made the men physically stronger and thus more capable of engaging in sexual intercourse. This exercise program also had a positive impact on the self-image of the men.

Another important area to be considered is the impact of drugs on sexual activity. As we saw in the last section, drugs can adversely affect sexual performance. There are, however, some drug therapies that may restore sexual capabilities. Hormone replacement therapy (HRT) has been examined as one possibility. HRT in women can prevent many of the changes associated with a decrease in estrogen (e.g., hot flashes and flushes, changes in vagina, urinary tract, and bones). Estrogen treatments can also relieve the painful orgasmic contractions that some aged women experience (Burnside, 1975a; Weg, 1983b). In postmenopausal women, HRT can increase the sex drive. The Brecher study (1984) found that women taking estrogen were more likely to be sexually active (93 percent) than those not taking estrogen (80 percent). They also found that among sexually active women those taking estrogen had higher levels of sexual functioning on eight out of ten measures: higher enjoyment of sex, higher frequency of sex, more likely to wake up sexually aroused, higher probability of having an orgasm when asleep, strong interest in sex, and the "right amount" of vaginal lubrication, more likely to masturbate, and more likely to reach orgasm when masturbating.

Although HRT with estrogen appears to resolve the negative consequences of estrogen deficiency, there are concerns about its safety (see Bergkvist et al., 1989; Gambrell, 1987). Specific concerns are an increased risk of uterus and breast cancer, and gall bladder disease. Additionally, some women may experience less hazardous but nonetheless distressing symptoms such as "nausea, vomiting, abdominal cramps, bloating, headache, dizziness, water retention, breast engorgement and tenderness, and increase in the size of preexisting . . . benign tumors of the uterus'' (Brecher, 1984).

There are ways to minimize the risks: minimum dosage, intermittent use, in combination with progestin, and frequent medical examinations (see Weg, 1983*b*). There are additional ways that women can compensate for some of the changes that affect sexual functioning. For example, some women will find that as they age the amount of lubrication secreted in the vagina will decrease. In Brecher's study of women over 50 years of age, 40 percent noted that the vagina did not secrete enough lubrication. This can cause pain when the penis is inserted into the vagina. However, it can be corrected through the use of an artificial lubricant.

For men, HRT has not been proven effective to overcome the physical declines that frequently accompany aging. Its benefits are psychological not physiological (Weg, 1983*b*).

Psychological Techniques

Sexual problems in the aged are caused primarily by social and psychological factors. The negative stereotypes of the aged combined with the lack of trained professionals to handle their problems create an atmosphere of sexual restrictions and discrimination. Sviland (1975) has designed a program to help sexually liberate the aged. The program is designed to assist the aged in once again regaining some of the positive aspects of the sexual experience. Basically, the program helps aged couples to understand the cultural pressures placed on them, to recognize their own and their partner's values and abilities, and to adjust and expand their repertoire of sexual behavior.

Sviland (1975) found that the therapy was generally very successful. She did, however, notice several potential problem areas. For example, sometimes older persons experienced depression and avoided sexual intercourse after therapy. This situation came about when individuals found themselves sexually liberated but unable to respond physically to the new liberation. The author concluded that it was important to continue the therapy until the individuals could adjust to their own limitations.

Masters and Johnson (1970) found that they were able to help about 70 percent of older persons who came to their clinic for therapy. This rate is high considering that there were years of sexual learning, behavior, and values to modify, societal attitudes to expose, physical limitations to work with, and often long periods of sexual abstinence to deal with.

Several writers have pointed out that satisfying sexual behavior does not have to cease with advancing age. If a couple has effective communication and adequate sexual knowledge, there are few reasons why sexual relations cannot be continued almost indefinitely. However, there may have to be some modifications in technique, frequency, and expectations. Sexual dysfunctioning in older persons should not be ignored simply because of the age of the afflicted.

The most effective way of eliminating sexual problems in older persons is by disseminating information in this area to professionals, the general public, and the aged. According to Burnside (1976), professionals who work with the aged would do the following:

1 Openly discuss sexuality with their peers and colleagues. This openness will provide the professional with a learning experience and also make them less inhibited or embarrassed to discuss sexuality with a patient or client.

2 Make an effort to learn about sexuality in the aged, especially the therapeutic aspects.

3 Try to develop empathy with the life-style of the aged. This effort will involve an attempt to understand their attitudes and values toward sexuality. Ideally, the professional will then develop respect and tolerance toward the sexuality of the aged.

4 Become aware of the societal attitudes toward sexuality in the aged. The professional should try to become aware of how these attitudes influence older persons.

5 Consider the environment in which the client or patient lives. Is it conducive to sexual expression? If not, what can be done about it?

6 Develop a professional approach to working with the sexual problems of the aged. The professional might also consider the therapeutic effects of such affective responses as touching, caring, or friendship.

Thus, if the sexual problems of the aged are to be helped, professionals must be aware of the various "causes" of sexual dysfunctioning; they must be aware of the various modes of treatment; and they must be willing to see sexuality as an important component of the life-cycle for most older persons.

The general public also must be informed of the importance of sexuality in old age. Currently, there are many myths surrounding this area. These myths are damaging to older persons because they may believe and respond as though the myths were true. However, they are also damaging to the young because they respond to the sexuality of the aged with laughter or disgust and because they are also predisposed to believe the myths and thus may reduce their frequency of sexual expression when they, too, become aged.

The third group is the aged themselves. They must be informed about some of the normal changes brought about by aging and about how these changes affect sexual performance. Most older persons expect certain physical changes to take place with increasing age. However, because information is not available on how these changes affect sexual expression, many do not know what to expect. Thus, normal changes are often interpreted as pathological, with the result that individuals experience anxiety about their sexuality or cease all sexual expression.

SEXUAL LIBERATION OF OLDER PERSONS

As we have already seen, older persons are sexually discriminated against in our society. Our society considers sex to be the domain of the young, not of the old. Very likely this attitude will change in the next several decades since more research in the area of human sexuality is about "sexual evolution" than the "sexual revolution." Also, researchers are establishing the importance of sexuality at all ages (see Horn, 1974).

One of the changes that will probably take place in the future will be more sanctioned sexual expression in nursing homes (see Fox, 1980; Kaas, 1978; Kassel, 1983). Currently, most nursing homes do not allow or encourage sexual expression. In many nursing homes males and females are separated. Sexuality is further discouraged by the lack of privacy. Moreover, many married couples are separated and placed in different rooms, at a time when they may need one another the most (see White, 1982).

Before there can be "sexual liberation" of older persons, several groups will have to be liberated. First, the adult children of older persons will have to change many of their preconceived ideas. It is generally difficult for them to see their parents, especially their aged parents, as individuals possessing sexual drives and desires. It is even more difficult for them to see a widowed parent having sexual feelings for someone other than the deceased spouse. Thus, if a nursing home offers "privacy" as a feature of the home, this might be the very reason the adult children would not allow their parents to go to that home.

The second group that will need to be liberated is nursing home administrators and staff. It has been mentioned that sexuality among residents in nursing homes takes on the aura of incest (see Glass et al., 1986), and the prevailing attitude is to discourage, punish, or ridicule any resident sexual activity. One of the consequences may be little intermingling between the sexes. The staff in nursing homes need to be instructed about the importance of sexuality for older persons and should try to keep the staff from discouraging "normal" sexual expression. Lobsenz (1974) reports an account of a horrified nurse running into the nursing home administrator's office and asking what she should do about a couple she had just discovered making love. The administrator replied that she should see to it that they are not disturbed. To encourage sexuality, as well as other factors such as socialization, beauty parlors should be established for the women and barber shops for the men. Information on grooming and sex should be provided to all residents who are capable of responding and who want the information. If possible, patients should have some privacy in their rooms, at least during certain hours (see Fox, 1980).

The third group involved in the sexual liberation of older persons is once again that of older persons themselves. As we saw in the last section, if older persons are to continue with sexual expression, their concepts, values, and norms will also have to change. They will have to realize that very often the only factor preventing them from engaging in sexual expression is the attitude of others (see West, 1983). Additionally, older persons have been raised with many myths about the sexuality they are now experiencing. They may misinterpret normal changes, or overreact to the changes. Education can teach them that many changes are normal and that they can learn new sexual techniques that will make sexual activity as enjoyable as in the past.

It should be noted that sexual liberation of older persons is not an attempt to force sexuality on them. Nor is it an attempt to say that a sexual way of life is better than a nonsexual way of life. It is recognized that there are many aged who are happy to be finished with certain forms of sexuality and many more who are debilitated physically and mentally and who cannot participate in sexual activity.

In an interesting article, "Sexuality and Aging: Essential Vitamin or Popcorn,"

Thomas (1982) has noted that recently writers have come to portray sex as an essential component of a healthy old age. He says that this may be nothing more than the projection of the values of a younger generation on older persons, perhaps in an attempt to deny aging.

If sexual liberation does become a desired feature of old age, there is still one major problem to overcome if it is to be heterosexual. This problem is that there are far more eligible aged women than aged men. Kassel (1966) had suggested polygyny (one man having several wives) as a solution to this problem. He sees several benefits in this type of relationship: (1) with a family unit of one man and two or more wives a true family group could develop and thus alleviate isolation and loneliness; (2) diet might become better since there would be at least three people capable of preparing food and monitoring each other's food intake; (3) living conditions would improve since several individuals could pool their money in order to buy food and pay rent; (4) the family unit could take turns nursing the sick and thus reduce the need for impersonal care; (5) the living environment would be cleaner since several individuals could pool their energies in maintaining the household; (6) many unmarried women could once again have a socially sanctioned sex partner; (7) appearance would be improved since there would be others to prod an individual into keeping fit and clean and looking attractive; (8) loneliness and depression would be less likely to occur since there would be others with whom to socialize and since there would be important roles to fill in the family unit; (9) the family unit would be able to obtain group medical insurance at a reasonable rate.

In addition to polygyny as a possible solution to the decline in sexuality that many women undergo, other writers have made other suggestions. For example, Starr (1985) has noted that masturbation may become a more frequent sexual outlet for older women. He pointed out that although this may have the benefit of the release of sexual tension, for many it may only intensify the lack of a sexual partner and the sharing and intimacy that often accompanies that relationship. The possibility of increasing bisexuality or homosexuality, sharing partners, or of more affairs was also mentioned by Starr (1985) as possible future trends.

SUMMARY

Traditionally, sexuality has been viewed as an important component of early life periods; now sexuality is recognized as an important part of all life periods, including old age. This chapter examined sexuality in old age.

In the first section three of the methodological problems in studying the sexuality of older persons were discussed. First, it was noted that much of what has been written is based on moral or personal beliefs, not scientific research. Second, that researchers are inconsistent in the way they present information. For example, one researcher may collect information on sexual intercourse, another on sexual activity. This makes comparison of results difficult. Third, until recently little research was conducted on the sexuality of the aged.

The second section reviewed the early research on the sexuality of older persons. It was noted that before the research by Kinsey and his associates little empirical research existed. Although Kinsey's work is widely cited and quoted, it does have several methodological limitations and Kinsey's sample of older persons was very small. However, Kinsey did dispel several myths about the sexuality of older persons: that they are asexual, that sexual dysfunctioning is irreversible, that rapid sexual declines take place on reaching old age, that sexual thought and activities are abnormal, and that sexual activity is dangerous.

The Duke Longitudinal Studies were better from a methodological perspective. These studies noted that although generally sexual activity declines with increasing age there are many exceptions, with some individuals' levels of sexual activity actually increasing.

The work by Masters and Johnson ushered in a new era in the study of human sexuality: the measurement of sexual response. For aging men the researchers concluded that aging brings about a decline in sexual responsiveness with increasing age; for women aging per se has little or no impact on the ability to maintain earlier levels of sexual activity. Their research noted that the most important factor in maintaining sexual functioning in old age is regular sexual activity throughout life.

The next major study of aged sexuality was conducted by Starr and Weiner. One important dimension of this study was its emphasis on the inner or personal experience of sex. Rather then simply quantifying the number of sex acts, or orgasms, they asked older persons about their enjoyment of sex. They reported that most older persons found their sexual activity either as pleasant or more pleasant than when younger.

The last major study was by Brecher who again reported that sexual activity declines with increasing age.

The third section noted that sexuality is important to the aged. It was also pointed out that sexuality is often equated with sexual intercourse, which is a limited perspective. It should include many forms of sexual expression including holding, touching, or even talking.

In the fourth section several factors that influence sexual expression were discussed. First, the physiological factors were examined. For men there are several physiological changes that occur with increasing age (e.g., increased time to achieve an erection, more time between erections, increase in prostate problems). Essentially, the physical ability to continue to be sexually active declines from previous levels in most older males. For females there are also physical changes that influence sexual expression (e.g., changes in the vagina, less vaginal lubrication secreted upon sexual stimulation). However, aging does not bring about a decline in their ability for sexual expression. Second, the sociopsychological factors influencing sexual expression were discussed: Those who are married tend to be more sexually active than those who are not married; those in the higher social classes are more sexually active than those in the lower social classes; males are more sexually active than females, primarily because males are more likely to have a partner; previous sexual activity correlates positively with sexual expression in old age.

The next section, the fifth, examined different forms of sexual expression: heterosexual, solitary (masturbation), and homosexual. Basically, the frequency of heterosexual activity and masturbation for both males and females declines with increasing age, although there are exceptions. Very little is known, at this time, about aged homosexuals.

The sixth section examined sexual problems of older persons. It was reported that the major reasons married females discontinued sexual activity was the death or illness of a spouse. The major reason married males discontinued sexual activity was the inability to perform sexually. Several factors contributed to the reduction or discontinuation of sexual activity. Older persons who have been abstinent, for reasons such as widowhood, often find that the resumption of sexual activity is difficult. Aging also causes changes which can make sexual activity more difficult. The use of alcohol, drugs, or tobacco also negatively influence sexual activity. The attitude of society toward the sexuality of older persons (i.e., seeing them as nonsexual or asexual) also contributes to sexual problems. Many older persons become bored with the same partner or the same acts. Illness, both acute and chronic, can directly prevent sexual activity, or indirectly through the consequences of drugs or surgery.

The seventh section discussed ways to treat the sexual dysfunctioning of older persons. Medical techniques, such as hormone replacement theory or surgery, can correct certain problems. Since sexual dysfunctioning is often psychological in origin, psychological techniques have also been utilized and found to be effective.

In the last section the sexual liberation of older persons was discussed. Here it was noted that more studies are needed on sexual evolution. The issue of sexual expression in nursing homes was discussed, as well as sexual expression in the future.

REFERENCES

Allen, C. (1961). The aging homosexual. In I. Rubin (Ed.), *The third sex*. New York: New Book.

Andrews, J. (1989). Anti-ageists unite. *Nursing Times*, **19**(29): 22.

Arluke, A., Levin, J., & Suchwalko, J. (1984). Sexuality and romance in advice books for the elderly. *The Gerontologist*, **24**(4): 415–418.

Ashikari, R. H. (1984). Modified radical mastectomy. *Surgical Clinics of North America*, **64**(6): 1095–1102.

Bachmann, G. A. (1987). Another perspective on osteoporosis. *Medical Aspects of Human Sexuality*, **21**(3): 21–28.

Berezin, M. A. (1969). Sex and old age: A review of the literature. *Journal of Geriatric Psychiatry*, **17**(2): 131–149.

Bergkvist, L., Adami, H-O., Persson, I., Hoover, R., & Schairer, C. (1989). The risk of breast cancer after estrogen and estrogen-progestin replacement. *New England Journal of Medicine*, **321**(5): 293–297.

Brecher, E. M. (1984). *Love, sex, and aging*. Boston: Little, Brown.

Broderick, C. (1975). Sexuality and aging. In I. M. Burnside (Ed.), *Sexuality and aging* (pp. 1–6). Los Angeles: University of Southern California Press.

Brower, H. T., & Tanner, L. A. (1979). A study of older adults attending a program on human sexuality. *Nursing Research*, **28**(1): 36–39.

Budoff, P. W. (1984). Breast cancer as viewed by the family physician. *Surgical Clinics of North America*, **64**(6): 1209–1212.

Burnside, I. M. (1975a). Sexuality and the older adult: Implications for nursing. In I. M.

Burnside (Ed.), *Sexuality and aging*. Los Angeles: University of Southern California Press.

Burnside, I. M. (1975*b*). Sexuality and aging. In I. M. Burnside (Ed.), Sexuality and aging (pp. 43–53). Los Angeles: University of Southern California Press.

Burnside, I. M. (1976). Sexuality and the aged. In I. M. Burnside (Ed.), *Nursing and the aged* (pp. 452–464). New York: McGraw-Hill.

Bush, J. F. (1987). Osteoporosis: When first-line treatment fails. *Medical Aspects of Human Sexuality*, **21**(10): 28–34.

Busse, E. W., & Maddox, G. L. (1985). *The Duke Longitudinal Studies of Normal Aging, 1955–1980*. New York: Springer.

Butler, R. N., & Lewis, M. I. (1976). *Love and sex after sixty*. New York: Harper and Row.

Butler, R. N., & Lewis, M. I. (1982). *Aging and mental health* (third edition). St. Louis: Mosby.

Catalano, D. J., & Schmidt, R. M. (Eds.) (1989). AIDS and an aging society. *Generations*, **13**(4): 1–88.

Catania, J. A., Turner, H., Kegeles, S. M., Stall, R., Pollack, L., & Coates, T. J. (1989). Older Americans and AIDS: Transmission risks and primary prevention research needs. *The Gerontologist*, **29**(3): 373–381.

Comfort, A. (1974). Sexuality in old age. *Journal of the American Geriatrics Society*, **22**(10): 440–442.

Covey, H. C. (1989). Perceptions and attitudes toward sexuality of the elderly during the middle age. *The Gerontologist*, **29**(1): 93–100.

Damrosch, S. P. (1982). Nursing students' attitudes toward sexually active older persons. *Nursing Research*, **31**(4): 252–255.

Damrosch, S. P. (1984). Graduate nursing students' attitudes toward sexually active older persons. *The Gerontologist*, **24**(3): 299–302.

deNigola, P., & Peruzza, M. (1974). Sex in the aged. *Journal of the American Geriatrics Society*, **22**(8): 380–382.

Dennerstein, L., Wood, C., & Burrows, G. D. (1977). Sexual response following hysterectomy and oophorectomy. *Obstetrics and Gynecology*, **49**(1): 92–96.

Dinner, M. I. (1984). Postmastectomy reconstruction. *Surgical Clinics of North America*, **64**(6): 1193–1207.

Ellenberg, M. (1977). Sexual aspects of the female diabetic. *Mount Sinai Journal of Medicine*, **44**(5): 495–500.

Felstein, I. (1983). Dysfunction: Origins and therapeutic approaches. In R. B. Weg (Ed.), *Sexuality in the later years: Roles and behavior* (pp. 223–246). New York: Academic Press.

Finkle, A. L., & Finkle, P. S. (1977). How counseling may solve sexual problems of aging men. *Geriatrics*, **32**(11): 84–89.

Fisher, J. J. (1987). Is there sex after prostatic cancer. *Medical Aspects of Human Sexuality*, **21**(6): 32–37.

Fox, N. L. (1980). Sex in the nursing home? For lord's sake why not? *RN*, **43**(10): 95–98.

Gambrell, R. D. (1987). Estrogen replacement therapy for the elderly woman. *Medical Aspects of Human Sexuality*, **21**(5): 81–93.

George, L. K., & Weiler, S. J. (1981). Sexuality in middle and late life: The effects of age, cohort, and gender. *Archives of General Psychiatry*, **38**(8): 919–923.

Gingrich, D. 91987). Preventing recurrent urinary tract infections in the elderly. *Medical Aspects of Human Sexuality*, **21**(11): 34–45.

Glass, J. C., Mustian, R. D., & Carter, L. R. (1986). Knowledge and attitudes of healthcare providers toward sexuality in the institutionalized elderly. *Educational Gerontology,* **12**(5): 465–475.

Glover, B. (1975). Sex in the aging. *Postgraduate medicine,* **57**(6): 165–169.

Goldberg, R. L. (1987). Sexual counseling for the stroke patient. *Medical Aspects of Human Sexuality,* **21**(6): 86–92.

Gray, H., & Dressel, P. (1985). Alternative interpretations of aging among gay males. *The Gerontologist,* **25**(1): 83–87.

Gregory, J. G. (1982). Impotence: The surgical approach. *Surgical Clinics of North America,* **62**(6): 981–998.

Griggs, W. (1978). Sex and the elderly. *American Journal of Nursing,* **78**(8): 1352–1354.

Harris, R. (1988). Exercise and sex in the aging patient. *Medical Aspects of Human Sexuality,* **22**(1): 148–159.

Harry, J., & DeVall, W. (1978). Age and sexual culture among homosexually oriented males. *Archives of Sexual Behavior,* **7**(2): 199–209.

Horn, P. (1974). Newsline: Rx: Sex for senior citizens. *Psychology Today,* **8**(1): 18–20.

Kaas, M. J. (1978). Sexual expression of the elderly in nursing homes. *The Gerontologist,* **18**(4): 372–378.

Kassel, V. (1966). Polygyny after 60. *Geriatrics,* **21**(3): 214–218.

Kassel, V. (1983). Long-term care institutions. In R. B. Weg (Ed.), *Sexuality in the later years: Roles and behavior* (pp. 176–182). New York: Academic Press.

Kelly, J. (1977). The aging male homosexual: Myth and reality. *The Gerontologist,* **17**(4): 328–333.

Kent, S. (1975a). Impotence: The fact versus the fallacies. *Geriatrics,* **30**(4): 164–171.

Kent, S. (1975b). Continued sexual activity depends on health and the availability of a partner. *Geriatrics,* **30**(11): 142–144.

Kent, S. (1975c). Being aware of a patient's sexual problems should be the concern of every physician. *Geriatrics,* **30**(1): 140–144.

Keyes, K., Bisno, B., Richardson, J., & Marston, A. (1987). Age differences in coping, behavioral dysfunction and depression following colostomy surgery. *The Gerontologist,* **27**(2): 182–184.

Kimmel, D. C. (1978). Adult development and aging: A gay perspective. *Journal of Social Issues,* **34**(3): 113–130.

Kimmel, D. C. (1979–1980). Life history interviews of aging gay men. *International Journal of Aging and Human Development,* **10**(3): 239–249.

Kinsey, A., Pomeroy, W. B., & Martin, C. E. (1948). *Sexual behavior in the human male.* Philadelphia: Saunders.

Kinsey, A., Pomeroy, W. B., Martin, C. E., & Gebhard, P. H. (1953). *Sexual behavior in the human female.* Philadelphia: Saunders.

Laury, G. V. (1987). Sexuality of the dying patient. *Medical Aspects of Human Sexuality,* **21**(6): 102–109.

Lemere, F., & Smith, J. W. (1973). Alcohol-induced sexual impotence. *American Journal of Psychiatry,* **130**(2): 212–213.

Libman, E., & Fichten, C. S. (1987). Prostatectomy and sexual function. *Urology,* **29**(5): 467–478.

Lobsenz, N. M. (1974). Sex and the senior citizen. *The New York Times Magazine,* **20**(January): 8.

Loughman, C. (1980). Eros and the elderly: A literary view. *The Gerontologist,* **20**(2): 182–187.

Ludeman, K. (1981). The sexuality of the older person: Review of the literature. *The Gerontologist,* **21**(2): 203–208.

Mandel, J. S., & Schuman, L. M. (1987). Sexual factors and prostatic cancer: Results from a case-control study. *Journal of Gerontology,* **42**(3): 259–264.

Martin, C. E. (1981). Factors affecting sexual functioning in 60– to 79–year-old married males. *Archives of Sexual Behavior,* **10**(5): 399–420.

Martin, M. B. (1987). Sexual dysfunction after surgery. *Medical Aspects of Human Sexuality,* **21**(9): 130–135.

Masters, W. H., & Johnson, V. E. (1966). *Human sexual response.* Boston: Little, Brown.

Masters, W. H., & Johnson, V. E. (1970). *Human sexual inadequacy.* Boston: Little, Brown.

Newman, G., & Nichols, C. (1960). Sexual activities and attitudes in older persons. *Journal of the American Medical Association,* **173**(1): 33–35.

Palmore, E. (1952). Published reactions to the Kinsey Report. *Social Forces,* **31**(2): 165–172.

Palmore, E. (Ed.) (1970). *Normal aging.* Durham, NC: Duke University Press.

Palmore, E. (Ed.) (1974). *Normal aging II.* Durham, NC: Duke University Press.

Palmore, E. (1981). *Social patterns in normal aging: Findings from the Duke Longitudinal Study.* Durham, NC: Duke University Press.

Palmore, E., Nowlin, J. B., Busse, E. W., Siegler, I. C., & Maddox, G. L. (Eds.) (1985). *Normal aging III.* Durham, NC: Duke University Press.

Peters, M. V. (1984). "Local" treatment of early breast cancer. *Surgical Clinics of North America,* **64**(6): 1151–1154.

Pfeiffer, E. (1974). Sexuality in the aging individual. *Journal of the American Geriatrics Society,* **22**(11): 481–484.

Pfeiffer, E., & Davis, G. C. (1972). Determinants of sexual behavior in middle and old age. *Journal of the American Geriatrics Society,* **20**(4): 151–158.

Pfeiffer, E., Verwoerdt, A., & Davis, G. C. (1972). Sexual behavior in middle life. *American Journal of Psychiatry,* **128**(10): 1262–1267.

Pietropinto, A. (1987). Sex and the elderly. *Medical Aspects of Human Sexuality,* **21**(6): 110–117.

Pocs, O., Godow, A., Tolone, W. L., & Walsh, R. H. (1977). Is there sex after forty? *Psychology Today,* **11**(1): 54–55, 87.

Polivy, J. (1977). Psychological effects of mastectomy on a woman's feminine self-concept. *Journal of Nervous and Mental Diseases,* **164**(2): 77–87.

Raphael, S., & Robinson, M. (1980). The older lesbian: Love relationships and friendship patterns. *Alternative Lifestyles,* **3**: 207–230.

Reyniak, J. V. (1987). Sexual and other concerns of the woman with osteoporosis. *Medical Aspects of Human Sexuality,* **21**(1): 16i–16j.

Riegle, G. D. (1987). Reproductive system. In G. L. Maddox (Ed.), *The encyclopedia of aging* (pp. 566–569). New York: Springer.

Riehle, R. A., & Vaughan, E. D. (1983). Genitourinary disease in the elderly. *Medical Clinics of North America,* **67**(2): 445–461.

Roberts, A. (1989). Sexuality in later life. *Nursing Times,* **85**(24): 65–68.

Robinson, P. K. (1983). The sociological perspective. In R. B. Weg (Ed.), *Sexuality in the later years: Roles and behavior* (pp. 82–104). New York: Academic Press.

Roff, L. L., & Klemmack, D. L. (1979). Sexual activity among older persons. *Research on Aging,* **1**(3): 389–399.

Rossman, I. (1975). Sexuality and the aging process: An internist's perspective. In I. M.

Burnside (Ed.), *Sexuality and aging* (pp. 18–25). Los Angeles: University of Southern California Press.

Runciman, A. (1975). Problems older clients present in counseling about sexuality. In I. M. Burnside (Ed.), *Sexuality and aging* (pp. 54–66). Los Angeles: University of Southern California Press.

Rykken, D. E. (1987). Sex in the later years. In P. Silverman (Ed.), *The elderly as modern pioneers* (pp. 158–182). Bloomington: Indiana University Press.

Shangold, M., & Mirkin, G. (1987). Fitness in postmenopausal women: How to motivate the patient. *Medical Aspects of Human Sexuality, 21*(2): 23.

Solnick, R. E., & Corby, N. (1983). Human sexuality and aging. In D. S. Woodruff & J. E. Birren (Eds.), *Aging: Scientific perspectives and social issues* (pp. 202–224). Monterey, CA: Brooks/Cole.

Sontag, S. (1972). The double standard of aging. *Saturday Review of the Society, 55*(39): 29–38.

Starr, B. D. (1985). Sexuality and aging. In C. Eisdorfer (Ed.), *Annual review of gerontology and geriatrics: Volume Five* (pp. 97–126). New York: Springer.

Starr, B. D. (1987). Sexuality. In G. L. Maddox (Ed.), *The encyclopedia of aging* (pp. 606–608). New York: Springer.

Starr, B. D., & Weiner, M. B. (1981). *The Starr-Weiner report on sex and sexuality in the mature years.* New York: McGraw-Hill.

Steinberg, M. D., Juliano, M. A., & Wise, L. (1985). Psychological outcome of lumpectomy versus mastectomy in the treatment of breast cancer. *American Journal of Psychiatry, 142*(1): 34–39.

Stimson, A., Wase, J. F., & Stimson, J. (1981). Sexuality and self-esteem among the aged. *Research on Aging, 3*(2): 228–239.

Sviland, M. A. (1975). Helping elderly couples become sexually liberated: Psychosocial issues. *Counseling Psychology, 5*(1): 67–72.

Teitelman, J. L. (1987). Homosexuality. In G. L. Maddox (Ed.), *The encyclopedia of aging* (pp. 329–330). New York: Springer.

Thomas, L. E. (1982). Sexuality and aging: Essential vitamin or popcorn. *The Gerontologist, 22*(3): 240–243.

Traupmann, J., Eckels, E., & Hatfield, E. (1982). Intimacy in older women's lives. *The Gerontologist, 22*(6): 493–498.

Travis, S. S. (1987). Older adults' sexuality and remarriage. *Journal of Gerontological Nursing, 13*(6): 9–14.

U.S. Bureau of the Census (1987). *Statistical abstracts of the United States: 1987.* Washington, DC: U.S. Government Printing Office.

U.S. Bureau of the Census (1990). *Statistical abstracts of the United States: 1989.* Washington, DC: U.S. Government Printing Office.

Verwoerdt, A., Pfeiffer, E., & Wang, H-S. (1969). Sexual behavior in senescence. *Journal of Geriatric Psychiatry, 2*(2): 163–180.

Weg, R. B. (1973). Changing physiology in aging. *American Journal of Occupational Therapy, 27*(5): 213–217.

Weg, R. B. (1975a). Physiology and sexuality in aging. In I. M. Burnside (Ed.), *Sexuality and aging* (pp. 7–17). Los Angeles: University of Southern California Press.

Weg, R. B. (1975b). Sexual inadequacy in the elderly. In M. Rockstein (Ed.), *The physiology and pathology of human aging* (pp. 203–228). New York: Academic Press.

Weg, R. B. (1976). Normal aging changes in the reproductive system. In I. M. Burnside (Ed.), *Nursing and the aged* (pp. 99–112). New York: McGraw-Hill.

Weg, R. B. (1978). The physiology of sexuality in aging. In R. L. Solnick (Ed.), *Sexuality and aging* (revised) (pp. 48–65). Los Angeles: University of Southern California Press.

Weg, R. B. (1983*a*). Introduction: Beyond intercourse and orgasm. In R. B. Weg (Ed.), *Sexuality in the later years: Roles and behavior* (pp. 1–12). New York: Academic Press.

Weg, R. B. (1983*b*). The physiological perspective. In R. B. Weg (Ed.), *Sexuality in the later years: Roles and behavior* (pp. 40–81). New York: Academic Press.

Weg, R. B. (1987). Menopause: Biomedical aspects. In G. L. Maddox (Ed.), *The encyclopedia of aging* (pp. 433–437). New York: Springer.

Weinberg, M. S. (1970). The male homosexual: Age-related variations in social and psychological characteristics. *Social Problems,* **17**(4): 527–537.

Weizman, R., & Hart, J. (1987). Sexual behavior in healthy married elderly men. *Archives of Sexual Behavior,* **16**(1): 39–44.

Wellisch, D. K., Jamison, K. R., & Pasnau, R. O. (1978). Psychological aspects of mastectomy: II. The man's perspective. *American Journal of Psychiatry,* **135**(4): 432–436.

West, H. L. (1983). Sexuality and aging: An innovative educational approach. *Gerontology and Geriatrics Education,* **4**(1): 61–66.

Wheeler, M. (1976). Osteoporosis. *Medical Clinics of North America,* **60**(6): 1213–1224.

White, C. B. (1982). Sexual interest, attitudes, knowledge, and sexual history in relation to sexual behavior in the institutionalized aged. *Archives of Sexual Behavior,* **11**(1): 11–21.

CHAPTER 8

PSYCHOLOGICAL ASPECTS

Deborah Kahn/Stock, Boston

INTRODUCTION

Major studies in the psychology of aging first appeared in the 1880s. Since that time the number of studies has increased substantially. This chapter examines speed of behavior, mental functioning, and mental disorders.

SPEED OF BEHAVIOR

Speed of behavior is unique in gerontology in that research results have been consistent for almost a century: with increasing age there is a slowing in speed of behavior (see Birren et al., 1980; Botwinick, 1984; Krauss, 1987; Salthouse, 1985). This has been shown in cross-sectional and longitudinal studies (Arenberg, 1982; Birren et al., 1963; Botwinick & Birren, 1965).

Much of the research has examined motor or psychomotor performance: learned responses made by the voluntary muscles. The voluntary muscles are those over which an individual has conscious control. An individual's motor performance is determined by a three-part process. The first is perception, in which the individual becomes aware of a stimulus in the environment; the second is information processing, in which the individual evaluates the stimulus and determines what response is necessary or appropriate; the third is responding, which generally involves motor performance. In this stage, the individual has processed the information and has made a decision to act and is therefore running, lifting, or engaging in some other response that involves the voluntary muscles.

There are two types of motor performance: simple and complex. Simple motor performance requires little information processing, decision making, or complex motor skills. Complex motor performance requires more information processing, decision making, and complex motor skills (Welford, 1977). Studies indicate that both types decline with increasing age, with the complex motor skills declining the most (Hale et al., 1987).

One frequent way of measuring the slowing of behavior has been through reaction time (RT). RT is the length of time between the onset of a stimulus and the execution of a measurable response to that stimulus. Studies indicate that RT increases with advancing age for both simple and complex motor performances. That is, it takes older persons longer than young adults to respond to a stimulus. According to Bischof (1976), there is an improvement in RT until about age 19. From ages 19 to 26, RT remains fairly constant. After age 26 there is a gradual but continual decline in RT. It has also been found that a weak stimulus, irrelevant stimuli, or a complex motor sequence that involves choices widens the gap between the RTs of young adults and those of older persons. However, studies also indicate that practice reduces the differences.

Among older persons there is a wide range of RTs. It has been found, for example, health and physical fitness play a role, with the healthiest and most physically fit having lower RTs than those who are in poor health and not physically fit (Botwinick & Thompson, 1968; Spirdiso, 1975, 1980; Spirdiso & Clifford, 1978). Exercise programs have also been found to improve RTs (Dustman et al., 1984). Still, however, the RTs of healthy, physically fit older persons will generally be slower than those of healthy, physically fit young adults. Thus, it is not only health or physical fitness that accounts for the differences.

The question of why there is a slowing of behavior is still being investigated. Researchers have examined a variety of possible explanations including the possibilities of physical changes, brought about by aging, declining health or senses, or cognitive changes in memory or speed of information processing. Currently, no definitive explanation exists (Krauss, 1987).

We will now examine the implications that the slowing of behavior has for older persons in everyday life. Birren (1964) has pointed out that although the RTs of older persons may be 10 to 20 percent slower than for young adults, the differences are generally not significant for everyday life. For example, the average RT of a 20-year-old to a visual signal might be 0.20 seconds; for a 65-year-old the visual signal might be 0.22 seconds. Although this represents a 10 percent difference, 0.02 of a second would generally not make much of a difference in everyday life.

However, there are some exceptions. A slowing of behavior or RT could, in certain situations, lead to a higher accident rate. For example, after slipping, older persons may not be able to regain their balance as rapidly as young adults, or while driving automobiles they may not be capable of responding as rapidly to a dangerous situation.

MENTAL FUNCTIONING

There are many variables that influence human behavior. Perhaps none is more important than mental functioning. Mental functioning is a broad term which deals with the processing of information through which the stimulus is interpreted and a response selected; that is, between the perception of a stimulus by the senses and the individual's response. This section will examine five of the areas of mental functioning: intelligence, learning, memory, creativity, and personality.

Intelligence

There are few concepts in psychology that have been studied as frequently, as thoroughly, or as widely as intelligence. However, there is still disagreement about what intelligence is, what intelligence tests measure, and what relevance intelligence test scores have to functioning and performance in the "real world." Because psychologists have different concepts of what intelligence is and because they use different testing devices, the resulting literature is often confusing and contradictory (see Woodruff, 1983).

Students need to understand that there are different models and theories of intelligence (see Birren et al., 1983; Botwinick, 1984; Cunningham, 1987). The model or theory can determine what aspects of intelligence are measured, and how they are measured.

A significant number of studies have used the Wechsler Adult Intelligence Scale (WAIS). The WAIS is separated into two major areas: verbal and performance intelligence (Horn, 1987). Verbal intelligence, which is measured by six separate subtests, concentrates on acquired knowledge; basically what individuals have learned. Performance intelligence, which is measured by five subtests, measures analytical or reasoning skills. Individuals are presented with "new" problems to solve.

The use of WAIS has contributed to the formation of two distinctive schools of thought concerning intelligence in old age. The first school of thought is what could be termed the "traditional school" in which psychologists have viewed intelligence as declining with increasing age. To date the majority of studies have demonstrated that a decline takes place in intelligence scores with increasing age. The studies have generally reported that the scores that decline the most are in the performance areas of the tests, which measure noncognitive functioning such as psychomotor skills, perception, and the senses. These sections usually involve speed, the ability to conceptualize an arrangement and then manipulate objects into that arrangement. Some believe that this measures "fluid intelligence," or the type of intelligence that is independent of education and experience. Older persons tend to compare equally with young adults on the vocabulary or verbal parts of intelligence tests. This fact indicates that verbal abilities and stored information decline relatively little, if at all, with increasing age. This measures "crystallized intelligence," or the type of intelligence that is determined by education and experience. This finding of significant declines in performance areas and small declines (or no decline) in verbal areas has been frequently documented and is called the "classic aging pattern" (Botwinick, 1967, 1977).

Although the overall conclusion that intelligence declines with increasing age has remained the same, the research results on the "classic aging pattern" has undergone some changes in the last two decades. First, the age at which the declines are believed to start have gradually increased. At one time it was believed that the declines started in the early twenties (see Kramer, 1987; Labouvie-Vief, 1985); then some of the early longitudinal studies found that the declines did not start until the fifties (Cunningham, 1987; Cunningham & Owens, 1983), or sixties (Schaie, 1983). More recently studies have found that the declines do not start until the seventies, and for some abilities until the eighties (Botwinick, 1977; Dixon et al., 1985; Schaie, 1970; Schaie & Hertzog, 1983; Schaie & Parham, 1976; Siegler, 1983; Wilkie & Eisdorfer, 1985; Willis & Baltes, 1980). Second, the declines are not as great as previously claimed, and may have little impact on functioning in the "real world" (Schaie & Parham, 1976). Third, the decline is no longer believed to be universal but rather, as noted above, specific to only certain intellectual abilities (see Botwinick, 1977; Cunningham, 1987).

The second school of thought challenges the traditional belief of declining intelligence with increasing age and states that with increasing age there is no decline as a result of senescence, and in fact there may even be an increase if individuals remain in good physical and mental health and are in stimulating environments. Support for the second school of thought comes primarily from criticisms directed against the methodology of the traditional school (see Baltes & Schaie, 1974).

The first criticism directed at the traditional school is that the declines in intelligence scores may not be an inevitable consequence of aging but a consequence of pathological conditions (Manton et al., 1986). That is, the lowered intelligence scores may not demonstrate the consequences of "normal" aging but the consequences of pathological conditions that interfere with intellectual functioning. There are several pathological conditions that can affect intellectual functioning. For example, a damaged cardiovascular system may reduce the blood flow to the brain causing declines in intellectual functioning. It has also been noted that sleep patterns found in older persons may be responsible for changes associated with a lower level of intellectual functioning (Prinz, 1977), although research has suggested that sleep will not influence cognitive functioning until the health status of the individual has significantly deteriorated (Berry & Webb, 1985). Hearing problems have also been found to contribute to decreased intellectual functioning (Sands & Meredith, 1989). Additionally, poor health in general may upset a number of bodily functions that could possibly affect intelligence or performance on intelligence tests (see Botwinick, 1984).

Second, most of the studies on intelligence have been cross sectional. That is, they have compared the scores of young adults with the scores of older persons. If the intelligence scores of the younger adults were higher than the scores of older persons the researchers often assumed that intelligence declined with increasing age. It has been previously pointed out that this assumption is incorrect. We cannot say that the intelligence scores of older persons have declined unless we have done a longitudinal study in which we have at least two sets of scores on the same individual at two or more time periods. Although young adults may score higher than older persons on intelligence tests, this could represent an age or cohort difference, not an age change. That is, the intelligence of older persons may have remained stable; the difference may be accounted for by the fact that the younger cohort is more intelligent as a result of more education, better nutrition, and greater stimulation.

Longitudinal studies do not necessarily resolve the problems noted above unless the researchers control for senescence, the environment, and pathological conditions. Additionally, there are other problems involved in certain types of longitudinal studies, such as obtaining the original participants of the study for the subsequent study. After 40 to 50 years it is obviously difficult to find the original participants in order to administer a second intelligence test. It has been found that there is generally a higher attrition rate among the less able participants (see Cooney et al., 1988; Siegler, 1983; Siegler & Botwinick, 1979), which tends to raise the total intelligence score of the group. Thus, those longitudinal studies that have shown either an increase in intelligence scores over time or a stability of intelligence scores, are often biased in that the most able participants are the ones most likely to be retested (see Botwinick & Siegler, 1980).

A third factor challenging the traditional belief of declining intelligence with increasing age is that intelligence tests and testing situations may be biased. In other words, the intelligence tests may be as biased against older persons as they are against certain ethnic or racial groups. We know that the psychomotor performance of older persons is not as fast as of younger persons, meaning that timed tests may discriminate against older persons. In fact, studies have found that by increasing the time available to older persons for taking intelligence tests, the gap is reduced between the scores of young adults and older persons. Also, older persons are generally not as "test wise" as younger adults who have grown up and recently experienced tests similar to intelligence tests. Rather, for most older persons, the style and format of intelligence tests is unfamiliar. Additionally, older persons tend to be more cautious in answering questions; they are less likely to guess at an answer.

The concept that intelligence tests discriminate against older persons is hardly new. In 1957 Demming and Pressey claimed that intelligence tests discriminated against older persons since the questions were generally more meaningful for children and young adults. They devised a test in which the questions were related more to the needs of older persons and found that the scores of older persons increased.

A fourth factor challenging the belief that intelligence declines with increasing age deals with education. We know that intelligence scores rise with increasing levels of education, and that young adults have higher levels of education than older persons. However, what we do not know is whether education makes you more intelligent or if more intelligent individuals go to school.

A fifth factor may be the nearness to death of many older persons (Riegel & Riegel, 1972; Wilkie & Eisdorfer, 1985). It will be pointed out in Chapter 17, "Dying and Death," that many, but not all, researchers believe that there is a relationship between nearness to death and cognitive functioning. Essentially, the closer to death, the more impaired the level of functioning; this is referred to as the terminal drop hypothesis. It has been suggested that if studies on intelligence excluded dying individuals the results would indicate no decline in intellectual functioning (see Cooney et al., 1988). Conceivably this would be done by eliminating all of the intelligence test scores of those who had died within 6 to 24 months of being tested. Current research indicates that while "terminal drop" exists, it appears to affect specific areas of intellectual functioning, not all areas (White & Cunningham, 1988).

The sixth factor deals with environmental stimulation. Researchers have noted that many older persons are subjected to less environmental stimulation than younger persons. This can be a result of declines in senses or because the individual lives in an environment that does not provide much stimulation. Schaie (1983) has noted that older persons who live in stimulating environments are more likely to exhibit stability or increases in intellectual functioning, while those who live in dull, mundane environments are likely to experience declines.

Seventh, studies have reported that through training and practice older persons can substantially increase their intelligence scores. Through experiential training Labouvie-Vief and Gonda (1976) found that performance scores increased. One longitudinal study reported that a cognitive training program reversed a pattern of intellectual decline in 40 percent of the participants and substantially reversed the decline in an additional 25 percent of the participants (see Willis & Schaie, 1983). Additional studies have also reported that training programs can reverse losses in fluid intelligence (Blackburn et al., 1988; Bliezsner et al., 1981; Plemons et al., 1978). These findings challenge the traditional belief that intelligence losses are irreversible or that older persons cannot increase their intelligence scores (see Baltes & Labouvie, 1973).

An eighth factor is that many older persons do not expect to do well on intelligence tests. This attitude can lead to a self-fulfilling prophecy that can lower performance and scores.

The ninth factor deals with motivation. Older persons often have little riding on the results of the tests. In contrast, young adults are often motivated to try harder since they see a link between test performance and future academic and work roles.

The tenth factor is fatigue. Many older individuals will become fatigued faster than younger individuals, and thus have a lower performance.

The eleventh, and last, factor notes that studies present average scores for age groups and that this does not indicate individual performance. Several of the factors just discussed would be expected to lower the overall intellectual functioning, and thus the average of the group. However, this does not necessarily mean that all individuals decline in intellectual functioning. Data from longitudinal studies have indicated that while some older persons experience a decline in intellectual functioning, for many individuals, even in their eighties, intellectual functioning remains at previous levels.

Critics of the second school have noted that there is a tendency among researchers to want to believe that a decline in intelligence does not take place with increasing age. It has been pointed out that this desire can make researchers see only what they want to see, which can lead to a distortion of the facts (Bischof, 1976; Horn & Donaldson, 1976; Labouvie-Vief, 1985). In rebuttal, those who support the second school of thought claim that early researchers had models of psychological growth that emphasized growth and development in the first few decades of life and decline in the last several decades of life, and as a result created measuring devices to support these models.

This issue is very much alive in psychology and gerontology. However, the complexity of the issue makes it unlikely that a definitive answer will be forthcoming.

Learning

Learning and memory are closely related and will be considered in sequence. If the learning process is ineffective, then there will be little to draw from the memory. On the other hand, if the memory is faulty, there will be no sign that learning has taken place (Botwinick, 1984). Learning refers to the acquisition of knowledge or of a skill, and memory refers to the retention and the ability to retrieve the knowledge or skill (Craik, 1977).

According to Botwinick (1984) the learning-memory sequence has three functions: learning, storage, and retrieval. The first, learning, which is also called encoding, is concerned with obtaining the information. The second and third parts of the sequence are concerned with memory: storage with keeping the information and retrieval with recalling it.

There are numerous definitions of learning. For our purposes, learning is considered to have taken place when the individual acquires a skill or some information that improves an overt response or performance. Learning is a psychological process and as such it is difficult to measure directly. In order to measure it, they must look at the individual's performance. As Botwinick (1984) has pointed out, the inference that learning has not taken place if there is not a change in the level of response or of performance may be erroneous. The learning ability of the individual may be adequate. However, there may be factors that are interfering with the performance

of the individual, such as lack of motivation, lack of confidence, or distracting environmental conditions. Additionally, the problem may not be in learning but memory.
The individual may have learned but be unable to retrieve the information from
memory.

For psychologists the goal has become to design experiments that will separate
learning from memory. Through a series of ingenious experiments they have done
this and most of the studies have indicated that learning performance declines with
increasing age.

Some of the major studies in the area of learning have examined pacing. Pacing
refers to the amount of time an individual has to perceive a stimulus or signal and
to make a response. Previously, many psychologists speculated that fast pacing was
inappropriate for older persons since they were used to functioning at a slower pace;
thus, perhaps they had learned but were not being given sufficient time to respond.
Numerous studies were conducted with a variety of pacing signals. For example,
some studies presented a signal very rapidly but allowed a slow response. Other
studies employed a pacing schedule in which individuals determined when the signal
was presented. It was generally found that the slower the pacing, the better the
learning performance of older persons. However, even though the learning performance
of older persons improved with slower pacing, it still did not equal that of young
adults (Canestrari, 1963; Eisdorfer, 1965; Hulicka et al., 1967; Kinsbourne & Berryhill,
1972; Monge & Hultsch, 1971).

A common belief is that older persons do worse in learning situations because of
a lack of motivation (Botwinick, 1984). However, studies have found that older
persons are as highly motivated as other age groups. In fact, their high motivation
can be detrimental to their learning since it leads to high levels of physiological
arousal, which interferes with the learning process. When older persons participating
in experimental learning experiments were given drugs to lower their level of physiological arousal, it was found that the learning performance increased but still did not
match that of young adults (Eisdorfer et al., 1970; Lair & Moon, 1972; Powell et
al., 1964; Ross, 1968). Other studies have indicated that when the tasks are made
meaningful, familiar, or not too abstract that the level of performance of older persons
increased, but still did not match that of young adults (Canestrari, 1966; Hulicka,
1967; Kausler & Lair, 1972; Zaretsky & Halberstam, 1968).

Older persons can learn to learn. One study reported that older persons do not
use mnemonics (i.e., something that will assist individuals in remembering) as frequently as young adults (Hulicka et al., 1967). In order to get them to utilize mnemonic
devices, one study had them take imaginary walks through their homes and stop at
sixteen familiar places. The experimenter then paired each stop with a word. The
study found that the use of familiar mnemonic devices substantially increased the
level of learning performance of older persons from previous levels (Arenberg, 1976;
Robertson-Tchabo et al., 1976).

Other studies found that the learning performance of older persons increased when
they were in supportive rather than challenging environments (Ross, 1968). It was
also found to increase when the information to be learned was presented through
two senses, for example, when the older person silently read words as the experimenter
read them aloud (Arenberg, 1968; McGhie et al., 1965).

The question of why older persons generally perform at lower levels in learning experiments has also been examined. The lower performance levels appear to result from interference. That is, one learning task interferes with another (see Arenberg & Robertson-Tchabo, 1977). Several studies have indicated that older persons are more vulnerable to interference than young adults (Arenberg, 1973; Inglis, 1965; Kausler, 1970).

Although most of the research on learning indicates that older persons perform at lower levels in learning experiments than young adults, there is still a great deal of research that needs to be done. Most of the current studies make no mention of variables that could influence learning, such as education or health.

Memory

Without memory we would only have knowledge of present, or what is currently happening. Memory allows us to have knowledge of the past, or to plan for the future. Researchers have conceptualized and used a variety of terms to describe memory. For this text we will use the terms sensory, primary, and secondary.

The sensory memory is the first step in the memory process. Here the senses acquire and briefly store information. Two types of sensory memory are iconic memory, which refers to visual information, and echoic memory, which refers to auditory information. Information in the sensory memory is held very briefly, from a fraction of a second to a maximum of 2 seconds. Because our senses are constantly bombarded, we do not concentrate or think about most of the information that comes into the sensory memory. However, when we do concentrate on certain sensory information, this information is transferred to the primary memory, which can be thought of as short-term memory or "temporary" reserve of information. A new telephone number would be an example. If someone tells you a phone number you will probably be capable of remembering the number long enough to dial it. However, if you get a busy signal or if later in the day you have to call the number again you will probably not remember the number; the number is gone from your primary memory. Primary memory can be thought of as having a limited storage capacity. As new information is acquired from the sensory memory, old information is pushed out of the primary memory. Most individuals can keep from five to ten items (such as names or numbers) in their primary memories. Information in this memory can be held for up to about 30 seconds. The third form of memory is secondary memory. If you rehearse or "learn" a telephone number then it can be "memorized" or transferred to the secondary memory (sometimes called long-term memory). The amount of information held in the secondary memory seems unlimited. The time this information remains in the memory and can be retrieved seems unlimited. There have been numerous studies that have tried to ascertain differences in memory by age. Studies on sensory memory are difficult to conduct and studies that have been done are inconclusive (see Walsh, 1983).

The results indicate that primary memory declines slightly with increasing age (see Poon, 1985). For example, in primary memory studies in which experimental subjects were asked to immediately repeat a series of letters, words, or numbers, the researchers generally found slight age decrements (see Shichita et al., 1986;

Taub, 1973; Watkins, 1974). Researchers disagree as to why this occurs. Some believe that the capacity of the primary memory declines with increasing age (Kausler, 1987), others disagree (Walsh, 1983) and suggest that the decline must be caused by different factors. There is agreement that retrieval of information from the primary memory is slower in older persons (Botwinick, 1984; Kausler, 1987; Poon, 1985; Walsh, 1983).

Because many older persons have an excellent recollection of events that happened decades ago, many researchers traditionally believed that secondary memory does not decline with increasing age. However, researchers began to discover that much of what was retrieved had been continually repeated or rehearsed. Most experimental studies indicate a decline in secondary memory with increasing age (Bahrick et al., 1975; Poon, 1985; Schonfield, 1972; Warrington & Silverstein, 1970). The decline in secondary memory can be because of problems in recall or recognition. Essay exams require recall memory. Essentially, here you have to search through the memory for certain information, such as the names of the states, or the dates of the Civil War. Recall memory bypasses retrieval. Examples would be multiple-choice exams where you have to recognize the correct answer from a list. Studies have consistently found that recall memory declines with increasing age; recognition memory remains fairly constant.

There have been several studies on the memory process to discover why older person do more poorly on secondary memory tests than young adults. Memory tests generally consist of three parts. The first measures the registration of information (learning), the second the storage of information, and the third the retrieval of information.

Older persons are believed to be deficient in all three of these areas. In regard to the registration of information or learning, the decline in the senses probably may have something to do with the deficiency. Also, over time the perception of older persons becomes more selective. This selectivity means that they are more likely to perceive familiar things. It has been found that the performance of older persons is considerably lower than young adults if they are distracted during the experiment (see Broadbent & Gregory, 1965; Broadbent & Heron, 1962; Craik, 1977; Kirchner, 1958).

In regard to the storage of information, Botwinick (1984) asserts that older persons do not do this as successfully as young adults. Some writers have suggested that there is a decay in the memory over time. That is, the longer material remains unutilized in the memory, the greater the decay (see Broadbent, 1963). Other researchers have also found that the major explanation for the differences between the memories of the old and the young relates to the storage areas (see Harwood & Naylor, 1969).

Concerning the retrieval of information, it has also been reported that old persons have more difficulties than younger age groups. Researchers have speculated that they have more information in their memories and that they therefore must go through a longer search process. Very often the concept of interference has been used to explain this phenomenon (see Guttentag & Hunt, 1988; Hultsch, 1975; Kausler, 1970; Schonfield, 1985). It has also been inferred that it is more difficult for older persons than for young adults to utilize new stimuli in order to retrieve old information.

There are a variety of factors that can account for the differences in memory other than age (see Perlmutter et al., 1987). There can be psychological variables influencing the scores of older persons such as expecting to do worse on memory tests, or mental health problems in areas such as depression, anxiety, or dementia. Older persons are more likely to have other conditions affecting memory such as poor physical fitness, inadequate nutrition, lowered senses, and drug ingestion that may interfere with perception, cognition, or alertness. Educational achievement is also lower and some of the tests may be measuring the consequences of a learning-memory sequence practiced in acquiring an education.

There are many ways to enhance memory. Different drugs have been tried but the results have not been encouraging (Kluger & Ferris, 1987). Other ways of aiding the memories of older persons are through external aids (e.g., notebooks, lists), or internals aids (e.g., rehearsing).

In conclusion, it should be pointed out that although most of the studies do demonstrate a difference in memory between young and old adults in certain areas, generally the differences are very small. Also, in a summary of research on memory, Botwinick (1984) noted that if only "bright" young adults and "bright" older persons are used in studies on memory, the results are often identical. Furthermore, if the material is made more "meaningful" for older persons, the differences in memory scores between the age groups often vanish. It has also been found that administering oxygen to older persons for a short period before testing negates memory differences. This discovery suggests that perhaps the decline in memory is not inevitable or permanent, but rather a function of a decreasing supply of oxygen to the brain because of some pathological condition such as poor circulation (see Botwinick, 1984).

Creativity

Another concept that we should examine in this section is creativity. Creativity is a highly ambiguous term and thus one that has received relatively little attention from gerontologists. Although creativity may appear to be an abstract term having little significance in the "real" world, it does have some important implications for everyday living. Individuals who are "creative" have a greater likelihood of finding new ways to adapt to losses or to some of the other changes that take place with increasing age.

Some of the earliest studies on age and creativity were done by Lehman (1953, 1956, 1958, 1963) who provided information on individuals who had been "creative" in the arts, sciences, and everyday life. Although he reported variations in different areas, fields, and disciplines, he concluded that the greatest amount of productivity of "quality" work took place between the ages of 30 and 39; thus, in general both the quality and quantity of work were diminished with increasing age.

Dennis (1956a, 1956b, 1958, 1966) criticized Lehman's methodology and conclusions. One of his primary criticisms was that many of those Lehman studied belonged to previous centuries when life expectancy was shorter than in the present; thus it only appeared that creativity was associated with young adults. Dennis controlled for this factor by studying only individuals who lived to old age. He found that "quantity" of output did not vary throughout the adult portion of the life span.

Bullough and his associates (1978) examined "intellectual achievers" in two periods: eighteenth-century Scotland and fifteenth-century Florence. Essentially the study reported that intellectual achievement continued throughout life. That is, there was not a peak or a leveling off, but rather that those who had produced early in life continued to produce later in life.

Cole (1979) created and conducted a more empirical study than earlier studies that dealt with the quantity and quality of research papers published by individuals in six disciplines. He found that age was related to quantity and quality of publications, in that there was an increase until the mid-forties, when a slight decline began. Consistent with the work of Dennis, and Bullough and his associates, Cole found that those who produced a high quantity and quality of work early in their careers tended to maintain this level throughout their careers.

Zuckerman's (1977) study of Nobel laureates also examined the question of creativity. She found that those who were 40 to 44 years of age when they received their awards represented 23 percent of all Nobel laureates, but only 14 percent of all scientists. Thus, this age category had a disproportionate percentage of Nobel laureates.

The debate continues with some implying that there may be a decrease in creativity with increasing age (see Ruth & Birren, 1985). Older persons may only appear to retain their creativity since it is older persons who control what research is done, operate as journal editors, monopolize graduate student research, and can get almost anything published by virtue of their status. Thus it may only appear that older persons retain their creativity or that they are more creative than young adults because it is older persons who have the power to appear to be creative (Crane, 1967; Zuckerman & Merton, 1972). Additionally, often discoveries, publications, or scientific awards occur years or even decades after the work has been done. Thus, although the recognition or publications may occur late in life, the majority of the work was done early in life.

However, others claim that there is no decline in creativity with increasing age. Although older persons may decline from prior levels in both the quantity and quality of previous research, it is because they have moved from positions involving research to positions involving administrative tasks and responsibilities. Additionally, the decline in productivity for some may be related to the "scientific reward system" which essentially operates to continually remove individuals from the research process, leaving fewer and fewer individuals in later ages (Cole, 1979).

To date, the evidence on whether individuals become more or less creative with advancing age is inconclusive. All of the studies have indicated that there are numerous older persons who demonstrate creativity; thus the issue is not the impact of senescence on creativity, but rather the impact of other variables, such as health or retirement, on creativity. In his excellent book *A Good Age,* Alex Comfort (1976) has pointed out numerous examples of older persons who have remained "creative" into old age.

Personality

We have probably all noticed that individuals respond in different ways to similar situations. Some of the different responses are caused by familiarity with the situation;

others by personality differences. it is personality that makes each of us unique; each an individual.

One of the problems in studying personality is that there are several major personality theories in psychology. Erickson, Kolberg, Freud, and Jung are just a few of many psychologists who have developed models of personality. In gerontology Neugarten (1968) has categorized personality types found in the Kansas City studies. The major question concerning personality is, "does the aging process bring about personality changes?"

The conclusions drawn by several recent longitudinal studies have been consistent in reporting that the aging process does not bring about personality changes (see Bengtson et al., 1985; Costa & McCrae, 1978; Eichorn et al., 1981; McCrae & Costa, 1984; Schaie & Parham, 1976; Siegler, 1987; Siegler et al., 1979). This does not necessarily mean that personality cannot change. Obviously there may be significant life events at any age that can have an influence on personality. However, the aging process does not appear to change personality.

MENTAL DISORDERS

The area of mental disorders and older persons is an emerging area in gerontology. It has been pointed out that this area has not been "fashionable nor lucrative" for scientists and researchers and as a result the quantity of scientific research has been slow to develop. Although in recent years more publications have appeared, many have had methodological limitations, thus limiting the data necessary to expand and clarify this subject (LaRue et al., 1985).

In addition to the lack of interest noted above, there are other problems that contribute to the lack of information. For example, there are relatively few longitudinal studies that examine the development of mental disorders and allow researchers to separate preexisting mental disorders from those that occur in old age. Additionally, diagnosis of disorders has been difficult, with qualified, experienced therapists often disagreeing on the category a patient should be placed in.

To an extent the diagnostic issue was aided with the publication of the *Diagnostic and Statistical Manual of Mental Disorders* (DSM) by the American Psychiatric Association; the third edition (1980) is known as DSM-III, and the revised third edition (1987) as DSM-III-R. This manual provided therapists with a more complete description of disorders and a multilevel evaluation with specific diagnostic criteria (Butler, 1987; Corsini, 1987). DSM-III is not without its critics (Foltz, 1980; Schacht, 1985), and even with the guidelines diagnosis can still be difficult and controversial.

Currently, research on the extent of mental disorders in old age vary somewhat. For example, LaRue and his associates (1985) have claimed that 10 percent have mental disorders that are serious enough to warrant medical intervention; for Kermis (1986) 15 to 25 percent have "significant mental health problems"; for others 10 to 30 percent have "mental health problems" (Waxman et al., 1984); some believe that the percentage is 25 percent (see Woodruff et al., 1988); 10 to 20 percent are "in need of mental health services" according to Lewinsohn and Tilson (1987); Waxman and Carner (1984) noted that "mild to moderate psychiatric impairment" was present in 22 percent of the aged population; others believe 15 to 20 percent are "in need of mental health care" (Ray et al., 1985).

There are two issues that have been challenged in recent years. First, traditionally it has been believed that the rates of mental disorders remained fairly constant throughout adulthood. Studies indicated that the rates of mental health problems were similar in young, middle-aged, and old adults (Allan & Brotman, 1981; Kay et al., 1964; Kay & Bergmann, 1980; Lowenthal & Berkman, 1967; Srole et al., 1962). Recent research has suggested that rates of mental disorders may be slightly lower in old age than for younger adult age groups (Feinson & Thoits, 1986; Weisman et al., 1985), although these studies have been criticized as focusing primarily on "healthy" community-dwelling older persons, and having a rigid diagnostic criteria that excluded many older persons with mental health problems (Blazer et al., 1987; Kermis, 1986). Second, traditionally it has also been believed that older women had higher rates of mental disorders than older men. A summary of recent studies has suggested that this belief may be incorrect (see Feinson, 1987).

The remainder of this section will examine three areas. First we will look at a frequent mental disorder in old age, namely depression. Here we will look into one possible consequence of depression, namely suicide. The treatment of depression will also be examined. Then we will examine psychological intervention and, finally, dementia.

Depression

Depression is believed to be one of the most frequent mental disorders of older persons (Blazer, 1982, 1989b; Botwinick, 1984; Butler & Lewis, 1982; Gurland & Toner, 1982; Thompson et al., 1987) with percentages varying from 2 to 7 percent (Thompson et al., 1987), 10 to 15 percent (Gurland & Toner, 1982) and 27 percent (Blazer et al., 1987). It has been pointed out that the term is not well defined and the difference in figures exist because of different types of samples, definitions, and measuring instruments.

Traditionally it has been believed that the rates of depression increased with increasing age. However, recent studies have suggested that the rates remain fairly constant throughout adulthood (Blazer, 1982; Boyd & Weissman, 1981; Craig & VanNatta, 1979; Hirschfield & Cross, 1982; U.S. Senate Special Committee on Aging, 1984).

Depression is different from occasionally "feeling low" or sad. This type of "depression" is part of life and is not considered a mental health problem. To distinguish the "normal" mood of "feeling low" from depression, the DSM-III lists several types of depression, along with the diagnostic criteria, although Blazer (1989b) noted that the definitions do not apply to most depressed older persons. Additionally, Thompson and his associates (1987) have provided information on several scales and instruments frequently used to clinically access depression.

The symptoms of depression can be varied and can include psychological symptoms such as apathy and loss of interest in everyday activities, feelings of guilt, helplessness and worthlessness, problems in cognitive functioning, inability to concentrate, irritability, as well as physiological symptoms such as excessive crying, or loss of appetite, weight, and energy. Sleep problems are also common (see Rodin et al., 1988).

In older persons depression is frequently not diagnosed or is misdiagnosed. Rapp and Davis (1989) found that physicians' knowledge of the causes, symptoms, and treatment of depression in older persons was limited. The lack of training in this area created problems in diagnosing and treating depression. They noted that even if depression was diagnosed, the lack of knowledge in this area often meant that ineffective modes of treatment would be prescribed. Some of the symptoms of depression, such as lack of energy or sleep disturbances, may be mistaken as "normal" consequences of aging or as normal reactions to losses experienced in old age. Additionally, there is "masked depression" where the older person in a clinical setting will minimize depressive symptoms and maximize physical complaints (Gurland & Toner, 1982; LaRue et al., 1985); thus the physician or therapist will focus on the physical complaints rather than exploring for depression. Other symptoms of depression, such as the inability to concentrate or forgetfulness, may be misdiagnosed as dementia, sometimes called pseudodementia. It is believed that this is a diagnosis made for about 15 percent of those with depression (Gurland & Toner, 1982; Thompson et al., 1987).

There is also concern that some "normal" symptoms such as occasional crying (see Hastrup et al., 1986) or physical complaints (see Berry et al., 1984) may be misdiagnosed as depression. An additional concern is that other pathological conditions, such as Parkinson's disease, cerebrovascular disorders, or disease of the pancreas, have symptoms which may be misdiagnosed as depression. As Blazer (1987) has pointed out, the advances in studying depression, especially in the area of psychobiology, now allow for a more accurate diagnosis of depression.

The causes of depression have been examined and more factors have been eliminated as causes than have been identified as causes. Although bereavement, isolation, retirement, and relocation have frequently been associated with depression, studies indicate that although temporary changes may occur, these are generally not responsible for long-term depression. Health problems have been associated with chronic depression. Additionally, the drugs used to treat health problems can cause depressive symptoms or depression. It has also been suggested that nondepressed older persons have developed more effective coping strategies than depressed older persons (Foster & Gallagher, 1986).

It appears that about half of those older persons with depression had it prior to age 65. Additionally, it appears that females have higher rates of depression than males until about age 75 (Gurland & Toner, 1982) to age 80 (LaRue et al., 1985) when a crossover takes place.

A consequence of depression is suicide. Although only a small percentage of those with depression attempt suicide, the "vast majority" of older persons who commit suicide suffer from depression; for many the depression was their first episode and was not "severe" (Gurland & Toner, 1982). Because suicide is so frequently associated with depression (see Blazer, 1987; Raskin, 1982), suicide will be discussed below.

Suicide   Suicide is listed as one of the ten leading causes of death in the United States. The figures indicate that 30,900 individuals committed suicide in the United States in 1986. This figure translates into a suicide rate (the number of suicides per 100,000 individuals) of about 12.8. Thus, for every 100,000 individuals in the United States in 1986, 12.8 committed suicide. Experts believe that this figure is conservative because many suicides are not detected and others, for a variety of reasons, are not reported.

Although the national suicide rate is 12.8, for those 65+ it is 21.5 (U.S. Bureau of the Census, 1990). The suicide rates for those 65–74, 75–84, and 85+ are: 19.7, 25.2 and 20.8. As with the total suicide rate, the rate for older persons is probably conservative. Because death in old age is expected, it is seldom that suicide will be sought as a cause of death, unless it is obvious.

There are two trends that can be found in the suicide figures. First, the suicide rate for aged white males is considerably higher than for aged white women or aged blacks. Second, there has been a decrease in the suicide rate for black females but an increase for black males (see Manton et al., 1987). There is more speculation than fact about the differences.

The difference in the rates between older males and females could be related to two factors: increasing physical dependency and social isolation. With increasing physical dependency males lose independence and control, both important components in the socialization of most males. The increasing loss of control and dependence may be too intolerable for some male egos, thus precipitating suicide. Second, through widowhood many males become socially isolated, since it was generally the wife that maintained social contacts. The loneliness that results could motivate suicide.

Part of the difference in suicide rates between black and white males may be due to differences in reporting. However, probably the reason for the difference is that it is more difficult for whites to adapt to becoming "second-class citizens" as they age. The white male has traditionally occupied a preeminent position in American society. Whites, however, often find that with increasing age they are downgraded in terms of both status and income. There is a considerable amount of discontinuity with the past. Thus, at least in part, the continuity and discontinuity hypothesis may explain why the suicide rates for black and white older males are so different (Kastenbaum, 1987).

Since most older blacks have been discriminated against all of their lives they find less discontinuity in their status simply because of increasing age. In fact, many older blacks may believe that their positions in society have improved in recent years. It has also been noted, however, that the suicide rate for black males is increasing. Although this trend is only beginning to emerge, and its cause is yet to be determined, the societal changes which are producing a breakdown of the traditional black extended family may be a cause. The traditional black family helped to provide a buffer against societal discrimination, provided a support network, and provided status for aged blacks.

Most suicide attempts by the young are unsuccessful. Most suicide attempts by older persons are successful. There appear to be four reasons for the difference. First, the methods used by older persons tend to be more lethal, probably because the motivation to die is stronger. That is, suicide is not an attempt by older persons to call attention to themselves or to make others feel sorry for them; rather, it is intended as a single lethal act (see McIntosh & Santos, 1985–1986). Second, older persons are generally physiologically weaker than the young and have potentially lethal coexisting chronic conditions. Thus, an attempted suicide may be too traumatic for the individual to survive. Third, because many older persons who commit suicide are cut off from work, family, friends, and the community, there are fewer chances of successful intervention. Fourth, older persons are expected to die, which when coupled with the low social worth many accord older persons, contributes to the fact that fewer attempts are made to revive older persons, especially those who are known to have attempted suicide.

Suicidal behavior consists of two types. The first is an overt singular act, such as jumping off a bridge or taking an overdose of pills. This type of suicidal behavior is intended to bring about immediate death. The second type of suicidal behavior consists of a general neglect of physical and mental well-being. This type of suicidal behavior is more common and in the end just as lethal. Both types will be discussed below.

There are a number of factors that contribute to the decision by older persons to commit an overt act of suicide. One such factor is widowhood. Bock and Webber (1972) have found that the widowed aged have a significantly higher suicide rate than the married aged. It should be noted that widowed men have a much higher suicide rate than widowed women. One explanation of the differences in suicide rates is that widowhood is more difficult for men than for women since men are being confronted by several major life changes, such as retirement, reduction in income, declines in health, and loss of wife. In contrast, many women have had major life events occur earlier, such as children leaving the home, and have thus adjusted to these changes and formed new roles.

Other factors involved in suicide include mental and physical illness. According to Resnik and Cantor (1973), there is a greater likelihood of suicide if psychiatric disorders are present. Physical illness may also be a factor in suicide. Physical illness can cause pain, loss of roles, dependence, and financial drain. An increased severity of physical illness has the potential of making suicide more likely (Resnick & Cantor, 1973). Benson and Brodie (1975) found that 60 percent of the aged who attempt suicide have severe physical disorders.

Earlier it was pointed out that there are two types of suicide. The first consists of a single overt act to end life. The second consists of a long, drawn-out process. This type of suicide can be accomplished through such methods as neglecting health or ignoring safety practices. In this second type, the dying process is not as fast as in the first, but it is just as deadly in the end. Many of the potentially lethal acts in which older individuals engage are not seen by others as suicidal. Thus, these types of acts have been referred to as "benign suicide," "subintentional suicide," "indirect self-destructive behaviors," or "passive suicide." For example, Burnside (1976) pointed out that if an older person refused medications, this behavior could be interpreted as the result of stubbornness or cantankerousness rather than as suicidal behavior. Or, if the older person took too much or too little of a certain medication, this behavior could be viewed as the result of confusion and not of any suicidal intent. The danger here is that the suicidal tendency in many older persons is not recognized and treated. Rather, the potentially lethal acts are interpreted as normal consequences of aging.

Patterson and his associates (1974) have noted several other examples of the second type of suicidal behavior. One type consists of behavior that will damage the individual's health. This type of behavior may take the form of ignoring a weight abnormality, avoiding a regular medical examination, heavy smoking or drinking, neglecting to obtain treatment for an illness, self-diagnosis or treatment of medical disorders, careless use of cigarettes, or neglecting to establish a medical emergency plan (see Gove, 1973; Kastenbaum & Mishara, 1971; Patterson et al., 1974).

Suicide is often predictable. McIntosh (1987) noted that suicide rates would decline if education and training included the elimination of myths (i.e., "those who talk about suicide don't commit suicide," or "suicide happens without warning"), the identification of high-risk older persons (i.e., white males, widowed, isolated, history of suicide attempts), developing and disseminating information of community resources in suicide prevention, and education on the different forms suicide can take (i.e., subintentional suicide).

Treatment of Depression   Depression is a very treatable disorder in old age, with rates of successful intervention being as high as 70 percent (Blazer, 1987, 1989*b*). Several forms of treatment are currently used.

Drug therapy is one of the most frequently used forms of intervention to treat depression (see Blazer, 1982, 1989*a*, 1989*b*; Raskin, 1982). Although drug therapy has been very successful, there have also been some problems, such as drug interactions. Certain drugs prescribed for depression have been found to increase the likelihood of stroke or heart attack. Because depression has a propensity to return, drug therapy may have to be long term.

Electroshock therapy has also been found to be effective with depressed individuals. Some believe that it may be safer than drugs. Also, the effects are immediate where it may take weeks for certain drugs to have a significant effect. There may be some memory loss with the use of electroshock therapy, although new methods reduce this risk (Blazer, 1989*b*; Gurland & Toner, 1982). Psychological therapy (e.g., psychoanalysis, behavioral therapy, group therapy) has also been widely used to treat depression, although currently data is lacking on its effectiveness (Gurland & Toner, 1982).

Psychological Intervention

We have discussed the treatment of depression but we should also briefly examine psychological intervention on a more global level (see Eisdorfer & Stotsky, 1977). We will examine three aspects of psychological intervention: effectiveness of psychological intervention, utilization of psychological intervention, and factors that influence use of psychological intervention.

Effectiveness of Psychological Intervention   This has been a very controversial area in psychology. Early psychologists believed that psychological intervention for older adults was essentially useless. It was believed that existing problems would be too difficult to treat, and even if they were treated, new problems associated with aging would nullify the benefits of the intervention.

However, different forms of psychological intervention were advocated for older persons (see Gatz et al., 1985). This, however, did not end the controversy. Some believed that specific techniques were needed to deal with older persons while others noted that general techniques were sufficient. For some, short-term therapy was more beneficial than long-term therapy; for others it was the reverse. Different forms of psychological intervention have also been recommended, such as individual or group therapy. In a summary of the literature Gatz and her associates (1985) noted that good empirical research in this area is just starting to emerge, but recent research demonstrates that older persons can benefit from different forms of psychological intervention. Some studies are reporting that older persons benefit more than younger persons (Knight, 1988).

Utilization of Psychological Intervention   There are many areas of disagreement in the area of mental disorders. However, most would agree that older persons have a lower rate of utilization of mental health services than other adults. One recent longitudinal study, from a community health center, reported that a significantly lower percentage of older persons with diagnosed mental disorders were treated than younger persons (Goldstrom et al., 1987). The study went on to note that even when older persons did see a mental health professional, the frequency of counseling sessions was lower than for young adults.

Kermis (1986) has also reported the underutilization of mental health services by older persons and found that only 15 percent of those needing services are receiving them. Other studies have noted that older persons represent about 4 to 6 percent of the clients in mental health centers (see Flemming et al., 1984; Woodruff et al., 1988), that 2.7 percent of "clinical services provided by psychologists" are for older persons (Gatz et al., 1985), and 4 percent of psychiatrists' patients are older persons (Schurman et al., 1985).

Factors Influencing Psychological Intervention   Gatz and her associates (1985) have summarized into three categories and provided information on the factors that have been identified as barriers to older persons obtaining mental health services: client variables, therapist variables, and mental health system variables. These will be examined below.

Client Variables   The first category is "client variables," which has three subcategories: psychological-mindedness, self-reliance, and age of therapist. Each of these will be examined below.

"Psychological-mindedness" refers to the fact that many older persons were raised in a cohort where mental health services were not available or were only available to "crazy" or mentally incompetent persons. Thus, many do not see that their problems warrant intervention or are afraid of being stigmatized or institutionalized. Although an interesting hypothesis, it has not been supported by much empirical research (see Waxman et al., 1984).

"Self-reliance" refers to the principle of "self-sufficiency and independence" that many older persons are believed to possess as a result of their socialization. Again, empirical research implicating this as a factor in the underutilization of mental health services is lacking.

"Age of therapist" is the third factor in this category and claims that most older persons are hesitant to see a mental health professional because most professionals are younger than those seeking assistance and cannot identify with the problems of old age. As with the other factors discussed in this category, this is an intriguing hypothesis, but unsupported by empirical research.

Therapist Variables The second category is called "therapist variables" and has four subcategories: worthiness and status, poor prognosis, misconceptions of the aged, and countertransference. This category was first discussed by Kastenbaum (1964) in an article called "The Reluctant Therapist." In the article Kastenbaum pointed out that for a variety of reasons, many psychotherapists avoided contact with older persons. Garfinkel (1975) reiterated this position a decade later and noted some of the misconceptions psychotherapists held about older persons. This category posits the reluctance of mental health professionals to treat older persons as the major reason for the underutilization of mental health services (see Ray et al., 1987).

"Worthiness and status" have been mentioned in this category since mental health professionals probably hold values similar to the general society. These values ascribe less status and social worth to older persons. In addition, older persons are more likely to have other characteristics that will lower their value even further, such as poverty and physical disabilities. This hypothesis is partially rejected because mental health professionals often treat "stigmatized" individuals (i.e., criminals) and there is little evidence to suggest that older persons have less value or worth than other groups.

"Poor prognosis" is also a factor in this category. Many early psychologists did not believe that older persons could benefit from psychological intervention. Essentially, older persons were seen as too inflexible or that new and inevitable conditions would simply exacerbate psychological problems. Gatz and her associates (1985) noted that several studies have reported that mental health professionals have lower expectations for successful psychological intervention for older persons than for young adults. It was also noted that this contributes to older persons being given less treatment, which allows their conditions to deteriorate, which then reinforces the belief that intervention is not successful with older persons. The status of this belief was discussed earlier in the section, "Effectiveness of Psychological Intervention."

"Misconceptions of the aged" is the third subcategory in this section and deals with the belief of many mental health professionals that highly specialized training is needed to deal with older persons. This was referred to as "therapeutic inhibition" and contributes to mental health professionals not seeking out or accepting older persons as clients.

"Countertransference" is the last subcategory in the "Therapist Variables" category associated with the underutilization of mental health resources by older persons. The belief is that many mental health professionals will be reluctant to treat older persons because the professional is confronted with his or her own aging, disability, and death. Again, although an interesting hypothesis, it is not supported by much empirical research (see Poggi & Berland, 1985).

Mental Health System Variables   This last category has three subcategories: reimbursement system, perceptions of needs, referral patterns. The basic premise is that it is the mental health system that results in the underutilization of mental health services by older persons.

"Reimbursement system" notes that the payment for mental health services is not as complete as the payment for physical health services. For example, medicare will pay for the diagnosis but not the treatment of Alzheimer's disease. Medicare has numerous other financial deterrents that prevent many older persons from using the mental health system. For example, it will generally not provide for payments to psychologists or social workers. Additionally, medicare will generally not provide payment for out-patient mental health services; thus, rather than treating the disorder at an early stage through less expensive out-patient mental health services, medicare requires that the disorder reach the point where more expensive in-patient services are necessary.

"Perceptions of needs" notes that service providers, clients, and families may have different ideas of what services are necessary. This can result in a service that clients and their families do not believe meets their needs.

The last subsection is "referral patterns." Gatz and her associates (1985) have noted that traditionally the referral of older persons to mental health agencies by physicians or aging organizations has not been very good. Waxman and Carner (1984) found this in their study when they reported that physicians had a low rate of diagnosis and referral of older persons with mental disorders.

Because of the underutilization of mental health centers by older persons, a variety of programs have been implemented to see if more of those needing services will seek them out. Realizing that for many individuals there is a stigma attached to mental health services, one program emphasized the educational and social services nature rather than the psychological or mental health nature of its services. For example, group sessions were labeled as "controlling your mood" or "skills training in problem solving" (Lewinsohn & Tilson, 1987). Another reason mental health services are underutilized is because of the cost involved. One way to reduce the cost is to use groups whenever possible. Another is to use paraprofessionals, graduate students, or trained older persons to provide some of the services, under appropriate supervision (Lewinsohn & Tilson, 1987). The delivery system can also be changed, and services may have to be provided in the individual's home. As Lewinsohn and Tilson (1987) have pointed out, this may provide the mental health professional with an indicator of how the individual functions in the community.

One study noted that the low utilization rate may be because most older persons do not know what services mental health professionals such as social workers, psychiatrists, counselors, or psychologists perform. This study produced short video tapes where mental health professionals explained some of their services. One group of older persons were shown the tapes on mental health professionals while a control group was shown a general tape on old age. Participants in each group were asked which of six responses they would select to solve a problem that was presented in a short vignette. The possible responses ranged from doing nothing to discussing the problem with family members or friends, mental health professionals, ministers, or physicians. Those who had seen the tape on mental health professionals were more likely to note that they would discuss the matter with mental health professionals. This study indicates the success that an outreach program can have in educating older persons about mental health resources (Woodruff et al., 1988).

Dementia

Of all the disorders that afflict older persons, perhaps none is feared as much as dementia or "senility." The term dementia is a very generic term that describes a group of symptoms rather than a specific disease. In fact, there are more than 100 diseases and conditions that can cause dementia or "senilitylike" symptoms. All of the conditions that produce dementia have one common characteristic: they cause brain damage and/or dysfunctioning. That is, there is an organic basis for the disorder; scientists can see the damage to the brain on x-rays or in tissue specimens or measure the dysfunctioning in areas such as metabolism or electrical activity. Dementia is different from functional disorders where no organic cause for the symptoms can be found.

The signs of dementia are declines in areas such as intellect, judgment, memory, abstract thinking, and orientation. Dementia is often said to be global, meaning that more than one area is affected. Dementia needs to be separated from other conditions such as mental retardation or delirium. A primary distinction between dementia and mental retardation is that those with dementia have suffered declines in areas such as intelligence and memory from previous levels. We will see shortly that delirium is characterized by a "clouded state of consciousness." It is the clouded state of consciousness that creates the mental impairment. With dementia there is generally clear consciousness, but mental impairment. Thus, even when the demented individual is awake and aware, there are problems in areas such as intellectual functioning or memory. This also helps to distinguish dementia from areas such as sleep, coma, or intoxication.

This section is separated into three subsections. The first will provide a brief historical perspective on dementia. The second examines delirium, which is often confused with dementia. The third, and last, will examine dementia, and is further subdivided into the two primary types of dementia: multi-infarct dementia and degenerative dementia. The subsection on degenerative dementia will focus on Alzheimer's disease.

Historical Concepts   Reisberg (1987) has presented a brief survey of some of the early writings on organic brain disorders. He noted that in 500 B.C. an Athenian poet and statesman named Solon wrote that after a man's death his heirs challenged his will, claiming that he made the will while suffering from the impaired judgment of old age. The will was invalidated. Plato made mention of certain criminals being excused from their crimes because of old-age diseases of the mind. In his 1793 textbook the famous American physician and psychiatrist Dr. Benjamin Rush briefly described a case of Alzheimer's disease, noting that it produced a second infancy with the accompanying loss of bowel and bladder control.

There has been a continual controversy over how to categorize dementia. In the late 1800s and early 1900s there were basically two types of dementia: cerebral arteriosclerosis and neurosyphilis. As researchers further investigated the area a third area of senile dementia was added to the list.

By the early 1950s DSM-I classified dementia as acute or chronic. In the late 1960s, with DSM-II, this classification system was revised to psychotic and nonpsychotic. In 1980 (DSM-III), dementia was included as one of seven organic brain syndromes: dementia, delirium, amnesic syndrome, organic hallucinosis, organic personality syndrome, organic delusional syndrome, and organic affective syndrome.

This classification scheme does not provide for the specific disease or condition causing the symptoms. There can be a variety of diseases and conditions producing symptoms such as acute illness, alcohol or drugs, brain tumor, head trauma, or degenerative diseases such as Alzheimer's disease. The amount and area of damage or dysfunction will determine the symptoms and their magnitude, and the course of the disorder.

Until recently dementia was separated into presenile dementia (dementia occurring before age 65), and senile dementia (dementia occurring from age 65 on). This distinction has been eliminated since the causes of the dementia occurring before and after age 65 are the same, as is the progression of dementia.

Of the descriptive organic brain syndromes, the two that are found the most frequently in older persons are delirium and dementia. Both will be examined below.

Delirium   Delirium has been previously called acute confusion, pseudosenility, acute brain failure, and acute brain disorder (see Gomez & Gomez, 1987, 1989; Lipowski, 1989). The disorder does produce dysfunctioning in the brain. Some of the causes are malnutrition, drug abuse, alcohol abuse, head trauma, cancer, stroke, dehydration, infection, or brain tumor. The symptoms are global and generally have a rapid onset of short duration which can include hallucinations, disorientation, memory loss, incoherent speech, confusion, restlessness (especially at night), altered consciousness, diminished attention span, and impairment of intellect. It is often characterized as a "clouded state of consciousness" (Gomez & Gomez, 1987, 1989). The disorder generally runs its course in a week. Although the distinction between delirium and dementia is fairly easy in younger individuals, it is more difficult in older persons (U.S. Congress, Office of Technology Assessment, 1987).

The care of patients with delirium can often be difficult because of factors such as hallucinations, which can make the patient aggressive toward a caregiver. Recovery depends on prompt and accurate diagnosis, and early treatment. However, because 30 to 50 percent of older hospitalized patients will experience some delirium from their conditions or treatments, it is often an "expected" consequence of hospitalization and thus not aggressively treated. This is especially true if the medical staff is unaware of the patient's previous mental status (Wills, 1986).

If the disorder is not treated early and aggressively it may result in permanent brain damage or death. The death rate for delirium can run as high as 40 percent even if there is a correct diagnosis and early aggressive treatment. This is in part because the disorder causing the delirium can be serious enough to produce death, and because the delirium is stressful to the patient (Butler & Lewis, 1982).

Dementia   In dementia there is permanent brain damage causing the symptoms. However, in some cases previous levels of functioning may be regained through rehabilitation and therapy. For example, individuals who have had strokes have permanent brain damage but some can, through rehabilitation and therapy, regain previous levels of functioning.

The causes of dementia are varied and can include metabolic disorders (e.g., liver or kidney problems), infections (e.g., syphilis), poisons (e.g., drugs, metals, carbon monoxide), degenerative diseases (e.g., Alzheimer's, Parkinson's, Pick's), vascular disease (e.g., strokes), accidents (e.g., head trauma), as well as other diseases and conditions (e.g., brain tumors) (see Thompson et al., 1987).

For years many individuals believed that dementia was an inevitable consequence of aging. As a result, many reversible conditions were diagnosed as a form of senility and thus not treated. These are sometimes referred to as the pseudodementias. Some of the conditions that were frequently misdiagnosed were depression, drug abuse, chemical imbalances, and heart and lung problems.

Definitive figures on the extent of dementia vary widely. This is because different samples will produce widely different figures. Also, different definitions either lower or raise the figure. For example, while some researchers count only those who are incapable of independent living others count all individuals with a form of dementia. The one consistent finding is that the rates of dementia go up with increasing age. According to the U.S. Congress (1987) the percentage of each age group with *severe* dementia is: 1 percent for those 65–74, 7 percent for those 75–84, and 25 percent for those 85+. In contemporary American society more than 3 million older persons are affected by dementia. It is estimated that more than 50 percent of those in nursing homes have a form of dementia (Weiler, 1987).

Alzheimer's disease accounts for from 50 to 60 percent of all dementia (U.S. Congress, 1987). Those who have had multi-infarcts account for another 12 to 20 percent. Another 25 percent are a combination of Alzheimer's and multi-infarct (see Thompson et al., 1987). In about 10 percent of the cases a specific diagnosis cannot be made. The remainder consists of a variety of other diseases and disorders (Reisberg, 1987; Weiler, 1987).

Although rarely listed as a cause of death, some believe that dementia is the third or fourth leading cause of death among older persons. As the percentage of old-old increase, both the incidence of dementia and the death rate are expected to increase (see Brody & Cohen, 1989; Katzman, 1976; Reisberg, 1987; Weiler, 1987). Descriptions of multi-infarct dementia and degenerative dementia follow.

Multi-Infarct Dementia   Cerebral arteriosclerosis was the term originally used to describe this disorder. This term was dropped because it was not the arteriosclerosis that was causing the dementia but the consequences of the disorder, namely strokes.

Until the 1960s multi-infarct dementia was believed to be the most common form of dementia. It was not until similar amounts of arteriosclerosis were found in autopsying demented and nondemented individuals that a "new concept of senility" was established, with Alzheimer's disease as the leading cause (Corsellis & Evans, 1965; Hachinski et al., 1974; Kent, 1983; Tomlinson et al., 1968; 1970; Worm-Peterson & Pakkenberg, 1968). Multi-infarct dementia is the second leading cause of dementia in older persons. It refers to brain damage through a series of strokes. Essentially, the blood flow to a certain part of the brain is reduced through a blood clot or hemorrhage of a blood vessel in the brain causing part of the brain to die, producing an area of coagulated blood and dead brain cells called an infarct. The consequences for the individual depend primarily on the size and the area affected. A small stroke may go largely unnoticed and produce few or no changes in behavior. When larger areas of the brain are involved the consequences for the individual are generally greater and can include death.

In most cases it is relatively easy to distinguish between patients whose dementia is caused by multi-infarcts and those where it is caused by Alzheimer's disease. Those who have had multi-infarcts have generally had a history of high blood pressure, vascular disease, and strokes. The disease also progresses in steplike fashion with each new stroke producing an abrupt change in functioning. Thus, the individual will stabilize at a certain level until there is another stroke when functioning will decline. There will then be a stabilization period until the next stroke. Additionally, since the strokes generally only affect one area of the brain the symptoms are generally limited. For example, only one side of the body or one facility such as language is affected.

Those with Alzheimer's disease may not have had the same history of high blood pressure, vascular disease, or stroke. Additionally, the decline is slow and continual. Also, the consequences of the disease are more global in nature, affecting several areas. From onset of symptoms until death averages 6.7 years; from diagnosis until death 2.6 years (U.S. Congress, 1987).

Degenerative Dementia   For those experiencing the signs of dementia society has created and assigned a variety of terms: senility, organic brain disorders, cerebral atrophy, organic brain syndrome, and senile dementia. The term dementia is now the most widely used. The word literally means "away mind." As noted earlier, the term describes the symptoms of a specific disease or condition, not the actual disease or condition. There are several categories of degenerative dementia such as multiple sclerosis, Parkinson's disease, Huntington's disease, Pick's disease, and Creutzfeldt-Jakob's disease. Although the outcomes are often similar each disease affects a different type of nerve cell or a different part of the nervous system.

Most dementing disorders have one common characteristic: the progression of the disorder cannot be stopped. Only 2 to 3 percent of the more than 100 conditions that cause or simulate dementia can be reversed. Thus, for most of those with dementia, it is a progressive disorder (U.S. Congress, 1987).

The stages or course varies depending upon the disorder producing the dementia and the individual. However, a general outline can be provided. The first signs of dementia are generally memory loss. Other early changes might be difficulty in mathematics. Handwriting will probably also start to deteriorate since there is early deterioration in rapid and fine motor functioning. Individuals often try to compensate for these early changes. Notes and lists compensate for memory losses, calculators for mathematical problems, and typewriters for handwriting difficulties. There may be mood swings, depression, or changes in personality. At this stage the individual will be able to work and live independently.

As the dementia progresses existing problems will intensify and new problems develop. Coordination will become more difficult. There will be problems with language, both in terms of understanding what others have said and in replying to what has been said. Working and living independently will become impossible. Individuals will need help with basic activities of everyday life, such as getting dressed, eating, bathing, or toileting. In addition to physical declines, there will also be psychological changes. Mood swings become more frequent and extreme; some individuals can become angry or violent; fear and suspicion are also frequent. In the last stages of dementia the individual is generally incontinent. Most are bedbound and will have to be fed. Most become mute. Pneumonia is a frequent cause of death.

The most common dementia is Alzheimer's disease. This disease was first described in 1906 by Dr. Alois Alzheimer, a German physician, at a convention of psychiatrists at Tubingen, Germany (Schorer, 1985). Alzheimer's disease will be discussed throughout the rest of this subsection.

Alzheimer's disease: The course of Alzheimer's can vary with the individual depending on the rate of progress and other physical conditions. Generally, the first symptoms are impairments in memory or personality. Ultimately there will be severe cognitive changes with patients being incapable of self-care or of orienting themselves to time, place, or other persons.

As was reported earlier, the number or percentage of the population with dementia varies from study to study. The same is true for the number or percentage of the population with Alzheimer's. One recent report published in the *Journal of the American Medical Association* on community-dwelling older persons said that Alzheimer's may be much more prevalent than previously reported. For those 65+ years of age the study reported that 10.3 percent probably had Alzheimer's. For the age categories 65–74, 75–84, and 85+ the percentages were 3, 18.7, and 47.2 percent (Evans et al., 1989).

Each form of dementia takes it own course. For Alzheimer's disease the number of years of survival from diagnosis to death can vary from 1 to 25 with an average for males of 2.7 and for females of 4.2 (Cohen, 1987; Katzman, 1985; U.S. Congress, 1987). Another source states that from the onset of symptoms until death averages 8.1 years; from diagnosis to death 3.4 years (U.S. Congress, 1987). It is estimated that Alzheimer's disease reduces the existing life expectancy by one-half (Katzman, 1985).

At autopsy the brains of Alzheimer patients show definite changes from normal brains. Some of the changes are the presence of senile plaques and neurofibrillary tangles. There is also a degeneration of neurons and a decrease in brain size and weight. Sometimes the damage to the brain appears severe, but the consequences for functioning were moderate; other times the brain damage appears modest, but there were severe consequences in functioning.

While the cost of a disease to a society is difficult to estimate, it is becoming increasingly important that this information be available so that it can be used in decisions that affect the funding of research as well as health care policy. The cost of Alzheimer's disease is estimated at from $28 to $31 billion a year (see Hay & Ernst, 1987; Huang et al., 1988). The cost of some other major causes of death are: heart disease $14.5 billion; cancer $13.1 billion; accidents $19.2 billion; stroke $5.1 billion (Coughlin & Liu, 1989; Weiler, 1987).

Major research efforts on Alzheimer's disease are of recent origin. In 1976 the federal outlay for research was $3.9 million; by 1987 it had increased to $67 million. In comparison, in 1983 the National Heart, Lung, and Blood Institute received $624 million and the National Cancer Institute $1 billion (Weiler, 1987).

Currently the diagnosis of Alzheimer's disease can only be made with microscopic examination of brain tissue (e.g., by biopsy or on autopsy). As a result, diagnosis is generally made after death, although a clinical assessment can generally rule other disorders and narrow the list of possibilities to Alzheimers (see Fischer et al., 1989; Price et al., 1985; U.S. Congress, 1987). The brain functioning of Alzheimer patients show abnormal functioning in areas such as oxygen metabolism, electrical activity, and endocrine functioning.

Research has been intensified as Alzheimer's has been identified as a major societal problem. In 1976 three federal research organizations (National Institute on Aging, National Institute of Neurological and Communicative Disorders and Stroke, and National Institute of Mental Health) began to coordinate their research on Alzheimer's. The increase in funding has also facilitated this research. One additional factor has facilitated research: new technology. Innovative technological developments such as positron emission tomography (PET) have allowed research to advance much more rapidly than previously.

There are currently several possible causes of Alzheimer's disease. Heredity has been investigated as a possible cause. The probability of developing Alzheimer's is three to fourfold for those having a first-degree relative (e.g., father, mother, brother, or sister) with the disease. It has been hypothesized that there is a gene on chromosome 21 that may stimulate the production of a chemical that contributes to the plaque formation in the brain. Huntington's disease, another form of dementia, appears to be genetically transmitted. The children of those with this disease stand a 50 percent chance of inheriting the disease (Cohen, 1987; Katzman, 1985). Down's Syndrome patients generally develop a form of Alzheimer's by age 40. Down's Syndrome is believed to be a genetic disease with the defective gene on chromosome 21 (Katzman, 1985). Additionally, first-degree relatives of Alzheimer's patients have an increased incidence of Down's Syndrome (Price et al., 1985).

Although studies in this area are yielding promising leads they are not conclusive. While some studies on identical twins have reported a genetic link, others have not (Katzman, 1985). Additionally, there may be some research bias in this area; researchers may be looking for and finding Alzheimer's more in certain families.

A second possible cause deals with slow-acting viruses. There appears to be a virus that affects the central nervous system of sheep causing a disease called scrapie. In female sheep naturally infected with the scrapie virus it was found that their lambs also had the virus, suggesting that the virus is passed on prior to birth via amniotic fluid or after birth via a contaminated environment. Additionally, exposing a culture of human brain tissue to extracts of brain tissue from an Alzheimer's patient causes the nerve fibers in the culture to become twisted, much like the neurofibrillary tangles seen in the brains of Alzheimer's patients. An infectious agent is also recognized as the cause of certain other forms of dementia such as Creutzfeldt-Jakob's disease. It is believed that this disease is caused by a virus that can lie dormant in the body for years. Once activated, the virus produces dementia very rapidly as well as other conditions such as muscle spasms.

Another avenue of research has dealt with the accumulation of metal, particularly aluminum, in the brain. Aluminum has been found in abnormally large amounts in the brains of many Alzheimer's patients. It is not known if the aluminum deposits are responsible for the neurofibrillary tangles or if the metal simply accumulates in the tangles after they have been formed. Individuals who live in areas where the aluminum content in the drinking water is high have not been found to have abnormally high levels of Alzheimer's disease (U.S. Congress, 1987).

Manganese has also been implicated as a possible causal agent. It is known that certain natives in Guam have a disproportionate percentage affected with a Parkinsonlike form of dementia. It is also known that the soil in this area has high concentrations of aluminum and manganese.

Neurochemical changes is another avenue of research. It is known that nerve cells secrete chemicals called neurotransmitters that transmit nerve signals from one cell to another. It is now known that Alzheimer patients either lack or have abnormally low amounts of an important enzyme needed to manufacture one important neurotransmitter.

Problems with the immune system have been investigated as a possible cause of Alzheimer's disease. It has been suggested that the plaque and tangles are the result of a defective immune system producing antibodies that attack and destroy brain cells. It has also been suggested that certain genes become damaged, through a variety of mechanisms, and as a result produce abnormal substances that cause the plaques and tangles.

Alzheimer's disease has been defined as a result of accelerated aging of the brain. Some of the microscopic changes of Alzheimer's patients can be found in the brains of most older individuals. As a result some have suggested that just as individuals age at different rates in terms of physiological functioning, individuals also age at different rates in terms of brain functioning.

The Alzheimer's patient: In addition to the mental deterioration, there are often other problems associated with Alzheimer's disease. They frequently have problems communicating with caregivers. Finding the right words or even understanding caregiver's questions can be difficult. Some may take items and hide or lose them and then not remember when or where the item was hidden or lost. Many, if left unsupervised, wander from their homes and become lost. Because during the day many patients lead sedentary lives, sleep disturbances are often present. Additionally, at night there is often increased agitation or confusion, perhaps caused by the increasing difficulty patients have in perceiving the environment.

Most Alzheimer's patients have other age-associated medical problems. If these problems are painful, patients may have difficulty in verbalizing the existence, nature, or location of the pain. The patient may become less coordinated, because of the disease, the aging process, and lack of exercise. This will increase the risk of falls. The simple inability to ask for a glass of water may lead to dehydration. Other medical conditions such as constipation, pressure sores, or dental problems also accompany Alzheimer's disease.

Reactions of caregivers: The primary victim is the individual with Alzheimer's disease. However, for each victim of the disease there are other individuals, generally close family members, whose lives are dramatically affected by the disease. They may end up as caregivers or participating in the financing of the care. The emotional burden of providing long-term support, directly or indirectly, can be a stressful experience. For many spouses, this occurs at a time when their physical health is declining; additionally, watching decades of savings depleted can add to the stress. For the adult children who provide direct care and financial support, they find that competing demands from their occupations and children impose many stresses on them. Although the "everyday" care is stressful, caregivers also often have to make "life-and-death" decisions for the patients, for example, whether to allow the patient to have an operation for a heart condition or chemotherapy for cancer (see Pratt et al., 1987).

The experiences and reactions to the caregiver role are determined by numerous variables. For example, the age of the caregiver. There may be one age group that is more willing to assume the responsibility than another. The relationship to the patient is also a variable: spouse, adult child, other relative. The health and financial status of the caregiver are other important variables that need to be considered. The length of time care has been provided and the amount of deterioration of the patient are other variables. One additional variable is that of support. The amount of support provided from other family members or community agencies can play a significant role in determining the experiences and reactions of caregivers.

Although it is difficult to provide one composite of caregivers, one study found that they were mostly married females, with an average age of 60 who had been providing care for approximately 4 years. For one-half of the caregivers, the amount of care averaged 16 hours per day (Caserta et al., 1987).

The caregivers, especially older spouses, have been called the "hidden patient" (Fengler & Goodrich, 1979). They have been seen as a group that will have a high degree of illness and early death caused primarily by the caregiver role; they will also have high rates of depression (Gallagher et al., 1989). Several studies have now empirically examined the caregiver role. The results will be reviewed below.

The caregivers first become aware of the dementia when they notice memory loss, disorientation, problems with work, and changes in personality. Initially the changes seem to be isolated incidents; however, eventually the incidents become more common and cannot be ignored. Often the changes are given interpretations other than dementia. For example, some thought that there were marital problems (Chenoweth & Spencer, 1986).

Once caregivers realize there is a problem they often face a difficult time convincing others. Chenoweth and Spencer (1986) found that frequently family members had difficulty in convincing a physician that something was wrong with the individual, especially in the early stages of the disease. Other caregivers noted that they had difficulty in convincing the demented individual to see a physician. Sometimes delays of weeks, months, or even years were reported.

The above researchers also asked the caregivers to relate what they were told about Alzheimer's disease after the diagnosis was made. There were five major responses given, and some provided more than one response. Fifty-four percent said that they were told there was no treatment, and that the condition was "hopeless." A factual explanation of Alzheimer's disease was provided to 28 percent. Twenty percent did not receive any information or explanation about the disease. Methods of coping with the patient or the role of caregiver were provided to 16 percent. None of the 289 caregivers in this sample were given information about services or resources within the community that might be capable of providing information or assistance.

The gerontological literature uses the term "caregiver burden" to refer to the problems that family caregivers confront (George & Gwyther, 1986). The problems can be social in terms of severed or reduced social interaction with friends and other family members; reduction in social activities such as church participation or hobbies is also experienced. The problems can be financial in terms of lost incomes of patients who can no longer work and caregivers who must provide intensive supervision. There are also costs associated with the disease such as medical costs or the cost for sitters. There are physical problems such as the inability of caregivers to attend to their own health needs or in terms of lifting or restraining the patient. There are also frequent sleep interruptions. The psychological problems are in the areas of stress and anxiety, frequently over some of the other problems mentioned (see Gaynor, 1989).

Studies have supported many of these observations. For example, it has been reported that in the psychological area caregivers report higher stress symptoms, lower life satisfaction, and a greater frequency to use psychotrophic drugs (George & Gwyther, 1986). This study also reported numerous social problems such as a reduction in visits with family and friends, less time spent on hobbies, less time relaxing, and fewer club activities.

The above study did not find health or finances differed from other community residents. This sample, however, may have been unique in that it was well off financially and that about 50 percent of the caregivers did not live with the patient. The study did note that this is an "at-risk" group especially in the area of mental health.

Although studies are limited, one study has suggested that the response of husbands and wives to the caregiver role may differ. Female caregivers noted that their relationship with their demented spouse deteriorated, that they were more distressed, and that they felt constrained by their caregiver role. Unexpectedly, male caregivers reported improved relationships with their spouses. The researchers hypothesized that for female caregivers it was the resumption of a role they had abandoned in middle age when their children had left home; for most males it was assuming a new role, and often provided a substitute for lost work roles (Barusch & Spaid, 1989; Fitting, Rabins et al., 1986; Motenko, 1989; Pruchno & Resch, 1989; Quayhagen & Quayhagen, 1988).

The age of the caregiver has also been reported to be a variable in how the role is perceived and responded to. Fitting and her associates (1986) found that younger caregivers were more "resentful of their plight." The researchers hypothesized that these individuals may have other responsibilities, such as a job and dependent children, that create additional stress.

Some studies have pointed out that a few caregivers have noted that the disease had brought the family closer together. By sharing in the responsibility of care, the family found new strength from the challenge and new pride in meeting the challenge (Chenoweth & Spencer, 1986).

As noted earlier, many caregivers literally "burn out" from providing intensive care over long periods of time. For some, the "burnout" may occur because they are not aware of community services that can assist them (Caserta et al., 1987; Moritz et al, 1989).

Time is the caregiver's biggest enemy. In the first few months of caregiving, the patient often needs less intensive care and the caregiver has time to maintain health and other outside activities. After 2 years caregiving began to take a toll. Patients become more demanding and difficult to care for, especially at night. Caregivers also have to do more physically for patients, such as lifting (Gaynor, 1989).

There are many ways that caregivers can be provided with assistance that will ease the "caregiver burden." Programs that offer assistance are one of the best ways of preventing burnout, although much of the research showing positive results is based on studies that have methodological problems (Toseland & Rossiter, 1989). The assistance provides the caregiver with some relief from responsibilities, perhaps during the day or at night. The assistance can come in many forms, such as a surrogate caregiver, or someone to assist with cleaning, cooking, shopping, or other responsibilities of the caregiver. Support groups have also been found to be effective. Here caregivers often learn that they are not alone, and can obtain information from others on how to handle the Alzheimer patient. One other form of assistance is in information on programs that might have some form of assistance for the caregiver or patient. The programs can range from financial assistance to psychological support. It should be noted that there is often difficulty in finding and identifying caregivers. Many caregivers do not have contact with social service agencies and if contacted will not accept assistance, preferring to remain independent (Greene & Monahan, 1989; Haley, 1989; Montgomery & Borgatta, 1989; Toseland et al., 1989; Zarit & Toseland, 1989).

Family caregivers have the potential to provide both a valuable service and to save their families thousands of dollars in nursing home costs. However, if the caregiver "burns out," there are two individuals in need of care. One way of preventing caregiver burnout is to assess the source and amount of stress the caregiver roles place on the caregiver. In this way others can design a program to reduce the stress for the caregiver. Several caregiver stress and hassle scales have been developed to assist in this area (see Kinney & Stephens, 1989).

Most caregivers have to make a decision at some point to institutionalize those they are caring for. The most frequently cited reasons for institutionalization were difficulty of constant care, illness of caregiver, behavioral problems of the patient, incontinence, violent or combative behavior. The most frequent reason, difficulty of constant care, was cited by 72 percent of the caregivers. The second reason was cited by 21 percent of the caregivers. Basically, the caregivers "couldn't take it any more." Most noted that they were "worn out" (Chenoweth & Spencer, 1986; Silliman & Sternberg, 1988).

The decision to institutionalize is generally not made easily. It also does not always indicate the end of caregiving. Very often caregivers want to continue to assist in providing certain forms of care, especially if they find them lacking in the institution. Many institutions have involved caregivers in enrichment and activity programs, especially during times, such as weekends, when the staff does not offer these programs (see Hansen et al., 1988).

Research on stress and caregivers is continuing. As Zarit (1989) has pointed out, many of the studies have had methodological limitations and in the future, research needs to change from descriptive studies to more controlled studies.

Treatment: There is no cure for Alzheimer's disease. On almost a weekly basis one hears of "new promising research" that may prevent the disease, stop the progression of the disease, or even cure the disease. However, to date the promising new research has not lived up to its expectations.

Currently, most of the treatment deals with controlling the symptoms. Certain drugs may lessen emotional or violent outbursts. An exercise program can lead to better sleeping habits and fewer pressure sores; likelihood of constipation is also reduced. it is also important to ascertain if the symptom is a cause of the dementia or some other disorder. For example, incontinence is a frequent consequence of dementia. However, rather than accepting the incontinence as another "step down" for the patient, the cause of the symptom should be thoroughly evaluated. The cause may be a urinary tract infection, which is easily treated by antibiotics (see Berger, 1985; Rabins et al., 1982).

Learning mnemonic aids may initially delay some of the declines in memory. Although it will not slow the rate of the disease, care from medical and nursing professionals, family members, and friends can also be an effective mode of treatment. One current trend is the development of "special units" in nursing homes to treat Alzheimer patients. There are several types of these units with different philosophies and treatments (see Rabins, 1986). To date there is little empirical evidence as to their effectiveness (Ohta & Ohta, 1988).

One study reported on the results of one of these special units for Alzheimer's patients which emphasized "reduced stimulation." For many Alzheimer's patients memory losses, coupled with the intensive stimulation of most institutions, exacerbate the losses. Factors such as a continual flow of patients, staff and visitors, phones ringing, the noise from televisions and radios, announcements over the PA system, and other forms of stimulation all impact on a deficient memory. This unit was somewhat isolated and the decor selected to be pleasing but not confusing or disorienting. There was a planned schedule that included activities and rest. The small number of patients made adherence to the schedule relatively easy. Positive benefits included less agitation, less use of restraints, more patient-to-patient interaction, and stabilization of weight. The isolation of the patients was not upsetting to friends and relatives of the patients (Cleary et al., 1988; see Kromm & Kromm, 1985; Maas, 1988; Peppard, 1985; Schafer, 1985).

Caregiver education has also been stressed (Glosser & Wexler, 1985; Rabins et al, 1982). Devices such as the "Alzheimer's Disease Knowledge Test" can be used in a variety of ways to enhance caregiver education (Dieckmann et al., 1988). One study examined the impact of an eight session caregiver education program that provided information on Alzheimer's disease, and skills for managing some of the legal, financial, social, and behavioral problems caregivers are faced with. The majority of participants found the education very useful. Many learned practical everyday skills by listening to how others dealt with demented individuals. Additionally, the caregivers received support from others. For many it was valuable to know that they were "not alone" and that some frustrations, guilt, and anxiety were common to caregivers (Glosser & Wexler, 1985).

SUMMARY

This chapter was separated into three sections: speed of behavior, mental functioning, and mental disorders.

As we have noted throughout this book, there are many areas of disagreement in gerontology. There is one area where there is agreement: with increasing age there is a slowing in the speed of behavior. Complex behavior declines more than simple behavior. Although there are declines, many are so small that they will have little or no impact on functioning in everyday situations.

The second section examined mental functioning. This section was separated into five subsections: intelligence, learning, memory, creativity, and personality.

Intelligence has received a great deal of attention from gerontologists and the research results have been mixed. To an extent this is because there are many models or theories of intelligence. The majority of studies have used the Wechsler Adult Intelligence Scale (WAIS) which is separated into verbal and performance areas. One school of thought believes that verbal intelligence, which can be conceptualized as "crystallized intelligence" (i.e., acquired knowledge) declines little with increasing age. Performance intelligence, which can be conceptualized as "fluid intelligence" (e.g., psychomotor skills, senses), declines with increasing age. This is sometimes called the "classic aging pattern." A second school of thought challenges the belief that intelligence declines with increasing age. This school of thought claims that the studies that show declines in intelligence are not measuring the results of an inevitable aging process but disease, different cohorts, age-biased tests, lower levels of education, the nearness to death and hence decreased physiological functioning, lack of environmental stimulation, lower performance expectations and the self-fulfilling prophecy, intelligence score averaging which negates individual performance, and fatigue. This group notes that studies have indicated that older persons can increase their performance on intelligence tests. Learning appears to decline with increasing age.

Memory can be separated into sensory memory, primary memory and secondary memory. Sensory memory is the information the senses acquire. Information remains in this memory for a very short period of time where it is either lost or transferred to the primary memory. The primary memory has a limited storage capacity and information is rapidly replaced by new information. Some information that is rehearsed is transferred to the secondary memory. The consequences of aging on the sensory memory are unclear. Primary memory appears to decline slightly with increasing age. Secondary memory does show distinctive declines with increasing age.

There have been relatively few studies on creativity in old age. The results are inconclusive. Aging does not appear to change personality. However, other life events, such as widowhood, poverty, chronic illness, may change personality.

The third section is on mental disorders. This is an emerging area in gerontology. Studies have found that older persons have rates of mental disorder equal to or below that of the general population. Two specific disorders were examined: depression and dementia.

Depression is believed to be one of the most frequent mental disorders in old age. The symptoms of depression can vary but often include feelings of guilt, and weight and energy loss. Depression is often misdiagnosed or underdiagnosed.

One possible consequence of depression is suicide. Although only a small percentage of depressed individuals attempt or commit suicide, most suicides suffered from depression. The suicide rate for older persons is high, especially for white males. This may relate to social isolation and feelings of powerlessness and dependency. Suicide consists of two types. The first type consists of a single act obviously intended to end life. The second is more hidden and generally takes longer to accomplish. Sometimes it is called "passive suicide" and examples would be ignoring health problems, or engaging in behaviors that endanger health and life.

Psychological intervention was also examined and it was noted that depression is one of the most treatable mental disorders in old age. However, many older persons do not use mental health services.

The second mental disorder that was examined was dementia, which is a general term describing a group of symptoms, not one of the 100+ diseases and conditions that cause the symptoms. With dementia there is an organic basis for the symptoms. Some of the signs of dementia are a global impairment of intellect, memory, abstract thinking, and orientation.

Dementia has often been confused with delirium, which generally has a rapid onset of short duration. With delirium there is a "clouded consciousness." In dementia the onset is generally slower and the individual is alert but mental functioning in areas such as memory is impaired. There are two frequent forms of dementia: multi-infarct and degenerative dementia.

Multi-infarct refers to a series of strokes that affect mental functioning. The individual's level of functioning goes through a pattern of stabilization then rapid decline (after a stroke). Degenerative dementia refers to a series of diseases, the most frequent being Alzheimer's disease, the cause of which is currently unknown. The Alzheimer's patient will undergo gradual but progressive deterioration that will probably start with minor memory loss and progress to complete dependence on others for the most basic needs. In addition to the Alzheimer's patient there are also "hidden victims," namely the patient's family who are often caregivers. Currently there is no treatment for Alzheimer's disease; some of the symptoms can be treated.

REFERENCES

Allan, C., & Brotman, H. (1981). *Chartbook on aging in America.* Washington, DC: White House Conference on Aging.

American Psychiatric Association (1980). *Diagnostic and statistical manual of mental disorders: DSM-III* (third edition). Washington, DC: American Psychiatric Association.

American Psychiatric Association (1987). *Diagnostic and statistical manual of mental disorders: DSM-III-R* (third edition, revised). Washington, DC: American Psychiatric Association.

Arenberg, D. (1968). Modality in short-term retention. *Journal of Gerontology,* **23**(5): 462–465.

Arenberg, D. (1973). Cognition and aging: Verbal learning, memory, and problem solving. In C. Eisdorfer & M. P. Lawton (Eds.), *The psychology of adult development and aging* (pp. 74–97). Washington, DC: American Psychological Association.

Arenberg, D. (1976). The effects of input conditioning on free recall in young and old adults. *Journal of Gerontology,* **31**(5): 551–555.

Arenberg, D. (1982). Changes with age in problem solving. In F. I. M. Craik & S. Trehub (Eds.), *Aging and cognitive process.* New York: Plenum.

Arenberg, D., & Robertson-Tchabo, E. (1977). Learning and aging. In J. E. Birren & K. W. Schaie (Eds.), *Handbook of the psychology of aging* (pp. 421–449). New York: Van Nostrand Reinhold.

Bahrick, H. P., Bahrick, P. O., & Wittlinger, R. P. (1975). Fifty years of memory for names and faces: A cross-sectional approach. *Journal of Experimental Psychology,* **104**(1): 54–75.

Baltes, P. B., & Labouvie, G. V. (1973). Adult development of intellectual performance: Description, explanation, modification. In C. Eisdorfer & M. P. Lawton (Eds.), *The psychology of adult development and aging* (pp. 157–219). Washington, DC: American Psychological Association.

Baltes, P. B., & Schaie, K. W. (1974). Aging and IQ: The myth of the twilight years. *Psychology Today,* **7**(10): 35–40.

Barusch, A. S., & Spaid, W. M. (1989). Gender differences in caregiving: Why do wives report greater burden. *The Gerontologist,* **29**(5): 667–676.

Bengtson, V. L., Reedy, M. N., & Gordon, C. (1985). Aging and self-conceptions: Personality processes and social contexts. In J. E. Birren & K. W. Schaie (Eds.), *Handbook of the psychology of aging* (second edition) (pp. 554–593). New York: Van Nostrand Reinhold.

Benson, R. A., & Brodie, D. C. (1975). Suicide by overdose of medicines among the aged. *Journal of the American Geriatrics Society,* **23**(4): 304–308.

Berger, E. Y. (1985). The institutionalization of patients with Alzheimer's disease. *Nursing Homes,* **34**(6): 22–29.

Berry, D. T. R., & Webb, W. B. (1985). Sleep and cognitive functions in normal older adults. *Journal of Gerontology,* **40**(3): 331–335.

Berry, J. M., Storandt, M., & Coyne, A. (1984). Age and sex differences in somatic complaints associated with depression. *Journal of Gerontology,* **39**(4): 465–467.

Birren, J. E. (1964). *The psychology of aging.* Englewood Cliffs, NJ: Prentice-Hall.

Birren, J. E., Butler, R. N., Greenhouse, S. W., Sokoloff, L., & Yarrow, M. R. (1963). *Human aging: A biological and behavioral study.* Washington, DC: U.S. Government Printing Office.

Birren, J. E., Cunningham, W. R., & Yamamoto, K. (1983). Psychology of adult development and aging. In M. R. Rosenzweig & L. W. Porter (Eds.), *Annual review of psychology: Volume 34* (pp. 543–576). Palo Alto, CA: Annual Reviews.

Birren, J. E., Woods, A. M., & Williams, M. V. (1980). Behavioral slowing with age: Causes, organization, and consequences. In L. W. Poon (Ed.), *Aging in the 1980s: Psychological issues* (pp. 293–308). Washington, DC: American Psychological Association.

Bischof, L. J. (1976). *Adult psychology* (second edition). New York: Harper and Row.

Blackburn, J. A., Papalia-Finlay, D., Foye, B. F., & Serlin, R. C. (1988). Modifiability of figural relations performance among elderly adults. *Journal of Gerontology: Psychological Sciences*, **43**(3): P87–89.

Blazer, D. G. (1982). The epidemiology of late life depression. *Journal of the American Geriatrics Society*, **30**: 581–592.

Blazer, D. G. (1987). Depression. In G. L. Maddox (Ed.), *The encyclopedia of aging* (pp. 169–170). New York: Springer.

Blazer, D. G. (1989*a*). Depression in late life: An update. In M. P. Lawton (Ed.), *Annual review of gerontology and geriatrics: Volume Nine* (pp. 197–215.

Blazer, D. G. (1989*b*). Depression in the elderly. *New England Journal of Medicine*, **320**(3): 164–166.

Blazer, D. G., Hughes, D. C., & George, L. K. (1987). The epidemiology of depression in an elderly community population. *The Gerontologist*, **27**(3): 281–287.

Blieszner, R. S., Willis, L., Baltes, P. B. (1981). Training research in aging on the fluid ability of inductive reasoning. *Journal of Applied Developmental Psychology*, **2**: 247–265.

Bock, E. W., & Webber, I. L. (1972). Suicide among the elderly: Isolating widowhood and mitigating alternatives. *Journal of Marriage and the Family*, **34**(2): 24–31.

Botwinick, J. (1967). *Cognitive processes in maturity and old age*. New York: Springer.

Botwinick, J. (1977). Intellectual abilities. In J. E. Birren & K. W. Schaie (Eds.), *Handbook of the psychology of aging* (pp. 580–605). New York: Van Nostrand Reinhold.

Botwinick, J. (1984). *Aging and behavior: A comprehensive integration of research findings* (third edition). New York: Springer.

Botwinick J., & Birren, J. E. (1965). A follow-up study of card-sorting performance in elderly men. *Journal of Gerontology*, **20**(3): 208–210.

Botwinick, J., & Siegler, I. C. (1980). Cross-sectional and longitudinal patterns of intellectual ability. *Developmental Psychology*, **16**(1): 49–53.

Botwinick, J., & Thompson, L. W. (1968). Age differences in reaction time: An artifact? *The Gerontologist*, **8**(1): 25–28.

Boyd, J. H., & Weissman, M. M. (1981). Epidemiology of affective disorders: A re-examination and future directions. *Archives of General Psychiatry*, **38**: 1039–1047.

Broadbent, D. E. (1963). Flow of information within the organism. *Journal of Verbal Learning and Verbal Behavior*, **2**(1): 25–28.

Broadbent, D. E., & Gregory, M. (1965). Some confirmatory results on age differences in memory for simulation. *British Journal of Psychology*, **56**(1): 77–80.

Broadbent, D. E., & Heron, A. (1962). Effects of a subsidiary task on performance involving immediate memory in younger and older men. *British Journal of Psychology*, **53**(2): 189–198.

Brody, J. A., & Cohen, D. (1989). Epidemiologic aspects of Alzheimer's disease. *Journal of Aging and Health*, **1**(2): 139–149.

Bruce, P. R., & Herman, J. F. (1986). Adult age differences in spatial memory: Effects of distinctiveness and repeated experience. *Journal of Gerontology*, **41**(6): 774–777.

Bullough, V., Bullough, B., & Mauro, M. (1978). Age and achievement: A dissenting view. *The Gerontologist*, **18**(6): 584–587.

Burnside, I. M. (1976). Depression and suicide in the aged. In I. M. Burnside (Ed.), *Nursing and the aged* (pp. 165–181). New York: McGraw-Hill.

Butler, R. N. (1987). Mental health and illness. In G. L. Maddox (Ed.), *The encyclopedia of aging* (pp. 439–440). New York: Springer.

Butler, R. N., & Lewis, M. I. (1982). *Aging and mental health* (third edition). St. Louis: Mosby.

Canestrari, R. E. (1963). Paced and self-paced learning in young and elderly adults. *Journal of Gerontology,* **18**(2): 165–168.

Canestrari, R. E. (1966). The effects of commonality on paired-associates learning in two age groups. *Journal of Gerontology,* **108**(1): 3–7.

Caserta, M. S., Lund, D. A., Wright, S. D., & Redburn, D. E. (1987). Caregivers to dementia patients: The utilization of community services. *The Gerontologist,* **27**(2): 209–214.

Cavanaugh, J. C., Dunn, N. J., Mowery, D., Feller, C., Niederehe, G., Fruge, E., & Volpendesta, D. (1989). Problem-solving strategies in dementia patient-caregiver dyads. *The Gerontologist,* **29**(2): 156–158.

Chenoweth, B., & Spencer, B. (1986). Dementia: The experience of family caregivers. *The Gerontologist,* **26**(3): 267–272.

Cleary, T. A., Clamon, C., Price, M., & Shullaw, G. (1988). A reduced stimulation unit: Effects on patients with Alzheimer's disease and related disorders. *The Gerontologist,* **28**(4): 511–514.

Clemente, F., & Hendricks, J. (1973). A further look at the relationship between age and productivity. *The Gerontologist,* **13**(1): 106–110.

Cohen, G. D. (1987). Alzheimer's disease. In G. L. Maddox (Ed.), *The encyclopedia of aging* (pp. 27–30). New York: Springer.

Cole, S. (1979). Age and scientific performance. *American Journal of Sociology,* **84**(4): 958–977.

Comfort, A. (1976). *A good age.* New York: Crown.

Committee on an Aging Society (1985). *America's aging: Health in an older society.* Washington, DC: National Academy Press.

Cooney, T. M., Schaie, K. W., & Willis, S. L. (1988). The relationship between prior functioning on cognitive and personality dimensions and subject attrition in longitudinal research. *Journal of Gerontology: Psychological Sciences,* **43**(1): P12–17.

Corsellis, J. A. N. & Evans, P. H. (1965). The relation of stenosis of the extracranial cerebral arteries to mental disorders and cerebral degeneration in old age. *Proceedings of the Fifth International Congress on Neuropathology.*

Corsini, R. J. (1987). Diagnostic and statistical manual of mental disorders. In G. L. Maddox (Ed.), *The encyclopedia of aging* (p. 179). New York: Springer.

Costa, P., & McCrae, R. (1978). Objective personality assessment. In M. Storandt, I. Siegler, & M. Elias (Eds.), *The clinical psychology of aging.* New York: Plenum.

Coughlin, T. A., & Liu, K. (1989). Health care costs of older persons with cognitive impairments. *The Gerontologist,* **29**(2): 173–182.

Craig, T. J., & VanNata, P. A. (1979). Influence of demographic characteristics on two measures of depressive symptoms: The relation of prevalence and persistence of symptoms with sex, age, education, and marital status. *Archives of General Psychiatry,* **36**: 149–154.

Craik, F. I. M. (1977). Age differences in human memory. In J. E. Birren & K. W. Schaie (Eds.), *Handbook of the psychology of aging* (pp. 384–420). New York: Van Nostrand Reinhold.

Crane, D. (1967). The gatekeepers of knowledge: Some factors affecting the selection of articles for scientific journals. *American Sociologist,* **2**(November): 195–201.

Cunningham, W. R. (1987). Intellectual abilities and age. In K. W. Schaie (Ed.), *Annual review of gerontology and geriatrics: Volume Seven* (pp. 117–134). New York: Springer.

Cunningham, W. R., & Owens, W. A. (1983). The Iowa State study of the adult development of intellectual abilities. In K. W. Schaie (Ed.), *Longitudinal studies of adult psychological development* (pp. 20–39). New York: Guilford.

Demming, J. A., & Pressey, S. L. (1957). Tests indigenous to the older years. *Journal of Counseling Psychology,* **2**(2): 144–148.

Dennis, W. (1956a). Age and achievement: A critique. *Journal of Gerontology,* **11**(4): 331–333.

Dennis, W. (1956b). Age and productivity among scientists. *Science,* **123**: 724–725.

Dennis, W. (1958). The age decrement in outstanding scientific contributions: Fact or artifact. *American Psychologist,* **12**(5): 457–460.

Dennis, W. (1966). Creative productivity between ages 20 to 80 years. *Journal of Gerontology,* **21**(1): 1–8.

Dieckmann, L., Zarit, S. H., Zarit, J. M., & Gatz, M. (1988). The Alzheimer's disease knowledge test. *The Gerontologist,* **28**(3): 402–407.

Dixon, R. A., Kramer, D. A., & Baltes, P. B. (1985). Intelligence: Its life-span development. In B. B. Wolman (Ed.), *Handbook of intelligence: Theories, measurements, and applications.* New York: Wiley.

Dustman, R. W., Ruhling, R. O., Russell, E. M., Shearer, D. E., Bonekat, H. W., Shigeoka, J. W., Wood, J. S., & Bradford, D. C. (1984). Aerobic exercise training and improved neuropsychological function of older individuals. *Neurobiology of Aging,* **5**: 35–43.

Eichorn, D., Clausen, J., Haan, N., Honzik, M., & Mussen, P. (1981). *Present and past in middle life.* New York: Academic.

Eisdorfer, C. (1965). Verbal learning and response time in the aged. *Journal of Genetic Psychology,* **107**(1): 15–22.

Eisdorfer, C., Nowlin, J., & Wilkie, F. (1970). Improvement of learning in the aged by modification of autonomic nervous system activity. *Science,* **170**: 1327–1329.

Eisdorfer, C., & Stotsky, B. A. (1977). Intervention, treatment, and rehabilitation of psychiatric disorders. In J. E. Birren & K. W. Schaie (Eds.), *Handbook of the psychology of aging* (pp. 724–751). New York: Van Nostrand Reinhold.

Evans, D. A., Funkenstein, H. H., Albert, M. S., Scherr, P. A., Cook, N. R., Chown, M. J., Hebert, L. E., Hennekens, C. H., & Taylor, J. O. (1989). Prevalence of Alzheimer's disease in a community population of older persons. *Journal of the American Medical Association,* **262**(18): 2251–2256.

Feinson, M. C. (1987). Mental health and aging: Are there gender differences? *The Gerontologist,* **27**(6): 703–711.

Feinson, M. C., & Thoits, P. A. (1986). The distribution of distress among elders. *Journal of Gerontology,* **41**(2): 225–233.

Fengler, A. P., & Goodrich, N. (1979). Wives of elderly disabled men: The hidden patients. *The Gerontologist,* **19**(2): 175–183.

Fischer, L., Visintainer, P. F., & Schulz, R. (1989). Reliable assessment of cognitive impairment in dementia patients by family caregivers. *The Gerontologist,* **29**(3): 333–335.

Fitting, M., Rabins, P., Lucas, M. J., & Eastham, J. (1986). Caregivers for dementia patients: A comparison of husbands and wives. *The Gerontologist,* **26**(3): 248–252.

Flemming, A. S., Buchanan, J. G., Santos, J. F., & Rickards, L. D. (1984). *Mental health services for the elderly: Report on a survey of mental health centers.* Washington, DC: White House Conference on Aging.

Foltz, D. (1980). Judgment withheld on DSM-III. *APA Monitor* **11**(1): 1, 33.

Foster, J. M., & Gallagher, D. (1986). An exploratory study comparing depressed and nonde-pressed elders' coping strategies. *Journal of Gerontology*, **41**(1): 91–93.

Gallagher, D., Rose, J., Rivera, P., Lovett, S., & Thompson, L. W. (1989). Prevalence of depression in family caregivers. *The Gerontologist*, **29**(4): 449–457.

Garfinkel, R. (1975). The reluctant therapist 1975. *The Gerontologist*, **15**(2): 136–137.

Gatz, M., Popkin, S. J., Pino, D. D., & VandenBos, G. R. (1985). Psychological intervention with older adults. In J. E. Birren and W. K. Schaie (Eds.), *Handbook of the psychology of aging* (second edition) (pp. 755–782). New York: Van Nostrand Reinhold.

Gaynor, S. (1989). When caregiver becomes the patient. *Geriatric Nursing*, **10**(3): 121–123.

George, L. K., & Gwyther, L. P. (1986). Caregiver well-being: A multidimensional examination of family caregivers of demented adults. *The Gerontologist*, **26**(3): 253–259.

Glosser, G., & Wexler, D. (1985). Participants' evaluation of educational/support groups for families of patients with Alzheimer's disease and other dementias. *The Gerontologist*, **25**(3): 232–236.

Goldstrom, I. D., Burns, B. J., Kessler, L. G., Feuerberg, M. A., Larson, D. B., Miller, N. E., & Cromer, W. J. (1987). Mental health services use by elderly adults in a primary care setting. *Journal of Gerontology*, **42**(2): 147–153.

Gomez, G. E., & Gomez, E. A. (1987). Delirium. *Geriatric Nursing*, **8**(6): 330–332.

Gomez, G. E., & Gomez, E. A. (1989). Dementia or delirium? *Geriatric Nursing*, **10**(3): 141–142.

Gove, W. R. (1973). Sex, marital status, and mortality. *American Journal of Sociology*, **79**(1): 45–67.

Greene, V. L., Monahan, D. J. (1989). The effect of a support and education program on stress and burden among family caregivers to frail elderly persons. *The Gerontologist*, **29**(4): 472–477.

Gurland, B. J., & Toner, J. A. (1982). Depression in the elderly: A review of recently published studies. In C. Eisdorfer (Ed.), *Annual review of gerontology and geriatrics: Volume Three* (pp. 228–265). New York: Springer.

Guttentag, R. E., & Hunt, R. R. (1988). Adult age differences in memory for imagined and performed action. *Journal of Gerontology: Psychological Sciences*, **43**(4): P107–108.

Hachinski, V. C., Lassen, N. A., & Marshall, J. (1974). Multi-infarct dementia: A cause of mental deterioration in the elderly. *Lancet*, **II**: 207–209.

Hale, S., Myerson, J., & Wagstaff, D. (1987). General slowing of nonverbal information processing: Evidence for a power law. *Journal of Gerontology: Psychological Sciences*, **42**(2): 131–136.

Haley, W. E. (1989). Group intervention for dementia family caregivers: A longitudinal perspec-tive. *The Gerontologist*, **29**(4): 478–480.

Hansen, S. S., Patterson, M. A., & Wilson, R. W. (1988). Family involvement on a dementia unit: The resident enrichment and activity program. *The Gerontologist*, **28**(4): 508–510.

Harwood, E., & Naylor, G. F. K. (1969). Recall and recognition in elderly and young subjects. *Australian Journal of Psychology*, **21**(3): 251–257.

Hastrup, J. L., Baker, J. G., Kraemer, D. L., & Bornstein, R. F. (1986). Crying and depression among older adults. *The Gerontologist*, **26**(1): 91–96.

Hay, J. W., & Ernst, R. L. (1987). The economic cost of Alzheimer's disease. *American Journal of Public Health*, **77**(9): 1169–1175.

Hirschfield, R. M. A., & Cross, C. K. (1982). Epidemiology of affective disorders: Psychosocial risk factors. *Archives of General Psychiatry*, **39**: 35–46.

Horn, J. L. (1987). WAIS test. In G. L. Maddox (Ed.), *The encyclopedia of aging* (pp. 688–689). New York: Springer.

Horn, J. L., & Donaldson, G. (1976). On the myth of intellectual decline in adulthood. *American Psychologist,* **31**(10): 701–719.

Huang, L-F., Cartwright, W. S., & Hu, T-W. (1988). The economic cost of senile dementia in the United States, 1985. *Public Health Reports,* **103**(1): 3–7.

Hulicka, I. M. (1967). Age differences in retention as a function of interference. *Journal of Gerontology,* **22**(2): 180–184.

Hulicka, I. M., Sterns, H., & Grossman, J. (1967). Age-group comparisons of paired-associates learning as a function of paced and self-paced association and response time. *Journal of Gerontology,* **22**(3): 274–280.

Hultsch, D. F. (1975). Adult age differences in retrieval: Trace-dependent and cue-dependent forgetting. *Developmental Psychology,* **11**(2): 197–201.

Inglis, J. (1965). Sensory deprivation and cognitive disorders. *British Journal of Psychiatry,* **111**(3): 309–315.

Institute of Medicine (1985). *Health in an older society.* Washington, DC: National Academic Press.

Kastenbaum, R. (1964). The reluctant therapist. In R. Kastenbaum (Ed.), *New thoughts on old age* (pp. 139–145). New York: Springer.

Kastenbaum, R. (1971). Use of psychological and social data: A need for researchers as a springboard for action. In J. J. Jackson (Ed.), *Proceedings of research conference on minority group aged in the south* (pp. 107–116). Durham, NC: Duke University Press.

Kastenbaum, R., & Mishara, B. (1971). Premature death and self-injurious behavior in old age. *Geriatrics,* **26**(1): 70–81.

Katzman, R. (1976). The prevalence and malignancy of Alzheimer's disease. *Archives of Neurology,* **33**(April): 217–218.

Katzman, R. (1985). Aging and age-dependent disease: Cognition and dementia. In Committee on an Aging Society (Ed.), *Health in an older society* (pp. 129–152). Washington, DC: National Academy Press.

Kausler, D. H. (1970). Retention-forgetting as a nomological network for developmental research. In L. R. Goulet and P. B. Baltes (Eds.), *Life-span developmental psychology: Research and theory* (pp. 305–353). New York: Academic Press.

Kausler, D. H. (1987). Memory and memory theory. In G. L. Maddox (Ed.), *The encyclopedia of aging* (pp. 429–432). New York: Springer.

Kausler, D. H., & Lair, C. V. (1972). Associative strength and paired-associate learning in elderly subjects. *Journal of Gerontology,* **21**(3): 278–280.

Kay, D. W. K., Beamish, P., & Roth, M. (1964). Old age mental disorders in Newcastle-upon-Tyne: Part I. *British Journal of Psychiatry,* **110**: 146–159.

Kay, D. W. K., & Bergmann, K. (1980). Epidemiology of mental disorders among the aged in the community. In J. E. Birren & R. B. Sloane (Eds.), *Handbook of mental health and aging.* Englewood Cliffs, NJ: Prentice-Hall.

Kent, S. (1983). What causes Alzheimer's? *Geriatrics,* **38**(2): 33–41.

Kermis, M. D. (1986). The epidemiology of mental disorders in the elderly: A response to the Senate/AARP report. *The Gerontologist,* **26**(5): 482–487.

Kinney, J. M., & Stephens, M. A. P. (1989). Caregiver hassle scale: Assessing the daily hassles of caring for a family member with dementia. *The Gerontologist,* **29**(3): 328–332.

Kinsbourne, M., & Berryhill, J. L. (1972). The nature of the interaction between pacing and the age decrement in learning. *Journal of Gerontology,* **27**(4): 471–477.

Kirchner, W. K. (1958). Age differences in short-term retention of rapidly changing information. *Journal of Experimental Psychology,* **55**(4): 352–358.

Kluger, A., & Ferris, S. H. (1987). Drug treatment for memory dysfunction. In G. L. Maddox (Ed.), *The encyclopedia of aging* (pp. 195–197. New York: Springer.

Knight, B. (1988). Factors influencing therapist-rated change in older adults. *Journal of Gerontology: Psychological Sciences,* **43**(4): P111–112.

Kramer, D. A. (1987). Cognition and aging: The emergence of a new tradition. In P. Silverman (Ed.), *The elderly as modern pioneers* (pp. 114–132). Bloomington: Indiana University Press.

Krauss, I. K. (1987). Reaction time. In G. L. Maddox (Ed.), *The encyclopedia of aging* (pp. 556–557). New York: Springer.

Kromm, D., & Kromm, Y-H. N. (1985). A nursing unit designed for Alzheimer's disease patients at Newton Presbyterian Manor. *Nursing Homes,* **34**(3): 30–31.

Labouvie-Vief, G. (1985). Intelligence and cognition. In J. E. Birren & K. W. Schaie (Eds.), *Handbook of the psychology of aging* (second edition) (pp. 500–530). New York: Van Nostrand Reinhold.

Labouvie-Vief, G., & Gonda, J. N. (1976). Cognitive strategy training and intellectual performance in the elderly. *Journal of Gerontology,* **31**(3): 327–332.

Lair, C. V., & Moon, W. H. (1972). The effects of praise and reproof on the performance of middle-aged and older subjects. *Aging and Human Development,* **3**(3): 279–284.

Lair, C. V., Moon, W. H., & Kausler, D. H. (1969). Associative interference in the paired-associates learning of middle-aged and old subjects. *Developmental Psychology,* **1**(6): 548–552.

LaRue, A., Dessonville, C., & Jarvik, L. F. (1985). Aging and mental disorders. In J. E. Birren & K. W. Schaie (Eds.), *Handbook of the psychology of aging* (second edition) (pp. 664–702). New York: Van Nostrand Reinhold.

Lehman, H. C. (1953). *Age and achievement.* Princeton, NJ: Princeton University Press.

Lehman, H. C. (1956). Reply to Dennis' critique of age and achievement. *Journal of Gerontology,* **11**(4): 333–337.

Lehman, H. C. (1958). The influence of longevity upon curves showing man's creative production rate at successive age levels. *Journal of Gerontology,* **13**(2): 187–191.

Lehman, H. C. (1963). Chronological age versus present-day contributions to medical progress. *The Gerontologist,* **3**(1): 71–75.

Lewinsohn, P. M., & Tilson, M. D. (1987). Psychotherapy services for older adults: Innovative roles for the clinical geropsychologist. *Gerontology and Geriatrics Education,* **7**(3/4): 111–123.

Lipowski, Z. J. (1989). Delirium in the elderly patient. *The New England Journal of Medicine,* **320**(9): 578–582.

Lowenthal, M. F., & Berkman, P. L. (1967). *Aging and mental disorder in San Francisco: A social psychiatric study.* San Francisco: Jossey-Bass.

Maas, M. (1988). Management of patients with Alzheimer's disease in long-term care facilities. *Nursing Clinics of North America,* **23**(1): 57–68.

McCrae, R. R., & Costa, P. T. (1984). *Emerging lives, enduring dispositions: Personality in adulthood.* Boston: Little, Brown.

McGhie, A., Chapman, J., & Lawson, J. S. (1965). Changes in immediate memory with age. *British Journal of Psychology,* **56**(1): 69–75.

McIntosh, J. L. (1987). Suicide: Training and education needs with an emphasis on the elderly. *Gerontology and Geriatrics Education,* **7**(3/4): 125–139.

McIntosh, J. L., & Santos, J. F. (1985–1986). Methods of suicide by age: Sex and race differences among the young and old. *International Journal of Aging and Human Development,* **22**(2): 123–139.

Manniche, E., & Falk, G. (1957). Age and the Nobel Prize. *Behavioral Science,* **2**(3): 301–307.

Manton, K. G., Blazer, D. G., & Woodbury, M. A. (1987). Suicide in middle age and later life: Sex and race specific life table and cohort analyses. *Journal of Gerontology: Social Sciences,* **42**(2): 219–227.

Manton, K. G., Siegler, I. C., & Woodbury, M. A. (1986). Patterns of intellectual development in later life. *Journal of Gerontology,* **41**(4): 486–499.

Monge, R., & Hultsch, D. (1971). Paired-associates learning as a function of adult age and the length of the anticipation and inspection intervals. *Journal of Gerontology,* **28**(1): 63–67.

Montgomery, R. V., & Borgatta, E. F. (1989). The effects of alternative support strategies on family caregiving. *The Gerontologist,* **29**(4): 457–464.

Moritz, D. J., Kasl, S. V., & Berkman, L. F. (1989). The health impact of living with a cognitively impaired elderly spouse: Depressive symptoms and social functioning. *Journal of Gerontology: Social Sciences,* **44**(1): S17–27.

Motenko, A. K. (1989). The frustrations, gratifications, and well-being of dementia caregivers. *The Gerontologist,* **29**(2): 166–172.

Neugarten, B. L. (1968). Adult personality: Toward a psychology of the life cycle. In B. L. Neugarten (Ed.), *Middle age and aging: A reader in social psychology* (pp. 137–148). Chicago: University of Chicago Press.

Ohta, R. J., & Ohta, B. M. (1988). Special units for Alzheimer's disease patients: A critical look. *The Gerontologist,* **28**(6): 803–808.

Patterson, R. D., Abrahams, R., & Baker, F. (1974). Preventing self-destructive behavior. *Geriatrics,* **11**: 115–121.

Peppard, N. R. (1985). Alzheimer special-care nursing home units. *Nursing Homes,* **34**(5): 25–28.

Perlmutter, M., Adams, C., Berry, J., Kaplan, M., Person, D., & Verdonik, F. (1987). Aging and Memory. In K. W. Schaie (Ed.), *Annual review of gerontology and geriatrics: Volume Seven* (pp. 57–92). New York: Springer.

Plemons, J. K., Willis, S. L., & Baltes, P. B. (1978). Modifiability of fluid intelligence in aging: A short-term longitudinal training approach. *Journal of Gerontology,* **33**(2): 224–231.

Poggi, R. G., & Berland, D. I. (1985). The therapists' reactions to the elderly. *The Gerontologist,* **25**(5): 508–513.

Poon, L. W. (1985). Differences in human memory with aging: Nature, causes, and clinical implications. In J. E. Birren & K. W. Schaie (Eds.), *Handbook of the psychology of aging* (second edition) (pp. 427–462). New York: Van Nostrand Reinhold.

Powell, A. H., Eisdorfer, C., & Bogdonoff, M. D. (1964). Physiologic response patterns observed in a learning task. *Archives of General Psychiatry,* **19**(2): 192–195.

Pratt, C., Schmall, V., & Wright, S. (1987). Ethical concerns of family caregivers to dementia patients. *The Gerontologist,* **27**(5): 632–638.

Price, D. L., Whitehouse, P. J., & Struble, R. G. (1985). Alzheimer's disease. *Annual Review of Medicine: Selected Topics in the Clinical Sciences,* **36**: 349–356.

Prinz, P. N. (1977). Sleep patterns in the healthy aged: Relationship with intellectual functioning. *Journal of Gerontology,* **32**(2): 179–186.

Pruchno, R., & Resch, N. L. (1989). Husbands and wives as caregivers: Antecedents of depression and burden. *The Gerontologist,* **29**(2): 159–165.

Quayhagen, M. P., & Quayhagen, M. (1988). Alzheimer's stress: Coping with the caregiver role. *The Gerontologist,* **28**(3): 391–396.

Quayhagen, M. P., & Quayhagen, M. (1989). Differential effects of family-based strategies on Alzheimer's disease. *The Gerontologist,* **29**(2): 150–155.

Rabins, P. V. (1986). Establishing Alzheimer's disease units in nursing homes: Pros and cons. *Hospital and Community Psychiatry,* **37**(2): 120–121.

Rabins, P. V., Mace, N. L., & Lucas, M. J. (1982). The impact of dementia on the family. *Journal of the American Medical Association,* **248**(3): 333–335.

Rapp, S. R., & Davis, K. M. (1989). Geriatric depression: Physicians' knowledge, perceptions, and diagnostic practices. *The Gerontologist,* **29**(2): 252–257.

Raskin, A. (1982). Psychopharmacology of depression in the elderly. In C. Eisdorfer (Ed.), *Annual review of gerontology and geriatrics: Volume Three* (pp. 266–296). New York: Springer.

Ray, D. C., McKinney, K. A., & Ford, C. V. (1987). Differences in psychologists' ratings of older and younger clients. *The Gerontologist,* **27**(1): 82–86.

Ray, D. C., Raciti, M. A., & Ford, C. V. (1985). Ageism in psychiatrists: Associations with gender, certification, and theoretical orientation. *The Gerontologist,* **25**(5): 496–500.

Reisberg, B. (1987). Senile dementia. In G. L. Maddox (Ed.), *The encyclopedia of aging* (pp. 594–600). New York: Springer.

Resnick, H. L. P., & Cantor, J. M. (1973). Suicide and aging. In V. M. Brantl & M. R. Brown (Eds.), *Readings in gerontology* (pp. 111–117). Saint Louis: Mosby.

Riegel, K. F., & Riegel, R. M. (1972). Development, drop, and death. *Developmental Psychology,* **6**(2): 306–319.

Robertson-Tchabo, E. A., Hausman, C. P., & Arenberg, D. (1976). A classic mnemonic for older learners: A trip that works. *Educational Gerontology,* **1**(3): 215–226.

Rodin, J., McAvay, G., & Timko, C. (1988). A longitudinal study of depressed mood and sleep disturbances in elderly adults. *Journal of Gerontology: Psychological Sciences,* **43**(2): P45–53.

Ross, E. (1968). Effects of challenging and supportive instructions on verbal learning of older persons. *Journal of Education Psychology,* **59**(3): 261–266.

Ruth, J. E., & Birren, J. E. (1985). Creativity in adulthood and old age: Relations to intelligence, sex, and mode of testing. *International Journal of Behavioral Development,* **8**(1): 99–109.

Salthouse, T. A. (1985). Speed of behavior and its implications for cognition. In J. E. Birren & K. W. Schaie (Eds.), *Handbook of the psychology of aging* (second edition) (pp. 400–426). New York: Van Nostrand Reinhold.

Sands, L. P., & Meredith, W. (1989). Effects of sensory and motor functioning on adult intellectual performance. *Journal of Gerontology: Psychological Sciences,* **44**(2): P56–58.

Schacht, T. E. (1985). DSM-III and the politics of truth. *American Psychologist,* **40**: 513–522.

Schafer, S. C. (1985). Modifying the environment. *Geriatric Nursing,* **6**(3): 157–159.

Schaie, K. W. (1970). A reinterpretation of age-related changes in cognitive structure and functioning. In L. R. Goulet & P. B. Baltes (Eds.), *Life-span developmental psychology: Research and theory* (pp. 486–562). New York: Academic Press.

Schaie, K. W. (1983). Age changes in adult intelligence. In D. S. Woodruff & J. E. Birren (Eds.), *Aging: Scientific perspectives and social issues* (second edition) (pp. 137–148). Monterey, CA: Brooks/Cole.

Schaie, K. W. (1984). Midlife influences upon intellectual functioning in old age. *International Journal of Behavioral Development,* **7**(5): 463–478.

Schaie, K. W., & Hertzog, C. (1983). Fourteen-year short-sequential analysis of adult intellectual development. *Developmental Psychology,* **19**(4): 531–543.

Schaie, K. W., & Parham, I. (1976). Stability of adult personality traits: Fact or fable? *Journal of Personality and Social Psychology,* **34**(2): 146–158.

Schneider, E. L., & Emr, M. (1985). Alzheimer's disease: Research highlights. *Geriatric Nursing,* **6**(3): 136–138.

Schonfield, D. (1972). The nuances and practical old questions: The psychology of aging. *Canadian Journal of Psychology,* **13**(3): 252–266.

Schonfield, D. (1985). Memory changes with age. *Nature,* **208**: 918.

Schorer, C. E. (1985). Historical essay: Kraepelin's description of Alzheimer's disease. *International Journal of Aging and Human Development,* **21**(3): 235–238.

Schurman, R. A., Kramer, P. D., & Mitchell, J. B. (1985). The hidden mental health network. *Archives of General Psychiatry,* **42**: 89–94.

Shichita, K., Hatano, S., Ohashi, Y., Shibata, H., & Matuzaki, T. (1986). Memory changes in the Benton Visual Retention Test between ages 70 and 75. *Journal of Gerontology,* **41**(3): 385–386.

Siegler, I. C. (1983). Psychological aspects of the Duke longitudinal studies. In K. W. Schaie (Ed.), *Longitudinal studies of adult psychological development* (pp. 136–190). New York: Guilford Press.

Siegler, I. C. (1985). Mental performance in the young-old versus the old-old. In E. Palmore, E. W. Busse, G. L. Maddox, J. B. Nowlin, & I. C. Siegler (Eds.), *Normal aging III* (pp. 232–237). Durham, NC: Duke University Press.

Siegler, I. C. (1987). Personality. In G. L. Maddox (Ed.), *The encyclopedia of aging* (p. 520). New York: Springer.

Siegler, I. C., & Botwinick, J. (1979). A long-term longitudinal study of intellectual ability of older adults. *Journal of Gerontology,* **34**(2): 242–245.

Siegler, I. C., George, L. K., & Okun, M. (1979). Cross-sequential analysis of adult personality. *Developmental Psychology,* **15**(4): 350–351.

Silliman, R. A., & Sternberg, J. (1988). Family caregiving: Impact of patient functioning and underlying causes of dependency. *The Gerontologist,* **28**(3): 377–382.

Spirduso, W. W. (1975). Reaction and movement time as a function of age and physical activity level. *Journal of Gerontology,* **30**(4): 435–440.

Spirduso, W. W. (1980). Physical fitness, aging and psychomotor speed: A review. *Journal of Gerontology,* **35**(6): 850–865.

Spirduso, W. W., & Clifford, P. (1978). Neuromuscular speed and consistency of performance as a function of age, physical activity level and type of physical activity. *Journal of Gerontology,* **33**(1): 26–30.

Srole, L., Langner, T. S., Michael, S. T., Opler, M. K., & Rennie, T. A. C. (1962). *Mental health in the metropolis: The midtown Manhattan study.* New York: McGraw-Hill.

Taub, H. A. (1973). Memory span, practice, and aging. *Journal of Gerontology,* **28**(3): 335–338.

Thompson, L. W., Gong, V., Haskins, E., & Gallagher, D. (1987). Assessment of depression and dementia during the late years. In K. W. Schaie (Ed.), *Annual review of gerontology and geriatrics: Volume Seven* (pp. 295–324). New York: Springer.

Tomlinson, B. E., Blessed, G., & Roth, M. (1968). Observations on the brains of nondemented old people. *Journal of Neurological Science,* **7**(3): 331–356.

Tomlinson, B. E., Blessed, G., & Roth, M. (1970). Observations on the brains of demented old people. *Journal of Neurological Science,* **11**(2): 205–242.

Toseland, R. W., & Rossiter, C. M. (1989). Group interventions to support family caregivers: A review and analysis. *The Gerontologist,* **29**(4): 438–448.

Toseland, R. W., Rossiter, C. M., & Labrecque, M. S. (1989). The effectiveness of peer-led and professionally led groups to support family caregivers. *The Gerontologist,* **29**(4): 465–471.

U.S. Bureau of the Census (1990). *Statistical abstracts of the United States: 1990.* Washington, DC: U.S. Government Printing Office.

U.S. Congress, Office of Technology Assessment (1987). *Losing a million minds: Confronting the tragedy of Alzheimer's disease and other dementias.* Washington, DC: U.S. Government Printing Office.

U. S. Senate Special Committee on Aging (1984). *Aging America: Trends and projections.* Washington, DC: U.S. Government Printing Office.

Walsh, D. A. (1983). Age differences in learning and memory. In D. S. Woodruff & J. E. Birren (Eds.), *Aging: Scientific perspectives and social issues* (second edition) (pp. 149–176). Monterey, CA: Brooks/Cole.

Warrington, E. K., & Silverstein, M. (1970). A questionnaire technique for investigating very long term memory. *Quarterly Journal of Experimental Psychology,* **22**(6): 508–512.

Watkins, M. J. (1974). Concept and measurement of primary memory. *Psychological Bulletin,* **81**(7): 695–711.

Waxman, H. M., & Carner, E. A. (1984). Physicians' recognition, diagnosis, and treatment of mental disorders in elderly medical patients. *The Gerontologist,* **24**(6): 593–597.

Waxman, H. M., Carner, E. A., & Klein, M. (1984). Underutilization of mental health professionals by community elderly. *The Gerontologist,* **24**(1): 23–30.

Weiler, P. G. (1987). The public health impact of Alzheimer's disease. *American Journal of Public Health,* **77**(9): 1157–1158.

Weismann, M. M., Myers, J. K., Tischler, G. L., Holtzer, C. E., Leaf, P. J., Orvascel, H., & Brody, J. A. (1985). Psychiatric disorders (DSM-III) and cognitive impairment among the elderly in a U.S. urban community. *Acta Psychiatrica Scandinavica,* **71**: 366–379.

Welford, A. T. (1977). Motor performance. In J. E. Birren & K. W. Schaie (Eds.), *The handbook of the psychology of aging* (pp. 450–496). New York: Van Nostrand Reinhold.

White, N., & Cunningham, W. R. (1988). Is terminal drop pervasive or specific. *Journal of Gerontology: Psychological Sciences,* **43**(6): P141–144.

Wilkie, F., & Eisdorfer, C. (1985). Intellectual changes. In E. Palmore, E. W. Busse, G. L. Maddox, J. B. Nowlin, & I. C. Siegler (Eds.), *Normal aging III* (pp. 190–195). Durham, NC: Duke University Press.

Willis, S. L., & Baltes, P. B. (1980). Intelligence in adulthood and aging: Contemporary issues. In L. W. Poon (Ed.), *Aging in the 1980s: Psychological issues* (pp. 260–272). Washington, DC: American Psychological Association.

Willis, S. L., & Schaie, K. W. (1983). Can decline in adult intellectual functioning be reversed? *Developmental Psychology,* **22**(2): 223–232.

Wills, R. (1986). Cognitive changes of normal aging and the dementias. In D. L. Carnevali & M. Patrick (Eds.), *Nursing management for the elderly* (pp. 241–256). New York: Lippincott.

Windom, R. E. (1988). An aging nation presents new challenges to the health care system. *Public Health Reports,* **103**(1): 1–2.

Woodruff, D. S. (1983). A review of aging and cognitive processes. *Research on Aging,* **5**(2): 139–153.

Woodruff, J. C., Donnan, H., & Halpin, G. (1988). Changing elderly persons' attitudes toward mental health professionals. *The Gerontologist,* **28**(6): 800–802.

Worm-Peterson, J., & Pakkenberg, H. (1968). Atherosclerosis of cerebral arteries, pathological and clinical correlations. *Journal of Gerontology,* **23**(4): 445.

Zacks, R. T., Hasher, L., Doren, B., Hamm, V., & Attig, M.S. (1987). Encoding and memory of explicit and implicit information. *Journal of Gerontology,* **42**(4): 418–422.

Zaretsky, H. H., & Halberstam, J. L. (1968). Age differences in paired-associate learning. *Journal of Gerontology,* **23**(2): 165–168.

Zarit, S. H. (1989). Do we need another "stress and caregiving study?" *The Gerontologist,* **29**(2): 147–148.

Zarit, S. H., Todd, P. A., & Zarit, J. M. (1986). Subjective burden of husbands and wives as caregivers: A longitudinal study. *The Gerontologist,* **26**(3): 260–266.

Zarit, S. H., & Toseland, R. W. (1989). Current and future direction in family caregiving research. *The Gerontologist,* **29**(4): 481–483.

Zuckerman, H. (1977). Scientific elite: Nobel laureates in the United States. New York: Free Press.

Zuckerman, H., & Merton, R. K. (1972). Age, aging, and age structure in science. In M. W. Riley, M. Johnson, & A. Foner (Eds.), *Aging and society: Volume Three: A sociology of age stratification* (pp. 292–356). New York: Russell Sage Foundation.

PART THREE

THREE

SOCIETAL ASPECTS

Emillio A. Mercado/The Picture Cube

CHAPTER **9**

FAMILY AND FRIENDS

Mike Button/EKM-Nepenthe

INTRODUCTION

We all belong to groups. In fact, if one were to list the groups one currently belongs to, most could easily list 15 to 30 groups. We spend most of our lives playing, working, and living in groups. Although there are some groups that we belong to for a long period of time, such as the family, our membership in many groups is of relatively short duration. In fact, life is a succession of memberships in different groups. For example, traditionally individuals have left high school groups and joined college groups, and then left the college groups to join work groups. Once in the work force, groups are entered and left through promotions and transfers. New family groups are formed through marriage, and additional groups through children's marriages. While new family groups are continually forming, others are dissolving through factors such as death and divorce.

In this chapter we will examine two groups that generally have the greatest amount of influence on us: family and friends. These groups can influence our behavior, values, beliefs, and aspirations. In addition, these groups are the most likely to provide us with affection and support.

This chapter is separated into two sections, the first will examine the family, the second friends.

THE FAMILY

As noted above, most individuals belong to several groups. Of all the groups we belong to, the family is generally the most important and influential group. Although the family is important, traditionally most textbooks on the family have focused on the family that still had young children living at home (see Dressel & Avant, 1978). There was relatively little research or writing on the aged postparental family or its relationship to other family members. While the amount of research has increased, there are still many areas where further research is needed (see Blieszner, 1986).

In this section, we will examine several aspects of the family in old age. First some definitions will be provided, followed by a discussion of the family life cycle. This will be followed by information on older persons who are married, widowed, and divorced. Remarriage and those who have never married are also discussed, as well as the relationship between older persons and their adult children, which examines the role of adult children as caregivers. The role of grandparent will also be examined, as will the relationship of older persons with their siblings. In the last two subsections we will look at alternative family forms and elder abuse.

Definition of Terms

The academic study of the family involves a number of terms that deal with factors such as types of marriages, mate selection, rules of inheritance, or place of residence for new families. In this chapter we will examine several relevant terms.

The first term that needs to be defined is **family.** According to the U.S. Bureau of the Census (1990), a family ". . . refers to a group of two or more persons related by blood, marriage, or adoption and residing together in a household.'' This is a fairly broad definition of the term and readily encompasses the family that still has young children living at home and the family in which the spouses are older and whose children are now adults and living independently.

The second and third terms are **family of orientation** and **family of procreation.** We are born or adopted into a family of orientation where our major roles are as a son/daughter or brother/sister. When we marry we form a second family, called the family of procreation, where our major roles change to husband/wife and father/mother. Thus, throughout most of our lives we maintain membership in two families.

The next two terms are **nuclear family** and **extended family.** The term ''nuclear family'' refers to two adults of the opposite sex living together with their children in a ''socially approved'' sexual relationship. In essence, the nuclear family has traditionally consisted of a mother, father, and their children. There can be some variations in a nuclear family, such as no children, or an absent parent because of factors such as widowhood, separation, or divorce. Also, an elderly couple whose children have left home would constitute a nuclear family. The term has been extended by some writers to include cohabiting heterosexual and homosexual couples. An extended family consists of two or more nuclear families living together in one household. In the extended family there may be three or more generations living in one household; for example, there may be a married couple with young children who have a parent living with them.

The general belief is that historically the extended family was the typical family setting. That is, most families had several generations living in one household. Although this is a ''romantic'' image, few historians believe that it is accurate (see Hagestad, 1987; Tibbitts, 1968; Treas, 1983).

A next term is **modified extended family.** This term has been used to refer to related nuclear families living in separate households but maintaining strong kinship ties and having frequent social interactions.

The last term is **filial responsibility.** This term refers to the belief that adult children should provide care and assistance to their aged parents (see Borgatta, 1987; Brubaker, 1985).

The Family Life Cycle

Family researchers have conceptualized a family life cycle that most newly married couples move through. Although several researchers have set forth family life cycles, the one that is probably the most well known and accepted is that of Duvall (1977), which has eight stages:

1 Establishment (those who are newly married and childless)
2 New parents (children 1 to 3 years of age)
3 Preschool family (children 3 to 6 years of age)
4 School-age family (oldest child 6 to 12 years of age)
5 Family with teenagers (oldest child 13 to 19 years of age)

6 Family with young adult (oldest 20+ years of age)
7 Family as launching center (first child leaves home)
8 Postparental family (all the children have left the home)

Admittedly, this represents an "ideal" family. It assumes that there are children, and that death and divorce do not interrupt the cycle. In this family life-cycle model we are most interested in the last two stages. The "family as a launching center," also called middle-aged parents, encompasses the period of time during which all of the children leave home and retirement occurs. The last stage, also called the aging family, encompasses the retirement period and the death of a spouse. Ultimately the family life cycle ends with the death of the second spouse.

In examining the family life cycle, researchers have found that social changes sometimes add new stages to the family life cycle or that certain events may occur during different stages. For example, in the 1940s researchers conceptualized four stages in the family life cycle, while current researchers have noted that more stages are needed (Glick, 1989).

Some of the changes in the last stages of the family life cycle are that the last child leaves the home when the parents are younger. This is because most families currently have fewer children spaced more closely together. This fact, coupled with an increased life expectancy, gives many older couples more than a decade together before widowhood. Previously, the death of the husband generally occurred before the last child had left home. It is interesting that currently most couples have more years "alone" after their children have left home than when they were first married.

Married

As can be seen in Table 9-1, most older men are married; most older women are not married.

For those who are married, about 2 percent of older persons are separated from their spouses. The percentage of both males and females who are married declines steadily with increasing age. For males the percent married for the age categories

TABLE 9-1
MARITAL STATUS, 1988

	Males, %	Females, %
Single	4.6	5.3
Married	77.7	41.5
Spouse present	75.1	39.9
Spouse absent	2.5	1.6
Widowed	13.9	48.7
Divorced	3.9	4.5

Source: U.S. Bureau of the Census, 1990.

65–74 and 75+ are 81.9 and 69.7 percent. For females the percentages are 53.3 and 24.9 (U.S. Bureau of the Census, 1990).

There are three reasons for the difference in percentage of married males and females. First, on average, males have a shorter life expectancy than females. Thus, the husbands die while still married leaving their wives in the widowed category. Second, the general pattern is for an older male, with a shorter life expectancy, to be married to a younger female, who has a longer life expectancy. Again, this means that females are likely to experience several years of widowhood before death. Third, widowed or divorced males are more likely to remarry than females. In fact they are eight times more likely to remarry. As can be seen from the figures in Table 9-1, widowed or divorced older males have a large pool of single, widowed, or divorced females as potential marriage partners. For nonmarried females the likelihood of remarriage is relatively small because there are not very many "eligible" males in the same age category and because males tend to marry females from "younger" age categories (or females tend to marry males from older age categories). That aged males often marry females from younger age cohorts can be seen by examining the average number of years grooms are older than their brides. The average age difference between a groom and bride is 5.3 years; however, for those 65+ years of age it is 12.1 years (U.S. Bureau of the Census, 1990). It is still probably more socially acceptable for an older male to marry a younger female than for an older female to marry a younger male.

Marital Satisfaction   Studies on marital satisfaction have been ongoing for several decades. Although there is a great deal of research, there are few definitive conclusions. The studies on marital satisfaction in the aging family can be separated into those which have found that with increasing age marital satisfaction increases, decreases, or remains about the same (see Brubaker, 1985; Montgomery, 1987). The studies have varied because of methodological differences. For example, researchers have used several different instruments to measure marital satisfaction. Another factor is that there have been relatively few longitudinal studies (see Brubaker, 1985; Markides, 1987; Montgomery, 1987).

The majority of studies have reported that marital satisfaction is high in the early years of marriage. It then declines during the childbearing and childrearing years. The postparental years are followed by an increase in marital satisfaction (see Anderson et al., 1983; Blieszner, 1986; Blood & Wolfe, 1960; Burr, 1970; Pineo, 1961; Rollins & Cannon, 1974).

The decline in marital satisfaction in the early years of marriage probably stems from several sources of stress. Some of the stress is associated with simply making a living. Other sources of stress are family related. For example, children bring stress into most marriages. Young children are demanding and often require a stressful reallocation of roles and time for couples. As the children age the types of stress change. For example, adolescents and teenagers bring new sources of stress in many areas, such as life-style selection. About the time the children are becoming more independent and less stressful a new source of stress is placed on many marriages when the aged parents of married couples need assistance. As aged parents die, couples are finally freed from many sources of family stress. During the postparental years, husbands and wives generally have more free time, more money to spend on themselves, less housework, fewer responsibilities that tie them down, and more opportunities to relax.

One study on marital satisfaction followed recently married couples for 20 years (Pineo, 1961). In general, the study found continual drops in marital adjustment and marital satisfaction. Specifically there were declines in areas such as happiness, sexual adjustment, the sharing of interests and activities, the frequency of kissing, the exchange of confidences, sexual intercourse, and egalitarianism. The author of the article concluded that the first 20 years of marriage are characterized by "disenchantment." At the time of the marriage there was a "good fit" between most couples; however, over time changes in each partner served to separate them and allowed disenchantment to occur. Additionally, various stresses associated with factors such as careers, childrearing, financial matters, or anticipated or actual caregiving of parents all served to create disenchantment.

A study by Blood and Wolfe (1960) came to conclusions similar to those of Pineo when they reported that after 2 years of marriage the percentage of wives who were satisfied with their marriages decreased while the percentage who were dissatisfied increased. This study found that marital satisfaction generally declined for at least the first 30 years of a marriage. There have been several other studies that have demonstrated that the childrearing years of a marriage are often characterized by disenchantment (Anderson et al., 1983; Burr, 1970; Dizard, 1968; Paris & Luckey, 1966; Rollins & Cannon, 1974; Safilios-Rothschild, 1967; Townsend, 1957).

The Empty Nest It was previously believed that the disenchantment period extended into the postparental years because of the "empty nest" or "postparental syndrome." The prevalent belief was that older couples, especially women, had difficulty in adjusting to the role losses that occurred when their adult children left home. However, there is little evidence to support the belief that the postparental years are detrimental to marital adjustment or satisfaction (Axelson, 1960; Blieszner, 1986; Deutscher, 1964; Glen, 1975; Harkins, 1978; Mancini & Blieszner, 1989; Rollins & Cannon, 1974; Troll, 1971). In fact, most studies demonstrate the opposite. In fact, the children's leaving tended to have a slightly positive effect on the mother's happiness and enjoyment of life, while fathers remained constant in happiness and enjoyment. This study is in contrast to what many expect. Most believe that a child's leaving home represents a major role loss for mothers (see Axelson, 1960; Clausen, 1972; Harkins, 1978).

The adjustment to the "empty nest" is probably mitigated by several factors. First, the process of children leaving home is often gradual. That is, not all of the children leave at once; the parents therefore have an opportunity to make adjustments gradually and to anticipate what life will be like without any children permanently at home. Also the transition to a postparental family is usually not abrupt because it has been eased by the children's temporary departures for camps, long weekends with friends or relatives, college, or the armed services.

A "new" trend that is emerging in the literature is the "refilling" of the empty nest which occurs when an adult child returns to the parental home to live (see Mancini & Blieszner, 1989). This often occurs when the adult child needs emotional support, such as after a divorce or widowhood, or when the adult child needs financial support, such as after the loss of a job. It has been speculated that this refilling of the empty nest would create stress and hence a decline in marital satisfaction for the aged parents. However, preliminary studies indicate that this is not true (Suitor & Pillemer, 1987, 1988). Part of the explanation may be that many of the stress-producing aspects of parenting are no longer present now that the child is an adult. Additionally, generally the parents have some choice in whether the adult child returns to the empty nest.

Consequences of Marriage Marriage appears to be a state that is beneficial to older persons. It has been found that married individuals find life more satisfying than those who are not married (Gove, 1973). It has also been reported that those who are married have fewer feelings of loneliness (Tibbitts, 1977). Gove (1973) found in his survey of the literature that married older persons have lower rates of mental illness than those who were not married, and that the factors associated with psychological well-being, such as willingness to seek and accept necessary medical treatment, were found more commonly among the married. Studies have shown that married older persons are happier, less lonely, live longer, and have better physical and mental health than their nonmarried counterparts. However, one cautionary post-script should be added. It may be that married older persons are a select group from which many physically and psychologically unstable individuals are excluded (see Brubaker, 1985).

Although generally considered to be beneficial, there have been suggestions that marriage may be detrimental in three situations. The first situation concerns caregiving. Caregiving typically involves a wife providing care for her husband. This can be a stressful experience psychologically, socially, and financially. Caregivers often find that they have difficulty with the physical aspects of care, such as the "bed and body work." The relationship between the couple often changes in that their roles go from husband and wife to patient and nurse. In addition, the caregiving responsibilities often mean that many social ties of the caregiver are severed, often creating loneliness. This severing of social ties can have significant consequence if the caregiver becomes widowed because a support network is no longer available. Also, caregivers often neglect or do not have time for their own health needs (see Barusch, 1988). Additional stress and anxiety are created when caregivers are caught between the conflicting demands of the care receiver and the instructions of professionals (Hasselkus, 1988), as well as their personal needs and responsibilities (Stone et al., 1987).

The second situation where marriage may be detrimental concerns widowhood. Many have believed that widowed individuals are at an increased risk of illness and death. Although the death rate may be higher for the widowed, it cannot be demonstrated that widowhood is causing the increase. The third and last area concerns social class. It has been reported that marriage does not appear to be beneficial for those in the lower social classes (Brubaker, 1985), although the reasons have not been investigated.

Widowed

A frequent partnerless state for many older persons is widowhood. Because widowhood primarily affects women, most of the literature deals with "widows" not "widowers."

As with dying, numerous stage theories exist on widowhood. DeSpelder and Strickland (1987) reviewed five stage theories of grief and noted that the number of stages ranged from 3 to 7. They also noted certain similarities between the theories, which they summarized into four stages or **tasks of mourning:** "accepting the reality" of the death; "experiencing the pain" of the death; "adjusting to a changed environment"; and "withdrawing emotional energy" from the relationship with the deceased and depositing it in new relationships. As with the stages of dying, this is an ideal model, and not a rigid sequence of events.

The impact of widowhood can vary. Several variables, such as social class, age, the nature of the death (i.e., expected or unexpected), and social support have been suggested as factors that impact on adjustment to widowhood. Social class impacts on the adjustment to widowhood. Since middle and upper class couples tend to do more activities together, their lives are more interwoven, initially, making the death of a spouse more disrupting to individuals in these social classes. However, these social classes also have access to more resources to help them recover from the death.

In the factor of age, many believe that adjustment is easier for older persons since they have had more time to "rehearse" for widowhood. They have seen the spouses of their friends die, and have had time to conceptualize their own widowhood. They have also often assisted their bereaved friends. However, others believe that adjustment is more difficult for older persons since they are usually experiencing multiple losses (i.e., friends, health, savings, etc.), and their support network is generally smaller.

The nature of the death, expected or unexpected, is also a factor. Some believe that there is better adjustment when the death was expected. This is because anticipatory grief will take place; research in this area is inconclusive. Others believe that there are two factors that reduce the likelihood of adjustment when the death was expected. The first is that an expected death often means that prior to death the survivor was a caregiver. This may have diminished the survivor's health and social network. The second factor is that after the death the caregiver has suddenly lost a major role that probably consumed a significant amount of time. Thus, there are two role losses which have to be adjusted to: spouse and caregiver.

The last factor that will be examined is the social support network. Although it would be hypothesized that the greater the support the greater the adjustment to widowhood, studies have not always reported this finding. Part of the explanation may be that those receiving the most support are those having the greatest difficulty adjusting to widowhood. Studies indicate that "intense grief" is generally gone after 6 weeks, and by 6 months grief is usually "minimal" (Brubaker, 1985).

In the past the gerontological literature almost universally assumed that widowhood brought low morale. Studies have now reported that it may not be widowhood in and of itself but factors associated with widowhood. Morgan (1976) found that widowhood is associated with a loss of income, social-class standing, and for some self-image. When Morgan controlled for these factors it was found that the morale scores of the widowed were no different from those of their nonwidowed counterparts.

There are several factors that can help the widowed recover from their losses. Two of the most obvious are an adequate financial income and good health. However, one factor that is difficult to measure deals with the replacement of lost roles, which ties in with the last stage of widowhood involving the withdrawal from the role with the decreased and the establishment of new roles. Widowhood either changes or truncates a number of roles. For example, the role of sexual partner, companion, or spouse have all, at least temporarily, been eliminated. It has been found that the widowed who have fewer roles to replace or who quickly reestablish lost roles are less likely to suffer adjustment problems than those who cannot make role substitutions or role adaptations (Shulman, 1975).

Divorced

Divorce is a neglected area in gerontology (Cooney, 1989; Troll, 1976; Uhlenberg et al., 1990). As was seen earlier in Table 9-1, the percentage of divorced older persons is relatively small, about 4 percent. The figure for the total adult population is 7.8 percent. Additionally, the divorce rate (per 1000 married population) for those 65+ years of age is lower than for other age categories: 1.5 for females and 2.0 for males. The figures for the adult population are 19.0 for females and 19.2 for males (U.S. Bureau of the Census, 1990).

The divorce rate among older persons is lower than for other age categories for several reasons. First, the marriages that survive to old age are generally stable. Couples have established effective methods of dealing with marital stress and anxiety. Second, many older couples were socialized in an era when divorce was unacceptable. As a result, they accept and tolerate disenchanted marriages. Third, it is generally not marriage that is the problem but the marital partner. Thus, remarriage would be the desired outcome of the divorce. However, many realize that their options for remarriage are limited. This is especially true for females, and those with health or financial problems. As a result, many do not seek divorce. Fourth, those thinking of divorce and remarriage are confronted with anxieties associated with areas such as dating. Fifth, there is often an investment in the existing relationship that is too great to jeopardize through divorce. The investment can be in financial areas such as pensions, investments, or homes, or in personal relationships with adult children and grandchildren. Sixth, with the empty nest, marital happiness may increase, thus reducing the risk of divorce.

More studies are needed on how divorce in old age impacts on the filial responsibilities of adult children. One study has indicated that divorced males are more isolated from their families than widowed or married males (Keith, 1986). More research is also needed on how divorce in old age will influence the assistance older persons provide to their adult children. Studies are also starting to emerge on the consequences of divorce for older persons. Although limited, the studies indicate the likelihood of severe economic problems for older women, even more severe than for the widowed (Uhlenberg et al., 1990).

Some have noted that the divorce rate in old age may increase in the future because many individuals will be in remarriages which have a higher probability of divorce, more females will have been in the work force and economically independent of their husbands (Giordano, 1988), and divorce will be more socially accepted. In fact, some have projected that divorce will replace widowhood as the major marital status of older women (Uhlenberg et al., 1990). Cooney (1989) has suggested that in the future, older women will spend more time divorced than widowed.

Remarriage

Many widowed or divorced older persons had grown accustomed to and had enjoyed marriage. They had become used to the companionship, interdependence, and other positive features of marriage. Thus, for many of them, remarriage is a desirable alternative.

Although remarriage may be a desirable alternative for many divorced and widowed older persons, it is not a realistic aspiration for most of them, especially females. The remarriage rate declines progressively with increasing age, as is shown by Table 9-2.

As was mentioned earlier, while most older males are married, most older females are widowed. This creates a large pool of eligible females but only a small pool of eligible males. For females the likelihood of remarriage decreases even further because traditionally it has been more acceptable for males to marry younger females, than for females to marry younger males.

TABLE 9-2
REMARRIAGE RATES: 1984
(Per 1000 Widowed and Divorced)

Age	Rate	
	Males	Females
20–24	241.8	244.4
25–29	223.1	186.8
30–34	206.0	140.0
35–39	175.8	92.3
40–44	143.4	63.3
45–49	120.8	46.9
50–54	77.0	26.1
55–59	66.3	13.7
60–64	49.1	9.7
65+	18.9	2.2

Source: National Center for Health Statistics, 1989.

There are several variables that influence older persons' probability of getting remarried (Bulcroft et al., 1989). The first is the number of years the individual has been widowed or divorced. The greater the amount of time not married the less likely the individual is to get remarried. The second variable is living arrangement; others in the household decrease the probability of remarriage. Three additional factors are education, health, and income, with higher levels being associated with a greater probability of remarriage. The reactions of adult children to remarriage is another factor; if adult children are against remarriage, its probability is reduced. Adult children can be against remarriage because of their concerns about their inheritance, or in the case of widowhood, they consider the remarriage inappropriate because it devalues the dead parent. The last factor is the opportunity to meet individuals. Those who are housebound or who have limitations of mobility because of physical or financial factors have few opportunities to meet potential marriage partners.

In terms of the probability of remarriage, it appears that the divorced are more likely to remarry than the widowed, perhaps because another person was the cause of the divorce and thus a quick remarriage is possible. It may also be because the divorced tend to be younger than the widowed, and they are not expected to postpone dating or marriage out of respect for the deceased spouse (Treas & VanHilst, 1976).

The remarriages of older persons generally appear to be successful. Treas and VanHilst (1976) found that remarriages of older persons that were contracted on the basis of affection, financial security, and their children's approval were generally successful. Moreover, Vinick (1978) found that remarriages among older persons that were formed on the basis of companionship, the desire for care from, the personal qualities of, or a deep emotional attachment to the spouse were also successful. Other factors that contribute to "successful" remarriages among older couples are knowing each other for a long period of time, good health, and residing in a "new" home. The remarriages were generally not successful if they were forced or if they were contracted out of desperation because of financial need (Bulcroft et al., 1989; Silverman, 1987).

Although many widowed and divorced older persons want to remarry, there are also many who prefer the status of "not married." Widowed older persons who have had to provide caregiving for a spouse in declining health, because of factors such as Alzheimer's disease, are often reluctant to remarry because of the fear they may have to repeat these duties. Divorced individuals are sometimes afraid of being "trapped" in another "bad" marriage.

One additional aspect of remarriage should be mentioned: dating. Although there is an abundance of material on the dating patterns and behaviors of young adults, very little exits on older persons. One study found that the divorced dated more frequently than the widowed, probably for reasons discussed earlier such as fewer social sanctions applied to dating among the divorced than the widowed. Many dated as an alternative to marriage and it provided them with long-term, monogamous relationships, equivalent to "going steady." Companionship was one of the major reasons for dating. For many older women, status with their friends increased because they were dating. Older males enjoyed having a confidant. Most were sexually active (Bulcroft & O'Connor, 1986).

The remarriage rate of older persons may decline in the future. The life expectancy of males is increasing, meaning that females will be older when widowed, thus perhaps further decreasing their chance for remarriage. Many may also believe that at a more advanced age there is little reason to remarry. Additionally, just as cohabitation has become more acceptable among younger age groups, it will probably become more acceptable among older persons. A last factor that may lower the remarriage rate among older persons in the future is that private pension plans, for both males and females, will make the desire for remarriage for economic security less necessary (Giordano, 1988).

It has also been suggested that the remarriage rates for older persons will increase, in large part because a larger segment of the population will have a cycle of marriage, divorce, and remarriage, and that this cycle will continue into old age.

Never-Married

About 5 percent of older persons have never married. This low percentage has made research on this group sparse, and generally researchers have grouped the never-married, divorced, and widowed into the generic category of "not married." The current research that is emerging is challenging what had previously existed. One of the first reports on the never-married elderly (Gubrium, 1974) pictured them as lifelong isolates who constituted a distinctive "social type." However, it was noted that they were no more lonely in old age than other older persons, and that being single was an advantage in that they did not have to confront caregiving responsibilities or widowhood.

Two studies have challenged some of these assertions (Rubinstein, 1987; Stull & Scarisbrick-Hauser, 1989). It does not appear that the never-married are lifelong isolates. Rubinstein (1987) found that while about one-third fit this pattern, the remaining two-thirds had either generally lived with someone else, or had alternated between living alone and with someone else.

Although it is widely believed that the never-married elderly are more likely to be living with their very old parents than any other marital category, this was not found to be true. They did have a greater likelihood of living with a nonrelative, sibling, or other relative (Stull & Scarisbrick-Hauser, 1989). The image of the never-married as lifelong isolate was also shattered when the inner circle of family and friends and social interaction was examined. While there were some never-married older persons who did not have any close friends or family members, most had close friends with whom they interacted in a variety of settings. In fact, the never-married elderly were more likely to have "close" friends than the married or widowed. It was reported that the family networks of the never-married were not, however, as extensive as those of the married or widowed (Rubinstein, 1987). One consistent finding is that the never-married do not appear to be any more lonely than other marital groups. It was also found that never having married did not necessarily protect individuals from bereavement. Many reported that the deaths of parents, coresidents, siblings, friends, or others with whom they had had long-term relationships was

TABLE 9-3
MARRIAGE RATES FOR THOSE 65+ YEARS OF AGE

Marital status	Males	Females
Single	2.9	0.9
Previously divorced	26.2	4.9
Previously widowed	16.6	1.9

Source: National Center for Health Statistics, 1989.

difficult. Rubinstein (1987) revealed one other interesting finding, namely that about half of the never-married regretted not having married.

The never-married elderly do no constitute one social type but are as diverse and heterogeneous as other marital groups (see Keith & Nauta, 1988).

As can be seen in Table 9-3, the marriage rate for the never-married is lower than for other marital categories. It appears that the factors that precluded marriage in their younger years are still operating in their later years.

One area that has been examined on the never-married deals with social support in old age. Because a spouse and adult children are a source of support in old age, the never-married have been pictured as a group in jeopardy. However, it has been found that the never-married establish helping networks of other family members and friends (Rempel, 1985).

Older Persons and Their Adult Children

Until recently, gerontologists believed that the family in American society was an isolated nuclear family. They believed that the extended or multigenerational family rarely existed for three reasons. First, there were fewer children to form extended families. Second, industrialization forced many adult children to move away from parents to new locations. Third, local, state, and federal programs assumed traditional family responsibilities to older relatives, thus eliminating the need for an extended family. Thus, to "early" gerontologists, the belief of the isolated nuclear family seemed to be adequate and correct (see Hess & Waring, 1978). However, about 1950, studies began to appear that contradicted this belief (see Shanas, 1979; Sussman, 1965; Sussman & Burchinal, 1962). Essentially, the studies indicated that "a modified extended family" was in existence. The modified extended family is composed of several nuclear families living in independent households in close physical proximity with strong ties of affection and assistance.

The early gerontologists were wrong when they speculated that fewer children, industrialization, and social programs for older persons would bring about the end of the extended family. Although married couples are having fewer children than in the past, more of the children survive to adulthood. Thus, the number of adult children is not a major factor in the existence or nonexistence of the extended family. Unquestionably, industrialization did create a need for geographical mobility. However, industrialization also facilitated the existence of the modified extended family by creating "better," faster, and less expensive modes of transportation and communication. By using the products of industrialization, families were able to maintain family ties. Industrialization also created a large number of jobs in a relatively small area. Whereas in the past some young adults had to leave certain areas because there were not enough jobs, with the advent of industrialization and its creation of jobs they were able to stay near their family of orientation. Furthermore, although some children of older persons moved away, others did not. Also, often older persons chose to relocate close to one of their adult children. The last factor believed to eliminate the extended family was the creation of social programs for older persons. Although many of these programs have substituted for adult children as caregiver, the programs often have numerous limitations that still mandate that adult children provide some caregiving responsibilities.

About 82 percent of older persons have living children (Brody, 1978; Brubaker, 1985; Rempel, 1985; U.S. Bureau of the Census, 1989). Of those older persons with children, about 10 percent live in the same household with their adult children. Older women are almost twice as likely to live with their children than older men (Johnson & Bursk, 1977). Generally, widowed older women in poor health are the most likely to live with adult children. Older married couples are seldom found living with their adult children. Most older persons who reside with an adult child do so in a two-generation family. Kaplan (1975) reported that only about 3 percent of older persons residing with an adult child also lived in a household with grandchildren.

When asked about preferred living conditions, most older persons prefer to live close by, but in separate households from their adult children. It has been found that the relationships between the generations are generally better and more stable when separate households are maintained (Johnson & Bursk, 1977). The ability of aged parents and their adult children to maintain close emotional ties and high levels of involvement is called "intimacy at a distance" (Treas, 1983).

The myth of the isolated nuclear family was also shattered when studies began to appear on the amount of contact older persons had with their adult children. It was found that for older persons who had adult children, 41 percent generally saw at least one child daily. An additional 20 percent reported seeing at least one of their children once a week. Only 6 percent said that they never or only occasionally saw their children (U.S. Bureau of the Census, 1990). The frequency of interaction with children did not vary if the older person lived alone or with others.

The amount of face-to-face contact is facilitated by the fact that most older persons live fairly close to at least one adult child. This can be seen in the amount of time it takes for an adult child to get to a parent. About 25.6 percent live within 10 minutes. An additional 28.6 percent live within 10 to 29 minutes. It takes 11.6 percent from 30 to 59 minutes. The percentages for 1 to 2 hours, 3 to 24 hours, and 24+ hours are 13.2, 13.8, and 7.3 (U.S. Bureau of the Census, 1990). Although there is the belief that rural older persons have more contact with their adult children, studies have not supported this belief. In fact, studies have found similar levels of contact between older persons and adult children who live in rural and urban areas (Krout, 1988).

Still other studies on the amount of intergenerational assistance have negated the myth of the isolated nuclear family. In fact, Johnson and Bursk (1977) found that reciprocal patterns of assistance existed in 93 percent of the aged who had adult children. Assistance was found to take many forms, with one of the most common providing gifts and financial aid. Other forms of assistance were helping out when someone was sick, babysitting grandchildren, giving advice, running errands, and fixing things around the house. Lower levels of assistance from older persons to their children and grandchildren were found in each successive older birth cohort. It is not known if this is related to age, if older birth cohorts have different attitudes about exchange and assistance, or if they are less able to give because of health or financial limitations (see Dewit et al., 1988; Hays, 1984).

Studies also have indicated that about 70 percent of older persons receive assistance from their adult children. This assistance from children to parents may take the form of housework, transportation, meal preparation, or information about such matters as medical care, nutrition, housing, or pension plans. Also, 13 percent of adult children contribute financially to their aged parents, generally in a reversal of previous roles (Seccombe, 1988). The reversal takes place because of the reduced incomes of the older parents and the increased incomes of the adult children (Johnson & Bursk, 1977; Sussman, 1970, 1976; Tibbitts, 1977).

Racial and ethnic differences in families have been examined with conflicting reports emerging, in large part because it is often difficult for researchers to obtain "good" samples. Also, it is often difficult to separate out the effects of race or ethnicity from the effects of income. Research in this area has either assumed an assimilation model, which holds that families lose their uniqueness and become assimilated into mainstream American society, or the inequity model, which holds that the group is different because of prejudice and discrimination. Attempts to test the models have produced conflicting results. This is not surprising given the diversity of the racial and ethnic groups that have been studied.

Many of the early studies held to the inequity model and presented idealized racial and ethnic families. High levels of support and social contact were reported. As more studies appeared, the results became less clear (see Rosenthal, 1986). Some studies on Asian families have noted that high levels of international migration have severed family ties. Also, there are often large differences in language and culture between first and second generations that can create conflict. As younger individuals are assimilated, older individuals are left in racial or ethnic ghettos (see Liu, 1986; Osako & Liu, 1986). Similar results have been found with Puerto Ricans. It was assumed that an extended family of informal caregivers would exist to provide care for older persons. One recent study reported that this caregiving network did not exist (Espino et al., 1988).

It has been assumed that black older persons would have more contact with their children and grandchildren than white older persons. Studies have indicated that there does not appear to be a significant difference in this area, although the more important issue of "quality" of interaction has yet to be examined. This may represent a change from the past and reflect greater economic opportunities and hence greater mobility on the part of younger blacks. It has also been assumed that older blacks in the lower socioeconomic class would be more likely to live with adult children or grandchildren than those in the higher socioeconomic classes. In fact the reverse has been found. This probably indicates that those with the greatest resources are most likely to share those resources. In terms of assistance, it was found that aged blacks were more likely to receive assistance from adult children and grandchildren than aged whites. This may reflect a racial difference or a need difference (Mitchell & Register, 1984; Taylor, 1985).

Caregiving   One area where we are starting to see more literature is in the area of caregiving. In fact, the U.S. Select Committee on Aging (1987) has estimated that adults will spend more time caring for their parents than for their children. Shanas (1979) has pointed out, for example, that it is often the adult children who are responsible for keeping their aged parents out of nursing homes. As expected, the amount and type of care varies depending on the relationship between the caregiver and the care receiver. For example, caregivers generally provide a mother or father with more care than a mother-in-law or stepmother (see Finley et al., 1988; Matthews, 1987).

Providing care for parents is a controversial issue. Essentially, are older persons responsible for preparing and providing for themselves in old age, or is the family responsible for caregiving responsibilities for older persons? Or, is it the government's responsibility? Or, is there a shared responsibility, and if there is, what is the responsibility of each? Some claim that adult children are responsible for their parents; the parents took care of the children now it is time for the adult children to take care of their parents. In principle this sounds logical. In reality there are problems. For example, asking an 80-year-old woman to care for her 105-year-old mother presents a problem. Asking a child who was abused, or perhaps deserted, by a parent to provide care for that parent presents a problem. Additionally, with what member of the family does the responsibility cease: child, grandchild, great-grandchild, niece, cousin, or sibling?

Some have suggested strengthening, modifying, or enforcing "family responsibility laws." This suggestion has come about because of the high government costs associated with providing care to the aged. Laws mandating that the family would assume some of these expenses would cut governmental expenses in two ways. First, family members would assume some of the direct costs associated with the long-term care of aged relatives. Second, because the family of older persons would have to assume some health-related costs, such as for a nursing home, they would delay placing an aged relative in a nursing home. Currently about half the states have family responsibility laws that make family members responsible for the care of aged relatives. Although the laws differ, the intent is that it is the duty of the family to maintain aged relatives. The laws generally apply to adult children providing care, to the extent possible, to parents. The laws are seldom enforced in part because the enforcement has been expensive and in part because this is a politically volatile issue (see Borgatta, 1987; Gilliland, 1986; Lammers & Klingman, 1986).

As noted above, although controversial, most adult children provide assistance to their aged parents, with more assistance being provided to older females than older males. Part of this is explained by the fact that older males die younger, while older females have more time to develop a variety of debilitating chronic conditions. This also means that older females are less likely to have a caregiver. Additionally, older females have traditionally maintained family networks and thus family members feel more obligated to assist them (Blieszner, 1986; Spitze & Logan, 1989).

Becoming a caregiver to an older parent sounds in some ways idyllic. There is a reciprocity in that the adult child is now returning the care to those who provided care when the adult child was dependent. One has a picture of an adult child cheerfully delivering a loaf of bread, or feeding an aged parent. However, caregiving can be physically, financially, and emotionally demanding and stressful and can interfere in the daily life of the caregiver contributing to what has been called "caregiver burden" (Barusch, 1988; Brody, 1985; Jarrett, 1985; Kleban et al., 1989; Pearson et al., 1988). One study on adult child caregivers noted that 80 percent experienced emotional strain, 60 percent physical strain, and 54 percent financial strain. Additionally, 70 percent noted that caregiving interfered with their job and family obligations. Although the figures vary, about 31 percent of adult children who are caregivers are employed, while another 10 to 28 percent have had to quit their jobs to provide care (Scharlach & Boyd, 1989).

Although it can vary tremendously, the average number of hours per week adult children provide their parents as caregivers is between 6 to 10 (Creedon, 1988; Lang & Brody, 1983; Osterkamp, 1988; Scharlach & Boyd, 1989). Caregiving can involve personal care, transportation, meals, socialization, and home maintenance as well as the management of such personal affairs as social security, medicare, pensions, and taxes. In fact, as various governmental agencies assume roles previously held by the family, a new caregiver responsibility is to help aged parents understand or receive local, state, or federal resources. Fischer and Eustis (1988) noted this trend when new medicare regulations provided for shorter in-hospital stays, thus discharging a patient that needed more attention from caregivers. This contributed to an adult child assuming the role of parent advocate in areas such as hospital admission, care, discharge and posthospital services (see Blieszner, 1986).

Many adult children have seen the consequences of caregiving on their friends so that even the anticipated care of an aged parent can produce a type of stress called "filial anxiety" (Cicirelli, 1988). Although currently many adult children of older persons help their parents in numerous ways (Noelker & Bass, 1989), this pattern may change in the near future. Some of the reasons are outlined below (see Dewit et al., 1988; Fischer & Eustis, 1988; Pratt & Kethley, 1988; Rosenthal et al., 1989; Treas, 1983):

1 During the depression and World War II, many couples had small families. Thus, as these couples have entered old age they have fewer children than previous generations to provide assistance. One of the most significant differences between the institutionalized and the noninstitutionalized is family support. Small families also means that there will be fewer "other" family members, such as siblings, to provide support. Although family size increased after World War II with the "baby boom," the "baby boomers" have been the "baby bust" generation.

2 People are living longer today than in the past. Increasing longevity means that it will often be an "old" adult child, with health limitations, attempting to provide care for an even older parent.

One study on adult children providing care for their centenarian parents found that the average age of the caregiver was 70. Obviously the centenarians were a high need group that placed high demands in terms of time and resources from caregivers. Interestingly enough, this group of caregivers did not perceive caregiving as a high burden, in part because they involved others in the caregiving responsibilities (Sanders et al., 1987).

3 Traditionally, caregiving for parents has been a daughter's responsibility (Brody & Schoonover, 1986; Lang & Brody, 1983; Spitze & Logan, 1989). Three factors are changing this. First, in the past, with larger families there was often an unmarried daughter who could provide caregiving. Currently, families are smaller, and a greater percentage of women are marrying, thus reducing the pool of potential caregivers. Second, more women are entering the work force. Thus, there will be less time for caregiving activities. Third, women are postponing childbearing, thus increasing the risk of having to provide care for both children and parents. In fact, it is estimated that currently about 50 percent of adult children who are caregivers for parents have at least one dependent child living at home (Scharlach & Boyd, 1989).

A few exploratory studies have not supported the belief that working women will provide lower levels of care to their aged parents. They may provide different types of support, but their caregiving responsibility will still be met (see Brody & Schoonover, 1986; Lang & Brody, 1983; Matthews et al., 1989; Scharlach, 1987). Even adult children who are geographically distant from their parents often provide certain forms of care. These distant caregivers also expressed feelings of helplessness, indicating that even caregiving at a distance can be stressful (see Schoonover et al., 1988).

4 One factor that is an unknown quantity deals with the divorce rate and adult children. Divorce is in and of itself a difficult situation that will impact on the ability of the adult child to provide care. If the adult child remains single, the demands of a single parent may reduce the probability of aid and assistance to parents. For those who remarry, the demands of both new and ex-nuclear family members take time from caregiving. One possible outcome of remarriage is that a large "family" network is created with more potential caregivers.

One area that is being examined deals with the percentage of adult children who have assumed caregiver responsibilities for their parents. One study reported that 10 percent provide high levels of care and 30 percent low to moderate levels of care. This study reported that currently the percentage "sandwiched" between providing care for dependent children and dependent parents was very small (Rosenthal et al., 1989). One organization found that 20 percent of its employees provided care to their parents (Creedon, 1988). It has also been reported that working and being a caregiver results in a higher incidence of being late or leaving work early, using work time for caregiving responsibilities such as making phone calls, or taking days off to provide care.

A variety of programs to help adult children who are caregivers have been suggested and developed. Flexible work hours is one option. Providing some type of "elder care" counseling is another option (see Dusell & Roman, 1989).

Although the emphasis of this section has been on adult children providing care to their aged parents, the reverse also takes place. That is, in certain circumstances older persons must provide care to their adult children. Although research is limited, one area that has been investigated deals with physically or developmentally handicapped individuals who cannot live independently. This has been called "perpetual parenthood." Since the adult children will generally outlive their caregiving parents, the parents are faced with declining strength and increasing disability, and realize that arrangements will have to be made, although they are generally postponed until necessary. These families tend to be socially isolated and have had extra expenses. This is an area where more research is needed (Jennings, 1987).

Grandparents

Grandparents have not received much attention from gerontologists, probably because the concept of grandparent is complex (Troll, 1980). Although the definition of grandparent is fairly simple—a parent's parent—the complexity of the concept can be seen if we examine age. The average age one becomes a grandparent in contemporary American society is 45. Thus many individuals become grandparent in "middle age" and continue as grandparent throughout old age. The role of grandparent for someone who is 45, in the work force, and in good health is probably very different from someone who is 85, retired, and in poor health. Age must also be considered as it relates to grandchildren. We often think of grandchildren as young children, but obviously as grandparents age so do grandchildren. Thus, trying to conceptualize and research a topic that encompasses so many age ranges, for both grandparents and grandchildren, is difficult. The issue becomes even more complex when we examine factors such as social class, ethnicity and race, proximity of grandparents to grandchildren, and paternal and maternal grandparents (see Thomas, 1986).

Although a difficult issue, it is nonetheless an important one since 75 percent of those 65+ years of age have living grandchildren (Brubaker, 1985), and most see at least one grandchild on a weekly basis (Brubaker, 1985; Troll, 1980). Although research is sparse and inconsistent, it has taken two directions. Early research attempted to categorize the grandparent role into types. More recent research has focused on how the disrupted marriages of adult children influence the grandparent role. Both of these will be examined below.

The classic study on grandparent roles was done by Neugarten and Weinstein (1964), who separated the grandparent role into three categories, each of which was further subdivided: ease of role performance, significance of the role, and style of grandparenting.

The ease of role performance dealt with how comfortable older persons were in the role of grandparent. While most were comfortable in the role, about one-third of males and females felt some discomfort in the role. This is not surprising since for many it is a physically and emotionally exhausting role. Many grandparents find some of the life-style selections being made by older grandchildren objectionable. Others find, through the divorces and remarriages of their adult children, that "blood" grandchildren are no longer legally related to them, while the children brought into a new marriage by their adult child's new spouse become instant grandchildren. Great-grandparents have commented on how family characteristics disappear given the greater tendency toward racial and ethnic intermarriages. For example, certain ethnic characteristics often disappear so that the great-grandparents see few family resemblances in their great-grandchildren (see Doka & Mertz, 1988).

Neugarten and Weinstein also asked grandparents about the significance and meaning of the grandparent role. From the responses they developed five subcategories. The first was "biological renewal," in which grandparents saw a continuity of family lines, or felt rejuvenated by their grandchildren. The second was "emotional fulfillment," which allowed grandparents to be successful in a new role; it allowed them to do things for their grandchildren that they did not have the resources or time to do for their own children. Thus, while they may have "failed" as a parent they could now succeed as a grandparent. For a small percentage the role allowed them to either act as a "resource person," which could be providing a grandchild with knowledge, financial aid, or other resources, or to achieve some form of "vicarious achievement" through the grandchild, such as feeling proud over the accomplishments of the grandchildren. The last form was "remote" which means that the role of grandparent had little effect on their lives.

The study also found five styles of grandparenting: formal, fun-seeking, parent surrogate, reservoir of family wisdom, and the distant figure. The formal maintained a regimented role which distinguished between parenting and grandparenting and seldom ventured into the parent role. These grandparents had relatively little contact with their grandchildren. The fun-seekers were more informal and playful; grandchildren were part of leisure activities. The surrogate parent often cared for the grandchildren when the parents were absent or unable to care for the children. The reservoir of family wisdom, expressed by a very small percentage, had the grandparents disseminating special skills and knowledge. It could be that many of the skills or knowledge that grandparents transmit were not considered relevant by grandchildren. It has traditionally been believed that grandmothers had more skills and knowledge to share with granddaughters, such as sewing or cooking, than grandfathers with grandsons; however, with the changing roles of women in contemporary American society this may no longer be true. The last role, the distant figure, had the grandparents emerging only on special occasions, such as a birthday, Christmas, or some other special occasion.

It is doubtful if grandparents play just one of these roles. Rather, the role probably changes as they age and as their grandchildren age. Younger and healthier grandparents are probably more likely to play roles such as fun-seeker or surrogate parent; older grandparents are more likely to have the roles of formal or distant figure. Some grandparents may enact one role with grandchildren in one age category and a different role with grandchildren in another age category; there may also be different roles depending on whether the grandchild is paternal or maternal.

Recent research (Matthews & Sprey, 1984) had grandparents use the above styles to describe their style of grandparenting. Most selected more than one designation, with the most common designation being "fun person." Males selected "source of wisdom" more frequently than females, and those whose adult children had divorced were more likely to select "surrogate parent." This study did not find that age was an important variable in designation. Johnson's (1988) research has supported some of the above findings. She found that most did not want to repeat the parenting role with grandchildren. Rather, they preferred a "fun-loving" type of role. Johnson also reported that the grandparent role was less important than other roles (see Kivnick, 1982).

Relationships with the maternal grandmother appear to be closest followed by the maternal grandfather. The paternal grandmother and paternal grandfather follow. Although it may appear that the paternal grandparents are not favored, it must be remembered that they may be maternal grandparents to another set of grandchildren (Brubaker, 1985; Matthews & Sprey, 1985). Just as the age of grandparents probably has something to do with the grandparent role, the same is true for grandchildren. That is, the age of the grandchild is important in determining the relationship with grandparents. Preschool children are generally looking for grandparents who will indulge, spoil, and provide gifts. Older children are seeking grandparents who are "fun" to be with. Young adults want grandparents who are intelligent, understanding, with good senses of humor and communication skills (Kahana & Kahana, 1970; Robertson, 1976).

More recently a new line of research has emerged in the study of grandparents which has dealt with their role during and after the disrupted marriages of adult children. The majority of this research has focused on marriage disrupted by divorce and most of the research has used grandmothers. Given the rise in the divorce rate in recent years this has had profound consequences on the grandparent role and has led to what has been called a "kinship reorganization" (Johnson & Barer, 1987). Although the figures vary somewhat, it has been estimated that about 60 percent of couples obtaining divorces have minor children who are potential grandchildren (Matthews & Sprey, 1984).

One concern has dealt with the legal rights of grandparents (see Wilson & DeShane, 1982). Often in a divorce process the parents are concerned with their rights with their children, not the right of relatives such as grandparents. Grandparents have often found that they have been unintended losers in custody battles. If a parent gives up or loses custody or visitation rights to a child, then the grandparents on that side of the family would probably also lose those rights. As a result there have been several legal battles where grandparents have sought the right to have contact with their grandchildren. This is an emerging legal area in contemporary American society.

Another area that is emerging in the literature on grandparents is what happens to the grandparent role during or after the divorce of an adult child. One study found that for 40 percent of grandparents the divorce of an adult child came as a "complete surprise" and another 30 percent were somewhat surprised. To an extent this probably indicates that most grandparents are on the outer or peripheral edge of their adult children's marriages (Matthews & Sprey, 1984). As expected, parents experiencing divorce are likely to encounter stress and anxiety. Because of what they are experiencing, parents may neglect to deal with the stress and anxiety the divorce is causing for their children. It has been reported that during this time grandparents often provide emotional support for their grandchildren (Gladstone, 1988).

Interest in the relationship older persons have with former sons-in-law and daughters-in-law has also been expressed. About half retained "friendly" relations. In instances where the divorce had been unpleasant or where spouse abuse had been present, the percentage is lower. It was also reported that relationships with former daughters-in-law were more likely to be maintained than with former sons-in-law (Matthews & Sprey, 1984).

When asked about relationships with their grandchildren, it was found that maternal grandparents were more likely to maintain relationships with their grandchildren (Johnson, 1988; Johnson & Barer, 1987; Matthews & Sprey, 1984). In fact, a divorce may increase the contact between a grandchild and grandparent, especially if the grandparent lives fairly close to the grandchild, the grandchild is young, and the grandchild is in the custody of the grandparent's adult children (Gladstone, 1988). Stepgrandparents do not appear to see or develop strong relationships with their stepgrandchildren. This may be because the relationships are generally established when the grandchildren and grandparents are both older and have other interests (see Sanders & Trygstad, 1989).

When asked about intergenerational involvement it was reported that most grandparents offered assistance to their divorcing adult children in areas such as babysitting, advice, or gifts. It was found that the adult children who had disrupted marriages gave less support to their parents than those with intact marriages (Cicirelli, 1983). One additional area has recently surfaced: great-grandparents (Doka & Mertz, 1988; Wentowski, 1985). Perhaps because of declining health, and geographical and social distance, most of these relationships were characterized as "remote."

Siblings

Studies have reported that between 75 and 90 percent of older persons have living brothers or sisters (see Brubaker, 1985; Cicirelli, 1980; Riley & Foner, 1968). In fact, several studies have indicated that older persons are more likely to have living siblings than any other living relative (see Brubaker, 1985; Cicirelli, 1977). Generally the relationships individuals have with siblings will be the longest of all relationships. Although this is potentially an important area, it is one where research is very limited (Blieszner, 1986; Cicirelli, 1980). About 2 percent of older persons reside with a sibling. Studies on the interaction of aged siblings are scarce; most have indicated that it generally goes down with increasing age. It has been found that upon the death of a spouse, older persons often resume contact and interaction with siblings. It appears that the sister-sister attachment is stronger and more prevalent than the brother-sister or brother-brother attachment (Brubaker, 1985; Troll, 1971).

Alternative Forms of the Family

Just as many of the young have selected alternative life-styles, so have many older persons. One example, in Florida, is an association called ''share-a-home'' which is designed to provide older persons with an alternative family environment. Essentially, the share-a-home organization purchases larger homes and approximately twenty older persons live in each home. The homes are under professional management (see Streib, 1978; Streib & Streib, 1975). The share-a-home concept of communal living has the potential of being an important innovative family and living option for older persons. Currently, many older persons have few options available to them in terms of living environments. Many do not want to live independently, with their adult children, or in a nursing home. Because the participants pool their money, labor, resources, abilities, and knowledge, the share-a-home concept allows them to live more autonomous lives at a much higher standard of living than if they were living independently. Also, by living in a ''family-type'' setting there is a much greater opportunity of developing strong relationships with others (see Kellogg & Jaffe, 1977).

It has also been suggested that some unmet personal needs of older persons may be met through nonmarital cohabitation (see Cavan, 1973). Some sociologists have speculated that through group marriage, communal living, homosexual relationships, or extramarital relationships many of the unmet needs outside or within marriage could be met. Some of the needs that could be satisfied would be of a sexual nature, and some would be in the form of companionship. Conventional society does not offer many older persons realistic alternatives to their unmet needs. Cavan (1973) has noted that alternative life styles are more acceptable for younger than older persons; over time societal attitudes may change and create a more liberal and accepting atmosphere for older persons in terms of alternative family forms.

Elder Abuse

Elder abuse is a new and emerging topic in gerontology. While child abuse and spouse abuse emerged in the 1960s and early 1970s as major issues, elder abuse did not emerge until the mid-1970s with English articles on ''granny bashing'' (Illing, 1977; Walsh-Brennan, 1977). In fact, it was not until 1984 that elder abuse appeared as a heading in the computer database MEDLINE (Mowbray, 1989). While the amount of research in this area has increased, the research results have been inconsistent largely because of the variations in the definition of elder abuse, the variety or research methods used, and the nonrandom samples (see Bookin & Dunkle, 1985; Callahan, 1988; Floyd, 1984; Galbraith & Zdorkowski, 1984; Gold & Gwyther, 1989; Hamilton, 1989; Kosberg, 1988; Pillemer & Finkelhor, 1988).

The percentage of older persons being abused ranges from 4 percent to about 10 percent (Callahan, 1988; Council on Scientific Affairs, 1987; Crystal, 1987; Hudson & Johnson, 1986; Powell & Berg, 1987). As noted above, part of the variation is because researchers have used different definitions of elder abuse. A definition that includes only abuse will generally yield a lower percentage than a broader definition that includes both abuse and neglect. Also, factors such as the frequency and intensity of the abusive behavior will determine the percentages. For example, one angry verbal outburst of a temporarily stressed and tired caregiver 9 months earlier may constitute abuse in one study while it would not in a different study. The sample can also make a difference. The majority of the samples are nonrandom, and depending on the characteristics of those studied, the results can vary tremendously. Also, the differences are caused by the research techniques used, with some being based on self-report and others on medical examinations.

Even if there is a "good" working definition of elder abuse, it is frequently difficult to document. In fact, Kosberg (1988) has estimated that only one case in six is reported. The perpetrator will generally deny the abuse and the abused individual may be too ashamed, afraid, or embarrassed to admit being abused. Also, abused individuals may believe that occasional abuse is less harmful than the consequences of reporting the abuse, which might involve being taken from their homes and placed into nursing homes. There are also some abused individuals who believe that they "deserve" to be abused because of the problems they are causing caregivers. Isolation is another reason abuse is often underreported; older persons are often isolated from "mainstream" society and as a result abuse can go undetected. Additionally, many older individuals do not know how or where to report the abuse. One other reason elder abuse is underreported is that many professionals do not report suspected cases of abuse for two reasons. First, many of those who work with older persons are not aware of the existence of elder abuse. Thus, they do not look for signs or symptoms of elder abuse. Second, many are not aware of laws requiring that elder abuse be reported (see Daniels et al., 1989).

One study of physicians in states that had mandatory laws for reporting suspected elder abuse [37 states require that elder abuse and neglect be reported to the proper authorities (Quinn, 1987)] found that 71 percent of physicians were not aware that they had to file a report and 12 percent claimed that no report was necessary (Crystal, 1987). While some professionals are unaware of the laws, others do not report the abuse because they believe that there is no one to enforce the law. That is, although many states created laws they did not create the funding to enforce the laws. Thus, overburdened social services personnel do not have the time to investigate the reports (Callahan, 1988).

As noted earlier, the definition of elder abuse has varied according to the research and has been a subject of controversy (see Kosberg, 1988). The difficulty in arriving at one definition was seen recently at a conference on elder abuse where a panel of experts was unable to develop a working definition of elder abuse (see Pillemer & Finkelhor, 1988). The Council on Scientific Affairs of the American Medical Association (1987) summarized several studies and developed a classification system of elder abuse: abuse, exploitation, neglect, self-neglect, violation of rights, and medical. The council noted that there can be three types of abuse (physical, psychological, and sexual), two types of exploitation (financial and material), and two types of neglect (active and passive). The three types of abuse (i.e., physical, psychological, and sexual) are self-explanatory. Some studies consider sexual abuse to be a form of physical abuse; psychological abuse is frequently called "verbal or emotional abuse." Financial exploitation is the theft or misuse of an older person's money, and can involve coercing or forcing the older person to sign over social security or pension checks. Material exploitation would be the theft or misuse of an older person's possessions and assets. This can include selling an older person's belongings (see Weiler, 1989).

Neglect can be active or passive. In active neglect something is done purposely to harm the older person; the action is malevolent. In passive neglect (sometimes called benign neglect) caregivers are not aware that they are harming the older person; neglect in this case is often a result of caregiver ignorance. Self-neglect, which if used in the definition is the most widely reported form of elder abuse, has been included in some studies as an example of abuse although this is an area of controversy. If individuals are competent to make decisions, then even though they may be neglecting themselves, in areas such as health, they have the right to exercise this option (Salend et al., 1984). Some studies have used active and passive as the two major categories of abuse and neglect with physical, psychological, and exploitation as subcategories. For example, active physical abuse or neglect would occur as the result of an intentional act on the part of a caregiver; passive physical abuse or neglect would occur unintentionally.

The violation of personal rights has also been considered in some definitions. Examples would be withholding or denying certain rights such as the right to vote, participate in religious services, see or talk to friends, or even open their mail (Quinn, 1987). Medical abuse is defined as not meeting the medical needs of older persons, such as not providing medications or medical aids such as a wheelchair, hearing aid, cane, or false teeth (see Fulmer & Cahill, 1984).

One question that is being asked is who are the abused elderly? In other words, do these individuals have certain salient characteristics that would make them readily identifiable to those working with older persons, and that would make the creation of social policy and the formation of protective services easier. This is an area where the recent research results have changed and have challenged traditional thinking in gerontology (Pillemer & Finkelhor, 1988). The first area of challenge deals with those who are abused. Traditionally the abused older person was thought of as being an older, frail, minority female, who was dependent on the caregiver, who was usually an adult child. We now know that no category of older persons are immune from abuse. Elder abuse is prevalent in both sexes, and in all races, religions, and social classes.

A second area that is being challenged deals with the abuser. Many studies reported the popular belief that elder abuse is perpetuated primarily by the adult children of older persons. In terms of absolute numbers, more older persons are abused by their spouses than by their adult children. This is because those being abused are most likely to be abused by those living in the same household. More older persons live with spouses than with adult children. When we consider the rate of abuse, it is about equal for those who live with their spouses versus those who live with their adult children.

A third area where the recent literature is challenging the past literature deals with the sex of those being abused. Most research has reported that those being abused were female. Recent research indicated almost equal numbers of males and females being abused, which, because of the sex ratio, means that the actual rate of abuse is higher for males than for females. Although the abuse rate for males is higher, the abuse of males appears to be less serious. The higher abuse rate for males exists because males are more likely to be living with someone, and those living with someone have higher rates of abuse than those living alone. What has emerged from the recent literature is a very different picture of the abused older person. Old age, frail health, and minority status have not been found to be associated with abuse. Males have been found to have a higher rate than females, as have those living with someone.

A fourth area that is being challenged deals with the cause of elder abuse. There certainly is not one cause of elder abuse; it is multicausal. This is perhaps evident by the fact that many older persons are abused by more than one individual (Kosberg, 1988). Traditionally gerontologists have believed that older persons, because of their increasing dependency, have placed increasing demands on caregivers which have created caregiver stress resulting ultimately in the abuse of the older person. Changes in health care financing, which often means early discharge from hospitals, increased caregiver responsibility and stress have also been blamed. The increasing percentage of women, traditionally the caregivers, in the work force, and the demands this places on them have also been mentioned. Frequently gerontologists made mention of the "sandwich generation"—those individuals who were being called on for assistance from their parents and children. They are sandwiched between two generations that need their assistance.

Although the above "sounded good" in gerontological theory, and certainly some abuse is caused by caregiver stress, recent research has indicated that the reverse may be true. That is, the abuser is dependent on the person being abused. Abused older persons stay in the relationship for a variety of reasons: family obligation, fear of losing contact with grandchildren (Pillemer, 1985).

There are certainly other factors causing elder abuse. One would be a history of family violence. As noted earlier, in some families a history of spousal abuse becomes elder abuse. Nothing has changed other than a new law that defines the same abusive behavior in a different way. It has also been reported that abused children have a greater propensity to become abusive caregivers. Mental health problems of abusers have also been frequently cited. Alcoholism is another source of elder abuse in two ways. First, the alcoholism of the abuser may make them less rational and more violent, and second, the alcoholism of the victims may make them easier to victimize.

The question is what to do about elder abuse. At one level, many states have now created laws concerning elder abuse. The early formulations of these laws had numerous problems such as vague definitions and few resources to ensure enforcement (Salend et al., 1984). In fact, as a result of the lack of resources the laws have been called "symbolic" (Daniels et al., 1989). At a different level are those who actually work with older persons and have the greatest probability of identifying and correcting abuse (see Council on Scientific Affairs, 1987; Fulmer & Cahill, 1984).

Two approaches have been taken to deal with elder abuse. The first is to try and prevent it from occurring, the second is to prevent it from recurring. Gold and Gwyther (1989) have presented an educational program designed to prevent elder abuse. The program is designed to teach individuals, of all ages, about different sources of family conflict and stress and then teach them nonviolent and acceptable methods of dealing with the conflict and stress. The model can be presented in a number of ways, such as part of a church program, in a senior center, or to a fraternal organization (see Powell & Berg, 1987). Hamilton (1989) has designed and developed an instrument that will evaluate the "risk of elder abuse in the home." Ideally, intervention can take place before the abuse actually begins.

One example of an organizational response to elder abuse laws is Beth Israel Hospital (1986) which developed a twelve-member multidisciplinary Elder Assessment Team to deal with suspected cases of elder abuse and neglect. The team initially encouraged staff to "over report" suspected cases in an attempt to sensitize the staff to elder abuse. Once a patient is referred to the team, there is a process for determining if abuse exists. If abuse is suspected, a formal report is made to the appropriate agency. It was noted that even if abuse was not suspected, there were often some positive outcomes of the investigation. One outcome was that as a result of the investigation the team was often able to make suggestions that improved the care of the older person. While there were positive outcomes there were also some negative outcomes. The cognitive impairments of some older persons made them imagine abuse or neglect and the caregivers were often angry at the subsequent investigation. As a result of being accused, some caregivers either refused or were hesitant to provide further care.

FRIENDS

We have seen that the family can be very important in the lives of older persons. Between older persons and their spouses, children, grandchildren, and siblings there is a great deal of interaction and reciprocal assistance. However, the family members of many older persons are not present, or are not capable or willing to provide assistance, services, or companionship. Therefore, older persons seek to supplement or replace family interaction with the interaction of friends. Although an important area, until recently the study of friendships in old age has been a neglected area of research (Adams, 1989; Adams & Blieszner, 1989).

Although the relationship with the family is generally considered to be the most intensive and important one in the lives of older persons, this assumption has been challenged. Petrowsky (1976) found that high morale was associated more with having friends and neighbors than with having a considerable amount of interaction with adult children. He cited two reasons for this finding. First, it was hypothesized that because of the differences between older persons and their adult children in regard to values, hobbies, life-styles, interests, attitudes, and beliefs, the two age groups often do not make good companions or friends and the relationships are characterized by a "dissimilarity of experiences" and interests. Other than their family ties, older persons have relatively little in common with them. Thus, Petrowsky (1976) found that although family ties are unquestionably important in the lives of older persons, the interactions with friends and neighbors may be more important because of similarity of experiences and interests.

The second reason Petrowsky (1976) claimed that friends and neighbors are more important than adult children was that there is often an unequal exchange of goods and services between older persons and their adult children. As we have seen, with increasing age a role reversal often takes place in which older persons become dependent on their adult children for several types of assistance. Petrowsky claimed that older persons were generally unable to reciprocate in providing assistance to their adult children and that this inability brought about lowered morale (see Roberto & Scott, 1986).

The research reviewed above makes a strong case that friendship may in many ways be more important for older persons than family interactions. Friends have common interests, values, opinions, and life-styles. In her excellent book *The Unexpected Community,* Hochschild (1973) pointed out that the women she studied were very similar in many ways. For example, while riding on a bus they would all be aware of similar items or places, such as a minister's home, a church, a beauty shop, a nursing home, or a funeral parlor. In social interaction these women not only understood what the others were talking about but also generally enjoyed and participated in the conversations. Because they had lived through similar experiences and were currently facing similar situations such as widowhood, declining health, and financial difficulties, the women felt a special bond toward each other that the author called a "sibling bond." Their similarities made interaction more comfortable and less stressful or strained. Moreover, Hochschild noted that the women she studied exchanged similar items and services. For example, a loaf of bread might be exchanged for a jar of strawberry jam. Both of the women involved in the exchange had the ability to make both jam and bread and so the exchange was equal and reciprocal. Petrowsky (1976) found that older persons did not simply want to take from a relationship but also wanted to be able to give; this was easier to achieve with friends and neighbors than with family (Goodman, 1984; Ingersoll-Dayton & Antonucci, 1988).

The study by Petrowsky (1976) also found that having a neighbor or a friend in whom they could confide was more important to morale than having a family member nearby. Older persons who had someone to confide in were less likely to feel lonely and were more likely to feel useful. Frequency of interaction with friends and neighbors was not important in morale. The study found that it was not interaction in and of itself that was important for morale, but rather the knowledge that a friend or neighbor was close by and could be called on if needed (see O'Bryant, 1985).

Not all studies have been as positive, showing friendship patterns and informal sources of support. Sheehan (1986) examined informal support among older persons living in public housing and found that while it existed, it was not as extensive as previously believed, especially for the frail. This lack of assistance may have existed because both the frail and nonfrail pulled away from each other. The frail considered assistance a threat to their independence and integrity; the nonfrail recognized that they had limited strength and resources, and also that it would be more beneficial to form relationships with others who would be more capable of providing them with assistance if or when it was needed.

It appears that there are differences by gender in the frequency of interaction and in the intensity of friendships. Basically, males have many friends, but few intimate friends. Females have fewer friends than males, but more intimate friends (Powers & Bultena, 1976). In part, these differences may be explained by early socialization patterns and role expectations. In our society men are generally not expected to be emotional or to share their intimate problems with those outside the family. Thus, when males engage in social interaction with friends it is generally less affective, emotional, or intense than when women engage in social interaction. Women, however, are allowed and encouraged to express affective, emotional behavior. Part of the "feminine role" has "traditionally" included expressive behavior. With these options, the types of relationships that women develop with friends are often more intimate and expressive than those of men. In these types of relationships women can discuss more openly and freely some of the problems that they have. The research indicates that these patterns exist through later life periods. Since in contemporary American society wives can expect their husbands to die before them, they generally must have other intimate ties to help buffer the loss. Men, however, tend to rely more on their wives for an intimate relationship. The wife's death may leave the husband without anyone to turn to or confide in and may thus create great social disruption in his life (see Powers & Bultena, 1976).

Studies have also been conducted on the male friends of nonmarried aged females (Adams, 1985). Basically, older females seldom have male friends. In part this is because there are so few older males. However, friendships were also discouraged by their adult children and female friends. The friendships were discouraged in part because they were seen as "romantic," which was deemed inappropriate both by adult children and female friends.

SUMMARY

There are two groups that can have tremendous significance on individuals' lives: family and friends. Each of these was discussed in this chapter.

The section on the family is separated into several subsections. In the first section some definitions were provided. The second section discussed the family life cycle. Starting with a newly married couple the family progresses through eight stages: newly married (establishment of family), new parents, preschool family, school-age family, family with teenagers, family with young adults, family as launching center, and postparental family. This is an ideal type and there are many variations.

Married older persons were examined in the next subsection. Here it was reported that while most older men are married, most older women are not married (about 50 percent are widowed). Although studies have presented very different results, it is believed that marital satisfaction often declines shortly after marriage with the birth of the first child, and then remains down until the postparental years. It is believed that the stress associated with making a living, childrearing, and caring for aged parents lower marital satisfaction.

Although it had been assumed that the empty nest was a traumatic time for both aged mothers and fathers, research has not found this to be true. Research has also found that married older persons appear to be in better mental and physical health than their nonmarried counterparts. Thus, it has been assumed that marriage is beneficial to older persons.

Widowed older persons were examined in the next subsection. Widowhood primarily affects older women, not men. As with many other areas it is believed that there are stages to widowhood: mourning, accepting the death, experiencing the pain of grief, adjusting, forming new relationships. A variety of factors have been investigated as impacting on adjustment to widowhood: social class, age, the nature of the death, and social support. The results of these investigations are inconclusive.

In the next subsection divorce was examined. This is a neglected area in gerontology, probably in part because so few older persons are divorced. Some of the reasons for the low divorce rate among older persons are that couples that survive have worked out ways of dealing with their problems or were raised with the concept that divorce is unacceptable. Many realize that the opportunity for remarriage is limited and some considering divorce are anxious about factors such as dating. Also, with increasing age, marital satisfaction may start to increase. Since many nonmarried older persons want to remarry, it is not realistic for most, especially females. There is a large pool of eligible females for males, but only a small pool of eligible males for females. It appears that divorced older persons are more likely to remarry than the widowed. Remarriages are generally successful. The next subsection examined the never-married, which constitutes about 5 percent of older persons. Early gerontological writing assumed that the never-married aged were isolates; recent research has not confirmed this belief.

Older persons and their adult children were examined next. Here it was noted that the family type that exists in contemporary American society is the "modified extended family," where nuclear families maintain close emotional ties and high levels of involvement but live in separate households. This has been termed "intimacy at a distance." Older persons have a tremendous amount of contact with their adult children, with 41 percent seeing at least one child daily, and another 20 percent seeing a child weekly. Most older persons live within 1 hour of an adult child. There is a tremendous amount of intergenerational exchange and assistance. One area that was considered in this subsection was caregiving. It was noted that most adult children will be faced with having to provide care for their parents. This is a controversial issue, with debates over whose responsibility is it to provide care. Caregiving can be a very stressful experience and the terms "caregiver burden," or "caregiver stress" have been coined by gerontologists to describe what they have found.

The next subsection discussed grandparents. Here it was noted that most older persons are grandparents. There are many different roles that grandparents can play—from formal to fun-seeking. The role assumed probably depends on several factors such as age and relationship to grandchild. A new area of research deals with the impact of the divorce of adult children on the grandparents.

The research on siblings was discussed next. Most older persons have at least one living sibling. These relationships often increase in importance with increasing age. Discussed next were alternative forms of the family.

The last subsection to be discussed was elder abuse. This is an emerging area, and as such there are controversies over definitions and research results. Recent research is challenging older beliefs in this area. Early research assumed that the person most likely to be abused was an older, frail, minority female who was being abused by an adult child upon whom she was dependent. Current research has reported that males who are being abused by a spouse appears to be the norm.

The second section discussed friends. Although the family is unquestionably important in the lives of older persons so are friends. In fact, friends often share a common history as well as interests. Some studies have found friends to be more important in the lives of older persons than family.

REFERENCES

Adams, R. G. (1985). People would talk: Normative barriers to cross-sex friendships for elderly women. *The Gerontologist, 25*(6): 605–611.

Adams, R. G. (1989). Conceptual and methodological issues in studying friendships of older adults. In R. G. Adams & R. Blieszner (Eds.), *Older adult friendship: Structure and process* (pp. 18–44). Newbury Park, CA: Sage.

Adams, R. G., & Blieszner, R. (1989). Preface. In R. G. Adams & R. Blieszner (Eds.) *Older adult friendship: Structure and process* (pp. 12–16). Newbury Park, CA: Sage.

Anderson, S. A., Russell, C. S., & Schumm, W. R. (1983). Perceived marital quality and family life-cycle categories: A further analysis. *Journal of Marriage and the Family, 45*(2): 127–139.

Axelson, L. J. (1960). Personal adjustment in the postparental period. *Marriage and Family Living, 22*(February): 66–68.

Barusch, A. S. (1988). Problems and coping strategies of elderly spouse caregivers. *The Gerontologist, 28*(5): 677–685.

Beth Israel Hospital Elder Assessment Team (1986). An elder abuse assessment team in an acute hospital setting. *The Gerontologist, 26*(2): 115–118.

Blieszner, R. (1986). Trends in family gerontology research. *Family Relations, 35*(4): 555–562.

Blood, R. O., & Wolfe, D. M. (1960). *Husbands and wives: The dynamics of married living.* Glencoe, IL: Free Press.

Bookin, D., & Dunkle, R. E. (1985). Elder abuse: Issues for the practitioner. *Social Casework, 66*(1): 3–12.

Borgatta, E. F. (1987). Filial responsibility. In G. L. Maddox (Ed.), *The encyclopedia of aging* (p. 256). New York: Springer.

Brody, E. M. (1978). The aging family. *Annals of the American Academy of Political and Social Science, 438*(July): 13–27.

Brody, E. M. (1985). Parent care as a normative family stress. *The Gerontologist, 25*(1): 19–29.

Brody, E. M., & Schoonover, C. B. (1986). Patterns of parent care when adult daughters work and when they do not. *The Gerontologist, 26*(4): 372–381.

Brubaker, T. H. (1985). *Later life families.* Beverly Hills: Sage.

Bulcroft, K., Bulcroft, R., Hatch, L., & Borgatta, E. F. (1989). Antecedents and consequences of remarriage in later life. *Research on Aging, 11*(1): 82–106.

Bulcroft, K., & O'Connor, M. (1986). The importance of dating relationships on quality of life for older persons. *Family Relations, 35*(3): 397–401.

Burr, W. R. (1970). Satisfaction with various aspects of marriage over the life-cycle. *Journal of Marriage and the Family, 26*(1): 29–37.

Callahan, J. J. (1988). Elder abuse: Some questions for policymakers. *The Gerontologist, 28*(4): 453–458.

Cavan, R. S. (1973). Speculations on innovations to conventional marriage in old age. *The Gerontologist,* **13**(4): 409–411.

Cicirelli, V. G. (1977). Relationship of siblings to the elderly person's feelings and concerns. *Journal of Gerontology,* **32**(3): 317–322.

Cicirelli, V. G. (1980). Sibling relationships in adulthood. In L. W. Poon (Ed.), *Aging in the 1980s* (pp. 455–462). Washington, DC: American Psychological Association.

Cicirelli, V. G. (1983). A comparison of helping behavior to elderly parents of adult children with intact and disrupted marriages. *The Gerontologist,* **23**(6): 619–625.

Cicirelli, V. G. (1988). A measure of filial anxiety regarding anticipated care of elderly parents. *The Gerontologist,* **28**(4): 478–482.

Clausen, J. A. (1972). The life course of individuals. In M. W. Riley, M. Johnson, & A. Foner (Eds.), *Aging and society, Volume three: A sociology of age stratification* (pp. 457–514). New York: Russell Sage Foundation.

Cooney, T. M. (1989). Co-residence with adult children: A comparison of divorced and widowed women. *The Gerontologist,* **29**(6): 779–784.

Council on Scientific Affairs (1987). Elder abuse and neglect. *Journal of the American Medical Association,* **257**(7): 966–971.

Creedon, M. A. (1988). The corporate response to the working caregiver. *Aging,* **358**: 16–19, 45.

Crystal, S. (1987). Elder abuse: The latest crisis. *Public Interest,* **88**(Summer): 56–66.

Daniels, R. S., Baumhover, L. A., & Clark-Daniels, C. L. (1989). Physician's mandatory reporting of elder abuse. *The Gerontologist,* **29**(3): 321–327.

DeSpelder L. A., & Strickland, A. L. (1987). *The last dance: Encountering death and dying* (second edition). Palo Alto, CA: Mayfield.

Deutscher, I. (1964). The quality of postparental life. *Journal of Marriage and the Family,* **26**(1): 52–59.

Dewit, D. J., Wister, A. V., Burch, T. K. (1988). Physical distance and social contact between elders and their adult children. *Research on Aging,* **10**(1): 56–80.

Dizard, J. (1968). *Social change in the family.* Chicago: University of Chicago Press.

Doka, K. J., & Mertz, M. E. (1988). The meaning and significance of great-grandparenthood. *The Gerontologist,* **28**(2): 192–197.

Dressel, P. L., & Avant, W. R. (1978). Aging and college family textbooks. *Family Coordinator,* **24**(4): 427–435.

Dusell, C., & Roman, M. (1989). The elder-care dilemma. *Generations,* **13**(3): 30–32.

Duvall, E. M. (1977). *Marriage and family development* (fifth edition). Philadelphia: Lippincott.

Espino, D. V., Neufeld, R. R., Mulvihill, M., & Libow, L. S. (1988). Hispanic and non-Hispanic elderly on admission to the nursing home. *The Gerontologist,* **28**(6): 821–824.

Finley, N. J., Roberts, M. D., & Banahan, B. F. (1988). Motivators and inhibitors of attitudes of filial obligation toward aging parents. *The Gerontologist,* **28**(1): 73–78.

Fischer, L. R., & Eustis, N. N. (1988). DRGs and family care for the elderly: A case study. *The Gerontologist,* **28**(3): 383–389.

Floyd, J. (1984). Collecting data on abuse of the elderly. *Journal of Gerontological Nursing,* **10**(12): 11–15.

Fulmer, T. T., & Cahill, V. M. (1984). Assessing elder abuse: A study. *Journal of Gerontological Nursing,* **10**(12): 16–20.

Galbraith, M. W., & Zdorkowski, T. (1984). Teaching the investigation of elder abuse. *Journal of Gerontological Nursing,* **10**(12): 21–25.

Gilliland, N. (1986). Mandating family responsibility for elderly members: Costs and benefits. *Journal of Applied Gerontology,* **5**(1): 26–36.

Giordano, J. A. (1988). Parents of the baby boomers: A new generation of young-old. *Family Relations,* **37**(4): 411–414.

Gladstone, J. W. (1988). Perceived changes in grandmother-grandchild relations following a child's separation or divorce. *The Gerontologist,* **28**(1): 66–72.

Glenn, N. (1975). Psychological well-being in the postparental stage: Some evidence from national surveys. *Journal of Marriage and the Family,* **37**(1): 105–110.

Glick, P. C. (1989). The family life cycle and social change. *Family Relations,* **38**(2): 123–129.

Gold, D. T., & Gwyther, L. P. (1989). The prevention of elder abuse: An educational model. *Family Relations,* **38**(1): 8–14.

Goodman, C. C. (1984). Natural helping among older adults. *The Gerontologist,* **24**(2): 138–143.

Gove, W. R. (1973). Sex, marital status, and mortality. *American Journal of Sociology,* **79**(1): 45–67.

Greenberg, J. S., & Becker, M. (1988). Aging parents as family resources. *The Gerontologist,* **28**(6): 786–791.

Gubrium, J. (1974). Being single in old age. *Aging and Human Development,* **6**(1): 29–41.

Hagestad, G. (1987). Family. In G. L. Maddox (Ed.), *The encyclopedia of aging* (pp. 247–249). New York: Springer.

Hamilton, G. P. (1989). Prevent elder abuse: using a family systems approach. *Journal of Gerontological Nursing,* **15**(3): 21–26.

Harkins, E. B. (1978). Effects of empty nest transition on self-report of psychological and physical well-being. *Journal of Marriage and the Family,* **40**(3): 544–555.

Hasselkus, B. R. (1988). Meaning in family caregiving: Perspectives on caregiver/professional relationships. *The Gerontologist,* **28**(5):686–691.

Hays, J. A. (1984). Aging and family resources: Availability and proximity of kin. *The Gerontologist,* **24**(2): 149–153.

Hess, B. B., & Waring, J. M. (1978). Changing patterns of aging and family bonds in later life. *Family Coordinator,* **27**(4): 303–314.

Hochschild, A. R. (1973). *The unexpected community.* Englewood Cliffs, NJ: Prentice-Hall.

Hudson, M. F., & Johnson, T. F. (1986). Elder neglect and abuse: A review of the literature. In C. Eisdorfer (Ed.), *Annual review of gerontology and geriatrics: Volume Six* (pp. 81–134). New York: Springer.

Illing, M. (1977). Comment . . . on how we can identify those at risk. *Nursing Mirror,* **145**(25): 34–36.

Ingersoll-Dayton, B., & Antonucci, T. C. (1988). Reciprocal and nonreciprocal social support: Contrasting sides of intimate relationships. *Journal of Gerontology: Social Sciences,* **43**(3): 565–573.

Jarrett, W. H. (1985). Caregiving within kinship systems: Is affection really necessary. *The Gerontologist,* **25**(1): 5–10.

Jennings, J. (1987). Elderly parents as caregivers for their adult dependent children. *Social Work,* **32**(5): 430–433.

Johnson, C. L. (1988). Active and latent functions of grandparenting during the divorce process. *The Gerontologist,* **28**(2): 185–191.

Johnson, C. L., & Barer, B. M. (1987). Marital instability and the changing kinship networks of grandparents. *The Gerontologist,* **27**(3): 330–335.

Johnson, E. S., & Bursk, B. J. (1977). Relationships between the elderly and their adult children. *The Gerontologist,* **17**(1): 90–96.

Kahana, B., & Kahana, E. (1970). Grandparenthood from the perspective of the developing grandchild. *Developmental Psychology,* **3**(1): 98–105.

Kaplan, J. (1975). The family in aging. *The Gerontologist,* **15**(5; Part 1): 385.

Keith, P. M. (1986). Isolation of the unmarried in later life. *Family Relations,* **35**(3): 389–395.

Keith, P. M., Hill, K., Goudy, W. J., & Powers, E. A. (1984). Confidants and well-being: A note on male friendship in old age. *The Gerontologist,* **24**(3): 318–320.

Keith, P. M., & Nauta, A. (1988). Old and single in the city and in the country: Activities of the unmarried. *Family Relations,* **37**(1): 79–83.

Kellogg, M. A., & Jaffe, A. (1977). Old folks' commune. In S. H. Zarit (Ed.), *Readings in aging and death: Contemporary perspectives* (p. 247). New York: Harper and Row.

Kiefer, C. W., Kim, S., Choi, K., Kim, L., Kim, B-L., Shon, S., & Kim, T. (1985). Adjustment problems of Korean American elderly. *The Gerontologist,* **25**(5): 477–482.

Kivnick, H. Q. (1982). Grandparenthood: An overview of meaning and mental health. *The Gerontologist,* **22**(1): 59–66.

Kleban, M. H., Brody, E. M., Schoonover, C. B., & Hoffman, C. (1989). Family help to the elderly: Perceptions of sons-in-law regarding parent care. *Journal of Marriage and the Family,* **51**(2): 303–312.

Komarovsky, M. (1964). *Blue-collar marriages.* New York: Random House.

Kosberg, J. I. (1988). Preventing elder abuse: Identification of high risk factors prior to placement decisions. *The Gerontologist,* **28**(1): 43–50.

Krauskopf, J. M., & Burnett, M. E. (1989). When protection becomes abuse. In H. Cox (Ed.), *Aging* (sixth edition) (pp. 188–194). Guilford, CT: Dushkin.

Krout, J. A. (1988). Rural versus urban differences in elderly parents' contact with their children. *The Gerontologist,* **28**(2): 198–203.

Lammers, W. W., & Klingman, D. (1986). Family responsibility laws and state politics: Empirical patterns and policy implications. *Journal of Applied Gerontology,* **5**(1): 5–25.

Lang, A. M., & Brody, E. M. (1983). Characteristics of middle-aged daughters and help to their elderly mothers. *Journal of Marriage and the Family,* **45**(1): 193–202.

Liu, W. T. (1986). Health services for Asian elderly. *Research on Aging,* **8**(1): 156–175.

Mancini, J. A., & Blieszner, R. (1989). Aging parents and adult children: Research themes in intergenerational relations. *Journal of Marriage and the Family,* **51**(2): 275–290.

Markides, K. S. (1987). Marital satisfaction. In G. L. Maddox (Ed.), *The encyclopedia of aging* (pp. 420–421). New York: Springer.

Matthews, S. H. (1987). Provision of care to old parents. *Research on Aging,* **9**(1): 45–60.

Matthews, S. H., & Sprey, J. (1984). The impact of divorce on grandparenthood: An exploratory study. *The Gerontologist,* **24**(1): 41–47.

Matthews, S. H., & Sprey, J. (1985). Adolescents' relationships with grandparents: An empirical contribution to conceptual clarification. *Journal of Gerontology,* **40**(5): 621–626.

Matthews, S. H., Werkner, J. E., & Delaney, P. J. (1989). Relative contributions of help by employed and nonemployed sisters to their elderly parents. *Journal of Gerontology: Social Sciences,* **44**(1): S36–44.

Mercier, J. M., Paulson, L., & Morris, E. W. (1989). Proximity as a mediating influence on the perceived aging parent-adult child relationship. *The Gerontologist,* **29**(6): 785–791.

Mitchell, J., & Register, J. C. (1984). An exploration of family interaction with the elderly by race, socioeconomic status, and residence. *The Gerontologist,* **24**(1): 48–54.

Montgomery, R. J. V. (1987). Marriage. In G. L. Maddox (Ed.), *The encyclopedia of aging* (pp. 421–423). New York: Springer.

Morgan, L. A. (1976). A reexamination of widowhood and morale. *Journal of Gerontology*, **31**(6): 687–695.

Mowbray, C. A. (1989). Shedding light on elder abuse. *Journal of Gerontological Nursing*, **15**(10): 20–24.

National Center for Health Statistics (1985). Teenage marriages and divorces. *Vital and Health Statistics*, Series 21, No. 43.

National Center for Health Statistics (1989). Remarriages and subsequent divorces. *Vital and Health Statistics*, Series 21, No. 45.

Neugarten, B. L., & Weinstein, K. K. (1964). The changing American grandparent. *Journal of Marriage and the Family*, **26**(2): 199–204.

Noelker, L. S., & Bass, D. M. (1989). Home care for elderly persons: Linkages between formal and informal caregivers. *Journal of Gerontology: Social Sciences*, **44**(2): S63–70, 1989.

O'Bryant, S. L. (1985). Neighbors' support of older widows who live alone in their own homes. *The Gerontologist*, **25**(3): 305–310.

Osako, M. M., & Liu, W. T. (1986). Intergenerational relations and the aged among Japanese Americans. *Research on Aging*, **8**(1): 128–155.

Osterkamp, L. (1988). Family caregivers. *Aging*, **358**: 3–5.

Paris, B. L., & Luckey, E. B. (1966). A longitudinal study in marital satisfaction. *Sociology and Social Research*, **50**(January): 212–223.

Pearson, J., Verma, S., & Nellett, C. (1988). Elderly psychiatric patient status and caregiver perceptions as predictors of caregiver burden. *The Gerontologist*, **28**(1): 79–83.

Petrowsky, M. (1976). Marital status, sex, and the social networks of the elderly. *Journal of Marriage and the Family*, **38**(4): 749–756.

Pillemer, K. (1985). The dangers of dependency: New findings on domestic violence against the elderly. *Social Problems* **33**(2): 146–158.

Pillemer, K., & Finkelhor, D. (1988). The prevalence of elder abuse: A random sample survey. *The Gerontologist*, **28**(1): 51–57.

Pineo, P. (1961). Disenchantment in the later years of marriage. *Marriage and Family Living*, **23**(1): 3–11.

Powell, S., & Berg, R. C. (1987). When the elderly are abused: Characteristics and interventions. *Educational Gerontology*, **13**(1): 71–83.

Powers, E. A., & Bultena, G. L. (1976). Sex differences in intimate friendships of old age. *Journal of Marriage and the Family*, **38**(4): 739–747.

Pratt, C. C., Jones, L. L., Shin, H-Y., & Walker, A. J. (1989). Autonomy and decision making between single older women and their caregiving daughters. *The Gerontologist*, **29**(6): 792–797.

Pratt, C. C., & Kethley, A. J. (1988). Aging and family caregiving in the future: Implications for education and policy. *Educational Gerontology*, **14**(6): 567–576.

Quinn, M. J. (1987). Elder abuse and neglect. In G. L. Maddox (Ed.), *The encyclopedia of aging* (pp. 202–204). New York: Springer.

Rempel, J. (1985). Childless elderly: What are they missing? *Journal of Marriage and the Family*, **47**(2): 343–348.

Riley, M. W., & Foner, A. (1968). *Aging and society, Volume One: An inventory of research findings*. New York: Russell Sage Foundation.

Roberto, K. A., & Scott, J. P. (1986). Equity considerations in the friendships of older adults. *Journal of Gerontology*, **41**(2): 241–247.

Robertson, J. (1976). Significance of grandparents: Perceptions of young adult children. *The Gerontologist*, **16**(2): 137–282.

Rollins, B. C., & Cannon, K. L. (1974). Marital satisfaction over the family life cycle: A reevaluation. *Journal of Marriage and the Family,* **36**(3): 271–282.

Rollins, B. C., & Feldman, H. (1970). Marital satisfaction over the family life cycle. *Journal of Marriage and the Family,* **32**(1): 20–28.

Rosenthal, C. J. (1986). Family supports in later life: Does ethnicity make a difference. *The Gerontologist,* **26**(1): 19–26.

Rosenthal, C. J., Matthews, S. H., & Marshall, V. W. (1989). Is parent care normative? The experience of a sample of middle-aged women. *Research on aging,* **11**(2): 244–260.

Rubinstein, R. L. (1987). Never married elderly as a social type: Reevaluating some images. *The Gerontologist,* **27**(1): 108–113.

Safilios-Rothschild, C. (1967). A comparison of power structure and marital satisfaction in urban Greek and French families. *Journal of Marriage and the Family,* **29**(4): 345–352.

Salend, E., Kane, R. A., Satz, M., & Pynoos, J. (1984). Elder abuse reporting: Limitations of statutes. *The Gerontologist,* **24**(1): 61–69.

Sanders, G. F., Pittman, J. F., & Montgomery, J. E. (1987). Family caregivers of centenarians: Support for the very old. *Journal of Applied Gerontology,* **5**(2): 113–125.

Sanders, G. F., & Trygstad, D. W. (1989). Stepgrandparents and grandchildren: The view from young adults. *Family Relations,* **38**(1): 71–75.

Scharlach, A. E. (1987). Role strain in mother-daughter relationships in later life. *The Gerontologist,* **27**(5): 627–631.

Scharlach, A. E., & Boyd, S. L. (1989). Caregiving and employment: Results of an employee survey. *The Gerontologist,* **29**(3): 382–387.

Schoonover, C. B., Brody, E. M., Hoffman, C., & Kleban, M. H. (1988). Parent care and geographically distant children. *Research on Aging,* **10**(4): 472–492.

Seccombe, K. (1988). Financial assistance from elderly retirement-age sons to their aging parents. *Research on Aging,* **10**(1): 102–118.

Shanas, E. (1979). The family as a social support system in old age. *The Gerontologist,* **19**(2): 169–174.

Sheehan, N. W. (1986). Informal support among the elderly in public senior housing. *The Gerontologist,* **26**(2): 171–175.

Shulman, N. (1975). Life-cycle variations in patterns of close relationships. *Journal of Marriage and the Family,* **37**(4): 813–821.

Silverman, P. (1987). Family life. In P. Silverman (Ed.), *The elderly as modern pioneers* (pp. 205–233). Bloomington: Indiana University Press.

Spanier, G. B., Lewis, R. A., & Cole, C. L. (1975). Marital adjustment over the family life cycle: The issue of curvilinearity. *Journal of Marriage and the Family,* **37**(2): 263–275.

Spitze, G., & Logan, J. (1989). Gender differences in family support: Is there a payoff? *The Gerontologist,* **29**(1): 108–113.

Stone, R., Cafferata, G. L., & Sangl, J. (1987). Caregivers of the frail elderly: A national profile. *The Gerontologist,* **25**(5): 616–626.

Streib, G. F. (1978). An alternative family form for older persons: Need and social context. *Family Coordinator,* **27**(4): 413–420.

Streib, G. F., & Streib, R. B. (1975). Communes and the aging: Utopian dream and gerontological reality. *American Behavioral Scientist,* **19**(2): 176–189.

Stull, D. E., & Scarisbrick-Hauser, A. (1989). Never-married elderly: A reassessment with implications for long-term care. *Research on Aging,* **11**(1): 124–139.

Suitor, J. J., & Pillemer, D. (1987). The presence of adult children: A source of stress for elderly couples' marriages? *Journal of Marriage and the Family,* **49**(4): 717–725.

Suitor, J. J., and Pillemer, K. (1988). Explaining intergeneration conflict when adult children and elderly parents live together. *Journal of Marriage and the Family,* **50**(4): 1037–1047.

Sussman, M. B. (1965). Relationships of adult children with their parents in the United States. In E. Shanas & G. F. Streib (Eds.), *Social structure and the family: Generational relations* (pp. 62–92). Englewood Cliffs, NJ: Prentice-Hall.

Sussman, M. B. (1970). Family relations and the aged. In A. M. Hoffman (Ed.), *The daily needs and interests of older people* (pp. 300–326). Springfield, IL: Charles C Thomas.

Sussman, M. B. (1976). The family life of old people. In R. H. Binstock & E. Shanas (Eds.), *Handbook of aging and the social sciences* (pp. 218–242). New York: Van Nostrand Reinhold.

Sussman, M. B., & Burchinal, L. (1962). Kin family network: Unheralded structure in current conceptualizations of family functioning. *Marriage and Family Living,* **24**(3): 231–240.

Taylor, R. J. (1985). The extended family as a source of support to elderly blacks. *The Gerontologist,* **25**(5): 488–495.

Thomas, J. L. (1986). Age and sex differences in perceptions of grandparenting. *Journal of Gerontology,* **41**(3): 417–423.

Thomas, J. L. (1988). Predictors of satisfaction with children's help for younger and older elderly parents. *Journal of Gerontology: Social Sciences,* **43**(1): 59–64.

Tibbitts, C. (1968). Some social aspects of gerontology. *The Gerontologist,* **8**(2): 131–133.

Tibbitts, C. (1977). Older Americans in the family context. *Aging,* **270–271**(April/May): 6–11.

Townsend, P. (1957). *The family life of old people.* London: Routledge and Kegan Paul.

Treas, J. (1983). Aging and the family. In D. S. Woodruff and J. E. Birren (Eds.), *Aging: Scientific perspectives and social issues* (second edition) (pp. 94–109). Monterey, CA: Brooks/Cole.

Treas, J., & VanHilst, A. (1976). Marriage and remarriage rates among older Americans. *The Gerontologist,* **16**(2): 132–136.

Troll, L. E. (1971). The family of later life: A decade of review. *Journal of Marriage and the Family,* **33**(4): 263–290.

Troll, L. E. (Ed.) (1976). *Family issues in current gerontology.* New York: Springer.

Troll, L. E. (1980). Grandparenting. In L. W. Poon (Ed.), *Aging in the 1980s* (pp. 475–481). Washington, DC: American Psychological Association.

Troll, L. E., Miller, S. J., & Atchley, R. C. (1979). *Families in later life.* Belmont, CA: Wadsworth.

Uhlenberg, P., Cooney, T., & Boyd, R. (1990). Divorce for women after midlife. *Journal of Gerontology: Social Sciences,* **45**(1): S3–11.

U.S. Bureau of the Census (1990). *Statistical abstracts of the United States: 1990.* Washington, DC: U.S. Government Printing Office.

U.S. Select Committee on Aging (1987). *Exploding the myths: Caregiving in America.* Washington, DC: U.S. Government Printing Office.

U.S. Senate, Special Committee on Aging (1987–1988). *Aging America: Trends and projections.* Washington, DC: U.S. Government Printing Office.

Vinick, B. H. (1978). Remarriage in old age. *Family Coordinator,* **27**(4): 359–363.

Walsh-Brennan, K. (1977). Granny bashing. *Nursing Mirror,* **145**(25): 32–34.

Weiler, K. (1989). Financial abuse of the elderly: Recognizing and acting on it. *Journal of Gerontological Nursing,* **15**(8): 10–15.

Wentowski, G. J. (1985). Older women's perceptions of great-grandparenthood: A research note. *The Gerontologist,* **25**(6): 593–596.

Wilson, K. B., & DeShane, M. R. (1982). The legal rights of grandparents: A preliminary discussion. *The Gerontologist,* **22**(1): 67–71.

CHAPTER 10

RELIGION AND EDUCATION

Rick Smolan/Stock, Boston

INTRODUCTION

This chapter will consider two areas that have the ability to significantly influence the lives of older persons: religion and education. Religion has the potential to be an important variable in the lives of older persons, because it has the ability to shape beliefs, opinions, and values, and can provide individuals with a framework through which they perceive, interpret, and comprehend the world, others, and themselves. Education also has the potential to significantly influence the lives of older persons. In this section we will examine their educational attainment and the concept of education for older persons.

Because the two subject areas are different, the references are separated into two parts: religion and education.

RELIGION

Several aspects of religion and older persons will be examined. First, the methodological problems, and second the religious beliefs and behaviors of older persons will be examined. In the third section the functions that religion serves for older persons will be examined. The last section will examine the impact of religion on older persons.

Throughout this section certain terms will be used in a "generic" sense. For example, **church** will be used synonymously for synagogue or mosque, and **minister** will be used generically to refer to religious leaders such as rabbis or priests.

Methodological Problems

It was noted above that religion can be a very powerful factor in the lives of individuals. However, many students of gerontology have noted that in general, gerontology books and journals contain either no material on religion or at best provide a token reference (see Glass, 1988). Part of the explanation is because there are five major problems for researchers writing in this area.

First, there is very little "scientific writing" in the area of religion and the aged. Although it abounds with personal accounts and observations, there are few research reports that satisfy the curiosity of empirically-oriented researchers (see Johnson & Mullins, 1989; Maves, 1960). Second, many of the "scientific" studies that were published on religion and older persons are now quite old. Because of numerous social changes, many writers are hesitant to use these data. Third, most of the studies have been cross-sectional studies. There is little research showing the changes over time in birth cohorts in regard to such variables as religious behavior or religious attitudes. Additionally, the studies that have noted a change in religious behavior or attitudes have generally not controlled for other variables that might be producing the changes, such as cohort differences, widowhood, retirement, or declining health.

Fourth, many of the studies have had admitted limitations in their samples. Certain ethnic or racial groups, for example, have religious beliefs that are disproportionate to the general population. Hunsberger (1985) noted that the sample used may distort the results. He reported that samples of "relatively religious" individuals will report an increase in "religiosity" with increasing age while a study on a "less religious sample" will find either no relationship or a negative relationship. Fifth, researchers face difficulties in trying to define certain concepts in the area of religion. Researchers disagree on the definition of basic terms such as religiosity. Not only are the definitions of certain concepts in dispute, but even if there is agreement on the definition of the concepts, they are often difficult to measure (see Koenig, Kvale, & Ferrel, 1988). For example, religiosity was traditionally measured by the frequency of attending religious services. Some researchers have claimed that this way of measuring religiosity is too restricted and that other measures, such as praying or listening/watching electronic religious programs, need to be considered (see Ainlay & Smith, 1984; Mindel & Vaughan, 1978; Tellis-Nayak, 1982).

Many of the problems are now starting to be addressed as the interest in this area increases (see Seeber, 1988). In addition to an increase in articles in gerontology journals, there is a new journal called *The Journal of Religion and Aging,* and a recent issue of *Educational Gerontology* (Volume 14, Number 4) was devoted to religion and aging.

Religious Beliefs and Behaviors of Older Persons

As just noted, "religiosity" is at best a difficult concept to define much less measure. Researchers have taken a variety of positions in this area with some stating that with increasing age it increases, others that it decreases, and still others that there is no change. There is also a group that takes "no position" except that more research is needed. Rather than attempt to define some of these concepts, we will examine some of the more "empirical" aspects of religious behavior and beliefs. Specifically we will examine the importance of religion, the percentage who believe in a god, religious identification, and religious behavior.

The Importance of Religion How important is religion in the lives of older persons? We know that since the 1950s, the percentage of all age groups responding that religion is "very important" in their lives has declined. In 1952, 75 percent said that it was very important; in 1986 the percentage was 55 (Briggs, 1987). By age group, the percentage that believes religion is very important in their lives increases with each successive age group. For the age group 18–29, 44 percent claim that religion is very important; for the age group 65+ the figure is 67 percent (Briggs, 1987).

It should not automatically be assumed that religion becomes more important in the lives of individuals as they age. What we may be witnessing is a cohort difference; that is most of the older persons in this sample may have been raised to believe that religion was important in their lives; fewer younger individuals may have been raised with this belief.

Belief in the Existence of God The figures in this area vary. Recent studies have reported that between 90 and 95 percent of adults believe in the existence of a god (see Koenig, Kvale, & Ferrel, 1988; Koenig, Moberg, & Kvale, 1988; Payne,

1988). Another study reported the figure as 86 percent (Riley & Foner, 1968). It has also been noted that with each successive age cohort the percentage who believe in the existence of a god increases. One study reported the following percentages for the following age cohorts 18–24 (71 percent), 25–34 (80 percent), 35–44 (81 percent), 45–54 (83 percent), 55–64 (85 percent), 65$^+$ (86 percent) (Riley & Foner, 1968).

Religious Identification   The majority of individuals in the United States identify with a specific religion. The figures are presented in Table 10-1.

As is apparent, the majority of the population identifies itself as protestant. Catholics are the second largest group and Jews the third. There are significant differences by age category. For example, while 49 percent of those 18–29 identified themselves as protestant, 69 percent of those 65+ years of age do so. The figures for Catholics are 31 percent for those 18–29 and 23 percent for those 65+. The figures for Jews are the same, 2 percent, for younger and older age groups. Those reporting no religious preference go from 14 percent of those 18–29 to 4 percent for those 65+. Identification as a church/synagogue member is higher for each successive age category. For those 18–29 years of age, 63 percent are members of a church or synagogue. For the ages categories 30–49, 50–64, and 65+ years of age the percentages are 67, 74, and 77 (Briggs, 1987).

As noted earlier we cannot assume that differences between young and old are age-related; it cannot be assumed that membership increases with increasing age. It may be that the older group was raised with stronger religious values than the younger age groups; thus the differences reflect an age difference not an age change.

Religious Behavior   We will examine two forms of religious behavior: prayer and attendance at religious services.

Prayer   Again, the figures in this area vary. Studies report that between 72 and 95 percent of older persons pray on a daily basis, with many of those 65+ years of age praying three or more times per day (Koenig, Kvale, & Ferrel, 1988; Koenig, Moberg, & Kvale, 1988; Payne, 1988). In terms of those who pray, there appears to be little difference by age category. However, in terms of those who pray three

TABLE 10-1
RELIGIOUS PREFERENCE

	Protestant, %	Catholic, %	Jewish, %	Other, %	None, %
1957	66	26	3	1	3
1967	67	25	3	3	2
1975	62	27	2	4	6
1985	57	28	2	4	9
1988	56	28	2	2	9

Source: U.S. Bureau of the Census, 1990.

or more times a day the percentages increase with each successive age group, from a low of 12 percent for those 18 to 24 years of age to a high of 24 percent for those 65+ years of age (Briggs, 1987).

Attendance at Religious Services   Studies have varied on the percentage of older persons who attend church on a weekly basis (Koenig, Moberg, & Kvale, 1988; Markides, 1987). A recent Gallup Poll reported that 49 percent of older persons had attended church in the last 7 days. The percentages for those 18–29, 30–49, and 50–64 were 33, 39, and 45 percent.

Attendance at religious services is associated with several variables. One is gender. Studies have indicated that women of all ages attended religious services more frequently than men (see Bengtson et al., 1976; Koenig, Kvale, & Ferrel, 1988; Payne, 1988; Petrowsky, 1976; Riley & Foner, 1968). Studies have also indicated that there is a difference in attendance between white-collar and blue-collar workers. Wingrove and Alston (1971) found that 46 percent of white-collar workers and 38 percent of blue-collar workers claimed that they attended religious services. This result was confirmed by the Duke Longitudinal Studies, which found that those in manual occupations were less active in religion than those in nonmanual occupations (Blazer & Palmore, 1976). Differences by race show blacks with a higher rate of participation than whites (see Payne, 1988; Taylor, 1986). Ethnic group membership can also make a difference with Mexican-Americans having higher rates of participation than many other groups (see Markides et al., 1987; Payne, 1988).

There are many differences influencing attendance at religious services, with age as one of the variables. As noted earlier, readers must be careful not to assume that the differences are age-related. Many have assumed that as one ages and recognizes that maintenance of health and life is becoming more precarious, they turn to religion as a source of support and comfort (i.e., age change). Others, however, believe that the differences are merely cohort differences; essentially different religious socialization experiences and expectations have led to different patterns of religious participation (i.e., age difference). There have been relatively few longitudinal studies that have attempted to answer these questions. One retrospective study on attendance at religious services reported that 30 percent of those 60+ years of age claimed that over time their attendance had decreased, 23 percent reported their attendance had increased, and the remainder reported no change in their attendance patterns (see Riley & Foner, 1968). The Duke Longitudinal Studies noted a fairly constant decline over time in religious service attendance (Blazer & Palmore, 1976). These data and other data seem to indicate that the older one becomes after age 65, the greater the likelihood of reducing attendance at religious services. From age 65 on, the percentage reporting that they currently attend religious services more frequently than in the past or that they attend religious services about the same level as in the past goes progressively down.

Researchers have often examined attendance at religious services to ascertain if a predictable or developmental model could be created. In examining the literature, Wingrove and Alston (1971) found that researchers had created four models. A brief examination of the four models is presented below (see Palmore, 1987). The first model is called the "traditional model." This model maintains that church attendance is at its lowest point between the ages of 30 to 35. After age 35, there is a gradual increase in attendance of religious services until old age, when a decrease in attendance takes place. The second model is the "stability model," which claims that age and church attendance are unrelated. The proponents of this model claim that attendance at religious services remains constant throughout life.

The third model, the "family life model," perceives church attendance as tied to the ages of the children in a family. The model claims that there will be high attendance at religious services by the family when the children are young and are perceived as needing religious instruction and values. As the children become older and are considered to have their values formed, attendance at religious services declines. The fourth, and last, model is called the "disengagement model." This model claims that attendance at religious services becomes less frequent in middle age when some disengagement takes place and that it becomes even further reduced in old age when the separation between the individual and society increases (see Argyle & Beit-Hallahmi, 1975; Bahr, 1970).

Wingrove and Alston (1971, 1974) used data from the 1939–1969 Gallup Polls to test these four models. In all of the Gallup Polls the same question was asked, "Did you attend church or a synagogue in the last 7 days?" The data allowed the researchers to do a longitudinal study of changes in specific birth cohorts. They did not find support for any of the above models. They found that each birth cohort had its own religious attendance profile, with some reaching attendance peaks early in adulthood, others reaching attendance peaks later in adulthood. Not only were cohort differences found, but this study also demonstrated the influence of period effects or the effects of social forces and trends. For example, the study reported that all of the cohorts reached their peaks in attendance during the same time period (e.g., 1950–1960), and that all of the cohorts declined in attendance after 1965. This suggests that all of the cohorts responded in the same manner to social forces and trends.

Some new "models" are starting to emerge that examine both organized and nonorganized religious participation. Young and Dowling (1987), for example, have found that participation in organized religious activity is dependent on participation in other social activities. Generally, the higher the participation in other social activities the higher the participation in organized religious activities. As individuals reduce their involvement in social activities, organized religion is generally one of the areas affected. This study rejected poor health, low income, and living alone as being factors that reduced participation in formal religious activities.

Moberg (1970, 1972) noted that although church attendance or "external" religious practices declined with increasing age, "internal" religious practices increased with increasing age. For example, older persons are more likely to read religious books and publications at home, pray at home, or listen to or watch religious programs at home than are the young (Hammond, 1969; Kivett, 1979; Mindel & Vaughan, 1978; Young & Dowling, 1987). For example, 7 percent of those under 30 read the *Bible* daily compared to 13 percent of those 65+ years of age (Briggs, 1987). It has been reported that the percentage who watch religious television programs on a weekly basis for the age groups 18–29, 30–49, and 50+ years of age are 18, 22, and 33 percent (U.S. Bureau of the Census, 1990). These findings probably indicate that although attendance at religious services decreases with increasing age, older persons still maintain an active interest in religion. Mindel and Vaughan (1978) support this position and have found that although many older persons do not frequently attend religious services, they are "nonorganizationally" religious.

Older persons reduce their attendance at religious services for a number of reasons. One reason is health (Koenig, Moberg, & Kvale, 1988). Failing health makes it impossible for many older persons to attend religious services, although two studies have not supported this assumption (see Mindel & Vaughan, 1978; Young & Dowling, 1987). Another reason is the lack of transportation. It has also been found that some older persons do not attend religious services because they cannot afford to dress in a manner they believe is appropriate. Still others reduce or truncate their attendance because they believe that younger church members, or perhaps younger religious leaders, have pushed them aside and ignored their opinions (see Moberg, 1972, 1974).

Functions of Religion

There are many functions that a religious organization can perform in the lives of older persons, such as providing companionship and counseling (McDonald, 1973); giving meaning to individuals' lives; comforting the sick, suffering, bereaved, and dying (Ailor, 1973; Moberg, 1970); supplying social activities and functions (Jacobs, 1974); offering visiting programs and chapel services in institutions and hospitals; protecting basic human rights (Moberg, 1974); providing programs that stimulate individuals to come back into the church and community (Ailor, 1973); and sponsoring nursing homes (Netting & Wilson, 1986).

As we will see later in this book, there have been several national White House Conferences on Aging, involving thousands of participants, and held in an attempt to ascertain and solve some of the problems of the aged in the United States. All of the White House Conferences on Aging have suggested ways for religion to serve older persons. The 1961 conference suggested some of the following: provide part-time jobs in the church; provide preretirement and retirement counseling; supply legal services in the preparation of taxes and wills; have sickroom equipment on hand to loan to needy members; set up a visitation program for the sick; sponsor nursing homes; have chapel services within hospitals; sponsor clubs and activities; provide an outlet for the sale of crafts; and have pastoral counseling (see Hammond, 1969; White House Conference on Aging, 1973).

The 1971 White House Conference on Aging made 15 recommendations concerning what the government should do to help religions meet the religious needs of the aged (White House Conference on Aging, 1973). Among these fifteen recommendations were that the government cooperate with religious organizations in helping the aged meet their spiritual needs, cooperate with the appropriate agencies to help in the delivery of religious services to the aged, provide financial assistance to appropriate individuals to help them understand the spiritual needs of the aged, and provide chaplaincy services in licensed institutions providing care to the aged.

The 1981 conference (Mini-Conference on Spiritual and Ethical Value Concerns) reiterated some of the earlier concerns and also made a number of policy recommendations that were designed to "enhance the spiritual and ethical posture of national policy." The conference also noted that the spiritual aspect is a neglected area in gerontology; this is unfortunate since it is an area that has the resources to meet the needs of many older persons (White House Conference on Aging, 1981).

Religious organizations can provide a number of other services to their aged members. Some of these services might be the following: exert influence within the community to help bring about needed programs; establish programs and organize senior centers; supply transportation; provide counseling; sponsor facilities such as nursing homes or retirement villages; visit the homebound or those in hospitals or nursing homes; offer continuing education programs, especially on relevant issues; provide senior citizens clubs with meals; create a telephone reassurance program; train clergy and lay clergy to find and assist caregivers (see Buesching, 1974; Moberg, 1970; Sheehan, 1989; Stough, 1965).

Not only can the church provide "formal" services, but it can create many "informal" sources of services. For example, through the social relationships that are formed, church members will provide each other with services such as companionship, help during illness, advice, and moral support. A study of 212 churches and synagogues examined the role of the church in providing services to older persons (Sheehan et al., 1988). The average number of service programs for older persons was 4.41. The most frequently mentioned programs were visitation programs for the homebound, those in nursing homes, and hospitals. Approximately 70 percent of the sample mentioned that they had these programs. Transportation and telephone reassurance programs were mentioned by about one-third of the sample. Less than one-third of the sample had the following: social/recreational programs, food distribution, education, home-delivered meals, support groups, discussion groups on aging, or self-help groups for older persons. The researchers reported that several factors affected the likelihood of programs for older persons: an active lay ministry, joint sponsorship with community agencies, and frequency of being called on to provide support and services to older persons. Others have noted that the greater the percentage of aged parishioners the greater the ministries' interest in programs for older persons (Doka, 1985–1986).

As was seen above, a frequent activity consists of visitations to those who are homebound, or in hospitals or nursing homes. It has been estimated that one-third to one-half of ministers' counseling and pastoral time is devoted to the aged (Hammond, 1969; Moberg, 1975). The reasons are probably that older persons are more likely to have a greater frequency of problems to which the clergy can attend, and that they are more accustomed to utilizing the services of the clergy, rather than social services, to solve problems. Although much of ministers' time is spent with older persons, many ministers do not particularly enjoy this aspect of their ministry. A study by Longino and Kitson (1976) reported that ministers' attitudes toward their aged parishioners found that although ministering to the needs of older persons was not their most enjoyable activity, neither was it the "least enjoyable" activity. They also found that the clergy tended to be somewhat ageist in their attitudes and responses toward older persons. Monk and Kaye (1982) reported that students at a college of religious instruction had "negative biases toward the aged." Essentially this means that active ministers and students in religious programs are affected by the same stereotypes and biases as others in society. Traditionally, religious training has focused on "youth-oriented ministries." An attempt now needs to be made to train ministers in assisting older persons. One way that is proving successful is through workshops designed to present ministers with the special needs of older persons (see Custer, 1988; Klick et al., 1987; Oliver, 1988).

Church members represent a group of potential volunteers to assist church or community members. Filinson (1988) described a church-based "Alzheimer's support/ tender caregivers project" in which volunteers were educated to provide respite care to prevent premature or unnecessary institutionalization. In addition to respite care, the volunteers also provided such services as visiting, providing transportation, and telephone reassurance. The author noted that some problems were that the volunteers did not believe they were appreciated and some were not certain of the level of care to provide.

Impact of Religion

Obviously, religion is an important aspect in the lives of many older individuals. Because of its importance, religion can have both functional and dysfunctional impacts on older persons. The functional allows the individual to integrate into the society or to adapt to or adjust to the society. The dysfunctional is disruptive to the integration, adaptation, or adjustment of the individual to the society. Moberg (1970) pointed out that most activities, including religion, are neither totally functional nor dysfunctional. Most are mixed in their effects. Also, what may be functional for one individual or one group may be dysfunctional for another individual or another group. Moreover, researchers commonly disagree about whether something is functional or dysfunctional.

This section of the chapter will examine some of the functional and dysfunctional impacts that religion can have on older persons. It should be recognized that it is difficult to empirically measure many of the ways in which spiritual or religious factors influence the aged (Moberg, 1970). However, a few empirical studies have been completed and some impressionistic observations noted.

Functional Impact   As noted in the introduction, religion has the potential to be an important variable in the lives of older persons. Studies have indicated that most older persons consider their religious beliefs to be exceptionally important. One study reported 55 percent who said that their religious faith was the most important influence on their lives; another 27 percent were in close agreement with the statement. This same study reported that 66 percent said that God's guidance should be sought in all important decisions; another 20 percent were in close agreement (Koenig, Moberg, & Kvale, 1988).

A study by Wolff (1959) reported that religious beliefs, prayer, and faith in God all helped older persons to overcome many of the common problems in old age such as grief or unhappiness. The impact on well-being, morale, and life satisfaction have also been examined. As is known, many older persons are confronted with problems in the areas of health, income, and public image. Religion is one way of coping with some of these problems. In fact, religion has been consistently mentioned as the most important form of coping behavior (Conway, 1985–1986; Manfredi & Picket, 1987; Rosen, 1982). A study from the second Duke Longitudinal Study (Koenig, George, & Siegler, 1988) has also mentioned that religion is a frequently used coping strategy. The coping strategy might include placing one's trust and faith in God, prayer, reading the *Bible,* help from a minister or church friends. Women and blacks appeared to use religion the most frequently as a coping strategy. The authors hypothesized that religious activity or beliefs might facilitate coping because they provide distractions and needed social support from other church members. At the psychological level the stressors may become less stressful; through religious activity such as prayer individuals assume they have more control. Not all studies have found such positive results (see Moberg & Taves, 1965; Spreitzer & Snyder, 1974; Toseland & Rasch, 1979–1980).

One specific coping strategy has been examined: using religion to lessen the fear of death. It was found that those who held conservative religious views were less afraid of death than other groups (Blazer & Palmore, 1976; Swenson, 1959, 1961). Hinton (1967) found that religious individuals were relatively free of anxiety in regard to dying. Kubler-Ross (1974) has also claimed that individuals who are "intensely" religious accept death more easily than others. Both Hinton (1967) and Kubler-Ross (1974) have claimed that those who do not truly believe in a religious system or those who are "tepid" believers have greater difficulty in accepting death. Treanton (1961) has challenged the above conclusions noting that the differences in the fear of death are due to the fact that religious individuals are more likely to have a reference group that will support them when they are dying. Thus, it is the group, not religion itself, that makes the difference.

There are also studies indicating that older persons who are church members are better adjusted than nonmembers, and that there is better adjustment among church members who are leaders in the church than among church members who do not assume such roles. It has also been found that those who read the *Bible* and frequently attend religious services are better adjusted than those who do not. Riley and Foner (1968) and Moberg (1965, 1970, 1974) reported that religious indicators such as attending church frequently, reading the *Bible* at home, believing in an afterlife, listening to religious radio programs, or watching religious television programs correlated with high personal adjustment, high morale, and high life satisfaction. The Duke Longitudinal Studies have also confirmed that there is a strong relationship between religious activity and feelings of happiness, usefulness, and adjustment in old age (Blazer & Palmore, 1976). Other studies have reported that there is a positive relationship between religiosity and life satisfaction, well-being, or morale (Beckman & Houser, 1982; Blazer & Palmore, 1976; Hadaway, 1978; Hunsberger, 1985; Koenig, Kvale, & Ferrel, 1988).

Other researchers have questioned the above studies. They believe that it is not religion that is influencing factors such as life satisfaction, but health. They note that those in better health are still capable of attending religious services or of reading religious material (see Guy, 1982; Markides et al., 1987). It is, of course, possible that individuals who are "better" adjusted are also more likely to remain religiously active. Janeway (1972) observed that religion offers many individuals an "alternative reality," that is, a reality different from that forced on them by health or economic circumstances. An alternative reality may be necessary for those living in "desperate circumstances." Religion can offer these individuals an escape from earthly existence and the hope of a better life. In this way, religion may be a primary factor in having a happy old age (see Blazer & Palmore, 1976).

Holcomb (1975) noted that crisis situations were faced better by those with some type of religious orientation. The reason was that individuals could view and understand the crises from a religious framework. This framework allowed individuals to understand the crises more clearly and ultimately enabled them to survive the crisis with fewer emotional scars (see Moberg, 1953; O'Reilly, 1963). It has also been reported that participation in organized religious activities can provide individuals with a social support network. For example, it has been reported that one's friends are also frequently members of one's church. For an "at-risk" population this can provide an important social network if the need arises (Koenig, Moberg, & Kvale, 1988). Additionally, it has been reported that the social aspects of religion, such as attending services, is related to lower levels of loneliness (Johnson & Mullins, 1989).

Religion can also be functional for the aged for other reasons. For example, religion may offer an older person several important roles to play. Some of these religious roles might be the following: assisting the pastor, minister, or rabbi in worship services; teaching Sunday school classes; assisting at church projects; participating in visitation programs to sick or infirm members; maintaining the church; assisting in secretarial or clerical duties; or providing transportation to other members (see Dickerson, & Myers, 1988; Elias, 1988; Moberg, 1970). Religion can also offer numerous activities and programs that are designed to be stimulating for older persons and provide meaning in their lives. One such program was described by Ailor (1973). The program was called the XYZ Club for "xtra years of zest." The program brought many older persons out of seclusion and was termed a "life-saver program" by many of the older persons who participated. The program eventually blossomed into education, music, fun, and arts and crafts. The purpose of the program was not to find "busy work" for older persons, but to bring them back into the community by having them participate in activities they found interesting, enjoyable, and fulfilling. This program demonstrated that if the opportunities are present, there is an enormous potential for growth in the aged (Hogan, 1974; Stough, 1965).

Dysfunctional Impact The potential impacts that religion can have on the lives of older persons are not all functional. Several writers have hypothesized, through impressionistic observations, that religion may also have dysfunctional impacts on older persons. Hogan (1974) has noted that some church programs are harmful to older persons because these programs "make children" of them. The main purpose of many such programs is to keep older persons from boredom by having them engage in "busy work" or meaningless activity. Hogan has claimed that these programs do not contribute to the inner growth of individuals and may in fact prevent such growth.

Religion may be dysfunctional for some older persons because of the values it provides members. Values define for individuals what is right or wrong, moral or immoral. Individuals raised with conservative and rigid religious values may find many of the changes in contemporary society difficult to understand, tolerate, or cope with. The older person may be unable to change either his or her own firmly entrenched values or the opposite values of contemporary society. This inability can create stress and anxiety, both of which increase the probability of physical and mental illness or of death.

Religion may also cause certain types of fear in older persons (Moberg, 1970). As they near death, they may fear that they have not done enough to earn salvation, or they may fear eternal damnation. Religion may also cause guilt. Individuals suffering from various problems may wonder what they did to deserve such a "wretched old age." Certain religious views may also be considered dysfunctional by many since they are in conflict with contemporary scientific beliefs. For example, individuals who have an illness that they believe to be "God's will" (Larue, 1976) may not seek help for the illness. It was suggested by Moberg (1974), that in a few cases the visit of the clergy to a sick individual may be interpreted as "last rites."

Gray and Moberg (1962) have found another dysfunctional impact of religion. They noted that many older persons become disillusioned with their churches when they change long-established patterns. Very often programs or activities that the older persons helped establish or that they had become accustomed to were changed when new ministers assumed duties or younger church members took over administrative functions. Often these changes tended to make many older persons feel as if their opinions and years of faith and service meant nothing, which led to disillusionment with religion and the church.

Last, although there is no one "theology of aging" (Lyon, 1988), some religious literature may present a bleak and negative image of growing old. For example, Psalm 31:10–13 reads:

For my life is worn out with sorrow,
My years with sighs;
My strength yields under misery,
My bones are wasting away.
To every one of my oppressors
I am contemptible.
Loathsome to my neighbors,
To my friends a thing of fear,
Those who see me in the street
Hurry past me.
I am forgotten, as good as dead in their hearts,
Something to be discarded

It is important to state again that many of the dysfunctions are impressionistic rather than empirical observations. This area, as well as the entire area of religion, needs further exploration in the future by gerontologists.

EDUCATION

We will examine two areas of education and older persons: the educational attainment of older persons and education for older persons.

Educational Attainment of Older Persons

As would be expected, the educational attainment of older persons is lower than for younger adults. As Table 10-2 illustrates, those 65+ years of age are less likely to have completed elementary school, high school, or college than other adult age groups. In fact, almost 50 percent have not completed high school.

The median number of years of school completed is 12.1 for those 65+ years of age. For blacks and Hispanics 65+ years of age the figures are 8.4 and 7.5 years. For the general adult population 25+ years of age the figure is 12.7. Although still lower than the general adult population, the educational attainment of older persons has been increasing, substantially reducing the difference between the educational levels of young adults and the aged. For example, in the early 1970s, 72 percent of older persons did not have high school diplomas (Bouvier et al., 1975); as noted earlier, the figure is now about 50 percent (see Uhlenberg, 1987).

Education for Older Persons

The concept of "lifelong education" is an old one in the United States, but it has only recently been implemented to any extent, especially with older persons (McClusky, 1974, 1982; Moody, 1976). This has been changing and it is now recognized that education should be a lifelong process (see Peterson, 1987). However, this change came slowly and was fostered by a number of developments. In late 1940s the National Education Association's section of adult education created a committee on education and aging, which was chaired by Clark Tibbitts. This led into the 1950 White House

TABLE 10 2
YEARS OF SCHOOL COMPLETED BY AGE

| Age | Percent of population completing | | | | | | | Median years |
| | Elementary school | | | High school | | College | | |
	0 to 4 years	5 to 7 years	8 years	1 to 3 years	4 years	1 to 3 years	4+ years	
25–29	1.0	1.3	1.5	10.2	42.2	21.0	22.7	12.8
30–34	1.1	1.9	1.3	8.7	41.0	21.2	24.7	12.9
35–44	1.4	2.4	1.9	8.3	38.1	21.3	26.9	12.9
45–54	1.9	3.7	3.8	12.5	41.9	15.5	21.0	12.7
55–64	3.2	5.9	7.7	15.7	39.6	12.9	15.0	12.4
65+	5.7	10.4	14.4	15.7	33.0	10.2	10.6	12.1

Source: U.S. Bureau of the Census, 1990.

Conference on Aging, with a section which emphasized the importance of education for older persons. In the early 1950s the Adult Education Association (USA) created a committee on aging chaired by Wilma Donahue which published the first scholarly material in the area (McClusky, 1982). The 1961 White House Conference on Aging again emphasized the value of education for older persons, primarily social service-type programs (Peterson, 1987).

In 1965 the Older Americans Act was passed. This provided federal money for educational programs and research. In 1967 the first conference devoted entirely to older persons and education was held and interest in the area started to increase significantly. The year-long preparation for and the 1971 White House Conference on Aging further stirred interest in this area. At this conference, Dr. Howard Y. McClusky's opening remarks to the delegates of the section on education summarized the beliefs of many when he said:

> Education is a basic right for all persons of all age groups. It is continuous and henceforth one of the ways of enabling older people to have a full and meaningful life, and a means of helping them develop their potential as a resource for the betterment of society (White House Conference on Aging, 1971).

McClusky was one of the first to see education as a way of fulfilling the potential of older persons.

The 1970s saw tremendous growth in both the education of older persons and in educators' recognition of the needs of older persons. There were even doctoral degrees offered in educational gerontology. The 1981 White House Conference on Aging emphasized education that would foster "self-help." Self-help education programs would emphasize areas such as the ability to solve problems (Peterson, 1987).

Education can be beneficial in meeting the needs of older persons and this section of the chapter will examine the ways that education can meet those needs (see Leclerc, 1985). Dr. Howard Y. McClusky (1974) set forth five needs that most older persons experience: coping, expressive, contribution, influence, and transcendence needs. By examining each of these five needs, it will be readily seen how and why education is important for older persons. These needs have not been empirically validated, and there is overlap among some areas (see Lowy, 1983).

Coping Needs   Increasing age often brings about a number of undesirable and irreversible changes for most older persons. There are often changes in areas such as income, marital status, position in society, power, health, and occupation. In order to maintain adequate psychological and physical health, individuals must learn to cope with these changes. Courses in the psychological and physiological aspects of aging might help them to better understand both the internal and external changes that are taking place. Practical courses, such as those in health education (see Baker, 1989; Cox & Monk, 1989; Keintz et al., 1988), physical exercise, dealing with the death of a spouse (see Klick, 1985), how to live with a spouse after retirement, or caregiving responsibilities (Heagerty et al., 1988; Pratt et al., 1989; Shulman &

Mandel, 1988) can help older persons cope and adjust to the changing nature of their lives.

Expressive Needs   In fulfilling expressive needs individuals derive intrinsic enjoyment, satisfaction, meaning, or pleasure from the activity itself. That is, individuals derive pleasure simply from their ability to participate in certain activities. With more time, interests that could not be fulfilled when younger, because of work or family obligations, can be realized in old age. Individuals may derive enjoyment or meaning from such activities as social interaction, the use of the senses, or the use of muscles. Education can offer a wide variety of courses that will satisfy an individual's expressive needs. The "how-to" courses can help individuals to become competent in areas they value. Liberal education courses, arts and crafts, current affairs, and many others also have the ability to satisfy expressive needs.

One example of a large-scale program that would fulfill this need is Elderhostel. What started in 1975 as a small, inexpensive, program for older persons on college campuses has grown into a program that has over 160,000 participants a year. The basic format is for older persons to travel to college campuses to take short (generally 5-day) courses in certain subjects. There are no exams or grades. The participants stay in college dorm rooms and eat in the college dining facilities. Over 1000 colleges offer Edlerhostel courses in every state and some foreign countries. The Elderhostel program has been consistent in offering an excellent selection of courses at low prices. The success of Elderhostel shows the interest of older persons in education.

Contribution Needs   Many older persons feel the need to be able to give to others. The contribution need permits older persons the dual function of fulfilling a useful role while at the same time feeling wanted and needed. Once again, a wide variety of programs can be implemented to fill this need. Examples would be training widowed older persons to assist recently widowed individuals adjust to bereavement (Petty & Cusack, 1989; Redburn & Juretich, 1989), helping families participate in the care of a cognitively-impaired relative (Linsk et al., 1988), serving as mentors to young offenders (Platt, 1988) or prison inmates (Sklar, 1987), helping in elementary schools (Tierce & Seelbach, 1987), becoming foster grandparents (Walls, 1987), or working with youth who have a high risk of substance abuse or dropping out of school (Elder, 1987).

Influence Needs   Many older persons have the need to influence and control the direction and quality of their lives. They want to understand some of the major issues that they will confront and the options and alternatives they will have, as well as their consequences. A variety of educational programs in areas such as the rights of those in nursing homes, or the rights of the terminally ill could help to satisfy this need.

One example would be an education program for grandparents on how to be grandparents. While there are numerous courses on "parenting" there are few if any on "grandparenting." Strom and Strom (1987) have noted that the role of grandparent has undergone significant change in recent years and that grandparents are often not competent for this new and changing role. One aspect of this program would be learning to accept and understand the diverse life-styles of grandchildren. With some of the skills presented in the program, grandparents can become more involved and influential in the lives of their grandchildren.

Transcendence Needs   The basic concept of transcendence is that older persons have the need to feel that they are somehow better off or at a higher level than in the past. There are several ways for education to meet this need. One way is through meeting some of the other needs. For example, in meeting the expressive need individuals may believe that they transcended an earlier level artistically, educationally, or even physically.

Structuring Education for Older Persons

If education is going to succeed for older persons, courses and programs will have to be structured to meet the needs of older persons, not administrators and instructors. To facilitate entry and enrollment some of the following are recommended (see Versen, 1986). Generally, the class should be taken to older persons rather than requiring older persons to go to the class. This can generally be facilitated by offering the class at a senior center rather than at a college or university campus. The location should be readily accessible in terms of a short walking distance from where the participants park. Steps and stairs should be kept to a minimum; access for those with mobility limitations should be considered. Elevators should be available if needed. The class should be offered at a time that is most convenient for older persons, which might be during daylight, nonrush hours. The course should be inexpensive or free. The instructor should have had some experience in working with older persons and be attuned to their needs. The instructor should be able to establish trust and rapport with the class and to speak in a loud, clear, slow-paced voice. The instructor should also be acquainted with the methods by which older persons learn the best.

There are other factors that could be mentioned, but the major point is that the motivation and needs of older individuals are different from those of younger individuals and if courses and programs are going to be successful, these needs must be kept in mind. Too often organizational rhetoric is that programs and courses for older persons are offered but few attend. In actuality these organizations often create insurmountable barriers for interested older persons. For example, at many colleges and universities older persons can often attend courses free of charge. However, the registration process for the course may involve more than most are willing to tolerate. For example, older persons may go to one building to register for the course only to be told that they first have to get permission from a different office (in a different building, usually at the opposite end of the campus) to take the course free of charge. At that office they will be told that they have to show some official document demonstrating age, which they probably did not bring. After obtaining and producing the appropriate documents they then register for the course. Some will have had to obtain the instructor's permission to "sit in" on the course rather than take it for credit. They will then need to obtain campus identification cards and parking permits. For most it is easier to stay home!

SUMMARY

This chapter examined religion and education, and how each influences older persons. The section on religion noted that terms such as "church" or "minister" would be used in a generic sense (i.e., church refers to synagogue, mosque, etc.). Several methodological problems in examining religion were then noted, such as "scientific writing," many old studies, biased samples, and controversial terminology.

In the next subsection the religious beliefs and behaviors of older persons were examined. The first area that was examined was the importance of religion in individuals' lives. Here it was found there was often an increase with each successive age group. It was noted that this may not represent an age change but an age difference. The second area dealt with the belief in the existence of God. Again, with each successive age group the percentage that believed in the existence of God increased. The third area examined religious identification. Most older persons identify themselves as protestant; then Catholic and Jewish. There are differences in religious identification by age group. Two topics were examined in the area of religious behavior: prayer and attendance at religious services. The percent of the population that prays appears to be fairly constant; however, older persons are more likely to pray more often during the day than other age groups. There have been literally hundreds of studies on how age influences attendance at religious services, with at least four models proposed to explain the findings. It is believed that both cohort and period effects have a role here.

The next subsection examined the functions of religion. It was noted that religion can assist older persons in numerous ways. This can be done through the creation of "formal" functions, such as a program to visit the sick, or informally, through the friends one makes through church membership. Finally, the impact of religion was examined. Here it was noted that religion can have a functional (positive) or dysfunctional (negative) impact on older persons. There appear to be several functional impacts associated with religion. Some are in areas such as morale and life satisfaction. Some potential dysfunctional impacts were also examined.

The second section of the paper examined education. Here it was noted that in recent years the gap in the median number of years of school completed has been narrowing between young adults and older persons. The concept of education for older persons was also presented. Here it was noted that education is now being conceptualized as a life-long process. Originally the concept of education for older persons was tied into a social services model; now it is seen as a way of fulfilling the potential of older persons. Howard Y. McClusky's needs of older persons, and the ways in which education can fulfill these needs, was examined.

REFERENCES

Section on Religion

Ailor, J. W. (1973). The church provides for the elderly. In R. R. Boyd & C. G. Oakes (Eds.), *Foundations of practical gerontology* (second edition) (pp. 205–220). Columbia: University of South Carolina Press.

Ainlay, S. C., & Smith, D. R. (1984). Aging and religious participation. *Journal of Gerontology,* **39**(3): 357–363.

Argyle, M., & Beit-Hallahmi, B. (1975). *The social psychology of religion.* Boston: Routledge and Kegan Paul.

Bahr, H. M. (1970). Aging and religious disaffiliation. *Social Forces,* **49**(1): 59–71.

Beckman, L. J., & Houser, B. B. (1982). The consequences of childlessness on the social-psychological well-being of older women. *Journal of Gerontology,* **37**(2): 243–250.

Bengtson, V. L., Kassachau, P. L., & Ragan, P. K. (1976). The impact of social structure on aging individuals. In J. E. Birren & K. W. Schaie (Eds.), *Handbook of the psychology of aging* (pp. 327–354). New York: Van Nostrand Reinhold.

Blazer, D., & Palmore, E. (1976). Religion and aging in a longitudinal panel. *The Gerontologist,* **16**(1): 82–84.

Briggs, K. A. (1987). Religion in America. *Gallup Report,* **259**(April): 1–76.

Buesching, R. (1974). Successful aging: A religious viewpoint. In W. C. Bier (Ed.), *Aging: Its challenge to the individual and to society* (pp. 282–292). New York: Fordham University Press.

Conway, K. (1985–1986). Coping with the stress of medical problems among black and white elderly. *International Journal of Aging and Human Development,* **21**(1): 39–49.

Custer, C. E. (1988). Preparing lay persons to work with older adults in the local church. *Educational Gerontology,* **14**(4): 327–342.

Dickerson, B. E., & Myers, D. R. (1988). The contributory and changing roles of older adults in the church and synagogue. *Educational Gerontology,* **14**(4): 303–314.

Doka, K. (1985–1986). The church and the elderly: The impact of changing age strata on congregations. *International Journal of Aging and Human Development,* **22**(4): 291–300.

Elias, J. L. (1988). Religious education of older adults: Historical perspectives. *Educational Gerontology,* **14**(4): 269–278.

Filinson, R. (1988). A model for church-based services for frail elderly persons and their families. *The Gerontologist,* **28**(4): 483–486.

Glass, J. C. (1988). Introduction. *Educational Gerontology,* **14**(4): iii–iv.

Gray, R. M., & Moberg, D. O. (1962). *The church and the older person.* Grand Rapids, MI: Wm. B. Erdmans.

Guy, R. F. (1982). Religion, physical disabilities, and life satisfaction in older age cohorts. *International Journal of Aging and Human Development,* **15**(3): 225–232.

Hadaway, C. K. (1978). Life satisfaction and religion: A reanalysis. *Social Forces,* **57**(2): 636–643.

Hammond, P. E. (1969). Aging and the ministry. In M. W. Riley, J. W. Riley, & M. E. Johnson (Eds.), *Aging and society, Volume Three: Aging and the professions* (pp. 293–323). New York: Russell Sage Foundation.

Hinton, J. (1967). *Dying.* Baltimore: Penquin.

Hogan, W. F. (1974). The challenge of aging for contemporary religion. In W. C. Bier (Ed.) *Aging: Its challenge to the individual and to society* (pp. 26–34). New York: Fordham University Press.

Holcomb, W. L. (1975). Spiritual crises among the aged. In M. G. Spencer & C. J. Dorr (Eds.), *Understanding aging: A multidisciplinary approach* (pp. 235–278). New York: Appleton-Century-Crofts.

Hunsberger, B. (1985). Religion, age, life satisfaction, and perceived sources of religiousness: A study of older persons. *Journal of Gerontology,* **40**(5): 615–620.

Jacobs, J. (1974). *Fun City: An ethnographic study of a retirement community.* New York: Holt, Rinehart and Winston.

Janeway, E. (1972). Review of *The coming of age. Atlantic Monthly,* **229**(6): 94–98.

Johnson, D. P., & Mullins, L. C. (1989). Religiosity and loneliness among the elderly. *Journal of Applied Gerontology,* **8**(1): 110–131.

Kivett, V. R. (1979). Religious motivation in middle age: Correlates and implications. *Journal of Gerontology,* **34**(1): 106–115.

Klick, A. W., Ladrigan, P. M., & Fenity, N. D. (1987). Clergy request linkages: Implications for planning ministry with older adults. *Educational Gerontology,* **13**(5): 437–442.

Koenig, H. G., Kvale, J. N., & Ferrel, C. (1988). Religion and well-being in later life. *The Gerontologist,* **28**(1): 18–28.

Koenig, H. G., Moberg, D. O., & Kvale, J. N. (1988). Religious activities and attitudes of older adults in a geriatric assessment clinic. *Journal of the American Geriatrics Society,* **36**(4): 362–374.

Koenig, H. G., George, L. K., & Siegler, I. C. (1988). The use of religion and other emotion-regulating coping strategies among older adults. *The Gerontologist,* **28**(3): 303–310.

Kubler-Ross, E. (1974). *Questions and answers on death and dying.* New York: Macmillan.

Larue, G. A. (1976). Religion and the aged. In I. M. Burnside (Ed.), *Nursing and the aged* (pp. 573–575). New York: McGraw-Hill.

Longino, C. F., & Kitson, G. C. (1976). Parish clergy and the aged: Examining stereotypes. *Journal of Gerontology,* **31**(3): 340–345.

Lyon, K. B. (1988). Aging in theological perspective. *Educational Gerontology,* **14**(4): 243–254.

McDonald, J. (1973). Religious needs of older Americans. In J. G. Cull & R. E. Hardy (Eds.), *The neglected older American* (pp. 110–117). Springfield, IL: Charles C Thomas.

Manfredi, C., & Pickett, M. (1987). Perceived stressful situations and coping strategies utilized by the elderly. *Journal of Community and Health Nursing,* **4**(2):99–110.

Markides, K. S. (1983). Aging, religiosity, and adjustment: A longitudinal analysis. *Journal of Gerontology,* **38**(5): 621–625.

Markides, K. S. (1987). Religion. In G. L. Maddox (Ed.), *Encyclopedia of Aging* (pp. 559–561). New York: Springer.

Markides, K. S., Levin, J. S., & Ray, L. A. (1987). Religion, aging, and life satisfaction: An eight-year, three-wave longitudinal study. *The Gerontologist,* **27**(5): 660–665.

Maves, P. B. (1960). Aging, religion, and the church. In C. Tibbitts (Ed.), *Handbook of social gerontology* (pp. 698–752). Chicago: University of Chicago Press.

Mindel, C. H., & Vaughan, C. E. (1978). A multidimensional approach to religiosity and disengagement. *Journal of Gerontology,* **33**(1): 103–108.

Moberg, D. O. (1953). The Christian religion and personal adjustment in old age. *American Sociological Review,* **18**(1): 87–90.

Moberg, D. O. (1965). Religiosity in old age. *The Gerontologist,* **5**(2): 78–87.

Moberg, D. O. (1970). Religion in the later years. In A. M. Hoffman (Ed.), *The daily needs and interests of older persons* (pp. 175–191). Springfield, IL: Charles C Thomas.

Moberg, D. O. (1972). Religion and the aging family. *Family Coordinator,* **21**(1): 47–60.

Moberg, D. O. (1974). Spiritual well-being in late life. In J. F. Gubrium (Ed.), *Late life:*

Communities and environmental policy (pp. 256–280). Springfield, IL: Charles C Thomas.

Moberg, D. O. (1975). Needs felt by the clergy for ministries to the aging. *The Gerontologist,* **15**(2): 170–175.

Moberg, D. O., & Taves, M. J. (1965). Church participation and adjustment in old age. In A. M. Rose & W. A. Peterson (Eds.), *Older people and their social worlds* (pp. 113–124). Philadelphia: F. A. Davis.

Monk, A., & Kaye, L. W. (1982). Gerontological knowledge and attitudes of students of religion. *Educational Gerontology,* **8**(5): 435–445.

Netting, F. E., & Wilson, C. C. (1986). Educating professionals to understand religious sponsorship of long-term care facilities. *Gerontology and Geriatrics Education,* **7**(1): 25–35.

Oliver, D. B. (1988). Preparing clergy and professional religious educators to work with older adults. *Educational gerontology,* **14**(4): 315–326.

O'Reilly, C. T. (1963). Religious practice and personal adjustment of older people. In C. B. Vedder (Ed.), *Gerontology: A book of readings* (pp. 343–346). Springfield, IL: Charles C Thomas.

Palmore, E. (1987). Religious organizations. In G. L. Maddox (Ed.), *The encyclopedia of aging* (pp. 561–563). New York: Springer.

Payne, B. (1988). Religious patterns and participation of older adults: A sociological perspective. *Educational Gerontology,* **14**(4): 255–268.

Petrowsky, M. (1976). Marital status, sex, and the social networks of the elderly. *Journal of Marriage and the Family,* **38**(3): 749–756.

Riley, M. W., & Foner, A. (1968). *Aging and society, Volume One: An inventory of research findings.* New York: Russell Sage Foundation.

Rosen, C. E. (1982). Ethnic differences among impoverished rural elderly in use of religion as a coping mechanism. *Journal of Rural Community Psychology,* **3**(2): 27–34.

Seeber, J. (1988). Needed: A ministry trained in aging. *The Aging Connection,* **9**(4): 4.

Sheehan, N. W. (1989). The caregiver information project: A mechanism to assist religious leaders to help family caregivers. *The Gerontologist,* **29**(5): 703–706.

Sheehan, N. W., Wilson, R., & Marella, L. M. (1988). The role of the church in providing services for the aging. *Journal of Applied Gerontology,* **7**(2): 231–241.

Spreitzer, E., & Snyder, E. E. (1974). Correlates of life satisfaction among the aged. *Journal of Gerontology,* **29**(4): 454–458.

Stough, A. B. (1965). *Brighter vistas: The story of four church programs for older adults.* Washington, DC: U.S. Government Printing Office.

Swenson, W. M. (1959). Attitudes toward death among the aged. *Minnesota Medicine,* **42**(3): 399–402.

Swenson, W. M. (1961). Attitudes toward death in an aged population. *Journal of Gerontology,* **16**(1): 49–52.

Taylor, R. J. (1986). Religious participation among elderly blacks. *The Gerontologist,* **26**(6): 630–636.

Taylor, R. J., & Chatters, L. M. (1986). Church-based informal support among elderly blacks. *The Gerontologist,* **26**(6): 637–642.

Tellis-Nayak, V. (1982). The transcendent standard: The religious ethos of the rural elderly. *The Gerontologist,* **22**(4): 359–363.

Toseland, R., & Rasch, J. (1979–1980). Correlates of life satisfaction: An AID analysis. *International Journal of Aging and Human Development,* **10**(3): 203–211.

Treanton, J-R. (1961). Comments on Symposium on Attitudes toward Death in Older Persons. *Journal of Gerontology,* **16**(1): 63.

U.S. Bureau of the Census (1990). *Statistical abstracts of the United States*. Washington, DC: U.S. Government Printing Office.

White House Conference on Aging (1973). *Post-White House Conference on Aging reports: Toward a new attitude of aging*. Washington, DC: U.S. Government Printing Office.

White House Conference on Aging (1981). *Spiritual and ethical value system concerns in the 1981 White House Conference on Aging*. Washington, DC: U.S. Government Printing Office.

Wingrove, C. R., & Alston, J. P. (1971). Age, aging, and church attendance. *The Gerontologist*, **11**(4; Part 1): 356–358.

Wingrove, C. R., & Alston, J. P. (1974). Cohort analysis of church attendance, 1939–1969. *Social Forces*, **53**(2): 324–331.

Wolff, K. (1959). Group psychotherapy with geriatric patients in a state hospital setting: Results of a three-year study. *Group Psychotherapy*, **12**(2): 218–222.

Young, G., & Dowling, W. (1987). Dimensions of religiosity in old age: Accounting for variation in types of participation. *Journal of Gerontology*, **42**(4): 376–380.

Section on Education

Baker, J. A. (1989). Breast self-examination and the older woman: Field testing an educational approach. *The Gerontologist*, **29**(3): 405–407.

Bouvier, L., Atlee, E., & McVeigh, F. (1985). The elderly in America. *Population Bulletin*, **30**(3).

Cox, C., & Monk, A. (1989). Measuring the effectiveness of a health education program for older adults. *Educational Gerontology*, **15**(1): 9–23.

Elder, J. K. (1987). The role of intergenerational programs in The Youth 2000 Campaign. *Aging*, **356**: 17–19.

Heagerty, B., Dunn, L., & Watson, M. A. (1988). Helping caregivers care. *Aging*, **358**: 7–10.

Keintz, M. K., Rimer, B., Fleisher, L., & Engstrom, P. (1988). Educating older adults about their increased cancer risk. *The Gerontologist*, **28**(4): 487–490.

Klick, A. W. (1985). Issues of widowhood: Implications for continuing education program planning. *Educational Gerontology*, **11**(2/3): 155–159.

Leclerc, G. J. (1985). Understanding the educational needs of older adults: A new approach. *Educational Gerontology*, **11**(2/3): 137–144.

Linsk, N. L., Miller, B., Pflaum, R., & Ortigara-Vicik, A. (1988). Families, Alzheimer's disease, and nursing homes. *Journal of Applied Gerontology*, **7**(3): 331–349.

Lowy, L. (1983). Continuing education in the later years: Learning in the third age. *Gerontology and Geriatrics Education*, **4**(2): 89–106.

McClusky, H. Y. (1974). Education for aging: The scope of the field and perspectives for the future. In S. Grabowski & W. D. Mason (Eds.), *Learning for aging* (pp. 118–129). Washington, DC: Adult Education Association.

McClusky, H. Y. (1982). Education for older adults. In C. Eisdorfer (Ed.), *Annual review of gerontology and geriatrics: Volume Three* (pp. 403–428). New York: Springer.

Moody, H. R. (1976). Philosophical presuppositions of education for old age. *Educational Gerontology*, **1**(1): 1–16.

Peterson, D. A. (1987). Adult education. In G. L. Maddox (Ed.), *The encyclopedia of aging* (pp. 9–10). New York: Springer.

Petty, B. J., & Cusack, S. A. (1989). Assessing the impact of a seniors' peer counseling program. *Educational Gerontology,* **15**(1): 49–64.

Platt, B. (1988). Retirees serve as mentors to young offenders. *Aging,* **357**: 14–16.

Pratt, C., Nay, T., Ladd, L., & Heagerty, B. (1989). A model legal-financial education workshop for families caring for neurologically impaired elders. *The Gerontologist,* **29**(2): 258–262.

Redburn, D. E., & Juretich, M. (1989). Some considerations for using widowed self-help group leaders. *Gerontology and Geriatrics Education,* **9**(3): 89–98.

Shulman, M. D., & Mandel, E. (1988). Communication training of relatives and friends of institutionalized elderly persons. *The Gerontologist,* **28**(6): 797–799.

Sklar, E. (1987). Foster grandparents go inside prison walls. *Aging,* **356**: 20–22.

Strom, R., & Strom, S. (1987). Preparing grandparents for a new role. *Journal of Applied Gerontology* **6**(4): 476–486.

Tierce, J. W., & Seelbach, W. C. (1987). Elders as school volunteers: An untapped resource. *Educational Gerontology,* **13**(1): 33–41.

Uhlenberg, P. (1987). A demographic perspective on aging. In P. Silverman (Ed.), *The elderly as modern pioneers* (pp. 183–204). Bloomington: Indiana University Press.

U.S. Bureau of the Census (1990). *Statistical abstracts of the United States.* Washington, DC: U.S. Government Printing Office.

White House Conference on Aging (1971). *Proceedings of the 1971 White House Conference on Aging: Final report, Volume II.* Washington, DC: U.S. Government Printing Office.

Versen, G. R. (1986). Senior adults in the undergraduate classroom. *Educational Gerontology,* **12**(5): 417–428.

Walls, N. (1987). Three generations of love: Foster grandparents and teenage parents are a natural combination. *Aging,* **355**: 2–5.

CHAPTER **11**

ECONOMICS

Steven Stone/The Picture Cube

INTRODUCTION

The economic aspect of aging is one of the most important in the lives of older persons. The amount of money older persons have access to can determine not only the length of their lives but also the quality of their lives. In examining the economic aspect of aging this section is divided into five sections. In the first we will examine the image of the economic status of older persons. The second will consider the actual economic status of older persons. In the third we will examine the income of older persons. The fourth will discuss the various sources of income for older persons. And last, older persons as consumers will be considered.

THE IMAGE OF THE ECONOMIC STATUS OF OLDER PERSONS

Only a decade ago the public image of the economic status of older persons was one of older persons rummaging through garbage cans for food or eating dog food to survive. Their housing was seen as dilapidated, dirty, overcrowded, single-room-occupancy hotel rooms in run-down, crime-ridden sections of cities.

The image has changed, perhaps because significant changes have been made in their economic status; perhaps because "old age" is no longer an "in-vogue" topic; perhaps because of misconceptions of how benefits for older persons are financed (Schultz, 1985; Uhlenberg & Salmon, 1986). The change can best be represented by one recent magazine cover with the heading "Greedy Geezers" (Fairlie, 1988); the story went on to claim it is wrong for a society to spend the bulk of its resources on an unproductive segment of society. Fairlie noted that while on the one hand magazines for older persons have advertisements for expensive housing in retirement communities or lavish vacations, they also muster reader support for a variety of age-based programs that include tax breaks and other economic benefits for older persons. Other articles have also noted that poverty among older persons is now largely a myth, and that the percentage of the federal budget supporting older persons could go from the current figure that approaches 30 percent to more than 70 percent by 2025 (Flint, 1980; see Califano, 1979; Peterson, 1987; Smeeding, 1982; Torrey, 1982). As Moon (1988) has noted, the image of older persons is changing from that of the "deserving poor to the undeserving rich." Older persons are seen as the winners in a battle with other age groups, especially children, for limited societal resources (Preston, 1984).

One consequence was the formation in 1985 of an organization called Americans for Generational Equity, which essentially believes that too much of the nation's resources are being spent on older persons (Wisensale, 1988). Some gerontologists had foreseen this trend (see Binstock, 1983; Hudson, 1978). In an attempt to forestall the trend the Gerontological Society of America issued a report in 1986 called "Ties That Bind: The Interdependence of Generations" (Kingson et al., 1986) which was designed to dispel certain myths about the amount being spent on older persons and to show the interdependence of the generations (see Kingson, 1988). The "truth" is often elusive. The reader will have to decide if the federal budget is ". . . increasingly being mortgaged for the use of a single group within our country: the elderly" (Broder, 1973), or if older persons have simply become a "scapegoat in contemporary American society" (Binstock, 1983; see Minkler, 1989).

ECONOMIC STATUS OF OLDER PERSONS

The economic status of older persons is difficult to determine for a variety of reasons (see Binstock, 1986; Uhlenberg & Salmon, 1986). First, there are several organizations that gather and publish reports on the economic status of older persons. Some of the major organizations are the Bureau of the Census, the Department of Labor, the Bureau of Labor Statistics, the Social Security Administration, the Administration on Aging, and the Congressional Budget office. The types of individuals studied, the research methodologies employed, and the terminology used by these organizations is often different, thus producing different trends and conclusions. Second, much of the data is old. By the time the data is collected, analyzed, and published it is often 3 to 4 years old. Given the rapidly changing nature of society, the data may reflect a historical rather than a current trend.

Third, the heterogeneity of older persons makes it difficult to take one set of figures as representative of older persons in general. That is, one figure, such as a mean or median income level, can be misleading when trying to make an assessment about all older persons. Even comparing the average income of older persons with another age group has problems. For example, a lower income for some older persons may not be detrimental if their home mortgages have been paid off and other costs associated with raising children have ceased. However, the same income may be insufficient for older persons with medical expenses not covered by insurance or for those who are making financial contributions to their adult children and their aged parents. Fourth, the way an organization collects information on the economic status of older persons may hide or disguise their actual economic status. Some organizations only collect income data on older persons who "head" households. Individuals who have the economic resources to maintain a household are more likely to have incomes above the poverty level. Individuals who are too poor to maintain a household and forced to live with others, would not be considered in this type of study. This type of study would overestimate the income of older persons and underestimate poverty. There is another way to hide the poverty of older persons that allows all older persons to be part of a study. These studies use the total income of households with older persons, not just the incomes of older persons living in the households. Thus, an older person who is forced to live with someone because of poverty has his or her income combined with the owner of the household. As a result, the study would indicate that the older person had an income that placed him or her above the poverty level.

The fifth reason it is difficult to determine the economic status of older persons is because income levels, such as poverty, are artificial (see Cook & Kramek, 1986; Schultz, 1988). For example, the poverty threshold determines an individual's eligibility for many benefits. The poverty threshold is set by well-paid federal bureaucrats who often have little conception of the needs of poor older persons. Many gerontologists believe that the poverty threshold is set too low, in part to save money, in part because the "government" will appear to be effective in eliminating poverty, and in part because an affluent society would be embarrassed by an excessive number of older persons living in poverty.

The economic status of older persons can be examined from different perspectives. First we will examine the statistics from a historical perspective. Second we will examine the poverty statistics in contemporary American society from three perspectives: the percentage of each age cohort that lives in poverty, the total population that lives in poverty, and the subjective observations of older persons. Table 11-1 examines poverty historically. It examines, for several years, the percent of those age 18–64 and those 65+ years of age living in poverty. As can be seen, both the percentage of the total population and the percentage of older persons that are below the poverty line have declined since 1959. In 1959 more than one-third of older Americans lived below the poverty line, a figure almost double that of the general population. By 1988 the figure had dropped substantially for both groups. One of the major reasons for the drop in the percentage of older persons living in poverty was the increase in social security benefits. Between 1969 and 1971, social security benefits were increased by 43 percent while the cost of living increased 27 percent. In 1972 benefits increased by another 20 percent. Changes in the Social Security Act brought about automatic cost-of-living increases in 1975. Given the two recessions and high inflation rates during the last half of the 1970s and early 1980s this narrowed the gap between the incomes of the aged and nonaged.

One additional factor has also resulted in higher incomes and lower poverty rates for older persons; namely more older persons have higher social security and private pension benefits. The higher social security benefits are not just from the cost-of-living increases but from older persons having worked in higher paying jobs for longer periods of time covered by social security (U.S. Senate Special Committee on Aging, 1987–1988). Essentially, the "old-old" who are the least well off financially are dying and being replaced by the "young-old" who are better off financially. Thus, much of the improvement in economic status is related to the natural attrition and replacement of those 65+ years of age by a younger cohort.

We have examined the percentage of older persons living in poverty from a historical perspective. As mentioned earlier, there are three ways of examining poverty among older persons in contemporary society. The first is to examine the total population of the United States and then the percentage within selected age groups that are below the poverty line. Table 11-2 presents this information. As we can see, in

TABLE 11-1
PERCENT BELOW THE POVERTY
LEVEL

	All ages	65+
1959	22.4	35.2
1970	12.6	24.6
1980	13.0	15.7
1985	14.0	12.6
1986	13.6	12.4
1988	13.1	12.0

Source: U.S. Bureau of the Census, 1980, 1990.

TABLE 11-2
PERSONS BELOW POVERTY
LEVEL, 1988

Age	Percentage
Total	13.1
<16	20.4
16–21	15.7
22–44	10.5
45–64	7.7
65+	12.0

Source: U.S. Bureau of the Census, 1990.

1988 12.0 percent of older persons 65+ years of age lived below the poverty line. This is slightly less than the figure for all age groups, 13.1 percent, and significantly less than the two youngest age groups, many of whom are students or just entering the job market (see Cook & Kramek, 1986). Older persons, however, have a higher percentage than adults 22 to 44 and 45 to 64 years of age.

As is noted in Chapter 16, "Minorities," poverty is not equally distributed among older persons. While about 6.1 percent of older males who live in family households are below the poverty line the figure for females is 13.7 percent (U.S. Bureau of the Census, 1990). Because of the higher figure for females, gerontologists now discuss the "feminization of poverty and older women" (Minkler & Stone, 1985; see Hess, 1986; Holden et al., 1986; Warlick, 1985). The factors contributing to the higher incidence of poverty for older women are discussed in greater detail in Chapter 16. Briefly they are, first, that older women are more likely to have a history of economic dependency. That is, they are less likely to have worked outside the home than succeeding generations and are dependent on the incomes of spouses. Second, a longer life expectancy increases health care costs with the likelihood of exhausting income and savings. Third, widowhood is associated with economic problems for women. There are probably several reasons for this, that deal with unfamiliarity with financial matters, pension plans of deceased husbands that do not have survivors benefits, and the fact that social security survivors benefits are only about 66 percent of a couple's benefits even though government reports indicate that surviving spouses need about 80 percent of the predeath benefit to live the same life-style (Warlick, 1985). Fourth, many women who did work often did so intermittently. Additionally, they were often in positions that had low salaries, and which did not generate high social security benefits or offer pension benefits. The fifth, and last, factor contributing to the feminization of poverty is social policy. In an excellent article Warlick (1985) noted that the *major* factor responsible for the feminization of poverty in old age is the treatment of older women in American society. The financial problems of older women are well-documented; the decision to not address these problems has been a conscious and intentional policy decision.

Another factor that is related to poverty in old age is age. Essentially, increasing age brings about increasing levels of poverty. Table 11-3 presents the figures for 1986.

Race and ethnicity are also variables that need to be considered. Older persons who are black or Hispanic are over-represented among those in poverty; the percentages

TABLE 11-3
PERCENTAGE BELOW POVERTY BY AGE: 1986

	65+	65–74	75–84	85+
Both	12.4	10.3	15.3	17.6
Male	8.5	7.0	10.7	13.3
Female	15.2	13.0	18.1	19.7

Source: U.S. Bureau of the Census, 1987.

are 33.9 for blacks and 27.4 for Hispanics. The overall figure for aged whites is 10.1 percent (U.S. Bureau of the Census, 1990).

Although the specific percentages will change, it is unlikely that the poverty trend for blacks and Hispanics will change. Markides and Levin (1987) have pointed out that American society is changing from an industrial-based society to a high technology-based society. This they believe will do little to increase the economic status of minority groups (see Dressel, 1986; Torres-Gil, 1986; Watson, 1986). Others are not as pessimistic about the future economic status of aged minority groups (see Kutza, 1986).

Other factors are also important in poverty. Table 11-4 shows the percentage of older persons below the poverty level by selected characteristics for 1986.

One other way of examining poverty in old age is to examine those who are above but "near" to the poverty line. The category most commonly used is for those who are 24 percent above the poverty level. Essentially, this examines those who are not technically in poverty but "near" to poverty. The figures are presented in Table 11-5. As can be seen, the figures for those in "near poverty" are higher for older persons. Thus, the cumulative figures for those below poverty and in near poverty are greater for older persons, 20.0 percent, than for those under age 65, 17.5 percent.

Earlier we noted that there were three ways of examining poverty among older persons in contemporary American society. The first way, which we have just finished, was by examining the total aged population and accessing the percentage of this aged population that lived in poverty. The second is to look at the entire population of those in poverty and then determine the percentage that is 65+ years of age.

TABLE 11-4
PERCENTAGE OF OLDER PERSONS BELOW
THE POVERTY LEVEL BY SELECTED
CHARACTERISTICS: 1986

All persons	12.4
Didn't work last year, 65+	13.8
Women, 65+	15.2
All persons, 85+	17.6
Nonmetropolitan, 65+	17.9
Widowed women, 65+	21.0
Central city poverty areas, 65+	21.6
Hispanics, 65+	22.5
Living alone, 65+	24.7
Less than 8 years of school, 65+	26.8
Social security sole source of income, 65+	28.9
Black, 65+	31.0
Black, didn't work last year, ill/disabled, 65+	45.8
Black women living alone, 72+	63.7

Source: Senate Committee on Aging, 1987–1988.

TABLE 11-5
ELDERLY AND NONELDERLY PERSONS BY POVERTY LEVEL: 1988

	Percent	
Income	Under 65	Over 65
Below poverty	13.1	12.0
Below 125 percent of poverty level	17.5	20.0

Source: U.S. Bureau of the Census, 1990.

Here the total population base becomes the poverty population and we are interested in the percentage of this total poverty population that is 65+ years of age. We can then determine if older persons are over-or underrepresented in comparison to their percentage in the total poverty population. In 1988, 31.8 million individuals lived in poverty, about 3.5 million of them were 65+ years of age. Thus, about 11 percent of those living in poverty were 65+ years of age. This is a decrease from the past. For example, in 1977 the aged were overrepresented in this category. While they composed 10 percent of the population they composed almost 13 percent of those living in poverty.

The third way to examine economic status of older persons in contemporary society is more subjective and involves asking older persons to assess the quality of their lives. Cook and Kramek (1986; Strate & Dubnoff, 1986) conducted a telephone survey of Chicago area residents, both young and old, to determine economic hardship in the areas of food, housing, and medical care. In all three areas older persons were less likely than younger persons to state that they were experiencing a hardship. They were less likely to have been unable to purchase food, to have been evicted from their housing, have had utilities cut off, or to have gone without needed medical care because of lack of health insurance. There were some racial differences, with blacks noting more difficulties than whites. However, the researchers concluded that older persons were ''no more likely to suffer hardships than adults of other ages.'' The reasons for this were probably threefold. First, through experience, older persons had become better managers of limited resources. Second, older persons had accumulated more resources, such as extra money. Third, older persons were entitled to more noncash benefits such as subsidized housing or meals.

One other area needs to be briefly explored before leaving this section, namely, a longitudinal examination of those in poverty. The majority of studies on poverty have been cross sectional. That is, a figure on the percentage living in poverty is obtained at one period in time. It has been assumed that yearly cross-sectional studies on older persons essentially reported on the same individuals year after year. The belief was that once in poverty it was difficult, if not almost impossible, for older persons to get out of poverty. However, recent longitudinal observations have challenged this belief. Coe (1988) found that there was considerable turnover among the older poverty population. In fact, in 1 year 42 percent went from poverty to nonpoverty status. The study noted that the longer an older person was in poverty the less the likelihood of escaping. For example, if an older person had been in poverty for 3 years only 5 percent went to a nonpoverty status. Also, women had more difficulty escaping poverty.

INCOME OF OLDER PERSONS

Income figures, as we saw with poverty figures, can differ significantly depending on what figures one is examining. Tables 11-6 and 11-7 will present income from two perspectives. In Table 11-6 we can see the percentage of each age category that is in each income category. Excluding the youngest age category, 15–24, which has a high percentage of individuals who are in school or beginning their careers, we find that older persons are overrepresented in the lowest income category and under-represented in the highest income category.

Table 11-7 has income for households, not individuals. We can see two trends. First, after the youngest age category there is an increase in income until 55–64 years of age, when early retirement and death reduces the incomes in many households. There are further drops after age 65. The second trend is that blacks and Hispanics have significantly lower incomes at all ages than whites.

We can also examine the income of the aged by age category. This is done in Table 11-8. We can see the same trend that we have seen earlier: the old-old have less income than the young-old. There are at least two possible explanations for the young-old having more income than the old-old. First, income drops with increasing age. That is, the young-old are more likely to be in the work force and to have more income from savings or investments. Over time, these sources of income have vanished for the old-old. For example, as individuals age they may be forced to stop working and to rely on savings and investments. The drain on savings and investments would reduce interest from the savings as a source of income. A second possible explanation of why the young-old have more income than the old-old is that the young-old have earned larger social security and private pension benefits.

TABLE 11-6
MONEY INCOME OF HOUSEHOLDS
(Percent Distribution by Households by Income Level)

Age	Under $5,000	$5,000 to $9,999	$10,000 to $14,999	$15,000 to $24,999	$25,000 to $34,999	$35,000 to $49,999	$50,000 to $74,999	$75,000 and over
15–24	13.8	11.6	15.8	25.6	15.8	8.1	3.6	0.9
25–34	5.7	7.8	9.6	22.2	20.3	20.4	10.9	3.0
35–44	4.3	6.1	6.6	15.7	17.5	23.5	17.5	8.9
45–54	4.9	5.6	6.6	14.0	15.3	20.5	20.0	13.1
55–64	7.5	9.9	9.5	18.8	15.2	17.0	13.7	8.3
65+	9.9	24.5	17.8	22.1	11.5	7.9	4.1	2.3

Source: U.S. Bureau of the Census, 1990.

TABLE 11-7
MONEY INCOME OF HOUSEHOLDS: 1987
(Mean Income in Dollars)

Age	White	Black	Hispanic
15–24	$20,630	$12,573	$18,601
25–34	31,913	19,277	23,473
35–44	41,154	26,647	28,737
45–54	45,997	27,689	30,631
55–64	36,445	20,174	24,474
65+	21,029	12,622	15,332

Source: U.S. Bureau of the Census, 1990.

In this case, the difference in level of income would occur not because the level of income has dropped with increasing age but because the young-old have earned higher benefits.

One quick note on the depletion of savings noted above. Most gerontologists have held the ''life-cycle hypothesis of savings'' (Ando & Modigliani, 1963) which claimed that with increasing age there was a tendency to ''dissave'' or deplete saving. This hypothesis has seemed logical and was accepted based mostly on cross-sectional data. New evidence is starting to appear suggesting that rather than dissave, continual saving takes place for many older persons (see Stoller & Stoller, 1987). More research in this area is needed.

As we have seen, a large percentage of older persons live below or near the poverty line. In recent years, there has been improvement in this area, although there has been fluctuation. The future financial outlook for older persons is, of course, unknown. There are two differing opinions. The first claims that in the near future older persons

TABLE 11-8
MEDIAN INCOME OF AGED FAMILIES AND
UNRELATED INDIVIDUALS: 1985

Families	Median income
65–74	$20,354
75–84	16,412
85+	15,111

Unrelated individuals	Median income
65–74	$ 8,160
75–84	7,186
85+	6,400

Source: U.S. Senate Committee on Aging, 1987–1988.

will not substantially improve their financial status. The second claims the opposite. Each of these opinions will be discussed briefly below.

Some believe that the financial status of older persons will not improve very much in the near future. One reason is that social security benefits will probably not substantially increase. Although social security benefits now increase automatically to keep pace with the cost of living (unless there is congressional action to delay the increase), there will still not be any increases in "real income." Other reasons advanced for the opinion that there will not be an increase in the financial position of the aged are that few of those nearing old age are actively preparing for old age, and that many still do not have private pension plans.

Others argue that the financial position of older persons will improve in the near future. These individuals note that in recent years there has been a general trend toward improvement in the financial position of older persons. They also note that older persons are becoming more educated and have higher occupational levels which are associated with maximum social security benefits, private pensions, savings, and assets. Additionally, social security benefits, because they are tied to increases in the cost of living, will increase faster than salaries.

SOURCES OF INCOME FOR OLDER PERSONS

Older persons generally have more than one source of income. This section will examine the composition and sources of their income. Table 11-9 indicates the major sources of income for older persons. As can be seen, social security is the major source of income for older persons. More than 90 percent of older persons are eligible for social security benefits; for 14 percent of older persons social security is their only source of income and for 31 percent it accounts for 80 percent of their income (Special Committee on Aging, 1988). As would be expected, social security makes up a larger percentage of total income for those with lower incomes (77 percent for those with incomes under $5000) than for those with larger incomes (21 percent for those with incomes above $20,000) (U.S. Senate Committee on Aging, 1987–1988).

Income from assets was the second major source of income. Assets have only recently become a major source of income. In 1962 assets accounted for 16 percent

TABLE 11-9
INCOME SOURCES FOR OLDER PERSONS: 1987

Source	Percentage
Social security	40
Asset income	26
Earnings	15
Pensions	16
Other	2
Supplemental security income	1

Source: Special Committee, 1988.

of income. Although assets are growing they are still unevenly divided among older persons with 33 percent having no asset income, 26 percent reporting less than $500 per year, 8 percent reporting between $500 and $4999, and 33 percent reporting more than $5000 per year (U.S. Senate Committee on Aging, 1987–1988). Earnings were the next major source of income. As expected, this differs with age, with the youngest age group, 65–69, receiving 30 percent of their income from earnings, while those 80+ years of age received 4 percent from earnings (U.S. Senate Committee on Aging, 1987–1988). The last major source of income is pension benefits. Currently approximately 40 percent of older persons receive pension benefits. Again, the percentage decreases with increasing age. The young-old are more likely to have higher pension benefits than the old-old.

There have been changes in the composition of the income sources for older persons. For example, in the 1960s about half of the income of older persons living in families came from earnings. As can be seen in Table 11-9, this has dropped significantly. In the 1960s social security composed about 22 percent of income. Again, we can see the increase in this area in Table 11-9. Early retirement is possible because more workers are covered by social security benefits and because they have earned higher benefits. Also, increases in the number of older persons with pensions, as well as increased benefits, and an increase in assets helps compensate for the loss of income through earnings.

We will now consider several of the specific sources of income for older persons in more detail. Work, as a source of income, is considered in Chapter 13, "Work, Retirement, and Leisure."

Social Security

Social security was instituted as a relatively modest, federally run, old-age pension or unemployment insurance program (OAI) in 1935. The social security program has since undergone a number of modifications that have made it one of the most extensive social insurance programs in existence. For example, survivors' benefits were added to the program in 1939 (OASI). In 1956, disability insurance was added (OASDI). In 1965, with the enactment of medicare, a health program was added (OASDHI). Additionally, over time, more workers have been brought into the social security system: 93.8 percent as of 1986. This subsection will deal with OASI.

Social security operates on several principles. First, participation in the system is compulsory for most workers. Most workers cannot choose whether or not to belong to the system, nor can they leave the system prior to death, disability, or retirement. Second, social security is a type of "insurance," protecting workers against unemployment in old age and spouses against loss of income through widowhood. It is for the "good" of all individuals, although not necessarily "fair" for all. For example, although some individuals may pay large amounts into the system, they may get very little or nothing out of the system. Others may pay little into the system and get a great deal out of the system in return. It is essentially an "insurance" policy for workers and their families against unemployment because of disability, retirement, or death. It is not a savings or pension plan. Third, social security is not welfare.

In order to receive social security benefits, individuals or their spouses or parents must have paid into the system. The amount of monthly benefits received depends on the amount the worker paid in. Thus, benefits are an earned right. Fourth, because it is a national program, the tax rates and benefits are the same nationally. Fifth, social security includes an income redistribution factor by which those at the lower income levels receive back proportionally more in retirement benefits than those at the higher income levels. Sixth, the program is supposed to be self-supporting. That is, income is supposed to meet expenditures. The system operates on a "pay-as-you-go" basis, with current income being used to meet current expenses. The original philosophy was that current workers would pay more into the system than retired workers or widowed spouses would draw out of the system.

As was noted at the beginning of this section, social security has gone from a relatively modest supplemental income plan for workers from sudden loss of wages due to disability, retirement, or death to a very comprehensive social insurance plan protecting not only workers but also their families. It is a form of insurance in that each generation of workers supports retired workers, in exchange for the guarantee that the next generation will do the same for them. It is also a form of insurance for workers against having to provide for parental support. As a result, the cost of the program for workers has grown. For example, in 1950 the social security tax was 1.50 percent on the first $3000 of income for both the employer and the employee. In 1990 it was 7.65 percent for both the employee and employer on the first $48,000.

In addition to adding survivors benefits, disability insurance, and health insurance, there have been numerous other changes to the original Social Security Act. One of the most recent and dramatic deals with the decision to increase the age at which full retirement benefits can be obtained from 65 to 67 for those born after 1960. This is recognition that early retirement and increased life expectancy were placing a heavy financial drain on the social security system (see Hayward et al., 1988).

Even after more than 50 years, social security is still a controversial program, with many believing that it is a drain on the economy (see Quadagno, 1987). Although there have been concerns about the financial stability of the social security system, it appears to be stable through the next half-century. As long as the federal government has the ability to increase the social security tax, there is little risk of financial problems.

Income from Assets

Other persons as a group have assets worth more than the nonaged. The median net worth for those 35+ years of age is $32,667; for older persons it is $60,266. The bulk of this, $46,192, is in home equity. Excluding home equity the figures for those 35+ and 65+ are $7,783 and $17,025. Many older persons may be "house rich" and "cash poor" (U.S. Bureau of the Census, 1987; U.S. Senate Committee on Aging, 1987–1988).

While as a group older persons hold more assets than adults in general, there are many older persons who have few assets. In fact, 28.5 percent have assets of under $25,000 and 15.4 percent a net worth of under $5000. For nonhome assets, 40 percent have assets worth less than $10,000.

As noted, one of the larger noncash assets of most older persons are their homes. Most have paid off mortgages and many others are close. New ways of turning this noncash asset into a cash asset, such as through reverse mortgages or home equity conversion, are starting to emerge (see Chapter 14, "Home and Community") (Jacobs, 1986).

Pensions

There are several types of employee pensions, which can be separated into private and public. Private plans would include plans of companies and unions, and public plans those of federal, state, and local governments, the U.S. military and the National Guard. This section will examine only private pension plans.

At the turn of the century there were only about ten private pension plans in the United States (see Schultz, 1988). Currently there are 1.2 million private pension plans (U.S. Bureau of the Census, 1990). According to Schultz (1985) and others the increase in private pension plans took place for several reasons:

1 The change from an agricultural society to an industrial society created the need for options for funding retirement, other than savings and the family.

2 The increase in life expectancy created a longer period when individuals were retired because of inability to work, inability to find work, or desire not to work.

3 Some employers created private pensions so that workers would not shift jobs; many early pensions were only granted after a significant number of years of employment and only if the employee was a certain age.

4 There were times when it was easier for a company to give pension benefits than increase wages.

5 The federal government has created several acts that have provided tax incentives to companies offering private pension plans.

6 A 1949 decision by the Supreme Court that made private pensions a negotiable issue in collective bargaining.

7 The increasing belief by employees that companies had a "social obligation to provide workers with pensions."

8 The realization by several segments of society that social security benefits were an inadequate source of retirement income.

9 The creation of "multiemployer" pension plans that made it easier for employers to create and manage pension funds.

Approximately 40.8 percent of all wage and salary workers are covered by private pension plans. Those who are covered tend to have higher salaries, work for organizations that employ more than 100 individuals, and have union status. The increase in coverage was rapid from 1950 to the early 1980s, when it slowed and even declined slightly because of the recessions and the job losses in manufacturing (Special Committee on Aging, 1988; U.S. Bureau of the Census, 1990).

There have been serious problems with private pension plans. Many of the early plans were created and funded by employers. Because there was little governmental regulation, in difficult economic times employers drew on the pension funds to cover costs or neglected to place money in the funds to cover an increasing future liability.

For the companies that went bankrupt, workers were often left with no pension benefits or a fraction of what they expected.

Other problems were also encountered in private pension plans that dealt with vesting and portability. Vesting refers to the amount of time employees have to work before they will receive pension benefits, even if the employee leaves the organization prior to retirement. Many of the early pension plans required an extensive number of years of service before employees could receive benefits. Employees who left organizations prior to being vested were not entitled to any pension benefits. There were numerous reports of companies attempting to reduce costs by firing employees shortly before they became eligible for pension benefits, sometimes after decades of service.

Portability refers to the ability of employees to take the pension money accumulated in one pension fund and move it to another pension fund; this generally occurred when workers left one organization for another. While many individuals had gained vested rights to benefits, often the benefits were "frozen" when employees left an organization and did not earn interest. Thus, the earlier rules on vesting and portability meant that the higher the job turnover rate the lower the pension benefits (Clark & McDermed, 1988).

Since the 1950s there has been concern over private pensions by the federal government. In 1959 it passed the Welfare and Pension Plan Disclosure Act to help prevent some of the problems noted above. However, this act did not have the power necessary to bring about significant changes. Thus, in 1974 the Employee Retirement Income Security Act (ERISA) was passed. This act was a much stronger act in protecting the private pension benefits of employees. In fact, some have claimed that it is the most important "pension legislation since the Social Security Act" (see O'Rand, 1987).

ERISA had many provisions, some of which have been modified by subsequent acts. Essentially the act made vesting mandatory according to one of three options: (1) 100 percent vesting after 10 years; (2) 25 percent vesting after 5 years, with additional vesting per year with 100 percent reached by 15 years; (3) 50 percent vesting when age and years of service equal 45, with 100 percent within 5 years. An insurance program which is monitored by the Pension Benefit Guaranty Corporation, a nonprofit federal corporation, was created to cover workers whose private pension plans went bankrupt. The insurance is funded by an employer fee on each covered employee. In 1986 it was $8.50 per employee. Minimum funding standards for pension plans were established. The act dealt with the diversification of assets and the portability of vested benefits.

There have been several other changes since 1974: 1982 the Tax Equity and Fiscal Responsibility Act (TEFRA); 1984 Retirement Equity Act (REA); 1986 Title XI of the Tax Reform Act.

Other Sources of Income

There are some other frequent sources of income that need to be examined: other government programs and family. Each will be examined below.

Supplemental Social Welfare Income Sources   As noted earlier, social security is a type of insurance that was established to supplement income in old age, not be the sole source of income. For many older persons social security is the only or the primary source of income. Also, there have been numerous individuals not covered by social security. Because of these factors, the federal government enacted two programs to help meet the economic needs of certain "needy" aged. The first was the Old Age Assistance Act of 1950. This act recognized that many of the aged needed financial assistance either because they had not been covered by social security, or because their time in social security did not permit them an adequate income. Through this act, certain aged individuals became eligible for monthly payments. This program, aid to the blind (AB), and aid to the permanently and totally disabled (APTD), were replaced in 1972 by supplemental security income (SSI).

For older persons to qualify for SSI they must be at least 65 years of age and have an income that is below a certain level; generally an income that is below the poverty level. Essentially, if the total income of an older person is below a specified amount, then the individual will receive the difference through SSI. SSI is a form of welfare and its funds come from the general revenues of the federal government. Because it is a form of welfare, there is an eligibility requirement in the form of an assets test.

Indirect Sources of Income   Although older persons have less income than the nonelderly, they do have certain advantages in terms of noncash benefits that reduce the economic differences between the groups. For example, older persons receive certain types of nonincome and noncash benefits such as low rent through subsidized housing, tax advantages (see Bell et al., 1987), medicare, food stamps, energy assistance, and access to nutrition programs. Although these are not a "direct" source of income, they can save many older persons large amounts of money.

For example, there are several provisions in the federal tax code that assist older persons in paying a smaller percentage of their total income in taxes. Thus, although older persons receive less income, they are able to "keep" a larger percentage than the nonelderly. Government-sponsored benefits such as energy assistance, food stamps, public housing, or rent assistance are other forms of noncash or nonincome indirect sources of financial support.

It should be noted that many of these potential sources of noncash or nonincome benefits are underutilized by older persons. For example, only about one-half of older persons who are eligible for food stamps actually receive them. This is because many do not know that they are eligible, others are embarrassed to enroll in the program, and for others transportation problems prevent them from enrolling in the program (Hollonbeck & Ohls, 1984). The rate of utilization for many benefits is low for older persons: energy assistance 7 percent; food stamps 6 percent; public housing 4 percent; rental assistance 2 percent (U.S. Senate Special Committee on Aging 1987–1988).

OLDER PERSONS AS CONSUMERS

Relatively little attention has been given to the role of older persons as consumers (Mertz & Stephens, 1986). This lack of attention seems strange since older persons

TABLE 11-10
EXPENDITURES BY AGE
(Percentage)

Type of expenditure	Under 65	65–74	75+
Shelter/furnishings	22.9	20.2	23.8
Utilities	7.3	10.4	11.7
Food	15.3	17.8	17.1
Clothing	5.7	4.5	3.1
Health care	3.3	8.4	13.3
Transportation	20.5	19.2	13.0
Pension and life insurance	10.0	4.9	2.0
Entertainment	5.0	3.8	2.6
Cash contributions	7.0	6.0	5.6
Other	3.1	4.8	7.8

Source: U.S. Senate Special Committee on Aging, 1987–1988.

constitute a significant percentage of the population, and many of them have extra disposable income. Although marketers are beginning to take into account the growing population of older persons, they are still underrepresented in areas such as television commercials (Swayne & Greco, 1987). This may soon change as corporations began to realize the size and purchasing power of older persons (see Hartman, 1988; Marken et al., 1989; Todd, 1989).

Table 11-10 shows the consumption patterns of different age groups. Older persons have a higher expenditure on essentials than nonaged. For example, the percentages for shelter, utilities, food, and health care increase with each age group. For those under age 65 the percentage is 48.8. For those age 65–74 and 75+ the percentages are 56.8 and 65.9. We can also see that older persons spend less in other areas: clothing, transportation, pensions and life insurance, and entertainment.

SUMMARY

The economic aspect of aging is important in that it has a significant bearing on both the quality and quantity of life in old age. This chapter was separated into five sections.

In the first section it was noted that the economic image of older persons has undergone a dramatic change in recent years. In many segments of society they have gone from the "deserving poor" to the "undeserving rich." There are several reasons, one of which is competition with other age groups for limited societal resources. The second section examined the actual economic status of older persons. A variety of factors, such as several organizations collecting information, make the determination of their actual economic status difficult. In 1988, 12.0 percent of older persons lived below the poverty line. In 1959 the figure was 35.2 percent. Poverty is not distributed equally: minorities and women are overrepresented in the poverty statistics.

In the third section the income of older persons was discussed. It was noted that older persons tend to be overrepresented in the lower income category and underrepresented in the highest income category. The fourth section examined the composition of income for older persons. It was noted that social security composes the largest percentage, followed by asset income, earnings, pensions, other, and SSI. Social security was instituted in 1935 and has grown significantly in terms of its coverage and cost. Pensions have also become more important as a source of income for older persons.

The last section examined older persons as consumers. It was noted that more attention is being focused on older persons as consumers.

REFERENCES

Ando, A., & Modigliani, F. (1963). The life-cycle hypothesis of savings. *American Economic Review*, **53**(1): 55–84.

Bell, W. G., Serow, W. J., & Shelley, W. J. (1987). Measuring the economic impact of a state's tax structure on an elderly population. *The Gerontologist*, **27**(6): 804–808.

Binstock, R. H. (1983). The aged as scapegoat. *The Gerontologist*, **23**(2): 136–143.

Binstock, R. H. (1986). Perspectives on measuring hardship: Concepts, dimensions, and implications. *The Gerontologist*, **26**(1): 60–62.

Broder, D. S. (1973). Budget funds for elderly grow rapidly. *The Washington Post*, January 30: 11–16.

Califano, J. A. (1979). Testimony. In U.S. Senate Special Committee on Aging, *Retirement, work, and lifelong learning*. Washington, DC: U.S. Government Printing Office.

Clark, R. L., & McDermed, A. A. (1988). Pension wealth and job changes: The effects of vesting, portability, and lump-sum distributions. *The Gerontologist*, **28**(4): 524–532.

Clark, R. L., & Sumner, D. A. (1985). Inflation and real income of the elderly: Recent evidence and expectations for the future. *The Gerontologist*, **25**(2): 146–152.

Coe, R. D. (1988). A longitudinal examination of poverty in the elderly years. *The Gerontologist*, **28**(4): 540–544.

Cook, F. L., & Kramek, L. M. (1986). Measuring economic hardship among older Americans. *The Gerontologist*, **26**(1): 38–47.

Dressel, P. L. (1986). An overview of the issues. *The Gerontologist*, **26**(2): 128–131.

Dressel, P. L. (1988). Gender, race, and class: Beyond the feminization of poverty in later life. *The Gerontologist*, **28**(2): 177–180.

Fairlie, H. (1988). Whatever happened to a dignified old age? Talkin' 'bout my generation. *The New Republic*, **198**(13): 19–22.

Flint, J. (1980). The old folks. *Forbes*, **125**(4): 51–56.

Hartman, C. (1988). Redesigning America. *Inc.*, **10**(6): 58–74.

Hayward, M. D., Grady, W. R., & McLaughlin, S. D. (1988). Recent changes in mortality and labor force behavior among older Americans: Consequences for nonworking life expectancy. *Journal of Gerontology: Social Sciences*, **43**(6): S194–199.

Hess, B. B. (1986). Antidiscrimination policies today and the life chances of older women tomorrow. *The Gerontologist*, **26**(2): 132–135.

Holden, K. C., Burkhauser, R. V., & Myers, D. A. (1986). Income transitions at older stages of life: The dynamics of poverty. *The Gerontologist*, **26**(3): 292–297.

Hollonbeck, D., & Ohls, J. C. (1984). Participation among the elderly in the food stamp program. *The Gerontologist*, **24**(6): 616–621.

Hudson, R. (1978). The graying of the federal budget and the consequences for old-age policy. *The Gerontologist,* **18**(5): 428–440.

Jacobs, B. (1986). The national potential of home equity conversion. *The Gerontologist,* **26**(5): 496–504.

Kingson, E. R. (1988). Generational equity: An unexpected opportunity to broaden the politics of aging. *The Gerontologist,* **28**(6): 765–772.

Kingson, E. R., Hirshorn, B. A., & Cornman, J. M. (1986). *Ties that bind: The interdependence of generations.* Cabin John, MD: Seven Locks Press.

Kutza, E. A. (1986). A policy analyst's response. *The Gerontologist,* **26**(2): 147–149.

Marken, E. W., Pratt, F., & Taylor, S. (1989). Teaching gerontology to the business community: Project older consumer. *Educational Gerontology,* **15**(3): 285–295.

Markides, K. S., & Levin, J. S. (1987). The changing economy and the future of the minority aged. *The Gerontologist,* **27**(3): 273–274.

Mertz, B., & Stephens, N. (1986). Marketing to older American consumers. *International Journal of Aging and Human Development,* **23**(1): 47–58.

Minkler, M. (1989). Gold in gray: Reflections on business' discovery of the elderly market. *The Gerontologist,* **29**(1): 17–23.

Minkler, M., & Stone, R. (1985). The feminization of poverty and older women. *The Gerontologist,* **25**(4): 351–357.

Moon, M. (1988). The economic situation of older Americans: emerging wealth and continuing hardship. In G. L. Maddox & M. P. Lawton (Eds.), Annual review of gerontology and geriatrics: Volume 8 (pp. 102–131). New York: Springer.

O'Rand, A. M. (1987). Employee Retirement Income Security Act. In G. L. Maddox (Ed.), *The encyclopedia of aging* (pp. 205–206). New York: Springer.

Peterson, P. G. (1987). The morning after. *The Atlantic,* **260**(4): 43–69.

Preston, S. H. (1984). Children and the elderly in the U.S. *Scientific American,* **251**(6): 44–49.

Quadagno, J. (1987). The Social Security program and the private sector alternative: Lessons from history. *International Journal of Aging and Human Development,* **25**(3): 239–246.

Schulz, J. H. (1985). To old folks with love: Aged income maintenance in America. *The Gerontologist,* **25**(5): 464–471.

Schulz, J. H. (1988). *The economics of aging* (fourth edition). Dover, MA: Auburn House.

Smeeding, T. M. (1982). Alternative methods for valuing selected in-kind transfer benefits and measuring their effect on poverty. Technical Paper 50, Washington, DC: U.S. Bureau of the Census.

Special Committee on Aging, United States Senate (1988). *Development in aging: 1987.* Washington, DC: U.S. Government Printing Office.

Stoller, E. P., & Stoller, M. A. (1987). The propensity to save among the elderly. *The Gerontologist,* **27**(3): 315–320.

Strate, J. M., & Dubnoff, S. J. (1986). How much income is enough? Measuring the income adequacy of retired persons using a survey-based approach. *Journal of Gerontology,* **41**(3): 393–400.

Swayne, L. E., & Greco, A. J. (1987). The portrayal of older Americans in television commercials. *Journal of Advertising,* **16**(1): 47–54.

Todd, B. (1989). Marketing to older people: Quality International's prime-time travel program. *Generations,* **13**(3): 58–60.

Torres-Gil, F. (1986). An examination of factors affecting future cohorts of elderly Hispanics. *The Gerontologist,* **26**(2): 140–146.

Torrey, B. B. (1982). Guns vs. canes: The fiscal implications of an aging population. *American Economic Association Papers and Proceedings,* **24**(May): 309–313.

Uhlenberg, P., & Salmon, M. A. P. (1986). Change in relative income of older women, 1960–1980. *The Gerontologist,* **26**(2): 164–170.

U.S. Bureau of the Census (1990). *Statistical abstract of the United States.* Washington, DC: U.S. Government Printing Office.

U.S. Bureau of the Census (1987). *Statistical abstract of the United States.* Washington, DC: U.S. Government Printing Office.

U.S. Senate Special Committee on Aging (1987–1988). *Aging America: Trends and projections (1987–1988 edition).* Washington, DC: U.S. Department of Health and Human Services.

Warlick, J. L. (1985). Why is poverty after 65 a woman's problem? *Journal of Gerontology,* **40**(6): 751–757.

Watson, W. H. (1986). Crystal ball gazing: Notes on today's middle aged blacks with implications for their aging in the 21st century. *The Gerontologist,* **26**(2): 136–139.

Wisedale, S. K. (1988). Generational equity and intergenerational policies. *The Gerontologist,* **28**(6): 773–778.

CHAPTER 12

POLITICS AND SOCIAL POLICY

Jim Anderson/Stock, Boston

INTRODUCTION

All societies are continually changing. For some societies the process of change is very rapid and dramatic. For others, change may be slow and barely noticeable. In a democratic society the degree, type, and amount of change are often determined by the political process. Individuals or groups that can utilize political power to elect certain politicians, influence the platform of a political party, or influence the voting of a politician on a specific issue are more likely to influence the political process. The reverse is also true. Thus, the political sphere is one of tremendous importance to almost every segment of society that desires to regulate change. In this chapter we will examine politics and social policy.

POLITICS

This section is separated into four subsections: political views, party affiliation, participation in politics, and political power.

Political Views

A common belief was that with increasing age individuals became more conservative. This belief was based on cross-sectional research which indicated that older persons were more conservative than younger individuals.

This belief has been frequently examined and found to be false (Cutler & Kaufman, 1975; Glenn, 1974). Even if older persons were found to be more conservative it would not necessarily follow that the aging process was the cause. It could, for example, indicate that older individuals were raised with more conservative beliefs than young adults. Part of the explanation of the difference might also be accounted for by education, not the aging process. In general older persons have less formal education than young adults and it is known that increasing levels of education are associated with increasing liberalism. In fact, Glamser (1974) found that the level of education was twice as important as age in explaining political views. Glamser's study suggested that many of the differences in the political views between young adults and older persons were not caused by differences in age but by differences in levels of education.

Research also indicates that older persons are more conservative on some issues, and more liberal on others. They are more conservative in areas that have an impact on them, for example law and order issues or those that threaten traditional values (i.e., abortion, drugs). On other issues they are found to be more liberal. For example, older persons were more likely to oppose the Vietnam War (a liberal stance), which may reflect an "isolationist" upbringing (see Campbell, 1971; Campbell & Strate, 1981; Douglass et al., 1974; Glamser, 1974).

Obviously political views can influence voting. One hypothesis that has recently been examined is the "gray peril hypothesis" which stated that older persons are politically active and will organize and vote primarily for issues that benefit them and against issues that do not benefit them. One specific area frequently mentioned

378

is school taxes, with the hypothesis stating that since school taxes do not directly benefit older persons they will vote against them. This is especially believed to be true for older persons who have left communities where they lived for many years and migrated to retirement communities. Recent research has challenged this hypothesis (Button & Rosenbaum, 1989; Rosenbaum & Button, 1989).

Although difficult to measure, in all probability most older persons become more liberal with increasing age, even though they are not as liberal as young adults. A subjective way to test this would be to ask older persons to compare their current views with what they believe their views were 50 years ago on issues such as civil rights, premarital sex, drugs, women in the work force, or living together before marriage. The results would most likely indicate that with increasing age most older persons have become more liberal (see Glenn & Hefner, 1972).

Political Party Affiliation

Generally, it has been believed that with increasing age individuals shift from the liberal Democratic party to the conservative Republican party. This belief was based on studies published during the 1960s which indicated that there were more older Republicans than Democrats, but that for younger adults the figures were reversed. The assumption was that as individuals grew older they became more conservative and shifted from the more liberal Democratic party to the more conservative Republican party. A 24-year study of political party affiliation by Glenn and Hefner (1972) found no support for the belief that as individuals aged they shifted from the Democratic to the Republican party (see Hudson & Strate, 1985). In fact, this study reported that party affiliation tended to remain stable.

There is one other area that needs to be examined dealing with party affiliation: strength of party ties and loyalties. Studies have also reported that younger individuals generally have weaker party ties and loyalties than older adults. Two explanations have been used to account for these differences. The first is the life-cycle explanation, which claims that the political inexperience of young adults contributes to their weak ties and loyalties, but that increasing age will bring about a strengthening in both areas (Converse, 1969, 1976, 1979). The generational explanation for the weak party ties and loyalties states that the differences are caused by differences in socialization; the older voters were socialized to have stronger ties and loyalties than younger voters (Abramson, 1976, 1979). The generational explanation appears to be the stronger of the two positions. Longitudinal studies have not reported the increase in party ties and loyalties projected by the life-cycle explanation (Abramson, 1976, 1979; Glenn & Hefner, 1972).

Based on some erroneous assumptions and beliefs about political party affiliation, there were projections that the increasing size of the older population would make the Republican party a powerful force composed primarily of older persons. What has emerged is very different. Essentially, the studies in the 1960s, which indicated that a large percentage of older persons were Republican, were merely noting the early political socialization of the older cohort. What is currently emerging is an older cohort that was socialized during the depression when there was a significant shifting of political alliance by young adults from the Republican party to the Democratic party. These individuals have entered old age and have shifted the traditional tendency of older persons as Republicans to older persons as Democrats. One other trend is an increasing percentage of independent voters. In the past there was a greater likelihood of belonging to a political party, and of keeping this identification throughout life. Young adults are more issue-oriented than party-oriented. Future studies will reveal the extent and the impact of this change.

Participation of Older Persons in Politics

Participation in politics can take several forms. Joining interest groups, becoming members of political parties, holding political office, or voting represent forms of political participation. In this section of the chapter we will examine the participation of older persons in three areas of politics: voting, holding political office, and other forms of political activity.

Voting   Certainly one basic American right deals with voting. Through the ballot, voters have the right to vote for the political candidates and issues they believe will best represent their interests.

Voting behavior over the life cycle has been conceptualized as being similar to a normal curve, with voting at the lowest level for the youngest age cohorts, and then rising gradually through middle age where it peaks, and then starting to decline in old age. Most studies have reported this trend; the differences have dealt with when and why the decline takes place. For some researchers the decline starts in the fifties or early sixties (see Cutler, 1983), while for others it does not start until the mid-seventies (Hill & Kent, 1988).

Although the trend in voter participation is clear, the reasons for the trend are not. Some writers have attributed the low voter turnout of young adults to age-related issues. For example, younger adults are less likely to vote because they have age-related concerns such as completing educational programs and starting careers and families. These concerns draw their attention and time from political issues. Additionally, many younger adults do not have as much invested in the outcomes of political elections. For example, young adults are less likely to own homes or have children in schools and as a result are not as concerned about the outcomes of political elections (see Cutler, 1983; Hudson & Strate, 1985). The decline in voting among older persons is seen as the result of disengagement from the political process for a variety of social and health reasons.

Others attributed the voting curve primarily to cohort effect. The belief is that cohorts are politically socialized into patterns of voting that persist over time. Glenn and Grimes (1968) found that this was true for the voter participation rates of six cohorts over 20 years. This and other studies (see Hout & Knoke, 1975) suggested that cohorts develop and maintain patterns of voting participation. The voting curve may also have been influenced by sex. The traditional model had males voting more frequently than females. Part of the explanation dealt with the early political socialization of females. It must be remembered that the Nineteenth Amendment, which gave women the right to vote, was passed in 1920. Even though it passed, many women of this era had been socialized to believe that voting was essentially a "male right." Many of these women either did not vote or mimicked the voting behavior of their husbands (Wolfinger, 1980). When husbands died many older females stopped voting.

We are starting to see a different voting trend for older persons emerge. First, the increase in the percentage of women 75+ years of age who vote. For example, in the presidential elections of 1972 49 percent of these women voted; by 1984 the percentage was 57 (Hill & Kent, 1988). A second pattern deals with the increased age at which voting starts to decline due to increased health and life expectancy of both males and females. The trend now is for voting to continue until very old age. Much of the decline noted in the past was probably attributed more to widowhood than any other factors. The age at which the "decline" in voting starts to take place has increased because most women have become politically independent of their husbands, and for those dependent on their husbands, increasing life expectancy will delay widowhood and the cessation of voting.

Third, education is going to influence frequency of voting. There is no doubt that education influences voting behavior. For example, of those voting in the 1984 presidential elections 36.7 percent of those with 8 or fewer years of education voted in comparison with 79.1 percent of those with 4 or more years of college. For the 1986 congressional elections the percentages were 32.7 and 65.2 (U.S. Bureau of the Census, 1990). Part of the differences in the voting between the middle-aged and aged reflects differences in education, with younger cohorts being more educated than older cohorts. The lower percentage of aged individuals voting was assumed to be an aging effect; however it was probably an education effect. As the education levels become more similar we will probably see similar levels of voting.

A fourth pattern deals with the percentage of all males and females who vote. Until recently a greater percentage of males than females voted. This changed in the national election of 1980 when 59.4 percent of females and 59.1 percent of males voted. The same pattern has been repeated in the 1986 congressional elections and the 1984 and 1988 presidential elections (U.S. Bureau of the Census, 1990). Voting will be discussed later in this chapter when we discuss the political power of older persons.

Political Office   A common belief is that older persons are overrepresented in many political offices. In certain areas this is true (e.g., ambassadors, supreme court justices, mayors, and governors). To be appointed to many political positions, individuals must have either the experience or the power to be elected or appointed. Generally, it is through time that experience and power are acquired. Thus, it is no surprise that many elected and appointed officials are older. We will examine the age composition of two areas: Congress and the presidency.

Congress   Table 12-1 has the median age of senators and representatives from 1799 to 1985.

Another way of examining the age composition of Congress is to examine the

TABLE 12-1
MEDIAN AGE OF SENATORS AND REPRESENTATIVES

	1799	1925	1978	1985
Representatives	43.5	53.5	50.0	49.7
Senators	45.3	55.0	55.0	54.2

Source: Cutler & Schmidhauser, 1975; Congressional Quarterly, 1985.

percentage in each age category, as is done in Table 12-2. To help understand Table 12-2 it needs to be pointed out (as we will see shortly in Tables 12-5 and 12-6) that older persons compose 16 percent of the voting population. With this in mind we can then see if older persons are over- (above 16 percent) or underrepresented (below 16 percent) in the 60+ years of age categories. Two observations can be made. First, in the 101st Congress they are overrepresented in the House of Representatives where 22 percent are 60+ years of age (17 percent age 60–69; 5 percent age 70–79); older persons are overrepresented in the Senate where 30 percent are 60+ years of age (22 percent age 60–69; 6 percent age 70–79; 2 percent age 80+). Second,

TABLE 12-2
CONGRESSIONAL REPRESENTATION BY AGE CATEGORY

	40 %	40–49 %	50–59 %	60–69 %	70–79 %	80+ %
Representatives						
92d Congress 1971	9	31	35	20	4	1
93d Congress 1973	10	30	36	18	5	0
94th Congress 1975	16	32	31	17	3	0
95th Congress 1977	19	28	34	16	3	0
96th Congress 1979	19	28	35	14	3	0
97th Congress 1981	22	33	30	12	3	0*
98th Congress 1983	20	33	30	13	3	0*
99th Congress 1985	16	35	30	14	4	0†
100th Congress 1987	15	36	32	13	3	0†
101st Congress 1989	9	38	31	17	5	0†
Senators						
92d Congress 1971	4	24	32	23	16	1
93d Congress 1973	3	25	37	23	11	1
94th Congress 1975	5	21	35	24	15	0
95th Congress 1977	6	26	35	21	10	2
96th Congress 1979	10	31	33	17	8	1
97th Congress 1981	9	35	36	14	6	0
98th Congress 1983	7	28	39	20	3	3
99th Congress 1985	4	27	38	25	4	2
100th Congress 1987	5	30	36	22	5	2
101st Congress 1989	0	30	40	22	6	2

* Indicates one representative.
† Indicates two representatives.
Source: U.S. Bureau of the Census, 1990.

TABLE 12-3
MEAN AGE FOR PRESIDENTS AT
INAUGURATION BY TIME PERIOD

Time period	Mean age
1789–1849	59.06
1849–1901	52.81
1901–1949	54.60
1949–1989	60.08

from the data it is difficult to determine if Congressional representatives are becoming older or younger.

On a related note, one recent study examined "congressional perceptions of the elderly" (Lubomudrov, 1987). Some have assumed that the perception of older people held by congressional representatives will determine, to a large extent, their voting on issues related to older persons. Utilizing material from various congressional committees and reports, Lubomudrov found that there were many stereotypes of older persons, with the majority being negative stereotypes. The senators and representatives who had the most negative stereotypes appeared to be the most likely to vote against legislation that would reduce social security benefits for older persons. Lubomudrov noted the "irony" of having those who have the greatest misperceptions about older persons their strongest supporters.

Presidency As with the ages of those in Congress, it has been speculated that the age of a president would be an important variable in determining policy toward older persons, with older presidents being more favorably predisposed to older persons. Table 12-3 has the mean age for the Presidents of the United States (age at inauguration was used). Since 1949 there have been 11 presidential elections. The President, term of service, and age at inauguration are reported in Table 12-4. In the time

TABLE 12-4
PRESIDENTS SINCE 1949 AND AGE AT INAUGURATION

President	Term of service	Age at inauguration
Harry S Truman	1-20-49 to 1-20-53	64
Dwight D. Eisenhower	1-20-53 to 1-20-57	62
Dwight D. Eisenhower	1-20-57 to 1-20-61	66
John F. Kennedy	1-20-61 to 11-22-63	43
Lyndon B. Johnson	11-23-63 to 1-20-65	55
Lyndon B. Johnson	1-20-65 to 1-20-69	56
Richard M. Nixon	1-20-69 to 1-20-73	56
Richard M. Nixon	1-20-73 to 8-09-74	60
Gerald R. Ford	8-09-74 to 1-20-77	61
Jimmy Carter	1-20-77 to 1-20-81	52
Ronald Reagan	1-20-81 to 1-20-85	69
Ronald Reagan	1-20-85 to 1-20-89	73
George H. W. Bush	1-20-89 to	64

period from 1949 to the present, the United States has had its second youngest President, John F. Kennedy (the youngest was Theodore Roosevelt who was elected at 42), and its oldest President, Ronald Reagan. It is difficult to distinguish a trend from the available data.

An assumption is that the "older" the president, the more favorably predisposed he or she would be toward policies that would benefit older persons. One set of studies examined this assumption by investigating economic hardship among older persons during Ronald Reagan's first 4 years in office (Binstock, 1986; Cook, 1986; Cook & Kramek, 1986; Crystal, 1986; Moon, 1986; Storey, 1986; Uehara et al., 1986). The studies noted difficulties in separating some of the different factors that determine economic hardship. For example, a president's proposal may be overridden by a congressional veto; or economic decisions and conditions may be dictated by national or international economic conditions. The difficulty in defining "economic hardship" was also discussed (Binstock, 1986; Crystal, 1986). The articles indicated that in Reagan's first 4 years cuts in benefits and programs hurt older persons less than younger persons (Cook & Kramek, 1986; Moon, 1986; Uehara et al., 1986). Storey (1986) stated that upper- and middle-income elderly benefited the most from lower inflation rates and tax cuts, while the lower-income elderly suffered the most because of cuts in benefits and social programs.

Before concluding this section one other point needs to be made. As noted above, there is an assumption that "older" politicians will do more for older persons in terms of legislation and benefits than "younger" politicians. This is not necessarily true. There are many "older" politicians who do not perceive themselves as old; nor do they identify with the economic, health, and social problems of many older Americans. Because of money, power, prestige, good health, and education many politicians do not share the characteristics or problems of most older Americans. Also, many politicians may not want their constituents to see them as old, perhaps because they fear that they will be seen as ineffective or obsolete. Also, a major goal of politicians is to be reelected and many believe that older persons as a group do not have much political power; thus, most do not want to be seen as representing primarily "age-related" issues. It is also likely that politicians realize that their positions on matters that relate to older persons will not cause a significant number of older persons to switch from one political party to another.

Political Activities

There have been several "common sense" approaches on how aging influences participation in political activities. One approach, disengagement theory, suggested that with increasing age political activities declined. Several cross-sectional studies, coupled with common sense observations of the declining physical and mental abilities of older persons, confirmed this view. Others took a "selective withdrawal" approach claiming that older persons become more selective in their political activities, shifting mostly to activities that benefit their age group. Studies have supported both perspectives.

A recent study has examined this issue from a longitudinal perspective (Jennings & Markus, 1988). This study noted that part of the conflict in research findings is a result of how researchers have defined political activity or political involvement.

These researchers separated passive, or less demanding forms of political involvement (i.e., reading about politics) from active, or more demanding forms of political involvement (i.e., attending political meetings). What they found was little change in the passive activities and an overall decline in the active activities; however, there was an increase in activities related to the problems of older persons.

Political Power of Older Persons

At first glance, it might appear that older persons have a great deal of political power for four reasons. First, many political leaders are old; second, older persons represent a large segment of the voting society; third, older persons vote with greater frequency than younger age groups; and fourth, older persons have a number of pressing issues that could serve as a common cause to unite them. This section will examine older persons as a political force in the past, present, and future.

The Past According to Carlie (1969), there were few old-age organizations prior to 1935, and those that did exist had little or no influence on the passage of old-age legislation. There are several reasons for this lack of influence. First, older persons were too heterogeneous a group to rally in force behind one leader or issue. Second, the groups that existed were weak in their organizational structure. It was difficult for them to organize effective membership drives or to have an effect on politicians. Third, the groups that did exist had very little money. Their memberships were not large enough or wealthy enough to contribute as much money as required for advertising or for other publicity-seeking drives. Fourth, most of the old-age associations were unrealistic in their demands and were thus avoided by politicians and potential members who saw the goals of the groups as too far-fetched. Fifth, many of the groups were strife-ridden internally. Sixth, the groups were inept and inexperienced at lobbying. Seventh, many of the groups depended for their existence on charismatic leaders. When the leaders died or left the groups, the groups generally disbanded or became smaller and less powerful (see Carlie, 1969; Pratt, 1974).

There were several age-based groups that existed during the 1930s, many of which attracted large memberships. For example, the Utopian Society had one-half million members at its peak during the depression. Upton Sinclair started a movement called "End Poverty in California" that was almost as popular as the Utopian Society. The McLain movement came into existence in the 1930s to bring about improved conditions for older persons. This movement claimed about 250,000 members nationally. The improved economic conditions of the 1940s brought an end to all of these movements.

The movement that attracted the most attention and the largest membership was the Townsend Plan, which called for a $200 a month pension to be paid to nonworking individuals 60+ years of age (see Cain, 1987; Pratt, 1976). By 1936, the movement had 1.5 million members. Essentially, older persons were to "work" as consumers by spending their $200 a month "salary" which would help create prosperity and end the depression. The plan was to be financed by a tax on business transactions. The basic premise was that the monthly "salary" was a debt owed older persons for decades of work, paying taxes, and raising children. Thus, the Townsend Plan was not seen as welfare but an *earned* right. The Townsend Plan also deviated from the prevailing view of working hard and saving for old age. Some of the plan's supporters were elected to the U.S. Congress, but the plan failed for a variety of reasons, one being the passage of the Social Security Act, even though social security would be paying only about $12 a month. The influence of the Townsend Plan on the passage of the Social Security Act has been vigorously debated (see Hudson & Strate, 1985). Pratt (1976) does not believe it had much influence because it did not begin until 1934, after the development of social security was well underway. A convention in the 1950s still attracted 1500 participants (Cain, 1987).

Most of the existing old-age legislation came into existence because of organizations that were not primarily based on age. For example, passage of the Social Security Act of 1935 was in part the result of two sources: unions and the children of older persons. Unions are not generally age-based organizations, but are structured to meet various needs and to accommodate different age groups. Unions became extremely powerful and influential in part through contributions to political campaigns and promises to deliver large blocks of votes for political favors. Because many retired union workers complained of inadequate pensions and paltry social security benefits, those still in the labor force who anticipated retirement made income security and adequacy important priorities. The backing of unions had an influence on the initial passage of social security, as well as subsequent amendments.

More recently Hudson and Strate (1985) have noted that some of these groups, such as unions, have had a "marginal influence" in policy development in the areas of social security, age discrimination, supplemental security income, and medicare. A criticism of some of these groups is that they are interested primarily in changes that benefit them, rather than changes that benefit older persons. Thus, there have been claims that some of the groups are self-serving (see Hudson & Strate, 1985).

A second factor that helped to bring about the Social Security Act of 1935 was the desire to win the vote of the adult children of the elderly. Older persons were the "hardest hit" of all age groups by the depression. They lost their savings and found it difficult to get jobs because of the high unemployment rate. Thus, many older persons were forced to become dependent on their adult children. The passage of old-age legislation was in part an attempt to win the votes of the adult children of older persons who would then be freed of the economic burden of caring for their aged parents (see Pratt, 1976).

The Present   There are several ways of measuring the political power of older persons. We will examine organizations, conferences, political action, and voting.

Organizations   One way of measuring the political power of older persons is to examine the increase in the number of organizations that represent older persons or the increase in the number of organizations that deal directly or indirectly with older persons. There are several types of organizations: public-affiliated aging organizations; nonprofit health-related organizations; consumer-oriented membership (Kerschner, 1987). Some organizations fall into more than one category. The next section will briefly review some of these organizations.

Public-affiliated aging organizations: This category does not have individuals as members but rather organizations, which obtain their funding generally from public sources. One example would be the National Association of Area Agencies on Aging (NAAA) which represents the 700 area agencies on aging (AAA). AAAs act as advocates for older persons at the local level and plan and implement services to meet local needs. AAAs are funded by state and federal funds. The purpose of the NAAA is to attempt to maintain or increase funding to area agencies on aging by convincing members of Congress that the funding is needed. Other examples are the National Association of Retired Senior Volunteer Programs (RSVP) and the National Association of State Units on Aging (NASUA).

Nonprofit health-related organizations: There are numerous nonprofit organizations that are involved in health-related issues. These organizations may seek to change national policy or to provide guidelines to improve health care in a certain area, such as nursing home care or care of the dying. Examples of organizations would be the National Hospice Organization, the American Association of Homes for the Aged, or the National Citizens Coalition for Nursing Home Reform.

Consumer-oriented membership: There are now numerous organizations that are centered around consumer-related issues, such as health care or income maintenance. One example would be the National Association of Retired Federal Employees (NARFE). This organization publishes a magazine called *Retirement Life* with articles noting legislation that would affect areas such as retirement income. A list of how politicians voted, with pluses and minuses, on matters relating to retired federal employees is published prior to elections.

Another organization is the American Association of Retired Persons or the AARP. This is by far the largest organization of older persons with over 28 million members (Brickfield, 1987; Smith, 1988). AARP lobbyists frequent Capitol Hill for age-related issues and in the 1988 elections spend over $8 million (Smith, 1988). In addition, AARP has developed a number of services for its members, such as a mail-order pharmacy, travel services, and various types of insurance. AARP publishes *Modern Maturity*, which has the third largest magazine circulation in the United States. In addition it has the Andrus Foundation which provided grants to researchers primarily in social gerontology.

The Gray Panthers was founded in 1970 by Margaret E. Kuhn. Originally called the Consultation of Older and Younger Adults for Social Change, the organization was labeled the "Gray Panthers" by the media because of its ". . .dramatic and sometimes radical tactics. . . ." (Kuhn, 1987), a name that was officially adopted in 1971. The Gray Panthers is an organization for all ages and is devoted to a variety of projects all of which are aimed at increasing the quality of life for older persons. They have more than 60,000 members. Although not as large as other national organizations, the members tend to be more articulate, vocal, and organized than many other organizations. As a result, the Gray Panthers have become a powerful force both nationally and internationally in improving conditions for older persons (see Kuhn, 1987).

Older women's movements have also emerged, which is not surprising given the fact that women compose the majority of the aged population and that many of the social problems of the aged are disproportionately experienced by females. To an extent in the 1960s and early 1970s older women were seen as an "invisible minority" in American society. Currently one of the largest organizations for older women is the Older Women's League (OWL) which is an advocate group for older women. OWL currently has over 10,000 members. The small membership is probably due to the politically conservative nature of many older women as well as the lack of recognition of their common concerns. One significant change is that in 1981 the White House Conference on Aging had a committee on the concerns of older women.

Essentially, there is no shortage of organizations willing to stand in line to take credit for policy decisions that benefit older persons. The actual influence of these organizations in bringing about benefits can be debated. In a summary of the literature, Hudson and Strate (1985) said that while at one time these age-based groups were believed to have been very powerful, more recent analyses have attributed much less power and influence to them.

Conferences The increasing interest in older persons can also be seen in the number of conferences that focus on older persons. The number of conferences currently being held not only demonstrates the increasing interest, but also generates more interest, in older persons. This section will examine one of the most important conferences, the federally-funded White House Conferences on Aging.

The first, which was not designated a White House Conference, was held in 1950 by the National Security Agency, predecessor of the Department of Health, Education, and Welfare (currently Health and Human Services), and was designed to examine the problems of older persons. This 3-day conference attracted 800 delegates who advocated that increased national attention be paid to the problems of older persons and that state agencies on aging be created. The groundwork for the National Institute on Aging was also laid.

In 1958 the White House Conference on Aging Act was passed by Congress. This act was designed to create a national forum of citizens to discuss both the problems and potential of older Americans. Planning for the 1961 White House Conference on Aging started in 1959 with the Secretary of Health, Education, and Welfare calling the meeting. The January 1961 conference was attended by 2500 to 3000 delegates and produced more than 900 recommendations, many of which had a significant impact in several areas. For example, the recommendations contributed to increases in social security benefits and created special allowances for older persons in the 1961 Housing Act. There was also a recommendation that a federal agency be created to serve as a national focal point for the concerns and needs of older persons. A recommendation for a program to support health care for older persons was also made which assisted in the passage of medicare.

In 1968, Congress passed another bill requesting the President to call another White House Conference on Aging in 1971. This conference had three stages: first, community forums; second, state and regional meetings; and third, the national meeting. The 1971 conference had 4000 delegates attending, over 35 percent of whom were 65+ years of age, and made over 700 recommendations, some of which were acted on. For example, there was again an increase in social security benefits as well as the creation of automatic increases according to increases in the cost of living; the creation of supplemental security income, the creation of the House Select Committee on Aging; the creation of the Federal Council on Aging. There was also the recommendation that more money be spent on research and training in the biomedical, social, and behavioral aspects of old age.

In 1977 legislation was passed calling for a 1981 White House Conference on Aging (see Laurie, 1987). Again, local and state committees met to plan for the national conference. Thousands of issues were generated as potential topics. This conference had more than 3000 individuals attending and took on more of a "political" atmosphere and generated more controversy than the previous conferences. Controversy emerged over the selection of delegates and the priority of issues. After the conference there were charges that certain groups manipulated the discussion of selected issues and that some of the final reports issued did not reflect what the participants had recommended (Torres-Gil, 1987).

Revisions to the Older Americas Act in 1987 authorized the President to hold a White House Conference on Aging in 1991 "to increase public awareness of the contributions of older individuals to society, to identify problems as well as the well-being of older individuals, to develop recommendations for the coordination of federal policy with state and local needs, to develop specific and comprehensive recommendations for both executive and legislative action to maintain and improve the well-being of older individuals, and to review the status of recommendations adopted at previous White House conferences on aging (Special Committee on Aging, 1988).

Political Action   The increasing political power of older persons can be seen in the establishment of four committees by the United States Congress to study the problems of older Americans. They are the Senate Special Committee on Aging, the Subcommittee on Aging of the Senate Committee on Labor and Public Welfare, the House of Representatives Select Committee on Aging, and the Federal Council on Aging. Their growing influence can also be seen in the establishment of the National Institute on Aging (NIA). The NIA was established as the eleventh National Institute of Health by the passage of the Research on Aging Act of 1974. The Act called for a multidisciplinary study of aging. Dr. Robert Butler was the first director of the NIA; Dr. T. Franklin Williams succeeded him in 1982. The NIA had a budget of $19.2 million in 1976; by 1985 the budget had increased to $143 million; and by 1989 to $222.6 million. The NIA has expanded into several areas including research, education, and training (see Butler, 1987).

Voting   One way that a group can exercise political power is through the ballot. There are two factors that appear to indicate that older persons have the potential of wielding significant power in this area: an increasing percentage of older persons and increasing percentage of older persons voting. Table 12-5 provides information on voting in the 1988 presidential election. The table has two aspects that need to be examined. The first deals with the percentage of those voting. As can be seen in the third column, the two youngest age groups have the smallest percentages voting. For those age 18–20, 33.2 percent voted; for those age 21–24, 38.3 percent voted. The highest percentage is for those 45–64 and those 65+ years of age, 67.9 and 68.8 percent. Thus, we see a greater percentage of voting in the two oldest age categories.

TABLE 12-5
PERCENTAGE OF POPULATION VOTING BY AGE CATEGORY IN THE 1988 PRESIDENTIAL
ELECTION

Age group	Total number	Percent voting	Number voting	Percent of total votes	Percent of total voting population
18–20	10,700,000	33.2	3,552,400	3	6
21–24	14,800,000	38.3	5,668,400	6	8
25–34	42,700,000	48.0	20,496,000	20	24
35–44	35,200,000	61.3	21,577,600	21	20
45–64	45,900,000	67.9	31,166,100	30	26
65+	28,800,000	68.8	19,814,400	19	16

Source: U.S. Bureau of the Census, 1990.

The second aspect of the table that needs to be examined deals with the last two columns: percent of total votes and percent of total voting population. The percent of total votes is simply a breakdown, by age group, of the percent of the total votes. We can see, for example, that those 65+ years of age cast 19 percent of all votes. Those in the two youngest age groups, 18–20 and 21–24, cast 9 percent of all votes. The last column has the percentage of the total voting population by age group. We know that those 65+ years of age compose about 12.3 percent of the *total* population. However, the total population cannot vote and thus we are interested in the percentage of older persons in the total voting population. As can be seen, those 65+ years of age make up 16 percent of the total voting population. We can see that while those 65+ years of age compose 16 percent of the voting population they cast 19 percent of all votes. The two youngest age groups compose 14 percent of the population but only 9 percent of all votes. If we examine the two oldest age groups we find that they compose 42 percent of the total voting population but 49 percent of all votes.

We can also examine this same impact in the 1986 congressional elections. In congressional elections the voter turnout is generally lower than for presidential elections. However, voter turnout for older persons is generally higher than for other age groups. Data on the 1986 congressional elections is presented in Table 12-6. What is interesting in this table is that in "off-year" elections older persons have significantly more "clout." As noted above, in the presidential election older persons composed 16 percent of the voting population and 19 percent of the total vote. In the congressional elections they still composed 16 percent of the population but 21 percent of the vote. If we combine the two oldest age groups their percent of total votes was 49 percent in the 1988 presidential election but 54 percent in the 1986 congressional election.

The Future   It is, of course, difficult to speculate on how powerful older persons will become as a political force in the future. Currently, gerontologists appear to be split into two groups on this issue. One group does not perceive a considerable

TABLE 12-6
PERCENTAGE OF POPULATION VOTING BY AGE CATEGORY IN THE 1986 CONGRESSIONAL ELECTION

Age group	Total number	Percent voting	Number voting	Percent of total votes	Percent of total voting population
18–20	10,700,000	18.6	1,990,200	2	6
21–24	15,700,000	24.2	3,799,400	5	9
25–34	41,900,000	35.1	14,706,900	18	24
35–44	33,000,000	49.3	16,269,000	20	19
45–64	44,800,000	58.7	26,297,600	33	26
65+	27,700,000	60.9	16,869,300	21	16

Source: U.S. Bureau of the Census, 1990.

increase in power in the future, while the other anticipates a substantial increase. The rationale of both groups will be examined.

No Gain in Political Power   Binstock (1972, 1974), Campbell (1971), and Cameron (1974) are a few of the gerontologists who have presented the case against older persons gaining any political power in the future. Their reasons are stated below. First, older persons are a heterogeneous group representing a variety of socialization experiences. They will be divided because of racial, ethnic, geographic, economic, and health factors. In other words, age will not be a uniting factor.

Second, many older persons do not classify themselves as "old." Culter and Schmidhauser (1975) reported that individuals 65+ years of age who identified themselves as "old" differed significantly in responses from those who identified themselves as "not old." Thus, it will be difficult for some older persons to identify with the causes of other older persons. Third, many older persons are retiring with more than adequate pensions and in better health than in the past. If this segment of the aged population enlarges, then many of the issues that currently serve to unite older persons will vanish.

Fourth, the organizations that represent older persons have not been very militant in the past, and it is doubtful that they will be militant in the future. The reason is that they simply do not have any power; that is, they cannot guarantee a large voting bloc nor can they threaten a work slowdown or strike. Fifth, older persons are fairly evenly split between the two major political parties. We also know that older persons are the least likely of any age group to change party affiliation. Politicians realize that with the even split and the lack of movement between parties, the votes of older persons tend to cancel each other out. For these reasons, it is difficult for the organizations of older persons to have much influence.

Sixth, older persons are competing with an ever-increasing number of "other" groups for a limited amount of money. Very often, the other groups are more organized and influential because of money or other sources of power. Seventh, we are a society dominated by the values of youth. Generally, politicians are affected by ageism as much as other segments of society. Ageism can negatively influence the views of politicians toward older persons.

Gain in Political Power There are other gerontologists who believe that older persons will gain more political power in the future than they currently have (see Butler, 1974; Cutler, 1983; Peterson et al., 1976; Ragan & Dowd, 1974). Some of the reasons follow: First, the percentage of older persons is growing in this country, and they constitute a significant percentage of the voting population. The percentage will probably increase, as will their political power. Second, in the future older persons will be better educated and wealthier. Better education leads to higher voter turnout. Thus, with a greater voter turnout older persons may become a more influential voting bloc. Income is also a predictor of political participation; the higher the income the greater the participation (see Miller et al., 1980).

Third, as society as a whole grows older, the negative stereotypes and disregard for older persons will be lessened. This change in attitude will probably come about for at least two reasons. First, older persons will have better health and more income than their predecessors. These advantages will make them more a part of the mainstream of society and less likely to be ostracized. Second, there will probably be some guilt over the "poor" treatment of older persons in the past. Thus, compensatory measures may result. Fourth, younger individuals are far less likely to belong to a political party than their aged predecessors. In other words, voters are becoming more independent. Rather than being influenced by partisan politics, voters will be more sensitive to the candidates and the issues in the future. Thus, politicians who cater to the needs of older persons could obtain a sizable swing vote in the future.

Fifth, older persons may become more homogeneous in the future. Many of the older persons in contemporary American society were foreign-born. They had a variety of socialization experiences. Language barriers have restricted the political participation of many of these individuals. Because of restricted immigration and the socialization of the mass media, we may find more similarities among older persons in the future. Sixth, older person may also gain political power with the help of unions. More and more unions are becoming concerned with what happens to their members after they retire. The unions have the money, power, and effective organizations to bring about changes for older persons. Because of the early retirement plans of many unions, there will be a large, powerful, and vocal segment of retired workers urging their unions to obtain benefits for them.

Seventh, the future aged voters will be post-World War II generation that grew up during the 1960s and 1970s with "protest politics" and will be more militant and more willing to use alternative approaches to gain power than voters in previous generations. They have witnessed mobilized efforts on behalf of civil rights, ecology, peace, and the rights of women. If this politically active birth cohort stays that way, then perhaps older persons in the future will use more radical and diverse means to bring about change.

Eighth, a variety of factors, such as age segregation, may create a "common consciousness" or a strong identity among older persons. If large numbers of similarly deprived individuals lived in age-segregated housing, they would see that others were equally deprived and equally desirous to change their living conditions. In other words, older persons would become more aware of the disadvantaged situation of older persons as a group, not as individuals. This awareness could create a strong group identity and a strong and effective social movement.

Although the temptation is to think of disadvantaged older persons developing this group consciousness, it may be, as Robert B. Hudson (1987) has suggested, the "able elderly" who develop this consciousness. Hudson noted that the resources of the able elderly would make them an "awesome" political force. To an extent this can be seen in some existing racial, ethnic, and women's groups. Although these groups had many heterogeneous segments, they still found common elements upon which they could create a group consciousness.

SOCIAL POLICY

This section will examine one of the major consequences of the political process, namely the creation of social policy. Think for a minute of what you would do to make society "better" if you had a significant amount of money. It does not take long to create a list of what needs to be done to make society better. Your list might include meeting the needs of the poor, a strong national defense, a national health care system, cleaning up the environment, ending illiteracy, increasing the "war" on drugs, or finding cures for AIDS, cancer, and heart disease.

Just as you can create a list so do legislative bodies. There are two differences between your list and the lists of legislative bodies. First, many of the items on your list are either not found or have a different priority than the lists of legislative bodies. Second, and most important, legislative bodies have money—through taxation and the ability to increase the national debt—to actually do something about the items on a list. Social policy refers to the prioritization of issues and the allocation of resources (i.e., money) to the issues by legislative bodies.

Social policy can be determined in many ways and there is a great deal written in this area. Understand that there are billions of dollars and millions of jobs at stake. As a result, there are literally thousands of lobbyists who try to influence the prioritization of issues by legislators. Even after policy decisions have been made there can be problems. For example, we saw earlier that until the 1980s research on Alzheimer's disease was not considered to be an important issue, and as a result there was not much funding in this area. While research on Alzheimer's disease currently receives considerably more funding, there are other policy decisions over the amounts that should be directed into areas dealing with the Alzheimer's victim (i.e., prevention, cause, or "cure" for the disease), and into areas dealing with the caregivers of Alzheimer's victims (i.e., respite care). In other areas, policy decisions will determine if resources are directed into building nursing homes and paying for the medical care of those in them, or into programs that support maintaining older persons in their homes. The potential list of policy issues in gerontology is obviously extensive.

One area of controversy is over whether policy should be age-based or need-based. That is, should programs be developed on the basis of age or need? Social security payments to retirees, for example, are age-based. That is, those who have paid into the system are eligible to collect social security payments at a certain age. Under an age-based system, money is paid if it is needed or not. Medicaid is need-based. That is, individuals must have income below a certain level to be eligible for medicaid. It is an income level that determines eligibility. Some programs have characteristics of both age- and need-based policy. For example, to an extent supplemental security income (SSI) is both need and age based. That is, individuals must be 65 years of age (or be blind or disabled) and demonstrate the need to be eligible for SSI. Those who believe in age-based policy claim that age is a good predictor of life events, and by making programs age-based there are fewer administrative problems and less intervention into individuals' lives. Those who believe programs should be need-based claim that resources should be directed at those who need them. This section will examine social policy from two perspectives. First we will look at federal outlays for older persons, and second at some specific legislation.

Federal Outlays for Older Persons

One way to examine social policy is to examine federal outlays benefiting older persons. In 1960 about 15 percent of the federal budget went to older persons. By

TABLE 12-7
FEDERAL OUTLAYS BENEFITING OLDER PERSONS: 1986

Type of outlay	Amount (dollars in millions)	% of total budget for older persons	% of total federal budget
Medicare	$ 64,417	23.90	6.21
Medicaid	8,878	3.29	0.86
Other federal health	4,662	1.73	0.45
Health subtotal	$ 77,957	28.92	7.52
Social security	$146,235	54.26	14.11
Supplemental security income (SSI)	3,719	1.38	0.36
Veterans compensation-pensions	6,113	2.27	0.59
Other retired, disabled, and survivor benefits	25,863	9.60	2.50
Retirement/disability subtotal	$181,930	67.51	17.55
National Institute on Aging	$ 132	0.05	0.01
Older American volunteer programs	106	0.04	0.01
Senior community service employment	323	0.12	0.03
Administration on Aging	836	0.31	0.08
Subsidized housing	4,870	1.81	0.47
Section 202 elderly housing loans	490	0.18	0.05
Farmers Home Administration Housing	84	0.03	0.01
Food stamps	612	0.23	0.06
Social services (Title XX)	369	0.14	0.04
Low income home energy assistance	606	0.22	0.06
Other miscellaneous	1,193	0.44	0.12
Other subtotal	$ 9,622	3.57	0.93
Total older persons outlays	$269,508		
Percent of total federal outlays			26.00

Source: U.S. Bureau of the Census, 1990.

1986 the percentage was 26, which was down from the high of 28 percent in 1984. The figures for 1986 are in Table 12-7.

As was mentioned in Chapter 11, "Economics," there is concern over the "graying of the federal budget." In other words, many persons are concerned that 26 percent of the budget is being devoted to 12.3 percent of the population. However, as many have noted, the major proportion of the federal budget for older persons is entitlement programs such as social security. Entitlement programs are financed through the collection of dedicated taxes for these benefits. Thus, individuals have paid for and are entitled to these benefits. If we combine entitlement programs such as social security, medicare, and veterans pensions we find that over 80 percent of the federal budget for older persons is for earned entitlements! For example, for every dollar spent by the federal government on older persons $0.54 went to Social Security and $0.24 to medicare. If we look at the percentage of the federal budget for older persons for nonentitlement programs, it composes less than 1 percent of the total federal budget!

Social Policy Legislation

Health Care   In this subsection we will examine medicare and medicaid. However, we should first briefly examine health care policy and costs from a historical perspective.

In the 1950s and 1960s health care policy was concerned with improving and expanding access to health care. Current policy is directed at containing health care costs. The reason for the concern over cost is simple: health care costs have increased dramatically. In 1965 health care expenditures were 5.9 percent of the gross national product (GNP). By 1986 they had increased to 10.9 percent. They are expected to reach 15 percent by 2000. Not only have costs increased, but so has the role of the federal government in paying for health care costs. In 1965 the federal government paid $5.5 billion (13.2 percent of the nation's health bill); by 1986 the figure was $134.7 billion (29.4 percent of the nation's health bill). By 2000 the cost is estimated at $498.6 billion dollars (33 percent of the nation's health bill) (Special Committee, 1988).

To contain health care costs the prospective payment system was introduced (PPS) in the early 1980s. Under this system hospitals are paid a specific amount based on a patient's diagnosis. PPS uses what are called diagnosis-related groups (DRGs) to categorize patients. Based on a patient's DRG, a specific reimbursement, based on the average cost to treat that diagnostic category, is made to health care providers. This was to discourage the "overuse" of services. For example, if a hospital can treat a patient for less than the DRG amount, then the hospital can make money; if, however, it costs more to treat the patient, then the hospital must absorb the loss.

Medicare   Medicare was enacted in 1965 (under Title 18 of the Social Security Act) to assist in covering acute health care costs. Medicare was never intended to cover ALL health care costs. It was created primarily as an insurance against short-term acute illnesses. Medicare has two parts: Hospital Insurance Program (Part A), and Supplementary Medical Insurance (Part B).

Part A is to cover the cost of hospitalization and related costs. This is financed by a special payroll tax on both employees and employers. This tax is often considered part of the total social security payroll tax. Currently this fund is solvent, although a 25-year projection indicates that to maintain solvency expenditures will have to be reduced or income increased 13 to 15 percent.

Although the rules and dollar amounts change yearly, in 1988 they were as follows. Under medicare, coverage is based on a "benefit period." A benefit period starts with hospitalization and ends when an individual has not been in a hospital or skilled nursing facility for 60 consecutive days. In a benefit period an individual is entitled to 90 days of inpatient hospital care (with a $540 deductible and a daily copayment for days 61 to 90 of $135), and 100 days of posthospital skilled nursing facility care (with a daily copayment for days 21 to 100 of $67.50). If an individual exceeds 90 days of hospital care a lifetime reserve of 60 days may be drawn on (with a daily copayment of $270). In addition, medicare will provide individuals with coverage for home health care and hospice services for the terminally ill.

Part B is a voluntary program, costing about $25 per month in 1988. The income from this fee covers about 25 percent of the total cost; the remaining money comes from the federal government's general fund. Part B pays for 80 percent of "reasonable charges" for the following: physician services, diagnostic tests, medical devices, outpatient hospital services, and laboratory fees. Enrollees must pay the first $75. It should be repeated that medicare was never intended to cover all medical care costs. Currently, it is believed that medicare covers about one-half of the medical care costs of the noninstitutionalized age (Special Committee, 1988). It has been a very controversial program. On the one hand it is criticized for not covering many forms of health care and for shifting more expenses to enrollees. On the other hand the costs of the program are criticized, especially in an era of an increasing national debt.

Medicaid   Medicaid was enacted in 1965 (Title 19 of the Social Security Act). Medicaid was designed to provide low-income Americans with medical care. Medicaid is a joint federal-state program, with states having some discretion over who is served. While federal law requires that certain individuals be served (i.e., persons receiving assistance under aid to families with dependent children, and individuals receiving SSI), states can cover other categories at their discretion. For older persons medicaid has become a major source of support for those in nursing homes. In fact, medicaid financed 42 percent of all nursing home expenditures.

Older Americans Act   The Older Americans Act (OAA) was enacted in 1965 and has since been revised 11 times, most recently in 1987 (Public Law 100–175). The importance of this act was that it created specific programs to meet the needs of older persons. Prior to the act the trend had been to create programs that were need-based rather than age-based. Although many aspects of the act have been changed, the goals of the OAA have remained the same: "To provide a wide array of social and community services to those older persons in the greatest economic and social need in order to foster maximum independence" (Special Committee, 1988). The goals of the OAA were larger than its initial funding, which was $6 million in 1965, but had increased to $71 million by 1971, and $1.2 billion by 1988. It is best understood by examining its different titles.

Title I: Declaration of Objectives Title I is more or less a policy statement surrounding the purpose of the act, which is "aimed at improving the lives of all older Americans in a variety of areas such as income, health, housing, and long-term care" (Special Committee, 1988). In the last revision of the act the protection of older persons, from abuse, neglect, and exploitation, was added to this section

Title II: Administration on Aging Title II established the Administration on Aging (AOA) to manage and administer OAA programs. The AOA, which is located within the Department of Health and Human Services and directed by the U.S. Commission on Aging, was also established to be the federal agency that would advocate for the needs of older persons. Amendments to this title in 1973 created the Federal Council on aging to "review and evaluate" federal programs for older persons, and to advise the President, Congress, and the Secretary of Health and Human Services of the needs of older persons. The fifteen-person council also was to act as a spokesperson for older people. The council became operational in 1974 (Special Committee, 1988; Torres-Gil, 1987).

Title III: Grants for State and Community Programs on Aging Title III is the largest and probably the most important part of the OAA. There are several parts to Title III:

Part A: Administrative operations
Part B: Supportive services
Part C–1: Congregate nutrition services
Part C–2: Home-delivered nutrition services
Part D: Nonmedical in-home services for the frail elderly
Part E: Services to meet the special needs of the elderly
Part F: Health education and promotion
Part G: Elder abuse prevention activities

The services under Title III are provided by state units on aging (SUAs) which designate the approximately 700 local area agencies on aging (AAA).

Title IV: Training, Research, and Discretionary Projects and Programs Under Title IV the AOA commissioner is authorized "to award funds for a broad array of training, research, and demonstration programs in the field of aging" (Special Committee, 1988). In the 1987 amendments to the act several new demonstration programs were added in areas such as health education and promotion, volunteerism, and consumer protection activities in long-term care (Special Committee on Aging, 1988).

Title V: Community Service Employment for Older Americans Title V has funds to subsidize part-time community service jobs for those 55+ years of age who are unemployed or at low incomes. There are also some funds available to make workers aware of age discrimination and aware of their rights under the Age Discrimination in Employment Act.

Title VI: Grants for Native Americans Title VI was added to the OAA in 1975 and originally called Grants for Indian Tribes. Basically, it was felt that under Title III Native Americans were not receiving their share of resources. Additionally, the minimum age for services was set at 60 when Native American life expectancy was 48 years of age. The act now allows tribes to determine the age at which individuals will receive services, which most have set at 55. Revision in the OAA in 1987 included lowering the number of individuals a tribe must have to receive services, and expanding the services to Native Hawaiians. Tribes are not eligible for funds under both Title III and Title VI.

Title VII: Older Americans Personal Health Education and Training Program This title was added in 1984 but never received funding and was repealed in 1987. However, there was an amendment to Title IV which preserved the intent which was to fund colleges and universities to develop model health education programs for older persons.

Social, Community, and Legal Services   There are many federal social service programs that offer services to older persons. The majority of these programs are designed to help individuals become self-sufficient, prevent abuse and neglect, and reduce the need for institutionalization. Several of these programs will be examined below.

Block Grants   Block grants are used for a wide range of activities such as "child day care, home-based services for the elderly, protective and emergency services for children and adults, family planning, transportation, staff training, and program planning" (Special Committee, 1988). There are different types of block grants such as social services block grants (SSBG) and community services block grants (CSBG). Block grants now allow states to determine what services to provide as well as the eligibility requirement for services.

Because states can determine how block grant funds will be spent, the amount of funding reaching older persons varies state by state. One survey found that forty-seven states used at least some of their SSBG funds for services for older persons, with the amount varying from 1 to 50 percent (Special Committee on Aging, 1988).

Action Programs   The action programs are aimed primarily at reducing poverty and helping physically and mentally disabled individuals. These programs are administered by Action, which was established in 1971 to coordinate several volunteer programs such as Volunteers in Service to America (VISTA), and the National Student Volunteer Program. Action also administers the older American volunteer programs which will be described below.

Older American Volunteer Programs   There are three programs in this area: Retired Senior Volunteer Program (RSVP), Foster Grandparents Program (FGP), and the Senior Companion Program (SCP). All of these programs provide older persons (60+ years of age) with an opportunity for part-time work in various local organizations. Funding is awarded to private or public sponsoring organizations that organize and supervise older persons.

Retired Senior Volunteer Program: This program was first created in 1969 as part of the Older Americans Act. Originally administered by the AOA, this program was transferred to Action in 1971. Volunteers in this program serve in areas such as "youth counseling, literacy enhancement, long-term care, crime prevention, refugee assistance, and housing rehabilitation" (Special Committee, 1988). In 1988, 392,000 older persons participated in this program. RSVP volunteers are not paid a salary or stipend but are reimbursed for any "out-of-pocket" expenses incurred while participating in the program. Funding for 1988 was $30.6 million.

Foster Grandparent Program: This program started in 1965 as a joint effort of the Office of Economic Opportunity and the AOA. In 1971 the program was transferred to Action.

This program is for low-income older persons to assist children with mental, physical, emotional, or social disabilities. Volunteers are placed in schools, hospitals, day care centers, or institutions. Foster grandparents work 20 hours a week and are paid a stipend, which is exempt from taxation. In addition to the stipend foster grandparents also receive an allowance for transportation, a free annual physical examination, some insurance benefits, and free meals while serving. In 1987 there were 23,400 foster grandparents who assisted 81,900 children. Funding in 1988 was $57.4 million.

Senior Companion Program: The SCP was authorized in 1973 to provide low-income older persons with part-time opportunities to assist frail, dependent, homebound elderly in maintaining independent living. Senior companions serve 20 hours a week and receive the same stipend and benefits as those participating in the FGP. In 1987 there were 9500 senior companions serving 33,350 individuals. Funding in 1988 was $23.1 million.

Transportation   As will be pointed out in Chapter 14, "Home and Community," transportation is important in the lives of older persons. Transportation is often the link with family, friends, medical resources, shopping, and social services as well as other valuable resources. The federal government has been active in three ways in making transportation available to older persons: funding the cost of transit systems, reimbursing older persons for transportation costs, and reducing fares. These programs have been funded under the OAA (Title III), block grants, and medicaid which offer fare reimbursement.

Amendment in 1970 to the Urban Mass Transit Act of 1964 added a section that called for modifying transportation facilities to improve access by the elderly and handicapped. Essentially this amendment stated that the elderly and handicapped have the same rights as others to use mass transportation. The National Mass Transportation Act of 1974 further amended the Urban Mass Transit Act to provide funding for both urban and nonurban areas through block grants. The Surface Transportation Assistance Act of 1978 increased assistance in nonurban areas.

Transportation is receiving a higher priority than in the past. It is recognized that creating medical and social services does not have the desired effect if individuals cannot gain access to those services because of the lack of transportation. Both the rural and suburban elderly have received increased attention.

Currently approximately $35 million is authorized for elderly and handicapped innovative research programs. Additionally, the Federal Mass Transportation Act of 1987 provides 95 percent of the funding for projects designed to improve the access of the elderly and handicapped to mass transportation. The Highway Safety Act of 1987 has specific provisions to commission a study of the safety problems of older drivers and to create a program to improve the driving of older drivers.

Housing   The last area that will be examined is housing. The federal government has had a significant role in housing since building low-rent housing during the depression era. This role was expanded in 1949 when Congress passed a national housing policy which stated that every American was entitled to a suitable living environment. The 1950 White House Conference on Aging noted the special needs of older persons in the housing area. Although not specifically intended for older persons, the 1937 Housing Act provided for low-income persons, many of whom were aged. In 1959 the first legislation for housing for the aged was passed under Section 202 of the 1937 Housing Act. This was eliminated in 1969 and then reinstated in the 1970s as Section 8. In 1987 Congress passed the Housing and Community Development Act which included funds for low-income housing.

Under Section 202 the federal government financed loans to private and nonprofit sponsors who were willing to build rental housing for older and handicapped persons. During this 10-year period about 45,000 units were constructed. A 1985 survey of residents found that most were single, white, with an average age of 73, and incomes of $6600. The average rent was $480 per month, of which they paid $146, the remainder being paid through Section 8 rental assistance payments. In 1986, $631 million was allocated for Section 202 for 12,000 housing units; for 1987 the figure was $593 million (Special Committee, 1988).

Public housing has been another option for older persons. As noted, public housing emerged during the depression and currently includes 1.4 million units housing 3.5 million individuals. Currently about 44 percent of public housing is occupied by older persons. Funded through the Low-Rent Public Housing Program the program is operated by local public housing authorities (PHAs). Each PHA can build or obtain housing. Section 8 was implemented in 1974 and was designed to provide low-income families with decent subsidized housing in the private sector. Sponsors agreed to keep rents low in a certain number of housing units and the federal government would make up the difference between what the family could afford to pay and the fair market rent. Vouchers, similar to food stamps, have also been used in this area.

In 1987 the Housing and Community Development Act was passed with some difficulty because of the federal budget deficit. This act authorized $15 billion for 1988 and $15.3 billion for 1989, and included provisions for Section 202 and Section 8. This appears to be an area with a decreasing federal commitment, perhaps because this area has been plagued with problems, and perhaps because of the current "problems" in HUD. In 1986 it was estimated that there were still 700,000 elderly poor who needed housing assistance. There are other areas related to housing that could be discussed, for example, energy assistance and weatherization. One of the major points is that housing has been a major social policy area.

SUMMARY

This chapter was separated into two sections: politics and social policy.

In the first section we found that with increasing age individuals do not become more conservative, and that there is not a shift from the Democratic to the Republican party. Studies have also reported that participation in voting is low in early adulthood, and rises to a peak in late middle age when a drop starts. Most studies have reported this trend, with differences being reported in the age at which the drop occurs and why it occurs. Some changes are being reported in voting trends, with later age being reported. Older persons tend to be overrepresented in some political offices because these offices are based on knowledge and experience. The age composition of Congress was examined where it was noted that older persons were not overrepresented in the House of Representatives but were over-represented in the Senate. The aged as a political force was also discussed, where it was noted that they did not have much power in the past, and their power in the present is controversial.

The last section discussed social policy, or essentially the allocation of governmental resources. Although older persons are often blamed for consuming a disproportionate amount of the federal budget, the majority of the federal budget directed at older persons is for entitlement programs such as social security. Several specific government programs for older persons were discussed.

REFERENCES

Abramson, P. R. (1976). Generational change and the decline of party identification in America: 1952–1974. *American Political Science Review,* **70**(2): 469–478.

Abramson, P. R. (1979). Developing party identification: A further examination of life-cycle, generational, and period effects. *American Journal of Political Science,* **23**(1): 78–96.

Binstock, R. H. (1972). Interest-group liberalism and the politics of aging. *The Gerontologist,* **12**(3): 266–280.

Binstock, R. H. (1974). Aging and the future of American politics. *The Annals of the American Academy of Political and Social Science,* **415**(September): 199–212.

Binstock, R. H. (1986). Perspectives on measuring hardship: Concepts, dimensions, and implications. *The Gerontologist,* **26**(1): 60–62.

Brickfield, C. F. (1987). American Association of Retired Persons. In G. L. Maddox (Ed.), *The encyclopedia of aging* (pp. 31–32). New York: Springer.

Butler, R. N. (1974). Pacification and the politics of aging. *International Journal of Aging and Human Development,* **5**(4): 393–395.

Butler, R. N. (1987). National Institute on aging. In G. L. Maddox (Ed.), *The encyclopedia of aging* (pp. 468–470). New York: Springer.

Button, J. W., & Rosenbaum, W. A. (1989). Seeing gray: School bond issues and the aging in Florida. *Research on Aging,* **11**(2): 158–173.

Cain, L. D. (1987). Townsend Movement. In G. L. Maddox (Ed.), *The encyclopedia of aging* (pp. 671–672). New York: Springer.

Cameron, S. W. (1974). The politics of the elderly. *The Midwest Quarterly,* **15**(2): 141–153.

Campbell, A. (1971). Politics through the life cycle. *The Gerontologist,* **11**(2; Part 2): 112–117.

Campbell, J. C., & Strate, J. (1981). Are old people conservative? *The Gerontologist,* **21**(6): 580–591.

Carlie, M. K. (1969). The politics of age: Interest group or social movement. *The Gerontologist,* **9**(4): 259–263.

Clark, P. G. (1985). The social allocation of health care resources: Ethical dilemmas in age-group competition. *The Gerontologist,* **25**(2): 119–125.

Congressional Quarterly (1985). *Members of Congress since 1789.* New York: Congressional Quarterly.

Converse, P. E. (1969). Of time and partisan stability. *Comparative Political Studies,* **2**(July): 139–171.

Converse, P. E. (1976). *The dynamics of party support: Cohort-analyzing party identification.* Beverly Hills: Sage.

Converse, P. E. (1979). Rejoinder to Abramson. *American Journal of Political Science,* **23**(1): 97–100.

Cook, F. L. (1986). Introduction. *The Gerontologist,* **26**(1): 25–26.

Cook, F. L., & Kramek, L. M. (1986). Measuring economic hardship among older Americans. *The Gerontologist,* **26**(1): 38–47.

Crystal, S. (1986). Measuring income and inequality among the elderly. *The Gerontologist,* **26**(1): 56–59.

Cutler, N. E. (1983). Age and political behavior. In D. S. Woodruff & J. E. Birren (Eds.), *Aging: Scientific perspectives and social issues* (second edition) (pp. 409–442). Monterey, CA: Brooks/Cole.

Cutler, N. E., & Schmidhauser, J. R. (1975). Age and political behavior. In D. S. Woodward & J. E. Birren (Eds.), *Aging: Scientific perspectives and social issues* (pp. 374–406). New York: Van Nostrand.

Cutler, S. J. (1973). Perceived prestige loss and political attitudes among the aged. *The Gerontologist,* **13**(1): 69–75.

Cutler, S. J., & Kaufman, R. L. (1975). Cohort changes in political attitudes: Tolerance of ideological nonconformity. *Public Opinion Quarterly,* **39**(1): 69–81.

Douglass, E. B., Cleveland, W. P., & Maddox, G. L. (1974). Political attitudes, age, and aging: A cohort analysis of archival data. *Journal of Gerontology,* **29**(6): 666–675.

Glamser, F. D. (1974). The importance of age to conservative opinions: A multivariate analysis. *Journal of Gerontology,* **29**(5): 549–554.

Glenn, N. D. (1974). Aging and conservatism. *Annals of the American Academy of Political and Social Science,* **415**(September): 176–186.

Glenn, N. D., & Grimes, M. (1968). Aging, voting, and political interest. *American Sociological Review,* **33**(4): 563–575.

Glenn, N. D., & Hefner, T. (1972). Further evidence on aging and party identification. *Public Opinion Quarterly,* **36**(Spring): 31–47.

Hanham, R. A. (1975). Aging in America: The White House Conference of 1981 in retrospect. *American Journal of Public Health,* **73**(7): 799–801.

Hill, D. B., & Kent, M. M. (1988). Population trends and public policy. *Election Demographics* (January).

Hout, M., & Knoke, D. (1975). Change in voting turnout, 1952–1972. *Public Opinion Quarterly,* **39**(1): 52–68.

Hudson, R. B. (1987). Tomorrow's able elders: Implications for the state. *The Gerontologist,* **27**(4): 405–409.

Hudson, R. B., & Strate, J. (1985). Aging and political systems. In R. H. Binstock & E. Shanas (Eds.), *Handbook of aging and the social sciences* (second edition) (pp. 554–586). New York: Van Nostrand Reinhold.

Jennings, M. K., & Markus, G. B. (1988). Political involvement in the later years: A longitudinal survey. *American Journal of Political Science,* **32**(2): 302–316.

Kerschner, P. A. (1987). Membership organizations. In G. L. Maddox (Ed.), *The encyclopedia of aging* (pp. 424–427). New York: Springer.

Kuhn, M. E. (1987). Gray Panthers. In G. L. Maddox (Ed.), *The encyclopedia of aging* (p. 297). New York: Springer.

Laurie, W. F. (1987). White House Conference on Aging, 1981. In G. L. Maddox (Ed.), *The encyclopedia of aging* (pp. 691–692). New York: Springer, 1987.

Lewis, M. I., & Butler, R. N. (1972). Why is women's lib ignoring old women? *Aging and Human Development,* **3**(3): 223–231.

Lubomudrov, S. (1987). Congressional perceptions of the elderly: The use of stereotypes in the legislative process. *The Gerontologist,* **27**(1): 77–81.

Markson, E. (1987). Older women's movement. In G. L. Maddox (Ed.), *The encyclopedia of aging* (pp. 502–504). New York: Springer.

Miller, A. H., Gurin, P., & Gurin, G. (1980). Age consciousness and political mobilization of older Americans. *The Gerontologist,* **20**(6): 691–700.

Moon, M. (1986). Impact of the Reagan years on the distribution of income of the elderly. *The Gerontologist,* **26**(1): 32–37.

Peterson, D. A., Powell, C., & Robertson, L. (1976). Aging in America: Toward the year 2000. *The Gerontologist,* **16**(3): 264–269.

Pratt, H. J. (1974). Old age associations in national politics. *The Annals of the American Academy of Political and Social Science,* **415**(September): 106–119.

Pratt, H. J. (1976). *The grey lobby.* Chicago: University of Chicago Press.

Ragan, P. K., & Dowd, J. J. (1974). The emerging political consciousness of the aged: A generational interpretation. *Journal of Social Issues,* **30**(2): 137–158.

Rosenbaum, W. A., & Button, J. W. (1989). Is there a gray peril?: Retirement politics in Florida. *The Gerontologist,* **29**(3): 300–306.

Smith, L. (1988). The world according to AARP. *Fortune,* **117**(5): 96–98.

Special Committee on Aging (1988). *Development in aging: 1987, Volume One.* Washington, DC: U.S. Government Printing Office.

Storey, J. R. (1986). Policy changes affecting older Americans during the first Reagan administration. *The Gerontologist,* **26**(1): 27–31.

Torres-Gil, F. M. (1987*a*). White House Conferences on Aging. In G. L. Maddox (Ed.), *The encyclopedia of aging* (pp. 692–693). New York: Springer.

Torres-Gil, F. M. (1987*b*). Federal Council on Aging. In G. L. Maddox (Ed.), *The encyclopedia of aging* (pp. 254–255). New York: Springer.

Uehara, E. W., Geron, S., & Beeman, S. K. (1986). The elderly poor in the Reagan era. *The Gerontologist,* **26**(1): 48–55.

U.S. Bureau of the Census (1990). *Statistical abstract of the United States.* Washington, DC: U.S. Government Printing Office.

Wolfinger, R. E. (1980). *Who votes?* New Haven: Yale University Press.

PART FOUR

ISSUES IN GERONTOLOGY

Jeff Albertson/Stock, Boston

CHAPTER 13

WORK, RETIREMENT, AND LEISURE

Alan Carey/The Image Works

INTRODUCTION

This chapter is separated into three sections, each examining an important area for older persons. The first is work. As we will see, with increasing age a decreasing percentage of the population is in the work force. The second deals with retirement, where we will examine certain aspects of retirement, including why individuals retire and their adjustment to retirement. The last section will examine leisure. We will explore how older persons use their leisure time.

WORK

In the next section it will be pointed out that retirement in old age, on a large scale, is of relatively recent origin. In the past, few older persons had the financial resources to retire in old age. As a result, most individuals worked until they became unable to work or until they died. Recently the need to work in old age has been offset for many older persons by pension plans: federal plans, such as social security, and private plans. The need to work in the past, because of the lack of pension plans, and the impact of pension plans can be seen in Table 13-1.

As can be seen, in 1930 almost 60 percent of older males were in the work force. The figure is currently 16.5 percent. Not only can we see the consequence of "retirement" for the traditional age group of 65+, but we can also see the effects of "early retirement." For example, in 1930 90.2 percent of those 55 to 64 years of age were in the work force. By 1988 the percentage had dropped to 67.0. While retirement and early retirement are part of the explanation, for the decline in the older persons in the work force, the drop in self-employment also accounts for part of the decline (U.S. Senate, 1987–1988). Self-employed individuals were less subject to factors that forced individuals out of the work force, such as mandatory retirement, and were more capable of modifying their work schedules to meet their needs.

The percentages for older females are somewhat different. In examining the percentage of females in the work force we can clearly see an overall increase. By examining the age categories, and then the percentage of females in the work force from 1930 to 1988, we see that in almost every instance there is an increase. For example, in 1930 42.4 percent of those age 20–24 were in the work force; by 1988 the percentage was 72.7. In 1930 20.4 percent of females age 45–54 were in the work force; by 1988 the percentage was 69.0. A variety of social and economic factors, which are beyond the scope and purpose of this book, have brought about this change.

The figures for females 65+ years of age have remained "fairly" consistent, especially in comparison to the figures for males. For example, 8 percent of females 65+ years of age were in the work force in 1930; in 1988 the percentage was 7.9. This seems inconsistent since more women have entered the work force, and we might anticipate that the percentage would have increased. There are four factors that have helped to keep the percentage of older females in the work force fairly constant. First, just as males in the age group 55–64 have elected early retirement so have females. Second, many women leave the work force when their husbands retire. Since husbands are generally older than their wives (or wives younger than

TABLE 13-1
CIVILIAN LABOR FORCE PARTICIPATION RATES
Participation = %

Age	Male						Female					
	1930	1950	1960	1970	1980	1988	1930	1950	1960	1970	1980	1988
20–24	89.9	81.9	88.9	83.3	85.9	85.0	42.4	43.2	46.1	57.7	68.9	72.7
25–34	97.3	92.1	96.4	96.4	95.2	94.3	27.8	31.8	35.8	45.0	65.5	72.7
35–44	97.6	94.5	96.4	96.9	95.5	94.5	22.6	35.0	43.1	51.1	65.5	75.2
45–54	96.5	92.0	94.3	94.3	91.2	90.9	20.4	32.9	49.3	54.4	59.9	69.0
55–64	90.2	83.4	85.2	83.0	72.1	67.0	16.1	23.4	36.7	43.0	41.3	43.5
65+	58.3	41.5	32.2	26.8	19.0	16.5	8.0	7.8	10.5	9.7	8.1	7.9

Source: U.S. Bureau of the Census, 1955, 1978, 1990.

their husbands), with working married couples there is generally an older male and a younger female leaving the work force. Third, as we will see shortly, age discrimination is widespread; females also have to contend with sex discrimination. Thus, older women have two forms of discrimination that effectively remove many from the work force. Fourth, although as we will see in Chapter 16, "Minorities," older women are one of the most financially disadvantaged groups in America, their condition has improved. Thus, fewer older women are continuing to work in old age.

We can also examine the percentage of the work force that is aged. Table 13-2 has information on the percentage of the work force by age category for selected years. In 1960, 4.6 percent of the work force was 65+ years of age. By 1988 the percentage had dropped to 2.7 percent. Although the percentage of the population that is aged has been increasing, the percentage of the work force that is aged has been declining. There are several reasons for this that include both voluntary and nonvoluntary reasons for older persons leaving the work force. The primary reason for voluntarily leaving the work force is that retirement income is seen as adequate. Some nonvoluntary reasons for leaving the work force are declining health, job termination, or forced retirement. Many older workers who desire to return to the work force find numerous barriers such as the lack of skills, obsolete skills, or intimidating technological changes in the workplace (see Brady et al., 1988).

The 1967 Age Discrimination in Employment Act made it illegal to discriminate by age in areas such as hiring, pay, and discharge. Originally the act covered those 45 to 65 years of age. In 1978 the age was extended to 69; in 1986 the act was again amended, this time removing an upper age limit for most occupations. However, age discrimination against older persons is said to be "widespread" (U.S. Senate, 1987–1988). Age discrimination can take many forms. First, an employer may offer *only* younger workers training opportunities. As a consequence, older workers will find that younger workers are suddenly "passing them" in terms of salary and rank within the organization. Second, an organization that would like an older person to take an early retirement may "reorganize" and either demote the older person to a lower position, at a lower salary, or claim that the reorganization has made it necessary for the older persons to relocate. Third, older persons seeking work are told

TABLE 13-2
CIVILIAN WORK FORCE: PERCENTAGE DISTRIBUTION

	Age						
	16–19	20–24	25–34	35–44	45–54	55–64	65+
1960	7.0	9.6	20.7	23.4	21.3	13.5	4.6
1970	8.8	12.8	20.6	19.9	20.5	13.6	3.9
1980	8.8	14.9	27.3	19.1	15.8	11.2	2.9
1988	6.6	11.9	29.2	24.2	15.7	9.7	2.7

Source: U.S. Bureau of the Census, 1990.

that they are "overqualified" for the position and that they wouldn't be happy in it.

There are probably many factors in age discrimination. The basis is from the "decrement theory of aging" (see McEvoy & Cascio, 1989) which claims that with increasing age there is a decrement or decline in areas such as reaction time, senses, and strength. The assumption is that there must also be a decrement in work performance. As a result, managers are less likely to hire older persons, and more likely to employ age discrimination to remove older workers (see Blocklyn, 1987). The research has consistently demonstrated that there is little factual basis for the decrement theory of aging as it relates to job performance. Most studies have shown no differences in productivity levels between older and younger workers. In a recent analysis of the literature McEvoy and Cascio (1989) reported that there was little relationship between age and job performance. The literature has been very consistent in demonstrating that older workers have a lower accident rate than younger workers. Their absenteeism rate is also lower. They have a higher commitment to the organization and higher job satisfaction. In addition, their turnover rate is lower (Krauss, 1987; McEvoy & Cascio, 1989).

Although it is difficult to predict the future, we may see an increase in the percentage of older persons who are employed. This is for four reasons. First, myths about the poor performance of older workers have been shattered by industrial gerontologists (see Sterns & Alexander, 1987a, 1987b). Second, many organizations are finding that older employees are a valued asset that needs to be maintained. To do this, organizations are creating new programs to either reemploy their retired workers, or make older workers continue in the work force. The programs to attract or maintain older workers can include job sharing, flexible work hours, or part-time work. Third, the number of young workers is starting to decline because the "baby boom" generation produced the "baby bust" generation. Thus, the number of young workers entering the work force will decline in future decades. As a result, organizations will try to keep older workers longer or hire "new" older workers. To an extent this can be seen in entry-level positions in fast food restaurants that used to be filled by high school and college students, but declines in this segment of the population have led the industry to recruit older persons (see Jessup & Greenberg, 1989). Fourth, labor-saving devices have been incorporated into many jobs that formerly required brute strength and stamina. As a result, youth, physical strength, and stamina are no longer a prerequisite for these jobs.

Second careers as a work option for older persons is an area that has been frequently mentioned but largely ignored by gerontologists. Leslie and Leonard Lieberman (1983) examined one type of second career, namely that of artists and craftspersons who participated in arts and crafts fairs. The study found several types of participants, such as those who had made a midlife career change and those who were looking for something to do after a "normal" retirement. They also found different rates of involvement for the different types of participants. For many their second career gave them an opportunity for creativity and independence that they had not had in their first careers. Income and satisfaction with income from the second careers seemed to vary by type of participants and retirement status.

Unemployment

We have examined work, we will now briefly look at unemployment. Table 13-3 has the unemployment figures by sex for those age 55–64 and 65+. The unemployment rate for older persons is about one-half that of young adults. However, the actual rate does not accurately represent older unemployed individuals since many older persons need work but become discouraged and drop out of searching for work. These individuals often need and want to work, but cannot find it. It is estimated that if these individuals were included in the unemployment figures, the percentages would double (U.S. Senate, 1987–1988).

Unemployed older persons have greater difficulty finding work than younger adults. In fact, in comparison to younger workers, older workers are unemployed almost twice as long (e.g., 9.5 weeks for those age 20–24, 23.2 weeks for those age 55–64) (Special Committee on Aging, 1988). In addition, once older workers become reemployed, they suffer a greater loss of income from their previous employment than younger workers.

RETIREMENT

Retirement is a relatively recent mass phenomenon (Fischer, 1977). Although individuals have been retiring for centuries, it is only recently that it has become an activity of the masses. In the past, only the rich and powerful could afford to retire. Retirement on a mass scale was made possible largely by several factors associated with industrialization. The first factor was a greater probability of people reaching old age. In the past, disease and famine contributed to a comparatively short life expectancy (see Chapter 3). In modern industrial society expanded medical knowledge, improved sanitation, and better food production and distribution significantly reduced disease and starvation, thus increasing life expectancy and allowing more individuals to reach old age.

Second, modern industrial society made it possible to support a large nonworking segment of the population. In the past, survival of the group was dependent on almost every member contributing economically to the group. Both the young and the old were responsible for producing and gathering food, finding shelter, and perform-

TABLE 13-3
UNEMPLOYMENT BY AGE AND SEX
(Percentage Unemployed)

Age 55–64		Age 65+	
Male	Female	Male	Female
3.5	2.7	2.5	2.9

Source: U.S. Bureau of the Census, 1990.

ing other tasks important to the survival of the group. Industrialization made it possible to support a large surplus of labor in retirement. Third, in industrial society there was often very little demand for the skills, knowledge, or labor of older persons. In fact, the skills and knowledge of older persons were often obsolete. Thus, older persons were often encouraged or forced to leave the labor force in order to make room for younger workers. Originally, retirement pension plans were viewed by many as financial incentives to remove older workers and replace them with younger workers.

Fourth, the rise of the industrial society also gave rise to social security systems, as well as the bureaucratic structures to support them, and private pension plans that made retirement financially possible. In the past it was difficult for most workers to save enough money for retirement. Also, because workers could seldom project the length of their retirements, they did not know when they had saved enough money to guarantee a financially secure old age. Today, most workers are guaranteed an "adequate" retirement income for life through a system of forced saving (see Atchley, 1982b; Pincus & Wood, 1973). Fifth, the concept of retirement changed in industrial society. As noted earlier, at one time retirement was conceptualized as something for those who were "used up" or worn out. It is now seen as an earned right (see Atchley, 1982b).

This section will examine several aspects of retirement. We will first consider the definition of retirement and then look at some statistics on retirement. Next we will discuss how retirement fits into the life cycle as well as the decision to retire. The last two subsections will consider retirement options and the consequences of retirement.

Definition of Retirement

Initially the concept of retirement may seem rather easy to define. However, like many concepts it can be defined in several ways (see Lipman & Osgood, 1982). For example, ask yourself if the following individuals, who are 65+ years of age, are retired or not retired:

Working part-time for 6 months out of the year
Working at a job that is very different from the type of job held prior to age 65
Working only for "something to do"
Working for a nonprofit organization that does not provide a salary
Working 4 to 5 hours a day to maintain a home
Providing care to an impaired spouse and parent

Some studies identify individuals as retired if they are drawing social security or private pension benefits, even if they are working "full time" at second careers. Some studies have eliminated the difficulty by identifying those who are "employed," "unemployed" and "not employed." There is no "one" definition of retirement and researchers currently use a variety of definitions. The definition that a researcher uses is important since the parameters of the definition will be inclusive and exclusive of certain types of individuals. Depending on the definition, the percentage of those retired and their characteristics can vary tremendously, those making the "facts" of retirement vary greatly from one article to another.

Retirement can and has been viewed in at least three ways. First, retirement can be seen as an event. Although usually conceptualized as an event that happens once in an individual's life, changes in contemporary society have made it an event that frequently happens more than once. Many individuals retire from one career or job after 20 or 30 years and then enter a second career or job, from which they will again ultimately retire. Second, retirement can also be viewed as a role. After retirement, individuals may adopt a number of new retirement roles such as senior-center participant or leisure participant. Third, retirement can be viewed as a developmental process or as a series of stages. Just as there is a developmental process in other segments of the life cycle, such as marriage or work, there is also a developmental process in retirement.

It is difficult to provide a single, exhaustive definition of retirement. Generally, individuals are considered retired if they are not working full time or year-round, if they are drawing social security or private pension benefits, and if they are considered to be retired by themselves or by society.

Statistics on Retirement

Retirement is becoming more prevalent for older persons in American society. In 1870, 25 percent of those 65+ years of age were retired. By 1950 the percentage was 40 percent (Fischer, 1977). The figures from 1960 to the present are in Table 13-4. One trend is toward early retirement, with the current median age 60.6 years (U.S. Senate, 1987–1988). Many organizations have encouraged older workers to retire early because of the false belief that older persons are less productive than younger persons. Additionally, organizations have encouraged early retirement to replace higher income older workers, with lower-income younger workers. Early retirement also created positions for younger workers (see Bell & Marclay, 1987; Mirkin, 1987).

TABLE 13.4
THOSE 65+ NOT IN LABOR FORCE

	Male	Female
1960	66.9	89.2
1970	73.2	90.3
1980	81.0	91.9
1988	83.5	92.1

Source: U.S. Bureau of the Census, 1990.

Although the trend is toward early retirement, concerns about the financial stability of the social security trust fund have brought about policy changes at the federal level in an attempt to increase the age at retirement. In 1983 there were amendments to the Social Security Act aimed at increasing the retirement age (see Herz & Rones, 1989). One change was the gradual increase from age 65 to age 67 when full benefits can be received. Another change is the removal of certain disincentives for older persons to remain in the work force (Boaz, 1987). Other policy decisions to keep individuals in the work force have been job discrimination legislation to protect older workers and the elimination of the mandatory retirement age for most private sector jobs. One additional change dealt with the pension regulations of some organizations that prevented workers past the age of 65 from accumulating further pension benefits. Recent legislation now prevents this. While some believe that the federal government's attempts to legislate retirement age through social policy decisions will be successful, others believe that the retirement age will continue to decline (Anderson et al., 1986).

Life-Cycle Approach to Retirement

The life cycle encompasses all of the life periods, from the first to the last. The significance of retirement in the life cycle can clearly be seen if we examine different segments of the life cycle, the average number of years individuals spend in each, and the percentage of the total life cycle each represents.

Table 13-5 shows the changing nature of retirement. The first part of the table has the average number of years males and females spent in retirement/working at home, the labor force, and education. The second part of the table has the total percentage of the life cycle each of these activities represents. If we examine the percentage part of the table we can see, as expected, that total life expectancy equals 100 percent of the life cycle. By looking at males we can see that retirement/working at home has gone from 3 percent of the total life cycle to 19 percent. In 1900 an average of 1.2 years were spent in retirement/working at home compared to 13.6 years in 1980. At the same time the percentage of the life cycle spent in the labor force declined. In 1900 69 percent of the total life cycle was spent in the work force; by 1980 the percentage had declined to 55 percent. As can be seen, although the percentage declined the actual number of years in the work force increased (e.g., 32.1 years in 1900 and 38.8 years in 1980), because life expectancy increased. We can also see that although the number of years of education increased, the percentage of the life cycle spent in education remained stable.

For females we can see the impact of working outside the home. For females the percentage of the life cycle spent in retirement/working at home decreased from 60 percent to 40 percent. We can also see that labor force participation increased from 13 percent of the total life cycle in 1900 to 38 percent in 1980. Males and females are spending more years in school, the work force, and retirement. However, when we examine these as a percentage of the life cycle we find that males now spend more time in school and retirement, but less in the work force. Females spend more

TABLE 13-5
LIFE-CYCLE DISTRIBUTION OF EDUCATION, LABOR FORCE PARTICIPATION, RETIREMENT,
AND WORK IN THE HOME: 1900–1980

	Number of years spent in activity					
	1900	1940	1950	1960	1970	1980
Male						
Average life expectancy	46.3	60.8	65.6	66.6	67.1	70.0
Retirement/work at home	1.2	9.1	10.1	10.2	12.1	13.6
Labor force participation	32.1	38.1	41.5	41.1	37.8	38.8
Education	8.0	8.6	9.0	10.3	12.2	12.6
Preschool	5.0	5.0	5.0	5.0	5.0	5.0
Female						
Average life expectancy	48.3	65.2	71.1	73.1	74.7	77.4
Retirement/work at home	29.0	39.4	41.4	37.1	35.3	30.6
Labor force participation	6.3	12.1	15.1	20.1	22.3	29.4
Education	8.0	8.7	9.6	10.9	12.1	12.4
Preschool	5.0	5.0	5.0	5.0	5.0	5.0

	Percent distribution by activity type					
	1900	1940	1950	1960	1970	1980
Male						
Average life expectancy	100	100	100	100	100	100
Retirement/work at home	3	15	15	15	18	19
Labor force participation	69	63	63	62	56	55
Education	17	14	14	15	18	18
Preschool	11	8	8	8	7	8
Female						
Average life expectancy	100	100	100	100	100	100
Retirement/work at home	60	60	58	51	47	40
Labor force participation	13	19	21	27	30	38
Education	17	13	14	15	16	16
Preschool	10	8	7	7	7	6

Source: U.S. Senate, 1987–1988.

years in education and the labor force. As a percentage of the total life cycle, females now spend more of the life cycle in the work force.

The Decision to Retire

The decision to retire is seldom determined by one factor, but by the relationships among factors such as anticipated retirement income, job satisfaction, personal health, and health of spouse. Although some of these factors are difficult to control for, it has been reported that about 66 percent of males accurately predicted when they would retire (Ekerdt et al., 1989). Currently, one of the primary reasons for retirement is a perceived adequate retirement income. This generally means that those considering retirement are eligible for social security or private pension benefits, since few individuals have the economic resources to retire without them. Increasing levels of household wealth, in the form of savings, also encourage retirement (Clark, 1988).

Two comments are necessary on perceived retirement income as a cause of retirement. The first deals with the adequacy of the retirement income. Peterson's classic (1972) study demonstrated that the percentage of retired older persons who considered their incomes "adequate" declined the longer they had been in retirement. Essentially, Peterson's study demonstrated that many individuals underestimated their economic needs in retirement or overestimated retirement income. Although Peterson's study is dated and has not been replicated, one recent study did examine the extent and causes of poverty after retirement (Burkhauser et al., 1988). The study followed nonpoverty preretirement couples for 10 years after retirement. While the majority did not go below the poverty line after retirement, certain groups had different probabilities of encountering poverty. The percentage of each group living in poverty after 8 years follows: intact couples with private pensions, 5 percent; intact couples without private pensions, 18 percent; women who became widowed after retirement with private pensions, 15 percent; women who became widowed after retirement without private pensions, 30 percent. We can clearly see that lack of private pensions and widowhood are associated with a higher risk of poverty. More importantly, however, this confirms Peterson's study and suggests that many older persons do not enter retirement with the financial resources to prevent poverty. Even financial planning among professionals is often inadequate. Kilty and Behling (1986) noted that although this is the group with the greatest financial resources to prepare for retirement, after retirement many will face financial problems because of poor planning.

The second comment on adequate income as a cause of retirement deals with benefits. This is a relatively new area of study and not much exists on its impact on retirement. Essentially, many organizations are now offering certain benefits to their retirees, with one of the most popular being an employer-sponsored health plan. Unless retirees purchase expensive health insurance, early retirement is often risky because most early retirees are not covered by a health plan until they reach 65 years of age and are eligible for medicare (Anonymous, 1987; Clark & Kreps, 1989).

A second reason frequently cited for retirement is poor or declining health, although some studies have suggested that health may be used more as a reason to justify retirement than as the real reason; further research is needed (see Ekerdt, 1987; Muller & Boaz, 1988; Palmore et al., 1984). Poor or declining health can obviously make work more difficult. Additionally, poor or declining health of a spouse or parent can place demands on a worker that may force retirement, although some workers are also forced to stay in the work force to maintain employer-sponsored health insurance.

Another factor that influences retirement is the labor supply. When there is a surplus of labor, organizations will offer incentives to get older workers out of the work force; when there is a shortage of labor, older workers will be encouraged to remain in the work force. If an organization is having a difficult time financially, it may encourage early retirement to reduce the higher salaries of older workers and prevent layoffs of younger workers. Additionally, overt or covert pressure may be applied to older workers to "step aside" to make room for younger workers.

Technological obsolescence is another reason for retirement. Many occupations and jobs have changed significantly in a short period of time with the skills and knowledge of older workers becoming obsolete.

Retirement Options

Traditionally, once the decision to retire has been made, the actual act of retirement is abrupt. That is, one day the individual is working, the next day the individual is retired. This is starting to change as many organizations recognize that retirement does not have to be abrupt, and it does not have to be an "all or nothing" approach. Two examples, out of several that could be provided, are provided below to illustrate some of the changes that are starting to be implemented. The first is phased retirement where the individual retires in phases or stages. For example, individuals may reduce the number of hours they work per day, or the number of days they work per week. Thus, individuals may, over a period of months or years, phase out of the work force by reducing the number of weekly hours from 40 to 32, then from 32 to 24, then from 24 to 16, and finally to 0. Additionally, the time between each stage can vary depending on the needs of the organization or the worker. This allows individuals to gradually move into retirement. The social, psychological, and financial changes are less abrupt. It also allows an organization to use the most valuable resources of the individual for a longer period of time.

The second retirement option is sometimes called rehearsal retirement where individuals have the opportunity to take unpaid leaves of absence for a specified period of time to see if they want to make the absence permanent. This can be done on a yearly basis, where individuals take unpaid leaves for a certain number of months each year, or provided as a one-time opportunity for individuals who are thinking about retirement. There are other retirement options. The major point is that many organizations are beginning to conceptualize retirement from different perspectives.

Consequences of Retirement

There are two major theories dealing with the consequences of retirement. The first theory is called the crisis or trauma theory of retirement and states that retirement is a traumatic and degrading experience. Proponents claim that although it is generally accepted that individuals have "earned" the right to a comfortable retirement, there also exists a belief that individuals retire when they can no longer perform adequately in their work roles. Thus, retirement is problematic because it means the loss of a work identity which leads to feelings of inadequacy. These theorists believe that work identity is a major source of identity that leisure roles cannot replace. This is because society does not consider leisure to be a legitimate source of identity. In other words, leisure as a retirement activity cannot replace work identity. The only exception would be leisure activities that would be similar to work.

The loss of a work identity stigmatizes retired individuals with the "inadequate" label. Retired individuals are perceived as no longer having the ability to perform work-related functions. This stigma can lead to a breakdown in an individual's identity. Because of the stigma and the breakdown in identity, the individual is embarrassed and tends to withdraw or disengage from society (Burgess, 1960; Miller, 1965; Rosow, 1962).

The second theory, referred to as continuity theory, suggests that retirement is not the trauma suggested above, but rather after retirement there is a continuity in areas such as life satisfaction and most roles (Atchley, 1976a; Palmore, 1981). Continuity theory claims that while work roles are major sources of identity, that they are not the only sources of identity. Thus, after retirement individuals continue in other roles that can be used for identity. Additionally, there are other factors that allow for a continuity of identity. First, individuals tend to select their friends from among those of a similar cohort. Thus, individuals tend to grow old and retire together. Because they have known each other for long periods of time, they are familiar with factors that contributed to each other's preretirement identity such as prestige, esteem, and status. This preretirement identity is thus carried into retirement for most retired individuals, thus allowing for a continuity in identity. Second, even with retirement, many other important roles continue. For example, individuals still have family, religious, or community roles which can be important sources of identity. Moreover, although the work role is important, it is by no means the "major" source of identity for many individuals. That is, many individuals do not base their identities on only one role. Third, retirement and leisure are becoming socially acceptable in contemporary American society. In fact, we are becoming a leisure-oriented society with shorter work weeks and longer vacation. Fourth, the crisis theory leaves little room for individuals to adapt to their situation. Even if identity is closely associated with work roles, this can change before or after retirement. A major limitation of continuity theory is that it does not recognize that retirement may be traumatic for some individuals.

Although both of these theories have been widely cited, both have also been deemed too simplistic and general (see Palmore et al., 1984). Additionally, the research on the consequences of retirement has often been flawed in that researchers assumed that postretirement characteristics, such as poor health, were caused by retirement when in fact they may have existed prior to retirement. It is now believed that the consequences of retirement depend on a variety of variables such as pre- and postretirement income, health, marital status, as well as race, gender, and whether retirement occurred "on-time" or "off-time." Although retirement has often been associated with an increasing risk of illness and death, studies have consistently refuted this belief (Ekerdt, 1987). This belief is discussed in greater detail in Chapter 17, "Dying and Death."

One study on the consequences of retirement reported that retirement had little impact on life satisfaction, activity, or health (Palmore et al., 1984). This study found that those who retired "off-time" or early had more negative aspects such as lower incomes, health, and happiness than those who retired "on-time."

Studies have been conducted to ascertain if retirement is more difficult for males or females. A variety of studies have reported that retirement is more difficult for females (Atchley, 1976*b*; Atchley & Corbett, 1977; Jaslow, 1976; Johnson & Williamson, 1980; Streib & Schneider, 1971), while other studies have reported that it is more difficult for males (Aitken, 1982; Blau, 1973; Elwell & Maltbie-Crannell, 1981; Palmore et al., 1984). The common reasons used to explain why retirement is more difficult for females is widowhood and lower incomes. For males it deals with the importance of the work role (see Davidson, 1982).

This is an emerging area where the research is becoming more complex. As in most areas in gerontology, the questions are not as simple as, ''Who has a better adjustment to retirement, males or females?'' Rather a variety of factors need to be examined such as health, income, and marital status. For example, if females who were widowed before retirement are asked about the impact of retirement they will generally report that it is relatively minor; in fact, the role changes associated with retirement are minor in comparison to the role changes associated with the death of a spouse. However, married females who have not experienced as traumatic a life event as widowhood may find retirement to be difficult (see Gratton & Haug, 1983; Matthews & Brown, 1987; Meade & Walker, 1989).

It has been reported that older persons who retired voluntarily had more positive postretirement feelings about retirement than those who retired involuntarily or unexpectedly (Matthews & Brown, 1987). Preliminary evidence suggests that more females may retire involuntarily or unexpectedly because of the failing health of a spouse or other family member. Health is also a prevalent factor in satisfaction with retirement, with those in better health defining the experience more positively than those in poor health. Obviously, lower levels of health can restrict the ability to participate and enjoy retirement (Beck, 1982; Elwell & Maltbie-Crannell, 1981; George & Maddox, 1977; Gratton & Haug, 1983; Hartman et al., 1981; Matthews & Brown, 1987; Riddick, 1985).

Another factor that has been associated with more positive adjustment to retirement is income, with higher incomes being correlated with higher levels of satisfaction (Hartman et al., 1981), although not all studies have reported this finding (Keith, 1985). Those with the lowest preretirement incomes generally have the lowest percentage of decline in income after retirement because of eligibility for income-maintenance programs. Those with the highest preretirement incomes suffer larger percentages of declines in income after retirement, but have generally sufficient resources to meet their needs. The group that appears to suffer the most is the middle group, who are not eligible for income-maintenance programs and who do not have the economic reserves to meet their needs (Fillenbaum et al., 1985).

Two additional areas have been associated with satisfaction with retirement. The first is marital status. It has generally been reported that the married are more satisfied than the nonmarried. Assumptions have been that the spouse is a companion, helper, friend, lover, and resource. The second area deals with preretirement occupation. The belief has been that the higher the occupation the higher the satisfaction with retirement. Part of this belief has been tied to income and health; those in higher occupations generally have higher incomes and better health which makes retirement satisfaction higher, and also have more social skills that help them adapt to retirement.

A new area of research deals with the retirement satisfaction among unmarried males and females (Keith, 1985). It has been assumed that work roles are more important to unmarried individuals because of the financial aspects and also as the primary source of identification and satisfaction. Additionally, it has been assumed that after retirement the lack of a spouse would make adjustment to retirement more difficult. Initial studies do not support these assumptions for most unmarried older persons. One exception was formerly married females, who defined the retirement experience more negatively than unmarried males and never-married females.

Another area that is being investigated is the impact that preretirement programs have on retirement (see Kleiber, 1982; Mangum, 1982; Palmore, 1982; Slover, 1982; Tedrick, 1982). Preretirement programs have been in existence since the 1940s with the intent of preparing individuals for retirement financially, psychologically, and socially. The programs have consisted of various types, such as individual counseling by someone from an organization's personnel department, to several group sessions where different aspects of retirement are discussed (see Tiberi et al., 1978). Although the figures vary, about 15 percent of companies have formal preretirement programs (Glamser, 1981), and about 4 percent of retired workers participated in programs (Beck, 1984).

Although there have been a number of studies on the consequences of preretirement programs, most have had methodological limitations. For example, to determine their effectiveness most of the preretirement programs did an immediate postprogram evaluation asking participants to rate how valuable they thought the program would be, rather than an examination of the actual value of the preretirement program after retirement. A study by Glamser (1981; see also Glamser & DeJong, 1975) examined the impact of two preretirement programs 6 years after they were given. The first program consisted of eight 90-minute discussion sessions, the second individual briefings by a personnel officer that lasted approximately 30 minutes. A control group, which constituted a third group, was also used. In terms of life satisfaction, preparedness for retirement, and adjustment to retirement there were no significant differences among the three groups. This does not mean that preretirement programs are of little or no value. It probably means that the duration and intensity of many programs is not sufficient. Additionally, new areas need attention, such as women and retirement (see Meade & Walker, 1989) and minorities and retirement. One limitation is that those who would benefit the most from preretirement programs are the least likely to participate or to have the opportunity to participate (Beck, 1984; Campione, 1988).

Although the variables that determine the consequences of retirement are varied and often interdependent, the vast majority of individuals, about 75 percent, are happy with retirement (Atchley, 1982a; Beck, 1982; Matthews & Brown, 1987; Palmore et al., 1984).

LEISURE

We have just examined retirement and found that a variety of factors have increased the percentage of the life cycle that older persons spend in retirement. In this section we want to examine what older persons do with that extra time; we will examine leisure. This area has not received the research attention that it deserves. Perhaps because studying a "fun-" type of voluntary activity seems insignificant in comparison to studying other issues such as income, health, and death.

There is little doubt that we are becoming a leisure-oriented society. Shorter work weeks—in 1870 the average work week was 60 to 72 hours (Havighurst, 1970; Howe, 1988; Osgood, 1982; Peacock & Talley, 1985)—better health, greater life expectancy, more income, coupled with the fact that we now spend about one-fifth of our lives in retirement, allows more time for leisure-related activities. There are a number of different definitions of leisure; in fact, leisure is as ambiguous a term as retirement (see Gunter, 1987; Kelly, 1982; McGuire, 1982). In this book, leisure will be considered an activity that one engages in on a voluntary basis for intrinsic enjoyment and that is not necessary for subsistence (see Peppers, 1976).

Leisure has a tremendous potential associated with it. However, the potential is two-sided. For example, leisure can be a growth experience. If individuals are willing to try new activities or continue old ones, leisure can be a stimulating and challenging experience that enables individuals to grow. Daily there are examples of individuals who utilize leisure in this manner. For example, newspapers and magazines often have stories about older persons who have completed high school, college, or even professional degrees. Many others have started new careers or have hobbies that are a source of pleasure and enjoyment. However, there is another side to leisure. Rather than being a growth experience, leisure can also have a darker side. There are examples of older persons who are lonely, isolated, bored, and unhappy with leisure. They sit alone or in silent groups in parks, shopping malls, or hotel lobbies and wait for sleep or death to release them from chronic boredom. Many of these individuals found that planned leisure activities turned out to be boring or too expensive or impractical because of financial or health limitations. Some have found that the health declines of a spouse impact on their leisure plans. Other individuals stopped certain leisure activities when they found them too difficult for their talents, abilities, or patience. For example, a person who had planned to write the "great American novel" may find that he or she does not have the ability or the talent to do so. Unfortunately, many of these individuals "give up" on leisure. They become bitter dropouts who speculate about what might have been rather than attempt to find alternative forms of leisure that might make life more enjoyable. This section of the book will examine the concept of leisure among older persons. Specifically, we will examine the types of leisure activities in which older persons participate.

Leisure Activities

Leisure activities are determined by variables such as health, race, education, income, and sex (Kelly et al., 1986; Lawton et al., 1986–1987). This section will examine some of the more prevalent leisure activities of older persons.

Television is unquestionably a major source of leisure activity for older persons. Ninety-five percent claim that they watch television, which is the highest for the adult-age categories surveyed (U.S. Bureau of the Census, 1990). The amount they watch depends on the study and can vary from an average of 5 to 40 hours per week. Because television is an important leisure-time activity for older persons, it should be briefly examined from two perspectives. The first perspective claims that television can be an important component in the lives of older persons for several reasons.

1 Television keeps individuals informed of local, state, national, and world events. Rather than allowing older persons to lapse into living in the past, television can keep them current and up to date.

2 Television is a source of entertainment. It has special advantages for older persons in that it is readily available, relatively inexpensive, and very accessible to those with mobility and hearing limitations.

3 As a source of entertainment, television offers the viewer an opportunity to escape from everyday life. It also offers variety and stimulation.

4 Just as there are specific programs designed for specific age groups such as children or adolescents, there can be specific programs designed for older persons. Network, cable, PBS, or even closed-circuit television programs in nursing homes or retirement communities could broadcast programs of interest to older persons. Programs might include discussions of social security, health care, estate planning, or social services programs for older persons.

5 Television can also bring meaning into the lives of older persons. Davis (1975) cited an example of an older person who said that television brought people and music into his life. Without television, the man continued, he would be ready to die. An older woman noted that television gave her something to talk about with friends and neighbors.

6 Many older person become ''personally'' involved with the characters or entertainers they watch on television. Thus, television can provide surrogate human contacts that might be missing in real life.

7 Television also has the opportunity to modify the negative image of older persons. This can be accomplished by avoiding the assignment of derogatory roles to older persons. Aged entertainers also present a positive image of older persons.

Not all gerontologists believe that television is a beneficial medium for older persons. The major complaints against television are listed below.

1 Television does not provide much mental or physical stimulation. Because the audience is sedentary and because it has a mesmerizing effect, it can be detrimental to both physical and mental development.

2 Television has also been criticized in the way it portrays older persons. Some believe that older persons are portrayed as pathetic, debilitated, or helpless individuals who are dependent on younger persons for assistance. There have also been complaints that older persons are assigned one-dimensional roles too frequently.

3 Television may also serve to sever human contact. Instead of being forced to create or to find human contacts, many older persons become satisfied with their ''friends'' on television.

The other media sources are used less frequently than television by older persons. Only about 66 percent listen to the radio, the lowest percentage of the adult-age categories surveyed. For newspapers the percentage is 82, again the lowest of the adult-age groups surveyed (U.S. Bureau of the Census, 1990). Reading can be a major source of leisure-time activity. One national study found that about 30 percent of the older persons surveyed had read one or more books during the previous 6 months, the lowest percentage of the adult-age categories listed. About 10 percent had not read books, magazines, or newspapers during the last 6 months (U.S. Bureau of the Census, 1990). The decline in reading is due to the increase in visual problems (see Heinemann et al., 1988), as well as different levels of education (see Fisher, 1988; Scales & Biggs, 1987).

Exercise or sporting activities also take up leisure time. A study on individuals 65+ years of age found the following percentages of sports/exercise activities participated in: exercise walking 32, fishing 11, swimming 13, bicycle riding 10, camping 8, golf 8 (U.S. Bureau of the Census, 1990). The percentages engaging in ''vigorous'' physical activity are somewhat misleading. To be included as a participant in some of the activities, individuals only had to engage in the activities six times per year. A more recent report has examined if the amount of physical activity is sufficient to prevent coronary heart disease and found that for those age 18–65 only 10 to 17 percent fell into this category (Brooks, 1987).

There have been few studies on specific leisure athletic or sporting activities. One report has examined shuffleboard as a leisure activity of older persons (Snyder, 1986). Because of shuffleboard's association with older persons it will be briefly examined. Shuffleboard or ''shuffling'' can have a variety of meanings for older persons. For some, it is an infrequent, casual, social activity. For these individuals shuffling does not have any special meaning or significance. It is a way of meeting others, and a place for social interaction to take place. For others its is a frequent, intensive, competitive activity. Many of these individuals compete in local, and even state or national tournaments. For these individuals shuffling takes on tremendous significance. The game is viewed as ''skill and strategy.'' Competitive players visit other courts to take notes on the characteristics of shuffleboard courts, such as how smooth or level the court is, which will determine the speed and drift of the disc.

Education, especially adult education [i.e., ''part-time organized educational activities such as college courses, employee training, continuing education, and private instruction'' (U.S. Bureau of the Census, 1990)], is another potential leisure-time activity of older persons. Currently about 0.5 percent participate in adult education (see Moyer & Lago, 1987).

A variety of other leisure activities can also be engaged in. Some of them, and the percentage of those 65+ years of age who engage in them are socializing with friends, 47 percent; caring for younger or older family members, 27 percent; sitting and thinking, 31 percent; gardening or raising plants, 39 percent; sleeping, 16 percent; participating in fraternal or community organizations or clubs, 17 percent; doing volunteer work, 8 percent; participating in political activities, 6 percent (Harris & Associates, 1975).

SUMMARY

This chapter was separated into three sections: work, retirement, and leisure. In the section on work it was pointed out that over time the percentage of the older population in the work force has gone progressively down. For example, in 1930 almost 60 percent of those 65+ years of age were in the work force; by 1987 it was about 16 percent. The percentage of older women in the work force has remained relatively constant.

The percentage of the work force that is aged has also declined. For example, in 1960 4.6 percent of the work force was composed of individuals 65+ years of age; in 1988 it was 2.7 percent. Age discrimination was briefly discussed, and it was noted that it is "widespread," in part because of prevalent myths about older workers. While unemployment among older persons is about half the figure for younger workers, it is believed that the low figure does not accurately reflect the true unemployment rate.

In the second section retirement was examined. Retirement is a relatively recent mass phenomenon, made possible by several aspects associated with industrialization: greater life expectancy, ability to support a large nonworking segment of the population, obsolescence of skills and knowledge of older workers, retirement income systems, and the concept of retirement as an earned right. The definition of retirement can vary. Also, retirement can be seen as an event, a role, or a series of developmental stages.

Currently the trend is toward early retirement, with an average age of 60.6 years. Currently individuals spend more years and a greater percentage of their lives in retirement. The decision to retire is seldom prompted by one factor, but several. One of the primary reasons is a perceived adequate retirement income. Another is declining health.

Many organizations are realizing that retirement does not necessarily have to be an "all or nothing process." Because of this several retirement options are being offered, such as phased retirement or rehearsal retirement. Two major theories have frequently been cited to explain the consequences of retirement, one of the theories concentrating on the negative aspects, the other positive. Both are probably too simplistic, and more research is needed in this area.

The third and last section dealt with leisure. Although an important area, relatively little research exists. Several forms of leisure activity were examined.

REFERENCES

Aitken, L. R. (1982). *Later Life*. New York: Holt, Rinehart and Winston.

Anderson, K. H., Burkhauser, R. V., & Quinn, J. F. (1986). Do retirement dreams come true? The effect of unanticipated events on retirement plans. *Industrial and Labor Relations Review*, **39**(4): 518–526.

Anonymous (1987). Employee-sponsored health insurance for retirees: The need and the cost. *Monthly Labor Review*, **110**(5): 38.

Atchley, R. C. (1976a). *The sociology of retirement*. New York: Schenkman.

Atchley, R. C. (1976*b*). Orientation toward the job and retirement adjustment among women. In J. Gubrium (Ed.), *Time, roles, and self in old age* (pp. 199–208). New York: Human Sciences Press.

Atchley, R. C. (1982*a*). The process of retirement: Comparing men and women. In M. Szinovacz (Ed.), *Women's retirement: Policy implications of recent research* (pp. 153–168). Newbury Park, CA: Sage.

Atchley, R. C. (1982*b*). Retirement as a social institution. *Annual Review of Sociology,* **8**: 263–287.

Atchley, R. C., & Corbett, S. L. (1977). Older women and jobs. In L. E. Troll (Ed.), *Looking ahead: A woman's guide to the problems and joys of growing older* (pp. 121–125). Englewood Cliffs, NJ: Prentice-Hall.

Beck, S. H. (1982). Adjustment to and satisfaction with retirement. *Journal of Gerontology,* **37**(5): 616–624.

Beck, S. H. (1984). Retirement preparation programs: Differentials in opportunity and use. *Journal of Gerontology,* **39**(5): 596–602.

Bell, D., & Marclay, W. (1987). Trends in retirement eligibility and pension benefits, 1974–1983. *Monthly Labor Review,* **110**(4): 18–25.

Blau, Z. S. (1973). *Old age in a changing society.* New York: New Viewpoints.

Blocklyn, P. L. (1987). Consensus on. . .the aging workforce. *Personnel,* **64**(8): 16–19.

Boaz, R. F. (1987). The 1983 Amendments to the Social Security Act: Will they delay retirement? A summary of the evidence. *The Gerontologist,* **27**(2): 151–155.

Brady, E. M., Palermino, P., Scott, D., Fernandez, R., & Norland, S. (1988). Barriers to work among the elderly: A Connecticut study. *Journal of Applied Gerontology,* **6**(4): 415–428.

Brooks, C. M. (1987). Leisure time physical activity assessment of American adults through an analysis of time diaries collected in 1981. *American Journal of Public Health,* **77**(4): 455–460.

Burgess, E. (1960). Family structure and relationships. In E. Burgess (Ed.), *Aging in western societies.* Chicago: University of Chicago Press.

Burkhauser, R. V., Holden, K. C., & Feaster, D. (1988). Incidence, timing, and events associated with poverty: A dynamic view of poverty in retirement. *Journal of Gerontology: Social Sciences,* **43**(2): S46–52.

Campione, W. A. (1988). Predicting participation in retirement preparation programs. *Journal of Gerontology: Social Sciences,* **43**(3): S91–95.

Clark, R. L. (1988). The future of work and retirement. *Research on Aging,* **10**(2): 169–193.

Clark, R. L., & Kreps, J. M. (1989). Employer-sponsored health care plans for retirees. *Research on Aging,* **11**(2): 206–224.

Davidson, J. (1982). Issues of employment and retirement in the lives of women over age 40. In N. J. Osgood (Ed.), *Life after work: Retirement, leisure, recreation, and the elderly* (pp. 95–118). New York: Praeger.

Davis, R. H. (1975). Television communication and the elderly. In D. S. Woodruff & J. E. Birren (Eds.), *Aging: Scientific perspectives and social issues* (pp. 315–335). New York: Van Nostrand.

Ekerdt, D. J. (1987). Why the notion persists that retirement harms health. *The Gerontologist,* **27**(4): 454–457.

Ekerdt, D. J., Vinick, B. H., & Bosse, R. (1989). Orderly endings: Do men know when they will retire? *Journal of Gerontology: Social Science,* **44**(1): S28–35.

Elwell, F., & Maltbie-Crannell, A. D. (1981). The impact of role loss upon coping resources and life satisfaction of the elderly. *Journal of Gerontology,* **36**(2): 223–232.

Fillenbaum, G. G., George, L. K., & Palmore, E. B. (1985). Determinants and consequences of retirement among men of different races and economic levels. *Journal of Gerontology* **40**(1): 85–94.

Fischer, D. H. (1977). *Growing old in America.* New York: Oxford University Press.

Fisher, J. C. (1988). Older adult readers and nonreaders. *Educational Gerontology,* **14**(1): 57–67.

George, L. K., & Maddox, G. L. (1977). Subjective adaptation to loss of the work role: A longitudinal study. *Journal of Gerontology,* **32**(4): 456–462.

Glamser, F. D. (1981). The impact of preretirement programs on the retirement experience. *Journal of Gerontology,* **36**(2): 244–250.

Glamser, F. D., & DeJong, G. F. (1975). The efficacy of preretirement preparation programs for industrial workers. *Journal of Gerontology,* **30**(5): 595–600.

Gratton, B., & Haug, M. R. (1983). Decision and adaptation: Research on female retirement. *Research on Aging,* **5**(1): 59–76.

Gunter, B. G. (1987). The leisure experience: Selected properties. *Journal of Leisure Research,* **19**(2): 115–130.

Harris, L., & Associates (1975). *The myth and reality of aging in America.* Washington, DC: The National Council on the Aging.

Hartman, C. (1988). Redesigning America. *Inc.,* **10**(6): 58–74.

Hartman, C., Foner, A., & Schwab, K. (1981). *Aging and retirement.* Monterey, CA: Brooks/Cole.

Havighurst, R. J. (1970). Leisure and aging. In A. M. Hoffman (Ed.), *The daily needs and interests of older people* (pp. 165–174). Springfield, IL: Charles C Thomas.

Heinemann, A. W., Colorez, A., Frank, S., & Taylor, D. (1988). Leisure activity participation of elderly individuals with low vision. *The Gerontologist,* **28**(2): 181–184.

Herz, D. E., & Rones, P. L. (1989). Institutional barriers to employment of older workers. *Monthly Labor Review,* **112**(4): 14–21.

Howe, C. Z. (1988). Selected social gerontology theories and older adult leisure involvement: A review of the literature. *Journal of Applied Gerontology,* **6**(4): 448–463.

Jaslow, P. (1976). Employment, retirement, and morale among older women. *Journal of Gerontology,* **21**(2): 212–218.

Jessup, D., & Greenberg, B. (1989). Innovative older-worker programs. *Generations,* **13**(3): 23–27.

Johnson, E. S., & Williamson, J. B. (1980). *Growing old: The social problems of aging.* New York: Holt, Rinehart and Winston.

Keith, P. M. (1985). Work, retirement, and well-being among unmarried men and women. *The Gerontologist,* **25**(4): 410–416.

Kelly, J. R. (1982). Leisure in later life: Roles and identities. In N. J. Osgood (Ed.), *Life after work: Retirement, leisure, recreation, and the elderly* (pp. 268–293). New York: Praeger.

Kelly, J. R., Steinkamp, M. W., & Kelly, J. R. (1986). Later life leisure: How they play in Peoria. *The Gerontologist,* **26**(5): 531–537.

Kilty, K. M., & Behling, J. H. (1986). Retirement financial planning among professional workers. *The Gerontologist,* **26**(5): 525–530.

Kleiber, D. A. (1982). Optimizing retirement through lifelong learning and leisure education. In N. J. Osgood (Ed.), *Life after work: Retirement, leisure, recreation, and the elderly* (pp. 319–329). New York: Praeger.

Krauss, I. K. (1987). Employment. In G. L. Maddox (Ed.), *The encyclopedia of aging* (pp. 206–208). New York: Springer.

Lawton, M. P., Moss, M., & Fulcomer, M. (1986–1987). Objective and subjective uses of time by older people. *International Journal of Aging and Human Development*, **24**(3): 171–188.

Lieberman, L., & Lieberman, L. (1983). Second careers in art and craft fairs. *The Gerontologist*, **23**(3): 266–272.

Lipman, A., & Osgood, N. J. (1982). Retirement: The emerging social institution. In N. J. Osgood (Ed.), *Life after work: Retirement, leisure, recreation, and the elderly* (pp. 29–64). New York: Praeger.

McEvoy, G. M., & Cascio, W. F. (1989). Cumulative evidence of the relationship between employee age and job performance. *Journal of Applied Psychology*, **74**(1): 11–17.

McGuire, F. A. (1982). Leisure time, activities, and meaning: A comparison of men and women in late life. In N. J. Osgood (Ed.), *Life after work: Retirement, leisure, recreation, and the elderly* (pp. 132–151). New York: Praeger.

Mangum, W. P. (1982). Retirement and leisure: A life course perspective. In N. J. Osgood (Ed.), *Life after work: Retirement, leisure, recreation, and the elderly* (pp. 295–314). New York: Praeger.

Matthews, A. M., & Brown, K. H. (1987). Retirement as a critical life event. *Research on Aging*, **9**(4): 548–571.

Meade, K., & Walker, J. (1989). Gender equality: Issues and challenges for retirement education. *Educational Gerontology*, **15**(2): 171–185.

Miller, S. (1965). The social dilemma of the aging leisure participant. In A. Rose & W. Peterson (Eds.), *Older people and their social world* (pp. 77–92). Philadelphia: F. A. Davis.

Mirkin, B. A. (1987). Early retirement as a labor force policy: An international overview. *Monthly Labor Review*, **110**(3): 19–23.

Moyer, I., & Lago, D. (1987). Institutional barriers to older learners in higher education: A critique of fee-waiver programs. *Educational Gerontology*, **13**(2): 157–169.

Muller, C. F., & Boaz, R. F. (1988). Health as a reason or a rationalization for being retired. *Research on Aging*, **10**(1): 37–55.

Osgood, N. J. (1982). Work: Past, present, and future. In N. J. Osgood (Ed.), *Life after work: Retirement, leisure, recreation, and the elderly* (pp. 3–28). New York: Praeger.

Palmore, E. B. (1981). *Social patterns in normal aging*. Durham: Duke University Press.

Palmore, E. B. (1982). Preparation for retirement: The impact of preretirement programs on retirement and leisure. In N. J. Osgood (Ed.), *Life after work: Retirement, leisure, recreation, and the elderly* (pp. 330–341). New York: Praeger.

Palmore, E. B., Fillenbaum, G. G., & George, L. K. (1984). Consequences of retirement. *Journal of Gerontology*, **39**(1): 109–116.

Peacock, E. W., & Talley, W. M. (1985). Developing leisure competence: A goal for late adulthood. *Educational Gerontology*, **11**(4/6): 261–276.

Peppers, L. G. (1976). Patterns of leisure and adjustment to retirement. *The Gerontologist*, **16**(5): 441–446.

Peterson, D. A. (1972). Financial adequacy in retirement: Perceptions of older Americans. *The Gerontologist*, **12**(4): 379–383.

Pincus, A., & Wood, V. (1973). Retirement. In R. Morris (Ed.), *Encyclopedia of social work* (pp. 1125–1135). Washington, DC: National Association of Social Workers.

Riddick, C. C. (1985). Life satisfaction of older female homemakers, retirees, and workers. *Research on Aging*, **7**(3): 383–393.

Rosow, I. (1962). One moral dilemma of an affluent society. *The Gerontologist*, **2**(2): 189–191.

Scales, A. M., & Biggs, S. A. (1987). Reading habits of elderly adults: Implications for instruction. *Educational Gerontology*, **13**(6): 521–532.

Slover, D. (1982). Preparation for retirement: The impact of preretirement programs. In N. J. Osgood (Ed.), *Life after work: Retirement, leisure, recreation, and the elderly* (pp. 342–350). New York: Praeger.

Snyder, E. E. (1986). The social world of shuffleboard: Participation by senior citizens. *Urban Life*, **15**(2): 237–253.

Special Committee on Aging, United States Senate (1988). *Development in aging: 1987.* Washington, DC: U.S. Government Printing Office.

Sterns, H. L., & Alexander, R. A. (1987a). Industrial gerontology: The aging individual and work. In K. W. Schaie (Ed.), *Annual review of gerontology and geriatrics: Volume Seven* (pp. 243–264). New York: Springer.

Sterns, H. L., & Alexander, R. A. (1987b). Industrial gerontology. In G. L. Maddox (Ed.), *The encyclopedia of aging* (pp. 349–351). New York: Springer.

Streib, G. F., & Schneider, C. J. (1971). *Retirement in American society: Impact and process.* Ithaca, NY: Cornell University Press.

Tedrick, T. (1982). Leisure competency: A goal for aging Americans in the 1980s. In N. J. Osgood (Ed.), *Life after work: Retirement, leisure, recreation, and the elderly* (pp. 315–318). New York: Praeger.

Tiberi, D. M., Boyack, V. L., & Kerschner, P. A. (1978). A comparative analysis of four preretirement education models. *Educational Gerontology*, **3**(4): 355–374.

U.S. Bureau of the Census (1955). *Statistical abstract of the United States.* Washington, DC: U.S. Government Printing Office.

U.S. Bureau of the Census (1978). *Statistical abstract of the United States.* Washington, DC: U.S. Government Printing Office.

U.S. Bureau of the Census (1990). *Statistical abstract of the United States.* Washington, DC: U.S. Government Printing Office.

U.S. Senate, Special Committee on Aging (1987–1988). *Aging America: Trends and projections (1987–1988 edition).* Washington, DC: U.S. Department of Health and Human Services.

CHAPTER **14**

HOME AND COMMUNITY

Mike Mazzaschi/Stock, Boston

INTRODUCTION

It is only recently that the environment has become an important variable in the social sciences (see Howell, 1980; Lawton, 1983, 1985). In the past, the environment was generally ignored or simply considered to be a backdrop against which individuals lived their lives. However, studies have now demonstrated the influence that environmental variables can have on the physical, psychological, and social functioning of older persons. This chapter is divided into two major sections. The first section will focus primarily on older persons living independently in their communities. The second section will examine aspects of the community that are important for older persons. The next chapter will examine one additional environment, namely nursing homes.

THE HOME

This section is separated into five subsections. The first will begin by examining the living arrangements of older persons. In the second we will examine economic impact of housing on older persons. The third subsection covers housing options for older persons. There will be a separate area on retirement communities. Fourth, we will examine the concept of the prosthetic environment. The fifth, and last subsection, is about the homeless.

Living Arrangements of Older Persons

Table 14-1 shows the living arrangements for males and females for the noninstitutionalized aged population. As can be seen, significantly more females than males live alone. Much of this is related to the fact that males tend to die earlier than females, thus leaving a greater percentage of females living alone. This fact can also be seen in the next figure on the percentage with a spouse present. The vast majority of males have a spouse present; the majority of females do not have a spouse present. The next figure, living with someone else, is also higher for females. Because of their greater life expectancy, women have a greater likelihood of being widowed and of developing disabilities. This frequently means that they need assistance, which necessitates living with someone else, such as adult children.

TABLE 14-1
LIVING ARRANGEMENTS FOR NONINSTITUTIONALIZED OLDER
PERSONS: 1988

	Male, %	Female, %
Living in household	99.5	99.5
Living alone	14.7	40.6
Spouse present	75.0	39.9
Living with someone else	9.8	19.0
Not in household	0.5	0.5

Source: U.S. Bureau of the Census, 1990.

Economic Impact of Housing

Housing is a major expense for older persons, and they tend to spend a greater percentage of their total income on housing costs than those under age 65. Table 14-2 shows the percentage of income spent on housing by different age groups by type of housing. As can be seen, those who own mortgage-free homes pay a smaller percentage of their total incomes for housing costs (i.e., taxes, utilities, maintenance, etc.). Two other trends are clear. First, those over 65 years of age, for all types of housing, spend more of their income on housing than those under 65 years of age. Second, with each successive age group housing represents a greater percentage of total income.

Owning a home in old age can be a blessing or a curse. On the one hand many older persons have paid off their mortgages and housing costs can be low, thus leaving a greater percentage of income for other expenses. On the other hand, many of the homes of older persons are in deteriorating neighborhoods, with increasing crime rates and dropping property values. Additionally, increasing property taxes and expensive repairs can be an economic burden for many aged home owners.

The largest investment most older persons have are their homes. Many older persons are faced with the dilemma of needing greater income in old age, which could be obtained by selling their homes, but at the same time wanting to stay in their homes. To an extent a new concept called "home equity conversion" or "home equity liquefying plans" (HELP) have been created to assist in resolving this dilemma. This is an emerging concept, and there are several forms, which have been described by Chen (1987). The basic concept is to provide the homeowner with cash from the equity in the home. One method makes monthly payments, or loans, to the homeowner. The size of the payments is determined by the equity the homeowner has in the house, the value of the house, and the number of payments (i.e., often based on homeowners projected life expectancy). When the homeowner dies or the loan period ends, the loan must be repaid, generally through the sale of the home. There are obviously problems with these plans, especially if the homeowner outlives the payment period.

Housing Options for Older Persons

A variety of housing options exist for older persons that range from expensive condominiums on Florida's gold coast, to single-room-occupancy (SRO) hotel rooms—which

TABLE 14-2
PERCENTAGE OF INCOME SPENT ON HOUSING BY AGE AND TYPE OF HOUSING

	Under 65	65–69	70–74	75+
Owned without mortgage	9.9	13.5	15.4	17.2
Owned with mortgage	19.8	22.7	24.4	28.6
Rented	27.9	31.2	31.3	33.3

Source: U.S. Senate Special Committee on Aging, 1987–1988.

are generally in rundown, crime-ridden, downtown areas of large cities. Lawton has classified the options into planned and unplanned (1985, 1987). Unplanned housing was not built specifically for older persons. Planned housing was built for older persons. There are some options that fall between the two, such as a mobile home that was not built specifically for older persons, but is located in a mobile home park that was designed for older persons. The major source of unplanned housing is, of course, individual single-family homes. Other unplanned housing can include mobile homes, apartments, or condominiums. It is estimated that 88 percent of older persons live in unplanned housing. Another 7 percent live in planned housing, which again can assume several forms. The remaining 5 percent are in long-term care facilities, such as nursing homes. We will examine several forms of planned housing.

Shared housing, of which there are several forms, is one example of planned housing. The key ingredient of shared housing is a home large enough to house several older persons who are capable of living independently. Sometimes the house is owned by one of the residents and an organization will attempt to find compatible boarders. Other times an organization will own the house and place boarders. Often housing units in the shared housing concept are managed by an outside agency. This type of housing is not without its problems (Pritchard, 1983). For example, the personalities of the residents may clash. Accessory apartments is another option that is becoming popular. Here a single family home is remodeled to include a separate and complete living unit. This living unit has its own entrance, bath, kitchen, living, and sleeping areas. Although accessory apartments are often used as rental housing, they are also used by caregivers of older persons. With accessory apartments both the caregiver and the older person can maintain independence and privacy; as an added feature the caregiver is close by.

ECHO housing (i.e., elder cottage housing opportunity) is another housing concept for older persons. These are sometimes known as ''granny flats'' and are separate single-family units designed with the needs of older persons in mind. They are small (i.e., 500 to 800 square feet), inexpensive (i.e., $15,000 to $25,000) factory-made homes that can be easily erected next to the home of a caregiver. As a result, the older person and caregiver have privacy, but the proximity makes caregiving somewhat easier. These have become popular in England and Australia (Lawton, 1985).

The last form of planned housing to be examined is retirement communities.

Retirement Communities   Retirement communities can generally be thought of as age-segregated communities for older persons. They are, in some ways, specialized environments for older persons in terms of structure and facilities. About 1 to 2 percent of older persons live in retirement communities (Blank, 1988). The term retirement community can be defined in a variety of ways and can include variables such as amount of planning, size, location (e.g., rural, urban, suburban), type of housing (e.g., high-rise apartments, cottages, individual single-family dwellings, etc.), or purpose (i.e., leisure or nursing care). Longino (1981) defines retirement communities by two characteristics: retirement and relocation. That is, most of those in the community must have retired from a major occupation, although they may work part-time, and they must have moved into the community.

As we will see shortly, some retirement communities are planned for older persons. As a result, the transportation, shopping, medical resources, and recreational options are built into the surrounding community. Other retirement communities are not planned, but seem to occur naturally. Because of climate or networking among friends, more and more older persons move into certain areas; as a result services develop to meet the needs of the area residents. Although an increasing percentage of older persons live in retirement communities, there is a surprising lack of research in this area since the first article appeared in the 1950s (Hoyt, 1954). Some of this may be because some residents in retirement communities are suspicious of or uncooperative with researchers (Streib et al., 1984).

This segment of the text will examine several specific retirement communities. The major point is to examine options. Just as there is not one housing option that is "right" for older persons, there is not one retirement community that is right. Some retirement communities are created and others emerge to meet the needs of different types of older persons. In reading about the different retirement communities ask what type of community is it. Think about the type of older person who would be best suited to the community. Now think about those who would be ill-suited. Ask yourself why older persons are in certain retirement communities: security, recreational opportunities, lack of other options. What resources are present or absent? Last, ask yourself if you would want to live there.

Two of the communities, Fun City and High Heavens, were described by Jacobs (1974a, 1974b, 1975) who used ethnographic research. This is a research technique frequently used by anthropologists, and consists of researchers' impressionistic observations of the communities they are studying. Although this research technique does not gather "hard" scientific data, such as self-concept or intelligence scores, it does report on the more personal, everyday lives of the people under study. Ethnography is an important and valuable research technique that is often undervalued. Hochschild (1973a, 1973b) also used this technique in her classic study of Merrill Court, as did Longino (1981) in his studies on Ozark Lakes, Horizon Heights, and Carefree Village.

Nancy Osgood (1982), in her excellent book *Senior Settlers: Social Integration in Retirement Communities,* used a technique called "the community study method" to study three retirement communities that will also be examined in this section: Hidden Valley, Ridgeview, and the Jamaica Club. This method is similar to the ethnographic studies above in that it is field-based, and relies on interviews and observation. The one difference is that it collects more "hard" data. That is, certain aspects of the study are less "impressionistic" and rely more on factual data.

All of these researchers have been important in the development of gerontology. Not only has the information contributed to our knowledge of older persons, but the researchers have also provided insight into the research process that will facilitate future studies.

Fun City Jacobs (1974a, 1974b, 1975) conducted a detailed ethnographic study of a retirement community in the 1970s he called Fun City (pseudonym). Fun City was a retirement community of about 6000 residents. The average age of the residents was 71 years. It was primarily a white, middle-to-upper class community. Fun City was located about 90 miles from a large metropolitan area. Geographically, Fun City was described as an isolated and rural community.

Fun City was a "planned" retirement community. In many ways it was a self-sustained community. Nearby there was a shopping center that had about 40 businesses which catered mostly to the needs of Fun City residents. There was also an activity center within Fun City that housed 92 Fun City clubs and organizations. The clubs and organizations included hobby clubs, sports clubs, service clubs, fraternal and political clubs, and church groups.

At first glance the brochures of Fun City made it seem as if it represented the activity or golden-years theory of aging. The large number of events, clubs, and organizations appeared to have something for almost everyone. However, Jacobs found that of the nearly 6000 residents only 200 to 300 per day participated in events; generally the same individuals participated in different events on different days. Thus, disengagement or nonparticipation seemed the norm for Fun City residents. Jacobs found several reasons for nonparticipation.

First, the lack of transportation. Many Fun City residents could not drive. Upon arrival at Fun City most could drive or were physically capable of walking to activities within Fun City; they thought nothing of the fact that there was no public transportation system. After living in Fun City many experienced declines in health that prevented them from driving or walking; as a result transportation to various activities became more difficult. Those who could walk often avoided doing so because of the exceptionally hot weather. Jacobs noted that the streets were deserted and that sports, such as golf, were generally finished by noon to escape the blistering afternoon sun.

Second, many did not participate because of poor health. A bad heart, severe arthritis, and other conditions, that had generally developed or grown worse after moving to Fun City, made many inactive. Air conditioning was a third factor. Some individuals found that the air conditioning of the activity center aggravated their arthritis and they had to stop going to the center. A fourth condition related to the previous occupations of Fun City residents. For example, physicians, lawyers, and accountants found that other residents called on them for their advice so frequently that they stayed at home. In fact, it was estimated that as many as 25 percent of the residents seldom left their homes.

When asked why they had moved to Fun City, the residents generally cited the safety of the streets, the healthy climate, the lack of congestion, the plethora of activities, and the geographical location. However, Jacobs became convinced that these were not the "real" reasons for living in Fun City. First, there was no police force in Fun City; the only protection from crime that Fun City residents had was its isolation. Additionally, residents did not feel as safe as they indicated since they engaged in numerous precautionary behaviors.

Second, although the hot, dry weather may have been "healthy" for certain conditions, there were unquestionably other climates or other areas that would have been just as healthy without some of the drawbacks of the climate in Fun City. For example, the excessive heat and the air conditioners were not healthy for some residents.

Also, there were no major medical facilities nearby. Other areas had major medical centers that might have better served the residents.

Third, although Fun City was not congested, there was also a restricted range of events. There were no concerts, movies, or many of the events that individuals had previously taken for granted. Also, the lack of public transportation made those who did not drive dependent on others. This forced dependency often turned nondrivers into shut-ins.

Fourth, although there were many activities in which to participate, most residents engaged in a passive way of life. Thus, the claim that they had moved because of all the activities at Fun City seemed a false reason.

Fifth, although Fun City was "well-suited" in relation to beaches, mountains, and a major metropolitan area, many of the residents could not drive to these areas. Often those who could drive did not like to drive on the freeways that connected Fun City to these areas.

After setting aside the reasons that the residents originally cited, Jacobs then tried to ascertain the "real" reasons. He felt that some had bought the land as an investment and because of the inability to sell the land or the convenience of ownership, they decided to settle at Fun City.

The Jacobs study was an important one on life in a retirement community. Although Fun City has almost certainly changed from the 1970s when this study was done, the study still shows some of the problems of developing retirement communities.

Hidden Valley Hidden Valley, 25 miles south of Tucson, Arizona, stands in stark contrast to Fun City. Hidden Valley was originally built in the mid-1960s as a planned total retirement community that would have ideal living conditions for older persons. In many ways the original developers saw their goals fulfilled.

The climate in Hidden Valley appears to be near perfect. The days are generally warm and sunny with low humidity while the nights are cool and comfortable. The real estate development was planned in terms of zoning, streets, and other aspects that often happen in a haphazard manner in many communities. In addition, at the time of the study there was a rapidly expanding shopping mall with more than 60 businesses, and many different churches and organizations. Hidden Valley was age-segregated; in each household at least one full-time resident had to be 50 years of age for a family to live in the community. As a result, the researcher noted the absence of certain features that we have come to take for granted in society, such as fast food restaurants, schools, and movie theaters.

Hidden Valley had many of the same features as Fun City. However, the utilization was very different. The recreation center that houses a variety of activities was busy with activities. In fact, the researcher noted the continual difficulty of finding a parking space near the center. Approximately 80 percent of the residents participated in at least one organized activity, with golf and bridge being the most popular. Hidden Valley was described as a very "social" community with much of the activity starting or ending with late afternoon "cocktail parties" that were very prevalent.

Most of the residents stated that they had more friends now than in the past and noted that they engaged in many activities with their friends. It was also noted that the small size of the community created a strong support network in times of sickness and death. When a friend was sick or bereaved all other activities were dropped to help that individual.

The difference between Hidden Valley and Sun City is startling. Part of the difference may be due to the climate; Hidden Valley's climate appears to be more pleasant, and allows for greater participation in activities. Part of the difference may have also been due to some factors that forced the residents of Hidden Valley to band together. For example, a private development company initially financed Hidden Valley with a loan from the federal government. The development company declared bankruptcy and the government became the owner. When the government attempted to prevent the residents from using certain facilities, such as the recreation center and the golf course, the residents formed a committee to resolve the problems associated with the bankruptcy and having the government as landlord. Basically, the problems were resolved and the committee continued to function.

Since that time there were several additional committees formed to resolve problems. For example, when water rights became a problem a committee was formed which resulted in the creation of a Hidden Valley Water Company. In addition to specialized committees to investigate and solve problems, there was also a general governing organization called the Coordinating Committee. This committee was to protect the rights of residents, owners, and investors. It was a powerful force in shaping the community. There were also ongoing committees such as the City Beautification Project.

When asked why they moved to Hidden Valley the residents cited reasons such as the healthy climate, the beauty of the region, the quality of life, the low cost of living, the lack of crime, and the activities. This does not mean that Hidden Valley was without problems, most of which were not unique to being a Hidden Valley resident. Some residents developed financial problems and could not maintain their homes or lawns in the manner required. Others found that they missed their families and old friends. Widowhood made others depressed and lonely. Others feared illness and death; this fear may have been exacerbated by the amount of illness and death seen in an age-segregated community. Other problems dealt with the rapid growth of the area. Some residents noted that their homes had at one time been the only ones in what had become a highly developed area. Others noted the noise of constant construction, traffic problems, long lines in stores, and the wait to get onto the golf course. More recently the issue of whether to incorporate Hidden Valley created a very controversial issue within the community.

High Heavens Jacobs (1975) conducted a second study in a retirement community called High Heavens. High Heavens was a twenty-one-story apartment building that housed about 450 older persons. It was situated next to a university campus on one side and a black ghetto on the other. There was a specific purpose behind the physical location of High Heavens: to integrate the residents of High Heavens into the environment and activities of the university students. There was an attempt to break down the generation gap and to create a greater understanding and tolerance among the different age groups.

This program was never very successful. Although the program seemed to work well originally, whatever success there was diminished over time. There was a dedicated and involved staff called the "magnificent seven." This staff helped to facilitate social interaction and activities. The early efforts were "promising." The residents of High Heavens seemed to have high morale and good spirits. Although the age-integration concept was not working very well within High Heavens, a great deal of activity was still taking place. However, most attempts to increase interaction between the age groups generally failed. For example, residents were given the opportunity to eat in the student dining hall. Because it was more expensive than cooking in one's own apartment, only about 20 to 30 residents chose to do so. Those that did eat in the student dining area segregated themselves in a corner of the dining hall away from the students. There were also "potluck" suppers held by the residents. Although students were invited, few attended. Again there was a snackbar frequented by both students and High Heavens residents where the age groups rarely engaged in any interaction. The social events held at High Heavens to which the students were invited were also poorly attended by students.

Part of the reason for the lack of interaction was the age difference. In interviews with several students, Jacobs found that some were repulsed by the physical characteristics of the High Heavens residents and therefore refused to associate with them. There were other problems that made interaction difficult. The largest of these problems concerned differences in educational levels and social class. The residents of High Heavens were by and large unskilled, lower-class workers with little education. The students tended to be middle to upper middle class with some college. These social barriers, more than the age barriers created the lack of interaction. Because of the differences in social class and education, the students and residents felt that they had little in common.

Over time significant changes took place in High Heavens. The first was that the "magnificent seven" left. High Heavens was placed under the control of the housing authority which perceived it as simply another housing complex that was not to be given any special treatment. Originally High Heavens had been a facility for the mentally and physically able older person. Under the housing authority it also became a facility for the debilitated older person. The number of black residents also increased, much to the alarm of many residents who thought that High Heavens was supposed to be racially segregated. Under the new authority and new management many of the programs to increase student and resident interaction were abandoned. Other programs that were attempted were not successful.

Even though the original purpose of High Heavens was not successful, we still might ask what life was like at High Heavens. Originally, many of the High Heavens residents perceived the accommodations as luxurious. However, over time their impressions changed. A major complaint was that there was no air conditioning. In the summer, the building was 10 to 12 degrees hotter inside than outside. When the residents opened their windows, the noise from the freeway made conversation in the rooms impossible. In the winter the heat was too intense for many residents. There was also a lack of security in and around the building. The residents were easy prey for the many gangs that wandered out of the ghetto. Also, many residents complained about the increase in the number of black residents. They envisioned gangs of black youths wandering up and down the hallways waiting to commit crimes. Several other complaints were expressed. There were an increasing number of physically and mentally disabled individuals being placed in High Heavens. Elevators took long periods to arrive and then closed so quickly that they caught people in the doors. The equipment in the physical therapy room could be used only with a note from a physician and, therefore, went largely unused. The lack of an enclosed passageway between the university facilities and High Heavens made many university offerings, such as lectures and movies, inaccessible to the residents because they were afraid to go out at night.

Jacobs described several different groups of individuals at High Heavens. The first group consisted of those who rarely interacted with others. They generally sat and stared out the lobby windows. This group looked depressed and was depressing to look at. The second group was more animated but was constantly getting into verbal confrontations with other residents. The third group kept to themselves but had friends with whom they would interact. The fourth group consisted of the "go-getters" and included many of the long-time residents of High Heavens who had been responsible for many of the past activities. This group was decreasing in size. The last group was the shut-ins who rarely left their apartments. There was no way to assess the health or activities of this last group.

What we are presented with is a retirement community that at one time was fairly integrated, active, and alive, but had become strife-ridden and inactive.

Ridgeview: A Florida Mobile Home Community   Ridgeview is another community described by Osgood (1982). Ridgeview is on the southeast coast of Florida, about 90 minutes from Orlando and Miami. It is a little more than a mile from the Atlantic Ocean and close to the Intercoastal Waterway. Ridgeview is, as its name portrays, on a ridge, which is cooled by the Gulf Stream winds.

Ridgeview was created by a man who wanted to develop a peaceful retirement community for older persons. He bought 265 acres to fulfill his dream. His initial problem was to convince the zoning commission to allow him to build a mobile home community. The zoning board was afraid of a "junky trailer park" being developed. He convinced the board that this would not take place and sold 120 lots in the mid-1960s. While owner he selected the residents and most became his "friends." The original developer sold Ridgeview in 1968. The new owners continued the close relationship with the residents. At the time of the study there were about 700 occupied lots.

The residents were primarily white, middle-class individuals, most of whom had lived in large cities and worked in factories. They were described as having been hard-working individuals. Most did not have any advanced education. They tended to be conservative and somewhat biased against minority groups. The community was well-maintained, quiet, uncongested, and had an abundance of wildlife, especially birds. There was also a tremendous amount of activity, with walking being a popular form of activity. In addition, individuals were often seen working in their yards and gardens. There was a small clubhouse with a pool and shuffleboard courts, both of which were in almost constant use. The residents frequently left the community to attend religious, club, or other activities.

There were several organizations, the most important the Homeowners' Association which was to promote the welfare of the residents. In addition there was a recreation committee to plan events such as trips, a membership committee, which was a welcoming committee, a pool committee, a bingo committee, a Saturday night dance committee, and a singles club committee.

Most stated that they had several close friends within the community. Osgood noted that generally it was a homogeneous group with the residents sharing the same background and the same future. Most liked the area, the inexpensive living, the easy maintenance, and the friends.

There were problems, again most related more to aging than living in Ridgeview: financial, health, and loneliness. Lack of public transportation was also a problem. At the time of the study a problem had developed over the control of the clubhouse by two opposing groups.

Jamaica Club   The Jamaica Club was a 60-acre 972-unit condominium development located on Florida's southeast section, close to Fort Lauderdale and Miami Beach. It was located in a rapidly growing area of the state. The residents of Jamaica Club were mostly Jewish.

The Jamaica Club was composed of twenty-seven three-story buildings. There was a recreation building with a swimming pool and shuffleboard courts. Until 1976 the Jamaica Club was managed by the developer. In 1976 a volunteer management council was established. In addition, there were more than 20 committees that carried out the day-to-day operations of the club.

There were a variety of activities at the Jamaica Club. The recreation center was a hub of activities, many of them educational in nature, such as language classes. There was also an organization that planned activities outside of the club.

As with some of the other communities that we have examined, there appeared to be close bonds among many of the residents. This was probably for three reasons. First, they shared a common background, being older and Jewish. Thus, they had many of the same problems and could share in a common history as well as common holidays. Second, many had been friends prior to moving to the Jamaica Club. At Jamaica Club it appeared that friends followed one another into retirement. Thus, a cadre of friends simply transplanted from one area of the country to Jamaica Club. Third, the arrangement of the apartments had a walkway or catwalk in front of all of the apartments. Through windows, residents could see other residents walking to and from their apartments. Many felt that this increased the visibility of other residents and made it a friendlier environment.

The reasons for moving to Jamaica Club were the climate, the number of friends or relatives living in the area, the inexpensive living conditions, that it was a Jewish community, and that it provided a safe, clean and active way of life.

As with the other communities, there were some problems. Many residents faced financial problems. For some the increasing costs of living at Jamaica Club had exacerbated this problem. For others there were health problems. The lack of a nearby hospital or clinic made it so that residents often had to go to several physicians for medical purposes, rather than one clinic or hospital. As with most of the other communities we have examined, there was no public transportation, although the club had a minibus that made regular trips to certain areas of the nearby city. There was also concern that the Jamaica Club was ''couple-oriented.'' That is, singles noted that they did not fit into the social environment, that they were seen as ''fifth wheels.'' Also, as we have seen previously, there was increasing friction developing between two segments of the community. In the Jamaica Club a split had occurred between the management group and the group that ran the communities newspaper. The issue had spread to the entire community.

Merrill Court   Merrill Court was an apartment building housing forty-three retired older persons. Of the 43 residents in Merrill Court, thirty-seven were women. By and large the women were widowed, protestant, of lower-class origin, and of working-class background.

Hochschild (1973a; 1973b) worked in Merrill Court over a period of 3 years. One of her jobs was as assistant recreation director, and it was probably this job that helped to create the community she reported.

The one overriding characteristic of Merrill Court was that it was a community. There was a great deal of interaction and activity at Merrill Court, which appeared to have started when a coffee machine was placed in the recreation room. The residents began to gather around the coffee machine to talk. Eventually, the recreation director began to participate in the discussions, and as a result a number of clubs, events, and organizations were created. There were a large number of well-attended events at Merrill Court. The social interaction was facilitated by the architectural design. The building was five floors high with ten apartments on each floor. The first floor consisted of a recreation room, a mail room, and one apartment. On the other floors there was a long porch outside all of the apartments with an elevator in the middle of the porch. When residents looked outside their living-room windows, they could see their neighbors come and go, much like Jamaica Club.

Hochschild noted that when she visited the residents' apartments, they received an average of one phone call per hour. There was also a great deal of visiting among residents and between residents and their families. Merrill Court residents seemed to have strong links with their families. The closeness of the residents was also illustrated by the fact that when one of them was robbed, a collection committee gathered up money and pushed it under the victim's door. Hochschild called this the ''unexpected community.'' She had expected to find a disengaged, lonely group of individuals. Instead, she found an active, engaged, and apparently satisfied group of older persons.

Ozark Lakes   After World War II a series of dams in the Ozark area of Missouri, Arkansas, and Oklahoma created literally hundreds of miles of fishing lakes in what was a beautiful and relatively sparsely populated area. Entrepreneurs initially created a tourist industry. Many of those attracted to the area as tourists came back as retirees. The area which had seen an outflow of residents because of lack of jobs, now saw economic growth because of the increased population. Eventually in many areas the retired migrants outnumbered those born in the area. In fact, in certain sections of the area, the retired migrants became the dominant political force. There were many changes in the area with community resources being created and changing to meet the needs of an ever larger retired community.

Horizon Heights   Horizon Heights was built in 1969 as a planned, subsidized housing development. It is located in a large (pop. 170,000) midwest city. Horizon Heights is part of a public housing development consisting of nineteen buildings: twelve for low-income tenants, and seven for older persons. Rent is established at 25 percent of income. It is located in a deteriorating neighborhood close to the central business district. Horizon Heights has a high percentage of low-income blacks. The buildings are somewhat stark, as is the neighborhood.

Most of the older persons in Horizon Heights have "aged in place." That is, most lived in the immediate neighborhood before moving into Horizon Heights.

Horizon Heights is administered by staff that provides a number of social services, including a noon meal program. The relationship between the staff and residents appears somewhat strained. For example, the sign greeting residents as they walk into the office is "Wipe your feet," and a television set in the lobby says "Do not adjust." Words such as "please" and "thank you" are noticeably absent. Although the contact between the staff and residents was "pleasant" the staff seemed hurried or rushed, and intent on enforcing rules and regulations.

The author noted that with its stark outer appearance (i.e., concrete buildings), coupled with certain inner features (i.e., long polished tile floors), and the bureaucratic staff, Horizon Heights had the feeling of an institution.

Carefree Village   Carefree Village is a planned retirement community in the midwest housing over 3000 residents. It is a form of a "life care" community, having housing that will accommodate individuals capable of different levels of living. As we will see in the next chapter, in life care communities individuals purchase a membership which guarantees them housing and care for life. As their health needs change, individuals move to different levels of housing. For example, most start by living in separate cottages that allow for independent living. These individuals are generally the younger residents. When independent living becomes difficult they are moved into apartments that allow them to live independently, but with certain services such as home-delivered meals and housekeeping services. When health deteriorations increase, they are moved into a skilled nursing facility (i.e., nursing home).

The Prosthetic Environment

When considering the environment, gerontologists generally consider the relationship between the demands of the environment and the abilities of the individual. Obviously, there can be a range in both of these areas. That is, the demands of an environment on an individual to adapt, respond, or change can range from low to high. The demands the environment places on the individual are sometimes referred to as "environmental press" (Lawton & Nahemow, 1973). Just as the demands of the environment can vary, so can the abilities of individuals range from low to high, depending on the presence and extent of certain physical conditions.

The goal is to have a good match or fit between the abilities of the individual and the demands of the environment. The "best" match or fit is when the demands of the environment, or the environmental press, modestly exceeds the abilities of the individual. This creates an environment that challenges but does not overwhelm individuals. When the environmental press is too low, it overcompensates so that existing abilities are not used to their maximum and soon atrophy. This type of environment is often boring, and the individual soon becomes dependent on others. When the amount of environmental press is too high, older persons are confronted with so many difficulties that it is unsafe for them to continue in this environment. This is a very stressful environment.

It is commonly believed that environmental press has less impact on those who have high levels of functioning than on those with low levels of functioning. Essentially, individuals with low levels of abilities are more vulnerable to environmental influences. These individuals do not have the ability to respond, change, or adapt to the environmental press. In contrast, individuals with high levels of abilities are more capable of adapting, responding, or changing to meet the demands of the environment (Lawton & Nahemow, 1973). This is referred to as the "environmental docility hypothesis" (Lawton & Simon, 1968).

In the remainder of this subsection we will examine several aspects of the home environment. One concept that will be present throughout the discussion is that of a prosthetic, compensatory, or supportive, environment. As previously mentioned, the majority of older persons differ from the younger segments of the population in terms of their relationship to the environment. The special requirements of older persons have created specialists in gerontology who are interested in creating or manipulating the environment so that older persons can function effectively and safely. The new environment will be one in which older persons can move about safely; it will also be pleasing and stimulating to the senses. In essence, this prosthetic environment will take into account the losses of older persons.

Prosthetic or supportive environments have been utilized with the young for centuries. Because of size, strength, and coordination problems, young children have benefited from the construction of specialized environments. For example, there is furniture specifically constructed for children, with both safety and effective utilization the principal design features. There are also special foods, feeding utensils, clothing, books, and entertainment items for children. Prosthetic environments have also been designed for those with physical handicaps. In these environments such measures as handrails, ramps, color-coding, and elevators have helped to compensate for physical limitations.

Until recently, older persons have generally been forced either to subsist in their environments with multiple physical losses or try to adapt devices to compensate for their losses. Generally, this narrow range of choices led to a lowered level of independence and functioning and probably to lowered self-esteem. However, the increasing interest in older persons has led environmental gerontologists to attempt to design prosthetic environments for older persons that would prevent both normal and pathological physical losses from deterring effective and efficient functioning. The basic concept behind environmental engineering is the design of an environment that is not penalizing and that at the same time is not overly protective.

The following sections will examine several aspects of the home environment of older persons. There will be an emphasis on environmental engineering and the prosthetic environment. It should be noted that creating functional homes for older persons does not necessarily have to significantly increase the cost of a home. Costa and Sweet (1976) estimated that the additional expense involved is only about 1 percent of the total cost (see also Bayne, 1971; Beattie, 1970; Blank, 1988; Blenker, 1967; Bruck, 1975; Chapanis, 1974; Cluff & Campbell, 1975; Grant, 1970; Jordan, 1983–1984; Kahana, 1974; Lindsley, 1964; Lipman & Slater, 1977; Madge, 1969; Nasar & Farokhpay, 1985).

Stimulation   As we have already pointed out, many of the declines that occur with increasing age have an impact on the relationship between individuals and their environments. Declines in the senses mean that stimulation, in terms of factors such as colors, sounds, odors, or tastes must all be intensified if older persons are going to respond to them. If this does not happen, the lack of variation in the environment can cause a monotonous environment which can impair the thought process, cause childish emotional responses, disturb visual perception, and cause organic deterioration (Loew & Silverstone, 1971). The environmental gerontologist tries to create an environment that will stimulate the senses of older persons, as well as their social lives and psychological states. There are several ways to achieve this goal.

Since vision generally declines with increasing age, one of the first changes made is to improve the lighting. This generally means increasing the amount of lighting without increasing the glare. Better lighting can change a dark, drab room into a lighter, more attractive room. Certain rooms may be painted in bright, bold colors. This kind of visual stimulation is done because colors must often be bright and intense in order for older people to see them. What appears to be bright red to a younger person may appear to be dark red to an older person. For further stimulation an area in a room may be painted in several colors and designs. The contrasts can often be both striking and stimulating. Other forms of visual stimulation are mobiles, brightly colored curtains, pictures, and large calendars and clocks. Thus, an increase in the intensity and the variety of the visual stimulus can compensate for visual impairments.

There are several ways to compensate for hearing loss. A good hearing aid is one way. Talking directly to the individual is another way. Headphones for listening to the phonograph, the radio, or television enable older persons to hear programs without being disturbed by outside noises and without disturbing those around them. Using gestures when talking and speaking slowly are other ways to compensate for hearing losses. Extra-loud doorbells and fire alarms that are equipped with a flashing light can also help to compensate for hearing loss.

Because many older persons are on special diets, it is often difficult to compensate for a deceased sense of taste. Since many have to reduce certain food enhancers such as sugar, salt, and spices, it is often a challenge to prepare meals with a taste older persons can enjoy. Part of the problem is that after years of eating certain types of food prepared in certain ways, anything "different" does not taste quite right. Depending on the advice of the older person's physician, certain substitutes for "taboo" foods may be found or new recipes may be used. It is also important that the food is presented in an attractive manner and that the older person takes proper care of his or her mouth and teeth.

It is even more difficult to compensate for a diminished sense of smell. Excessive amounts of perfume or after-shave lotion, or the presence of body odor may be barely noticeable to an older person, and yet be so strong as to be offensive to a younger individual. Older individuals need to be sensitized to the fact that their sense of smell has diminished and that they need to pay special attention to such factors as personal cleanliness or the use of perfume or after-shave lotions. It is also difficult to compensate for a decreased sense of touch. On a personal level, you can make up for a diminished sense of touch by simply applying more pressure when touching an older person. For example, on entering a room you may make your presence known by touching the individual's shoulder or by gently squeezing the individual's arm. Extra pressure should not be applied when shaking hands since those with arthritis or other conditions may find the pressure painful.

Psychological and social stimulation are also important. To stimulate older individuals psychologically, researchers have employed such tactics as jigsaw puzzles and conversations in which the older person is required to name times, dates, places, people, and so on. Social stimulation can take the form of visits, eating together, games, and other events that bring individuals into social interaction. Loew and Silverstone (1971) constructed a prosthetic environment with sensory stimulation and social and psychological stimulation for the aged in an institution. They found that in 6 months positive changes took place in 63 percent of the men and in 100 percent of the women. In a similar group that was not exposed to the stimulation, no significant changes took place.

Mobility   The second aspect of the environment that should be considered in any home where an aged person lives is mobility. Unfortunately, many environments are not designed for the mobility of older persons. Many older persons find that moving about is difficult in their homes and in their communities. Mobility in the community will be discussed later in this chapter under transportation. Here we are concerned with mobility in the home.

Although it is not apparent to many younger individuals, many average homes have insurmountable and dangerous barriers for older persons. Homes can be designed that provide for maximum mobility and safety for older persons. To design such a home, the special limitations of older persons must be taken into account. The architect and interior decorator should include several features in the home.

First, it should be laid out on one level. There should not be any steps or stairs. Also, thresholds of different levels should be eliminated. All of these tend to limit the mobility of older persons and to increase the risk of accidents. In older homes, ramps or elevators that have a track on an existing staircase can compensate for existing stairs, or a ground-level room can be turned into a bedroom or a bathroom and can thus eliminate the necessity of using stairs. Every year there are thousands of accidents in which older persons fall down stairs. Therefore, if possible, the need to use stairs should be eliminated in the homes of older persons. Other safety features that can be employed are to color-code the bottom and top step in existing stairways, to put in good lighting over the stairs, and to install sturdy, well-anchored handrails with some type of indicator to inform individuals when they are at the top or at the bottom.

A second feature of homes designed specifically for older persons should be the provision of extra-wide doors to accommodate a wheelchair. These doors will enable people in wheelchairs to move about without limitation and without crushing their hands between the wheelchair and the door.

Third, houses for older persons should be designed to be as maintenance-free as possible. Therefore the house should generally be small; if it is large, it should have rooms that are easy to close off. To facilitate upkeep, the house might have aluminum or vinyl siding, metal storm windows, and a yard with a maximum of bushes, shrubs, and ivy to minimize yard work. To make the house cleaner an electric air cleaner could be installed on the furnace.

Fourth, as a safety feature and to increase mobility, the floors should not have any throw rugs or slippery surfaces. Deep-pile carpets can restrict mobility for both walkers and wheelchairs. Fifth, doors should have crank handles, not round knobs, on them. It is almost impossible to turn a slippery knob with a hand crippled by arthritis. However, it is fairly easy to push down on a crank handle with a closed hand or arm in order to open a door.

Sixth, those designing the home may want to take into account both existing physical limitations and potential future physical limitations. For an older couple with no current physical limitations the architect might design a larger house that could be reduced in size through closing off sections, and still be functional as the couple became increasing incapacitated. Most of the house could be closed off and only two or three rooms could be used. There would, for example, be a bath, bedroom, and kitchen that could become the living unit of the home with the rest closed off. Seventh, the furniture of the home also needs to be considered. For example, the height of a bed can make entrance or exit easier. A chair with a lift can also make getting up and down easier. Just the ability to more easily get out of bed or a chair can significantly increase the individual's mobility.

There are a number of other features an architect or interior decorator could incorporate into a new house to make it more functional for the mobility of an older individual. This section is not intended to be a complete list but only a brief survey (see Institute of Medicine, 1988; Monk, 1988; Office of Technology Assessment, 1985).

Safety It is perhaps obvious that many of the concepts discussed in the previous section on mobility also relate to safety. For example, stairs hinder the mobility of older persons and are also a safety hazard. There are many areas within a home that can be modified in order to make the home safer for older persons. For example, if stairs are necessary, they should be modified so that the treads are deeper and the rise shorter. As we have already mentioned, good lighting is essential for safety. It is especially important in dangerous areas such as the kitchen, the bathroom, and stairways. Sturdy well-anchored handrails throughout the house are also important; these are particularly important in stairways and in bathrooms. Since some older persons shuffle, it is important not to have anything on which they might catch their feet and trip, such as throw rugs, mats, or extension cords. Floors should not be slippery. Additionally, certain types of carpet can facilitate mobility and provide a cushion to protect against falls. All homes with older individuals should have smoke detectors that are equipped with loud alarms and flashing lights. Also appliances that older persons use, such as stoves, should have clear, large markings on them that are easy to read. If possible, the home should have several telephones, or perhaps a cordless phone that can be carried around. An emergency alarm system that is handheld or worn on the body that will alert a hospital, police department, or neighbor of an emergency is also important.

Certain areas need to be designed with the special needs of older persons in mind. For example, most bathrooms are dangerous places for older persons, because of slippery floors and hard surfaces. Well anchored grabbars beside the toilet and bathtub are an indispensable safety feature. Carpeting on the floor and rounding sharp corners and edges can also make a bathroom less dangerous. Specialized equipment, such as lifts for bathtubs or portable commodes can also decrease the risk of an accident.

Social Interaction The first factor in determining social interaction is mobility. The mobility of both older persons and their friends and relatives must be taken into account. The second factor in social interaction is the proximity of older persons to friends and relatives. Very often with increasing age, the older individual sees friends, relatives, and family members move away. A third factor is the neighborhood in which the older person lives. As we pointed out above, many older persons live in deteriorating neighborhoods. Social interaction may be truncated because the family, friends, and relatives are afraid to venture into the neighborhood or because the older individual is afraid of venturing outside. Thus mobility, proximity of visitors, and the community can all have an influence on the amount of social interaction in which older persons engage.

Within the home social interaction can be facilitated in several ways. For example, selecting a room where there is little outside noise can help. Or, using carpeting and curtains to help eliminate outside noise can make communication easier.

Privacy With increasing age, the personal or private life of the older person often comes to an end. Restricted finances may necessitate living with friends or relatives. Physical or mental problems may mean institutionalization. Both of these living arrangements can mean the end of privacy. The presence of a roommate or of a large number of other individuals close by, or the inability to lock a door or to predict when others will be entering one's room are all indicators of an end of privacy. Pastalan (1970) has noted that privacy is very important in individuals' lives. It is through privacy that dignity and individuality are maintained. It is in privacy that the individual can relax from the social demands of society and can cease role playing. Pastalan has further observed that continual social interaction is like an actor who is continually "on stage." Individuals need time "off stage" by themselves to rest, to reflect, to plan, to be alone, and to engage in behaviors they consider private. Attached to privacy is the concept of control. With control over their environment, individuals can decide which aspects they will make public and which they will keep private.

In the prosthetic environment privacy can be achieved in two ways: through physical barriers and through the establishment of social rules. Very often both ways are required in order to achieve privacy. For example, older individuals who live with adult children may set aside times when their rooms are "off limits." During this time they will expect not to be disturbed.

Comfort   The last feature of the home environment that will be discussed is comfort. The prosthetic environment should be comfortable to live in. Essentially, comfort means that the individual feels at ease and that the environment is not producing an excessive amount of stress. Very often if the other aspects of the home environment are not producing an excessive amount of stress individuals will then feel comfortable. That is, if the environment is appealing and stimulating to the senses, if the individual has mobility and feels safe, if the environment is conductive to social interaction, and if there is privacy, then comfort will naturally follow as a feature of the environment.

The above factors are primarily concerned with providing comfort in the sense of "peace of mind." There can also be comfort in a physical sense. For example, the prosthetic environment should be comfortable in terms of temperature. Older persons are more vulnerable to temperature extremes; therefore, if possible, the prosthetic environment should remain at a fairly constant temperature through an adequate heating and cooling system. Noise is also a factor to consider. Older persons do not sleep as well as the young, and a noisy environment can aggravate the problem. To be comfortable in one's environment the individuals must also feel safe. This can include feeling safe from crime, from the fear of a fire, and from the fear that others will not know if you are injured or sick.

Comment: Prosthetic Environment   Many of the features of the prosthetic environment rely on technological advancements. While technology can certainly improve the living conditions of older persons, there are some potential disadvantages. For example, there is the possibility of technological breakdown. That is, devices the individual needs for daily living break down. Although the devices can probably be "fixed" or replaced the cost may be prohibitive. A second possible problem with technology is that it may perform at a level that will allow the abilities of the individual to atrophy. That is, the technological innovations are so great and efficient that the individual finds it easier to push buttons rather than exercise remaining abilities. A third possible problem is that individuals will become socially-isolated by the technology. There is less need for relatives, friends, or neighbors to assist with certain activities. A last problem is that some older persons may fear the technology (Blank, 1988).

The Homeless

One new area of research deals with the homeless elderly (Doolin, 1986). Little research exists in this area, but what does exist suggests that homelessness for older persons represents a long-term pattern, not a sudden disruption in their lives. It has been found that the homeless older persons have a history of unemployment, unstable families, itinerant work behaviors, and propensity for certain deviant behaviors such as alcoholism and drug use. These individuals not only lack housing, but food, clothing, and medical care.

THE COMMUNITY

The second environment that is important to older persons is the community. As we have previously mentioned, about 95 percent of those 65+ years of age live in the community. Only about 5 percent are in long-term care facilities. Although the term community can take on several different definitions, for this book ''community'' refers to the area and the people that the individual lives near and interacts with. The type of community in which an individual lives can have a tremendous impact on that individual's life. This section will examine five aspects of the community that influence the lives of older persons: crime, transportation, community resources, and age integration/age segregation.

Crime

To date, relatively few studies have been done to assess the amount of crime against the elderly or the impact it has on them. Thus, much of the information that gerontologists have takes the form of hunches, assumptions, and educated guesses. One area that is significantly underreported in crime statistics, which was examined in Chapter 9, is elder abuse.

One of the reasons that gerontologists do not know very much about crime and the aged is that crime is underreported by older persons, probably more than any other age group except the very young. According to Malinchak and Wright (1978), many older individuals do not report theft because they believe that the police will be unable to recover their stolen property, especially if it has no identifying marks. Underreporting also takes place because they do not want others to know that they have been victimized. Many believe that by admitting they have been victimized, others will see them as incompetent to live in the community.

The statistics on crimes against older persons, as well as a comparison of crimes for the entire population are presented in Table 14-3. As can be seen from this table, older persons have a lower victimization rate than the general population for both crimes in the personal and household sector. There are at least two factors that make them less susceptible to crime than other age groups. They are:

TABLE 14-3
CRIME RATE (PER 1000) FOR SELECTED CRIMES FOR THE
AGED AND THE ENTIRE POPULATION

	Aged	Population
Crimes against the person		
Total personal sector	24.1	96.1
Rape	0.1	0.7
Robbery	1.8	5.2
Assault	3.6	22.7
Purse snatching	1.1	
Pocket picking	1.6	
Household crimes		
Total household sector	80.0	171.4
Burglary	33.2	61.3
Larceny	41.1	94.0
Motor vehicle theft	5.7	16.1

Source: U.S. Bureau of the Census, 1990.

1 As a group, older persons are economically disadvantaged. Generally speaking, most criminals realize that their profits from older persons are going to be small, thus criminals look for other victims.

2 Because of reduced finances and mobility, older persons do not go out in public as much as most other age groups. Thus, their exposure in public is less as is their opportunity for victimization.

Even though older persons have a lower victimization rate than the general population, there are several factors that predispose older persons to victimization. Some of the factors are:

1 The urban aged often live in deteriorating neighborhoods where there is a high crime rate.

2 The times when older persons are likely to receive social security, pension, or benefits checks are well known, thus alerting criminals to the times when older persons are likely to have money.

3 Older persons often have reduced strength and vision. Therefore, criminals know that an older person is less likely to resist or escape from victimization and will be less likely to be able to identify them.

4 Many older persons suffer from chronic disorders that the medical profession cannot correct. Con artists often use the pain and suffering of older persons to victimize them. In the search for relief from pain, for a cure for a terminal illness, or for a fountain of youth, older persons are often vulnerable to con artists.

5 Older persons are more likely to live alone than members of other age groups. Also, by living alone older individuals may be lonely and a con artist can capitalize on the loneliness of an older person in order to victimize them.

6 Older persons use public transportation frequently and are therefore in public areas. Thus, there is a greater opportunity for victimization.

It is perhaps obvious that all older persons are not equally susceptible to crime. Variables such as community size, age, marital status, race, income, and level of education have all been found to be related to likelihood of victimization. In a study on personal victimization of older persons, Liang and Sengstock (1981) found the size of the community to be the most important factor; in fact, holding other variables constant (i.e., race, sex, age, etc.), the likelihood that an older person in a urban area would be victimized was four times greater than for someone in a rural area. Marital status was also important, with the married having lower victimization rates than the widowed, divorced, separated, or single. Blacks also had a higher victimization rate, as do males, who had a 70 percent greater likelihood of personal victimization than females (see Malinchak & Wright, 1978).

For older persons who have been victimized, the impact of crime on them is generally more serious than on younger individuals for three reasons. First, older persons are generally weaker and more fragile physically than those in younger age groups. Thus, if it is a violent crime they have a greater likelihood of being injured, such as a purse snatcher pushing an older woman to the ground. If they are hurt during the commission of a crime, their already weakened state makes the injury that much more serious. Injuries are also much slower to heal in older individuals. Second, the psychological effect of victimization is generally more devastating in older persons than in younger individuals. The crime reinforces the helplessness of the individual. Third, older persons generally suffer more economically as a result of the crime than those in other age groups. They have fewer reserves to draw upon and fewer opportunities to regain their losses.

In addition to victimization, crime has another impact on older individuals: fear. The fear of crime is rampant among older persons (Harris & Associates, 1975; Janson & Ryder, 1983; Lee, 1983) and can result in what has been called "self-imposed house arrest," which is the curtailment of daily activities outside of the house because of the fear of crime (Goldsmith & Tomas, 1974). Although this belief has received considerable attention, and it certainly occurs to some extent, research has not supported it to any significant extent (Cutler, 1987).

However, the fear of crime can be so intense among some older persons that gerontologists have constructed and done studies on the "fear-victimization paradox" (see Lindquist & Duke, 1982). The paradox is that those who are the least likely to be victimized by crime are the most afraid of crime. For many this leads to a restricted and often isolated existence. Many individuals are literally afraid to leave their homes; these individuals also tend to be fearful of crime while at home. They interpret many "normal" sights and sounds outside their homes as being potentially threatening.

There is nothing abnormal about being concerned with victimization and taking preventative measures. In fact, no doing so would be abnormal. However, for some older persons the potential threat of victimization becomes the major controlling factor in their lives. Several variables account for this, the first being previous victimization or knowing someone who was victimized. This personal knowledge of victimization appears to significantly increase the fear of crime. Those in poor physical health also appear to have an exaggerated fear of crime. Low levels of formal education were also correlated with a high fear of crime. Lee (1982) hypothesized that these individuals may believe they have less control over their lives.

Transportation

In American society there is an extensive reliance on mechanized transportation. Because of the diffuse nature of our society some form of mechanized transportation is almost essential for individuals if they are going to fully participate in the community and with family and friends. Very few individuals, especially those who live in rural areas or suburbs, live within short, easily accessible distances to such facilities as hospitals, churches, shopping centers, theaters, or the homes of family and friends. The lack of adequate transportation may force individuals to limit health care because they cannot get to a physician's office, a clinic, or a hospital. In fact, medicare's prospective payment system (PPS) has made transportation more important as a factor in the medical care of older persons. Under PPS there are incentives for hospitals to cut costs. One way hospitals do this is by releasing patients from hospitals earlier, while patients still need additional follow-up care. Thus, while hospitals costs are reduced, transportation costs for patients obtaining follow-up care are increased.

There are several modes of transportation available to older persons. Walking is perhaps the most obvious. However, Carp (1971) found that most older individuals did not find walking to be a desirable mode of transportation for several reasons. First, very often the distance that has to be covered is too great for them to cover by walking. Second, many older persons fear being victimized when they are walking. Third, physical limitation can make walking difficult and painful. Fourth, poor eyesight makes it difficult to see curbs, breaks in the sidewalk, traffic lights, and oncoming traffic. Fifth, if the older person is out on a shopping trip, carrying heavy purchases home can be exhausting.

The automobile is another mode of transportation. However, it is estimated that only about one-half of those 65+ own and operate automobiles. Many older persons find it too expensive to do so. Others have physical limitations that make driving difficult or impossible, especially at night. Additionally, many who drive limit their driving to certain daylight hours and certain areas. Another way to be transported is to be a passenger in an automobile. In a study of aged nondrivers, Carp (1971) found that many older persons relied on the generosity of family, friends, and neighbors for their transportation needs. It was reported that 87 percent were occasionally offered rides, that 50 percent could count on weekly rides, and that only 3 percent could rely on daily rides. As expected, it was also found that most nondrivers preferred private automobiles as a source of transportation over public transportation because of the speed, convenience, and sociability. There were, however, some drawbacks to being an automobile passenger: nervousness created by driving ability of driver, infrequency of rides, indebtedness to the driver.

Another kind of transportation is mass transit. Unfortunately, mass transit presents several problems for older persons. First, it is often expensive. For many older persons on limited budgets even "modest" rates are too expensive. Second, mass transit vehicles are generally poorly designed for older persons. For example, buses often have a series of high, steep steps that make entry and exit difficult and dangerous for older persons, especially if they are carrying packages and if it is "rush hour." Third, mass transit is frequently poorly routed for older persons. They may have to take several buses to get where they want to go. Also, mass transit involves a walk to the pick-up site and generally a walk from the exit site to one's destination. Again, this can be exhausting for some older persons. Fourth, many older persons do not like the crowds or the feeling of being rushed that is often associated with mass transit.

Some communities have tried to facilitate the mobility of older persons through methods designed to reduce or eliminate some of the problems mentioned above, for example, buses routed past senior housing projects that run past facilities utilized frequently by older persons such as clinics. Fares on mass transit have also been reduced for "senior citizens." Some cities have introduced special fares during nonrush hours.

Two areas that have started to receive more attention deal with the transportation needs of those who live in rural areas and the suburbs. The dispersion of rural older persons makes it difficult to have an efficient, cost-effective transportation system. Additionally, in rural areas communities may not have the funding to subsidize public transportation or to acquire a vehicle that is designed for older persons. A high user cost coupled with a poorly designed vehicle can result in little or no utilization by older persons.

To an extent the suburbs are suffering some of the same problems as rural areas. The suburbs, which were developed primarily after World War II, were originally composed primarily of young, upwardly mobile middle-class and upper-middle-class families. Many of the families aged and we are now seeing a "graying of the suburbs." In fact, more older persons now live in suburbs than in central cities (U.S. Senate, 1988). As with rural areas, public transportation systems often tend to be limited in suburban areas. The cost of developing and operating such systems is prohibitive.

Transportation is important to the life satisfaction of older persons. Essentially it has been found that those with access to transportation generally have higher life satisfaction scores than those without personal transportation (see Cutler, 1972, 1975). These same studies reported that those who lived the furthest away from the center of the community facilities and did not have transportation to them also had lower self-concept scores.

Community Facilities and Resources

Another aspect of the community that influences the lives of the aged is the availability or nonavailability of facilities or resources for older persons. Here we are talking about not only specialized facilities for older persons such as senior centers but also general facilities such as grocery stores, hospitals, or entertainment centers. As we pointed out in the last section, transportation for older persons is often a problem. According to Carp (1971), older persons did not like to walk. Regnier (1975) found that older persons seldom ventured outside a six-block radius from their homes for needed goods and services. Thus if a community is going to effectively serve the needs of its older persons, many facilities and resources will have to be concentrated in a relatively small area. Some of the facilities and resources that older persons need are bus stops, drug stores, variety stores, restaurants, educational facilities, legal services, leisure facilities, senior citizen centers, hospitals, parks, libraries, churches, and entertainment centers. Obviously, it is difficult for most communities to provide their elderly with all of these resources in a relatively small area.

In addition to the services mentioned above, communities can also provide supportive services to older persons. About 21 percent use community services such as senior centers, congregate meals, public transportation, visiting nurses, home delivered meals, or home health aides (Fowles, 1987). Supportive services are services designed to compensate for the reduced functioning of older persons. By compensating for lost functioning, supportive services allow individuals to remain in the community. Otherwise, these same individuals would have to go to nursing homes or some other type of facility. Blonsky (1973) has pointed out that many older persons enter institutions not because they are physically ill, but because the community lacks the essential supportive services for them to remain independent. Blonsky described how one community started a supportive service program and what its effect was on older persons in that community. The program was based on the principle of using the strengths and resources of the aged to help the aged. A storefront office staffed by older persons was set up, and older persons in the community were informed of its existence in several ways. Among its many services were a bus service, a tenant-landlord complaint bureau, a neighborhood improvement association, a cooperative food service, and an information referral desk that directed all types of problems to an appropriate source. The program was effective in maintaining many older persons in the community who would otherwise have been forced to go to institutions.

Bricker and his associates (1976) reported on another type of supportive service widely available to older persons, namely, the home delivery of medical services. Very often individuals are institutionalized because they cannot receive the necessary medical services in their homes. In this study, to correct this problem, a medical team visited individuals in their homes. Bricker and his colleagues noted that this type of approach kept many individuals in the community who would otherwise have been institutionalized. The authors observed that by keeping older persons in their homes and providing medical services, there were positive results. First, this type of supportive service meant a substantial savings to the community. It is considerably cheaper to maintain individuals in their homes than to maintain them in institutions. Second, more hospital beds were freed up in the community, and older persons could stay in a familiar environment with the reassurance that medical care would be provided if needed. Although the home delivery of medical care is important it is underfunded; there is currently a bias in medicare and medicaid programs toward institutional care.

Bergman (1973) has noted that older persons have traditionally been seen as moving in one direction in terms of housing from home to institution. He pointed out that the reverse direction of institution to home is seldom considered. He believes this is an unfortunate situation since the majority of older persons would prefer to live in their own homes. He observes that with the supportive services of the community, it is feasible to have an institution-to-home move in some cases. In a study of patients discharged from an institution he found that the vast majority could live independent lives in the community if certain services were provided. Those living independently said they enjoyed the privacy, individualized food, friends, participation in the community, and the freedom. Of the 10 percent who went back into the institutions, the majority did so for health reasons (see Siegel & Lasker, 1978).

There are a number of other supportive services that communities can offer. Day-care centers for the aged are one such service (see Bell, 1973; Gustafson, 1974; Rathbone-McCuan, 1976; Weissert, 1976). The concept of day-care centers for older persons is the same as that of day-care centers for the young. That is, some individuals need certain types of care at least part of the time. Some individuals are not capable of living in complete independence without some supervision. Also, day-care centers give a spouse or relative an opportunity to work. Another supportive service is meals on wheels. This program delivers meals to the homes of older persons. A similar program is that of congregate meal programs. In the programs older persons gather in one central location such as a church or school to receive their meals.

There are several other possible supportive services that the community can offer to older persons. Visitation programs can relieve a sense of loneliness and boredom. Outreach programs are designed to seek out older individuals in the community who need help, who do not know of a program's existence, or who are too proud to ask for help. Telephone reassurance programs are similar to visitation programs in that loneliness can be lessened and reassurance given. Although telephone reassurance programs differ, the basic idea is that an older person is called daily at the same time. If the individual does not answer, then it is assumed that the individual cannot answer because of a medical emergency, and assistance is summoned. The individual making the phone call can also "visit" with those called. Many telephone reassurance programs have been replaced by electronic emergency alarm systems (e.g., Lifeline). Different organizations, both public and private, offer this type of program. Individuals wear an electronic transmitter on their bodies, usually attached to a belt. In an emergency the transmitter is activated, which sends a signal to a unit in the home which is connected to a telephone which automatically dials a central control center. At the control center the signal is received and decoded so that the source can be identified. Assistance is sent. Homemaker services provide for a competent person to come into the home and perform essential housekeeping duties for the older individual. Some duties of homemaker services are to clean the house, do the laundry, prepare the meals, and shop for food, as well as other tasks. Supportive community services may also include employment counseling to make certain that elderly individuals are receiving all the benefits to which they are entitled and that they are filling out their income tax forms correctly, and various types of protective services and crisis intervention counseling (see Estes, 1973; Fasano, 1976; Hall et al., 1973; Petty et al., 1976; Taietz, 1975).

One last community service that needs to be mentioned is senior centers. About 15 to 18 percent of older persons use senior centers (Krout, 1983; U.S. Senate, 1988). The first senior center was developed in New York City in 1943 by the welfare department. It was believed that older clients preferred the company of age peers. It is now believed that there are over 5000 senior centers (Havighurst, 1987), which serve a number of functions for older persons.

Age Segregation and Age Integration

The previous section brought up an important issue in gerontology, "Should older persons be concentrated in age-segregated or age-integrated communities?" We previously mentioned that it is important for older persons to have certain resources and facilities in close proximity to them if proper transportation is lacking. Older persons sometimes concentrate in areas that have these resources. This section will examine the issue of age segregation and age integration (see Brody, Kleban, & Liebowitz, 1975; Bronson, 1972; Schwartz, 1975; Winiecke, 1973).

The debate among gerontologists over the impacts of age-integrated and age-segregated environments has been going on for decades. The debate increased substantially when activity theorists began to question disengagement theorists. As would be expected, the disengagement theorists generally claimed that age segregation was best since a segregated environment would facilitate the disengagement process. The activity theorists claimed that an age-integrated environment was best because individuals would find it easier to maintain a middle-aged way of life. From the mid-1960s to the present there have been hundreds of studies conducted to ascertain the impact of living in age-integrated versus age-segregated environments. The results of the studies have been conflicting and inconclusive.

In the past research was concerned with ascertaining which environment was "right" for older persons. In 1954 Wilma Donahue summarized the current attitude when she said that one formula could not be written concerning the best type of environment for older persons. The reason is that older persons represent a heterogeneous population. Because older persons are heterogeneous, there is not one type of environment that is best for all older persons. The reader should also realize that it is difficult for researchers to conduct studies on the impacts of age-integrated and age-segregated housing because there are so many confounding variables affecting the results of the studies. For example, there can be a number of environments very different from one another that can be classified as "age-segregated." Age-segregated housing can vary from a modern, expensive housing complex for older persons with many facilities to a slum hotel that houses mainly aged residents. Also, age segregation is seldom complete. Most older persons, even if they live in segregated housing units, still interact with the young. With these research problems in mind, let us examine a few of the studies on aged integration and age segregation (Sherman, 1975).

1 Those in age-segregated and age-integrated environments received about the same amount of help from their children.

2 Those in age-integrated environments were more likely to give help to their children. However, in this survey it appeared that those in age-integrated environments lived closer to their children.

3 Individuals in both age-integrated and age-segregated environments had the same pattern of assistance from their neighbors.

4 In both the age-integrated and the age-segregated groups it was found the greater the frequency of mutual assistance between the aged and their children, the greater the frequency of mutual assistance between the aged and their neighbors.

5 Individuals in both age-integrated and age-segregated environments were satisfied if they chose their environment according to their needs and preferences.

6 The aged who lived in age-integrated environments had relatively little intergenerational contact.

7 Individuals in age-segregated environments usually interacted less with their children, grandchildren, and relatives. They also had fewer younger friends than those in age-integrated environments.

8 Individuals in age-segregated environments had more new friends and visited more with neighbors and peers than those in age-integrated environments.

Fishbein (1975) and Winiecke (1973) found that the aged individuals whom they studied liked age-segregated housing because of the following factors: companionship, a monitoring or "buddy" system, safety and convenience, social activities and contacts, improved living conditions, lower rent.

Sherman et al. (1968) and Messer (1967) found that the morale of those in age-segregated environments was higher than those in age-integrated environments. Messer noted that older persons in age-segregated environments also had higher levels of interaction than those in age-integrated communities. According to Sherman and her associates, most individuals in age-segregated environments said that others did not pressure them to join club and activities, and that other people minded their own business. Harel and Harel (1978) drew the following conclusions about age-segregated public housing.

1 It provided the necessary facilities for continued community living.
2 It was important for the development of mutual support networks.
3 It facilitated utilization of health and social services.
4 It contributed to the well-being of the older person.

A similar study on age-segregated public housing by Teaff and his associates (1978) came to the following conclusions:

1 Those living in age-segregated environments participated more frequently in organized activity.
2 There was higher morale in age-segregated environments.
3 There was higher housing satisfaction in age-segregated environments.

According to the Teaff study, there are two possible explanations of why age-segregated public housing has positive effects on older persons. First, in a group homogeneous in age there are less likely to be negative stereotypes and negative opinions expressed about the aged. Second, in such a group there is greater personal security. It is easier for the aged, who are often anxious about crime, to monitor strangers in this type of environment.

On the negative side of age segregation, Sherman and her associates (1968) found that only 38 percent of the residents said that they liked living in a place where there were few young people, and 34 percent said that they did not see young people often enough.

A study by Kennedy and DeJong (1977) examined the question of whether United States cities were remaining the same or whether they were becoming more-or-less age concentrated. In examining the 1960 and 1970 census data from ten United States cities they found virtually no change in concentrations of the aged. There was a slight lessening of segregation for aged in older cities and a slight increase of segregation in younger cities.

The literature on age-integrated and age-segregated environments is abundant and seems to suggest that there is not one environment that is "best" for the aged. There are "good" and "bad" aspects associated with each type of environment. Furthermore, if as gerontologists we are concerned with concepts such as life satisfaction and morale, the heterogeneity of the aged would suggest that both environments should be viable options for the aged. Sherman (1975b) concluded that the aged can find either an age-segregated or an age-integrated environment satisfactory, depending on whether or not their needs are met.

SUMMARY

It is only recently that gerontologists have started to examine the environments of older persons. The environments examined in this chapter are the home and the community. The section on the home was separated into five subsections: living arrangements, economic impact of housing, housing options, prosthetic environment, and the homeless.

The most frequent living arrangement for males was living with a spouse; for females it was living alone. It was also observed that older persons spend a larger percentage of their income on housing than younger persons. Since many older persons are "house rich" but "cash poor," programs, sometimes called "reverse mortgages," have been created to assist older persons. There are a variety of housing options for older persons. Often the options are grouped into planned and unplanned. Unplanned housing was not designed specifically for older persons; planned housing was designed with the needs of older persons in mind. There are several types of planned housing, such as shared housing, accessory apartments, and ECHO housing. Retirement communities can also generally be considered a type of planned housing. Most of those in retirement communities have two characteristics. First, they are retired and second they have relocated to the community. Several retirement communities were examined. The prosthetic environment was also examined. The basic concept is to design an environment that is not stressful for the individual.

The last area examined was the homeless aged. This is a new area of research. Preliminary data suggests that homelessness is a long-term pattern for most older persons who are homeless.

The second part of the chapter examined the community and was separated into the following subsections: crime, transportation, community resources, and age integration/age segregation.

The crime statistics indicate that older persons have a lower victimization rate than the general population. Crime against older persons is not equally distributed, with certain groups having higher victimization rates. Transportation is essential for the health and well-being of older persons. This is a major problem for many older persons since they do not drive or own motor vehicles, and mass transit is either too expensive or poorly designed for their needs. Transportation is an especially critical problem for those living in rural areas or the suburbs.

The services a community offers for older persons can have a significant impact on the well-being of older persons. Support services, such as meals on wheels, can help older persons maintain independent living. The availability of recreational services can also be important in the lives of older persons. The last area examined dealt with age integration and age segregation. Here it was pointed out that each can have advantages and disadvantages for older persons.

REFERENCES

Anonymous (1978). Crime and apprehension plague the elderly: Four federal agencies try to help. *Aging,* **281–282**: 26–31.

Antunes, G. F., Cook, F. L., Cook, T. D., & Skogan, W. G. (1977). Patterns of personal crime against the elderly. *The Gerontologist,* **17**(4): 321–327.

Arnone, W. J. (1978). Mobilizing the elderly in neighborhood anticrime programs. *Aging,* **281–282**: 23–25.

Ashford, N., & Holloway, F. M. (1972). Transportation patterns of older people in six urban centers. *The Gerontologist,* **12**(1): 43–47.

Bates, A. P. (1964). Privacy—a useful concept. *Social Forces,* **42**(May): 429–434.

Bayne, J. R. D. (1971). Environmental modification for the older person. *The Gerontologist,* **11**(4; Part 1): 314–317.

Beattie, W. M. (1970). The design of supportive environments for the life span. *The Gerontologist,* **10**(Autumn): 190–193.

Bell, W. G. (1973). Community care for the elderly: An alternative to institutionalization. *The Gerontologist,* **13**(3; Part 1): 349–354.

Bell, W. G., & Olsen, W. T. (1974). An overview of public transportation and the elderly: New directions for social policy. *The Gerontologist,* **14**(4): 324–330.

Bergman, S. (1973). Facilitating living conditions for aged in the community. *The Gerontologist,* **13**(2): 184–188.

Blank, T. O. (1988). *Older persons and their housing: Today and tomorrow.* Springfield, IL: Charles C Thomas.

Blenker, M. (1967). Environmental change and the aging individual. *The Gerontologist,* **7**(2): 101–105.

Blonsky, L. E. (1973). An innovative service for the elderly. *The Gerontologist,* **13**(2): 189–196.

Bricker, P. W., Janeski, J. F., Rich, G., Dugue, T., Starita, L., LaRocco, R., Flannery, T., & Werlin, S. (1976). Home maintenance for the housebound aged: A pilot program in New York City. *The Gerontologist,* **16**(1): 25–29.

Briggs, J. C. (1968). Ecology as gerontology. *The Gerontologist,* **8**(1): 78–79.

Brody, E. M., Kleban, M. H., & Liebowitz, B. (1975). Intermediate housing for the elderly: Satisfaction of those who moved in and those who did not. *The Gerontologist,* **15**(4): 350–356.

Bronson, E. P. (1972). An experiment in intermediate housing facilities for the elderly. *The Gerontologist,* **12**(1): 22–26.

Bruck, C. (1975). Designs for aging. *Human Behavior,* **2**(April): 25–27.

Bruhn, J. G. (1971). An ecological perspective of aging. *The Gerontologist,* **11**(4): 318–321.

Carp, F. M. (1967). The impact of environment on old people. *The Gerontologist,* **7**(2): 106–108, 135.

Carp, F. M. (1971). Walking as a means of transportation for retired people. *The Gerontologist,* **11**(1): 104–114.

Carp, F. M. (1972). Retired people as automobile passengers. *The Gerontologist,* **12**(1): 66–72.

Carp, F. M. (1977). Impact of improved living environment on health and life expectancy. *The Gerontologist,* **17**(3): 242–249.

Carriere, M. (1983–1984). Memphis share-a-home program. *Aging,* **342**: 26–27.

Chapanis, A. (1974). Human engineering environments for the aged. *The Gerontologist,* **14**(3): 228–235.

Chen, Y-P. (1987). Home equity conversion. In G. L. Maddox (Ed.), *The encyclopedia of aging* (pp. 323–324). New York: Springer.

Clemente, F., & Kleiman, M. B. (1976). Fear of crime among the aged. *The Gerontologist,* **16**(3): 207–210.

Cluff, P. J., & Campbell, W. H. (1975). The social corridor: An environmental and behavioral evaluation. *The Gerontologist,* **15**(6): 516–523.

Costa, F. J., & Sweet, M. (1976). Barrier-free environments for older Americans. *The Gerontologist,* **16**(5): 404–409.

Cutler, S. J. (1972). The availability of personal transportation, residential location, and life satisfaction among the aged. *Journal of Gerontology,* **27**(3): 383–389.

Cutler, S. J. (1975). Transportation and changes in life satisfaction. *The Gerontologist,* **15**(2): 155–159.

Cutler, S. J. (1987). Crime (against and by the elderly). In G. L. Maddox (Ed.), *The encyclopedia of aging* (pp. 155–156). New York: Springer.

Donahue, W. (1954). Where and how older people wish to live. In Wilma Donahue (Ed.), *Housing the aged* (pp. 21–40). Ann Arbor: University of Michigan Press.

Doolin, J. (1986). Planning for the special needs of the homeless elderly. *The Gerontologist,* **26**(3): 229–231.

Duncan, L. E. (1972). Ecology and aging. *The Gerontologist,* **8**(2): 80–83.

Ehrlich, I. F. (1972). Life-styles among persons 70 years and older in age-segregated housing. *The Gerontologist,* **12**(1): 27–31.

Estes, C. L. (1973). Barriers to effective community planning for the elderly. *The Gerontologist,* **13**(2): 178–183.

Fasano, M. A. (1976). Community resources. In I. M. Burnside (Ed.), *Nursing and the aged* (pp. 504–519). New York: McGraw-Hill.

Fishbein, G. (1975). Congregate housing—with a difference. *Geriatrics,* **30**(9): 124–128.

Fowles, D. G. (1987). The use of community aging services. *Aging,* **355**: 36–37.

Goldsmith, J., & Tomas, N. E. (1974). Crimes against the elderly: A continuing national crisis. *Aging,* **236**(June/July): 10–13.

Graney, M. (1974). The aged and their environment: The study of intervening variables. In J. F. Gubrium (Ed.), *Late life: Communities and environmental policy* (pp. 5–17). Springfield, IL: Charles C Thomas.

Grant, D. P. (1970). An architect discovers the aged. *The Gerontologist,* **10**(Winter): 275–281.

Gross, P. J. (1976). Law enforcement and the senior citizen. *The Police Chief,* **24**(February): 24–27.

Gubrium, J. F. (1970). Environmental effects on morale in old age and the resources of health and solvency. *The Gerontologist,* **10**(Winter): 294–297.

Gubrium, J. F. (1972). Toward a socioenvironmental theory of aging. *The Gerontologist,* **12**(Autumn): 281–283.

Gubrium, J. F. (1974). Victimization in old age. *Crime and Delinquency,* **20**(3): 245–250.

Gustafson, E. (1974). Day care for the elderly. *The Gerontologist,* **14**(1): 46–49.

Haber, P. A. L. (1986). Technology in aging. *The Gerontologist,* **26**(4): 350–357.

Hall, G. H., Mathiasen, G., & Ross, H. A. (1973). *Guide to development of protective services for older people.* Springfield, IL: Charles C Thomas.

Harel, Z., & Harel, B. B. (1978). On-site coordinated services in age-segregated and age-integrated public housing. *The Gerontologist,* **18**(2): 153–157.

Harris, C. S. (1978). *Fact book on Aging: A profile of America's older population.* Washington, DC: The National Council on the Aging.

Harris, L., & Associates (1975). *The myth and reality of aging in America.* Washington, DC: The National Council on the Aging.

Havighurst, R. J. (1987). Senior centers. In G. L. Maddox (Ed.), *The encyclopedia of aging* (p. 600). New York: Springer.

Hochschild, A. R. (1973a). *The unexpected community.* Englewood Cliffs, NJ: Prentice-Hall.

Hochschild, A. R. (1973b). Communal life-styles of the old. *Society,* **10**(5): 50–59.

Howell, S. C. (1980). Environments and aging. In C. Eisdorfer (Ed.), *Annual review of gerontology and geriatrics* (pp. 237–260). New York: Springer.

Hoyt, G. C. (1954). The life of the retired in a trailer park. *American Journal of Sociology,* **59**: 361–370.

Institute of Medicine (1988). *The social and build environment in an older society.* Washington, DC: National Academy Press.

Jacobs, J. (1974a). *Fun City: An ethnographic study of a retirement community.* New York: Holt, Rinehart & Winston.

Jacobs, J. (1974b). An ethnographic study of a retirement community. *The Gerontologist,* **14**(6): 483–487.

Jacobs, J. (1975). *Older persons and retirement communities.* Springfield, IL: Charles C Thomas.

Janson, P., & Ryder, L. K. (1983). Crime and the elderly: The relationship between risk and fear. *The Gerontologist,* **23**(2): 207–212.

Jordan, J. J. (1983–1984). The challenge: Designing buildings for older Americans. *Aging,* **342**: 18–21.

Kahana, E. (1974). Matching environments to needs of the aged: A conceptual scheme. In J. F. Gubrium (Ed.), *Late life: Communities and environmental policy* (pp. 201–214). Springfield, IL: Charles C Thomas.

Kennedy, J. M., & DeJong, G. F. (1977). Aged in cities: Residential segregation in 10 USA central cities. *Journal of Gerontology,* **32**(1): 97–102.

Krout, J. A. (1983). Correlates of senior center utilization. *Research on Aging,* **5**(3): 339–352.

Lawton, M. P. (1970a). Assessment, integration, and environments for older people. *The Gerontologist,* **10**(1): 38–46.

Lawton, M. P. (1970b). Ecology and aging. In L. A. Pastalan & D. H. Carson (Eds.), *Spatial behavior of older people* (pp. 40–67). Ann Arbor: University of Michigan Press.

Lawton, M. P. (1974). Social ecology and the health of older people. *American Journal of Public Health,* **64**(3): 257–260.

Lawton, M. P. (1983). Environment and other determinants of well-being in older persons. *The Gerontologist,* **23**(4): 349–357.

Lawton, M. P. (1985). Housing and living environments of older people. In R. H. Binstock & E. Shanas (Eds.), *Handbook of aging and the social sciences* (pp. 450–478). New York: Van Nostrand Reinhold.

Lawton, M. P. (1987). Housing. In G. L. Maddox (Ed.), *The encyclopedia of aging* (pp. 333–336). New York: Springer.

Lawton, M. P., & Nahemow, L. (1973). Ecology and the aging process. In C. Eisdorfer & M. P. Lawton (Eds.), *The psychology of adult development and aging* (pp. 619–674). Washington, DC: American Psychological Association.

Lawton, M. P., & Simon, B. B. (1968). The ecology of social relationships in housing for the elderly. *The Gerontologist,* **8**(1): 108–115.

Lee, G. R. (1982). Sex differences in fear of crime among older people. *Research on Aging,* **4**(3): 284–298.

Lee, G. R. (1983). Social integration and fear of crime among older persons. *Journal of Gerontology,* **38**(6): 745–750.

Liang, J., & Sengstock, M. C. (1981). The risk of personal victimization among the aged. *Journal of Gerontology,* **36**(4): 463–471.

Lindquist, J. H., & Duke, J. M. (1982). The elderly victim at risk: Explaining the fear-victimization paradox. *Criminology,* **20**(1): 115–126.

Lindsley, O. R. (1964). Geriatric behavioral prosthetic. In R. Kastenbaum (Ed.), *New thoughts on old age* (pp. 41–60). New York: Springer.

Lipman, A., & Slater, R. (1977). Homes for old people: Toward a positive environment. *The Gerontologist,* **17**(2): 146–156.

Loew, C. A., & Silverstone, B. M. (1971). A program of intensified stimulation and response facilitation for the senile aged. *The Gerontologist,* **11**(4; Part 1): 341–347.

Longino, C. F. (1981). Retirement communities. In F. J. Berghorn, D. E. Schafer, & Associates (Eds.), *The dynamics of aging: Original essays on the processes and experiences of growing old* (pp. 391–418). Boulder: Westview.

Madge, J. (1969). Aging and the fields of architecture and planning. In M. W. Riley, J. W. Riley, & M. E. Johnson (Eds.), *Aging and Society: Aging and the professions* (pp. 229–273). New York: Russell Sage Foundation.

Malinchak, A. A., & Wright, D. (1978). The scope of elderly victimization. *Aging,* **281–282**: 11–16.

Mangum, W. P. (1988). Community resistance to planned housing for the elderly: Ageism or general antipathy to group housing. *The Gerontologist,* **28**(3): 325–329.

Messer, M. (1967). The possibility of an age-concentrated environment becoming a normative system. *The Gerontologist,* **7**(3): 247–251.

Monk, A. (Ed.) (1988). Technology and aging. *American Behavioral Scientist,* **31**(5): 515–613.

Montgomery, J. E. (1972). The housing patterns of older people. *The Family Coordinator,* **21**: 37–46.

Nasar, J. L., & Farokhpay, M. (1985). Assessment of activity priorities and design preferences of elderly residents in public housing: A case study. *The Gerontologist,* **25**(3): 251–257.

Newcomer, R. (1973). Environmental influences on the older person. In R. H. Davis (Ed.), *Aging: Prospects and issues* (pp. 79–89). Los Angeles: University of Southern California Press.

Newcomer, R. J., & Caggiano, M. A. (1976). Environment and the aged person. In I. M. Burnside (Ed.), *Nursing and the aged* (pp. 559–572). New York: McGraw-Hill.

Office of Technology Assessment (1985). *Technology and aging in America.* Washington, DC: U.S. Government Printing Office.

Osgood, N. J. (1982). *Senior settlers: Social integration in retirement communities.* New York: Praeger.

Pastalan, L. A. (1970). Privacy as an expression of human territoriality. In L. A. Pastalan & D. H. Carson (Eds.), *Spatial behavior of older people* (pp. 88–101). Ann Arbor: University of Michigan Press.

Petty, B. J., Moeller, T. P., & Campbell, R. Z. (1976). Support groups for elderly persons in the community. *The Gerontologist,* **16**(6): 522–528.

Pritchard, D. C. (1983). The art of matchmaking: A case study in shared housing. *The Gerontologist,* **23**(2): 174–179.

Rathbone-McCuan, E. (1976). Geriatric day care: A family perspective. *The Gerontologist,* **16**(6): 517–521.

Regnier, V. (1975). Neighborhood planning for the urban elderly. In D. S. Woodruff & J. E. Birren (Eds.), *Aging: Scientific perspectives and social issues* (pp. 295–314). New York: Van Nostrand.

Rich, T. A. (1968). Ecological psychology and aging. *The Gerontologist* **8**(1): 116–120.

Schwartz, A. N. (1975). Planning microenvironments for the aged. In D. S. Woodruff & J. E. Birren (Ed.), *Aging: Scientific perspectives and social issues* (pp. 279–294). New York: Van Nostrand.

Sherman, S. R. (1975a). Mutual assistance and support in retirement housing. *Journal of Gerontology,* **30**(4): 479–483.

Sherman, S. R. (1975b). Patterns of contact for residents of age-segregated and age-integrated housing. *Journal of Gerontology,* **30**(1): 103–107.

Sherman, S. R., Mangum, W. P., Dodds, S., Walkley, R. P., & Wilner, D. M. (1968). Psychological effects of retirement housing. *The Gerontologist,* **8**(2): 170–175.

Siegel, B., & Lasker, J. (1978). Deinstitutionalizing elderly patients. *The Gerontologist,* **18**(3): 293–300.

Streib, G. F., Folts, W. E., & LaGreca A. J. (1984). Entry into retirement communities. *Research on Aging,* **6**(2): 257–270.

Taietz, P. (1975a). Community complexity and knowledge of facilities. *Journal of Gerontology,* **30**(3): 357–362.

Taietz, P. (1975b). Community facilities and social services. In R. C. Atchley (Ed.), *Environments and the rural aged* (pp. 145–156). Washington, DC: The Gerontological Society.

Teaff, J., Lawton, M. P., Nahemow, L., & Carlson, D. (1978). Impact of age integration on the well-being of elderly tenants in public housing. *Journal of Gerontology,* **33**(1): 126–133.

U.S. Bureau of the Census (1990). *Statistical abstract of the United States.* Washington, DC: U.S. Government Printing Office.

U.S. Senate Special Committee on Aging (1988). *Developments in aging: 1987.* Washington, DC: U.S. Government Printing Office.

Weissert, W. G. (1976). Two models of geriatric day care: Findings from a comparative study. *The Gerontologist,* **16**(5): 420–427.

Winiecke, L. (1973). The appeal of age segregated housing to the elderly poor. *Aging and Human Development,* **4**(3): 293–306.

CHAPTER 15

NURSING HOMES

Gale Zucker/Stock, Boston

INTRODUCTION

The last chapter examined the home and community as two important environments of older persons. This chapter will examine one additional environment, nursing homes. It is difficult to conceptualize a topic in gerontology that has generated as much literature or controversy as nursing homes. Nursing homes represent an area in which many gerontologists set aside scientific objectivity and launch into an emotional verbal assault against the horror, abuse, and neglect they have seen and heard about.

This chapter will examine a very emotional and controversial area in gerontology in a scientific and objective manner. The purpose of this chapter is not to castigate, condemn, praise, defend, or apologize for nursing homes but rather to objectively examine the scientific literature. The chapter is separated into the following sections: definition, historical perspective, nursing homes in America, older persons in nursing homes, the decision to seek admission to a nursing home, the life cycle of a nursing home resident, the abilities of older persons in nursing homes, the life of older persons in nursing homes, care in nursing homes, consequences of institutionalization, rehabilitation of older persons in nursing homes, and alternatives to institutionalization.

DEFINITION

Although the term **nursing home** is frequently used in gerontology, it has a variety of meanings. Nursing homes can be differentiated by type of ownership and level of care. In terms of ownership, nursing homes can be classified as proprietary, nonprofit, or governmental. Proprietary nursing homes are "for profit." That is, they are run as a business to make a profit. The nonprofit nursing homes are generally run by religious or fraternal organizations. Governmental nursing homes are managed by a state or the federal government.

Nursing homes can also be separated by the level of care provided. A variety of terms are used here but the most frequently used terms are skilled nursing facility (SNF), intermediate care facility (ICF), and residential care facility (RCF). The SNF provides the most intensive level of care. SNFs have the look and feel of a hospital with nurse stations and unlocked patient doors. Individuals in these facilities need a wide range of nursing care—such as intravenous injections, catheterization, or nasal feeding—which must be provided by registered nurses. The residents in SNFs are the least able physically and mentally and need to be closely supervised. In addition to needing medical care, most are unable or limited in their ability to provide personal care in areas such as eating, using toilet facilities, dressing, or bathing. Residents are generally dressed in hospital gowns rather than personal clothing.

The RCFs are at the opposite end of the continuum of nursing homes; they service older persons who need minimum assistance in daily living and who do not need skilled nursing care. Essentially, individuals in RCFs need supervision and room and board. Supervision can be provided by aides, rather than nurses. These facilities often have a more "homelike" atmosphere and the residents dress in their own clothing and can lock the doors to their rooms. RCFs were previously called adult foster homes or congregate living facilities (see Mor et al., 1986).

In between SNFs and RCFs are the ICFs. ICFs are for those who do not need as intensive or complex nursing care as those in SNFs but more nursing care than can be provided by RCFs. Individuals may need help with daily living in the area of eating, bathing, dressing, as well as in having someone monitor their medications.

Obviously the composition of a nursing home's staff is determined by the level of care provided. A SNF will have a greater percentage of registered nurses than an ICF. RCFs will generally not have nurses. Some facilities serve as SNFs and ICFs and the term "nursing home" has come to be a generic term representing both types of facilities. This author prefers the term nursing home to either SNF or ICF simply because of the term "home." We need to remember that for many individuals who enter SNFs or ICFs this will not be a temporary stop, such as a hospital, but their home until they die. Thus, the personal possessions they use to personalize their rooms, and the care and treatment they receive, are all reflective that this is more than a facility: it is a home for the residents.

The distinction between SNFs and ICFs may soon be eliminated, and both will fall under one set of medicaid and medicare regulations.

The term "institution" is also frequently used in gerontology and technically can refer to a variety of settings, such as a university, prison, hospital, or mental hospital; for this text the term institution will refer to a nursing home.

Long-term care facility is another term that is frequently used as a synonym for nursing home. In fact, this is an emerging term for two reasons. First, nursing homes have taken on a negative connotation in contemporary society; long-term care facility has less negativism connected to it. Second, the term long-term care facility can be used to describe the whole spectrum of services for older persons with chronic care needs, ranging from home support and day care, to skilled nursing care. This chapter will cover both spectrums of long-term care, with the first few sections of the chapter examining nursing homes, and the last section reviewing alternatives to nursing homes.

HISTORICAL PERSPECTIVE

The primary purpose of nursing homes is to provide long-term care for individuals who are not capable of certain aspects of self-care. Nursing homes are a relatively recent phenomenon in American society, emerging in the 1930s. Prior to the existence of nursing homes older persons who lacked the capability for self-care were dealt with in several ways. First, many were boarded out to families that agreed to provide needed levels of care; many were boarded in the homes of retired nurses. Payment for this service could be private—provided by an individual or family, or public—provided by the community or state. Prior to the depression eighteen states had enacted old age assistance or old age relief policies which provided funds to care for the destitute aged (U.S. Senate Special Committee, 1987–1988). Second, alms-houses, or homes for the poor also housed many older individuals. In fact, it is estimated that in the early part of this century 60 to 90 percent of those in almshouses were 65+ years of age (Fischer, 1978). Third, for those who were well off financially "old age homes" did exist; many were run by religious or fraternal organizations. Fourth, mental institutions became repositories for many older persons who had "no place to go.'' Most of those placed in mental institutions did not have mental problems; often they had financial or physical conditions that made independent living impossible. However, the mental institutions were, at the time, the only facilities that could provide care.

With the depression most of the old age assistance and old age relief acts that states and communities had created were reduced or eliminated. States and communities started to look to the federal government for assistance in meeting more of the problems they were facing, including care of older persons. The Social Security Act of 1935 established a practice, which would later be expanded, of federal government "obligations" toward older persons. The initial obligation of the government was to provide an adequate retirement income to retired workers. The initial Social Security Act created a public expectation about the role of the federal government in providing for the needs of older persons.

The original Social Security Act did not provide funds to residents of public institutions. Thus, even if an individual was "entitled" to payments, if that individual was a resident in a public institution, probably a "poor house," that individual would not receive payment from social security. As a result, a number of private facilities emerged to meet a developing need. In 1950 the Social Security Act was amended so that beneficiaries in public institutions could receive payments; it also allowed for direct payment to health care providers. The amendment also recommended that standards be established for nursing homes, although specific standards were not recommended.

In 1956 there was an amendment to the Social Security Act to increase federal spending for social security, including funding for medical services to public assistance recipients, even those in nursing homes. This was replaced in 1960 with the Kerr-Mills Act which created medical assistance for the aged designed to provide funding for the medically needy. By 1965 forty-seven states had provisions for this act and it had 300,000 recipients.

In 1965, with the passage of medicare (Title 18) and medicaid (Title 19) of the Social Security Act, the nursing home industry changed. Essentially, more government money was provided for long-term care. While medicare was restricted primarily to acute care, medicaid became the primary provider for long-term care. Medicaid was under both federal and state administration and linked to welfare programs. Basically, it paid for long-term care for individuals who qualified under a state's welfare program. Medicaid was designed as a third party insurance program to pay medical costs for eligible low-income individuals of all ages. For older persons, it provided long-term care *if* they qualified financially. This often meant exhausting savings and assets until they qualified, or "spent down" to the poverty level. The Senate Special Committee on Aging (U.S. Senate Special Committee, 1988*a*, 1988*b*) noted that one-third of those who enter nursing homes end up impoverished.

Having to impoverish oneself to qualify for medicaid is of course controversial. Recent studies have questioned the one-third figure provided by the federal government. One study reported that 7 percent "spent down" to the poverty level. This study found that 2.5 percent of those who stayed 2 months or less spent down to impoverishment; for those who stayed 2 or more years the figure was 13.5 percent (Liu et al., 1990). It has also been reported that many older persons anticipating long-term care have found ways of sheltering their income and assets. These individuals believe, correctly or incorrectly, that it is the government's responsibility to provide the funding for their long-term care, and that their income and assets are for their heirs (Moses, 1990; Smeeding, 1990).

Because of the increased role of the federal government in providing payment for nursing home care the Department of Health, Education, and Welfare (HEW) (now the Department of Health and Human Services) was authorized to set standards for nursing homes. During its first year, 6000 nursing homes applied for certification; 740 met the standards and were approved. By 1971 an HEW study found that 50 percent of nursing homes were in violation of medicaid standards in areas such as nursing staff-to-patient ratio, number of physician visitations, or fire/safety standards. Since the inception of medicaid there have been numerous changes in the rules and regulations. The basic premise, however, remains the same: medicaid will pay for long-term care only for beneficiaries of the social security system and only for individuals who qualify under a state's welfare criteria.

NURSING HOMES IN AMERICA

In 1986 there were 25,646 nursing homes (16,388 SNFs and ICFs and 9258 RCFs) in America with 1,553,000 residents. There were 20,223 proprietary homes, 4378 nonprofit homes, and 1045 government homes. The majority of those in nursing homes are white, 65+ years of age, without a spouse, and female. Currently about 93 percent of those in nursing homes are 65+ years of age (National Center for Health Statistics, 1987). The occupancy rate nationally is about 90 percent (U.S. Bureau of the Census, 1990).

Certain groups are not equally represented in nursing homes. For example, 93 percent of those in nursing homes are white, 6 percent are black, and 1 percent are "other" races. If we examine the percentage of older persons by race in nursing homes we find that 5 percent of whites 65+ years of age are in nursing homes; for blacks it is 4 percent, and for "other" races it is 2 percent. It has been assumed that the lower percentage of nonwhites in nursing homes has been because they have a shorter life expectancy and because they receive greater support from family and friends (U.S. Senate Special Committee, 1987–1988). We have examined this assumption in Chapter 9, "Family and Friends."

The payment of nursing home costs are presented in Table 15-1. As can be seen, 51 percent of nursing home costs were paid by individuals in 1987. It is sometimes said that these individuals pay "out-of-pocket" or "privately." There is no third-party paying for the cost of the nursing home. Table 15-1 also clearly points out that medicare does not cover long-term care cost. It also demonstrates that medicaid is covering a smaller percentage of total costs than in the past. Private insurance policies cover about 1 percent of the total cost (U.S. Senate Special Committee, 1988*b*).

TABLE 15-1
NURSING HOME COSTS BY
SOURCE OF PAYMENT

	1980	1987
Out-of-pocket	44%	51%
Medicaid	48%	42%
Other	6%	6%
Medicare	2%	2%

Source: U.S. Senate Special Committee, 1988a.

Nationally the cost of nursing home care is expensive. In 1986 the cost was estimated at $38.1 billion, with the government share approximately $18 billion (U.S. Bureau of the Census, 1989). The average cost per year for a resident is $25,000 (U.S. Senate Special Committee, 1988b). SNFs cost more than RCFs.

Because of the increasing cost of long-term care coverage, some private insurance companies are now offering long-term care insurance policies. A study that reviewed thirty-one long-term care policies found several limitations in existing policies such as high cost, stringent eligibility requirements, failure of the policy to account for inflation, and limited coverage for certain services. Part of the reason for these limitations is that the companies do not have much experience with this type of coverage and as a result are taking a conservative financial approach. As their experience increases, the limitations may decrease making long-term care coverage a more realistic option for older persons (Wiener et al., 1987; see also Anonymous, 1989). An additional factor that may make the policies "better" for older persons will be increased competition among insurance companies (see Branch, 1987).

Another area that is receiving increasing attention in reducing the personal cost of long-term care is life-care or continuing care contracts. Historically life care has both secular and religious roots. In the past older persons would give all their worldly goods to a community or a religious organization that agreed to provide life care in exchange. In contemporary society, the concept has emerged with for-profit organizations developing communities to provide life care. These retirement communities provide residents with housing and services at several levels. For example, there are housing units for residents capable of independent living. As physical and mental problems develop, services are provided to residents, such as home delivered meals or housekeeping services. As health further deteriorates the resident may need to be transferred from an independent living facility to some type of intermediate care facility, where supervision can be provided. Eventually the individual may have to be transferred to a skilled nursing facility. Generally, there is one complex or "campus" that has all of these facilities. Individuals transfer among the facilities with changes in health status. Depending on the specific contract, the individual may need to provide additional funding for more intensive forms of care.

Generally the life-care and continuing care contracts require a large "up-front" fee and then monthly fees. The "up-front" fee is often possible because those seeking admission have just sold their homes; the monthly fee is often paid through social security and pension checks. In a life-care contract the monthly fee remains the same, even if more intensive health needs develop. In a continuing care contract, individuals pay an increased amount for additional health services, although the amount may be less than the total cost of the services.

There have been many problems with this emerging industry, such as bankruptcies. Additionally, many of these communities do not appear to be very strong financially, both in terms of short- and long-range projections (see Ruchlin, 1988). Because of these problems, legislation has been developed or proposed in about half of the states that would provide more regulation of this emerging industry. However, a study of the legislation on life-care and continuing care contracts found many problems with the legislation. For example, there was inadequate funding for enforcement of the regulations, and even confusion over the agency or person in the state responsible for enforcing the regulations (Netting & Wilson, 1987; see also Feinauer, 1987).

OLDER PERSONS IN NURSING HOMES

About 4.5 percent of older persons are in nursing homes. About another 1/2 percent are in other long-term care facilities such as VA hospitals, mental institutions, or facilities for the mentally handicapped. For convenience we will use the figure 5 percent. The current percentage of those in nursing homes represents an increase over 1960 when the percentage was 2.4 (Palmore, 1976), or 1967 when the figure was 3.3 percent (National Center for Health Statistics, 1987).

Since 1960 both the percentage and number of older persons in nursing homes has increased. The increase does not necessarily reflect the fact that the physical and mental health of older persons is getting worse. In fact, as was pointed out in Chapter 6, "Physical Health," the physical health of older persons is improving. Rather, there are several variables that account for the increase. First, there has been a tremendous increase in the number of nursing homes available for the placement of older persons. In the past other facilities, such as mental institutions or almshouses, had to accommodate older persons who could not live independently. Second, the increase is also accounted for by the fact that families who would ordinarily have kept their aged members at home now have the option of providing care through placement in a nursing home. Additionally, currently most families are less capable of providing long-term care because they are smaller, and because most women, who have been the traditional caregivers, are in the work force.

Third, nursing home care is available to older persons who are destitute, since medicaid will pay the nursing home bills. Fourth, the increase in the percentage of older persons in nursing homes is due to major illnesses that have changed from acute to chronic. Fifth, the "old-old" segment of the population, which is most in need of nursing home care, is rapidly increasing in size. Sixth, in the last 15 to 20 years nursing homes have become a normative aspect of American life and are becoming an accepted mechanism to provide care during old age. Just as industries have evolved to take care of the needs of other age groups (e.g., day-care centers and schools), so an industry has now emerged to take care of certain needs of older persons.

As noted above, about 5 percent of older persons reside in nursing homes. Most individuals assume from this figure that their lifetime risk of ever being in a nursing home is only about 5 percent. However, as several studies have demonstrated, this is incorrect; this has been referred to as the "5 percent fallacy." Essentially, the 5 percent figure represents the percentage of older persons in nursing homes at a particular time. Generally, these are the "old-old"; those who have chronic problems which restrict independent living. As these individuals die they are replaced by other older persons who have gone from the ranks of "young-old" to "old-old." Thus, older persons move from a healthy and independent old age to one where there are an increasing number of medical problems and dependencies. Several studies, which have used methods as diffuse as examining place of death on death certificates to mathematical models, have examined the increased risk of becoming a nursing home resident (Cohen et al., 1988; Ingram & Barry, 1977; Kastenbaum & Candy, 1973; Lesnoff-Caravaglia, 1978–1979; Liang & Tu, 1986; McConnel, 1984; Vicente et al., 1979; Wershow, 1976; Wingard et al., 1987). The National Nursing Home Survey reported 30 percent of the deaths of those 65+ years of age and 55 percent of deaths of those 85+ years of age occurred in or following a stay in a nursing home (U.S. Senate Special Committee, 1988a). Although the figures vary, the lifetime risk of being a nursing home resident is between 36 to 65 percent, with females having a higher percentage, 52, than males, 30 (U.S. Senate Special Committee, 1987–1988).

This 5 percent fallacy can also be seen if we examine the percentage of older persons who are in nursing homes by specific age category. While about 5 percent of the total aged population is in nursing homes the percentages for the age categories 65–74, 75–84, and 85+ are 1 percent, 6 percent, and 22 percent (U.S. Senate Special Committee, 1988a). If we examine the total nursing home population for older persons, the percentages for the age groups 65–74, 75–84, and 85+ are 16.1, 38.7, and 45.2 (U.S. Senate Special Committee, 1987–1988).

THE DECISION TO SEEK ADMISSION TO A NURSING HOME

Many older persons will never become residents in nursing homes. Even though they may be confronted with a variety of disabilities, they will continue to age and to eventually die in their own homes or in the homes of friends or relatives. This is apparent since there are twice as many severely disabled aged who are living in their homes or in the home of friends or relatives as there are living in institutions. Families do not automatically "dump their aged relatives" into nursing homes at the first sign of weakness or disability, but explore a variety of long-term care alternatives in an attempt to avoid institutionalization. In fact, about 30 percent of the older persons in nursing homes were living with their families prior to admission (York & Calsyn, 1977). Thus, for most families the decision to place an aged member into a nursing home is a last, reluctant alternative (Brody, 1978).

One extensive study examined the lives of nursing home residents prior to admission.

The study reported that prior to admission 88 percent of the residents had health problems that had existed for more than 1 year. The main sources of support were adult children and spouses. The decision to place the individual into a nursing home came when the caregiver role became too great, often due to a greater demand for services by the care receiver due to declining health, or due to the exhaustion or illness of the caregiver. The researcher concluded that there was a substantial amount of care provided prior to admission into a nursing home (Smallegan, 1985).

A question that naturally comes to mind is, ''Are the aged who become residents in nursing homes different from those who do not?'' This question is important and has both policy and planning implications. In an early investigation of this question Tobin and Lieberman (1976) in their book *Last Home for the Aged* explored common assumptions such as:

1 Institutional care is sought out by those with dependent personalities.
2 The lack of a confidant precipitates nursing home admission.
3 Physical, economic, and social losses increase the likelihood of an individual seeking nursing home admission.

Their research focused on two groups of individuals living in the community: those awaiting admittance to a nursing home and those not awaiting admittance to a nursing home. The research rejected the three hypotheses above and found that three variables were responsible for seeking admission to a nursing home.

1 The inability or unwillingness of others to provide the care that the individual perceived as necessary.
2 Increasing physical deterioration.
3 The lack of community services to help provide independent living.

A recent review of the literature has supported and extended the above findings (Wingard et al., 1987). The review reported that the following were ''repeatedly'' found to be associated with nursing home utilization.

1 Age: The data indicates that with increasing age utilization increases. It was reported that about 1 percent of those age 65–69 are in nursing homes compared to 20+ percent of those 85+ years of age.
2 Sex: Nursing home utilization is higher for females. Some of the studies reported a utilization rate that was twice as high for females. The difference was not simply because there are more older females. The explanation is that women generally live longer than men, and thus have a greater opportunity of developing health problems but are less likely to have a caregiver available.
3 Availability of caregiver: This factor was again found to be significantly related to nursing home admission. The availability of a caregiver, whether it be a spouse, adult child, or other family member, decreased the risk of nursing home utilization.
4 Functional Status: The loss of the ability to perform activities of daily living was consistently found to increase the likelihood of institutionalization. The reduction in functional status could result from either physical or mental problems.

The authors of the above article noted that many of the articles in this area have deficiencies and that further research is needed in this important area (see Cohen et al., 1988; Vicente et al., 1979).

A study by Shapiro and Tate (1988) examined the probability of institutionalization of individuals with multiple high-risk characteristics. Based on certain characteristics they projected the probability of institutionalization within a 2.5- or 7-year period. This study was more complex than most in that it noted the cumulative effect of multiple risk factors.

For three age categories, 65–74, 75–84, and 85+, they noted that the overall probability of institutionalization within 2.5 years based on age alone for each age category was 2 percent, 6 percent, and 16 percent. For 7 years the percentages were 5 percent, 19 percent, and 37 percent.

However, when they included other risk factors the percentages changed significantly. For example, the risk of someone 85+ being institutionalized within 2.5 years went from 16 percent based on age alone, to 19 percent if the spouse was not at home; to 31 percent if there had also been a recent hospitalization; to 44 percent if the individual also lived in retirement housing; to 53 percent if the individual had one or more problems with activities of daily living; to 62 percent if the individual also had mental problems.

For an individual 85+ who had a spouse at home the probability of institutionalization was 7 percent; if in addition there had not been a recent hospitalization it decreased to 5 percent; if in addition they did not live in retirement housing it remained at 5 percent; if in addition they did not have any difficulties with activities of daily living it decreased to 4 percent; if in addition they also did not have any mental problems it remained at 4 percent.

THE LIFE CYCLE OF A NURSING HOME RESIDENT

In 1976 Wershow provided an alarming statistic; namely that 3 percent of those admitted to nursing homes were dead within 24 hours and 44 percent within 30 days. The high mortality rate after admission did not necessarily reflect poor care or postrelocation mortality but simply the fact that these individuals were admitted to a nursing home because they had suffered a decline of some type that made self-care or home care difficult or impossible. Thus these individuals were admitted to the nursing home in a weakened and debilitated state, and their deaths "may" have been due to their physical state prior to admission and not to nursing home care or relocation stress.

Lewis and her associates (1985) have provided further information on what might be called the life cycle of a nursing home patient. This was an elaborate and well-designed study that followed 197 residents for 2 years after being discharged from a nursing home. Discharge could be to a hospital, home, another nursing home, or because of death. By the end of the study they found that 72 percent had died; 15 percent were living at home; the remainder were still living in a nursing home. They also reported that during the first 30 days after admission 28 percent of the residents died; during the next 30 days an additional 15 percent died. The major cause of death in nursing homes is "infections," most caused by pneumonia (Weinberg et al., 1989). The study reported that a "ping-pong" pattern developed for many residents, e.g., being transferred to a nursing home, a hospital, and another nursing home; the authors believed this was a result of reimbursement policies.

National statistics on length of time in a nursing home are 163 days for those who are discharged dead and 70 days for those who are discharged alive (U.S. Bureau of the Census, 1990).

ABILITIES OF OLDER PERSONS IN NURSING HOMES

Many individuals have never been inside a nursing home. These individuals might naturally ask, "What abilities do older persons in nursing homes have?" That is, are all of the aged in nursing homes senile and in wheel chairs, or do some retain both mental and physical abilities? One way of examining the abilities of nursing home residents is to look at the percentage who require assistance in certain activities of everyday life. Table 15-2 presents the dependency status of aged nursing home residents. We can see two trends from Table 15-2. First, the percentage needing assistance increases with increasing age for each of the activities. Second, the percentage of females needing assistance is higher than for males in all activities. This is primarily because the average age of females in nursing homes is higher than for males.

In terms of the mental status of nursing home residents Gottesman and Bourestom (1974) found that 47 percent were alert, 28 percent were moderately alert, and 25 percent were confused. Another study on the mental status of nursing home residents came up with similar results. When asked if they knew their roommate's full name, 80 percent of the residents studied were aware of the full name, 13 percent knew a partial name, and 7 percent were completely unaware of a name (Miller & Beer, 1977).

TABLE 15-2
DEPENDENCY STATUS OF NURSING HOME RESIDENTS BY AGE AND SEX
(Percentage Requiring Assistance)

	65–74	75–84	85+	Male	Female
Bathing	84.8	90.3	94.1	86.9	92.6
Dressing	70.2	75.9	81.9	71.5	79.7
Using toilet	56.6	60.3	68.2	56.2	65.7
Transferring	52.1	59.7	69.0	55.3	65.2
Eating	33.4	39.1	44.0	34.8	42.3
Continence	42.9	55.0	58.1	51.9	55.3

Source: U.S. Bureau of the Census, 1990.

THE LIFE OF OLDER PERSONS IN NURSING HOMES

There have been many sensational articles and books describing life in nursing homes. There have been relatively few that have quantified the life of a nursing home resident. One study reported that 56 percent of the time residents are awake is spent in passive or null activity. Passive or null activity can best be described as "doing nothing." About 23 percent was spent in bathing, dressing, and engaging in personal-care activities. A further analysis showed that 5 percent of personal-care activity was spent with staff members. Twenty percent of residents' spare time was spent watching television and 3 percent was spent with staff members (Gottesman & Bourestom, 1974).

In an attempt to obtain more data on the life of a nursing home patient, Gubrium (1975) became a participant observer while he worked in several occupations in a nursing home. He found that there was a daily cycle that revolved around meals. Certain types of activities would start or stop before or after meals. Generally the busiest time of the day came after breakfast when the residents engaged in personal behaviors such as reading, washing articles of clothing, or writing checks to pay bills. About 1 hour before lunch the residents had usually finished with these activities and began to wait for lunch. After lunch came the "longest part of the day." For many it was simply a matter of waiting for dinner. It was generally during this part of the day that the residents had to find ways to "pass the time."

There were several ways to pass the time. One of the most frequent ways was walking. The residents not only considered walking to be good exercise but also a good way to pass time. Another frequent way of passing time was sleeping. Residents could be found sleeping in their beds, in wheelchairs, in the lounge, in the television room, or even in other residents' rooms. Still another form of passing time was watching. Watching consisted of being aware of both internal and external events. The last form of passing time was talking. Talking consisted of current gossip, discussion of the past, news from family and friends, or an analysis of current events.

Other studies have tried to ascertain the amount of companionship or friendships older persons have in nursing homes. The general belief is that residence in a nursing home discourages friendships. This is because of the physical design which may discourage mobility, the confused mental status of some residents, as well as other factors. A study by Retsinas and Garrity (1988) examined factors that were conducive to forming friendships. The study reported that the majority of residents had at least one friend in the nursing home. The major factor that appeared to impact on friendships was the ability to communicate. Those who had lost the ability to communicate coherently had the least number of friends. The researchers noted that the friendships that developed in nursing homes may be more extensive than previously reported.

In addition to friends inside the nursing home, residents also had friends outside the nursing home. About 62 percent of nursing home residents receive visitors from the outside, on a daily or weekly basis; 13 percent had not received a visitor in over 1 year (Institute of Medicine, 1986). The frequency of visitations appears to decline over time. This decline probably occurs because friends die or are themselves institutionalized and because others move from the area (Miller & Beer, 1977). For other residents of nursing homes contact with friends and relatives is continued through the mail. Miller and Beer (1977) found that 63 percent of those they studied received personal correspondence: 33 percent weekly, 38 percent monthly; and 29 percent occasionally.

Another source of activity for nursing home residents is leaving the home to visit friends or relatives. The Miller-Beer study found that 68 percent had the opportunity to leave the home: 42 percent weekly, 42 percent monthly, 16 percent occasionally.

CARE IN NURSING HOMES

During the late 1950s through the 1970s the nursing home industry was characterized by scandals, numerous investigations by private and governmental organizations, and increasing regulation. As early as 1956 the Commission on Chronic Illness issued a report on nursing homes, citing low standards of care including untrained staff and fire and safety hazards. In 1959 the U.S. Senate established the Senate Subcommittee on Problems of the Aged which noted that only a few nursing homes had high standards; most were substandard with poorly trained or untrained staff and few services, such as rehabilitation. The subcommittee also noted that because of the shortage of nursing home beds most states were reluctant to create new standards of care or to even enforce existing standards since the majority of nursing homes would be closed, and the states would then be faced with providing the funding and creating the facilities to care for those removed from substandard nursing homes.

In 1961 the Senate created the Special Committee on Aging which studied nursing homes. The committee's report again noted that many substandard nursing homes were allowed to continue operating since there were no other facilities for residents if they were closed. The committee's report also stated that one of the only weapons to bring a home into compliance with regulations was the threat to take away the home's license, which took months or years, and which most judges were reluctant to do, especially if the nursing home operator claimed that the problems were being corrected. The report also claimed that inspectors generally examined the physical plant of the nursing home, not the actual care of patients (Institute of Medicine, 1986).

Several books provided an expose on the nursing home industry, that portrayed it very negatively. For example, Ralph Nader's group report on nursing homes *Old Age: The Last Segregation* (Townsend, 1970), Mary Adelaide Mendelson's *Tender Loving Greed* (1974) and Bruce C. Vladeck's *Unloving Care: The Nursing Home Tragedy* (1980) all provided graphic material on the abuse, lack of care and caring, and neglect in America's nursing homes. Books by nursing home residents also provided graphic examples of abuse and neglect (Horner, 1982; Laird, 1979; Tulloch, 1975; see Berdes, 1987), as did government investigations and reports (U.S. Senate, 1974). More recently Steven Long's book *Death Without Dignity* (1987) documented the first criminal prosecution of a nursing home corporation, and its top executives, for the murder of residents through neglect.

Unquestionably, many changes have to be made in the nursing home industry. The abuses in nursing homes have been sufficiently reported for decades. These are not victimless crimes. The money that nursing home profiteers steal is at the expense of the residents. Critics of the nursing home industry have charged that the Senate subcommittee investigations of nursing home abuses were not intended to bring about any "real" changes but only to temporarily quell the concern by appearing to do something, or to create campaign publicity. Some have charged that the nursing home industry is immune from regulation since many powerful politicians protect the industry for a variety of reasons. For example, some protect the nursing home industry because of "kickbacks" while others realize that correcting the problems would mean closing many proprietary homes and creating more governmental or state-owned homes, which would mean a tremendous expense while not necessarily increasing the level of care.

The issue of the "quality of care" has become a major issue in gerontology (see Applebaum, 1989). Some of the original components of this issue centered around defining and measuring the quality of care. The Institute of Medicine's (1986) book *Improving the Quality of Care in Nursing Homes* (see Butler, 1989) was one of the first to suggest some of the ways quality care can be empirically measured. They suggested eleven "key indicators" of quality care that could be measured, which dealt with areas such as medications; decubitus ulcers; urinary tract infections; management of urinary incontinence; dehydration; medical, nursing, and rehabilitative care indicators; nursing and personal care; mental status; diet and nutrition; activities and social participation; and quality of life.

While abuse in nursing homes has been well-documented, there have been few scientific attempts to ascertain what percentage of the care the abuse represents (see Pillemer, 1988; Pillemer & Moore, 1989). In a 1977 study Kahn and his associates assessed patient care in nursing homes. They found that documentation on patients was inadequate in 36 percent of the cases examined. They also found that often the diagnosis of a resident's condition was incomplete and that in 50 percent of the cases the medical diagnosis was not reflective of an individual's problems. This kind of inaccuracy may be due to the fact that 50 percent of nursing home residents do not receive a physical examination upon entrance into a nursing home (Linn & Gurel, 1972). Moreover, the researchers discovered there were too many medical diagnoses and too few psychological and social diagnoses, and that very often there was no correlation between the residents' level of functioning and the services received. Finally, they found that the drugs administered were inadequate in 36 percent of the cases.

A recent survey of nursing home staff reported that 36 percent had seen at least one resident physically abused within the last year, with the most frequent forms of abuse being excessive use of restraints, pushing, grabbing, shoving, pinching, slapping, or hitting. Ten percent admitted physically abusing residents. In terms of psychological abuse, 81 percent had seen it in the last year, the most frequent form was yelling at a resident. Forty percent admitted psychologically abusing residents (Pillemer & Moore, 1989). Residents in the same nursing home can receive very different treatment and care. Gottesman and Bourestom (1974) found that the residents who received the greatest amount of overall quality nursing care generally had personal possessions in their rooms, had their fees privately paid, had at least one visitor a month, were white, and were in a nursing home where the staff was expected to have had prior nursing home experience (see Pillemer, 1988).

Type of ownership of nursing homes has also been investigated. Lemke and Moos (1989) reported that nonprofit homes provided a higher quality of care in most cases than proprietary homes, but an earlier review of the literature noted that no such conclusion could be formed (O'Brien et al., 1983).

As would be expected, even in a nursing home, social status can make a difference in the type and amount of care and treatment. Those who are financially well-off can pay or can arrange for their families to pay in order to make certain that they receive somewhat better treatment than the rest of the residents. Kosberg (1973) noted that wealthy older persons receive better treatment than the nonwealthy aged. It has been observed that the care of welfare residents is generally "inferior" to those who pay privately (Pillemer, 1988).

Nursing homes that are more expensive generally have a more pleasant atmosphere, greater communication between residents and staff, a cleaner environment, more physical facilities, better food, and a higher staff-to-resident ratio. As a result they can provide "better" care (Pillemer, 1988).

Placement of an older relative in a nursing home does not mean the end of caregiving responsibilities. It has been reported that those who have caregiver responsibilities prior to institutionalization continue to provide care after institutionalization (Bowers, 1988). While caregivers do not continue to provide "bed and body" work after institutionalization, they do evaluate and monitor the care their relatives receive. Many believe that the quality of care is dependent on their monitoring the performance of the nursing home staff. A caregiver may instruct the staff on how to perform certain types of caregiving for a resident. They may also try to inform the staff member of the resident's unique traits, in an attempt to "personalize" the care. Staff turnover or changes made this a continual process. With the resident they may attempt to cope with depression and to preserve the individual's dignity.

A great deal has been written about the staff in nursing homes. Some of the articles portray the staff as uncaring, insensitive, and often cruel. Other articles portray them as caring individuals who are overworked, poorly paid, and untrained. Both are probably true. Below we will examine some of the more objective reports on nursing home staff.

The turnover rate of nursing home staff, especially the nursing staff (RNs, LPNs, and aides) is very high, with rates between 55 to 100 percent being reported (see Halbur, 1986; Waxman et al., 1984). For the aides, who have the highest turnover rate, the reasons are generally low status, low pay and benefits, exhausting work both physically and mentally, and a low staff-to-patient ratio. Management style has also been found to be a very important factor, with an authoritarian management style contributing to a high turnover rate and a more "informal" management style contributing to a low turnover rate (Waxman et al., 1984). It has been reported that much of the turnover by aides is due to "burnout" (Hare & Pratt, 1988). Methods to lower the turnover through increasing benefits, advancement opportunities, and participation in decision making have been recommended (Brannon et al., 1988; Halbur, 1986).

One recently developed instrument measured employee's communication skills, interpersonal skills, attitudes toward providing nursing home services, and their willingness to assist other nursing home staff members. The instrument was found to have high reliability in predicting turnover rates (Beach, 1988). Traditionally it has been believed that high turnover rates are dysfunctional to an organization. However, Halbur and Fears (1986) have noted that there may be some benefits to the high turnover in nursing homes. For example, there may be new staff with fresh ideas (see Beach, 1988).

Aides in a nursing home have more contact with the residents than the professional staff. In fact, it is estimated that aides provide 90 percent of resident care (Waxman et al., 1984). In an analysis of nursing home aides, Handschu (1973) found that 49 percent were high school graduates, that 81 percent were under 25 years of age, and that 51 percent had received no formal training for their current jobs as nursing home aides. Most of the training that did take place was on-the-job training with another aide and the teaming generally lasted only 2 to 3 days. Stannard (1973) has noted that the aides in many nursing homes occupy marginal positions in the labor market. Most have little in the way of training, skills, or education. Very few have a strong commitment to their jobs or the nursing home where they are employed. Low pay and few benefits perpetuate this system. In communities with high unemployment, nursing home administrators can be selective in the aides they hire; in communities with low unemployment they cannot be as selective (Pillemer, 1988).

It is unfortunate that aides receive so little education. Because they have the greatest amount of contact with the residents, aides have the greatest opportunity of effecting beneficial changes in residents. Unfortunately, it has been found that the nonprofessional staff in nursing homes is more likely than the professional staff to hold negative views on the rehabilitation potential of the aged. Expressions such as, "Don't let him try—he's too far gone" reflect this negativity. Such attitudes can impede rehabilitation (Kosberg & Gorman, 1975) and result in "learned helplessness" or "induced dependency" (Baltes, 1987). Very often these negative attitudes simply result from lack of education. The way in which the staff interacts with the residents does not necessarily spring from maliciousness or hatred but from "good intentions."

One recent study has demonstrated the importance of education on the quality of care. The study provided staff with course work on mental health in old age, and had excellent results in improving the communication skills of the staff with residents, the way the staff dealt with "difficult" residents, and the morale of the staff (Chartock et al., 1988).

The group that has the second greatest amount of contact with nursing home residents is nurses. One program was designed to improve the quality of care for nursing home residents through the education and placement of geriatric nurse practitioners (Kane et al., 1988). Over the course of this program 120 nurses were involved in becoming geriatric nurse practitioners. Although many found their new roles unstructured and undefined in nursing homes and thus somewhat difficult to implement, most soon created important roles for themselves that dealt directly with improving resident care.

Although stress and burnout have traditionally been identified with the nursing staff of nursing homes, administrators also encounter considerable stress. One study on nursing home administrators identified several sources of stress such as the inconsistency among inspectors in terms of their interpretation of rules and regulations, the negative public image of nursing homes, patient problems (such as runaway patients), staff turnover and absenteeism, and negative employee attitudes (Mullen, 1985).

To improve care there have been a variety of recommendations (see Anderson, 1974). Blatz and Turner (1977) suggested that the time has come to focus on the personalities of the individuals who work with the aged in nursing homes. They have recommended that a screening device be created to eliminate those individuals who would probably not work well with the aged. In a pilot study they developed such an instrument.

The Institute of Medicine (1986) made several recommendations focused on care that concerned the rights of nursing home residents. The report noted that residents have civil and personal rights unless they are not legally competent. Some of the rights are:

1 To be informed of one's rights (in a language other than English if necessary).

2 To have access to the name, address, and phone number of the state's nursing home ombudsman. The role of the ombudsman is to investigate and resolve complaints made by or concerning residents in nursing homes.

3 To see the nursing home policies.

4 To have access to one's medical records.

5 To be notified of impending transfers.

6 To meet with visitors for political and social reasons as long as the visitations do not interfere with the rights of other residents.

It is generally believed that a "good" nursing home should include the following: a program of rehabilitation, recreation workers, an occupational therapist, a physical therapist, a staff of volunteers to provide entertainment and stimulation, hobbies, crafts, clubs, exercise programs, religious services, movies, music, discussion groups, and educational programs. It should also provide excellent medical and dental care. There should be a library with large-print books or books on tape, a beauty salon, a barber shop, and a store where residents can purchase personal items and clothing at reasonable prices.

In addition there should be mental-health services for residents of nursing homes (see Freedberg & Altman, 1975). It is now widely recognized that many of the problems of older persons in nursing homes are psychological in origin and thus cannot be treated successfully by a regular physician. Unfortunately, the psychological problems are often considered to be part of a physical problem or a part of the aging process (see Power & McCarron, 1975). Today there is evidence not only of the need of mental health services for residents but also of the benefits such services can provide. Unfortunately, it appears that mental health services for older persons will not be available in nursing homes on a regular basis for some time since many community mental health facilities have little interest in developing ties with nursing homes. Furthermore, many nursing homes do not want ties with mental health clinics (Winn & Kessler, 1974).

Care in nursing homes is currently a major concern of gerontologists, of older persons, of those who provide support for older persons in the community, and of those who provide services for older persons in nursing homes. Nursing homes will generally not improve unless there is public pressure to do so. Perhaps as more Americans learn that they stand an excellent chance of being placed in a nursing home at some point during their lives, public pressure will increase. Perhaps one way of quantifying care is to examine the consequences of placement in a nursing home.

CONSEQUENCES OF INSTITUTIONALIZATION

One indicator of the quality of care is to examine the consequences of institutionalization. This is a difficult research issue since the prognosis for most nursing home residents is toward progressive decline, not caused by the quality of care but their medical conditions and the limits of medical technology to slow or prevent the decline.

One innovative study by Retsinas and Garrity (1988) tested the hypothesis of nursing home iatrogenesis. Iatrogenesis refers to a condition being caused by medical personnel or medical care. Nursing homes are frequently charged with providing a level of care that will increase dependency and exacerbate existing physical and mental conditions. For example, a staff member may push a resident in a wheelchair rather than allowing the resident to walk, or feed the resident rather than allowing the resident to feed himself or herself.

This study examined the prognosis of newly admitted nursing home residents. One way of determining the amount of iatrogenesis was to examine what happened to residents whose prognosis was eventual discharge back into the community. If most of the residents who were projected to be discharged into the community were discharged then this would indicate that iatrogenesis was not a major problem. This study did not support the concept of nursing home iatrogenesis. Eighty-four percent of those who were supposed to return to the community did so. The 16 percent who did not return to the community stayed in the nursing home for reasons unrelated to nursing home iatrogenesis. For example, some decided they liked the security of the nursing home. Others had caregivers who became unable or unwilling to provide further care. Some of the others had a change in physical or mental functioning, unrelated to nursing home care, that prevented them from leaving the nursing home.

Another "classic" article has discussed the "positive consequences of institutionalization" (Smith & Bengtson, 1979). In a 2-year study with residents of a nursing home and their adult children, the researchers found that some of the widespread negative beliefs about nursing homes were not supported by empirical research. This study was interested in the consequences of institutionalization on the relationships between nursing home residents and their adult children. What the researchers found was that 70 percent of the relationships could be characterized as positive; 30 percent were negative. The positive relationships were characterized by a "renewed closeness and strengthening of family ties," a "discovery of new love and affection," and a "continuation of closeness." The positive relationships emerged for several reasons. First, there had been preadmission stress. Often prior to institutionalization there was a period of continued deterioration where the resident had placed increasing demands on the caregiver. As the care receiver deteriorated in health and placed further demands on the caregiver, the relationship often deteriorated into one where the caregiver had little time, energy, or patience for a "close" relationship but spent his or her time engaged in caring for the care receiver. With institutionalization, the bed and body tasks were assumed by the staff and the care receiver and adult child had more time to renew and strengthen, as well as to discover, new relationships. Second, institutionalization often resulted in improved mental status for the resident. This often came about because of a greater intensity of care, and a better monitoring of drugs and nutrition. Third, many residents formed new relationships with other residents. This growth in relationships seemed to strengthen family closeness.

The researchers did not find that all relationships improved. For some there was a "continuation of separateness" that institutionalization did not change and others found frequent contact without quality interaction. In the second category the researchers reported that there were often "negative feelings . . . beneath the surface" between the resident and adult child. The resident may feel resentment at being in an institution while the adult child feels guilt. Pearlman and Uhlmann (1988) have also noted that many nursing home residents do not rate their quality of life any lower than community residents. The nursing home residents have accepted their limitations and often see the nursing home as an environment suited to their needs. For many there was security in knowing that medical help was near; for others institutionalization may have provided a cleaner, healthier, and safer environment; some found new friends. This did not mean that there were not complaints about the cost, lack of privacy, or food.

Although it may be difficult for a young, healthy individual to conceptualize that the quality of life in a nursing home could be rated as high, we need to consider it from the perspective of an older person who has gradually experienced physical and mental losses, has found everyday activities more and more difficult, and has worried about having a medical emergency with no one to assist. Although nursing homes are often looked upon as warehouses for the dying, in actuality many individuals come to nursing homes for therapy and rehabilitation.

REHABILITATION AND THERAPY OF OLDER PERSONS IN NURSING HOMES

In the past, the majority of nursing home directors and staff perceived nursing homes as custodial institutions. The staff saw themselves as custodians whose function was merely to maintain the lives of the residents at continually decreasing levels of functioning (see Citrin & Dixon, 1977; Harris & Ivory, 1976).

In a custodial institution, the degree of functioning that an older person has upon entrance or the degree of functioning that they can achieve is often soon lost. When the individuals are treated like infants whose every need is taken care of by the staff, existing abilities that could lead to independence or semi-independence soon atrophy. When no demands are made on the residents, and when they are not allowed to engage in independent behaviors that they are still capable of performing, dependency soon results. It should be noted that dependency can be forced on nursing home residents by a "well-meaning" staff or by a staff that is interested only in expediency.

For example, aides in a nursing home may force dependency on aged individuals since it is often easier and faster for the aides to feed, dress, and bathe residents than for residents to do these activities by themselves. Other aides may force dependency on aged residents because they do not want to embarrass or humiliate them by requiring them to perform tasks that they either cannot do or that they can do only at reduced levels. The aides may also be unaware that certain individuals have the potential or the ability to perform particular tasks by themselves.

Some nursing home directors claim that they do not have rehabilitation or therapy programs because of the cost involved. Other nursing home directors believe that the additional cost of rehabilitation and therapy are not warranted because of the limited improvements that can be expected and because of the limited life expectancies of the residents.

In his excellent essay, "The Elderly Mystique," Cohen (1988) discusses the societal attitudes toward older persons with disabilities. He noted that unlike other groups with disabilities, such as the mentally or physically handicapped, older disabled persons are not seen as having the potential for growth and development. The goal for disabled older persons is not functioning at a higher level of development, but preventing present functioning from deteriorating to the point where nursing home placement is necessary.

Many of the studies that we will be examining in this section challenge these societal attitudes. These studies indicate that significant improvements can be brought about in aged nursing home residents if existing staff is trained in therapeutic and rehabilitation techniques. The extra time involved is usually minimal since many of the techniques involve nothing more than altering the ways in which the staff interacts with the residents. The cost of educating the staff and the time involved are usually modest and can often be done with required in-service training.

The studies that we will be examining in this section also indicate that it is misleading to state that the benefits older persons gain through therapy or rehabilitation would be overshadowed by their limited life expectancies. It is difficult to say how long anyone is going to live or to measure their "quality of life." It should also be stressed that greater independence could increase the "will to live" and lead to improved health, thus increasing life expectancy.

In the last few decades gerontologists have been involved in testing a number of different therapy and rehabilitation programs for older persons. The goals and methods of these programs have varied. Generally speaking, rehabilitation and therapy in nursing homes have had three goals. The first goal was to make residents less dependent on the staff. This was achieved by increasing both the physical and mental abilities of the residents. The second goal was to help the residents maintain contact with reality. This was attained by stimulating and challenging the existing abilities of the residents. The third goal was to raise residents' morale and self-concept levels and was often obtained if the first two goals were reached. Some rehabilitation and therapy programs have the ultimate goal of raising the functioning of residents to the level at which they can leave nursing homes and return to their communities. As we shall see, some of the programs have been very successful.

The results of the rehabilitation and therapy programs in nursing homes have not been universally successful. However, the results do indicate that, in general, therapy and rehabilitation can and do work with older persons in nursing homes. This conclusion represents a dramatic departure from the past when older persons were considered too old, too "senile," or too sick to benefit from rehabilitation and therapy programs. It should also be pointed out that many of the programs that were not successful were often conducted by poorly motivated and inadequately trained "therapists" over too short a time span, or were attempted with those nursing home residents who had been devoid of stimulation for so long that the programs were not intensive enough to have an impact. Nevertheless, it appears that nursing homes can be more than "warehouses for the aged." The vast majority of nursing home residents can still progress from "doing nothing" to pass the time to leading "active" and "meaningful" lives. Several of the rehabilitation and therapy programs that have been used by gerontologists in nursing homes will be described below.

The rehabilitation and therapy program that has achieved the greatest amount of attention from gerontologists is reality orientation (see Drummond et al., 1978). Although many different techniques exist to implement reality orientation, the basic purpose of the program is to truncate and try to reverse the physical and mental deterioration in nursing home residents. One of the basic assumptions behind reality orientation in nursing homes is that deterioration of mental and physical function is intensified by the environment commonly found in nursing homes (see Barnes, 1974).

Generally speaking, reality orientation is carried out through the use of one or more of three techniques. The first technique is staff contact, the second environmental stimulation, and the third the classroom technique. The use of the first two of these techniques together is sometimes called 24-hour reality orientation. The purpose of 24-hour reality orientation is to try to continually present a therapeutic and rehabilitative environment—not one that lasts for only 30 minutes a day 5 days a week.

In the first technique, staff contact, the residents are helped to maintain contact with reality through everyday interaction with the staff. The typical nursing home "script" will include many of the following: "Ask your doctor," "And how are we today," "It's time for your pill," "You're looking well today," or "It's time to eat." All of these statements are generally delivered in an impersonal, brief, and emotionless manner. In the staff-contact technique, aides are instructed on how to deal with the residents in order to help them maintain contact with reality. Through conversation an attempt is made to make residents aware of their environment (see Taulbee, 1976). For example, a resident's attention might be brought to objects in the environment through such statements as, "Did you notice the new picture in the dining room?" or "Have you noticed that the leaves are turning color early this fall?" The second technique commonly used in reality orientation is environmental stimulation and can be achieved through such items as large clocks or bulletin boards listing such information as the date, day of the week, weather, and name of the nursing home.

The third technique is that of the classroom setting. In this technique, a small group of residents gather and a staff member directs discussion. In their study on the effects of the classroom technique of reality orientation, Harris and Ivory (1976) observed groups of four residents who met for 30 minutes a day for 5 months.

They found that by the end of the study, 76 percent of the residents showed improvement. The residents displayed greater self-pride, socialized more frequently with others, had improved manners, demonstrated more interest in radio and television, showed more concern with their personal appearance, talked more, had more awareness of the names of the staff and of the residents, engaged in less "crazy talk," and showed less withdrawal. Citrin and Dixon (1977) used 24-hour reality therapy and the classroom technique in their study. It incorporated the staff-resident interaction and environmental-stimulation concepts. They found positive results in their subjects after only 2 months.

Another research project involved 24-hour reality orientation and a policy whereby the staff was told not to "overnurse." Residents were required to perform as many of their daily activities as they could. The staff was constantly reminded not to intervene unless necessary by posters that carried such banners as, "Let us do things by ourselves even if it takes us longer." The program brought about both positive psychological and physical changes in the residents. Some of the physical changes were relearning how to walk and talk, regaining control over bowel and bladder functioning, and relearning how to dress. Some of the psychological improvements noted were less confusion, greater awareness of the environment, greater interaction with other residents, and greater motivation (Salter & Salter, 1975).

There are numerous other studies on the positive effects of reality orientation. However, as we previously pointed out, not all of the studies have had positive outcomes. Gubrium and Ksander (1975) raised some serious questions about the outcomes of reality orientation. In some cases it might be more detrimental than rehabilitative. For example, a bulletin board might list the date, day of the week, next holiday, and weather. The board might indicate that the weather was sunny, but a lazy, noncommitted, or overworked staff might not have noticed that the weather had changed. Thus the board would be giving out faulty information, which could conceivably lead to greater confusion and disengagement from reality because residents would no longer be certain if they were perceiving reality correctly. Gubrium and Ksander also found that many residents and staff instructors involved in the classroom technique did not take reality orientation seriously and the sessions turned into shams. Thus many of the studies that showed little change in behavior may have been due to improper use of the techniques of reality orientation by the staff.

In defense of some of the studies that indicated "no change in behavior after reality orientation," it should be noted that some of the effects are difficult to empirically measure. For example, Barnes (1974) found that in using the classroom technique of reality orientation there were no significant changes in the measured variables. However, impressionistic observations by the staff indicated that significant changes had taken place. For example, the residents were less confused and more manageable. Most other forms of rehabilitation and therapy use some of the concepts involved in reality orientation. The techniques may differ slightly, but the goal is the same, namely, to increase the independence, the contact with reality, and the morale of residents.

In an attempt to minimize the dependence of residents in one nursing home, Lipman and Slater (1977) used three techniques. First, they used activity. They noted that the activity in many nursing homes was regimented; that is, residents "came alive" only during specified segments of the day, generally around the breakfast, lunch, and dinner hours. They felt that one way to decrease dependence was to increase activity, and that one way to increase activity was to turn certain behaviors into social activities. For example, they noted that many residents went down to the dining area an hour or more before meals were served. Rather than letting the residents sit passively during that time, the researchers tried to involve them in setting the tables, serving the food, and helping other residents to eat. At the end of the meal the residents were also encouraged to help in clearing the tables and washing the dishes.

The second factor used to help minimize dependence was privacy. Many researchers believe that privacy is a right of all nursing home residents, at least during certain parts of the day, and that privacy can help achieve resident independence in several ways and might encourage residents to perform more activities by themselves. As a motivating factor to increase independence, privacy will work only if the resident's room has certain features. For example, the room should have a small sitting area, a bathroom, and perhaps a hot plate and small refrigerator. A handrail in the room will facilitate independent mobility. Handrails in the bathroom will make toileting and bathing easier for the resident.

The third factor used in the study to help minimize dependence was integration. Residents were not segregated by "condition." That is, different wings or floors of the nursing home did not have different types of residents. Rather, the confused and the coherent, along with the mobile and the immobile, were in adjoining rooms. The basic idea here was that the independent would use their resources to help the dependent. A mobile individual would take an immobile individual down to the lounge or to the television room. A mentally coherent resident might talk to and thus stimulate a mentally incoherent resident. It was believed that all the residents would benefit from this type of arrangement. The immobile, incoherent residents would probably receive more attention, stimulation, and care than they would otherwise receive. The independent and coherent residents would be given an opportunity to exercise their abilities and play important and challenging roles.

The three techniques employed above were not intended to recruit "slave labor" from the ranks of nursing home residents. Nor were the three factors intended to replace or to supplement staff members. The basic ideas were to help create resident independence and to prevent the atrophy of existing functioning.

There have been two studies that have supported the above concepts. Both studies were built on the hypotheses that if nursing home residents could maintain important and useful roles in the nursing home, they would keep or develop a positive sense of self and would have greater independence. Many gerontologists have commented on the fact that nearly all of the nursing home residents' previous roles are truncated upon entrance into a nursing home. Each resident is forced into playing the role of nursing home resident, a role that may entail a range of behaviors considered to be undesirable. If the residents can maintain other roles, then the atrophy of abilities, skills, and functioning may not be as rapid.

Studies now seem to indicate that older persons who have not lost major social roles maintain higher morale than those who have lost these roles (Rosow, 1967). In one study residents of a nursing home could take on the role of "parent," "grandparent," "counselor," and "friend" to a group of mentally retarded adults. The results of the study indicated that the residents who participated in the program showed improved morale and improved social-interaction patterns (Kalson, 1976).

A similar program was conducted at the Philadelphia Geriatric Center. Here residents were given the opportunity to assume a role that would allow them to be part of a welcoming committee for new residents. The role involved offering the new residents social and emotional support in orienting them to the facility. The welcoming committee met frequently with the staff to discuss the problems of both old and new residents. The program was judged effective for both those on the welcoming committee and the new residents, whose stress at relocation was reduced (Friedman, 1975). This type of program can increase morale and can also increase satisfaction with the nursing home as a permanent home. Both of these variables have been found to be predictors of survival among aged nursing home residents (Noelker & Harel, 1978).

In a similar approach, Scharlach (1988) constructed a study to empirically measure the consequences of a "peer counselor" program (see Priddy & Knisely, 1982). The "counselors," all residents in nursing homes, received 8 hours of training that would assist them in "orienting" new residents to the nursing home in areas such as coping and adjusting to institutional life. The study found that the "counselor" role benefited the residents in terms of their appearance and grooming, and positively influenced new residents in such areas as social functioning.

In order to foster residents' independence and to keep morale high, Hirsch (1977) conducted a study in which she tried to construct a "humane" environment in a nursing home. A humane environment was seen as one that resembled a conventional and "meaningful" way of life. One way of bringing about the humane environment was to avoid the severing of residents' ties with the community. If possible, residents should have a sense of continuity with the community. Such continuity can be achieved by having the residents frequently visit the community and engage in community activities and programs. This prescription was followed in Baltimore, Maryland, through a project called Centercare, which involved stimulation at senior centers. The nursing-home residents were allowed to participate in programs to which the noninstitutionalized aged had access, such as educational programs, arts-and-crafts programs, and physical-fitness programs. These programs also gave the residents opportunities to expand their friendships. Many of the residents who took part in the programs benefited from their participation. However, some of the residents who originally participated found that they were too exhausted or that activities at the senior centers were not interesting to them. It is also significant that the majority of nursing homes contacted refused to participate in the Centercare project. They cited the lack of free transportation, inadequate transportation for those in wheelchairs, or lack of staff support as their objections.

Maintaining ties with the community may also help bridge the "gap" between residents and staff. Residents are less likely to be seen as useless and to be treated as dependent by the staff. Residents and staff may engage in some of the same activities and may thus bridge even more gaps between them (see Kahana, 1973). It has also been found that when the community is involved in a nursing home through volunteer projects the residents generally receive better care (Barney, 1974).

Another form of therapy or rehabilitation is visitations from outsiders. In one research program college students visited withdrawn and uncooperative residents for about 2 hours a week for 10 weeks. At the end of the study significant improvements were found in the morale scores for residents receiving visitations (Arthur et al., 1973; Newman et al., 1985). Moss and Pfohl (1988) examined the impact of a staff visitation program on nursing home residents. The researchers noticed that several staff members were regularly visiting patients and decided to examine the impact. They found that the residents benefited through increases in self-concept; they also had someone to discuss problems with. The staff members also benefited in their understanding of the aging process as well by seeing positive benefits to the residents.

Other programs have sought to establish resident independence. For example, one study found that an effective program could be established to change residents' eating behavior from a dependent pattern to an independent one (Baltes & Zerbe, 1976). Other types of programs have found that some residents who had been judged wheelchairbound for life could regain the ability to walk (MacDonald & Butler, 1974); others have changed patterns of continual wandering to a positive form of behavior (Snyder et al., 1978). With an increase in independence residents will also likely increase their contact with reality, morale, life satisfaction, self-concept, and sense of usefulness. Some of the long-term programs have been so effective that up to 61 percent of the nursing home residents have been released back into the community (Kaplan & Ford, 1975; U.S. Senate Special Committee, 1988a).

Some studies have attempted to increase social interaction among nursing home residents. It is widely believed that by increasing social interaction much of the apathetic, withdrawn behavior of residents can be modified. In an attempt to discover an activity that would increase social interaction, one group of researchers established a "coffee hour." They found that the coffee hour significantly increased the amount of social interaction among residents (Blackman et al., 1976). However, not all of these studies have had positive results. One study found that increasing the amount of social interaction among residents through recreational therapy also increased the amount of conflict in the nursing home. Researchers noted that there appeared to be a great deal of mistrust and hostility among residents (Jones, 1972). This finding probably indicates that older persons need not only rehabilitative programs, but also mental-health therapy or programs to help them adjust to life in a nursing home and their own losses in areas such as health, independence, and privacy.

All the above programs and therapies to increase activity are important since inactivity can lead to physical problems such as muscle atrophy, osteoporosis, pressure sores, and bowel and bladder dysfunction. Also, once started, social isolation and inactivity are difficult to reverse (McClannahan, 1973) and can lead to increased dependence, a loss of contact with reality, and decreased morale.

Inactivity or lack of social interaction in nursing home residents may very well be caused by the fact that the residents are not aware of when events are occurring. To test this hypothesis a group of researchers established a program in which a small amount of money was given to residents if they would interact briefly with a researcher during a certain time period each day. The program was publicized by posters, announcements at lunch, and messages over the loudspeaker. The researchers found that each of the methods of announcement was effective in itself and that a combination of methods produced only a slightly greater attendance. When the announcements of the regularly scheduled event were stopped, attendance declined by 50 percent. This finding indicates that regularly scheduled events in nursing homes must be announced if attendance by residents is desired (McClannahan & Risley, 1974).

To increase the probability of resident participation in social interaction there should be ample aids to locomotion. The list would include handrails, canes, crutches, wheelchairs, ramps, braces, the absence of barriers, and the assistance of others if needed. It has also been found that long corridors with hard floors that intensify sounds make residents more likely to stay in their rooms. Shorter hallways with carpeting are more conducive to social interaction and independence (McClannahan, 1973). Even residents with limitations can be encouraged to maintain independence and social contacts if a few changes in the environment are made. McClannahan (1973) listed several examples.

1 The transfer of an individual from a wheelchair to a bed or vice versa is made easier if the seat of the wheelchair and the level of the bed are at the same height. If they are of different heights, transfer will become more difficult.

2 If light switches are placed at a lower level, residents will not have to call an aide to turn the lights on or off.

3 Closets should be designed so that the clothing and shelves are within the reach of those in wheelchairs.

4 Residents in wheelchairs can often function independently if the wash basin is lowered, and if there is enough room for them to maneuver in the bathroom. It is also convenient to have a mirror tilted to enable wheelchair residents to see themselves.

5 Facilities within the nursing home such as the lounge, television room, or bathroom should be clearly marked with large signs, symbols, and bright colors. There might be colored lines leading to certain facilities or rooms. For example, a blue dotted line might lead to the dining area, a yellow solid line might lead to the lounge, and a red line composed of dashes might lead to the television room.

6 Being dressed by an aide is often a humiliating experience for the residents. Residents' independence can be facilitated by having clothing that is easy to put on and take off. If there are buttons or zippers, they should be in front. Ideally, instead of buttons or zippers there should be a pressure strip.

A number of studies have found that exercise is important for both physical and mental functioning at all ages. Although more research is appearing on exercise for noninstitutionalized older persons, relatively little has appeared on institutionalized older persons. One study examined the impact of setting goals for residents, providing them feedback on meeting their goals, and the use of contingent reinforcement. The form of exercise used was riding a stationary bicycle. All of those involved in the study had several "major" physical and mental disorders. Weekly goals for each resident were established during weekly meetings. The new goals were 10 percent higher in terms of miles ridden than the previous week. Goals were posted for each resident in the physical therapy room. After 4 weeks of continued increases the goal remained constant. If residents achieved their weekly goals, they were awarded a gold star which was placed on a chart next to their names. Verbal praise was also provided. For those who continued to progress, colored buttons and t-shirts were awarded. Additionally, a newsletter describing the program and the participants was distributed to all residents in the nursing home.

After 30 weeks the tangible rewards were discontinued. That is, there were no more t-shirts, buttons, or gold stars. Goals were still posted and verbal praise provided. The study reported that establishing goals and acknowledging performance enhanced the performance of the participants. As the goals were increased the distance ridden increased. The average increase was 74 percent over the baseline distance. Even after the discontinuation of tangible rewards the riding distances remained the same for most of the participants, thus indicating that once exercise had been established as a regular behavior the tangible rewards could be discontinued (Perkins et al., 1986).

Programs have also examined the impact of mental health programs. One study examined the impact of volunteer mental health workers (Crose et al., 1987). The study noted that many nursing home patients have mental problems and examined the impact of a low-cost program in which adults received mental health training and were then assigned to visit nursing home residents with specific mental health problems. The study reported that although there were some problems, the patients benefited from the assistance they received. The important point is that many of the aged residents in nursing homes can be rehabilitated. Some can be rehabilitated enough to enable them to leave the nursing home. Others can live more independent lives with greater satisfaction through rehabilitation.

ALTERNATIVES TO NURSING HOMES

Generally, when we think of long-term care we think of nursing homes. However, it is estimated that 60 to 80 percent of all the long-term care needs of older persons are provided by family members or friends for no compensation (U.S. Senate Special Committee, 1988a). This means that there are far more older persons receiving long-term care outside of nursing homes than inside.

Nursing home care has generated a great deal of concern in this country for several reasons. One reason is the cost. The cost of nursing home care has increased significantly. It is estimated that 26 percent of the health care costs in this country are for nursing home care (Knight & Walker, 1985). The projections for an increase in the segment of the population 65+ years of age also projects an increase in nursing home care costs. In addition to the cost factor there is also concern over the care issue. Many believe, correctly or incorrectly, that the quality of nursing home care is not very good. A third issue relates to the loss of freedom; there is generally a greater loss of freedom in nursing homes than with other forms of care. This has generated a search for alternatives, other than home care by family and friends, to placing older persons in nursing homes. Three of these alternatives will be presented below.

Respite Care

One of the major reasons older persons are eventually placed in nursing homes is that the caregivers can no longer provide 24-hour-a-day care, 7 days a week; essentially, caregivers "burnout." In respite care, caregivers are temporarily relieved of their caregiving responsibilities for a certain time period, which can be in a variety of combinations such as for a certain number of hours per day, a certain number of days per week, or a certain number of consecutive days per month. In respite care a substitute caregiver may come and provide care in the home or the care receiver may temporarily be placed in a nursing home.

The concept behind respite care is that many family caregivers become overburdened with caregiving responsibilities. It must be remembered that the "only" difference between many of those who are at home and those who are in institutions is that those at home have a caregiver willing to provide care and supervision. Respite care provides the caregiver with some relief, which may extend the amount of time the caregiver provides care to the impaired individual at home. Being a primary caregiver to an impaired older person can be very demanding. Studies have reported that some caregivers cannot leave those for whom they provide care for more than 1 hour at a time. Other studies have noted that too often care recipients do not allow caregivers uninterrupted sleep. A study on California caregivers found that many had not had relief from their caregiving responsibilities for 3 to 12 years (see Scharlach & Frenzel, 1986). Essentially it is believed that respite care can relieve the caregiver burden thus delaying nursing home admission. It can be provided by another family member, friends, community support, as well as by local, state, or federally funded programs and can be provided in several locations, such as day-care centers, nursing homes, or the individual's home.

Several factors have been identified as critical in assisting caregivers in maintaining care recipients at home (Berman et al., 1987):

1 Caregiver health: Many caregivers are also "old" and have chronic health problems. Respite care allows caregivers time for the treatment of their health problems as well as time to recuperate.

2 The strain created by the behavior of the patient and the caregiver role: Many patients have problems that can make their care stressful. For example, those with mental problems may be confused or disoriented making constant supervision necessary. Others may be violent. Additionally, there is the strain of the caregiver role. The caregiver has several new roles which can be stressful. For example, the caregiver often assumes a nursing function and must do bed and body work as well as administer medications and manage incontinence.

3 Marital history: There are two factors that appear to be important here: length of marriage and strength of marriage. There is a positive relationship between the length and the strength of the marriage and the duration and intensity of caregiving the caregiver is willing to tolerate.

4 Social supports: The caregiver burden is often shared by other family members, friends, and neighbors. The greater the social support the less the amount of caregiver strain.

5 Financial resources: Home care can be expensive, especially to those on a fixed income. There are frequently medical expenses not covered by medicare or other forms of insurance. The greater the financial stress of home care, the less likely the caregiver is to continue with home care.

6 Availability of respite care: Most of the caregivers in this study noted that the availability of respite care was essential in allowing them to continue with the caregiving role.

7 Residence appropriateness: Another factor that was important in maintaining someone at home was the appropriateness of the residence. There are many homes, especially older homes, that need expensive renovations to make them practical for home care.

8 Beliefs: There are certain belief systems, which can be based on religious beliefs or personal beliefs, that define marriage or family relationships in a manner that makes home care more likely to occur.

This study also reported three factors that respite care offered caregivers:

1 Time for personal care: The caregivers used this time in a variety of ways such as vacations, medical care and treatment, rest, community activities, home improvements.

2 Providing care to the patient: Although the patient was in respite care, some caregivers still went to the institution and provided care. This was beneficial in that the staff could show the caregiver how to provide care in a more efficient manner.

3 The development of formal and informal support systems: The article noted that those who provide acute care are often provided with "a landslide" of support. When the problem becomes chronic the support often declines and then stops. In this article the staff of the respite institution assisted the caregiver in building or rebuilding a support system.

Scharlach and Frenzel (1986) examined the impact of a respite service provided by a VA hospital where care receivers could stay for up to 14 continuous days for a total of 28 days a year. The study examined the impact of this program on the caregivers as well as the care recipients.

The major reasons for using the respite service by caregivers were the need for emotional and physical rest. The caregivers had the opportunity to visit family members, acquire solitude, complete household tasks, visit friends and neighbors, or have certain medical needs attended to. The results indicated that 72 percent of the caregivers said that their health improved as a result of the relief from caregiving responsibilities. A subjective report from the staff of the VA nursing home was that the caregivers "looked" younger as a result of their rest (see Seltzer et al., 1988).

Another potential impact was on the caregiver-care recipient relationship. Now that the caregivers had time off from their responsibilities, would they be "refreshed" or would they have found a relief and be hesitant to resume caregiver responsibilities? Also, would the care recipients be bitter, hostile, or fearful about the temporary institutionalization? Thirty-eight percent of the caregivers noted a deterioration in their relationship with the care recipient. This was generally because care recipients were angry at being taken from their homes or fearful of being abandoned. When asked about the likelihood of institutionalization 33 percent of caregivers said that respite care made it less likely; 30 percent said it was more likely. Those that found it more likely said that respite care in a nursing home had shown them that nursing homes were not as bad as they had envisioned; others found that the nursing home had several options that could benefit the care of the recipient; others found that the care recipient could manage without their constant care. Not all studies on respite care have had positive results. One study reported that respite care only delayed institutionalization about a month (Lawton et al., 1989).

One form of respite care is day care. Just as respite care can take several forms so can day care. It has been estimated that over 1000 day-care centers exist for adults in the United States (see Cherry & Rafkin, 1988) and that day care can significantly delay institutionalization (see Zimmerman, 1986). The cost can vary, depending on the needs of the older person. One study found that costs ranged from $10 to $105 per day, with an average of about $30 per day. It was noted in this study that those receiving day care tended to be younger, married, and with fewer disabilities than nursing home residents (Weissert et al., 1989; see Capitman, 1989).

Community-Based Long-Term Care Projects

In addition to respite care, there have also been some community-based projects designed to reduce long-term care utilization. One of these projects has been described by Nocks and his associates (1986). This project studied individuals eligible for medicaid-sponsored nursing home care. Those eligible were randomly separated into control and experimental groups. The experimental group was provided with a number of community-based services such as personal care, day medical care, home-delivered meals, home-based therapies, and respite care. After 18 months it was found that nursing home utilization was significantly less in the experimental group.

Greene and Monahan (1987) described a federally-funded project that provided professionally guided support and education groups for caregivers. The purpose of the project was to ascertain the effectiveness of these groups in reducing institutionalization rates. There was a control group that did not participate in the meetings. The treatment group attended a series of 3-hour sessions divided into three components. The first component allowed caregivers to vent some of their feelings about being a caregiver. The group leader assisted the caregivers in "constructively" handling their negative emotions. The second component was education; the caregivers learned specific techniques to assist them in their caregiving responsibilities. The last component was relaxation training. The program reported a significant difference in the institutionalization rates: control group 8.6 percent; treatment group 3.8 percent.

Agency-Assisted Shared Housing

Some institutionalized older persons could live independently if they had assistance in their homes. The assistance levels would vary according to the needs of the older person. For those with minimum levels of physical and mental deterioration the assistance provided would be minimal, perhaps maintenance around the home and errands. For those with increasing levels of physical and mental deterioration the assistance needed would be greater.

One way older persons might stay in their own homes and receive assistance is through older persons sharing their homes in exchange for certain caregiver services. Essentially an older person provides room, board, and perhaps a stipend, in exchange for certain caregiver services. The advantages to older persons are that they can continue to live in their own homes while receiving the assistance they need. At the state or national level it can mean lower medicaid costs. In the past, older persons have had to make private arrangements in this area. More recently community agencies have established programs to assist older persons in obtaining caregivers. The belief is that an agency may be capable of matching more individuals with greater compatibility than older persons working independently.

Jaffe and Howe (1988) have examined agency-assisted shared housing. They have noted that there are many different programs with many different structures. They noted that the ''typical'' older client is someone who because of certain physical and/or mental changes finds independent living difficult. Most of these individuals are initially reluctant to share their housing. The authors also reported that the agency-assisted housing programs noted that matches between older persons needing assistance and caregivers were very difficult to make in large part because the older persons had ''unrealistic expectations about homesharing.'' Jaffe and Howe also found that most matches did not last very long; most had ended within 3 months. This was in part because of incompatibility between the older person and the housemate, and because most of the housemates were in a transition period, such as students who needed temporary housing or unemployed individuals who were looking for other employment.

SUMMARY

Nursing homes are a very emotional and controversial topic in gerontology. They are designed to provide for the long-term nonacute health needs of individuals who either cannot cope with or have difficulty in everyday living. Nursing homes can be differentiated by type of ownership and level of care. Ownership can be proprietary, nonprofit, and governmental. Level of care can be skilled nursing, intermediate care, or residential care. Long-term care, although frequently equated with nursing homes, has a much broader definition than nursing home and encompasses a spectrum of chronic-care needs, ranging from home support and day care, to skilled nursing care in a nursing home.

In the past there were few nursing homes. Those needing long-term care were often placed in mental institutions or almshouses. The Social Security Act of 1935 established the obligation of the federal government toward older persons, and laid the groundwork for the development of federal funds to assist the nursing home industry. About 5 percent of the aged are in nursing homes. Most are white females. Although at any one time only about 5 percent of older persons are in nursing homes, the lifetime risk of becoming a nursing home patient is much higher.

Nursing homes are expensive, averaging about $25,000 per year, the majority of which is paid by individuals, often called "out-of-pocket" expenses. Medicaid will pay for an individual's nursing home expenses only under certain conditions, generally impoverishment.

The decision to seek admission to a nursing home is associated with advanced age, being female, not having a caregiver, and reduced functional status. The abilities of those in nursing homes are markedly different from those not in nursing homes. Those in nursing homes are more likely to require assistance in the activities of daily living such as bathing, dressing, toileting, or eating.

Care in nursing homes has been a major issue for decades. Some believe that a low quality of care is pervasive. Others believe that although poor care exists, it is the exception that receives a disproportionate amount of publicity. There have been many recommendations on improving care in nursing homes. One way of examining care has been to observe the consequences of institutionalization. Many studies have reported positive consequences in terms of improved abilities of residents and discharge back into the community. Other studies have reported an improved relationship between older persons and their family caregiver. Many of the positive consequences of institutionalization have come about because rehabilitation and therapy are used more frequently in nursing homes. Most studies have had positive results with rehabilitation programs.

The last area examined was alternatives to nursing homes. As mentioned at the beginning of this chapter, long-term care covers a spectrum of services. Nursing homes are at one end of the spectrum. At the other end are some long-term care alternatives primarily designed to prevent institutionalization. One is respite care which is designed to prevent caregiver burnout. Respite care provides caregivers temporary relief from caregiving responsibilities for a certain time period, which can be in a variety of forms such as a certain number of hours per day, or of a certain number of consecutive days per month. One form of respite care is day care for older persons.

A second alternative to institutionalization is community-based long-term care projects. These projects can assume a number of forms such as home-delivered meals and medical services. The last alternative was agency-assisted shared housing. Again, this can take a variety of forms. The basic concept is to provide those still living independently in the community, but in need of assistance, with a caregiver. In exchange for caregiving responsibilities the caregiver receives free room and board.

REFERENCES

Anderson, N. A. (1974). Approaches to improving the quality of long-term care for older persons. *The Gerontologist,* **14**(6): 519–524.

Anonymous (1989). New report and developments on nursing home insurance. *Aging*, **359**: 39–40.

Applebaum, R. (1989). What's all this about quality. *Generations*, **13**(1): 5–7.

Arthur, G. L., Donnan, H. H., & Lair, C. V. (1973). Companionship therapy with nursing home aged. *The Gerontologist*, **13**(2): 167–170.

Baltes, M. M. & Zerbe, M. B. (1976). Independence training in nursing-home residents. *The Gerontologist*, **16**(5): 428–432.

Baltes, P. B. (1987). Learned helplessness. In G. L. Maddox (Ed.), *The encyclopedia of aging* (pp. 379–380). New York: Springer.

Barnes, J. A. (1974). Effects of reality orientation classroom on memory loss, confusion, and disorientation in geriatric patients. *The Gerontologist*, **14**(2): 138–142.

Barney, J. L. (1974). Community presence as a key to quality of life in nursing homes. *American Journal of Public Health*, **3**(3): 265–268.

Beach, D. A. (1988). A new procedure in the evaluation of nursing aide applicants. *Nursing Homes*, **37**(2): 17–18.

Berdes, C. (1987). The modest proposal nursing home: Dehumanizing characteristics of nursing homes in memoirs of nursing home residents. *Journal of Applied Gerontology*, **6**(4): 372–388.

Berman, S., Delaney, N., Gallagher, D., Atkins, P., & Graeber, M. P. (1987). Respite care: A partnership between a veterans administration nursing home and families to care for frail elders at home. *The Gerontologist*, **27**(5): 581–584.

Blackman, D. K., Howe, M., & Pinkston, E. M. (1976). Increasing participation in social interaction of the institutionalized elderly. *The Gerontologist*, **16**(1; Part 1): 69–76.

Blatz, T. M., & Turner, J. G. (1977). Development and analysis of a nursing home aide screening. *The Gerontologist*, **17**(1): 66–69.

Block, C., Boczkowski, J. A., Hansen, N., & Vanderbeck, M. (1987). Nursing home consultation: Difficult residents and frustrated staff. *The Gerontologist*, **27**(4): 443–446.

Booth, T. (1986). Institutional regimes and induced dependency in homes for the aged. *The Gerontologist*, **26**(4): 418–423.

Bowers, B. J. (1988). Family perceptions of care in a nursing home. *The Gerontologist*, **28**(3): 361–368.

Branch, L. G. (1987). Continuing care retirement communities: Self-insuring for long-term care. *The Gerontologist*, **27**(1): 4–8.

Brannon, D., Smyer, M. A., Cohn, M. D., Borchardt, L., Landry, J. A., Jay, G. M., Garfein, A. J., Malonebeach, E., & Walls, C. (1988). A job diagnostic survey of nursing home caregivers: Implications for job redesign. *The Gerontologist*, **28**(2): 246–252.

Brody, E. (1978). The aging of the family. *Annals of the American Academy of Political and Social Science*, **438**(July): 13–27.

Butler, P. A. (1989). New direction for nursing home regulation. *Generations*, **13**(1): 38–41.

Capitman, J. A. (1989). Day care programs and research challenges. *The Gerontologist*, **29**(5): 584–585.

Chartock, P., Nevins, A., Rzetelny, H., & Gilberto, P. (1988). A mental health training program in nursing homes. *The Gerontologist*, **28**(4): 503–507.

Cherry, D. L., & Rafkin, M. J. (1988). Adapting day care to the needs of adults with dementia. *The Gerontologist*, **28**(1): 116–121.

Citrin, R. S., & Dixon, D. N. (1977). Reality orientation: A milieu therapy used in an institution for the aged. *The Gerontologist*, **17**(1): 39–43.

Cohen, E. S. (1988). The elderly mystique: Constraints on the autonomy of the elderly with disabilities. *The Gerontologist*, **28**(Supplement): 24–31.

Cohen, M. A., Tell, E. J., & Wallack, S. S. (1988). The risk factors of nursing home entry among residents of six continuing care retirement communities. *Journal of Gerontology: Social Sciences,* **43**(1): S22–27.

Crose, R., Duffy, M., Warren, J., & Franklin, B. (1987). Project OASIS: Volunteer mental health paraprofessionals serving nursing home residents. *The Gerontologist,* **27**(3): 359–362.

Drummond, L., Kirchhoff, L., & Scarbrough, D. R. (1978). A practical guide to reality orientation: A treatment approach for confusion and disorientation. *The Gerontologist,* **18**(6): 568–573.

Feinauer, D. (1987). Movement of residents through multilevel lifetime care facilities: A Markovian matrix analysis. *Journal of Applied Gerontology,* **6**(3): 313–331.

Fischer, D. H. (1978). *Growing old in America* (expanded edition). New York: Oxford University Press.

Freedberg, L. E., & Altman, C. S. (1975). Psychiatric consultation in a nursing home: A two-year experience. *The Gerontologist,* **15**(2): 125–128.

Friedman, S. (1975). The resident welcoming committee: Institutionalized elderly in volunteer service to their peers. *The Gerontologist,* **15**(4): 362–367.

Gottesman, L. E. (1974). Nursing home performance as related to resident traits, ownership, size, and source of payment. *American Journal of Public Health,* **3**(3): 269–276.

Gottesman, L. E., & Bourestom, N. C. (1974). Why nursing homes do what they do. *The Gerontologist,* **14**(6): 501–506.

Greene, V. L., & Monahan, D. J. (1987). The effect of professionally guided caregiver support and education group on institutionalization of care received. *The Gerontologist,* **27**(6): 716–721.

Gubrium J. F. (1975). *Living and dying at Murray Manor.* New York: St. Martin's.

Gubrium, J. F., & Ksander, M. (1975). On multiple realities and reality orientation. *The Gerontologist,* **15**(2): 142–145.

Halbur, B. T. (1986). Managing nursing personnel turnover rates: Strategies for nursing home professionals. *Journal of Applied Gerontology,* **5**(1): 64–75.

Halbur, B. T., & Fears, N. (1986). Nursing personnel turnover rates turned over: Potential positive effects on resident outcomes in nursing homes. *The Gerontologist,* **26**(1): 70–76.

Handschu, S. S. (1973). Profile of the nurses's aide—expanding her role as psychosocial companion to the nursing home resident. *The Gerontologist,* **13**(3, Part 1): 315–317.

Hare, J., & Pratt, C. C. (1988). Burnout: Differences between professional and paraprofessional nursing staff in acute care and long-term care health facilities. *Journal of Applied Gerontology,* **7**(1): 60–72.

Harrington, C., Estes, C. L., Lee, P. R., & Newcomer, R. J. (1986). Effects of state medicaid policies on the aged. *The Gerontologist,* **26**(4): 437–443.

Harris, C. S., & Ivory, P. B. C. B. (1976). An outcome evaluation of reality orientation therapy with geriatric patients in a state mental hospital. *The Gerontologist,* **16**(6): 496–503.

Hirsch, C. S. (1977). Integrating the nursing home resident into a senior citizen center. *The Gerontologist,* **17**(3): 227–234.

Horner, J. (1982). *That time of year: A chronicle of life in a nursing home.* Amherst: University of Massachusetts Press.

Ingram, D. K., & Barry, J. R. (1977). National statistics on deaths in nursing homes: Interpretation and implications. *The Gerontologist,* **17**(4): 303–308.

Institute of Medicine, Committee on Nursing Home Regulation (1986). *Improving the quality of care in nursing homes.* Washington, DC: National Academy of Sciences.

Jaffe, D. J., & Howe, E. (1988). Agency-assisted shared housing: The nature of programs and matches. *The Gerontologist,* **28**(3): 318–324.

Jones, D. C. (1972). Social isolation, interaction, and conflict in two nursing homes. *The Gerontologist,* **12**(3; Part 1): 230–234.

Kahana, E. (1971). Emerging issues in institutional services for the aging. *The Gerontologist,* **11**(1): 51–58.

Kahana, E. (1973). The humane treatment of old people in institutions. *The Gerontologist,* **13**(3): 282–289.

Kahn, K. A., Hines, W., Woodson, A. S., & Burkham-Armstrong, G. (1977). A multidisciplinary approach to assessing the quality of care in long-term facilities. *The Gerontologist,* **17**(1): 61–65.

Kalson, L. (1976). M*A*S*H: A program of social interaction between institutionalized and adult mentally retarded persons. *The Gerontologist,* **16**(4): 340–348.

Kane, R. A., Kane, R. L., Arnold, S., Garrard, J., McDermott, S., & Kepferle, L. (1988). Geriatric nurse practitioners as nursing home employees: Implementing the role. *The Gerontologist,* **28**(4): 469–477.

Kaplan, J., & Ford, C. S. (1975). Rehabilitation for the elderly: An eleven-year assessment. *The Gerontologist,* **15**(5; part 1): 393–397.

Kastenbaum, R., & Candy, S. E. (1973). The 4 percent fallacy: A methodological and empirical critique of extended care facility population statistics. *Aging and Human Development,* **4**(1): 15–21.

Kenny, K., & Belling, B. (1987). Home equity conversion: A counseling model. *The Gerontologist,* **27**(1): 9–12.

Knight, B., & Walker, D. L. (1985). Toward a definition of alternatives to institutionalization for frail elderly. *The Gerontologist,* **25**(4): 358–363.

Kosberg, J. I. (1973). Differences in proprietary institutions caring for affluent and nonaffluent elderly. *The Gerontologist,* **13**(3; Part 1): 299–304.

Kosberg, J. I. (1974). Making institutions accountable: Research and policy issues. *The Gerontologist,* **14**(6): 510–516.

Kosberg, J. I., & Gorman, J. F. (1975). Perceptions toward the rehabilitation potential of institutionalized aged. *The Gerontologist,* **15**(5; Part 1): 398–403.

LaGreca, A. J., Streib, G. F., & Folts, W. E. (1985). Retirement communities and their life stages. *Journal of Gerontology,* **40**(2): 211–218.

Laird, C. (1979). *Limbo: A memoir about life in a nursing home by a survivor.* Novato, CA: Chandler and Sharp.

Lawton, M. P., Brody, E. M., & Saperstein, A. R. (1989). A controlled study of respite service for caregivers of Alzheimer's patients. *The Gerontologist,* **29**(1): 8–16.

Lemke, S., & Moos, R. H. (1989). Ownership and quality of care in residential facilities for the elderly. *The Gerontologist,* **29**(2): 209–215.

Lesnoff-Caravaglia, G. (1978–1979). The 5 percent fallacy. *International Journal of Aging and Human Development,* **9**(2): 187–192.

Lewis, M. A., Cretin, S., & Kane, R. L. (1985). The natural history of nursing home patients. *The Gerontologist,* **25**(4): 382–388.

Liang, J., & Tu, E. J-C. (1986). Estimating lifetime risk of nursing home residency: A further note. *The Gerontologist,* **26**(5): 560–563.

Linn, M. W. (1974). Predicting quality of patient care in nursing home placement. *The Gerontologist,* **14**(3):225–227.

Linn, M. W., & Gurel, L. (1972). Family attitude in nursing home placement. *The Gerontologist,* **12**(3; Part 1): 220–224.

Lipman, A., & Slater, R. (1977). Homes for old people: Toward a positive environment. *The Gerontologist,* **17**(2): 146–156.

Liu, K., Doty, P., & Manton, K. (1990). Medicaid spenddown in nursing homes. *The Gerontologist,* **30**(1): 7–15.

Long, S. (1987). *Death without dignity.* Austin, TX: Texas Monthly Press.

McClannahan, L. E. (1973). Therapeutic and prosthetic living environments for nursing home residents. *The Gerontologist,* **13**(4): 424–429.

McClannahan, L. E., & Risley, T. R. (1974). Design of living environments for nursing home residents: Recruiting attendance. *The Gerontologist,* **14**(3): 236–240.

McConnel, C. E. (1984). A note on the lifetime risk of nursing home admission. *The Gerontologist,* **24**(2): 193–198.

MacDonald, M. L., & Butler, A. K. (1974). Reversal of helplessness, producing walking behavior in nursing home wheelchair residents using behavior modification procedures. *Journal of Gerontology,* **29**(1); 97–101.

Manson, S. M. (1989). Long-term care in American Indian communities: Issues for planning and research. *The Gerontologist,* **29**(1): 38–44.

Mendelson, M. A. (1974). *Tender loving greed.* New York: Knopf.

Miller, D. B., & Beer, S. (1977). Patterns of friendship among patients in a nursing home setting. *The Gerontologist,* **17**(3): 269–275.

Miller, D. B., Brimigion, J., Keller, D., & Woodruff, S. (1972). Nurse-physician communication in a nursing home. *The Gerontologist,* **12**(3; Part 1): 225–229.

Miller, D., & Harris, A. P. (1972). Demographic characteristics of discharged patients in two suburban nursing homes. *The Gerontologist,* **12**(3; Part 1), 246–250.

Mor, V., Sherwood, S., & Gutkin, C. (1986). A national study of residential care for the aged. *The Gerontologist,* **26**(4): 405–417.

Moran, J. A., & Gatz, M. (1987). Group therapies for nursing home adults: An evaluation of two treatment approaches. *The Gerontologist,* **27**(5): 588–591.

Moses, S. A. (1990). The fallacy of impoverishment. *The Gerontologist,* **30**(1): 21–25.

Moss, M. S., & Pfohl, D. C. (1988). New friendships: Staff as visitors of nursing home residents. *The Gerontologist,* **28**(2): 263–265.

Mullen, W. E. (1985). Identification and ranking of stressors in nursing home administration. *The Gerontologist,* **25**(4): 370–375.

National Center for Health Statistics (1987). Health statistics for older persons, United States. *Vital and Health Statistics.* Series 3, No. 25.

Netting, F. E., & Wilson, C. C. (1987). Current legislation concerning life care and continuing care contracts. *The Gerontologist,* **27**(5): 645–651.

Newman, S., Lyons, C. W., & Onawola, S. T. (1985). The development of an intergenerational service-learning program at a nursing home. *The Gerontologist,* **25**(2): 130–133.

Nocks, B. C., Learner, R. M., Blackman, D., & Brown, T. E. (1986). The effects of a community-based long-term care project on nursing home utilization. *The Gerontologist,* **26**(2): 150–157.

Noelker, L., & Harel, Z. (1978). Predictors of well-being and survival among institutionalized aged. *The Gerontologist,* **18**(6): 562–567.

O'Brien, J., Saxberg, B. O., & Smith, H. L. (1983). For-profit or not-for-profit nursing homes: Does it matter? *The Gerontologist,* **23**(4): 341–348.

Palmore, E. (1976). Total chance of institutionalization among the aged. *The Gerontologist,* **16**(6): 504–507.

Pearlman, R. A., & Uhlmann, R. F. (1988). Quality of life in the elderly: Comparisons between nursing home and community residents. *Journal of Applied Gerontology,* **7**(3): 316–330.

Perkins, K. A., Rapp, S. R., Carlson, C. R., & Wallace, C. E. (1986). A behavioral intervention to increase exercise among nursing home residents. *The Gerontologist,* **26**(5): 479–481.

Pillemer, K. (1988). Maltreatment of patients in nursing homes: Overview and research agenda. *Journal of Health and Social Behavior,* **29**(3): 227–238.

Pillemer, K., & Moore, D. W. (1989). Abuse of patients in nursing homes: Findings from a survey of staff. *The Gerontologist,* **29**(3): 314–320.

Power, C. A., & McCarron, L. T. (1975). Treatment of depression in persons residing in homes for the aged. *The Gerontologist,* **15**(2): 132–135.

Priddy, J. M., & Knisely, J. S. (1982). Older adults as peer counselors: Considerations in counselor training with the elderly. *Educational Gerontology,* **9**(1): 53–62.

Retsinas, J., & Garrity, P. (1988). Going home: Analysis of nursing home discharges. *The Gerontologist,* **26**(4): 431–436.

Retsinas, J., & Garrity, P. (1988). Testing nursing home iatrogenesis. *International Journal of Aging and Human Development,* **26**(1): 57–69.

Rosow, I. (1967). *Social integration of the aged.* New York: Free Press.

Ruchlin, H. S. (1988). Continuing care retirement communities: An analysis of financial viability and health care coverage. *The Gerontologist,* **28**(2): 146–162.

Salter, C. L., & Slater, C. A. (1975). Effects of an individualized activity program on elderly patients. *The Gerontologist,* **15**(5; Part 1): 404–406.

Scharlach, A. E. (1988). Peer counselor training for nursing home residents. *The Gerontologist,* **28**(4): 499–502.

Scharlach, A. E., & Frenzel, C. (1986). An evaluation of institution-based respite care. *The Gerontologist,* **26**(1): 77–82.

Seltzer, B., Rheaume, Y., Volicer, L., Fabiszewski, K. J., Lyon, P. C., Brown, J. E., & Volicer, B. (1988). The short-term effects of in-hospital respite on the patient with Alzheimer's disease. *The Gerontologist,* **28**(1): 121–124.

Shapiro, E., & Tate, R. (1988). Who is really at risk of institutionalization. *The Gerontologist,* **28**(2): 237–245.

Smallegan, M. (1985). There was nothing else to do: Needs for care before nursing home admission. *The Gerontologist,* **25**(4): 364–369.

Smeeding, T. D. (1990). Toward a knowledge base for long-term care finance. *The Gerontologist,* **30**(1): 5–6.

Smith, K. F., & Bengtson, V. L. (1979). The positive consequences of institutionalization: Solidarity between elderly parents and their middle-aged children. *The Gerontologist,* **19**(5): 438–447.

Snyder, L. H., Rupprecht, P., Pyrek, J., Brekhus, S., & Moss, T. (1978). Wandering. *The Gerontologist,* **18**(3): 272–280.

Spence, D. A., & Wiener, J. M. (1990). Nursing home length of stay patterns: Results from the 1985 National Nursing Home Survey. *The Gerontologist,* **30**(1): 16–20.

Stannard, C. I. (1973). Old folks and dirty work: The social conditions for patient abuse in a nursing home. *Social Problems,* **20**(3): 329–342.

Steinberg, A., Fitten, L. J., Kachuck, N. (1986). Patient participation in treatment decision-making in the nursing home: The issue of competence. *The Gerontologist,* **26**(4): 362–366.

Taulbee, L. R. (1976). Reality orientation and the aged. In I. M. Burnside (Ed.), *Nursing and the aged* (pp. 245–254). New York: McGraw-Hill.

Tobin, S. S., & Lieberman, M. A. (1976). *Last home for the aged.* San Francisco: Jossey-Bass.

Townsend, C. (1970). *Old age: The last segregation.* New York: Grossman.

Tulloch, G. J. (1975). *A home is not a home: Life within a nursing home.* New York: Seabury.

U.S. Bureau of the Census (1990). *Statistical abstract of the United States*. Washington, DC: U.S. Government Printing Office.

U.S. Senate Special Committee on Aging (1987–1988). *Aging America: Trends and projections*. Washington, DC: U.S. Government Printing Office.

U.S. Senate Special Committee on Aging (1988*a*). *Developments in aging: 1987, Volume One*. Washington, DC: U.S. Government Printing Office.

U.S. Senate Special Committee on Aging (1988*b*). *Developments in aging: 1987, Volume Three*. Washington, DC: U.S. Government Printing Office.

U.S. Senate, Subcommittee on Long-Term Care (1974). *Nursing home care in the U.S.: Failure in public policy*. Supporting Paper No. 1. Washington, DC: U.S. Government Printing Office.

Vladeck, B. C. (1980) *Unloving care: The nursing home tragedy*. New York: Basic Books.

Vicente, L., Wiley, J. A., & Carrington, R. A. (1979). The risk of institutionalization before death. *The Gerontologist, 19*(4): 361–367.

Waxman, H. M., Carner, E. A., & Berkenstock, G. (1984). Job turnover and job satisfaction among nursing home aides. *The Gerontologist, 24*(5): 503–509.

Weinberg, A. D., Engingro, P. F., Miller, R. L., Weinberg, L. L., & Parker, C. L. (1989). Death in the nursing home: Senescence, infection and other causes. *Journal of Geriatric Nursing, 15*(4): 12–16.

Weissert, W. G., Elston, J. M., Bolda, E. J., Cready, C. M., Zelman, W. N., Sloane, P. D., Kalsbeek, W. D., Mutran, E., Rice, T. H., & Koch, G. G. (1989). Models of adult day care: Findings from a national survey. *The Gerontologist, 29*(5): 640–649.

Wershow, H. J. (1976). The four percent fallacy: Some further evidence and policy implications. *The Gerontologist, 16*(1; Part 1): 52–55.

Wiener, J. M., Ehrenworth, D. A., & Spence, D. A. (1987). Private long-term care insurance: Cost, coverage, and restrictions. *The Gerontologist, 27*(4): 487–493.

Wingard, D. L., Jones, D. W., & Kaplan, R. M. (1987). Institutional care utilization by the elderly: A critical review. *The Gerontologist, 27*(2): 156–163.

Winn, S., & Kessler, S. (1974). Community mental health centers and the nursing home patient. *The Gerontologist, 14*(4): 345–348.

Winston, C. T. (1981). Nonprofessional employee turnover in nursing homes. *Nursing Homes, 30*: 37–41.

York, J., & Calsyn, R. J. (1977). Family involvement in nursing homes. *The Gerontologist, 17*(6): 500–505.

Zimmerman, S. L. (1986). Adult day care: Correlates of its coping effects for families of an elderly disabled member. *Family Relations, 35*(2): 305–311.

CHAPTER **16**

MINORITIES

Hiroji Kubota/Magnum

INTRODUCTION

In Chapter 4, "Research and Theory in Gerontology," we pointed out that one of the current problems in gerontology is that relatively little information exists on minority aged. In this chapter we will examine minority aging. The reader should be aware that research is limited and that there are far more questions than answers. There are still some minority groups where there is very little material available on aged members.

Early gerontologists generally perceived the aged as a homogeneous group. Most of the studies conducted prior to the early 1950s indicated that older persons were a homogeneous group with common needs (see Bell, 1976). During this time most studies in gerontology did not distinguish their participants by race or ethnic group, thus ignoring the possibility that there might be differences in areas such as income, health, or life expectancy. In fact, in most research studies minority status was generally ignored as an independent variable. The concept of the homogeneity of older persons did not change until the early 1950s. At this time, many of the factors that make the aged a heterogeneous population were recognized. However, even with this recognition little research appeared on minority aged until the mid-1960s.

A recent issue of the *Journal of Gerontology* addressed the issue of the lack of research and noted the concerns and directions of the different sections (Anderson, 1989; Gibson, 1989; Jackson, 1989; Smith & Adelman, 1989). Anderson (1989) in the Medical Sciences section noted that a review of the major geriatrics and gerontology journals from the last 10 years had produced only nineteen articles on biomedical research and minority groups. He went on to note the large number of questions in this area, such as why there are life expectancy differences, how minority differences influence the aging process, and why there are differences in rates of diseases? It was noted that further research would be needed to answer some very basic questions.

Progress, although slow, is being made in this area. For example, in response to the need for more and better research on minority aging the Gerontological Society of America has created a task force on minority issues.

Research in this area has probably been slow to develop for five reasons. First, although many gerontologists recognize the lack of information in the area of minority aged, they also realize that other areas in gerontology are equally devoid of information. It appears that most gerontologists are more interested in these other areas. Second, many gerontologists may be interested in studying the minority aged, but they find that if they are not of the same ethnic or racial group that they want to study, that the aged members of these groups are suspicious of them. For example, one study noted that white researchers trying to complete studies on a racial minority group often found that as soon as they started asking questions, it was assumed that they were from the police department (Ransford, 1976) or from the welfare department. Most refused to answer questions. Moreover, in studying the black aged, it has been found that black researchers obtained very different answers to the same questions that white researchers asked (Ransford, 1976). Third, language may also be a problem for the gerontologist who wants to study the minority aged. For example, many Hispanics, as well as recent immigrants from countries such as Vietnam, have a limited understanding of English. Furthermore, many aged Native Americans speak their tribal language. Fourth, some researchers may want to study the minority aged but live a considerable distance from the group they want to study. For example, Native Americans are not represented randomly throughout the population but tend to be concentrated in certain rural areas. Thus, although a researcher may have an interest in studying the older persons in a certain minority group, that group may be so far removed geographically that the research becomes difficult to conduct. Fifth, until there are more gerontologists who are members of ethnic and racial minority groups more research is not likely to appear.

This chapter will examine older persons in several minority groups. Some material has also been "integrated" into other chapters. Material is often scanty, several years old, and based on small nonrandom samples. Additionally, studies are frequently conducted on large minority groups that needed to be broken down into separate groups. For example, Native Americans are not one group, but consist of different tribes with very different languages, customs, and beliefs. Studies on Hispanics could be separated into country of origin (e.g., Cuba, Mexico, Puerto Rico etc.). Even whites could be separated by ethnicity or by area of origin (e.g., western Europe, eastern Europe) (see Holzberg, 1982a, 1982b; Markides, 1982). The major point is that more research is needed. This chapter will be separated into two sections. In the first section some definitions will be provided. In the second several minority groups will be examined.

DEFINITION OF TERMS

Moore (1971b) has pointed out that in American society, minority groups are distinct from the majority group in several ways. Each minority group has a unique history, has suffered from discrimination and a stereotyped image, has developed a subculture, has evolved certain characteristics within that subculture to help it cope with the larger culture, and has been in a state of constant change.

Minority groups can be conceptualized as groups with limited access to power and certain opportunities in society. Moreover, because of their unique language, or cultural and physical characteristics, minority individuals stand out from the rest of society and collectively receive unequal treatment from those in higher and more powerful positions. Because of their exclusion from full participation in society, minority group members have generally developed an image of themselves and of their group as the targets of collective discrimination (Wirth, 1945).

It should be realized that in some instances a group may form a numerical majority and yet still be considered a minority. For example, in certain countries a group may represent a numerical majority, yet sociologically be considered a minority because it lacks access to power and to certain opportunities within the society. A minority can be formed on the basis of such criteria as "race," ethnicity, religion, or age (see Rose, 1965; Streib, 1965). In a sociological sense, to belong to a minority means that individuals must possess certain unique physical or social characteristics to which the society attaches values or beliefs.

As you read this chapter it is important to keep several things in mind. First, in examining the differences between whites and minority group members, you should remember that many of the differences, in areas such as life expectancy and health, may result more from differences in social class, income, or level of education than from racial or ethnic differences. Kalish (1971) has pointed out that even geographical differences may be important. Second, remember that although a group is classified as a minority, this fact does not necessarily imply that the individuals are homogeneous. For example, a study of aged Native Americans would have to take into account different tribes, cultures, values, and languages. In a study of Hispanics, country of origin would be important. Third, remember (again!) that information in this area is sparse, and that some of it is of questionable value because of the methods used or because the information is old.

One term that needs to be defined is that of "jeopardy." This term has been used to refer to individuals in contemporary society who experience discrimination and prejudice from the society at large because of traits or characteristics they possess. Because of the discrimination and prejudice to which minority group members are subjected, they are in jeopardy in areas such as physical and mental health, and employment opportunities. In fact, some of these individuals may find that their lives are in jeopardy because of the characteristics or traits that they possess. The term "double jeopardy" is applied to individuals who hold two characteristics or traits that the society at large finds undesirable such as advanced age and membership in a minority group. An example of triple jeopardy would be individuals who are old, poor, and members of a minority group. Quadruple jeopardy would refer to someone who was old, poor, a minority-group member, and female.

Hypothetically, an individual who is characterized by double jeopardy is "better off" than one who is characterized by quadruple jeopardy since the second is more likely to encounter discrimination and will often find that the discrimination is more intense because of the combination of characteristics and traits. Research in this area has produced mixed results. Some believe that with increasing age the differences between minority groups and whites increase in areas such as income and health. Others believe that increasing age reduces the differences between the minority groups and whites. Studies support both positions.

The research results are mixed because the definitions in this area vary. Originally the concept of double jeopardy was created to apply to aged blacks. Thus, the original definition had two characteristics, race and a lifetime of prejudice and discrimination. The first part of the definition, race, has been modified by some researchers to include other races, such as Chinese-Americans. Some have modified the definition to include ethnic groups, including white Hispanics. Others have modified the definition so that the second characteristic of lifelong prejudice and discrimination was absent. This allowed the definition to apply to the aged in minority groups such as recent Vietnamese immigrants to the United States. In their country of origin they were not subjected to prejudice and discrimination. However, as recent immigrants they are subjected to prejudice and discrimination. The concept of double or multiple jeopardy is important, and could have important consequences on social policy. However, as it currently exists, it has too many problems to be of much value.

MINORITY GROUP AGED

This section will examine the aged in several different minority groups. Aged women will be considered first. Then the "racial" and ethnic groups will be taken in order of their presence or arrival in this country. Thus, we will examine Native Americans, Hispanics, blacks, and Asian and Pacific Island Americans.

Women

It has been noted that although the roles of women, and the percentage of the life cycle spent in certain roles, have changed in the twentieth century, the overall status of women has changed relatively little (O'Rand, 1987). For example, women have experienced changes in life expectancy, fertility, participation in the labor force, and education, but overall they are still subject to considerable prejudice and discrimination, which results in high levels of poverty. Women have often been characterized as a minority group in contemporary American society since they have generally been excluded from full participation in the society, have been accorded an inferior position in society, and have lacked access to power.

According to Trager (1974) aged women in contemporary American society are at a disadvantage to aged men since aged women are often considered obsolete in terms of their roles as sex objects, workers, and childbearers. Until recently older women represented an invisible minority in America society. It was not until the mid-1970s that much research started to take place on them. In part, the increasing interest in aged women was generated by the 1973 conference, "Women: Life Span Challenges," held at the University of Michigan. Just prior to this conference Lewis and Butler (1972) pointed out that the women's movement had largely ignored older women by focusing on issues such as day care, abortion, and education—all issues that had little concern for most older women. Lewis and Butler (1972) also pointed out that the then newly formed Women's Political Caucus did not have any aged women on its policy council.

Other changes that have helped to focus attention on aged women were that the Baltimore longitudinal studies (see Chapter 4) included women for the first time in the 1970s, the Older Women's Caucus held a meeting at the 1975 annual meeting of the Gerontological Society of America, and in 1981 there was a special committee on older women at the White House Conference on Aging. One of the consequences is a new journal called the *Journal of Women and Aging*.

Many writers have noted that aging in contemporary American society is more difficult for women than for men. The reasoning here is that women have been subjected to economic discrimination, which precluded them from many employment opportunities and gave them a low status in society. Also, the concept of "attractiveness" seems to be more restrictive and narrow for women than men. For example, although the actor Cary Grant was capable of playing leading roles from the early 1930s until the mid-1960s, most of his early female costars had been relegated to matronly roles, B-grade movies, or forced retirement.

It has been suggested that in part the negative image of aged women that many individuals hold begins to form in early childhood and is reinforced by cultural stereotypes. The process starts with the negative way in which aged women are portrayed in fairy tales, where they are often depicted as witches and hags (Lewis & Butler, 1972). A study by Angello (1977) of children's books found that only about 16 percent contained older characters and that the characters were primarily male. Angello (1977a) concluded that aged females, when they were presented, were less active and verbal than aged males, but more likely to be tired, sick, or poor. This section will examine aged women as a minority group. Specifically, we will examine the following characteristics: demographic, health, housing, economic, and family.

Demographic Characteristics   In 1988 there were 30.4 million individuals 65+ years of age in the United States. Of that number 18.0 million were female, 12.4 million were male. This means that about 60 percent of the aged population is female. Aged females represent 14.3 percent of the total female population (for aged males the figure is 10.3 percent).

Health Characteristics   One indirect indicator of health is life expectancy. Women live longer than men. In 1988 the expectations of life were as presented in Table 16-1. As can be seen, women live longer than men. This is true for white and black women. As will be noted in Chapter 17, "Dying and Death," this is a result of life-style and genetics. Although women live longer it has been reported that they have more health problems. In Chapter 6, it was noted that many of the acute and chronic conditions they have are less life threatening than the conditions of males (see Verbrugge, 1984).

Housing Characteristics   Aged women are much more likely to live alone than are aged men. In 1988, 40.6 percent of aged women lived alone; the figure for aged males was 16.2 (U.S. Bureau of the Census, 1990). In large part the explanation is that older women are more likely to be widowed than are older men.

Economic Characteristics   It is well known that women are discriminated against economically in contemporary American society. Women, both in the past and present, have often been relegated to work that is "less desirable," at lower pay, with limited

TABLE 16-1
EXPECTATIONS OF LIFE IN YEARS
AT BIRTH

	Male	Female
White	72.1	78.9
Black	65.1	73.8

Source: U.S. Bureau of the Census, 1990.

opportunities for advancement, and frequently without the pensions and other benefits provided male workers. This has been called "occupational segregation," which can be demonstrated by the fact that 80 percent of women in the work force are in 20 of the 420 jobs listed by the Department of Labor (see Minkler & Stone, 1985). Although illegal to discriminate on the basis of sex or age, it is well known that this is both a sexist and ageist society, and that women in the work force, especially aged women, suffer from prejudice and discrimination.

This section will examine two aspects of the economic characteristics of aged women. The first will examine indicators of economic status and the second, factors that determine economic status. In the first part we will examine five indicators of the economic status of aged women.

First, the median income of aged year-round full-time workers in 1988 was $18,545 for females; for males the figure was $27,342 (U.S. Bureau of the Census, 1990). We can see a significant difference in income. Part of this difference may be explained by the fact that males have traditionally had more education, experience, and time on the job than women who were more likely to have had childrearing interfere with both education and continued employment. However, part of the difference is also explained by the fact that women are often forced to accept lower paying jobs with fewer advancement opportunities.

Second, the average social security payment is less for women than for men. The difference is partly explained by the fact that men have worked longer in the social security system than women and have retired at higher salaries. However, part of the explanation is that in the past the social security system chose not to cover many occupations traditionally held by employed women.

Third, women are less likely to have private pensions. Additionally, the average benefits paid to women are less than for men. Currently, 47 percent of males and 37 percent of females in the work force are covered by private pensions. Males are more likely to have worked in areas where pensions were available. They were also more likely to have worked more years at higher salaries and thus acquired higher benefits. Older women were more likely to be employed in jobs not covered by pension benefits, or to have worked part-time which reduced their likelihood of having a pension, or to have had a pattern of having worked intermittently, with time off for childrearing. The intermittent work pattern often meant that the women did not work long enough to acquire pension benefits (see Tracy & Ward, 1986).

Fourth, aged females are less likely to be employed than aged men. Currently about 7.9 percent of aged females and 16.5 percent of aged males are employed (U.S. Bureau of the Census, 1990). Part of the difference is explained by the fact that traditionally, many women have not gone into the work force and do not desire to do so after age 65. However, it is also partly explained by the fact that many women want to work but are prevented from doing so by ageism and sexism.

Fifth, aged females are more likely to live below the poverty line than aged males. For those living in a family household 6.1 percent of males and 13.0 percent of females live below the poverty line. For those living with unrelated individuals, 19.6 percent of males and 26.8 percent of females live below the poverty line. Poverty is not equally distributed among older persons. While about 6.0 percent of older males who live in family households are below the poverty line the figure for females is 13.7 percent (U.S. Bureau of the Census, 1990). Because of the higher figure for females, gerontologists now discuss the "feminization of poverty and older women" (Minkler & Stone, 1985; see Hess, 1986; Holden et al., 1986; Warlick, 1985). The premise is that women enter old age at an economic disadvantage and then as a result of widowhood, higher health costs, longer life expectancy, and pension inequities, the economic discrepancy between males and females widens.

There are a number of factors that contribute to the economic status of older women. First, many older women have a history of economic dependency. That is, they were less likely to work than succeeding generations and were dependent on the income of a spouse. With widowhood they often have to rely on inadequate survivor's benefits. Second, women have a longer life expectancy which increases health care costs and increases the likelihood of exhausting income and savings.

Third, widowhood is associated with economic problems for women. There are probably several reasons for this, the first being unfamiliarity with financial matters. Although studies have reported that older widowed women were not as naive about financial matters as previously believed, many, especially if financial matters were not discussed prior to widowhood and if they were not in the work force, were inexperienced in this area which may have contributed to their financial problems (Morgan, 1986). Another factor is that many pension plans of deceased husbands did not have survivor benefits or the male workers dropped the survivor benefits option for a larger pension while they were living. Yet another factor is that social security survivor benefits are only about 66 percent of a couple's benefits even though government reports indicate that surviving spouses need about 80 percent of the predeath benefit to live the same life-style (Warlick, 1985). It should be noted that although the percentage of older males living in poverty is lower than older females, widowhood has also been found to have a negative impact on the financial status of older males (Zick & Smith, 1986).

Fourth, many women who were in the work force often worked intermittently and were in positions that had low salaries, which did not generate high social security benefits or offer pension benefits. The fifth, and last, factor contributing to the feminization of poverty is social policy. In an excellent article Warlick (1985) noted that the *major* factor responsible for the feminization of poverty in old age is the treatment of older women in American society. The financial problems of older women are well documented; the decision to not address these problems has been a conscious and intentional policy decision. An example can be seen in the President's National Commission of Social Security Reform which, although recognizing the inequality to older women, said that it did not have the time to explore the problem (see Beattie, 1983; Binstock, 1986; Rodeheaver, 1987).

One response widowed women can make to poverty is to enter the work force. It has been reported that about 24 percent of nonworking recently widowed older women do search for and eventually find work. Those looking for work tend to be younger and have had a significant decline in their standard of living (Morgan, 1984). One major barrier to many women seeking work is discrimination. As Hess (1986) pointed out, although illegal, antidiscrimination policies are often not enforced for older women. In fact, violations are often ignored, and will continue to be ignored until there is a national commitment to resolve the economic problems of women (Hess, 1986). Warlick (1985) has echoed some of the same concern, and noted that the trend has been to place the blame for women's poverty on factors such as widowhood. She has eloquently, and correctly, replied that it is not widowhood that causes poverty, but the society's treatment of widowhood.

Some attempts have been made to "defeminize" poverty. For example, in 1972 there were changes in social security benefits that awarded a higher benefit to a surviving spouse. Additionally, pension reforms have made it mandatory that benefits be paid to a surviving spouse (see Holden, 1988).

Family Characteristics Aged women are much less likely to be married than aged men; 78 percent of aged males and 42 percent of aged females are married. Aged women are less likely to get remarried. At the family level women are the most likely to be caregivers to parents and spouse.

Native Americans

There is a great deal of literature on the history of Native Americans. However, less research exists on Native Americans in contemporary American society, and even less on aged Native Americans. It should be mentioned that Native Americans are a very diverse group, composing more than 400 tribes and 200 languages (National Indian Council on Aging, 1984).

Native Americans are unlike most other ethnic and racial groups in the United States since they have been physically and culturally isolated on reservations, thus decreasing their assimilation into mainstream society. This segregation, coupled with the small number of older Native Americans, makes them a low visibility group. Furthermore, Native Americans were denied full citizenship until 1924. Even after 1924, many states denied them access to voting and to white schools. Native Americans are also unique in that the federal government, in the form of the Bureau of Indian Affairs (BIA), has emerged as their "protector" and legal guardian. This bureaucracy designed to "protect" Native Americans has reached an enormous size, having one bureaucrat for every eighteen Native Americans (Cahn, 1969).

Demographic Characteristics Estimates of the size of the Native American population vary because there is no set of criteria for what constitutes a Native American. For example, is someone a Native American if he or she is one-half, one-fourth, or one-eighth Native American? Currently different organizations have different standards for determining whether an individual is a Native American. The federal government has a definition for eligibility for federal programs. Some states have different definitions for eligibility for state programs. Tribes can have definitions that differ from both federal and state definitions. The Administration on Aging (AOA) definition of Indian is someone who is a member of an Indian tribe. The Older Americans Act (OAA) also allows tribes to define "elderly." Traditionally it has been 60 years of age. However, in 1981 the OAA was amended so that tribes could define elderly; some now define it as 50 or 55 years of age.

In the last few decades the number of Native Americans has increased dramatically. One reason for the increase is that the birth rate has remained high (e.g., about 28 per 1000 in comparison to the total birth rate of 15.9) while the infant death rate has been lowered largely because of improvement in medical care and living standards. The number of Native Americans has also increased because of better reporting. In the past many Native Americans were not included in the census figures. In 1960 the census figures reported 523,591 Native Americans; by 1970 the figure was 792,730; and by 1988 it had increased to 1,699,000 (U.S. Bureau of the Census, 1970, 1977, 1990). Native Americans comprise about 0.6 percent of the total population (U.S. Department of Health and Human Services, 1985). Table 16-2 has a breakdown by age group for Native Americans, as well as the comparison percentages for the total population. As can be seen, Native Americans are overrepresented in the younger age categories, and underrepresented in the aged categories. Where 12.3 percent of the total population is 65+ years of age, it is 5.2 percent for Native Americans. The states with the largest numbers of Native Americans are California, Oklahoma, Arizona, New Mexico, North Carolina, Washington, South Dakota, Texas, and New York (U.S. Department of Health and Human Services, 1985). About 60 percent of Native Americans live on or near reservations, which is a significant decline from the past. Poverty and few economic opportunities have created a migration of primarily young Native Americans to urban areas.

Health Characteristics   Life expectancy for Native Americans is from 8 to 20 years shorter than for whites (Curley, 1987; National Tribal Chairman's Association, 1976; Seccombe, 1989). In 1979 the death rate for Native Americans was 770.2 per 100,000; the same rate for the total population in 1979 was 588.8 (U.S. Department of Health and Human Services, 1985). The major causes of death and disability

TABLE 16-2
PERCENTAGE OF NATIVE AMERICANS BY AGE GROUP

Age	Percentage Native American	Percentage Total population
<5	10.1	7.5
5–14	20.8	14.0
15–24	22.4	15.3
25–34	16.9	17.8
35–44	11.1	14.4
45–64	13.4	18.6
65–74	3.4	7.3
75+	1.8	5.1

Source: U.S. Bureau of the Census, 1990.

among Native Americans are very different from the society in general. For example, the death and disability rates for Native Americans from accidents, homicide, pneumonia and influenza, diabetes mellitus, suicide, and tuberculosis are much higher than for the general population. Health, in terms of functional ability, indicates that many Native Americans age "rapidly." For example, Curley (1987) noted studies reporting that by age 45 Native Americans have the functional ability of whites who are 65. Much of the difference is related to socioeconomic status and education, not race or ethnicity (Seccombe, 1989).

As we saw above, only 5.2 percent of Native Americans are 65+ years of age, less than half the percentage figure for whites. As with whites, older Native American women generally outnumber older Native American men. Life expectancy for most Native Americans is shorter because of decades of inadequate medical care, poor nutrition, and poverty, all of which tend to bring about cumulative damage. Many Native Americans prefer traditional health methods rather than those provided by the Indian Health Service (IHS). Often it is difficult and expensive to travel to IHS centers, and some have found that some IHS staff members are insensitive to their needs.

Housing Characteristics Housing is another area in which Native Americans suffer. In fact, the housing of most aged Native Americans is so substandard that the National Indian Conference on Aging named housing as the number one priority for aged Native Americans. The conference pointed out that individuals cannot find "peace of mind" in either an alien environment or in one that is substandard.

Most aged Native Americans live on reservations where housing is often inadequate and unsanitary. Although the BIA has appropriated funds for better housing, the maintenance costs of these housing units are often too high for aged Native Americans. A report by the U.S. Senate (1971) noted that often housing programs funded by the BIA did not take into consideration the needs or wishes of aged Native Americans in design, location, or construction. Thus, often new housing facilities created frustrations and added to already high economic liabilities. Furthermore, many aged Native Americans have strong ties to their traditional homes. Even though new homes may have many features that the older homes lack, many of the elderly still prefer to stay in their traditional homes or to have them renovated.

Another problem in housing for aged Native Americans is the lack of nursing homes that can effectively meet their needs. Nursing home admission can often produce a great deal of stress for aged Native Americans because there are very few homes for Native Americans, because admission often means being relocated a substantial distance from family and friends, because of language and cultural differences, and because of prejudice.

This is becoming an especially relevant issue since it is estimated that 13 percent of aged Native Americans are in nursing homes, in comparison to 5 percent of the total aged population. Currently the Indian Health Service has been reluctant to become involved in long-term care. Nonetheless, some changes in this area are being seen. For example, in 1969 the first Native American nursing home was built. Six more were built in the 1970s, and two more in the 1980s. These homes are capable of holding 435 residents. The majority of the staff in these homes are Native Americans (Seccombe, 1989). The residents in these homes tend to have a different profile from those in nursing homes in general. For example, males tend to outnumber females in Native American nursing homes, where in nursing homes in general we see the reverse. In large part this is because of the high incident of crippling accidents and alcohol-related impairments, which tend to affect Native American males more than females (Manson, 1989).

Economic Characteristics   Native Americans are one of the most economically deprived minorities in contemporary American society. Older Native Americans are especially vulnerable since few have earned social security or private pension benefits. The inadequate financial situation of aged Native Americans is intensified by the fact that the BIA has made little effort to inform them of the social services benefits to which they are entitled (U.S. Senate, 1971; National Tribal Chairman's Association, 1976). Also, many aged Native Americans do not know about programs or services for which they are eligible because they are physically isolated from the agencies that would dispense this information. Many of them make little use of even those services of which they are aware, because they live many miles away from the services and have no way of reaching them (Murdock & Schwartz, 1978). Also many do not use formal services because of the insensitivity of the bureaucrats (Dukepoo, 1980).

Many older Native Americans are concentrated on reservations because they have little economic success elsewhere. Most of the older Native Americans who have left their reservations have found that their low levels of education, few job skills, and susceptibility to discrimination make employment difficult or impossible to obtain on the outside (Benedict, 1972). Thus, most have returned to the reservation (Graves & Van Arsdale, 1966; Sorkin, 1969). Unfortunately, there are few jobs on or near most reservations and the unemployment rates reach 80 percent on some (Cahn, 1969). It is exceptionally difficult for most aged Native Americans to find work on reservations since traditionally jobs first go to the young. To help alleviate the high unemployment among aged Native Americans, it has been recommended that the federal government create jobs on reservations. Aged Native Americans could serve in such capacities as teachers of Indian dance, language, history, and customs. These types of jobs could fill two of their needs. First, the jobs could fill the need for more income, and second, they could fill the need to remain Native American and to disseminate the Native American way of life to their children and grandchildren (see Dukepoo, 1980; National Tribal Chairman's Association, 1976). Native Americans living in urban areas have been found to have higher incomes than those living in rural areas; however, the higher costs of living associated with urban areas often negate the income differences (Dukepoo, 1980).

Family Characteristics   Discrimination, prejudice, and physical isolation on reservations have generally created strong family bonds by which the family offers more support than found in society in general. Low incomes have forced extended families to pool resources. Often older persons, who might have some funds from social service agencies, can be a major source of financial support for a family. Also, in Native American societies there is generally more respect for the aged since there is often less emphasis on change (see Rogers & Gallion, 1978).

Other Characteristics Recreation is another limitation of the aged Native Americans. Few reservations have senior centers. Furthermore, senior centers that are close to reservations are seldom used. The use of senior center facilities in nearby communities is often hampered by the fact that the road systems around reservations are inadequate, or that the aged are widely scattered and do not have access to transportation. Prejudice is also a factor. Very often the whites in senior centers do not welcome aged Native American members.

Recreation was a major concern of the National Indian Conference on Aging. The participants at the conference felt that there was a need for a "happiness factor" for aged Native Americans. A paper presented at the conference pointed out that aged Native Americans are often idle and isolated from the rest of their society. The conference felt that these Americans should be able to share their knowledge and experience with others. Another problem is the low level of education which is around the eighth grade; the consequences are that about 50 percent of older Native Americans have difficulty reading English (Dukepoo, 1980). In 1976 the National Indian Council on Aging (NICOA) was created as an advocate for aged Native Americans. It has collected information and published several reports which have helped to direct attention and resources to aged Native Americans.

Hispanics

The term Hispanics refers to individuals, of any race, who have origins in a Spanish-speaking country. Obviously, the number of cultures that can be represented is enormous. Hispanics are one of the fastest growing minorities in the United States. They currently compose about 6.4 percent of the total population. It is estimated that by the year 2000 they will be larger than the black population (Markides, 1987), which currently composes 11.4 percent of the total U.S. population.

Generalizations about Hispanics would be that they are a young population, the median age is 25.8 in comparison to 33.3 for whites. The birth rate of Hispanics is higher than that of whites. The percentage of older persons is lower, about 5 percent, compared to 12.4 percent for whites. They are also more likely to be in poverty: 23.7 percent compared to 7.9 percent for whites (U.S. Bureau of the Census, 1990).

As noted above, Hispanics are not one homogeneous group, but several. Often the Hispanic population is separated into country of origin, and some brief statistics will show the tremendous differences. Currently Mexican-Americans represent about 60 percent of the Hispanic population in the United States, and tend to be concentrated in the American southwest. The second largest Hispanic minority is Puerto Ricans (14 percent), who are concentrated in the northeast, especially New York City. Cubans represent the third largest Hispanic group (about 6 percent), and are concentrated primarily in southern Florida. The remainder is composed of those from Central or

South America (about 7 percent), and "other" (13 percent) (U.S. Bureau of the Census, 1990). Although Hispanics are often treated as one group, they are very different in many ways. The basis for this ethnic category, origin in a Spanish-speaking country, is at best a weak one and few generalizations can be made about Hispanics at a whole. [Bastida (1987) would disagree and claim that similarities are more common than differences.]

The heterogeneity of Hispanics can be seen first by examining the birth rate. For Mexican-Americans it is 26.6, for Puerto Ricans it is 20.3, and for Cubans it is 9.6. As can be seen, it is substantially higher for Mexican-Americans. If we examine births to unmarried females we will also see tremendous differences. The births per 1000 unmarried females for Mexican-Americans is 54.5; for Puerto Ricans it is 74.5; for Cubans it is 9.3. Again, we can see large differences, which reflect different values and age structures. We can also examine some health characteristics for those 65+ years of age. The number of acute conditions per 100 persons per year for Mexican-Americans, Puerto Ricans, and Cubans are: 143, 100, 140. The number of days of restricted activity for those 65+ years of age for Mexican-Americans, Puerto Ricans, and Cubans are: 50.8, 39.1, and 33.3. The last example is the rate of Mexican-Americans, Puerto Ricans, and Cubans 65+ with an activity limitation due to a chronic condition: 143, 100, 140. One last area we can examine is education. Table 16-3 has the percent of individuals 65+ years of age who have less than 12 years of education and who have 4 or more years of college (U.S. Department of Health and Human Services, 1985).

The Mexican-Americans are hardly one homogeneous group. Some have ties in the United States that date back to when the American southwest was controlled by Spain. They have generally been integrated into the mainstream of American society. Others are recent illegal immigrants into the United States, many of whom speak only Spanish. Most of the material that exists has been conducted on Mexican-Americans. For this reason, the remainder of this subsection will look at Mexican-Americans.

Demographic Characteristics   After blacks, the Mexican-Americans are the second largest minority group in contemporary American society. There are currently about 12,110,000 Mexican-Americans in the United States (U.S. Bureau of the Census,

TABLE 16-3
EDUCATIONAL LEVEL BY MINORITY GROUP: 1988

	<12 years %	College + %
White	22.3	20.9
Black	36.7	11.3
Hispanic	49.0	10.0
Mexican	55.4	7.1
Puerto Rican	49.2	9.6
Cuban	39.5	17.2

Source: U.S. Bureau of the Census, 1990.

1990). In 1977 the median age for Mexican-Americans was about 18.8 years, about 12 years younger than the median age for the total population, which was 32.3 in 1977. Once again, the lower median age is due to a higher birth rate, and a shorter life expectancy. Only about 3.9 percent of Mexican-Americans are over 65 years of age (U.S. Bureau of the Census, 1990). Unlike the demographic profile of whites, the number of Mexican-American men and women remains fairly constant throughout life. In old age, the number of men is slightly higher than the number of women. This probably reflects a higher immigration rate (both legal and illegal) of males.

Health Characteristics   For a number of reasons, Mexican-Americans age faster than whites. Sanchez (1973) claims that a 48-year-old Mexican-American is physically similar to a 65-year-old white. Thus, the life expectancy of Mexican-Americans is shorter than for whites. Not only do Mexican-Americans tend to have a shorter life expectancy than whites but they also have poorer health. Even when the variables of socioeconomic status, gender, and income are controlled, aged Mexican-Americans rate their health as poorer than that of whites or blacks. The poor health and shorter life expectancy of Mexican-Americans stem from several factors. One factor is an inadequate income that leads to poor nutrition and unsanitary and overcrowded housing conditions. Also, there are relatively few Spanish-speaking physicians, thus increasing communication problems between physicians and patients.

Housing Characteristics   The housing of aged Mexican-Americans is less adequate than that of aged whites (Carp, 1968). However, one study found that the vast majority of aged Mexican-Americans did not want to move into ''better'' housing units that had been built for them by the federal government. Most aged Mexican-Americans have strong community ties, pride in home ownership, and close relationships with other family members who live nearby (Carp, 1969). The study also found that many aged Mexican-Americans did not wish to move into housing units that had not been designed with their needs and culture in mind. Many did not want to live in areas where whites lived, since they found the white life-style ''abhorrent.'' Many also feared that in a white-dominated housing unit they would be subjected to prejudice and discrimination.

Thus, although the housing of many aged Mexican-Americans is inadequate by government standards, many aged Mexican-Americans do not seem to mind. They appear to be comfortable in their homes and in their communities. A study on the underutilization of nursing homes by elderly Mexican-Americans supports the above conclusion. The study found that increases in the incomes of aged Mexican-Americans or of their adult children would result in less usage of nursing homes. Thus, the underutilization of nursing homes by aged Mexican-Americans is due primarily to their lower life expectancy and their desire to stay in the community (Eribes & Bradley-Rawls, 1978).

Economic Characteristics   About 28.3 percent of aged Mexican-Americans live in poverty (U.S. Bureau of the Census, 1990). The poverty of aged Mexican-Americans stems from several sources. First, only 59 percent of aged Mexican-Americans receive social security benefits because so many of them worked at jobs not covered by social security. Second, most have been employed at low-paying jobs and have not been able to save very much money for old age. Most of the men have worked in unskilled or semiskilled occupations and most of the women have been in domestic service (Carp, 1968; Moore, 1971a). Third, most aged Mexican-Americans cannot move up occupationally because of linguistic and educational limitations. Spanish is the primary language for many aged Mexican-Americans. Fourth, many aged Mexican-Americans did not want to advance occupationally because of their lack of United States citizenship. To advance would have increased their visibility and hence their risk of being deported. In fact, in the 1960s and 1970s studies indicated that about one-third of aged Mexican-Americans were not United States citizens (Carp, 1968; Sanchez, 1973).

Income declines for aged Mexican-Americans are much greater than for aged whites. A study by Dowd and Bengtson (1978) found that between the ages of 45 and 75 the incomes of Mexican-Americans declined 62 percent. For whites the figure was 36 percent. Even when the variables of socioeconomic status, gender, and health were held constant these differences were still found to exist.

Although future aged Mexican-Americans will probably have a better economic outlook than the current aged (Torres-Gil, 1986), they are still expected to have economic problems (Markides & Levin, 1987). Basically, most Mexican-Americans have moved to urban areas, which have traditionally been industrial areas that allowed limited upward mobility. However, urban areas are increasingly changing and becoming more areas for the distribution of information rather than production. This relegates Mexican-Americans to the lower positions in urban society since their levels of education have not kept pace with whites. Additionally, there are language barriers that need to be overcome. Many Mexican-Americans have Spanish as their sole or dominant language. This also will prevent increases in economic success. The last barrier is discrimination. It has been noted that civil rights legislation has been designed and been more beneficial for blacks than Hispanics (Torres-Gil, 1986).

Family Characteristics In the past there was an extended family among Mexican-Americans. In the extended family the aged were honored and cared for by a wide variety of relatives. Old age was seen as a time of retirement and rest, and as a time when the aged would be sought out for their wisdom and knowledge. In essence, old age for Mexican-Americans was a very comfortable time. The extended family took care of the aged individuals' physical needs, as well as their social and psychological needs (Leonard, 1967). Recent studies on the Mexican-American family are contradictory. Some studies have indicated that the extended family is still in operation while others have indicated that a change has occurred. The changes that have been noted are probably reflective of the fact that the Mexican-American population is heterogeneous and that in some parts of the American southwest different patterns have emerged. Both kinds of studies will be presented.

Several studies have reported that the Mexican-American aged live in an environment in which they receive a great deal of support and warmth from their family (Carp, 1968, 1970; Dowd & Bengtson, 1978; Moore, 1971a). For example, Carp (1970) found that the extended family was intact because of poverty and discrimination.

Poverty forced family members to rely on one another for goods and services. It was cheaper for individuals to live together in one household, rather than separately in different households. Discrimination also separated Mexican-Americans from the white community and made them dependent on one another. In this environment, the aged Mexican-Americans had many meaningful roles for which their families gave them both support and prestige. In fact, adult children often did not want their aged parents to move into new government housing because this would reduce the amount of contact and alter the close affectionate bonds between them (see Carp, 1968). Not only were these relationships close, but the relationships between aged Mexican-Americans and their grandchildren were also very close (Carp, 1968).

Studies have also indicated that the marriages of aged Mexican-Americans are more likely to remain intact than those of whites. Furthermore, aged Mexican-Americans are less likely to be living alone than are aged whites. The reasons are that the extended family often takes care of them, life expectancies of men and women are about the same, and they have more adult children to look after them than aged whites (Carp, 1968).

As we said above, not all of the recent studies indicate such a warm, supportive, extended family. Moore (1971a) claimed that writing on the Mexican-American family was highly romanticized; it has been noted that this could be detrimental in that social services would not be extended. A study by Crouch (1972) indicated that the family structure of Mexican-Americans has been changing. For example, Crouch found that 55 percent of the aged Mexican-Americans whom he studied perceived old as being undesirable. Only 13 percent felt that old age was a good time of life. These percentages do not coincide with the figures that researchers would expect if the supportive family system were in operation. In contrast to the above studies, Crouch found that the economic realities of membership in the lower class had truncated the obligations of the extended family to the aged. The majority of aged Mexican-Americans did not expect to receive any support from their families. When asked about other supportive organizations, 81 percent believed that the church did not have any special activities for them. Furthermore, many of them were not aware of governmental programs that might be supportive. Other researchers have also noted that a close relationship between young and old Mexican-Americans does not exist. Rather, these researchers have concluded that they live worlds apart and that they seldom interact.

In contrast, a more recent study (Markides et al., 1986) has reported that strong family networks of help and assistance exist. They concluded that the family is still a major source of support for all age groups and that contact and affection with grandchildren was a source of psychological well-being (see Markides & Krause, 1985).

Blacks

More has been written on aged blacks than on the aged in other minority groups. This is probably because interest and research started earlier than on the other groups discussed so far. For example, in 1971 the National Caucus on the Black Aged was formed (currently the National Center and Caucus of the Black Aged). Also, there was a session at the 1971 White House Conference on Aging on aged blacks. However, research on them is still limited (Jackson, 1987; Register, 1981). The one salient factor that has been noted is that aged blacks, like the other groups examined so far, are not a homogeneous group. Just as variables such as different life experiences, levels of income, levels of education, and social class have made the aged in other minority groups different, the same factors have operated among aged blacks to create a heterogeneous population.

Demographic Characteristics Blacks compose the largest ''racial'' minority in the United States. In 1988 there were 30,202,000 blacks in the United States. This figure represented 12.2 percent of the total population. Aged blacks compose about 5 percent of the total population 65+ years of age, and 8.3 percent of the total black population (U.S. Bureau of the Census, 1990).

The composition of the black population is shown in Table 16-4, which has the percentage in each age category. For comparison purposes, the percentage for the total population is also presented. As can be seen in two areas, blacks are a ''younger'' population than the total population. First, 27.2 percent of the total black population is under 15 years of age in comparison to 21.5 percent for the total population. Second, in 1988 the median age of blacks was 27.5, while for the total population the figure was 32.3. The difference in median age is due to the fact that blacks have a higher birth rate and a shorter life expectancy than whites. For example, in 1988 the birth rate (per 1000 population) of blacks was 21.6 while for whites the figure is 14.5. In terms of life expectancy the figures are 72.1 years for white males and 65.1 years for black males, and 78.9 years for white females and 73.8 years for black females.

Blacks still tend to be slightly more concentrated in the southern states. About 53 percent live in southern states; the percentages for the north, north central, and

TABLE 16-4
PERCENTAGE OF BLACKS BY AGE GROUP: 1987

Age	Percentage Blacks	Percentage Total population
<5	9.3	7.5
5–14	17.9	14.0
15–24	18.2	15.3
25–34	18.3	17.8
35–44	12.6	14.4
45–64	15.6	18.6
65–74	5.1	7.3
75+	3.2	5.1

Source: U.S. Bureau of the Census, 1990.

TABLE 16-5
EDUCATIONAL STATUS OF THOSE 25+ YEARS
OF AGE

Education	Blacks, %	Whites, %
0–8 years	18.0	11.2
High school 1–3 years	18.6	11.1
High school 4 years	37.1	39.5
College 1–3 years	15.0	17.2
College 4+ years	11.3	20.9

Source: U.S. Bureau of the Census, 1990.

west are 18, 20, and 9. There has been a shift from rural to urban areas. Studies indicate that since 1970 a majority of blacks have moved into metropolitan areas (Hill, 1978).

The educational status of blacks has been improving, but still lags behind whites, especially at the upper levels. Table 16-5 has the figures for those 25+ years of age. As can be seen, overall blacks have a lower level of educational achievement than whites. Additionally, much of the education that older blacks received was inferior to that of whites. Fewer years of education, coupled with education of lower quality had a cumulative effect on aged blacks, especially in opportunities in the work force.

Health Characteristics   We will examine four aspects of health: acute and chronic conditions, self-assessed health, death rate, and life expectancy.

Table 16-6 has certain types of acute conditions for whites and blacks by sex. The data here are mixed, with white males having higher rates of acute conditions in certain areas (i.e., respiratory or injuries), and black males having higher rates in other areas (i.e., digestive and other). The rates of acute conditions for white and black females are similar for respiratory and other; white females have higher rates for digestive and injuries.

TABLE 16-6
ACUTE CONDITIONS PER 100 FOR PERSONS 65+

	Respiratory	Digestive	Injuries	Other
White male	37.6	4.7	15.8	23.2
Black male	16.8	10.1	6.9	44.2
White female	40.5	7.5	26.4	36.1
Black female	41.1	1.6	16.4	33.2

Source: National Center for Health Statistics, 1986.

TABLE 16-7
RATES OF CHRONIC CONDITIONS BY RACE AND SEX FOR THOSE 65+
(Number per 1000)

	Ischemic heart disease	HBP*	Cerebro- vascular disease	Diabetes	Arthritis
White male	178.4	316.7	62.9	79.7	392.2
Black male	61.0	370.9	108.0	120.9	468.3
White female	118.6	428.8	50.4	85.2	540.4
Black female	76.6	642.7	75.8	211.1	639.6

* High blood pressure (hypertension).
Source: National Center for Health Statistics, 1986.

Table 16-7 examines the rates of chronic conditions by age and sex for those 65+ years of age. Again, the results are somewhat mixed, with white males having a higher rate of ischemic heart disease, and black males having higher rates of HBP, cerebrovascular disease, diabetes, and arthritis. With females, whites again have a higher rate of heart disease, with black females having higher rates of HBP, cerebrovascular disease, diabetes, and arthritis.

Table 16-8 examines self-assessed health and degree of activity limitation for those 65+ years of age. Whites, both males and females, are more likely to assess their health as being "excellent or very good" than blacks. Blacks, both males and females, are more likely to assess their health as being "fair or poor" than whites. In terms of activity limitation, whites, both males and females, are more likely to report no activity limitations. Blacks are more likely to report limitations in major activities.

TABLE 16-8
SELF-ASSESSED HEALTH STATUS AND DEGREE OF ACTIVITY LIMITATION FOR THOSE
65+ YEARS OF AGE BY RACE AND SEX
(Percent Distribution)

	Self-assessed health			Degree of activity limitation			
	Excellent or very good	Good	Fair or poor	No activity limitation	Limited but not in major activity	Limited in amount or kind of major activity	Unable to carry on major activity
White male	36.7	30.5	32.3	61.3	15.6	10.3	12.8
Black male	26.6	25.1	47.7	53.5	14.9	13.1	18.5
White female	36.8	32.5	30.1	61.2	14.0	16.4	8.3
Black female	24.1	21.2	53.0	47.4	14.5	24.1	13.9

Source: National Center for Health Statistics, 1986.

To examine the health of aged blacks we also need to examine the death rate. Table 16-9 has this information. As can be seen, white males have a lower death rate than black males at all ages except 85+. The same is true for white females and black females. The higher death rate for blacks results from a variety of conditions, most associated with a lower socioeconomic status.

For the age group 85+ we see what is referred to as the crossover effect, which has been reported since 1900 (Wing et al., 1985). That is, up until the age category 85+ black males have a higher death rate than white males; the same is true for black females and white females. However, after age 85 this trend reverses: blacks have a lower death rate than whites. Why this happens is not clear. Some even dispute that it happens, claiming that it is the result of faulty data. Those who claim that the figures are accurate have hypothesized that it is a select group of blacks reaching old age.

Earlier life expectancy was mentioned and we saw that black males lag behind white males, and black females lag behind white females. Still, however, blacks have made tremendous advances in life expectancy in recent years. This can be seen in Table 16-10 which has life expectancy figures for selected years. Again, whites are provided for comparison. In 1920 the difference in life expectancy between white males and black males was 8.9 years; by 1988 it had declined to 7.0 years. For females the 1920 difference was 10.4 years; the 1988 difference was 5.1 years. The gains in life expectancy from 1920 to 1988 for white males was 17.7 years; for black males it was 19.6 years. For white females the gain was 23.3 years; for black females 28.6 years. All of the groups have experienced significant gains in life expectancy, with black females experiencing the greatest gains. In fact, in 1920 white males lived almost 10 years longer than black females; in 1988 black fe-

TABLE 16-9
DEATH RATE BY AGE, SEX, AND RACE PER 100,000

	Males		Females	
	Whites	Blacks	Whites	Blacks
<1	938	2,197	693	1,860
1–4	52	83	43	49
5–14	29	39	19	38
15–24	144	214	52	74
25–34	170	405	61	143
35–44	255	704	123	287
45–54	573	1,294	314	596
55–64	1,557	2,416	866	1,399
65–74	3,534	4,527	1,993	2,887
75–84	8,235	9,360	5,145	5.998
85+	18,934	15,343	14,728	12,260

Source: U.S. Bureau of the Census, 1990.

TABLE 16-10
LIFE EXPECTANCY FOR SELECTED YEARS: 1988

	Males		Females	
	Whites	Blacks	Whites	Blacks
1920	54.4	45.5	55.6	45.2
1950	66.5	59.1	72.2	62.9
1988	72.1	65.1	78.9	73.8

Source: U.S. Bureau of the Census, 1990.

males lived almost 2 years longer than white males. Clearly significant gains have been made.

Housing Characteristics   Housing is a problem for many aged blacks. Much of the housing in which aged blacks live is substandard. However, even more important is the fact that many aged blacks live in the inner areas of cities, where the crime rate is very high. Thus, crime is a major concern of aged blacks (Dancy, 1977).

Blacks have another housing problem in that very few of them are found in nursing homes (National Center for Health Statistics, 1986). There are three reasons for this situation. The first is racial discrimination. Many nursing homes discourage blacks from using their facilities. When blacks do reside in nursing homes, they often receive a lower quality of care than that of whites (Gottesman & Bourestom, 1974). Jackson (1978) has pointed out that many aged blacks suffer special problems in nursing homes. One such problem is racism, directed at them from staff members. The second reason blacks are not found in nursing homes as frequently as whites is the cost. The third reason is the family support system of blacks, which will be discussed in more detail later in this subsection.

Economic Characteristics   Currently about 33.9 percent of aged blacks live in poverty, compared with 10.1 percent of aged whites. As Table 16-11 shows, the extent of poverty for both aged whites and blacks has been substantially reduced from the 1970s. Obviously there are still substantial differences between the incomes of blacks and whites. It also appears that with increasing age declines in incomes are greater for blacks than for whites. Although the rate of poverty has been reduced since 1970, blacks still have a significantly higher rate of poverty than whites. Even when aged whites and blacks with similar education are compared, blacks still have higher rates of poverty. This is the result of the old concept of ''separate but equal'' education which gave blacks a much lower quality of education, and discrimination which prevented blacks from achieving the same occupational levels as whites (Taylor & Chatters, 1988).

In the future the rate of poverty will probably decline. Many believe that the overall trend, of blacks having a higher rate of poverty, will not change. This is for the same reasons mentioned in the section on Hispanics. Basically, the economy

TABLE 16-11
POVERTY RATES FOR THOSE 65+
YEARS OF AGE

	1970	1988
All races	24.6	12.0
White	22.6	10.1
Black	47.7	33.9
Hispanic	—	27.4

Source: U.S. Bureau of the Census, 1990.

changes from an industrial-based economy to a knowledge-based economy, and many blacks will not possess the educational skills necessary to compete in the new economy (Markides & Levin, 1987).

Family Characteristics   Most of the information on aged blacks seems to indicate that strong kinship bonds exist into old age. A high percentage of aged blacks see at least one of their adult children on a weekly basis, although the percentage is slightly lower than for aged whites. Aged blacks are more likely to live with an adult child, probably because of economic necessity. Aged blacks are also more likely to receive assistance from adult children, which is probably a result of greater need. Aged blacks are also more likely to take grandchildren and other relatives into their homes to live (Mitchell & Register, 1984). This can be seen in Table 16-12 which indicates that aged blacks are more likely to be living with relatives than aged whites.

It has been found that aged blacks tend to have high levels of social interaction with their families, probably because in the extended family aged individuals are more likely to have important roles. Because of their importance in the family, aged blacks are often respected by younger family members. One characteristic of aged black families that distinguishes them from aged white families is the presence of young children. Most of these children are either the children or grandchildren of relatives.

TABLE 16-12
PERCENTAGE OF THOSE 65+ LIVING IN THE FOLLOWING

White			Black		
Alone	With spouse	With relative	Alone	With spouse	With relative
30.4	55.6	11.8	33.6	41.4	21.9

Source: U.S. Bureau of the Census, 1990.

Although the family is unquestionably important in the lives of aged blacks, it is not necessarily the most important factor in their lives. Jackson (1972a) found, for example, that aged blacks obtained greater satisfaction from interacting with friends than with adult children. This same trend has been found among aged whites. The explanation is probably that friends tend to have the same beliefs, values, problems, tastes, and life-styles. Thus, they see and interpret things from the same perspective. Although parents and their adult children belong to the same family, they often share little else in common. Jackson (1971c) also found that although adult children of aged blacks often give financial aid to their parents, neither the adult child nor the aged parents generally believe that the other provides much moral support. It was found that moral support generally comes from "within" the individual or from friends of the same age. Part of the explanation here may be that aged blacks want to lead independent lives and do not want to be a burden on their adult children (Golden & Weinstock, 1975).

Studies have also found that the matriarchy does not prevail among aged black families. It was found that aged black males tended to dominate areas that have "traditionally" been in the male domain and that aged black females dominated areas that have "traditionally" been controlled by women (Jackson, 1972b).

Although future changes in the family are difficult to predict, societal changes may lower the status of aged blacks. This is because the results of desegregation will mean that more younger blacks will be incorporated into mainstream society. As a consequence many will have the incomes to adopt "mainstream" life-styles and move to other areas. Aged blacks are likely to stay where their friends and church are located. Thus, we will see not only increasing distance in terms of social class but also geography.

Other Characteristics   Religion is also an important aspect in the lives of many aged blacks (Heisel & Faulkner, 1982; Taylor, 1986). Through religion, many aged blacks can have high-status roles in a white-dominated society. Furthermore, through religious belief many aged blacks can ease the burdens of old age and discrimination. Also, the church has frequently been a center for social and educational activities for blacks and serves as a source of social support (Taylor & Chatters, 1986).

Asian and Pacific Island Americans

There has been very limited research on Asian or Pacific Island Americans. The research that does exist suggests that there is tremendous intergroup as well as intragroup diversity. The intergroup diversity is easy to conceptualize with the many different Asian and Pacific Island nationalities (e.g., Chinese, Filipino, Japanese, Asian-Indian, Korean, Vietnamese, Hawaiian, Guamian, Samoan, etc.) each with its own national history, culture, language, immigration pattern, and assimilation history. Studies have also indicated that there is tremendous intragroup diversity. For example, it has been pointed out that there are differences between Chinese-Americans who are Cantonese, who came as laborers and planned to return to China, and those who are Mandarin, who came as political refugees (see Carp & Kataoka, 1976; Hsu, 1971; Lyman, 1974; Wu, 1975). It is now also suggested that there are significant differences between aged Japanese-Americans, depending on whether those being studied are first, second, or third generation (see Osako & Liu, 1986).

This is an area that is just beginning to be explored by gerontologists. The studies that exist are often limited in terms of sample size or representativeness. Additionally, many of the studies and statistics are old. It is not unusual to find a 20-year-old set of statistics or a 20-year-old study being cited because it is literally all that is available. Because this area of study is just emerging, this subsection will present a very general overview of Asian and Pacific Island Americans. Table 16-13 provides a breakdown by age category of several Asian and Pacific Island groups. As can be seen, the percentage of older persons is smaller than for the total society. The reasons vary by group.

Generally Asian and Pacific Island Americans have settled in urban areas, primarily in the west (e.g., Filipinos, Japanese, Korean, Vietnamese), or west and northeast (e.g., Chinese, Asian-Indians). The Chinese-Americans constitute the largest Asian minority group. This is in large part because they have been in this country the longest period of time. Traditionally Chinese-Americans have been slow to assimilate into mainstream society, which had severe economic consequences in old age in that few received social security. Additionally, many did not speak English, which made knowledge or delivery of social services difficult. Early studies on aged Chinese-Americans noted financial and health problems. Current studies are noting that Chinese-Americans have higher than average levels of education and income, and that their life expectancy may be longer than for whites (Liu, 1986b; Yu, 1986).

Filipino-Americans are the second largest group, and little is known except that males outnumber females and generally assimilation has been slow.

Japanese-Americans are the third largest group. Research on Japanese-Americans has concentrated on two groups: Issei or the first generation, and Nisei or the second generation who were primarily born in the United States. The Nisei generally assimilated

TABLE 16-13
PERCENTAGE OF ASIAN AND PACIFIC ISLANDERS

	Asian						Pacific Islanders		
	Chinese	Filipino	Japanese	Indian	Korean	Vietnamese	Hawaiian	Guamian	Samoan
<5	7.1	9.0	5.2	11.1	10.6	10.0	10.0	9.1	14.1
5–14	14.0	18.1	11.3	16.0	21.7	24.8	19.2	19.9	25.7
15–24	17.9	15.9	17.4	11.3	15.8	23.2	22.5	26.6	22.5
25–34	23.0	20.9	18.9	25.5	21.0	21.6	16.4	21.7	16.9
35–44	12.9	15.5	12.8	18.1	18.0	10.4	11.7	10.5	10.4
45–64	18.1	13.5	27.0	10.1	10.5	8.0	14.7	9.7	8.4
65+	6.9	7.2	7.3	8.0	2.4	1.9	5.6	2.4	2.0

Source: U.S. Bureau of the Census, 1990.

into mainstream society, which especially benefited their children, the Sansei or third-generation Japanese-Americans, in terms of education which has improved the economic standing of this group. Research noted large differences between first- and second-generation Japanese-Americans, the second generation becoming more assimilated into mainstream society. Preliminary research suggests that third-generation Japanese-Americans are rediscovering their past (Osako & Liu, 1986).

Although it is difficult to generalize about all groups, some common areas seem to exist. One deals with first-generation immigrants. Some of the literature on first-generation Chinese-Americans and Japanese-Americans who came to this country pre-1920 indicated that there was a low rate of assimilation. For example, by old age only a small percentage could speak English. These individuals had low levels of education and job skills. The first generation also relied on traditional health practices and healers since they found the practices familiar, the healers could speak the same language and were sensitive to the individual's cultural needs. There is also a tendency for first-generation immigrants to maintain religion beliefs from the Asian or Pacific Island country. They have also generally relied on extended families for assistance, rather than on social services, which they had come to distrust because of discrimination, lack of sensitivity to cultural differences, and fear of deportation.

There are some similarities being found with aged Vietnamese-Americans, most of whom are recent immigrants. They tend to stay primarily in Vietnamese enclaves, thus resisting assimilation. Again, a low percentage speak English (Die & Seelbach, 1988). With the Vietnamese we are seeing a slight change in that in certain areas, such as financial matters, they rely on social services rather than the extended family. This reliance on social services, rather than the extended family, has also been seen among Korean aged (Koh & Bell, 1987). Further research will be needed to ascertain how rapidly and in what areas assimilation will occur. In all probability we will see significant assimilation take place with young and middle-aged immigrants. Factors such as different educational levels between the young and old, coupled with social class differences, geographic mobility, and interracial marriage will probably decrease the differences between these groups and mainstream society.

SUMMARY

This is a difficult area since so little is known about minority groups in the United States, and even less is known about the aged in these minority groups. One danger of this is that myths will be perpetuated or generated that will be harmful to these groups. There are a variety of reasons research has been slow to develop, including the need for research elsewhere, and certain research difficulties in areas such as language or location.

Minority groups were conceptualized as groups with limited access to power and certain opportunities within their society. They also possess unique characteristics in areas such as language, or cultural or physical characteristics. Because of membership in a minority group, most are excluded from full participation in society. The concept of jeopardy was also examined. It is believed that some individuals possess characteristics that place them at greater risk in old age than others, for example, being old and female, or old and black. This is sometimes referred to as "double jeopardy." This concept, although interesting, needs further refinement.

Women were considered as a minority group since they have traditionally been excluded from full participation in society. In terms of health it was mentioned that women live longer than men, although they also report more health problems. Women are more likely to live alone, because more are widowed. Economically, women are more likely to find themselves living in poverty than men. At the family level women are more likely to be caregivers to parents and spouse.

Native Americans were the second group considered. There is relatively little information on aged Native Americans. It is believed that about 5.2 percent of Native Americans are 65+ years of age. Life expectancy is shorter than for whites. Native Americans also face significant problems in the areas of health, housing, and economic conditions.

Hispanics are those who have origins in Spanish-speaking countries. Hispanics have a lower median age than whites, primarily because of a higher birth rate. Hispanics are not one group but several, and differences among Cubans, Mexican-Americans, and Puerto Ricans were noted. The text examined Mexican-Americans, since they are the largest group. Again, the median age is lower than for whites, mostly because of a higher birth rate. About 3.6 percent of Mexican-Americans are 65+ years of age. It is believed that Mexican-Americans age rapidly, primarily because of social class, not ethnicity. As with Native Americans, aged Mexican-Americans also have numerous health, housing, and economic problems. Some studies on the Mexican-American family have supported the belief of an extended family that supports its aged members; other studies have claimed that this is a romanticized picture that does not exist.

There is more literature on aged blacks than the other minority groups. However, much of the literature is old and much has severe methodological limitations. About 8.1 percent of blacks are 65+ years of age. As with the other groups, blacks have more health, housing, and economic problems than whites.

Asian and Pacific Island Americans were also examined. Again, little research exists which makes it difficult to draw conclusions.

REFERENCES

Anderson, N. B. (1989). Health status of aged minorities: Directions for clinical research. *Journal of Gerontogy: Medical Sciences,* **44**(1): M1–2.

Angello. E. D. (1977*a*). Age and ageism in children's first literature. *Educational Gerontology,* **2**(3): 255–274.

Angello, E. D. (1977*b*). Old age and literature: An overview. *Educational Gerontology,* **2**(3): 211–218.

Bastida, E. (1987). Sex-typed age norms among older Hispanics. *The Gerontologist,* **27**(1): 59–65.

Beattie, W. M. (1983). Economic security for the elderly: National and international perspectives. *The Gerontologist,* **23**(9): 406–410.

Bell. B. D. (1976). *Contemporary social gerontology: Significant developments in the field of aging.* Springfield, IL: Charles C Thomas.

Benedict, R. (1972). A profile of Indian aged. In *Minority aged in America* (pp. 51–58). Ann Arbor: University of Michigan Press.

Binstock, R. H. (1986). Perspectives on measuring hardship: Concepts, dimensions, and implications. *The Gerontologist,* **26**(1): 60–62.

Cahn, E. S. (Ed.) (1969). *Our brother's keeper: The Indian in white America.* New York: A New Community Press Book.

Carp, F. M. (1968). *Factors in utilization of services by Mexican-American elderly.* Palo Alto: American Institute for Research.

Carp, F. M. (1969). Housing and minority group aging. *The Gerontologist,* **9**(1): 20–24.

Carp, F. M. (1970). Communicating with elderly Mexican-Americans. *The Gerontologist,* **10**(2): 126–134.

Carp, F. M., & Kataoka, E. (1976). Health problems of the elderly of San Francisco's Chinatown. *The Gerontologist,* **16**(1; Part 1): 30–38.

Crouch, B. M. (1972). Age and institutional support: Perceptions of older Mexican-Americans. *Journal of Gerontology,* **27**(4): 524–529.

Curley, L. (1987). Native American aged. In G. L. Maddox (Ed.), *The encyclopedia of aging* (pp. 471–472). New York: Springer.

Dancy, J. (1977). *The black elderly: A guide for practitioners.* Ann Arbor: University of Michigan Press.

Die, A. H., & Seelbach, W. C. (1988). Problems, sources of assistance, and knowledge of services among elderly Vietnamese immigrants. *The Gerontologist,* **28**(4): 448–452.

Dowd, J., & Bengtson, V. (1978). Aging in minority group populations: An examination of the double jeopardy hypothesis. *Journal of Gerontology,* **33**(3): 427–436.

Dressel, P. L. (1988). Gender, race, and class: Beyond the feminization of poverty in later life. *The Gerontologist,* **28**(2): 177–180.

Dukepoo, F. C. (1980). *The elder American Indian.* San Diego: Campanile Press.

Eribes, R. A. & Bradley-Rawls, M. (1978). The underutilization of nursing home facilities by Mexican-American elderly in the southwest. *The Gerontologist,* **18**(4): 363–371.

Ferraro, K. F. (1987). Double jeopardy to health for black older adults? *Journal of Gerontology,* **42**(5): 528–533.

Gibson, R. C. (1989). Minority aging research: Opportunity and challenge. *Journal of Gerontology: Social Sciences,* **44**(1): S2–3.

Golden, H. M., & Weinstock, C. S. (1975). The myth of homogeneity among black elderly. *Black Aging,* **1**(2 and 3): 1–11.

Gottesman, L. E., & Bourestom, N. C. (1974). Why nursing homes do what they do. *The Gerontologist,* **14**(6): 501–506.

Graves, T. D., & Van Arsdale, M. (1966). Values, expectations, and relocation: The Navaho migrant to Denver. *Human Organization,* **25**(4): 300–307.

Heisel, M. A., & Faulkner, A. O. (1982). Religiosity in an older black population. *The Gerontologist,* **22**(4): 354–358.

Hess, B. B. (1986). Antidiscrimination policies today and the life chances of older women tomorrow. *The Gerontologist,* **26**(2): 132–135.

Hill, R. (1978). A demographic profile of the black elderly. *Aging,* **287–288**: 2–9.

Holden, K. C. (1988). Poverty and living arrangements among older women: Are changes in economic well-being underestimated? *Journal of Gerontology: Social Sciences,* **43**(1): S22–27.

Holden, K. C., Burkhauser, R. V., & Myers, D. A. (1986). Income transitions at older stages of life: The dynamics of poverty. *The Gerontologist,* **26**(3): 292–297.

Holzberg, C. S. (1982*a*). Ethnicity and aging: Anthropological perspectives on more than just the minority elderly. *The Gerontologist*, **22**(3): 249–257.

Holzberg, C. S. (1982*b*). Ethnicity and aging: Rejoinder to a comment by Kyriakos S. Markides. *The Gerontologist*, **22**(6): 471–472.

Hsu, F. L. K. (1971). *The challenge of the American dream: The Chinese in the United States*. Belmont, CA: Wadsworth.

Jackson, J. J. (1971*a*). Negro aged: Toward needed research in social gerontology. *The Gerontologist*, **11**(1; Part 2): 52–57.

Jackson, J. J. (1971*b*). The blacklands of gerontology. *Aging and Human Development*, **2**(3): 156–171.

Jackson, J. J. (1971*c*). Sex and social class variations in black aged parent-adult child relationships. *Aging and Human Development*, **2**: 96–107.

Jackson, J. J. (1972*a*). Comparative lifestyles and family and friend relationships among older black women. *The Family Coordinator*, **21**(February): 477–485.

Jackson, J. J. (1972*b*). Marital life among aging blacks. *The Family Coordinator*, **21**: 21–27.

Jackson, J. J. (1978). Special health problems of aged blacks. *Aging*, **287–288**: 15–20.

Jackson, J. S. (1987). Black aged. In G. L. Maddox (Ed.), *The encyclopedia of aging* (pp. 71–73). New York: Springer.

Jackson, J. S. (1989). Race, ethnicity, and psychological theory and research. *Journal of Gerontology: Psychological Sciences*, **44**(1): P1–2.

Kalish, R. A. (1971). A gerontological look at ethnicity, human capacities, and individual adjustment. *The Gerontologist*, **11**(2; Part 2): 78–87.

Kii, T. (1984). Asians. In E. Palmore (Ed.), *Handbook on the aged in the United States*. Westport, CT: Greenwood.

Kim, P. (1983). Demography of the Asian-Pacific elderly: Selected problems and implications. In R. L. McNeely & J. L. Colen (Eds.), *Aging in minority groups*. Beverly Hills: Sage.

Kitano, H. H. L. (1976). *Japanese-Americans: The evolution of a subculture*. Englewood Cliffs, NJ: Prentice-Hall.

Koh, J. Y., & Bell, W. G. (1987). Korean elders in the United States: Intergenerational relations and living arrangements. *The Gerontologist*, **27**(1): 66–71.

Kurzeja, P. L., Koh, S. D., Koh, T-H., & Liu, W. T. (1986). Ethnic attitudes of Asian American elderly: The Korean immigrants and Japanese Niseis. *Research on Aging*, **8**(1): 110–127.

Leonard, O. E. (1967). The older rural Spanish-speaking people of the southwest. In E. G. Youmans (Ed.), *Older rural Americans: A sociological perspective* (pp. 239–261). Lexington: University of Kentucky Press.

Lewis, M. I., & Butler, R. N. (1972). Why is women's lib ignoring old women? *Aging and Human Development*, **3**(3): 223–231.

Liu, W. T. (1986*a*). Culture and social support. *Research on Aging*, **8**(1): 57–83.

Liu, W. T. (1986*b*). Health services for Asian elderly. *Research on Aging*, **8**(1): 156–174.

Lyman, S. M. (1974). *Chinese Americans*. New York: Random House.

Manson, S. M. (1989). Long-term care in American Indian communities: Issues for planning and research. *The Gerontologist*, **29**(1): 38–44.

Markides, K. S. (1982). Ethnicity and aging: A comment. *The Gerontologist*, **22**(6): 467–470.

Markides, K. S. (1987). Hispanic Americans. In G. L. Maddox (Ed.), *The encyclopedia of aging* (pp. 322–323). New York: Springer.

Markides, K. S., Boldt, J. S., & Ray, L. A. (1986). Sources of helping and intergenerational solidarity: A three-generations study of Mexican Americans. *Journal of Gerontology,* **41**(4): 506–511.

Markides, K. S., & Krause, N. (1985). Intergenerational solidarity and psychological well-being among older Mexican Americans: A three-generations study. *Journal of Gerontology,* **40**(3): 390–392.

Markides, K. S., & Levin, J. S. (1987). The changing economy and the future of the minority aged. *The Gerontologist,* **27**(3): 273–274.

Minkler, M., & Stone, R. (1985). The feminization of poverty and older women. *The Gerontologist,* **25**(4): 351–357.

Mitchell, J., & Register, J. C. (1984). An exploration of family interaction with the elderly by race, socioeconomic status, and residence. *The Gerontologist,* **24**(1): 48–54.

Moore, J. W. (1971*a*). Mexican-Americans. *The Gerontologist,* **11**(1; Part 2): 30–35.

Moore, J. W. (1971*b*). Situational factors affecting minority aging. *The Gerontologist,* **11**(1): 88–93.

Morgan, L. A. (1984). Continuity and change in the labor force activity of recently widowed women. *The Gerontologist,* **24**(5): 530–535.

Morgan, L. A. (1986). The financial experience of widowed women: Evidence from the LRHS. *The Gerontologist,* **26**(6): 663–668.

Murdock, S. H., & Schwartz, D. F. (1978). Family structure and the use of agency services: An examination of patterns among elderly native Americans. *The Gerontologist,* **18**(5): 475–481.

National Center for Health Statistics (1987). Health statistics for older persons, United States. *Vital and Health Statistics.* Series 3, No. 25.

National Indian Council on Aging (1984). Indians and Alaskan natives. In E. Palmore (Ed.), *Handbook on the aged in the United States.* Westport, CT: Greenwood.

National Tribal Chairman's Association (1976). *National Indian Conference on Aging.* Phoenix: National Tribal Chairman's Association.

O'Rand, A. M. (1987). Women: Changing status. In G. L. Maddox (Ed.), *The encyclopedia of aging* (pp. 697–699). New York: Springer.

Osako, M. M., & Liu, W. T. (1986). Intergenerational relations and the aged among Japanese Americans. *Research on Aging,* **8**(1): 128–155.

Ransford, H. E. (1976). On isolation, powerlessness, and violence. In M. P. Golden (Ed.), *The research experience* (pp. 305–314). Itasca, NY: Peacock.

Register, J. C. (1981). Aging and race: A black-white comparative analysis. *The Gerontologist,* **21**(4): 438–443.

Rodeheaver, D. (1987). When old age became a social problem, women were left behind. *The Gerontologist,* **27**(6): 741–746.

Rogers, C. J., & Gallion, T. E. (1978). Characteristics of elderly Pueblo Indians in New Mexico. *The Gerontologist,* **18**(5): 482–487.

Rose, A. M. (1965). The subculture of the aging: A framework for research in social gerontology. In A. M. Rose & W. Peterson (Eds.), *Older people and their social world* (pp. 3–16). Philadelphia: F. A. Davis.

Sanchez, P. (1973). The Spanish heritage elderly. In E. P. Stanford (Ed.), Minority aging (pp. 28–34). San Diego: San Diego State University Press.

Seccombe, K. (1989). Ethnicity or socioeconomic status? Health differences between elder Alaska natives and whites. *The Gerontologist,* **29**(4): 551–556.

Smith, L., & Adelman, R. C. (1989). Message to biologists from the GSA taskforce on minority issues in gerontology. *Journal of Gerontology: Biological Sciences,* **55**(1): B1–3.

Snyder, P. (1984). Health service implications of fold healing among older Asian Americans and Hawaiians in Honolulu. *The Gerontologist,* **24**(5): 471–476.

Sorkin, A. L. (1969). Some aspects of American Indian migration. *Social Forces,* **48**(2): 243–250.

Streib, G. F. (1965). Are the aged a minority group? In A. W. Gouldner & W. A. Peterson (Eds.), *Applied sociology* (pp. 311–328). New York: Free Press.

Tally, T., & Kaplan, J. (1956). The negro aged. *Gerontological Society Newsletter,* **3**(4).

Taylor, R. J. (1985). The extended family as a source of support to elderly blacks. *The Gerontologist,* **25**(5): 488–495.

Taylor, R. J. (1986). Religious participation among elderly blacks. *The Gerontologist,* **26**(6): 630–636.

Taylor, R. J., & Chatters, L. M. (1986). Church-based informal support among elderly blacks. *The Gerontologist,* **26**(6): 637–642.

Taylor, R. J., & Chatters, L. M. (1988). Correlates of education, income, and poverty among aged blacks. *The Gerontologist,* **28**(4): 435–441.

Torres-Gil, F. (1986). An examination of factors affecting future cohorts of elderly Hispanics. *The Gerontologist,* **26**(2): 140–146.

Tracy, M. B., & Ward, R. L. (1986). Trends in old-age pensions for women: Benefit levels in ten nations, 1960–1980. *The Gerontologist,* **26**(3): 286–291.

Trager, N. P. (1974). Introduction. In *No longer young* (ix–xv). Ann Arbor: University of Michigan Press.

Uhlenberg, P., & Salmon, A. P. (1986). Change in relative income of older women, 1960–1980. *The Gerontologist,* **26**(2): 164–170.

U.S. Bureau of the Census (1970). *Statistical abstract of the United States.* Washington, DC: U.S. Government Printing Office.

U.S. Bureau of the Census (1977). *Statistical abstract of the United States.* Washington, DC: U.S. Government Printing Office.

U.S. Bureau of the Census (1990). *Statistical abstract of the United States.* Washington, DC: U.S. Government Printing Office.

U.S. Department of Health and Human Services (1985). *Health status of minorities and low income groups.* Washington, DC: U.S. Government Printing Office.

U.S. Senate, 92 Congress, first session (1971). Special Committee on Aging: A statement by the members of the Advisory Council on the elderly American Indian, together with an analysis of Statistical Information and other Appendixes. Washington, DC: U.S. Government Printing Office.

Verbrugge, L. M. (1984). A health profile of older women with comparisons to older men. *Research on Aging,* **6**(3): 291–322.

Warlick, J. L. (1985). Why is poverty after 65 a woman's problem? *Journal of Gerontology,* **40**(6): 751–757.

Weeks, J. R. (1987). Asian-American aged. In G. L. Maddox (Ed.), *The encyclopedia of aging* (pp. 38–40). New York: Springer.

Williams, G. C. (1980). Warriors no more: A study of the American Indian elderly. In C. L. Fry (Ed.), *Aging in culture and society: Comparative viewpoints and strategies* (pp. 101–111). Brooklyn: Bergin.

Wing, S., Manton, K. G., Stallard, E., Hames, C. G., & Tryoler, H. A. (1985). The black/white mortality crossover investigation in a community-based study. *Journal of Gerontology,* **40**(1): 78–84.

Wirth, L. (1945). The problem of minority groups. In R. Linton (Ed.), *The science of man in the world crisis* (pp. 347–372). New York: Columbia University Press.

Wu, F. Y. T. (1975). Mandarin-speaking aged Chinese in the Los Angeles area. *The Gerontologist,* **15**(3): 271–275.

Yu, E. S. H. (1986). Health of Chinese elderly in America. *Research on Aging,* **8**(1): 84–109.

Zick, C. D. & Smith, K. R. (1986). Immediate and delayed effects of widowhood on poverty: Patterns from the 1970s. *The Gerontologist,* **26**(6): 669–675.

CHAPTER **17**

DYING AND DEATH

Robert V. Eckert, Jr./EKM-Nepenthe

INTRODUCTION

Dying and death are two events that all individuals eventually experience. Older persons, however, are more likely to confront dying and death than any other age group, both in terms of their own dying and death as well as that of a spouse or friends. This chapter will examine dying and death among older persons. It is divided into six sections. In the first section we will examine dying and death in American society. In the second section we will examine dying and death and older persons. This section is separated into four subsections: the attitudes toward dying and death in contemporary American society; the treatment of dying geriatric patients by the medical profession; the stages of dying; and the dying process. The third section will examine the statistics on death in contemporary American society. Here we will examine the death rates of various age groups and the causes of death. In the fourth section we will study life expectancy, examining the factors that have a consequence on length of life. The fifth section will examine three of the factors that are commonly associated with death in old age: bereavement, relocation, and retirement. The sixth, and last, section will examine contemporary issues in the area of dying and death. Specifically we will examine the definition of death, the removal of life-sustaining treatment, and euthanasia.

DYING AND DEATH IN CONTEMPORARY AMERICAN SOCIETY

Concepts change over time in meaning, significance, and purpose. For example, 100 years ago the concept of human sexuality was considered pornographic and was hidden by the veil of Victorianism. Sexuality now permeates our society in fashion, the mass media, the arts, language, as well as other areas. Not only has our "exposure" to sexuality increased, but the primary purpose of sex has changed from that of procreation to that of pleasure.

The concepts of dying and death have also changed in the last 100 years. Dying and death went from frequently encountered and discussed concepts, to concepts that were disguised, hidden, and seldom mentioned. Death became a taboo subject, a pornography that was as obscene to contemporary society as sexuality was to the Victorians (Feifel, 1963; Gorer, 1965). In the past, death was accepted as a natural, normal part of life. Death was not a stranger or a mystery for most individuals. High death rates brought on by famines, epidemics, wars, and accidents made individuals constantly aware of the inevitability of dying and death.

Because of the number of factors involved, it is difficult to say exactly when the concept of death began its transformation, but by 1865 the change was well under way. The common element in the factors is that they removed most individuals from dying and death. Previously, the living often had frequent contact with the dying; the dying were generally cared for in the home by family members. After the individual died it was the family that prepared the body for burial, organized and held a religious service, built a coffin, dug a grave, made the "tombstone," filled in the grave, and maintained the grave. Several factors changed this.

536

First, with medical advances sick or terminally ill individuals received better care from professionals in hospitals than from family members in homes. As a result, the family was removed from caring for the dying individual. Second, even if care could be provided in the home, smaller families coupled with many family members moving to other areas, created a situation where there were often not enough family members to provide care. Third, industrialization created highly specialized work roles. In the past work roles were less specialized and an individual could be nurse, physician, mortician, coffinmaker, grave digger, and even minister. In an industrial society most individuals assume highly specialized roles and no longer have most of the skills needed to care for the dying or dead. These roles are assumed by various occupations and professions. Fourth, laws were created governing the care of dying individuals and the burial of the dead. These laws were generally created to prevent the spread of contagious diseases. Essentially, laws created barriers to individuals caring for dying or dead family members. Fifth, with increasing urbanization many families no longer had ready access to burial space. Rural farm families often maintained sections of land as family cemeteries. However, those who lived in urban areas did not have access to land and had to rely on professionals. The intent is not to be critical of these changes; only to note that they had an impact on dying and death in American society. If there is a ''bottom line'' it is that all these changes made dying and death unfamiliar to most Americans.

Today very few Americans have ever witnessed a death. Most have had limited contact with the dying and dead. In contemporary American society dying individuals are often taken from their homes and placed in hospitals among white-robed, whispering, impersonal strangers. An additional barrier has been created through the use of euphemisms that shield most individuals from dying and death. For example, it is rare that anyone dies anymore, rather they pass on, join their forefathers, exit, become defunct, demise, cease, perish, pass away, lose vital signs, are lost, or have been taken away. Furthermore, biologists do not ''kill'' experimental animals but rather ''sacrifice'' them; radio stations do not have a daily ''death listing'' but rather ''special announcements.'' Family pets are ''put to sleep.'' Additionally, an industry has been created to make the dead look as much as possible as if they were sleeping. Funeral directors make it apparent that you are not going to look at a corpse in a coffin, but that you are going into the slumber room to have a visitation with the deceased.

We are witnessing the emergence of a ''death awareness movement'' which can be seen in the hospice movement, in the increase in the number of dying and death courses, and in the challenge to certain laws, medical procedures, and with issues such as ''the right to die.'' Although the ''death awareness movement'' is starting to alter the concepts of dying and death, there is still a great deal of ''ambivalence'' in this area at both the individual and societal levels (Wass & Myers, 1984).

In the near future there will probably be a significant change in the societal concepts of dying and death. More individuals will be unwilling to accept the idea that dying and death can only be dealt with by professionals. Just as people determine their life-styles, they now want the right to determine how and even when they will die.

DYING AND DEATH: OLDER PERSONS

This section is divided into four subsections. The first deals with attitudes toward dying and death, the second with the treatment of geriatric patients, the third with the stages of dying, and the fourth with the dying process.

Attitudes toward Dying and Death

Attitudes are shaped by numerous factors. The cultural context in which we are socialized has a great deal to do with the formation of our attitudes. Generally, individuals in our society are raised with "negative" attitudes of aging and the aged. Many are raised to believe that older individuals are "used up" or that in many cases they would be "better off dead." Several articles have noted that American society does not allocate much social worth to older persons (see Cumming, 1964; Kalish, 1965, 1968, 1971, 1972). The most highly regarded values in American society are generally those that are antithetical to old age. For example, there is an emphasis on the future, on productivity and achievement, and on "keeping up with the times." Older persons are often not seen as having a future, as being dependent on society, and of living in the past. Thus, the societal attitude toward older persons is in many cases negative.

In our society older persons are expected to die, in contrast to the past when children were expected to die. In our society death and dying are a normal and expected part of the role of the aged. Kastenbaum (1965) has found that although society may expect and even try to hasten the death of older persons through cursory medical care, there exists within most older persons a strong desire to live. Kubler-Ross (1974) has echoed this same sentiment. She has asserted that "old age is not synonymous with being glad to die." Thus old age is not necessarily a time when older persons believe that their lives have lost all meaning and that death is better than life.

There is a common belief that older persons fear death more than younger individuals. This belief seems logical since with increasing age there is a greater probability of death. However, studies contradict this belief. Marshall (1975) claimed that with increasing age the fear of death decreases and that older individuals generally face death with a calm, accepting attitude. Hinton (1967) noted that young terminal patients are much more anxious than older patients. A study by Templer, Ruff, and Franks (1971) found that older persons have normal death-anxiety scores. Kastenbaum (1969) and Kalish (1976, 1985, 1987) have both claimed that older persons, even those with terminal illnesses, possess fewer fears about death than other age groups (see Wass & Myers, 1984).

Kalish (1976) believes that the lower fear of death among older persons stems from three factors. First, they view themselves as having less value and fewer prospects for the future. Second, many have lived longer than they expected; therefore they believe that they are on "borrowed time." Third, older persons have had to deal with the deaths of friends, peers, family members, and colleagues and so have come to accept death as a natural, normal part of life. Beauvoir (1972) claimed that many older persons accept approaching death with a calm attitude because life has become meaningless to them. Therefore, Beauvoir said, they may welcome rather than fear death (see Christ, 1961; Jeffers et al., 1961; Rhudick & Dibner, 1961; Swenson, 1961).

The Treatment of Dying Geriatric Patients

A great deal has been written on the medical profession's treatment of the dying geriatric patient. The general belief has been that the dying geriatric patient has not fared very well.

The major reason the dying aged may not receive adequate medical care has been advanced by Kalish (1972). He pointed out that the responses of medical personnel toward a dying geriatric patient are determined by past socialization. Very often the geriatric patient's death is not deemed a social loss. In fact, it may be seen as a social gain in that valuable time and resources will no longer be spent on an individual of low social worth (see Carpenter & Wylie, 1974; Comfort, 1967; Kastenbaum, 1974). Glaser (1966) noted that the death of a geriatric patient does not constitute much of a social loss for many medical personnel. This death stands in contrast to a child's death, which would constitute a high social loss since the child would have an entire life yet to live. The highest social loss would be the death of a middle-aged or young adult. These individuals are seen as having a future ahead of them and an important past behind them that includes education, a family, and an occupation.

A number of writers have commented on the negative treatment geriatric patients often receive. Both Sudnow (1967) and Kastenbaum (1969) referred to a concept called "social death." This term means that terminally ill patients are treated and responded to as though they were dead, even though they are physically alive. This callous attitude resulted in cursory medical care at best. According to Glaser (1966), many medical personnel rationalize social death by such declarations as, "She is too old to resist the disease," or "People at his age often get this illness and there is nothing more to do for them," or "The individual has led a full life and has nothing more to live for."

Even more distressing was Sudnow's (1967) description of the treatment of an older individual who arrived at a hospital DOA (dead on arrival). The individual was pronounced dead after a cursory medical examination and no resuscitation attempt. However, when a young child was brought in DOA, the hospital staff worked feverishly for 11 hours trying to save the child. Sudnow noted that the effort to save DOA patients was clearly related to the patient's age and social status. LaSagna (1970) also noted that the quality of treatment appears to be inversely related to age, with lower age groups receiving higher levels of care and higher age groups receiving lower levels of care. He maintained that the charts of older persons were more likely to be "red tagged" or marked DNR (do not resuscitate) than the charts of those in younger age groups.

From the above, two points need to be made. First, the studies cited above are "fairly old." Sudnow's study is a classic, and as such it is frequently cited. However, it is more than two decades old. The research was done before the recent increase in courses, seminars, and publications on dying and death. Changes *have* been made in this area. For example, the number of death education courses has increased significantly in recent years in schools of medicine, nursing, and pharmacy (Dickinson et al., 1987).

Second, it is much easier to describe "poor care" than "good care." When death cannot be prevented, when pain or other physical symptoms cannot be controlled, and when the patient is depressed or anxious, it is easy to blame the medical staff rather than the state of knowledge of medicine. Also, it is often poor care that receives the greatest amount of publicity. For example, recently there have been several books that have dealt with dying individuals. The books are filled with page after page of the horrible care these dying individuals experienced, many of them upper-class, white males. Although the emphasis in the books is on the poor care of the dying, the authors have noted that poor care was the exception. These books are valuable and need to be read; we need to learn from them and make changes. However, examples of positive care also need to receive more emphasis.

Loomis and Williams (1983) have pointed out that it is often believed that the terminally ill are provided substandard care. To test this belief they designed a study where a group of individuals evaluated the care received by dying patients, most of whom were 60+ years of age. It was found that the patients received very good medical care. The areas most commonly criticized were in the areas of staff communication and emotional support with patients. This study refuted two common beliefs about terminal care. The first belief was that life is inappropriately prolonged through the use of drugs, surgical techniques, and medical technology. This was not found to be true in this study. The second refuted belief was that dying patients were abandoned. Again, this was not found to be true. Some support was found for a third common belief, namely that there is poor control of pain among terminally ill patients; however, a disproportionate number of those in this study were dying from cancer, which may have biased the results. The authors went on to present a model that would provide quality care to terminally ill patients (see Meyers et al., 1983).

One indication of the care of patients was presented in a study on healthcare workers (Lerea & LiMauro, 1982). The researchers examined grief among healthcare workers in a general hospital and in a skilled nursing facility. Almost all of those working in the general hospital had grieved in response to the death of a patient. For those working in a skilled nursing home the percentage was somewhat lower. The researchers noted that differences in grief response rate was because patients in a general hospital are generally there for acute conditions, thus making death more unexpected. These deaths were "off-time tragedies." Healthcare workers in a skilled nursing facility dealt more with "expected" death. The researchers pointed out that bereavement counseling is needed for healthcare workers. The major point is that if healthcare workers "care" enough to grieve then they probably also "care" enough to provide quality care.

One recent article addressed ways caregivers can help older persons face death (Billig et al., 1988). The article noted the importance of providing patients with current information on their disease and the treatment options. It was also emphasized that honesty was needed, and included a discussion of issues such as the use of "heroic measures."

A factor intended to bring about even better care of the dying is that of hospice. Hospices originally developed during the Middle Ages as places that assisted travelers, who were often in strange lands and faced with many hardships. Currently hospices assist individuals on the journey from life to death.

There are about 2000 hospices in the United States (Davidson, 1988). There can be several different types of hospices. One type is labeled ''volunteer'' which offers primarily information, bereavement support, equipment, and social and psychological support to the dying. There is no medical care provided. A second type would do all of the above and also provide some home medical care, often through a visiting nurse. A third type of hospice is ''hospital-based,'' which generally means that a wing or floor of a hospital has been transformed into a hospice. The last type is a ''free-standing'' hospice, which is a facility devoted to the medical, social, and psychological care of the dying. The medical care provided by hospices to the terminally ill is primarily directed at controlling pain and other symptoms (e.g., nausea, breathing difficulties) associated with the terminal illness. Unlike hospitals, hospices do not have life-sustaining equipment. They have the equipment that will relieve the distress of the dying, not prolong the dying process.

Most of the literature has emphasized the need for hospices on two fronts: care and cost. Concerning the first need, care, the belief is that hospitals are for those with acute illnesses, not the dying. Also, hospital staffs are accustomed to dealing with sick patients not dying patients; thus the interpersonal skills and the medical skills are often lacking. The second need, cost, deals with the fact that hospitals need expensive life-saving technology, the costs of which are passed on to all patients. Hospices do not need this equipment, thus the cost is lower. The studies are mixed on whether hospices provide better care at a lower cost (see Davidson, 1988).

While the majority of literature on hospices has been positive, some important concerns are being expressed. Gibson (1984) has summarized two common concerns. One concern is that selected patients could be singled out for hospice care if cost-cutting was necessary. Thus, life-sustaining technology would be terminated not because of individual conditions, but because of concerns about cost. Gibson also questioned if hospices are a necessary alternative or if hospitals are capable of responding to the concerns.

Important changes are taking place in this area. For example, many health insurance companies now provide coverage for hospice care. Also, standards for the accreditation of hospices are being established (Bulkin & Lukashok, 1988). Additionally, the Social Security Act now provides limited coverage for hospice care, which has made hospices a part of the American system of health care.

Stages of Dying

It was probably inevitable that a dying stage theory emerged. After all, there are stage theories surrounding most life periods. The stage theory that has achieved the greatest amount of attention is that set forth by Elisabeth Kubler-Ross.

Kubler-Ross grew up, went to medical school, and first practiced medicine in Europe. When she came to this country she was shocked at the differences in the way the dying were treated. She was accustomed to seeing people die in their homes, among friends and familiar surroundings, and to viewing death as an open and natural process. She found in America that the dying were shipped to hospitals to die in unfamiliar environments among indifferent and often uncaring strangers. She also found that dying in America was more difficult for the dying individual, for that individual's family and friends, and for hospital personnel than it was in Europe. This was because the avoidance of dying and death created an awkward system of communication between the living and dying. From her work with the dying Kubler-Ross formulated a six-stage theory of dying. The stages are listed and described below (Kubler-Ross, 1969, 1974).

1 Denial: When most individuals are informed that they are dying, their first reaction is to deny the diagnosis. They may say something like, "No, it can't be me—the lab must have mixed up my test results with those of someone else." At this stage individuals will usually seek a second opinion or have the tests repeated. According to Dr. Kubler-Ross, denial is an important stage because it allows patients time to gradually adjust to the reality of the diagnosis.

2 Anger: In this stage dying individuals ask, "Why me?" It is during this stage that dying individuals express behavior that is difficult for family and friends to understand and to cope with. Dying individuals are angry that they are dying. They feel cheated out of life. The anger becomes projected at almost everyone. Visitations often become one-sided battlegrounds with the dying individual venting fear, frustration, and anger.

3 Bargaining: In the bargaining stage dying individuals try to bargain for a longer life. The bargaining process generally takes place with either a physician or God. Patients will vow to physicians to be good patients and to donate their bodies to science, or to participate in experimental programs if they can be guaranteed more time. Bargains with God generally include various promises concerning future religious beliefs and behaviors. Kubler-Ross has observed that few dying patients keep their bargains.

4 Depression: The fourth stage is depression. There are two types of depression: reactive and preparatory. Reactive depression comes about when dying individuals contemplate past losses. For example, individuals become depressed over losses as a result of previous surgeries. Preparatory depression comes about when individuals start to conceptualize future losses, such as not being able to see their families grow and mature, or the knowledge that certain roles will soon be lost, such as mother or wife.

5 Acceptance: Many eventually reach this stage. During this stage there is no anger, bitterness, resentfulness, or depression. Individuals are generally very tired and weak, and often heavily drugged. It is not a happy time, only a time when individuals realize that death is near and accept the inevitability. For many, it is a peaceful time; for others it is devoid of emotions. It is during this time that the dying reduce their attachment to people and things. They focus on a few remaining people and things that are important in their lives. Some see this as a form of disengagement (Kalish, 1976).

6 Hope: Hope is not a separate stage in the dying process. Rather, it permeates all the other stages, from about halfway through denial to halfway through acceptance. Hope has two stages. In the first stage patients hope for a cure through new drugs, surgical techniques, or even a miracle. In the last stage hope is focused into areas such as a hope for life after death or hope for those they are leaving behind.

There has been a tremendous amount written on Kubler-Ross's stage theory of dying. While much of this writing has clarified her work, much is also misleading. Some of this is because writers have misunderstood her theory; some because as a scientific theory the theory is not well formulated; some of it is because Kubler-Ross has continually modified the theory.

A frequent belief is that dying individuals start in denial and work their way to acceptance. According to Kubler-Ross, individuals can start in any stage, and go in any direction. Also, individuals can be in more than one stage at a time. Another common misconception is that individuals should die in the stage of acceptance. Dr. Kubler-Ross does not believe that this is necessary. The appropriate stage depends on the individual. There are few, if any, who would criticize Kubler-Ross in terms of her enthusiasm, energy, concern, or care for the dying. To a large extent it was the work of Kubler-Ross that started the current "death awareness movement," and to a large extent it has been her books and lectures that have provided the movement with momentum. A modest woman, Kubler-Ross says that she does not understand all of the attention and honors that she has received; she noted that she has never discovered or invented anything, she has just listened to dying patients.

Her theory is not without its critics (Hinton, 1975; Kastenbaum, 1985; Metzger, 1979; Schultz & Anderman, 1974). First, the theory is not supported by much empirical data (Kalish, 1985). Information of how and why the transition from one stage to another takes place is lacking. Second, the theory is a "general" theory that claims to cover those dying from all causes. Many find it difficult to believe that there is one simple six-stage theory that will account for both sexes, as well as all races, ethnic groups, ages, backgrounds and the myriad of diseases and their consequences on dying individuals. Third, some claim that what Kubler-Ross is reporting is not a stage theory but emotions and that there are several emotions missing. For example, it would be easy to include stages of guilt, anxiety, struggle, or fear.

Some believe that the Kubler-Ross stage theory does not apply to older persons (Retsinas, 1988). They believe that the theory was developed more for middle-aged individuals who are involved with family and friends. An examination of the six stages noted that many stages do not appear to apply to older persons. Denial is generally not a factor since most older persons have had multiple life-threatening conditions for decades. Anger generally does not appear since many have seen their friends and spouse die; thus rather than anger there is acceptance that it is now their time to die. Bargaining for extra time may not occur because the extra time is seen as a curse, not a blessing. Depression may or may not be a consequence of the dying process; more likely it is a result of other factors, such as uncontrollable physical symptoms. Acceptance is not so much a stage as a natural, inevitable consequence of life. Older persons are more likely to accept their deaths as timely. Hope may not be so much for a cure but an ''easy'' death.

As noted earlier, many saw the Kubler-Ross stage of acceptance as the ultimate goal in the dying process. Weisman's (1972) concept of appropriate death relates to this ''ultimate goal concept,'' and needs to be briefly considered. An appropriate death is a death that we would select for ourselves. Generally, it consists of being provided with assistance to function at as high a level as possible. Distressing symptoms are reduced as much as possible. This means that to the extent possible, physical, social, and psychological distress are reduced or eliminated. Individuals, both the dying and survivors, are aware of the diagnosis and prognosis. Dying individuals maintain close, intimate relationships with family and friends. To a large extent the appropriate death is a way of living not of dying; while dying individuals accept death, they do not capitulate to it.

The Dying Process

The dying process is generally somewhat different for the old than the young. Older persons generally die from degenerative chronic conditions, often after years of gradual decline. For younger individuals the dying process is often much shorter, a result of accidents. For many older individuals mental conditions, such as Alzheimer's disease, or extensive medication, make them confused or comatose. For younger individuals this condition is much less prevalent. For many older persons their support networks have diminished due to factors such as death or incapacity. Younger individuals are more likely to have intact support networks.

There has been little research on older persons shortly before death. That is, what happens physically, psychologically, and socially prior to death. Studies that do exist suggest that measurable changes take place for many individuals as they approach death. The discovery that measurable changes take place is important in the life-periods concept, discussed in Chapter 1. In this chapter it was noted that the transition from one life period to another results because of noticeable social events, such as marriage or graduation, or because of physical changes, such as the onset of menstruation. It now appears that there are measurable changes that take place as individuals enter the dying process.

In terms of health, studies have reported that older persons who were within 1 year of dying were in worse health than the aged in general. The percent with certain chronic conditions such as heart disease, cancer, or circulation problems, who fell during the year, had urinary or bowel incontinence, or spent time in a hospital were all greater than for the aged population in general and indicated a segment of the population in failing health (Moss et al., 1985).

The above study also found that the ability to provide self-care activities (eating, bathing, dressing, etc.) also declined as death approached. One year prior to death, 65 percent were self-sufficient in self care; 1 month before death the figure was 39 percent. Social interaction remained relatively stable throughout the last year of life, with a decline in ability to leave the home but visits by family and friends remaining the same. About 12 percent reported a decline in contact with family and friends during their last year.

Many, but not all, studies have also found that cognitive functioning appears to decline shortly before death. Kleemeier (1962) presented some tentative data suggesting that older persons who were near death suffered a greater decline in intelligence than those who were not near death. He called this the "terminal drop" hypothesis. Berkowitz and Green (1965) demonstrated the same trend although the data were not statistically significant.

Lieberman (1965, 1966) also found changes in cognitive functioning that lessened the ability of dying individuals to cope with the demands of their environment. An increased sense of hopelessness, concern for and awareness of others, and a decreased preoccupation with death itself were also reported (see Lieberman & Coplan, 1969). Another study by Reimanis and Green (1971) found that those who died within a year of being tested had suffered a greater intellectual decline than those who survived.

The study cited the most frequently in this area was written by Riegel and Riegel (1972) who reported that decline in intellectual functioning occurs within 5 years of death. In examining the studies on terminal drop, Siegler (1975) concluded that there is strong evidence to support the hypothesis that intellectual declines in old age are related to dying rather than aging (Siegler, 1987).

Botwinick and associates (1978) also found that behavioral measures could be useful in predicating death. Their study employed twenty-six measures of demographic, cognitive, perceptual, psychomotor, personality, health, and social-activity variables. The researchers found that a number of these variables significantly distinguished between those who lived and those who died after 5 years. An important implication for the medical profession is that most of these tests can be given in a short period of time and are relatively easy to score. Thus, those aged who receive certain scores can be placed on medical alert. Moss and his associates (1985) also examined cognitive functioning and found that there was a decline during the year preceding death. One year before death 72 percent were "always alert." One month prior to death the figure was 62 percent. Other psychological areas declined. For example, there was more depression and less interest in the world.

Recent studies have started to ascertain if cognitive changes are global or specific. White and Cunningham (1988) have reported that only certain abilities, such as vocabulary, are affected, and that the impact may be restricted to 2 years before death. So the reader will not be lulled into believing that the psychological changes in older persons who are near death make them consistently confused or intellectually blank, it is relevant to bring in a study by Kastenbaum (1967*b*). In using the "psychological autopsy" technique (see Kastenbaum & Weisman, 1972) 49 percent of the deceased geriatric patients studied had consistent and clear mental status until death. Another 26 percent had fluctuated between confused and alert, while about 22 percent had only partial contact with reality. Three percent had been consistently confused. The study concluded that the majority of dying geriatric patients studied were aware and cognizant of their environment, at least part of the time, prior to death.

We have examined several aspects of the dying process: attitudes, treatment, stages, and process. We will now examine death rates and the causes of death.

DEATH RATES AND CAUSES OF DEATH

This section will examine the statistics on death. Readers should be aware that death statistics are a source of controversy. The death statistics that are compiled by the Bureau of the Census are the most commonly cited, and will be used in this section. This does not mean, however, that they are without their critics. For example, in examining the autopsy reports of 200 individuals 85+ years of age Kohn (1982) reported that 26 percent had no readily identifiable cause of death other than "complications of the aging" process, which is not currently an acceptable cause of death on death certificates. Others have also commented on the inaccuracy of death certificates (see Glasser, 1981; Percy et al., 1981).

Sorlie and Gold (1987) reported that significant changes in death rates can occur simply because of physician preference for one term over another. Sirken and his colleagues (1987) said that death statistics "would be greatly enhanced if more were known about their quality." Death statistics are important since they can help to determine governmental health-related policy in terms of the amount of funding that is allocated for research, prevention, and treatment (see Greenfield et al., 1988; Hopkins et al., 1989; Rosenberg, 1989).

This is not intended to diminish the quality of the statistics, only to make readers aware that questions exist and further research is needed. Two areas will be examined in this section: death rates and causes of death.

Death Rates

In contemporary American society, death is primarily something that happens in old age. In fact, 70 percent of all deaths occur among those 65+ years of age; 30 to 50 percent of all deaths occur among those 80+ years of age (J. A. Brody, 1989). Thus, we would expect the death rates to be very high for the 65+ age category.

When we examine death statistics several trends can be seen. The first set of statistics that we need to examine deals with death rates. Table 17-1 examines the death rates for several age categories; two trends need to be observed. First, as can be seen for 1988, after adolescence the death rate goes up with increasing age. This is what most people would expect to happen in contemporary American society: as one grows older there is an increased likelihood of death. This belief characterizes a modern society whose major causes of death are from degenerative diseases, that tend to kill in the later years, more than an underdeveloped country where the major causes of death are from contagious diseases, whose victims tend to be the young. It is interesting that in contemporary American society the aged, who are most often associated with death, are also the most undervalued segment, while in an underdevel-

TABLE 17-1
DEATH RATES BY AGE AND SEX: 1960 TO 1988
(Per 100,000)

	All ages	Under 1 year	1–4	5–14	15–24	25–34	35–44	45–54	55–64	65–74	75–84	85+
Male												
1960	1,105	3,059	120	56	152	188	373	992	2,310	4,914	10,178	21,186
1970	1,090	2,410	93	51	189	215	403	959	2,283	4,874	10,010	17,822
1980	977	1,429	73	37	172	196	299	767	1,815	4,105	8,817	18,801
1988	944	1,122	56	31	154	196	296	637	1,624	3,583	8,243	18,475
Female												
1960	809	2,321	98	37	61	107	229	527	1,196	2,872	7,633	19,008
1970	808	1,864	75	32	68	102	231	517	1,099	2,580	6,678	15,518
1980	785	1,142	55	24	58	76	159	413	934	2,145	5,440	14,747
1988	825	876	45	22	55	71	141	344	909	2,051	5,167	14,452

Source: U.S. Bureau of the Census, 1990.

oped society, where infectious diseases kill a high percentage of the young, it is the young who have little status or significance. In fact, because of the high death rate, some preliterate societies do not give infants and children names until adolescence, which minimizes or negates the grief process and the disruption to the society. Second, the death rate has generally decreased in recent years for all ages and for both sexes.

Cause of Death

The next area we need to examine is cause of death. Table 17-2 will examine causes of death in 1900 and in 1988. From this table, five trends need to be observed. First, the major causes of death have changed. In 1900 the major causes of death were from communicable diseases such as influenza, pneumonia, and tuberculosis. In 1988 the major causes of death were from degenerative diseases, such as heart disease and cancer.

Second, the magnitude of the leading causes of death has changed. For example, in 1900 the four major causes of death accounted for 39 percent of all deaths. In 1988 the two leading causes of death accounted for 50 percent of all deaths and the four leading causes of death 60 percent of all deaths. Thus, in the past, death seemed to be from a greater diversity of diseases and conditions. In present society, the major causes of death stem from two major diseases: heart disease and cancer.

Table 17-3 is a more detailed analysis of cause of death by age grouping, and presents the third trend: The major causes of death differ by age category. For example, for those age 15–24 the leading causes of death are accidents, suicide, and cancer. For those 65–74 the leading causes of death are heart disease, cancer, and cerebrovascular disease (stroke). Each age category is subjected to different risk factors, a different duration of exposure to risk factors, and thus, different rates of death from each disease and condition.

The fourth trend can be observed by referring back to Table 17-1: women have a lower death rate than men. Two explanations have been offered for this difference. The first explanation has a genetic component, the second a psychosocial component (Stillion, 1984, 1985; Waldron, 1981).

Essentially, some researchers have speculated that there are genetic reasons for the differential in death rates. They have noted that there are 115 to 120 males conceived for every 100 females. However, at birth, there are 105 males born for every 100 females. This is because male fetuses have a higher rate of spontaneous abortion than females fetuses. Additionally, male infants have a higher death rate than female infants (in Table 17-1 the death rate for males under one year of age is 1122; for females the rate is 876). What the researchers are noting is that before psychosocial factors can have much of an impact the genetic factors can clearly be seen.

Others believe that the difference in the death rates is caused by psychosocial variables. The belief is that males have traditionally been socialized into roles that are more hazardous to health. For example, traditionally males have smoked more

TABLE 17-2
MAJOR CAUSES OF DEATH IN THE UNITED STATES

	1900			1988	
	% of all deaths	Rate per 100,000		% of all deaths	Rate per 100,000
All Causes	100.00	1719.10	1. Diseases of the heart	35.36	873.20
1. Influenza and pneumonia	11.76	202.20	2. Malignancies	22.34	312.20
2. Tuberculosis	11.31	194.40	3. Cerebrovascular disease (stroke)	7.11	194.70
3. Gastritis, duodenitis, and enteritis	8.30	142.70	4. Obstructive pulmonary diseases	3.64	62.10
4. Disease of the heart	7.99	137.40	5. Pneumonia and influenza	3.32	31.80
5. Cerebrovascular disease	6.22	106.90	6. Accidents (motor)	2.28	29.00
6. Chronic nephritis	5.15	88.60	7. Accidents (not motor)	2.26	19.90
7. All accidents	4.21	72.30	8. Diabetes mellitus	1.76	19.70
8. Malignancies	3.72	64.00	9. Suicide	1.47	15.40
9. Early infancy diseases	3.64	62.60	10. Chronic liver disease and cirrhosis	1.25	12.80
10. Diphtheria	2.34	40.30			10.90
Total	64.65			81.02	

Source: U.S. Bureau of the Census, 1975, 1990.

TABLE 17-3
DEATH RATES BY SELECTED CAUSES AND CHARACTERISTICS: 1988
(Per 100,000)

Both sexes	Total	Disease of the heart	Malignant neoplasms	Accidents	Cerebro-vascular diseases	Chronic pulmonary disease	Pneumonia	Suicide	Diabetes mellitus	Chronic liver disease
15–24	104.8	2.8	5.0	51.3	0.9	0.4	0.5	12.8	0.4	0.2
25–34	133.6	7.3	10.8	37.3	2.1	0.6	2.1	15.5	1.7	2.4
35–44	217.6	33.0	44.3	32.1	7.1	1.8	3.6	14.3	3.7	10.3
45–54	486.4	131.4	157.2	31.2	20.4	8.8	7.3	14.8	9.3	20.0
55–64	1,246.3	405.6	456.5	34.4	51.9	50.2	19.3	15.7	26.4	30.1
65–74	2,731.2	985.6	845.4	50.8	155.7	151.6	60.7	16.8	62.3	35.7
75–84	6,324.4	2,554.4	1,324.8	110.8	544.4	301.3	263.5	28.9	127.8	31.0
85+	15,577.7	7,119.1	1,664.5	273.7	1,710.3	399.9	1,090.2	19.7	203.9	18.3

Source: U.S. Bureau of the Census, 1990.

than females. Since smoking is linked to the leading causes of death, this factor has accounted for the higher male death rate. Additionally, traditionally males have had occupations that placed them at higher risk of death. For example, working in industries where accidents or hazardous materials were present, or in dangerous jobs such as mining or as police or fire officers, have all increased the death rate. Another factor is that traditionally males have had greater freedom to engage in hazardous recreational activities such as mountain climbing, scuba diving, or hang gliding. They have also probably traditionally had less supervision. Another factor is alcohol consumption. Males consume more alcohol than women. This can contribute to medical problems, such as cirrhosis of the liver, as well as to accidents: automobile, industrial, recreational. Access to automobiles also plays a factor in the death rates. Not only have males traditionally driven more miles but they tend to drive faster, use seat belts less frequently, and drive while intoxicated more frequently. In terms of suicide, men have had greater socialization to firearms, which have a greater probability of producing death than the means women have been socialized to use, drugs, which allow for an increased probability of successful intervention. A last factor deals with health and has three components.

The first component is prevention. Women tend to utilize preventative services, such as annual physical exams, more than men. The second component deals with the fact that society has made women more conscious of their weight than men. The thin body for women came into vogue in the 1920s and has remained in fashion ever since. This has made women more weight and nutrition conscious than men. The third component is that women have probably benefited more from medical advances than men. This can be seen in areas such as childbirth where 150 years ago infections killed many women after giving birth (see Speert, 1973). With the advent of the knowledge of antiseptic as well as new drugs to fight infection the maternal mortality rate dropped to 376 per 100,000 women in 1940 and to 6.6 in 1987 (U.S. Bureau of the Census, 1980, 1990). Additionally, effective birth-control methods have given women greater choice in family planning, and women can plan childbearing when factors, such as health, are optimal.

One question that is likely to be asked deals with the amount of influence the biogenetic factors have in comparison to the psychosocial factors. It has been suggested that 25 percent of the difference is produced by genetic factors and the rest by psychosocial roles (Waldron, 1981). This is an estimate and a recent conference sponsored by the National Institute of Aging suggested while the difference in life expectancy exists the reasons remain elusive (Holden, 1987).

The fifth and last area that needs to be examined is cause of death by race (see Table 17-4). As can be seen, there are some significant differences by race. Black males and females have higher death rates from disease of the heart, cancer, cerebrovascular disease, diabetes, and homicide than whites. White males and females have higher rates of suicide than blacks.

We have examined the death rate and causes of death in contemporary American society. A question that frequently arises during this discussion deals with life expectancy, which will be examined in the next section.

TABLE 17-4
CAUSE OF DEATH BY RACE
(Per 100,000)

	Disease of the heart	Malignant neoplasms	Cerebro-vascular disease	Diabetes	Homicide	Suicide
Males						
White	225.9	158.4	30.3	9.5	7.9	20.1
Black	287.1	227.9	57.1	18.3	53.3	12.0
Females						
White	116.3	109.7	26.3	8.1	3.0	5.3
Black	180.8	132.0	46.7	21.3	12.6	2.1

Source: U.S. Bureau of the Census, 1990.

LIFE EXPECTANCY

Life expectancy is a frequently misunderstood concept in gerontology (Yin & Shine, 1985). Many confuse the terms life expectancy and life span. Life span deals with the maximum or potential number of years that an organism could live if life were not truncated by factors such as illness, disease, or accidents. Although figures vary, it is widely believed that the potential for human life is between 120 to 130 years. Life expectancy is the estimated number of years an individual at a certain age can expect to live. Table 17-5 presents the life expectancy figures for men and women from 1920 to 1988. There are three trends that need to be observed from this table. First, women live longer than men. This is to be expected given our discussion on death rates. The reasons are those that we just discussed and deal with both genetic and psychosocial factors. The second trend deals with the increase in the number of years an individual can expect to live. Since 1920 males have gained about 18 years; women 24 years.

TABLE 17-5
EXPECTATIONS OF LIFE AT BIRTH: 1920 TO 1988

Year	Total	Male	Female
1920	54.1	53.6	54.6
1930	59.7	58.1	61.6
1940	62.9	60.8	65.2
1950	68.2	65.6	71.1
1960	69.7	66.6	73.1
1970	70.8	67.1	74.7
1980	73.7	70.0	77.4
1988	74.9	71.4	78.3

Source: U.S. Bureau of the Census, 1990.

This is a remarkable increase in a short period of time. Life in the not too distant past was almost certainly characterized by the Hobbesian phrase "nasty, short, and brutish." Table 3-1 (in Chapter 3) presented the estimated life expectancies throughout history. Until the 1900s, life expectancy did not increase very much. In fact, the gains made in this century are as great, or greater, than those made during the entire span of human history.

To understand the increase we need to understand more about the concept life expectancy. The life expectancy figures are more or less an average age at death. A society that has a high infant, child, and adolescent mortality rate will have a low life expectancy rate. Although life expectancy at birth is the most frequently cited figure, there can be a life expectancy figure for any age. Table 17-6, which presents the average number of years of life remaining at selected ages, appears to indicate that the aged have benefited most from medical advances. However, in actuality the increase in life expectancy has not come about because of an extension of life for the aged, but mainly because of the decrease in the infant, child, and adolescent death rates.

We know that in the past the young had a high death rate as a result of birth-related complications and because of childhood diseases. In 1900 about one out of every six infants died during the first year of life (Yin & Shine, 1985). The childhood diseases then took their toll until the late teens. Until recently, the increases in life expectancy have been primarily because of lower infant, child, and adolescent death rates and not because of an extension of life for the aged.

As was noted in Chapter 6, "Physical Health," this is starting to change. Death rates for two of the leading causes of death for older persons (heart disease and stroke) are starting to decline. Although the death rate for cancer has been increasing, age at onset and survival time have been increasing (Soldo & Agree, 1988).

TABLE 17-6
EXPECTATIONS OF LIFE AT SELECTED AGES: 1986

Age	Total	White male	White female	Black male	Black female
At birth	74.8	72.0	78.8	65.2	73.5
1	74.5	71.5	78.4	65.5	73.7
10	65.7	62.7	69.6	56.8	65.0
20	56.0	53.1	59.8	47.3	55.3
30	46.6	43.9	50.1	38.5	45.7
40	37.2	34.6	40.4	30.3	36.6
50	28.3	25.7	31.2	22.7	28.0
60	20.3	17.9	22.6	16.1	20.3
70	13.5	11.5	15.1	10.8	13.9
80	8.1	6.9	8.8	6.8	8.5
85+	6.1	5.2	6.5	5.5	6.7

Source: U.S. Bureau of the Census, 1990.

The third observation can be made using Table 17-7. As can be seen, the gains for women have been much greater than the gains for men. In 1920 women lived 1 year longer than men. By 1970 it was 7.70 years longer. It is unlikely that a change that occurred this rapidly could not have resulted from genetic changes in women that increased life expectancy. However, since 1980 the difference has started to decrease, not increase. There are at least three possible explanations for this which will be discussed below.

First, changes in social roles. The rates of smoking are now nearly equal for men and women. This has unquestionably had an impact on women's death rates. Lung cancer now kills more women than breast cancer, and 75 percent of lung cancers are caused by smoking (Itri, 1987). Additionally, there are more women in what have been traditionally "men's roles," many of which have increased risks associated with them. A second explanation may be that women reached a "maximum" life expectancy sooner than men. That is, men lagged behind and are now just beginning to make the gains that women made earlier. A third possible explanation, also noted for the differential in death rates, is that earlier medical advances benefited women more than men. We will now briefly examine several factors that help to determine life expectancy.

Determinants of Life Expectancy

Health, illness, and death are not randomly distributed throughout the aged population. Rather, certain types of individuals have a greater likelihood of being healthy, or having certain illnesses, or of dying. This section will examine some of the variables that contribute to life expectancy. There were three major sources of information for this section. The first was the Center for the Study of Aging and Human Development studies that were conducted at Duke University (see Busse & Maddox, 1985; Palmore, 1980, 1981, 1982). The second was the Retirement Age Study by the Center for Health Statistics (Chapman et al., 1986). The third was a study by Kaplan and his associates (1987) on the aged in Alameda County, California.

This section will separate the determinants into two categories: determinants of

TABLE 17-7
CHANGES IN LIFE EXPECTANCY (WHITES)

	Males	Female	Difference
1920	53.6	54.6	1.00
1930	58.1	61.6	3.50
1940	60.8	65.2	4.40
1950	65.6	71.1	5.50
1960	66.6	73.1	6.50
1970	67.1	74.7	7.70
1980	70.0	77.4	7.40
1986	72.1	78.9	6.80

Source: U.S. Bureau of the Census, 1975, 1990.

life expectancy that can be controlled and determinants that cannot be controlled. Although all of the variables discussed below relate to older persons, the next section will discuss three additional variables, in greater detail, that are often associated with death in old age.

Determinants of Life Expectancy That Can Be Controlled

Diet   The studies at Duke University reported that "too much" and "too little" food can have an influence on life expectancy. Those under and overweight had more illnesses and a higher death rate than those that maintained normal weights for heights. As with most studies, however, there are confounding factors. For example, overweight individuals probably do not exercise and it is difficult to determine if it is being overweight or lack of exercise that produced the difference in life expectancy. Underweight individuals might have an illness that has produced the condition. The Alameda County study reported that those who did not eat breakfast had an increased risk of death. This study did not ascertain if socioeconomic or health factors played a role in the eating behavior.

Exercise   Numerous studies have indicated that exercise increases life expectancy. Part of the reason may be that those in better health are more capable of exercising (Buskirk, 1985). Certain segments of the population value exercise more than others (Chapman et al., 1986).

Smoking   Smoking is consistently identified as the major cause of premature death in American society. The mortality rate of smokers is 70 percent greater than for nonsmokers (Chapman et al., 1986). The studies at Duke University found smoking to be the greatest negative correlate of life expectancy.

Smoking is the most significant risk factor in lung cancer. It is a major risk factor in heart disease. Additionally, smoking acts synergistically with industrial and atmospheric pollutants and alcohol consumption to increase the incidence of disease (Kaplan et al., 1987). Smokers who work or live in polluted environments have a higher incidence of respiratory disease; smokers who consume alcohol have a higher incidence of mouth and throat cancer. As noted in the chapter on health, not only does smoking kill, but it also produces significant amounts of illness and disability.

There is, however, a confounding factor; those who smoke are probably less health conscious than those who do not.

Socioeconomic Status   Studies in this area have presented "mixed" results. The studies tend to find that death rates are higher for individuals in the lower socioeconomic classes, although over the last 40 years the death rates have become more similar. This is probably because many lower class jobs that previously had a high risk of death or which exposed the workers to life-threatening conditions (i.e., cancer-causing chemicals) have been eliminated, and because medical insurance now provides more equal medical care.

The confounding factor in this example is that an individual may belong to the lower social class because of a chronic illness which prevents him or her from obtaining a better paying job. Thus, social class is seen as the variable influencing life expectancy when in actuality it is a preexisting illness.

Determinants of Life Expectancy that Cannot be Controlled

Heredity   The other factors that we have discussed can be modified. Individuals can technically control and change all of them. Heredity is a variable that as of yet cannot be modified.

The studies at Duke University examined the hereditary or genetic factor. The belief has been that genetics play a large role in life expectancy. The Duke University studies did not confirm this belief. These studies reported that after age 60 there was no correlation between the life expectancy of parents and their offspring. The researchers concluded that hereditary factors have an influence early in life, with diseases such as sickle cell anemia, but in later years life style appears to override genetics. Not all studies have reported the same conclusion (see Rockstein & Sussman, 1979).

Sex   As we have noted earlier, females live longer than males. Part of the difference is genetic, and part is due to psychosocial variables. Table 17.1 noted that females have a lower death rate than males at all ages, and Table 17.5 noted their greater life expectancy.

Race   As was seen in Table 17.6, blacks have a shorter life expectancy than whites until late old age when there is a "cross-over effect" (see Wing et al., 1985). They also have a higher death rate at all ages except late old age. The differences in life expectancy and death rate throughout most of life are probably due in large part to socioeconomic differences, not racial differences.

In the last few decades the life expectancy rates of blacks have increased significantly. However, recently there have been some declines in their life expectancy. The reasons for the declines are not yet clear, but are probably related to a high death rate for young black males from violent death.

Intelligence   Those with higher levels of intelligence have greater life expectancy. There are three possible explanations for this. First, high intelligence may show a better level of physical functioning. Second, individuals with higher levels of intelligence may be able to solve problems and adapt to situations better than those with lower levels of intelligence. Third, those with higher levels of intelligence have higher socioeconomic positions.

Long-Lived Societies   One last issue needs to be addressed in this section: long-lived societies. There have been suggestions that there are certain nonindustrial societies where the life expectancy is significantly longer than in industrial societies. Societies in the Soviet Union and Ecuador have been the most frequently mentioned. Reasons for this extraordinary life expectancy have ranged from genetic superiority to diet (i.e., yogurt). The majority of these claims have been refuted. Among those claiming extraordinary longevity in Ecuador it was reported that most had exaggerated their ages (Mazess & Forman, 1979). The same was found to be true among the Abkhazians in the Soviet Union (Bennett & Garson, 1986). In a review of the literature, Palmore (1987) concluded that there are no "authenticated" societies that have extraordinary longevity.

As noted earlier, the next section is going to examine three factors that are often associated with death in old age: bereavement, retirement, and relocation.

DETERMINANTS OF DEATH IN OLD AGE

As we just saw in the section on life expectancy, death, at any age, is not a random event. Rather, there are a plethora of factors that increase or decrease the probability of death. This section will examine three factors that have frequently been assumed to predispose older persons to death: bereavement, relocation, and retirement.

Bereavement

The influence of bereavement on health is an issue that has been debated by gerontologists for decades. There is no doubt that bereavement brings about physical, psychological, and social changes. The questions that gerontologists have been asking is how do these changes influence health and death rates (see Bettis & Scott, 1981; Caserta et al., 1985; Gentry & Shulman, 1985).

Physically, bereavement can cause lack of energy, tightness in the chest, shortness of breath, frequent sighing, headaches, dizziness, a feeling of emptiness in the abdomen, loss of muscular strength, and stomach disorders (Kalish, 1976; Lindemann, 1979; Wass & Myers, 1984). It has also been suggested that bereavement can cause death. This type of death has been referred to as the "broken heart syndrome," or the "loss effect." Several researchers have suggested that during the first 6 months to 1 year after the death of a spouse, the death rate of the bereaved is as much as 40 percent higher than for the nonbereaved (Carpenter & Wylie, 1974; Hinton, 1967; Rees & Lutkins, 1967). Although few studies have found a death rate as high as 40 percent, most have found that the death rate of the bereaved is significantly higher than expected. For example, a study of 95,647 individuals widowed in Finland between 1972 and 1976 found that the widowed had a death rate that was 6.5 percent higher than what would be expected (Kaprio et al., 1987).

In recent years the literature in this area has become increasingly sophisticated and complex. Studies have attempted to ascertain if the higher death rate is caused by the physical, psychological, or social consequences of bereavement, or if it is caused by other factors that are associated with bereavement. For example, there may be a physical reaction to bereavement that brings about a coronary event (heart attack) or a psychological reaction that results in suicide or an increased probability of an accidental death. The death of a spouse may also bring about a lowered financial status that produces a change in health status, thus producing death. These are some of the confounding variables that recent studies have examined.

Two studies have examined and reviewed the literature in this area (Rowland, 1977; Stroebe et al., 1981–1982). Both of the studies have noted that although the death rate is higher among the bereaved, it cannot be demonstrated, at this time, that the higher death rate for the bereaved is being caused by bereavement. This is because there are several possible explanations for the higher death rate that research has not ruled out. Six of the possible explanations are presented below.

Health is a factor that is used in the first four explanations. The first explanation is what is known as the "selective remarriage" or "health as a preselector" explanation. There are several ways to conduct studies on the death rate among the bereaved.

One way is to examine the marital status of individuals who have died. The researchers in this area are interested in comparing the death rate of the recently widowed with the death rate for those who are married. Although this is an acceptable way of conducting this type of research, there is a limitation. The limitation is that there is a greater likelihood that the widowed who are in good health will remarry, while those in poor health will remain single. As a result, the healthy widowed are removed from the category of "widowed," leaving a disproportionate percentage of widowed individuals in poor health, presumably with a higher death rate. Thus, while the results appear to show that widowhood is causing death, it is in fact prewidowhood health status.

A second explanation, which also concerns health, is known as the "homogamy of health explanation." This explanation claims that just as individuals who are similar in terms of variables such as social class, religion, race, or educational background tend to marry, this is also true in the area of health: the healthy tend to marry the healthy and the sick tend to marry the sick. Thus, when examining the death rate of the married and bereaved, the bereaved have a higher death rate, again because of prebereavement health status.

The third explanation has been called the "joint unfavorable environment explanation." This explanation states that both spouses died at approximately the same time because they were in the same pathogenic or unhealthy environment. The unfavorable environment may have been unhealthy or substandard living conditions, the stress of poverty, or minority status.

"Mutual infection or accidents" is the fourth explanation. If one spouse died from an infectious disease it is reasonable that the other was infected and will die within a short period of time, not from widowhood, but from an infectious disease. Or, if a couple was in a catastrophic automobile accident, during which one died immediately, the other might live for a few days or months, but then also die as a result of the accident. Again, it appears that statistically there is a relationship between widowhood and death, when in fact the cause of the death was the accident.

Statistics have been used as a basis for the fifth possible explanation. Research studies often group individuals into age ranges such as 55–64 or 65–74. The death rates within these groups are then compared by marital status. For example, within the age group 65–69 the death rates of those who are married and those who are bereaved would be compared. It is possible that within each age group the average age of the widowed and married differ, with a higher average age for the widowed than the married. Since age is related to death, we would expect the group with the highest average age to have the highest death rate. Thus, the bereaved have a higher death rate than those who are married, but it is because they are older, not because they are bereaved. Stroebe and his associates (1981–1982) reported that at least two studies have found that when specific ages in age groups are examined, the widowed have an average age that is about 1 year higher than the married.

The sixth possible explanation deals with what has been termed "comparison group problems." The basic idea presented here is that widowhood produces many changes, all of which can affect health. For example, with widowhood may come a change in financial status. Thus, when comparing the death rates of the married and widowed, and noting the difference in death rate, it is difficult to determine if the higher death rate among the widowed is caused by the "broken heart" syndrome or by a lowered financial status (see Morgan, 1986). In addition to the six explanations for the higher death rate of the bereaved are a number of studies on death rate and marital status. Some of these studies will be reviewed below.

According to the "broken heart" explanation, the bereaved die because of health-related factors. Thus, we would expect to see the health of the bereaved gradually decline. Heyman and Gianturco (1973) studied widowed individuals who had a median age of 72. They found that after widowhood there was little health deterioration, and what had occurred was attributed to time-related health decreases. They noted that those in this study adapted very well to the death of a spouse. They attributed this adaptation to the fact that social pressures, in terms of family or career, were less pressing. Additionally, most were psychologically prepared for widowhood. Although Ferraro (1985–1986) found that perceived health declined immediately after the death of a spouse, he reported that the long-term effects were not significant.

The next area that needs to be examined is the psychological reaction to bereavement. Perhaps there are psychological changes that predispose the bereaved to death. Obviously there can be negative psychological reactions to the death of a spouse that can affect mental health and predispose an individual to death. The questions for researchers are whether these reactions are intense enough in a significant percentage of the bereaved to bring about a death rate that is significantly different from those who are married.

Psychological reactions to bereavement can include guilt, depression, anger, rage, stress, anxiety, distorted perceptions (i.e., seeing or sensing the presence of the person who died), and a preoccupation with or idealization of the deceased (Lopata, 1973; Parkes, 1972; Wass & Myers, 1984). Gallagher and her associates (1983) examined the mental health status of elderly widows and widowers. While they found that the bereaved had more psychological distress, most of the scores did not indicate that serious psychopathology was present. In fact, the researchers concluded by noting that the loss of a spouse may not be as much of a mental health problem as previously believed, although they noted that future studies would be needed to determine the ultimate consequences of the death of a spouse (see Lund et al., 1986).

Some researchers have speculated that the psychological reactions to grief may not be as severe as expected because of "anticipatory grief." Anticipatory grief occurs when individuals become aware of the impending death of a spouse, or significant other, and start the grief process before the death occurs (see Gerber et al., 1975). The survivors have an opportunity to prepare for the death so that when the death occurs they have worked through the grief process. Although this is an interesting hypothesis, research in this area is "inconclusive" (see Hill et al., 1988).

In contrast to the above, the study done in Finland on the widowed suggested that the psychological reaction to widowhood may be a serious mental health problem. In fact, it may be that the psychological reactions are causing the difference in the death rate. This study found that overall the death rate for the widowed was 6.5 percent higher than would be expected. However, when the figures were further analyzed it was found that deaths from natural causes accounted for 3.2 percent of all deaths while those from violent deaths, such as accidents and suicide, accounted for 93 percent of the deaths. Although death rates have frequently been compared, causes of death have not. This study suggests that the psychological consequences of bereavement are more devastating than the physical consequences (Kaprio et al., 1987).

The negative psychological impact of bereavement can also be seen in the literature that shows that married individuals are happier, are better off psychologically, have lower rates of mental illness, and have a greater chance of survival than their widowed, single, or separated counterparts (Gove, 1973). Gove found that those not married were more careless and reckless in their behavior than their married counterparts. They had more accidents and had more crimes committed against them than those who were married. Gove also found a higher incidence of cirrhosis of the liver, lung cancer, tuberculosis, and nontreatment for diabetes among those who were not married than among those who were married. In addition to physical and psychological changes, bereavement can also lead to social changes that might predispose an individual to death. Most widowed individuals receive little or no help in restructuring their lives. This lack of assistance can lead to role changes that involve alcohol abuse, excessive smoking, neglect of health, or lack of proper diet. Again, this is an area where further research is needed.

One other area needs to be discussed which deals with the continual debate over whether aged males or females will adjust better to bereavement. Some believe that males will adjust better than females because (Stillion, 1984, 1985):

1 Many women have an identity that is closely connected with the husband. When the husband dies, they lose this identity.

2 With increasing age, the sex ratio will dictate that most women will not remarry. Most men, however, will have ample potential partners to select from. This opportunity for future intimacy gives men a more optimistic outlook on the future.

3 With the death of the husband, women have many unfamiliar responsibilities in the area of decision making and finance that are stressful.

However, it has also been suggested that widowhood is more difficult for men than for women. Some of the following reasons have been provided (Kaprio et al., 1987; Stroebe & Stroebe, 1983):

1 Because of the higher death rate, men do not have as many friends to engage in leisure activities with.

2 The male is confronted with many unfamiliar household tasks with which he is uncomfortable.

3 Since husbands generally die before their wives, more men are not prepared psychologically to outlive their wives.

A study by Feinson (1986) reviewed the literature in this area and conducted a study on the mental health differences of aged widows and widowers. In his review of the literature, Feinson separated the studies into those showing behavioral, physiological, and psychological responses to bereavement. He concluded that based on the available studies, conclusions were premature because of methodological limitations inherent in the studies, and the scarcity of studies. Feinson's study found that the bereaved reported more mental health disorders than married couples. He did not find, however, gender differences. Scott and Kivett (1985) did not find a difference in morale in widowed males and females. They concluded that morale was determined more by the resources that were available rather than gender.

In a 2-year longitudinal study of 192 bereaved individuals, Lund and his associates (1986) did not find that males or females had a more difficult bereavement process in terms of the psychological and social outcomes that they examined. They did find that when asked the open-ended question, "What has been the single greatest difficulty that you have had related to your spouse's death?" the specific responses were different, although there was a similarity. The similarity was that each found the major difficulty was engaging in activities that had been the responsibility of the dead spouse. For women activities such as yard work, financial matters, or home repairs created problems; for men it was shopping, cooking, and cleaning that created problems. The study did report that social support networks, which were more developed among women, played a significant role in helping the bereaved to cope (see Dimond et al., 1987). The study continued by noting that at the end of 2 years, improvement in mental health areas, such as depression, were significant and that bereavement is a continual process.

Although it is difficult to quantify some of the consequences, bereavement does have an impact. Gass (1987) has reviewed the helpful and less helpful coping strategies of widows. Those that she found helpful included such activities as keeping busy, taking part in social groups, acquiring new skills, analysis of the death, use of religion and prayer, speaking to the dead spouse, and remembering pleasant memories. Coping strategies that Gass found less helpful included the use of drugs or alcohol (see Valanis et al., 1987), accusing oneself of the death, averting or becoming angry with others, and bargaining or compromising with God. Gass also reported that receiving detrimental information from others, such as "You will never get over widowhood, it is terrible" or "I was told time would heal but it doesn't," did not help the widow to cope with the loss (see Lund et al., 1985).

Relocation

Relocation is a sensitive issue among gerontologists. It is an emotional issue because relocation involves deep-rooted beliefs concerning life and death. Those in favor of relocation believe that the relocation of older persons is less detrimental than leaving them where they currently reside. For example, they believe that moving older persons from substandard facilities to facilities that meet codes will be beneficial. Those opposed to relocation assert that relocating older persons is traumatic and will generally increase their risk of death. Early studies reported "relocation trauma," "transportation shock," or "transfer trauma" which became translated into a "mortality hypothesis" which was widely accepted by the gerontological community in the 1960s (see Burnette, 1986). Essentially, this hypothesis noted the adverse consequences of relocation in such areas as a higher death and illness rate, increased mental confusion, and greater dependency on staff. As Coffman (1983) has pointed out, this hypothesis had far-reaching consequences for nursing home patients in facilities that did not meet health codes since nursing home administrators could argue that moving patients was more detrimental to their health than keeping them in a substandard facility.

Numerous studies reported that moving older persons from one environment to another caused a significantly higher mortality and morbidity rate (Aldrich & Mendkoff, 1963; Downey, 1974; Ferrari, 1963; Ferraro, 1982; Horowitz & Schulz, 1983; Isner, 1975; Killian, 1970; Lieberman, 1961, 1974; Miller & Lieberman, 1965). Some studies have indicated that as many as 50 percent of those relocated were negatively affected by the relocation (see Isner, 1975). Most of the authors studying relocation have emphasized the crisis that comes after leaving a familiar environment. The crisis is believed to cause stress and anxiety because of the disruption in environment and long-standing social ties (Elwell, 1986). It has even been reported that simply informing individuals of a future move increased the death rate (see Carpenter & Wylie, 1974). The "mortality hypothesis" was challenged by research of the 1970s and 1980s. Much of this research either found that relocation had no impact, or that it had a positive impact on physical and mental health.

While there is still controversy, the current trend is to believe that the threat of relocation has been exaggerated (Borup, 1982, 1983; Borup & Gallego, 1981; Borup et al., 1979; Coffman, 1983; Elwell, 1986; Kasl, 1972; Lawton & Yaffe, 1970; Mirotznik & Ruskin, 1985a, 1985b; Wittels & Botwinick, 1974). In an analysis of relocation studies Borup (1983) found that 75 percent of the studies reported that relocation had no impact on mortality while 14 percent said that it increased mortality. In some of the other studies the relationship between relocation and mortality could not be ascertained.

Part of the conflict in research is because of the multitude of variables that are involved in this research. Some of the research examined voluntary moves while other research looked at involuntary moves. Some examined intrainstitutional moves (from one part or wing of an institution to another) while other research examined interinstitutional moves (from one institution to another). Some examined moves from the community to an institution, others moves from institution to institution, and others moves from the institution to the community. Some of the moves were prompted by a change in health status, either better or worse, while others were prompted by other factors such as urban renewal. In some relocations the staff and other residents also made the move while in others this did not occur. In some studies special programs to prepare the residents took place; in other studies no such preparation took place (see Brody et al., 1974; Jasnau, 1967; Novick, 1967; Rosswurm, 1983; Zweig & Csank, 1975). One additional concern is that most of the studies have focused on mortality. More emphasis needs to be placed on "behavioral and mental changes" that occur after relocation (see Coffman, 1983; Elwell, 1986; Horowitz & Schulz, 1983; Schulz & Anderman, 1974).

The similarity between the two sides is that both care about the aged. Both sides in this issue believe that the views of the other side will harm the aged. For example, Bourestom and Pastalan (1981), who believe that the " . . . radical and involuntary relocation of frail elderly individuals carries with it potentially high risks," noted that one of their fears is that the current belief, of relocation not being harmful, will reduce the number of programs that prepare older persons for relocation. In other words, the mortality of relocated individuals may have dropped because of programs to assist in the relocation. Thus, if those working with older persons in nursing homes believe that relocation is not detrimental, they might eliminate their relocation programs.

Borup (1983), who does not believe that relocation is detrimental, recognizes that there are high-risk individuals and situations. Another factor Borup (1982) has mentioned is that there are many older persons (15 to 40 percent) living in nursing homes who could live in other "less restrictive" environments. Again, the myth of relocation mortality prevents many of these individuals from being relocated to homes or other less restrictive facilities where their physical and mental functioning might improve. Elwell (1986) has pointed out that while recent studies have not supported the relocation trauma theory, it cannot be discarded. However, he pointed out, more of the same type of research is *not* needed; rather, gerontologists need to improve "previous research designs and existing theory to clarify the empirical evidence."

Retirement

Retirement has frequently been seen as a "death sentence," especially if the retirement was forced. The gerontological literature does not support this position, although this belief is still prevalent. There are probably several reasons this belief persists, four of which will be discussed in this book (see Ekerdt, 1987). First, almost everyone has an example which he or she can point to. The examples may be personal, such as a friend or relative, or deal with a national figure who died shortly after retirement.

Second, retirement is seen as stressful. The "Social Readjustment Rating Scale" (see Eisdorfer & Wilkie, 1977; Holmes & Rahe, 1967) is a popular and frequently cited index of life stressors. Retirement is number 10 on the scale and worth 45 out of a maximum of 100 points (the three most stressful events are death of a spouse 100 points, divorce 73 points, and marital separation 65 points). Thus, those who hold this belief claim that the stress of retirement will kill retirees before they can adjust. In addition to retirement as a stressor, the event of retirement also produces other changes that are listed as stressful. For example, there are changes in financial status (38 points) and in social activities (18 points). Third, gerontological theory also played a role in the support of the belief that retirement is detrimental to health. For example, activity theorists often spoke of the negative consequences of retirement, especially if work roles were not replaced. Role theorists also discussed the belief that retirement was not a valued role in American society, thus the retired had low self-worth.

Fourth, the consequences of aging are often correlated with the event of retirement. Thus, if an individual died shortly after retirement, retirement, not aging, was blamed. The last factor that has contributed to the belief are studies indicating that the retired have higher illness and death rates than working individuals in the same age groups. However, what these studies did not take into account is that those with health problems were more likely to retire, while those in good health were more likely to continue working. Thus, it was age, not retirement status, that contributed to health problems. Ekerdt (1987) has noted that this is one of the most persistent myths in gerontology. He said that a review of the literature, from the 1950s to the present, revealed, almost without exception, that retirement, in and of itself, does not increase the risk of illness or death.

There have also been claims that retirement improves health, although these studies tended to be older and have numerous methodological problems. Ekerdt and his associates have recently investigated this claim (Ekerdt, Baden, Bosse, & Dibbs, 1983; Ekerdt, Bosse, & LoCastro, 1983). In a study of participants of the Veterans Administration Normative Aging Study they found that 38 percent claimed that their health improved after retirement. For many individuals this improvement seems logical. After all, they were removed from some of the physical and psychological aspects of work that were injurious to health. Additionally, they now had more leisure time to spend in health-related activities, such as exercise. The study did not support the claim of an improvement in medical status. It did find that functional health, or the perception that one has of his or her health, increased. The perception of an increase in health status may be because of fewer and less demanding roles that allow the same medical status to function more efficiently. The study noted that further research is needed in this area and that the importance of functional health should not be underestimated.

The next, and last, section will examine three contemporary issues in dying and death.

CONTEMPORARY ISSUES IN DYING AND DEATH

At the beginning of this chapter it was mentioned that concepts change over time. Some of the changes in the concepts of dying and death were discussed in the early part of this chapter. Not only do concepts change but so do the issues that surround concepts. The next section will examine three contemporary issues in the area of dying and death: the definition of death, the removal of life-sustaining treatment, and euthanasia.

Definition of Death

In the 1960s through the early 1980s the major issue in dying and death concerned the definition of death. The issue surfaced because technological innovations had blurred the traditional signs that distinguish life from death. Where at one time the absence of respiration and heartbeat signaled death, modern technology has created the ability to artificially maintain heartbeat and respiration even in individuals who will never regain consciousness because of extensive and permanent brain damage. In addition, intravenous hydration, nasogastric feeding, and antibiotics existed to assist in keeping these individuals "alive," sometimes for decades. In the past these individuals died fairly rapidly from dehydration, starvation, or infections. This is not intended as a criticism of modern technology. Rather, it is to demonstrate that modern technology created the need to change the concept and definition of death.

Although it may seem as though the diagnosis of death is a simple matter, in fact it has always been a difficult diagnosis, even though the direction of the problem has changed. In the past, there was a fear that the living would be misdiagnosed as dead and prematurely buried; today there is the fear that the dead will be misdiagnosed as living and artificially maintained. Through modern technology individuals who have no brain functioning and who can never regain consciousness can have machines simulate signs of life, such as respiration and heartbeat. This has created a new category of individuals who have generated medical, legal, and social problems. At the medical level are issues that deal with when to terminate and when to continue treatment. Legally there are issues such as life insurance and inheritance. For example, can a family collect an individual's life insurance and divide the estate. Socially there are issues that deal with questions for family members of patients such as whether a woman is a wife or widow.

The issue on the definition of death surfaced for four reasons. First, physicians wanted to know when they should or could legally and ethically terminate treatment. The second issue dealt with cost. The cost of maintaining someone in a hospital can be thousands of dollars a day. Again, a definition was needed that would allow physicians or a family member to know when to terminate treatment. Third, medical advances increased the need for donor organs for transplant. The sooner after death organs are transplanted the greater the likelihood of a successful transplant. Thus, a definition would allow physicians to remove an organ prior to the cessation of heartbeat and respiration which would increase the likelihood of a successful transplant. Fourth, certain cases, such as Karen Ann Quinlan and Nancy Cruzan, gained national attention for the need for a new definition of death.

The question was debated by physicians, lawyers, religious leaders, as well as others. There were literally thousands of articles written and published that ranged from philosophical statements to empirical research. In 1981 President Reagan created the President's Commission for the Study of Ethical Problems in Medicine and Biomedical and Behavioral Research. The interdisciplinary commission was to study "the ethical and legal implications of the matter of defining death, including the advisability of developing a uniform definition of death."

The commission was asked to develop a new standard of death that could be used when modern technology, such as mechanical ventilators, precluded the use of traditional methods of determining death. In its report, the commission pointed out that the definition of death has continually evolved because of medical advances; just as changes had been made in the definition in the past, changes were needed in the present and would be needed in the future. The commission noted the effect the stethoscope and EKG had on the definition of death, and that modern technology had made additional clarification necessary. The commission stated that it had examined three possible ways of determining death: death of part of the brain, death of the whole brain, or other nonbrain ways to determine death, such as absence of heartbeat. The commission decided on a definition of death that included the traditional nonbrain signs of death (cardiopulmonary) as well as a "whole brain" definition (neurologic). The commission developed the following proposal:

> *Determination of Death.* An individual who has sustained either (1) irreversible cessation of circulatory and respiratory functions, or (2) irreversible cessation of all functions of the entire brain, including the brain stem, is dead. A determination of death must be made in accordance with accepted medical standards.

The commission recognized that there could be "complicating conditions" such as drug and metabolic intoxication, hypothermia, for individuals in shock, and for children. These were also addressed in its report. The proposal was accepted by both the American Bar Association and the American Medical Association.

As can be seen in its definition of ''brain death,'' the commission took the more conservative approach by selecting the whole brain definition. A simplistic approach to the brain can conceptualize the brain as consisting of two parts: higher brain and lower brain. The higher brain (cerebrum) controls consciousness, thought, memory, and feelings. It is in this part of the brain that the ''personality'' resides. The lower brain (brainstem) controls certain biological functions, such as respiration. When the brain is deprived of oxygen it is the higher brain that is destroyed first. The extent and length of oxygen deprivation will determine the amount of brain damage. When the cerebrum is destroyed but part of the brainstem remains intact the individual is in a ''persistent vegetative state'' or ''persistent noncognitive state.'' These individuals can move, yawn, open their eyes, make facial grimaces, and may even breathe unassisted. However, without higher brain functioning, they are without awareness of their environment. They can be ''awake'' but not aware. The longest survival of a patient in a persistent vegetative state is 37 years (President's Commission, 1981). The commission was faced with the decision of deciding if someone with the loss of higher brain functioning or the whole brain was dead.

The commission rejected ''higher'' brain death as a definition of death since severely retarded or senile individuals could be classified in this category. Also, individuals whose higher brain is destroyed but whose brain stems remain functional can breathe unassisted. The commission rejected that individuals in these situations were dead. If both parts of the brain are destroyed then even modern technology can only keep individuals functioning for a relatively short period of time, usually only days or weeks.

The purpose of the proposal was to have one definition of death that would apply in all states. The majority of states have adopted the proposal or one similar in content.

Termination of Life-Sustaining Treatment

The President's Commission created a new concept of death which helped to resolve some complex issues in the area of dying and death. However, a second issue also needed attention: when to forego life-sustaining treatment. The commission (1983) also addressed this issue in its report *Deciding to Forego Life-Sustaining Treatment*. In addition, both the House and Senate Aging Committees requested the Office of Technology Assessment to further study this area and to issue a separate report for the elderly. It was believed that the elderly constituted a ''special'' population since individuals in this group are at greater risk of life-threatening illness, and often have other conditions that lead to a poor prognosis even with life-sustaining treatment. Additionally, it is this segment that makes the greatest use of medical resources in American society. The final report was called *Life-Sustaining Technologies and the Elderly* (U.S. Congress, 1987).

Life-sustaining technology is of relatively recent origin. Until this century, physicians had the ability to alleviate some symptoms, such as pain with opium, but had few skills, techniques, or drugs to sustain life. From the 1920s major advancements have been made in several areas that have given physicians the ability to sustain life. Without these advancements, individuals in need of them would die, generally within days. The common life-sustaining technologies are:

- Cardiopulmonary resuscitation
- Mechanical ventilation
- Renal dialysis
- Nutritional support and hydration
- Antibiotics

Of the five life-sustaining technologies listed, only one, antibiotics, can "cure" a disease or condition.

The need for these reports was fourfold. First, increasing medical knowledge had brought two basic medical goals into more frequent conflict with one another. The two goals are the extension of life and the relief of pain. Modern medicine could often extend life but it was a tortured existence for many, filled with drugs that produced unpleasant side effects, repeated and painful medical procedures, and the ravages and discomforts of the disease or condition. Associated with this is the question of "quality of life." Second, medicine now had more control over life and death. Applying certain medical techniques and knowledge could extend life; withholding them could hasten death. Thus, medical technology has acquired the ability, in most cases, to determine the "timing and circumstances of death." Third, although medicine has more options, patients are often in less of a position to make choices. Many patients are comatose or incompetent to make decisions because of the effects of drugs or the consequences of diseases. Thus, there was a need for physicians and family members to know when to truncate life-sustaining treatment. The fourth area concerns cost. The medical costs for the dying are very high. The medicare costs for those who died during a given year were four to six times higher than for those who used medicare but did not die (U.S. Congress, 1987). Realizing that there are limits to governmental spending in the health area, some have asked if it would not be "better" to spend on those who have an opportunity to live rather than those who are going to die.

This issue has been expanded by Daniel Callahan (1987) in his thought-provoking book *Setting limits: Medical goals in an aging society.* Callahan noted the high cost of medical care for older persons and said that while life is extended, the quality is often very low. He has noted that if this trend continues, in the next several decades the cost of medical care for the aged will consume 45 percent of the federal budget. He continued that this can only be done by taking resources away from other age groups. Callahan proposes that medical technology should not be directed at extending life; rather its direction should be focused on improving life throughout the "natural life span." This would allow individuals to accomplish what they need to accomplish during a "natural" life span. Thus, when they reached the end of the natural life span (probably somewhere around 80 years of age), they would have fulfilled their goals and obligations, and society's obligation to them would be completed, which would make them ineligible for life-extending medical treatment such as kidney dialysis or coronary bypass surgery.

The questions in this area are complex, and the answers—any answers—are almost certain to be controversial. Although in the future the determination of who receives what treatment may be clarified, currently there is a great deal of confusion.

One current question is who determines whether a patient receives life-sustaining treatment. The President's Commission noted that competent patients have the right to decide on life-sustaining technology. For incompetent patients surrogates were to be appointed. Additional guidelines in this area were presented in 1984 and 1989 when the *New England Journal of Medicine* published an article "The Physician's Responsibility toward Hopelessly Ill Patients" (Wanzer et al., 1984, 1989). The first article noted the difficulty of formulating "universally accepted guidelines for physicians" in treating the hopelessly ill. The article was written in an attempt to meet a need for "irreversibly ill" adults (treatment decisions on neonates and minors were not discussed). The second article noted significant changes that had taken place since the publication of the first article and mentioned the need for medical personnel to discuss with dying patients the prognosis of their disease, as well as the patients' directions on terminal care (see Hastings Center, 1987). Recommendations have also been made for those in long-term care facilities (Murphy, 1988).

There have been numerous studies on "do not resuscitate" (DNR) orders. A study by Zimmerman and his associates (1986) on the intensive care units at 13 hospitals found that 5.4 percent of patients had DNR orders, approximately one-half were 65+ years of age. Approximately 40 percent of those with DNR orders had been in "failing health" before they were admitted to the intensive care unit. The major reasons for admission were "failure or insufficiency of the cardiovascular system (37 percent), respiratory system (27 percent), or neurological system (19 percent)." Sixty percent of those admitted had at least one other organ system that was failing. As expected, these patients were more seriously ill than those who did not have DNR orders. The majority of patients with DNR orders died within 2 days or were transferred out of the intensive care unit, which was taken to mean that therapy was being withdrawn and the patient allowed to die.

A study by Wagner (1984) noted that while there is a great deal of discussion about issues such as cardiopulmonary resuscitation (CPR), there have been few studies that have asked those most likely to need it if they would want it. Wagner questioned 163 elderly women in a residential institution if they wanted CPR applied if they had an in-hospital cardiac arrest. The study found that 11 wanted CPR, 77 did not want CPR, 64 requested that the physician make the decision at the time, and the remaining 11 were either incompetent to decide or did not answer. It needs to be remembered that although life-sustaining technology exists, it is often ineffective, extending life for a matter of hours or days. One study on the effectiveness of CPR noted that it was originally developed for those with certain acute illnesses or disorders; however, it is now widely used on those with chronic disorders and illnesses. This study reported that only 5 to 23 percent of those who have in-hospital CPR are discharged alive. From CPR to death averages 2 to 14 days. The study also reported that there were certain conditions where CPR was applied but no patients were discharged alive (Blackhall, 1987). Taffet and his associates (1988) reported that few older patients were discharged alive after CPR (see Schiedermayer, 1988).

Another area to examine relates to "living will" legislation, which has become more popular in recent years. Currently, 41 states have living will legislation, although the legislation differs by state (J. E. Brody, 1989). The increase in the number of states that have legislation indicates the importance of this issue (between 1976 and 1980 ten states enacted legislation; between 1981 and 1984 thirteen states enacted legislation; from 1985 on seventeen states enacted legislation).

Generally, it is the individual, not a family member, who has the right to determine his or her medical care. However, if the individual is incapacitated and incapable of making a decision the physician will generally ask the family for instructions. If the instructions of the family violate the ethics of the physician or the policy of the health care institution (see Miles, Singer, & Siegler, 1989), there is often a conflict. Living wills are a way of planning for this possibility. Essentially, living wills provide instructions in the event of a terminal illness or conditions where the individual is unable or not competent to make a decision.

The living will allows individuals to state their wishes, while they are competent, concerning life-sustaining treatment if they become hopelessly ill and incompetent. If completed according to the guidelines of the state, the living will can be a valuable document for a physician if the patient is unable to communicate his or her intentions (see Society for the Right to Die, 1987). Generally, the living will provides instructions that life-sustaining technology not be utilized; that the process of dying not be artificially extended. Generally, the only medical care will be directed at relieving pain and other distressing symptoms, and maintaining dignity and personal hygiene (Mishkin, 1987).

Besides living wills there is a second option that is frequently being utilized: durable power of attorney. This was generally used in business, but is now being applied more to dying. Essentially, someone is appointed to make decisions on behalf of the individual. The durable power of attorney will designate an individual and the areas over which the individual has power (Mishkin, 1987). Although important in assisting surrogates and physicians in determining what life-sustaining treatment to apply in end-of-life medical decisions for individuals incapable of making decisions, only about 4 to 15 percent of the population have written plans in this area (Zweibel & Cassel, 1989). Although it is often assumed that family members "know" what the individual would want, studies have found that this is not the case (see Diamond et al., 1989).

One "new" issue has emerged in this area, namely, what constitutes "life-sustaining treatment," "extraordinary care" or "heroic measures" (see Dickey, 1988). For example, is artificial feeding an example of a life-sustaining treatment or an example of basic nursing care? There have been different guidelines used to define life-sustaining treatment. Some have considered life-sustaining treatment as invasive treatment; for others it dealt with the ability to make the patient "better"; for others the frequency of use was the guideline (see Steinbrook & Lo, 1988). The issues raised in the removal of life-sustaining treatment relate to the last issue, euthanasia.

Euthanasia

At the beginning of this section it was reported that during the 1960s to the early 1980s the major issue in dying and death was determined when someone was dead. The issue has now become when someone should die. Essentially, euthanasia has evolved around two issues; when does the agony of life outweigh the relief of death, and when does the quality of life dictate the termination of life-sustaining treatment.

Recently a third issue has emerged dealing with individuals who have chronic debilitating disorders that are not life-threatening who are requesting that life-sustaining treatment, such as feeding, be withdrawn. Thus, the removal of life-sustaining treatment and euthanasia are no longer centered only on the dying; rather, these issues have changed and now focus on quality of life issues. As the issues have changed, so have the number of court cases, and the groups involved. In the 1970s there were relatively few court cases. Now one can read about a different case on almost a weekly basis. The groups involved have also changed. The groups on both sides are now larger, more active, and more organized.

Much of the controversy around euthanasia is because it is not just one concept. Euthanasia has been defined in a variety of ways, usually according to whatever definition is "best" for the group. Generally it is interpreted by its supporters to mean a dignified, easy, or natural death. For those opposed to euthanasia, it is seen as murder or suicide. To define euthanasia we need to examine the two central issues: control and means. The first issue, control, deals with who determines if euthanasia is used. Two types of control are frequently discussed: voluntary and involuntary. Voluntary deals with the individual making the decision to die; involuntary is someone deciding for the individual that he or she will die. The second issue deals with the means used to induce death, and again two categories exist: active and passive, although positive and negative and direct and indirect have also been used. In active euthanasia direct action is taken to cause death, such as the injection of a lethal drug. In passive euthanasia there is no action taken to prolong life or to hurry death. The patient is allowed to die a "natural" death. Thus, drugs, surgery, or life-sustaining machinery are not employed to extend life, although they may be used to control pain or other distressing symptoms. The two issues, each with two types, create four possible forms of euthanasia:

1 Voluntary and passive: It is this form of euthanasia that proponents of euthanasia most often refer to. The patient has generally signed a "living will" and requested that at a certain stage in his or her illness life-sustaining treatment either not be employed or that it be withdrawn.

2 Voluntary and active: There are two distinct categories that fall under this heading. The first is suicide; the individual has voluntarily taken action to end his or her life. The second would be a terminally ill individual requesting that a physician or someone else take action that will end his or her life. An example would be someone, at the request of the patient, injecting the patient with a lethal drug.

3 Involuntary and passive: The individual has not requested death but nothing is done to extend life. The patient is "let go."

4 Involuntary and active: This could be labeled a "mercy killing," or murder. An action is taken, without the consent of the individual, to bring about his or her death.

Although these categories help to clarify the complexity of the term and show that it is not one but many concepts, in reality there are many cases that fall into a gray area (Devettere, 1989).

There appears to be increasing public support of voluntary passive euthanasia, with 60 percent of the public favoring euthanasia "under certain conditions" (Angell, 1988). This can also be seen in the increasing membership rolls of organizations such as Concern for the Dying and the Society for the Right to Die. Additionally, some states have had proposals to legalize certain forms of euthanasia. To date the proposals have been defeated but they will almost certainly return in states such as California and Florida. Also, certain western countries are changing their laws or policies in this area. In the Netherlands, for example, 6000 to 10,000 individuals are "euthanized" yearly (Kass, 1989; Meucci, 1988). Although it is technically a crime, case law and public support protects physicians (Angell, 1988).

As noted earlier, the issues are complex. Proponents stress a dignified, painless dying process, while opponents provide historical parallels with Nazi German (Meucci, 1988); others see a dehumanization of the dying taking place (Kass, 1988).

The controversy in this area can be seen by a recent article that appeared in the *Journal of the American Medical Association* called "It's Over Debbie" (Anonymous, 1988). The article was allegedly written by a resident who was called to the bedside of a young woman dying of ovarian cancer. The woman's weight was down to 80 pounds and she had not slept or eaten in 2 days; she was also having difficulty breathing. The young woman looked up at the resident and said, "Let's get this over with." The physician then administered a lethal dose of morphine. The responses to the article [see *Journal of the American Medical Association*, **259**(14):2094–2098; see also Gaylin et al., 1988; Vaux, 1988], which were both critical and supportive of the physician, indicated the emotionality in this issue, and that this is an issue that will continue to confront us.

SUMMARY

Dying and death are two events that older persons are more likely to experience than any other age group, in terms of their own dying as well as that of family and friends. In examining dying and death this chapter was separated into six sections.

The first section examined dying and death in contemporary American society. Here it was noted that dying and death went from frequently encountered events and discussed topics, to seldom encountered events and topics that were not discussed. In the distant past the family provided care to the dying and took care of the body after death. A high death rate meant that death was frequently encountered. Several factors brought about the change, such as better health care, which removed the dying from the care of the family. We are currently witnessing a "death awareness movement" which is reversing the earlier trend.

In the second section dying, death, and older persons were discussed in four subsections. The first subsection dealt with the fear of death and here it was mentioned that older persons fear dying and death less than younger individuals. This lower fear of death is probably because (1) older persons see themselves as having less value and fewer future prospects, (2) they have lived longer than expected, (3) through the death of family and friends they have come to accept death.

The second subsection discussed the treatment of dying geriatric patients. Traditionally, studies have indicated that older persons are perceived as having less social worth than younger patients and treated accordingly. However, many of these studies are old and have not been replicated. Recent research is inconclusive on this matter. Hospices were briefly discussed in this subsection, and it was noted that they came into existence because it was believed that they could provide better care at a lower cost than hospitals. This has not been demonstrated.

In the third subsection the stages of dying were examined, with the major emphasis on the stages of Kubler-Ross. It was pointed out that there is a great deal of misunderstanding of her stage theory. Also, many criticize her theory and claim that it does not apply to older persons. The fourth subsection discussed the dying process. Here it was noted that there are often changes that occur shortly before death. Changes take place in areas such as health and intellectual functioning.

The third section of this chapter examined death rates and causes of death. Here it was noted that in contemporary society death is something that happens primarily to older persons. Concerning the death rate it was noted that after adolescence it goes up; the death rate has declined in recent years; the major causes of death have changed from contagious diseases to degenerative diseases; the magnitude of the leading diseases has changed; the causes of death differ by age category; females have a lower death rate than males; blacks have a higher death rate than whites.

In the fourth section life expectancy was discussed. Essentially, life expectancy has increased significantly since the early part of this century. To a large extent, many of the earlier gains were in the reduction of infant, child, and adolescent death rates. Now, however, some gains are being made in life expectancy for older persons.

The life expectancy of females has increased faster than that of males. However, recently the differences have begun to narrow. There are several determinants of life expectancy, which can be categorized into factors that can be controlled and factors that cannot be controlled. Under the factors that can be controlled are diet, exercise, smoking, and socioeconomic status. Factors that cannot be controlled are heredity, sex, race, and intelligence. A last factor on longevity dealt with societies that appeared to have a disproportionate percentage of the population living to extreme old age. Studies have not supported any claims for extraordinary longevity in these societies.

The fifth section discussed three factors that are often associated with death in old age: bereavement, relocation, and retirement. Bereavement has often been assumed to be a cause of death in old age; it was called the "broken heart syndrome." The basic idea was that the death of a significant other was so traumatic and stressful that it caused the survivor to die within 6 months of being bereaved. Studies in this area are mixed. Several alternative explanations were offered for the studies that have found a higher death rate among the bereaved. This subsection also discussed the problems males and females face in bereavement.

Traditionally it has been believed that relocation is traumatizing to older persons, and results in a high postrelocation death rate. The majority of recent studies have not confirmed this belief. Retirement has also been seen as a "death sentence." In fact, this is one of the most persistent beliefs in gerontology. However, it is also one of the most consistently rebuked beliefs.

The last section examined three contemporary issues in dying and death: the definition of death, the termination of life-sustaining treatment, and euthanasia.

New medical technology has blurred the distinction between life and death; thus, a new definition was needed. The new definition has brought in the concept of brain death. Another issue that was considered is when to terminate life-sustaining treatment. Here it was noted that although the medical establishment has the ability to extend life, it is often a tortured existence. Both physicians and the dying have been asking at what point can life-sustaining treatment be terminated. Someone who is competent can make that determination. For someone who is not competent (i.e., comatose, advanced dementia, etc.) the issue is more complex. In some cases a surrogate is allowed to make medical decisions. Here the importance of living wills was discussed. The last subsection dealt with euthanasia. Euthanasia is not one concept it is many. For example, at one extreme an individual can elect not to have heroic measures; at the other extreme an individual is involuntarily killed. The issue of euthanasia is complex, controversial, and not likely to go away.

REFERENCES

Aldrich, C., & Mendkoff, E. (1963). Relocation of the aged and disabled: A mortality study. *Journal of the American Geriatric Society,* **11**(3): 185–194.

Angell, M. (1988). Euthanasia. *New England Journal of Medicine,* **319**(20): 1348–1350.

Anonymous (1988). It's over, Debbie. *Journal of the American Medical Association,* **259**(2): 272.

Beauvoir, S. (1972). *The Coming of Age.* New York: Putnam.

Bennett, N. G., & Garson, L. K. (1986). Extraordinary longevity in the Soviet Union: Fact or artifact. *The Gerontologist,* **26**(4): 358–361.

Berkowitz, B., & Green, R. F. (1965). Changes in intellect with age. *Journal of Genetic Psychology,* **107**(2): 179–192.

Bettis, S. K., & Scott, F. G. (1981). Bereavement and grief. In C. Eisdorfer (Ed.), *Annual review of gerontology and geriatrics: Volume Two* (pp. 144–159). New York: Springer.

Billig, N., Dickman, R. L., & White, L. (1988). Helping the older patient face death. *Patient Care,* **22**(January 15): 107–130.

Blackhall, L. J. (1987). Must we always use CPR? *The New England Journal of Medicine,* **317**(20): 1281–1285.

Borup, J. H. (1982). The effects of varying degrees of interinstitutional environmental change on long-term care patients. *The Gerontologist,* **22**(4): 409–417.

Borup, J. H. (1983). Relocation mortality research: Assessment, reply, and the need to refocus on the issues. *The Gerontologist,* **23**(3): 235–242.

Borup, J. H., & Gallego, D. T. (1981). Mortality as affected by interinstitutional relocation: Update and assessment. *The Gerontologist,* **12**(1): 8–16.

Borup, J. H., Gallego, D. T., & Heffernan, P. G. (1979). Relocation and its effect on mortality. *The Gerontologist,* **19**(2): 135–140.

Botwinick, J., West, R., & Storandt, M. (1978). Predicting death from behavioral test performance. *Journal of Gerontology,* **33**(5): 755–762.

Bourestom, N., & Pastalan, L. (1981). The effects of relocation on the elderly: A reply to Borup, J. H., Gallego, D. T., & Heffernan, P. G. *The Gerontologist,* **21**(1): 4–7.

Brody, E., Kleban, M., & Moss, M. (1974). Measuring the impact of change. *The Gerontologist,* **14**(4): 299–305.

Brody, J. A. (1989). Toward quantifying the health of the elderly. *American Journal of Public Health,* **79**(6): 685–686.

Brody, J. E. (1989). Most states recognize the legality of a "living will," but few invoke it. *New York Times,* September 21.

Bulkin, W., & Lukashok, H. (1988). Rx for dying: The case for hospice. *New England Journal of Medicine,* **318**(6): 376–378.

Burnette, K. (1986). Relocation and the elderly: Changing perspectives. *Journal of Gerontological Nursing,* **21**(10): 6–11.

Buskirk, E. R. (1985). Health maintenance and longevity: Exercise. In C. E. Finch & E. L. Schneider (Eds.), *Handbook of the biology of aging* (second edition) (pp. 894–931). New York: Van Nostrand Reinhold.

Busse, E. W., & Maddox, G. L. (1985). *The Duke longitudinal studies of normal aging.* New York: Springer.

Callahan, D. (1987). *Setting limits: Medical goals in an aging society.* New York: Simon and Schuster.

Carpenter, J. O., & Wylie, C. M. (1974). On aging, dying, and denying. *Public Health Reports,* **89**(5): 403–407.

Caserta, M. S., Lund, D. A., & Dimond, M. F. (1985). Assessing interviewer effects in a longitudinal study of bereaved elderly adults. *Journal of Gerontology,* **40**(5): 637–640.

Chapman, S. H., LaPlante, M. P., & Wilensky, G. (1986). Life expectancy and health status of the aged. *Social Security Bulletin,* **49**(10): 24–48.

Christ, A. E. (1961). Attitudes toward death among a group of acute geriatric psychiatric patients. *Journal of Gerontology,* **16**(1): 56–59.

Coffman, T. L. (1983). Toward an understanding of geriatric relocation. *The Gerontologist,* **23**(5): 453–459.

Comfort, A. (1967). On gerontophobia. *Medical Opinion Review,* **3**(1): 31–33.

Crandall, R. C. (1986). *Running: The consequences.* Jefferson, NC: McFarland.

Cumming, M. E. (1964). New thoughts on the theory of disengagement. In R. Kastenbaum (Ed.), *New thoughts on old age* (pp. 3–18). New York: Springer.

Davidson, G. W. (1988). Hospice care for the dying. In H. Wass, F. M. Berardo, & R. A. Neimeyer (Eds.), *Dying: Facing the facts* (pp. 185–200). New York: Hemisphere.

Devettere, R. J. (1989). Reconceptualizing the euthanasia debate. *Law, Medicine, & Health,* **17**(2): 145–155.

Diamond, E. L., Jernigan, J. A., Moseley, R. A., Messina, V., & McKeown, R. A. (1989). Decision-making ability and advance directive preferences in nursing home patients and proxies. *The Gerontologist,* **29**(5): 622–626.

Dickey, N. W. (1988). The ethics of heroic measures. *Patient Care,* **22**(1): 19.

Dickinson, G. E., Sumner, E. D., & Durand, R. P. (1987). Death education in U.S. professional colleges: Medical, nursing, and pharmacy. *Death Studies,* **11**(1): 57–61.

Dimond, M., Lund, D. A., & Caserta, M. S. (1987). The role of social support in the first two years of bereavement in an elderly sample. *The Gerontologist,* **27**(5): 599–604.

Doka, K. J. (1989). The awareness of mortality in midlife: Implications for later life. *Gerontology Review,* **2**(1): 19–28.

Downey, G. W. (1974). Must a transfer order be a death sentence for SNF patients? *Modern Health Care,* **3**(1): 44–47.

Eckert, J. K., & Haug, M. (1984). The impact of forced residential relocation on the health of the elderly hotel dweller. *Journal of Gerontology,* **39**(6): 753–755.

Eisdorfer, C., & Wilkie, F. (1977). Stress, disease, aging and behavior. In J. E. Birren & K. W. Schaie (Eds.), *Handbook of the psychology of aging* (pp.251–275). New York: Van Nostrand Reinhold.

Ekerdt, D. J. (1987). Why the notion persists that retirement harms health. *The Gerontologist,* **27**(4): 454–457.

Ekerdt, D. J., Baden, L., Bosse, R., & Dibbs, E. (1983). The effect of retirement on physical health. *American Journal of Public Health,* **73**(7): 779–783.

Ekerdt, D. J., Bosse, R., & LoCastro, J. S. (1983). Claims that retirement improves health. *Journal of Gerontology,* **38**(2): 231–236.

Elwell, F. (1986). The effect of single-patient transfers on institutional dependency. *The Gerontologist,* **26**(1): 83–90.

Farberow, N. L., Gallagher, D. E., Gilewski, M. J., & Thompson, L. W. (1987). An examination of the early impact of bereavement on psychological distress in survivors of suicide. *The Gerontologist,* **27**(5): 592–598.

Feifel, H. (1963). The taboo of death. *The American Behavioral Scientist,* **6**(1): 66–67.

Feinson, M. C. (1986). Aging widows and widowers: Are there mental health differences. *International Journal of Aging and Human Development,* **23**(4): 241–255.

Ferrari, N. (1963). Freedom of choice. *Social Work,* **8**(4): 104–106.

Ferraro, K. F. (1982). The health consequences of relocation among the aged in the community. *Journal of Gerontology,* **38**(1): 90–96.

Ferraro, K. F. (1985–1986). The effect of widowhood on the health status of older persons. *International Journal of Aging and Human Development,* **21**(1): 9–25.

Foster, D., Klinger-Vartabedian, L., & Wispe, L. (1984). Male longevity and age differences between spouses. *Journal of Gerontology,* **39**(1): 117–120.

Gallagher, D. E., Breckenridge, J. N., Thompson, L. W., & Peterson, J. A. (1983). Effects of bereavement on indicators of mental health in elderly widows and widowers. *Journal of Gerontology,* **38**(5): 565–571.

Gass, K. A. (1987). Coping strategies of widows. *Journal of Gerontological Nursing,* **13**(8): 29–33.

Gaylin, W., Kass, L. R., Pellegrino, E. D., & Siegler, M. (1988). Doctors must not kill. *Journal of the American Medical Association,* **259**(14): 2139–2140.

Gentry, M., & Shulman, A. D. (1985). Survey sampling techniques in widowhood research, 1973–1983. *Journal of Gerontology,* **40**(5): 641–643.

Gerber, I., Rusalem, R., Hannon, N., Battin, D., & Arkin, A. (1975). Anticipatory grief and aged widows and widowers. *Journal of Gerontology,* **30**(2): 225–229.

Gibson, D. E. (1984). Hospice: Morality and economics. *The Gerontologist,* **24**(1): 4–8.

Glaser, B. G. (1966). The social loss of aged dying patients. *The Gerontologist,* **6**(1): 77–80.

Glasser, J. H. (1981). The quality and utility of death certificate data. *American Journal of Public Health,* **71**(3): 231–233.

Gorer, G. (1965). *Death, grief, and mourning.* New York: Doubleday.

Gove, W. R. (1973). Sex, marital status, and mortality. *American Journal of Sociology,* **79**(1): 45–67.

Greenfield, S., Aronow, H. U., Elashoff, R. M., & Watanabe, D. (1988). Flaws in mortality data: The hazards of ignoring comorbid disease. *Journal of the American Medical Association,* **260**(15): 2253–2255.

Hastings Center (1987). *Guidelines on the termination of life-sustaining treatment and the care of the dying.* Bloomington: Indiana University Press.

Heyman, D. K., & Gianturco, D. T. (1973). Long-term adaptation by the elderly to bereavement. *Journal of Gerontology,* **28**(3): 359–362.

Hill, C. D., Thompson, L. W., & Gallagher, D. (1988). The role of anticipatory bereavement in older women's adjustment to widowhood. *The Gerontologist,* **28**(6): 792–796.

Hinton, J. (1967). *Dying.* Baltimore: Penguin.

Hinton, J. (1975). Facing death. *Journal of Psychosomatic Research,* **10**(1): 22–28.

Holden, C. (1987). Why do women live longer than men? *Science,* **238**(4824): 158–160.

Holmes, T. H., & Rahe, R. H. (1967). The social readjustment rating scale. *Journal of Psychosomatic Research,* **11**: 213–218.

Hopkins, D. D., Grant-Worley, J. A., & Bollinger, T. L. (1989). Survey of cause-of-death query criteria used by state vital statistics programs in the U.S. and the efficacy of the criteria used by the Oregon vital statistics program. *American Journal of Public Health,* **79**(5): 570–574.

Horowitz, M. J. & Schulz, R. (1983). The relocation controversy: Criticism and commentary on five recent studies. *The Gerontologist,* **23**(3): 229–234.

Isner, C. (1975). Reducing the risk of relocating the elderly. *RN,* **38**(4): 48–51.

Itri, L. (1987). Women's health: Cancer. *Public Health Report Supplement,* **102**(4): 92–96.

Jasnau, K. F. (1967). Individual versus mass transfers to nonpsychotic geriatric patients from mental hospitals to nursing homes, with special reference to death rates. *Journal of American Geriatrics Society,* **15**(3): 280–284.

Jeffers, F. C., Nichols, C. R., & Eisdorfer, C. (1961). Attitudes of older persons toward death: A preliminary study. *Journal of Gerontology,* **16**(1): 53–56.

Kalish, R. A. (1965). The aged and the dying process. *Journal of Social Issues,* **21**(4): 87–96.

Kalish, R. A. (1968). Life and death: Dividing the indivisible. *Social Science and Medicine,* **8**(3): 249–259.

Kalish, R. A. (1971). Social values and the elderly. *Mental Hygiene,* **55**(1): 51–54.

Kalish, R. A. (1972). Of social values and the dying: A defense of disengagement. *The Family Coordinator,* **21**(1): 81–94.

Kalish, R. A. (1976). Death and dying in a social context. In R. Binstock & E. Shanas (Eds.), *Handbook of aging and social sciences* (pp. 483–509). New York: Van Nostrand Reinhold.

Kalish, R. A. (1985). The social context of death and dying. In R. H. Binstock & E. Shanas (Eds.), *Handbook of aging and the social sciences* (pp. 149–170). New York: Van Nostrand Reinhold.

Kalish, R. A. (1987). Death. In G. L. Maddox (Ed.), *The encyclopedia of aging* (pp. 158–160). New York: Springer.

Kalish, R. A. (1988). The study of death: A psychosocial perspective. In H. Wass, F. M. Berardo, & R. A. Neimeyer (Eds.), *Dying: Facing the facts* (pp. 55–75). New York: Hemisphere.

Kaplan, G. A., Seeman, T. E., Cohen, R. D., Knudsen, L. P., & Guralnik, J. (1987). Mortality among the elderly in the Alameda County study: Behavioral and demographic risk factors. *American Journal of Public health,* **77**(3): 307–312.

Kaprio, J., Koskenvuo, M., & Rita, H. (1987). Mortality after bereavement: A prospective study of 95,647 widowed persons. *American Journal of Public Health,* **77**(3): 283–287.

Kasl, S. V. (1972). Physical and mental health effects of involuntary relocation and institutionalization on the elderly: A review. *American Journal of Public Health,* **62**(3): 377–384.

Kass, L. R. (1989). Neither for love nor money: Why doctors must not kill. *Public Interest,* **94**(Winter): 25–46.

Kastenbaum, R. (1965). The realm of death: An emerging area in psychological research. *Journal of Human Relations,* **13**(4): 538–552.

Kastenbaum, R. (1967a). Multiple perspectives on a geriatric death valley. *Community Mental Health Journal,* **3**(1): 21–29.

Kastenbaum, R. (1967b). The mental life of dying geriatric patients. *The Gerontologist,* **7**(2; Part 1): 97–100.

Kastenbaum, R. (1969). Death and bereavement in later life. In A. H. Kutscher (Ed.), *Death and bereavement* (pp. 28–54). Springfield, IL: Charles C Thomas.

Kastenbaum, R. (1974). On death and dying: Should we have mixed feelings about our ambivalence toward the aged? *Journal of Geriatric Psychiatry,* **7**(1): 94–107.

Kastenbaum, R. (1985). Do we die in stages? In S. G. Wilcox & M. Sutton (Eds.), *Understanding death and dying* (pp. 124–132). Palo Alto: Mayfield.

Kastenbaum, R. J., & Weisman, A. D. (1972). The psychological autopsy as a research procedure in gerontology. In D. P. Kent, R. J. Kastenbaum, & S. Sherwood (Eds.), *Research planning and action for the elderly* (pp. 210–217). New York: Behavioral Publications.

Killian, E. (1970). Effects of geriatric transfers on mortality rates. *Social Work,* **15**(1): 19–26.

Kleemeier, R. W. (1962). Intellectual changes in the senium. *Proceedings of the American Statistical Association,* **1**(2): 181–190.

Kohn, R. R. (1982). Cause of death in very old people. *Journal of the American Medical Association,* **247**(20): 2793–2797.

Kubler-Ross, E. (1969). *On death and dying.* New York: Macmillan.

Kubler-Ross, E. (1974). *Questions and answers on death and dying.* New York: Macmillan.

LaSagna, L. (1970). Physicians' behavior toward the dying patient. In O. Brim (Ed.), *The dying patient* (pp. 83–101). New York: Russell Sage Foundation.

Lawton, M., & Yaffe, S. (1970). Mortality, morbidity and voluntary change of residence by older people. *Journal of the American Geriatric Society,* **18**(10): 823–831.

Lerea, L. E., & LiMauro, F. (1982). Grief among health care workers: A comparative study. *Journal of Gerontology,* **37**(5): 604–608.

Lieberman, M. A. (1961). Relationship of mortality rates to entrance to a home for the aged. *Geriatrics,* **16**(10): 515–519.

Lieberman, M. A. (1965). Psychological correlates of impending death: Some preliminary observations. *Journal of Gerontology,* **20**(2): 181–190.

Lieberman, M. A. (1966). Observations on death and dying. *The Gerontologist,* **6**(1): 70–73.

Lieberman, M. A. (1974). Relocation research and social policy. *The Gerontologist,* **14**(6): 494–500.

Lieberman, M. A., & Coplan, A. S. (1969). Distance from death as a variable in the study of aging. *Developmental Psychology,* **2**(1): 71–84.

Lindemann, E. (1979). Symptomatology and management of acute grief. In L. A. Bugen (Ed.), *Death and dying: Theory, research, practice* (pp. 6–17). Dubuque, Iowa: Wm. C. Brown.

Loomis, M. T., & Williams, F. T. (1983). Evaluation of care provided to terminally ill patients. *The Gerontologist,* **23**(5): 493–499.

Lopata, H. A. (1973). *Widowhood in an American city.* Cambridge, MA: Schenkman.

Lund, D. A., Caserta, M. S., & Dimond, M. F. (1986). Gender differences through two years of bereavement among the elderly. *The Gerontologist,* **26**(3): 314–320.

Lund, D. A., Dimond, M., & Juretich, M. (1985). Bereavement support groups for the elderly: Characteristics of potential participants. *Death Studies,* **9**(3–4): 309–321.

McConnel, C. E., & Deljavan, F. (1982). Aged deaths: The nursing home and community differential, 1976. *The Gerontologist,* **22**(3): 318–323.

Marshall, J. R. (1975). The geriatric patients' fears about death. *Postgraduate Medicine,* **57**(4): 144–149.

Mazess, R. B., & Forman, S. H. (1979). Longevity and age exaggeration in Vilcabamba, Ecuador. *Journal of Gerontology,* **34**(1): 94–98.

Metzger, A. M. (1979). A Q-methodological study of the Kubler-Ross stage theory. *Omega,* **10**(4): 291–302.

Meucci, S. (1988). Death-making in the human services. *Social Policy* **18**(3): 17–20.

Meyers, A. R., Master, R. J., Kirk, E. M., Jorgenson, C., & Mucatel, M. (1983). Integrated care for the terminally ill: Variations in the utilization of formal services. *The Gerontologist,* **23**(1): 71–74.

Miles, S. H., Singer, P. A., & Siegler, M. (1989). Conflicts between patients' wishes to forgo treatment and the policies of health care facilities. *The New England Journal of Medicine,* **321**(1): 48–50.

Miller, D., & Lieberman, M. (1965). The relationship of affect state and adaptive capacity to reactions to stress. *Journal of Gerontology,* **20**(5): 492–497.

Mirotznik, J., & Ruskin, A. P. (1984). Interinstitutional relocation and its effects on health. *The Gerontologist,* **24**(3): 286–291.

Mirotznik, J., & Ruskin, A. P. (1985a). Interinstitutional relocation and its effects on psychosocial status. *The Gerontologist,* **25**(3): 265–270.

Mirotznik, J., & Ruskin, A. P. (1985b). Interinstitutional relocation and the elderly. *Journal of Long-Term Care Administration,* **13**(4): 127–131.

Mishkin, B. (1987). Living wills and other directives for health care. In G. L. Maddox (Ed.), *The encyclopedia of aging* (pp. 405–406). New York: Springer.

Morgan, L. A. (1986). The financial experience of widowed women: Evidence from the LRHS. *The Gerontologist,* **26**(6): 663–668.

Moss, M. S., Lawton, M. P., & Glicksman, A. (1985). The last year of life of elderly persons. Paper presented at the 38th Annual Meeting of the Gerontological Society of America, New Orleans.

Murphy, D. J. (1988). Do-not-resuscitate orders: Time for reappraisal in long-term-care institutions. *Journal of the American Medical Association,* **260**(14): 2098–2101.

Myers, G. C., & Manton, K. G. (1984). Compression of mortality: Myth or reality. *The Gerontologist,* **24**(4): 346–353.

Novick, L. (1967). Easing the stress of moving day. *Hospitals,* **41**(16): 64–74.

Palmore, E. B. (1980). Predictors of longevity. In S. G. Haynes & M. Feinleib (Eds.), *Epidemiology of aging* (pp. 57–64). Washington, DC: U.S. Government Printing Office.

Palmore, E. B. (1981). *Social patterns in normal aging: Findings from the Duke Longitudinal Study.* Durham, NC: Duke University Press.

Palmore, E. B. (1982). Predictors of the longevity differences: A 25–year follow-up. *The Gerontologist,* **22**(6): 513–518.

Palmore, E. B. (1987). Long-lived human populations. In G. L. Maddox (Ed.), *The encyclopedia of aging* (p. 409). New York: Springer.

Parkes, C. M. (1972). *Bereavement: Studies of grief in adult life.* New York: International Universities.

Percy, C., Stanek, E., & Gloeckler, L. (1981). Accuracy of cancer death certificates and its effect on cancer mortality statistics. *American Journal of Public Health*, **71**(3): 242–250.

President's Commission for the Study of Ethical Problems in Medicine and Biomedical and Behavioral Research (1981). *Defining death: A report on the medical, legal, and ethical issues in the determination of death*. Washington, DC: U.S. Government Printing Office.

President's Commission for the Study of Ethical Problems in Medicine and Biomedical and Behavioral Research (1983). *Deciding to forego life-sustaining treatment: A report on the ethical, medical, and legal issues in treatment decision*. Washington, DC: U.S. Government Printing Office.

Rees, W. D., & Lutkins, S. G. (1967). Mortality of bereavement. *British Medical Journal*, **4**(1): 13–16.

Reimanis, G., & Green, R. F. (1971). Imminence of death and intellectual decrement in the aging. *Developmental Psychology*, **5**(2): 270–272.

Remondet, J. H., & Hansson, R. O. (1987). Assessing a widow's grief: A short index. *Journal of Gerontological Nursing*, **13**(4): 31–34.

Retsinas, J. (1988). A theoretical reassessment of the applicability of Kubler-Ross's stages of dying. *Death Studies*, **12**(3): 207–216.

Rhudick, P. J., & Dibner, A. S. (1961). Age, personality, and health correlates of death concerns in normal and aged individuals. *Journal of Gerontology*, **16**(1): 44–49.

Riegel, K. F., & Riegel, R. (1972). Development, drop, and death. *Developmental Psychology*, **6**(2): 306–319.

Rockstein, M., & Sussman, M. (1979). *Biology of aging*. Belmont, CA: Wadsworth.

Rosenberg, H. M. (1989). Improving cause-of-death statistics. *American Journal of Public Health*, **79**(5): 563–564.

Rosswurm, M. A. (1983). Relocation and the elderly. *Journal of Gerontological Nursing*, **9**(12): 632–637.

Rowland, K. F. (1977). Environmental events predicting death for the elderly. *Psychological Bulletin*, **84**(2): 349–372.

Sanders, C. M. (1980–81). Comparison of younger and older spouses in bereavement outcome. *Omega*, **11**(3): 217–232.

Schiedermayer, D. L. (1988). The decision to forgo CPR in the elderly patient. *Journal of the American Medical Association*, **260**(14): 2096–2097.

Schulz, R., & Anderman, D. (1974). Clinical research on the stages of dying. *Omega*, **5**(2): 137–144.

Scott, J. P., & Kivett, V. R. (1985). Differences in the morale of older, rural widows and widowers. *International Journal of Aging and Human Development*, **21**(2): 121–135.

Siegler, I. C. (1975). The terminal drop hypothesis: Fact or artifact? *Experimental Aging Research*, **1**(2): 169–185.

Siegler, I. C. (1987). Terminal drop. In G. L. Maddox (Ed.), *The encyclopedia of aging* (pp. 664–665). New York: Springer.

Sirken, M. G., Rosenberg, H. M., Chevarley, F. M., & Curtin, L. R. (1987). The quality of cause-of-death statistics. *American Journal of Public Health*, **77**(2): 137–139.

Society for the Right to Die (1987). *Handbook of living will laws*. New York: Society for the Right to Die.

Soldo, B. J., & Agree, E. M. (1988). America's elderly. *Population Bulletin*, **43**(3): 1–51.

Sorlie, P. D., & Gold, E. B. (1987). The effect of physician terminology preference on coronary heart disease mortality: An artifact uncovered by the ninth revision. *American Journal of Public Health*, **77**(2): 148–152.

Speert, H. (1973). *Iconographia gyniatricia: A pictorial history of gynecology and obstetrics*. Philadelphia: F. A. Davis.

Steinbrook, R., & Lo, B. (1988). Artificial feeding—solid ground, not a slippery slope. *New England Journal of Medicine,* **318**(5): 286–290.

Stillion, J. M. (1984). Perspectives on the sex differential in death. *Death Education,* **8**(4): 237–256.

Stillion, J. M. (1985). *Death and the sexes.* New York: Hemisphere.

Stroebe, M. S., & Stroebe, W. (1983). Who suffers more? Sex differences in health risks of the widowed. *Psychological Bulletin,* **93**(2): 279–301.

Stroebe, M. S., Stroebe, W., Gergen, K. J., & Gergen, M. (1981–1982). The broken heart: Reality or myth? *Omega,* **12**(2): 87–105.

Sudnow, D. (1967). *Passing on.* Englewood Cliffs, NJ: Prentice-Hall.

Swenson, W. M. (1961). Attitudes toward death in an aged population. *Journal of Gerontology,* **16**(1): 49–52.

Taffet, G. E., Teasdale, T. A., & Luchi, R. J. (1988). In-hospital cardiopulmonary resuscitation. *Journal of the American Medical Association,* **260**(14): 2069–2072.

Templer, D. I., Ruff, C. F., & Franks, C. M. (1971). Death anxiety: Age, sex and parental resemblance in diverse populations. *Developmental Psychology,* **4**(1): 108.

U.S. Bureau of the Census (1975). *Historical abstracts of the United States, Colonial Times to 1970, Bicentennial Edition.* Washington, DC: U.S. Government Printing Office.

U.S. Bureau of the Census (1980). *Statistical abstract of the United States.* Washington, DC: U.S. Government Printing Office.

U.S. Bureau of the Census (1990). *Statistical abstract of the United States.* Washington, DC: U.S. Government Printing Office.

U.S. Congress, Office of Technology Assessment (1987). *Life-sustaining technologies and the elderly.* Washington, DC: U.S. Government Printing Office.

Valanis, B., Yeaworth, R. C., & Mullis, M. R. (1987). Alcohol use among bereaved and nonbereaved older persons. *Journal of Gerontological Nursing,* **13**(5): 26–32.

Vaux, K. L. (1988). Debbie's dying: Mercy killing and the good death. *Journal of the American Medical Association,* **259**(14): 2140–2141.

Venglarik, J. M., & Adams, M. (1985). Which client is a high risk? *Journal of Gerontological Nursing,* **11**(5): 28–30.

Wagner, A. (1984). Cardiopulmonary resuscitation in the aged: A prospective survey. *New England Journal of Medicine,* **310**(17): 1129–1130.

Waldron, I. (1981). Why do women live longer than men? In P. Contad & R. Kern (Eds.), *The sociology of health and illness* (pp. 45–66). New York: St. Martin's.

Wanzer, S. H., Adelstein, S. J., Cranford, R. E., Federman, D. D., Hook, E. D., Moertel, C. G., Safar, P., Stone, A., Taussig, H. B., & VanEys, J. (1984). The physician's responsibility toward hopelessly ill patients. *New England Journal of Medicine,* **310**(15): 955–959.

Wanzer, S. H., Federman, D. D., Adelstein, S. J., Cassel, C. K., Cassem, E. H., Cranford, R. E., Hook, E. W., Lo, B., Moertel, C. G., Safar, P., Stone, A., & Van Eys, J. (1989). The physician's responsibility toward hopelessly ill patients. *The New England Journal of Medicine,* **320**(13): 844–849.

Wass, H., & Myers, J. E. (1984). Death and dying: Issues for educational gerontologists. *Educational Gerontology,* **10**(1): 65–81.

Weisman, A. (1972). *On dying and denying: A psychiatric study of terminality.* New York: Behavioral Publications.

White, N., & Cunningham, W. R. (1988). Is terminal drop pervasive or specific. *Journal of Gerontology: Psychological Sciences,* **43**(6): P141–P144.

Wing, S., Manton, K. G., Stallard, E., Hames, C. G., & Tryoler, H. A. (1985). The black/

white mortality crossover: Investigation in a community-based study. *Journal of Gerontology*, **40**(1): 78–84.

Wittels, I., & Botwinick, J. (1974). Survival in relocation. *Journal of Gerontology*, **29**(4): 440–443.

Yin, P., & Shine, M. (1985). Misinterpretations of increases in life expectancy in gerontology textbooks. *The Gerontologist*, **25**(1): 78–82.

Youngner, S. J. (1988). Who defines futility. *Journal of the American Medical Association*, **260**(14): 2094–2095.

Zimmerman, J. E., Knaus, W. A., Sharpe, S. M., Anderson, A. S., Draper, E. A., Wagner, D. P. (1986). The use and implications of do not resuscitate orders in intensive care units. *Journal of the American Medical Association*, **255**(3): 351–356.

Zweibel, N. R., & Cassel, C. K. (1989). Treatment choices at the end of life: A comparison of decisions by older patients and their physician-selected proxies. *The Gerontologist*, **29**(5): 615–621.

Zweig, J., & Csank, J. Z. (1975). Effects of relocation on chronically ill geriatric patients of a medical unit: Mortality rates. *Journal of American Geriatrics Society*, **23**(2): 132–136.

GLOSSARY

activity theory   A theory maintaining that high life satisfaction in old age is achieved by retaining middle-age activity levels; the antithesis of disengagement theory.

acute condition   A condition, disorder, or disease that is temporary, such as a cut, flu, or cold.

age cohort   See birth cohort.

age effect   The impact of maturation or age on an individual's behavior or performance.

age grading   The social process whereby chronological age determines eligibility for certain rights, roles, or positions in society.

age-integrated environment   An environment in which individuals of all ages live and interact together.

age-segregated environment   An environment in which certain age groups live and interact outside the mainstream of society.

age-stratification model   A concept that perceives age as an important determinant of behavior. Chronological age is seen as a variable that separates the population into age strata, each of which has a set of rights, roles, obligations, and opportunities.

aged   A term that can be defined in many different ways. For example, an individual may be termed aged on the basis of social, physical, or psychological characteristics, as well as on the basis of chronological age. The designation of any chronological age or any specific characteristics as being distinguishing traits of the aged is, of course, arbitrary. In this book, the age group 65+ is considered to be aged.

ageism   The prejudice of discrimination of one age group against another on the basis of age.

aging   Technically, human beings can be considered to be aging from the moment of conception. In this book, aging refers to an individual's acquiring the social, physical, and psychological characteristics that society classifies as those of an aging individual.

anticipatory socialization   Learning about the expectations of future roles and positions.

asexual Being sexless; not having sexual feelings, desires, or sexual expression.

atrophy The wasting away of part of an organism through disease or nonuse. The term is also used by social scientists when they talk about concepts such as "will to live," family ties, or self-concept.

autoimmunity theory of senescence A theory maintaining that with increasing age there are more cell mutations in cell divisions, causing the body to produce antibodies. The result is that the body in essence destroys itself.

bereavement A stage of life that survivors experience after someone close to them has died. The stage of bereavement is characterized by certain physical symptoms (shortness of breath, headaches, muscular weakness, etc.), psychological distress, and changes in social roles.

birth cohort A group of individuals born in the same year or in the same grouping of years. Also commonly referred to as age cohort.

birth rate The number of children born per 1000 women of childbearing age.

causation Scientists do not believe that events simply happen. Rather, they are caused to happen; something makes them occur. For a variable to be the cause of an event, it must be both necessary for the event to take place and sufficient to produce that event.

cautiousness A term used in psychological experimental studies to denote a delay or withholding of a response.

chronic condition A condition, disorder, or disease that is permanent or that will incapacitate an individual for a long period of time.

cohort A group of individuals born in the same year (e.g., 1910) or in the same grouping of years (e.g., 1910–1920). Sometimes referred to as birth cohort or age cohort.

cohort effect Researchers believe that the birth cohort into which an individual is born influences that individual. Because every cohort is exposed to somewhat different socialization and educational experiences, as well as to the same historical events at different ages, each cohort is somewhat different from every other cohort. Because of these differences, cohorts perceive and interpret the same events differently. Different cohorts may believe or perform very differently from one another, not because of differences in age per se but because of cohort differences.

collagen theory of senescence According to this theory, aging is caused by the growing rigidity of collagen found in the connective tissues of the body. The progressive rigidity prevents the tissues of the body from absorbing nutrients and expelling waste products.

comatose An unconscious state resulting from an accident, disease, injury, or drug overdose. Although individuals who are comatose cannot respond to their environment, they are sometimes aware of what is going on around them (e.g., conversations and the presence of others).

compensatory environment See prosthetic environment.

creativity A term that is difficult to define but one that is generally used to denote originality or uniqueness of mental and physical works.

cross-sectional study A type of study that makes an observation at only one point in time.

cultural relativity The principle of understanding the behavior of individuals in a society other than your own by examining their values, beliefs, and culture.

culture The aspects of a society that are socially transmitted. The culture of a society includes its knowledge, arts, beliefs, morals, laws, customs, norms, etc.

custodial institution An institution that does not recognize or try to develop existing or potential abilities of residents. Rather, the institution tends to "overcare" for the residents and thus causes existing and potential abilities to atrophy.

death   The cessation of life. Although death may appear to be an easily definable state, there is considerable disagreement in contemporary American society as to when death has occurred. For example, has death occurred when the heart has stopped or when there are no brain waves? For further elaboration on this point, see *Death, dying, and the biological revolution: Our last quest for responsibility,* Veatch, R., New Haven: Yale University Press, 1976.

death rate   A figure representing the total number of individuals who have died in the total population, expressed per 100, 1000, 10,000, or 100,000 individuals in the society. Thus a death rate of 10 (per 1000) would mean that for every 1000 individuals in the society, 10 have died. Death rate is the same as mortality rate.

definition of the situation   Human beings do not always automatically respond when stimulated. Rather, they enter into a period during which they interpret the stimulus and then respond to it. This intermediate period between the stimulus and the response is called the definition of the situation.

demography   The study of the composition of a population. Such variables as the changing age, sex, racial, or geographic composition of the population are studied. Demographers examine such phenomena as the existing composition of a population and the variables that bring about changes in that composition.

dependency ratio   A figure that compares the number of economically productive individuals to the number of economically unproductive individuals in a society. The aged dependency ratio compares the number of individuals 65+ years of age (who are considered to be unproductive) to the number of individuals between the ages of 18 and 64 (who are considered to be productive).

dependent variable   The variable that is believed to be caused by the independent variable; the outcome or result of a study.

developmental psychology   That branch of psychology that is interested in examining the characteristics of the life periods and noting why changes come about and the impact of these changes on individuals.

disenchantment period   The period of time in a marriage occurring shortly after the birth of the first child and extending to the postparental period that is characterized by a lower level of marital satisfaction.

disengagement theory   A theory maintaining that high life satisfaction in old age is achieved when the aged individual gradually relinquishes roles and activities; the antithesis of activity theory.

double jeopardy   See jeopardy.

educational gerontology   A subfield of gerontology that examines the educational needs and wants of the aged and the development of programs and courses that will satisfy these needs and wants.

empty nest   The postparental period or the period of time after the children have left home. This term is generally used in connection with middle-aged women who no longer have children at home and who are incorrectly assumed to have a difficult time in adjusting to this fact.

ethnocentrism   The attitude that one's own culture is superior and that it should be used as a standard by which to judge the culture of another society.

extended family   Two or more nuclear families plus assorted relatives living together in one household.

family   Two or more individuals who are related by blood, marriage, or adoption and who are living together in the same household.

family of orientation   The family into which an individual is born.

family of procreation   The family that adults form at the time of marriage.

family life cycle   The continual process of birth, growth, maturation, and death in the extended family. The family life cycle examines the different ages at which these events occur and the length of time they last and does so for different historical periods.

fantasy death   Death that is presented in an unrealistic manner.

filial responsibility   The willing assumption of supportive or caretaking roles by adult offspring for their aged parents.

functional disorder   A psychological disorder that is diagnosed as not having an organic or physical origin.

geriatrics   The study of the medical aspects of old age.

gerontocracy   A society that is ruled by the aged.

gerontology   The study of the aged. The term gerontology is a very broad term and encompasses the study of the ages by many disciplines and professions.

gerontophobia   Fear of aging or of the aged.

Hawthorne effect   The distortion of an experimental study by the fact that the participants in the study know that they are being studied and therefore alter their behavior.

health   The World Health Organization has defined health as a ''state of complete physical, mental, and social well-being and not merely the absence of disease or infirmity.''

hormone theory of senescence   A theory maintaining that senescence is caused by the lack of a specific hormone. Proponents of this theory attempt to prevent or retard aging by administering hormonal supplements.

hospice   A facility that specializes in caring for and treating terminally ill patients. In the hospice the family plays an important part in providing care to the patient. Home care is encouraged. The hospice seeks to allow patients to have pain-free and alert lives.

hypochondria   A neurotic disorder in which afflicted individuals feel that they are physically ill or about to become physically ill in the absence of any measurable pathology.

hypothesis   An expectation, educated guess, or tentative answer as to the outcome of a study.

incontinent   Lacking voluntary control of both bowel and bladder functioning.

independent variable   A variable that is manipulated by the experimenter.

intelligence   A controversial term in psychology that refers to the score an individual achieves on an intelligence test.

interview   A method used by researchers in which the interviewer asks questions of the subject and then records the responses.

jeopardy   Many individuals find that society reacts negatively to certain traits or characteristics that they possess. In fact, their likelihood of achieving an adequate education, of having equal job opportunities, and of maintaining adequate health is in jeopardy because of the way society treats them and reacts to them. Individuals who possess two undesirable traits (i.e., advanced age and low financial status) are characterized by the term double jeopardy; individuals who possess three undesirable traits (i.e., advanced age, low financial status, and membership in a minority group) are characterized by triple jeopardy; and individuals who possess four undesirable characteristics (i.e., advanced age, low financial status, membership in a minority group, and female) are characterized by quadruple jeopardy. Individuals characterized by double, triple, or quadruple jeopardy find that the likelihood and intensity of discrimination increase proportionately with the number of negative characteristics they possess.

labeling theory   A theory maintaining that the identity others give us is often the identity we will assume.

learning   The acquisition of information that improves a response or performance.

leisure   An activity in which a person engages on a voluntary basis for intrinsic enjoyment and one that is not necessary for subsistence.

life expectancy The average number of years that an individual can expect to live from birth.

life period A particular segment of an individual's life that is different from all others because of physical, social, economic, and psychological factors.

life-period approach The categorization of individuals into several distinct groups on the basis of such variables as chronological age or social, psychological, or physiological characteristics. The different life periods have different demands and expectations placed on them. The life period into which individuals are categorized will often determine the roles and positions that they can hold.

life satisfaction The attitudes that individuals have about their lives in the past, present, and future.

life span The potential number of years that human beings could live if environmental variables such as disease and accidents did not cut that number short.

longitudinal study A type of study that makes the same observations at two different points in time. Generally, something has occurred between the first and second set of observations and the researcher is interested in seeing if that occurrence produced a difference between the observations.

looking-glass self The image that individuals form of themselves after interpreting the way other individuals respond to them.

manic reaction A neurotic disorder in which the individual's mood is one of elation.

master status The status that dominates all others.

memory The retention of learned information.

minority group A group within society that has limited access to equal opportunities or a power base and that generally experiences discrimination and prejudice.

modified extended family Several related nuclear families that do not live in the same household but maintain strong kinship ties and caring and helping patterns and have frequent social interaction.

monogamy The practice of having one spouse.

morale The emotional component of life satisfaction.

morbidity rate A figure derived from an examination of the total number of individuals who are physically or psychologically ill in the total population, and expressed as the number of ill individuals per 100, 1000, 10,000, or 100,000 individuals in the population. Often, both the morbidity and mortality rates focus on a specific population. For example, a researcher may focus on widows in a certain age group and observe that the morbidity rate is much higher than for nonwidows in the same age group.

mortality rate See death rate.

motor performance The learned responses that are made by the voluntary muscles; also referred to as psychomotor performance.

near-poverty level The Department of Health, Education, and Welfare recognizes that individuals whose incomes are only slightly above the poverty threshold cannot be recognized as having an adequate income. Therefore, they have created a near-poor category that is 25 percent higher than the poverty threshold.

neurosis A functional disorder in which the individual's ability to think clearly and to judge wisely may be impaired.

nomadic Wandering about from area to area, usually seasonally, in order to secure food supplies. Not having a settled place of residence.

nuclear family Two adults of the opposite sex living together in a socially approved sexual relationship with their children. However, children may or may not be present and a spouse may be absent because of death, separation, or divorce.

nursing home A facility that provides care for individuals who are incapable of self-care.

operational definition   A concrete, empirical definition of a term.

organic disorder   A disorder that has a biological or physical basis.

osteoporosis   The decrease in both the mass and density of bones.

pacing   Either having a fixed time when a response is required or allowing the individual to respond at his or her own rate.

participant-observer method   A research method whereby researchers go out into the field and participate in what they are observing. Researchers can engage in different levels of participation (active to passive) when conducting their observations.

patriarchal   Characterized by the supremacy of the oldest male member in the family.

patrilineal   Tracing family descent through the father's family.

period effect   The impact that the historical period under examination has on different birth cohorts being studied.

periodontal disease   A disease of the gums that often leads to loss of teeth.

peristaltic movement   The muscle movement that moves the feces from the stomach to the anus.

personality theory   A theoretical framework in gerontology maintaining that it is not the level of activity that determines life satisfaction but rather the level of activity coupled with personality type.

phenomenological theory   A theoretical framework that tries to understand human behavior through an analysis of the individual's perception and interpretation of the world.

polygamy   The practice of having more than one spouse at one time.

polytheistic   Believing in more than one god.

population   The entire group of individuals having the characteristics that the researcher is interested in studying. Since most populations are much too large to study, most researchers select only a part or sample of the population for study.

postparental   Occurring after parenthood.

poverty threshold   The level of income below which individuals are considered to be living in poverty and above which individuals are not considered to be living in poverty.

preliterate   Not having a written form of language.

presentation of self   A concept created by Goffman that claims that when we engage in social interaction, we manipulate or change the self we present. We have the option of presenting ourselves in a variety of ways, and we choose the self that we feel will best serve our needs in a particular social-interaction situation.

primary relationship   A relationship that endures over time, involves individuals interacting in a variety of roles, creates a strong "we" feeling, is not easily transferred to others, and has an emotional, intimate, and personal nature attached to it.

primitive   An ethnocentric term generally referring to a society that the evaluator feels is not as advanced as his or her own.

prostatectomy   The surgical removal of the prostate gland.

prosthetic environment   An environment that has been designed to compensate for certain physical disabilities.

psychosis   A functional disorder in which there is often some loss of contact with reality.

quadruple jeopardy   See jeopardy.

questionnaire   A written document that researchers give to subjects to fill out in order to solicit information from them.

reaction time   The time in between the onset of a stimulus and a measurable response to that stimulus.

realistic appraisal   Treating an age group according to one's real beliefs, despite contradictory verbal attitudes.

reality orientation A therapeutic technique that helps individuals maintain existing abilities and contact with reality.

reliability A test is reliable if it will consistently yield the same results on the same individual under the same conditions.

relocation Moving an individual from one place of residence to another.

retirement Individuals can be considered retired if they are not working fulltime or year-round, if they are drawing social security or private-pension benefits, and if they are considered to be retired by themselves or by society.

retirement community Generally, an age-segregated community that is composed almost entirely of retired individuals.

rite of passage An event that shifts an individual from one life period into another.

ritualistic deference Responding with an outdated societal belief when asked a question. Generally, actual behavior does not coincide with the statements made when using ritualistic deference. Actual behavior is an example of realistic appraisal.

role Individuals who hold certain positions or statuses in a society have certain behaviors expected of them. These behavioral expectations are called roles.

role theory A theory maintaining that one's behavior is determined in large part by one's interpretation of the components of one's role.

sample A group of individuals drawn from the population to study. A sample should be representative of the population.

sanctions Rewards (positive sanctions) given to individuals for behaving according to role or societal expectations or punishments (negative sanctions) given to individuals for not fulfilling these expectations.

science An empirical, orderly process of obtaining information about the world.

secondary relationships Relationships that are formalized, unemotional, impersonal, and highly specialized, and that involve individuals acting in only one role.

senescence The physical and biological process of growing old.

senility An all-too-frequently used term that refers to mental incapacities brought about by increasing age.

sex ratio The number of males per 100 females in a society.

social death Often before biological death, individuals are treated as if they were in fact dead. This attitude can result in the cessation of medical care and references to the individual in the past tense. For an excellent description of social death, see *Passing on,* Sudnow, D., Englewood Cliffs, NJ: Prentice-Hall, 1967.

social gerontology A specialized area within gerontology that studies the reciprocal relationship between the aged individual and society.

social security A general term referring to Old Age Survivors, Disability, and Health Insurance (OASDHI). Social security is a national social insurance program primarily designed to protect individuals against unemployment in old age.

socialization The process whereby the values, beliefs, and norms of a society are transmitted. Socialization is a process that starts with birth and does not end until death.

subculture Although individuals often speak of the American culture, most of us recognize that this society is not composed of one homogeneous group. Rather, it is composed of many groups. Although these groups may share some common characteristics, they nevertheless differ from one another in many respects. These groups are called subcultures.

subculture theory A theory maintaining that the behavior of the aged is caused by the fact that they belong to a subculture composed of other aged individuals. The subculture of the aged is alleged to have created a unique belief system in the aged individuals who belong to it.

suicide The taking of one's own life.

supplemental security income A welfare program that supplements the existing incomes of the eligible aged and attempts to bring these incomes up to the poverty threshold.

theory A statement of the relationship or common principle inherent in a number of observations.

valid An instrument is valid when it accurately reflects what it is supposed to be measuring.

values An individual's judgments or appraisals about what is important, right, moral, correct, proper, or desirable.

wear-and-tear theory of senescence The belief that senescence is the result of the body's wearing out after prolonged use or of the body's being exposed to an environment that is abusive to it.

AUTHOR INDEX

Riegel, R., 545, 579
Riegel, R. M., 254, 291
Riegle, G. D., 245
Riehle, R. A., 142, 148, 154, 235, 236, 245
Riggs, B. L., 154
Riley, J. W., 21, 37
Riley, M. W., 11, 21, 36, 37, 87, 91, 96, 99, 108, 117, 318, 331, 338, 339, 344, 354
Rimer, B., 355
Risley, T. R., 490, 500
Rita, H., 577
Rivera, P., 287
Rivlin, R. S., 145, 146, 154
Rizer, R. L., 154
Roberto, K. A., 24, 37, 144, 154, 324, 331
Roberts, A., 231, 245
Roberts, J., 204, 209
Roberts, J. C., 140, 143, 154
Roberts, M. D., 328
Roberts, S. L., 154
Robertson, B., 207
Robertson, J., 317, 331
Robertson, L., 403
Robertson-Tchabo, E., 283
Robertson-Tchabo, E. A., 256, 257, 291
Robins, L. N., 206
Robinson, M., 245
Robinson, P. K., 221, 245
Robinson, R., 202
Rockstein, M., 126, 127, 131, 141, 147, 154, 579
Rodeheaver, D., 510, 532
Rodgers, W. L., 88, 89, 115, 117
Rodin, J., 263, 291
Roe, B. B., 203
Roe, D. A., 185, 208
Roff, L. L., 218, 245
Rogers, A., 52, 57
Rogers, C. J., 515, 532
Rogosa, D., 87, 117
Rogot, E., 197, 208
Rollins, B. C., 301, 302, 332
Roman, M., 315, 328
Roman, P., 117
Rones, P. L., 415, 427
Rose, A. M., 37, 102, 105, 117, 118, 505, 532
Rose, J., 287
Rosen, C. E., 344, 354
Rosenbaum, W. A., 379, 401, 403
Rosenberg, H. M., 546, 579
Rosenberg, N., 206
Rosenthal, C. J., 311, 313, 314, 332
Rosenwaike, I., 46, 57
Rosow, I., 69, 80, 102, 106, 118, 419, 428, 488, 501
Ross, E., 256, 291
Ross, H. A., 462
Ross, K. M., 119
Rossiter, C. M., 279, 292
Rossman, I., 135, 143, 154, 229, 232, 245
Rosswurm, M. A., 562, 579
Rost, K., 173, 208
Roszman, T., 155
Roter, D., 173, 208
Roth, M., 288, 292
Roundtree, J. L., 192, 208
Rowe, J. W., 15, 23, 37, 144, 154
Rowland, K. F., 557, 579

Rozovski, S. J., 208
Rubinstein, R. L., 308, 332
Ruchlin, H. S., 16, 37, 501
Ruff, C. F., 538, 580
Ruhling, R. O., 286
Runciman, A., 228, 246
Rupprecht, P., 501
Rusalem, R., 575
Ruskin, A. P., 562, 578
Russell, C. S., 327
Russell, E. M., 286
Ruth, J. E., 260, 291
Ryan, A. J., 208
Ryder, L. K., 452, 462
Ryff, C. D., 10, 33
Rykken, D. E., 222, 228, 229, 232, 246
Rzetelny, H., 497

Sachs, L. A., 16, 37
Safar, P., 580
Safilios-Rothschild, C., 302, 332
Sager, K., 208
Salend, E., 321, 332
Salmon, A. P., 533
Salmon, M. A. P., 358, 359, 375
Salter, C. A., 486, 501
Salter, C. L., 486, 501
Salthouse, T. A., 118, 250, 291
Samet, J., 183, 208
Samorajski, T., 166, 204
Sanchez, J., 204
Sanchez, P., 517, 518, 532
Sanders, C. M., 579
Sanders, G. F., 318, 332
Sands, L. P., 95, 118, 253, 291
Sangl, J., 332
Santo-Novak, D., 172, 173, 208
Santos, J. F., 265, 286, 289
Saperstein, A. R., 499
Sargent, F., 125, 151
Satz, M., 332
Saxberg, B. O., 500
Scales, A. M., 424, 429
Scarbrough, D. R., 498
Scarisbrick-Hauser, A., 308, 332
Schacht, T. E., 291
Schafer, S. C., 280, 291
Schaie, K. W., 19, 31, 32, 87, 95, 99, 114, 118, 252, 254, 261, 283, 285, 291, 293
Schairer, C., 242
Scharf, M., 193, 204
Scharlach, A. E., 313, 314, 332, 488, 492, 493, 501
Scherr, P. A., 286
Scheve, A. S. S., 153
Schiedermayer, D. L., 579
Schiffman, S. S., 139, 154
Schimer, M. R., 16, 37
Schmall, V., 290
Schmidhauser, J. R., 382, 391, 402
Schmidt, D. H., 206
Schmidt, R. M., 47, 57, 226, 243
Schneider, C. J., 103, 119, 420, 429
Schneider, E., 128, 154
Schneider, E. L., 15, 23, 33, 37, 165, 185, 208, 291

SUBJECT INDEX

AARP, 387
Abraham, Karl, 18
Absorption, drugs, 172
Abstinence, effect on sexuality, 228
Abuse, elder, 319–323
Acceptance, stage of dying, 542
Action programs, 398
Activity theory, 103–104
Acute conditions, 159–160
Administration, occupation in gerontology, 27
Administration on Aging (AOA), 397
Age effect, 91–92
Age grading, 9–10
Age integration, 457–459
Age segregation, 457–459
Age-stratification model, 108–110
Aged:
    abuse, 319–323
    academic interest in, 13–21
    alcoholism, 166–171
    Asian and Pacific Island Americans, 526–528
    attitudes about death, 538–539
    bereavement, 557–561
    blacks, 50, 194–196, 311–312, 361–363, 452, 469, 519–526
    children of, 309–312
    community environment, 450–459
    consumers, 371–372
    creativity, 259–260
    crime, 450–453
    cross-cultural universals, 68
    death:
        attitudes toward, 538–539
        causes of, 548–550
        rates, 546–548
    defined, 7
    demographic profile, 48–55
        number of aged, 41
        percentage of aged, 41
    dependency ratio, 50–51
    divorced, 49, 305–306
    dying, treatment of, 539–541
    economic status, 50–51, 359–364
    education, 51, 347–351
    ethnic composition, 50
    friends, 323–325
    geographic distribution, 51–53
    grandparents, 315–318
    growth of aged population, 40–48

Aged (*Cont.*):
    Hispanics, 515–519
    home environment, 432–450
    income, 364–366
    income sources, 366–371
    increasing interest in, 60–64
    intelligence, 251–255
    labor force participation, 50, 408–411
    learning, 255–257
    leisure, 421–424
    life period approach, 8–13
    living arrangements, 54–55
    marital satisfaction, 301–302
    marital status, 49–50, 300–303
    married, 49–50, 300–303
    medical care of, 182–185, 477–482, 539–541
    memory, 257–259
    mental disorders, 261–281
    minority, 504–528
    Native Americans, 511–515
    never-married, 308–309
    nursing homes, 466–495
    past, American society, 73–77
    personality, 260–261
    political:
        activities, 384–385
        affiliation, 379–380
        power, 385–393
    population growth of, 40–48
    preliterate societies, 69–73
    race and ethnicity, 50
    racial composition, 50
    reaction time, 250–251
    religion, 336–346
    religious behaviors, 338–341
    religious beliefs, 337–338
    religious identification, 338
    relocation, 561–563
    remarriage, 49, 306–307
    remarried, 306–308
    retirement, 412–421, 563–564
    retirement communities, 434–443
    sex ratio, 48–49
    siblings, 318
    social support ratio, 53–54
    speed of behavior, 250–251
    transportation, 453–454
    widowed, 304–305
    women, 50, 55, 196–197, 220–225, 361, 381, 387–388, 408–410, 415–416, 507–511